I0105323

Modern France

MODERN FRANCE

Michael F. Leruth

Understanding Modern Nations

BLOOMSBURY ACADEMIC

NEW YORK • LONDON • OXFORD • NEW DELHI • SYDNEY

BLOOMSBURY ACADEMIC
Bloomsbury Publishing Inc
1385 Broadway, New York, NY 10018, USA
50 Bedford Square, London, WC1B 3DP, UK
29 Earlsfort Terrace, Dublin 2, Ireland

BLOOMSBURY, BLOOMSBURY ACADEMIC and the Diana logo
are trademarks of Bloomsbury Publishing Plc

First published in the United States of America by ABC-CLIO 2022
Paperback edition published by Bloomsbury Academic 2025

Copyright © Bloomsbury Publishing Inc, 2025

For legal purposes the Acknowledgments on p. xiii constitute an extension of this copyright page.

COVER PHOTOS: Acropolis, Athens, Greece. (Sven Hansche/Dreamstime);
Santorini, Village of Fira. (JOHN KELLERMAN/Alamy Stock Photo); Greek Presidential Guard.
(Stephen Hogg/Alamy Stock Photo); Crete Island. Greece, (Smallredgirl/Dreamstime)

All rights reserved. No part of this publication may be reproduced or
transmitted in any form or by any means, electronic or mechanical,
including photocopying, recording, or any information storage or retrieval
system, without prior permission in writing from the publishers.

Bloomsbury Publishing Inc does not have any control over, or responsibility for,
any third-party websites referred to or in this book. All internet addresses given
in this book were correct at the time of going to press. The author and publisher
regret any inconvenience caused if addresses have changed or sites have
ceased to exist, but can accept no responsibility for any such changes.

Library of Congress Cataloging-in-Publication Data
Names: Leruth, Michael F., author.
Title: Modern France / Michael F. Leruth.
Description: Santa Barbara, California : ABC-CLIO, [2022] | Series:
Understanding modern nations | Includes bibliographical references and index.
Identifiers: LCCN 2022012538 | ISBN 9781440855481 (hardcover) |
ISBN 9781440855498 (ebook)
Subjects: LCSH: France—History. | France—Civilization.
Classification: LCC DC38 .L478 2022 | DDC 944—dc23/eng/20220316
LC record available at https://lccn.loc.gov/2022012538

ISBN: HB: 978-1-4408-5548-1
PB: 979-8-7651-4114-4
ePDF: 979-8-2161-8631-1

Series: Understanding Modern Nations

To find out more about our authors and books visit www.bloomsbury.com
and sign up for our newsletters.

CONTENTS

SERIES FOREWORD

We live in an evolving world, a world that is becoming increasingly globalized by the minute. Cultures collide and blend, leading to new customs and practices that exist alongside long-standing traditions. Advancing technologies connect lives across the globe, affecting those from densely populated urban areas to those who dwell in the most remote locations in the world. Governments are changing, leading to war and violence but also to new opportunities for those who have been oppressed. The *Understanding Modern Nations* series seeks to answer questions about cultures, societies, and customs in various countries around the world.

Understanding Modern Nations is geared toward readers wanting to expand their knowledge of the world, ideal for high school students researching specific countries, undergraduates preparing for studies abroad, and general readers interested in learning more about the world around them. Each volume in the series focuses on a single country, with coverage on Africa, the Americas, Asia and the Pacific, and Europe.

Each country volume contains 16 chapters focusing on various aspects of culture and society in each country. The chapters begin with an Overview, which is followed by short entries on key topics, concepts, ideas, and biographies pertaining to the chapter's theme. In a way, these volumes serve as "thematic encyclopedias," with entries organized for the reader's benefit. Following a general Preface and Introduction, each volume contains chapters on the following themes:

- Geography
- History
- Government and Politics
- Economy
- Religion and Thought
- Social Classes and Ethnicity
- Gender, Marriage, and Sexuality
- Education
- Language
- Etiquette
- Literature and Drama
- Art and Architecture

- Music and Dance
- Food
- Leisure and Sports
- Media and Popular Culture

Each entry concludes with a list of cross references and Further Readings, pointing readers to additional print and electronic resources that might prove useful.

Following the chapters are appendices, including "A Day in the Life" feature, which depicts "typical" days in the lives of people living in that country, from students to farmers to factory workers to stay-at-home and working mothers. A Glossary, Facts and Figures section, and Holidays chart round out the appendices. Volumes include a Selected Bibliography, as well as sidebars that are scattered throughout the text.

The volumes in the *Understanding Modern Nations* series are not intended to be comprehensive compendiums about every nation of the world, but instead are meant to serve as introductory texts for readers, examining key topics from major countries studied in the high school curriculum as well as important transitioning countries that make headlines daily. It is our hope that readers will gain an understanding and appreciation for cultures and histories outside of their own.

ACKNOWLEDGMENTS

Without the love, support, encouragement, patience, and understanding of my wife, Angela, and our daughters, Sophie and Alice, this book would never have happened. The calming presence of our cat, Musette, helped a lot, too. *Modern France* is dedicated to them. I also acknowledge the support and inspiration for this project that has come from my institution, William & Mary, and from my colleagues and students in the Department of Modern Languages and Literatures and the French and Francophone Studies Program. Many of the ideas and analyses in this book came out of and have been tested in my French literature and culture classes at William & Mary. Two William & Mary people deserve special recognition for their vital contributions to this volume. The first is Joe Plumeri, the generous benefactor of the Plumeri Award for Faculty Excellence, which I am honored to have received in 2018. This award sustained me during part of the writing of this volume and funded travel to France for research. The second is my student, Sonali Gobin, who helped me with revisions for the semifinal version of the manuscript. I appreciate the professionalism of everyone at ABC-CLIO, especially that of the supportive and skillful editors who accompanied the manuscript through its various stages of writing and production: Kaitlin Ciarmiello, Erin Ryan, and Nicole Azze. Thank you for not giving up on me when this project started taking longer than planned. Kudos as well to Kousalya Devi Krishnamoorthy and Amnet for capably ushering this book through the final production phase. My own voyage of discovery of France began forty years ago to the sound of a cassette of Yves Montand's famous 1981 concert at L'Olympia playing on the car stereo of my French host, Alain Breton, who picked me and my three American program mates from Xavier University up at Paris Orly Airport. The fascination, and the fear, of those first moments are still palpable. Since then, I have come to consider France my second *patrie*, thanks in large part to Angela, *ma française*, and to her family. I wish I could keep on writing because I am still learning new things, and unlearning some old ones, every day about this complex, contradictory, and charming country. A final *merci* therefore goes to the people of France, past and present, for giving me so much to think about over the years. There is still a lot of *grandeur* in you. Don't let anyone tell you otherwise.

INTRODUCTION

General Charles de Gaulle, the leader of France's government-in-exile during the German occupation of France and later the first president of the French Fifth Republic, was famously possessed of a "certain idea of France" that included the conviction that "France cannot be France without greatness." The statesman's declaration can be interpreted as expressing three notions that still resonate among the French: first, the certitude that France was indeed a great nation in the past—a military, diplomatic, and colonizing power that often stood at the forefront of modern western civilization; second, the sobering realization that it was a diminished nation in the shifting geopolitical order of the latter half of the twentieth century—a middling power shorn of its empire and more reliant than it would care to admit on the United States and on its own European partners for the peace and prosperity that it craved; and third, a deep-seated dissatisfaction with this more modest station and a preternatural aspiration to be something more. Much nostalgic longing lurked below the surface of de Gaulle's proud statement.

In recent years, this nostalgia has morphed into gloom in the face of the major challenges that France faces as a nation:

1. An eroded industrial base coupled with chronically high unemployment, which have led to a widening gap between its haves and have-nots, often raucous social and political unrest (e.g., the Yellow Vest protests of 2018–2020), and fertile ground for populist ideologies with a strong undercurrent of xenophobic nationalism;
2. The stubborn difficulty France has had trying to reconcile the real multicultural diversity of French society with a venerable yet dated "republican ideal" of the French nation that places considerable emphasis on "indivisibility" and *Laïcité*, or strict secularism;
3. The acute socioeconomic disenfranchisement of minority youths from the sprawling suburbs (*banlieues*)—a situation that has produced its own spectacular instances of unrest (e.g., the riots/uprising of November 2005);
4. A presidential system of government that proved itself adept at ushering the nation through the period of unprecedented economic growth and social modernization known as the Thirty Glorious Years (1945–1975) and is still capable of churning out major structural reforms that experts deem necessary, yet that finds its

democratic legitimacy increasingly called into question (e.g., the high hopes that accompanied the stunning electoral triumph of Emmanuel Macron in 2017, quickly followed by an equally dramatic decline in the young president's popularity as he struggled to live up to expectations, then a mood of tense uncertainty as he started his second term in 2022 after defeating far right populist rival Marine Le Pen for the second straight time);

5. The mounting stress on the European Union (EU)—of which France is a founding member—caused by steady enlargement, increased skepticism about the EU's ability to ensure economic prosperity and function as a democracy in which the will of the people (and not just that of the financial markets) is taken into account, and disagreements among member states about how to handle certain major crises in the 2010s (e.g., the Greek sovereign debt crisis, the refugee crisis, and the consequences of the "Brexit" referendum in the United Kingdom);

6. A string of high-profile incidents of domestic terrorism (e.g., the *Charlie Hebdo/Hypercacher* attacks of January 2015, the November 2015 attacks in Paris, and the truck attack in Nice on Bastille Day in 2016); and

7. The effects of the global COVID-19 pandemic that raged throughout 2020 and 2021—forcing three nationwide lockdowns, infecting over 27 million French people, claiming the lives of over 144,000 by April 2022, and putting unprecedented stress on the already tepid French economy.

The combined effects of such challenges have found an echo in a steady stream of pessimistic and alarmist essays with provocative titles like *The Fall of France* (Nicolas Baverez, 2003), *The Unhappy Identity* (Alain Finkielkraut, 2013), and *The French Suicide* (Éric Zemmour, 2014).

Important as it is not to minimize the gravity of these and other challenges that France faces, it is also important to bear in mind France's many strengths, as well as the sometimes overlooked ways in which it is still a prominent and influential nation. There is France's advantageous geography. It is situated at the western extremity of the continental European landmass—midway between Europe's northern and southern regions—with thousands of kilometers of coastline (North Sea, English Channel, Atlantic Ocean, and Mediterranean Sea) and other natural borders (the Rhine River, and the Vosges, Jura, Alps, and Pyrenees Mountains) that give it the regular shape that is the basis for its nickname, *"L'Hexagone."* Moreover, the remnants of its former colonial empire—now overseas departments and semiautonomous "territorial collectivities"—give France a presence in North America (Saint Pierre and Miquelon), the Caribbean (Guadeloupe, Martinique), South America (French Guiana), the Indian Ocean (Réunion, Mayotte), and the South Pacific (French Polynesia, New Caledonia). By virtue of its area (552,000 km²) and population (65 million), mainland France is the largest and third largest country, respectively, in Western Europe. It has the seventh largest economy in the world, and is a leading exporter not only of wine, cheese, and luxury goods, but also of aircraft and aerospace technology, pharmaceuticals, and other agricultural products. Indeed, although agriculture accounts for under 3% of French jobs and a mere 1.5% of its GDP, France is a global agricultural powerhouse—it has the largest area of arable land in the EU, and leads in both crop and animal production; it is also the sixth largest producer and fifth largest exporter of agricultural products in the world. In terms of diplomatic and military clout, France may not be a superpower, but it is still a force to reckon with: in tandem with Germany, it has often been a driving force of EU politics; it has veto power as a permanent member of the United Nations Security Council; it is the home of important international organizations like the European Parliament (Strasbourg), UNESCO, and the Organisation for Economic Co-operation and Development (Doctors Without Borders, now headquartered in Geneva, Switzerland, was started by French doctors in 1971); and its military—active in overseas operations—boasts the largest active duty armed forces in the EU, the sixth largest defense budget in the world, the third largest arsenal of nuclear weapons in the world, formidable naval forces, and a fifth place ranking in the world in terms of overall military might.

France also continues to measure up in the cultural arena. Paris may no longer be the undisputed global capital of the arts that it once was (e.g., in the thirteenth, seventeenth, and eighteenth centuries, and between 1830 and 1930), but it still matters. French literary authors, philosophers, public intellectuals, visual and performing artists, composers, architects, filmmakers, chefs, and fashion designers still enjoy considerable international acclaim. Even as officials carry out ambitious reforms of the French educational system at all levels, France continues to excel in research. It has produced numerous winners of the Nobel Prize and Fields Medal (Mathematics); and its National Center for Scientific Research (CNRS) is the largest research organization in Europe and the fourth leading institutional source of scientific papers in the world. Moreover, thanks to the enduring allure of Paris, the natural beauty of the nation's countryside and varied topography, its attractive beach destinations, its charming and well-preserved villages, its regional cuisines and world-famous vineyards, its summer festivals to suit every taste in art and culture, and its forty-five UNESCO World Heritage Sites, France is the top tourist destination nation in the world in terms of total number of visitors. Finally, the French language is more than the native language of close to 90% of the population of France and of an admittedly modest 77 million people worldwide. If one also counts L2 speakers—including many who live in countries where French is one of the national languages (e.g., France's former African colonies)—there are 321 million Francophones in the world. By some estimates, French is the fifth most spoken language in the world, the second most learned foreign language in the world, the third most common language of international business, and the fourth language for internet content. Francophone solidarity and cooperation at the international level help enhance France's global cultural presence in spite of the fact that some critics call attention to the latent neocolonial connotations of "*La Francophonie.*"

Additional French strengths are to be found in what are often considered traits of the national character. The French people are considered to be steeped in "Cartesian" rationalism (i.e., methodological doubt, rigorous deductive reasoning, a fondness for conceptual abstraction, and insistence on "clear and distinct" ideas expressed in elegant language) and Enlightenment idealism (i.e., belief in scientific progress, free thought, liberal government, and universal human rights). However, they are equally devoted to *la joie de vivre* (the joy of living) and the pleasures of the senses, including a liberal attitude toward sexuality and seduction as a subtext of everyday interpersonal interactions. The French also have a well-known reputation for esthetic elegance and cultural refinement, and an exceptionally strong sense of history and tradition. The latter is not surprising when one considers how old the French nation is.

French national sentiment is traditionally thought to trace its origins back to 52 BCE, when the Arverni chieftain Vercingetorix established a fleeting military alliance of Gauls against Roman imperial forces. Following four centuries of Roman political and cultural hegemony, Roman Gaul begins to turn into "France" during the Merovingian and Carolingian periods against the backdrop of the symbiotic relationship between the Catholic Church and the Frankish monarchy. National milestones of this era include the Merovingian ruler Clovis's conversion to Christianity in order to consolidate his hold on power (496 CE) and Charles Martel's victory over the Muslim Saracens at the Battle of Tours (732 CE)—a military triumph traditionally seen as having "saved" western Christendom and paved the way for Carolingian Frankish rule (Martel was the grandfather of Charlemagne) over most of Western Europe. The three-and-a-half century-long reign of the Capetian royal dynasty—which began with Hugh Capet in 987—was also crucial insofar as it was during this era that the institutional and territorial foundations of the modern French nation-state were laid. The French nation reinvented itself as the French Republic during the French Revolution (1789–1799). The First Republic did not last long but a propensity to reinvent itself has been part of the French nation's political DNA ever since—two empires, two constitutional monarchies, the Vichy regime, and four more republics till the present. Another national character trait that was not an *ex nihilo* invention of the French Revolution but was given patriotic legitimacy by it is the fierce French attachment to civil liberties and social equality—the bases of a uniquely militant democratic ethos that is reflected in the famous French penchant for protest but does not preclude placing one's faith in state intervention to improve society (although it does involve a deep-seated wariness of elites both in and outside the government). The third term in the French Republic's motto—Liberty, Equality, Fraternity—is a bit fuzzier. It has been interpreted in recent times as synonymous with "social solidarity" and seen as the moral underpinning of France's generous social safety net and extensive public services (two pillars of the vaunted French social model), which enjoy solid support across the political spectrum. However, fraternity entails more than government programs and services. It ultimately involves a yearning for civic togetherness and national unity, and a corresponding desire to overcome cultural "particularisms" (past and present) and ideological fractiousness. There have been a number of spectacular displays of French *Fraternité* in recent years, in moments of great sorrow and joy—the massive rallies that took place in Paris and other French cities in 2015 in response to the *Charlie Hebdo* and Hypercacher terror attacks; the ecstatic celebrations that took place when the French men's national team won the 2018 FIFA World Cup in soccer, twenty years after the cup was first won by Les Bleus; the shared distress and outpouring of concern on display when fire ravaged and nearly destroyed Notre-Dame Cathedral in Paris—a cherished national monument that transcends both its Parisian location and its original religious function—on April 15, 2019; and a general willingness to band together in isolation to deal with the unprecedented challenges of the coronavirus pandemic of 2020–2022. Even in these moments, however, the French did not surrender their right to question and to quarrel—not everyone could reflexively and full-throatedly proclaim *Je suis Charlie* (sympathy for the victims, defense of free speech, and condemnation of violent extremism went hand in hand with criticism of the satirical newspaper's "stupid and nasty" style of humor and perceived prejudice against French Muslims); not everyone was a soccer fan or saw the national team's success as a vindication of the nation's de facto multiculturalism; not everyone was comfortable with the millions of euros pouring in from billionaire donors for the rebuilding of Notre Dame during a time of great social need. Not everyone applauded the government's handling of the pandemic or agreed with all stringent measures taken to limit its spread. In other words, the French appear to be instinctively familiar with American anthropologist David Kertzer's concept of "solidarity without consensus."

France is a diverse country. The most basic trope of French geographical and cultural diversity is the North-South divide, which formerly had significant political, linguistic, sociocultural, and even religious connotations, but now connotes primarily that there is a different "feel" to the France one encounters when one reaches the Massif Central highland region and heads deeper into the "Midi," or South of France. In the days of the monarchy, France was a patchwork of provinces with widely varying social structures, customs, and dialects. The French Republic was at first somewhat suspicious of this "archaic" diversity and opted to subdivide the national territory into smaller and more rational units—the departments (of which there are currently ninety-six in mainland France). Still, local identities were not suppressed altogether and even found expression in the naming of the departments for local rivers and mountains. An even more specific form of local identity centers on the concept of terroir, a term that is most commonly used to describe the unique character, quality, and traditional cultural value of food and drink produced in a small ecoregion. There is no commonly agreed way of dividing France into its constituent terroirs (different mapping schemes number them in the 400s or 500s), but locals in rural parts of France know what terroir they belong to and may even refer to it as *mon pays*. Since the 1980s, the French government has decentralized public administration and policy making to a considerable extent by transferring power (but neither sovereignty nor legislative authority) to the regional, departmental, and communal (municipal) levels. The biggest beneficiaries have been the administrative regions, created in 1956, given legal standing as "territorial collectivities" in 1982, and reorganized in 2016. France's thirteen mainland regions are Hauts-de-France, Normandy, Île-de-France, Grand Est, Brittany, Pays de la Loire, Centre-Val de Loire, Bourgogne-Franche-Comté, Nouvelle-Aquitaine, Auvergne-Rhône-Alpes, Occitanie, Provence-Alpes-Côte d'Azur (also called Sud), and Corsica. The reorganization also included the new administrative and territorial category of the *métropole*, or "metropolis," which reflects the increasing importance and dynamism of France's largest cities. Other than Paris—the nation's political, economic, and cultural capital—the most important urban areas (in order of size of population) are Lyon, Marseille, Toulouse, Bordeaux, Lille, Nice, Nantes, Strasbourg, Rennes, Grenoble, Rouen, Toulon, and Montpellier.

The French are connoisseurs of their regional and local diversity. There is no good reason why the same positive attitude shouldn't apply to its racial, ethnic, and religious diversity, which is the product of immigration. Accepted or not, the fact remains that France is a melting pot. There are close to 6 million immigrants (including both foreign-born naturalized citizens and noncitizen foreign-born residents) presently living in France—close to 9% of the population. If one goes back three generations, 40% of the population of France can be considered, at least partially, as products of immigration—a statistic known to demographers and sociologists but not yet fully part of common perception. While much of this diversity is connected to "postcolonial" immigration (i.e., the influx of workers from France's former colonies and, later, their families) in the 1950s, 60s, 70s, and 80s, the modern history of immigration in France reaches back to the nineteenth century and includes people from a wide range of countries. In descending order, the largest contingents of immigrants come from Algeria, sub-Saharan Africa (e.g., Mauritania, Senegal, Mali, Niger, Guinea, Côte d'Ivoire, Cameroon, Republic of Congo, Comoros, Madagascar), Morocco, Portugal, Italy, Spain, Turkey, Tunisia, and Southeast Asia (e.g., Vietnam). Eastern Europe and other parts of Asia (e.g., China) are also important sources of immigrants. Because of the prominence of immigrants from the Maghreb and sub-Saharan Africa, Islam is now the second leading religion in France after Roman Catholicism, counting between 4.5 and 5.5 million adherents (7.5%–8.0% of the population). France not only has the largest Muslim community in the EU but the largest Jewish one as well.

The purpose of this volume is to offer a current and encyclopedic survey of modern France that adheres to the general parameters of the Understanding Modern Nations series. Although special emphasis will be on France today—a complex, diverse, changing, and innovative nation that contradicts old reductive stereotypes and romantic clichés—a considerable amount of attention will nonetheless be devoted to situating the topics treated in a historical context. This approach extends to the concept of "modernity" itself since it will also consider the historical development of a French paradigm of modernity—one that is characteristically associated with the French Revolution, the Republic, industrial society, the twentieth century, and modernism—and then endeavor to explore how contemporary/present-day France (postcolonial, postindustrial, and postmodern) both continues to adhere to and departs from this French paradigm of modernity and its various social, economic, political, and cultural corollaries. Certain caveats about this volume's intended "encyclopedic" scope and "current" quality are to be kept in mind. First, the choice of topics covered is based on the personal criteria of the author. The reader should therefore bear in mind that different, equally justifiable choices could have been made that would have resulted in a somewhat different version of "Modern France" emerging from these pages. Second, while a concerted effort has been made to base this volume on the most current and accurate information available, France is a nation in flux—realities can be measured in different ways and statistics are constantly changing. In other words, this book is a snapshot. France has already changed since the time of its research, writing, and publication. This is particularly true of the ongoing COVID-19 (coronavirus) pandemic, which was beginning to spike again in France just as the manuscript was being finalized. It is the author's hope that the reader will pardon any inaccuracies that may have found their way into the book's pages and that they will use this book as a point of departure for further reading and research and thereby come to form their own more complete, current, and accurate image of France today and tomorrow.

Selected Bibliography

Asselin, Gilles, and Ruth Mastron. *Au Contraire!: Figuring Out the French*. 2nd ed. Brealey, 2010.

Barlow, Julie, and Jean-Benoît Nadeau. *Sixty Million Frenchmen Can't Be Wrong: Why We Love France but Not the French*. Sourcebooks, 2003.

Birnbaum, Pierre. *The Idea of France*. Trans. M. B. DeBevoise. Hill and Wang, 2001.

Braudel, Fernand. *The Identity of France*. Trans. Sian Reynolds. Collins, 1988–1990. 2 vols.

Chabal, Emile, ed. *France since the 1970s: History, Politics and Memory in an Age of Uncertainty*. Bloomsbury, 2015.

Chafer, Tony, and Emmanuel Godin, eds. *The End of the French Exception?: Decline and Revival of the "French Model."* Palgrave Macmillan, 2010.

Dumossier, Marion, et al., eds. *The Routledge Handbook of French Politics and Culture*. Routledge, 2019.

Godin, Emmanuel, and Tony Chafer, eds. *The French Exception*. Berghahn, 2005.

Gopnik, Adam. *Paris to the Moon*. Random House, 2000.

Granville, Brigitte. *What Ails France?* McGill-Queen's UP, 2021.

Hewitt, Nicolas, ed. *Cambridge Companion to Modern French Culture*. Cambridge UP, 2003.

Howarth, David, and Georgios Varouxakis. *Contemporary France: An Introduction to French Politics and Society*. New ed. Routledge, 2014.

Hughes, Alex, and Keith Reader, eds. *Encyclopedia of Contemporary French Culture*. Routledge, 1998.

Kidd, William, and Sian Reynolds, eds. *Contemporary French Cultural Studies*. Arnold, 2000.

Magny, Olivier. *WTF?!: What the French*. Berkeley, 2016.

Schwartz, Vanessa R. *Modern France: A Very Short Introduction*. Oxford UP, 2011.

Steele, Ross. *The French Way: The Keys to the Behavior, Attitudes, and Customs of the French*. 2nd ed. McGraw-Hill, 2006.

Waters, Sarah. *Between Republic and Market: Globalization and Identity in Contemporary France*. Continuum, 2012.

Zeldin, Theodore. *The French*. Pantheon, 1982; Vintage, 1996.

FRANCE

CHAPTER 1

GEOGRAPHY

OVERVIEW

With an area of 640,679 km² (247,368 mi²) and a population of 67.2 million, France (continental mainland + overseas departments and territories) is the forty-second largest country in the world in terms of surface area and the twenty-first largest in terms of population. France is the largest European Union (EU) country in terms of area and the second largest in terms of population. It is the third westernmost country in continental Europe. Its national capital, Paris, in the northern part of the country, is located at 48°51′ N latitude, 2°21′ E longitude. Continental France uses Central European Time (UTC+01:00) in the fall and winter and Central European Summer Time (UTC+02:00) in the spring and summer. France is bordered by Belgium, Luxembourg, and Germany in the north and northeast; Switzerland and Italy in the east; the Mediterranean Sea in the southeast; Spain in the south; the Atlantic Ocean (Bay of Biscay) in the west; and the English Channel and North Sea in the northwest. Natural borders consisting of mountains and seas along three-fourths of its perimeter have enhanced France's territorial security through history (with the notable exception of its northern and northeastern borders). Because of its regular six-sided shape, its residents commonly refer to France as "the Hexagon."

The French landscape is varied. Flat plains and gently rolling hills dominate the northern part of the country. The eastern, central, and southern parts are marked by a series of mountain ranges and massifs—the Vosges, Jura, and Alps in the east and southeast; the Massif Central in the south-central part of the country; and the Pyrenees in the south. Mainland France has 3,427 km (2,129 mi) of coastland. Its main rivers are the Seine, Loire, Rhine, Rhône, and Garonne. Its climate is temperate, with a combination of four different climate types—oceanic and semi-oceanic in the west and Paris region, Mediterranean in the coastal southeast, semi-continental in the northeast, and alpine in areas of higher elevation. France has warm and sunny beaches that are vacation meccas in the summertime, and several famous winemaking regions. Continental France does not have significant underground natural resources. However, French Guiana has oil reserves and New Caledonia has important deposits of nickel.

Continental France is divided into thirteen administrative regions, which are only loosely based on its historical regions. It is further divided into departments (96 in metropolitan France) and local communes (over 36,000 in metropolitan France). There is a moderately strong sense of regional and local identity in France that is deeply rooted in history, culture, and language. It tends to be more pronounced in the Midi (South) and in peripheral regions that became part of France later, such as Brittany and Alsace; however, except in the Basque Country and Corsica, where there are strong nationalist movements, regional identities are generally not a source of political tension. France's north-south divide is rooted in topography (for many, the south begins south of the Loire), history, and language (i.e., the *langue d'oc* romance dialects that evolved from Latin in the south, as opposed to the *langue d'oïl* dialects of the north, including what became modern French). There is thus a historical and cultural rivalry between the north and south. However, the south is well integrated into the national community and Occitan and other southern regional languages and dialects are not widely used on daily basis.

The legacy of its former colonial empires, France has far-flung overseas departments and territories located in twelve different time zones (more than any other nation). Integral parts of the French Republic, Guadeloupe and Martinique in the Caribbean, French Guiana in South America, and Réunion and Mayotte in the Indian Ocean have dual status as departments and regions (*départements et régions d'outre-mer*). In contrast, France's "overseas collectivities" (*collectivités d'outre-mer*) are not fully integrated parts of the French Republic and have varied administrative structures and degrees of autonomy. They include Saint Pierre and Miquelon in the North Atlantic, Saint Martin and Saint Barthélemy in the Caribbean, and French Polynesia and Wallis and Futuna in the South Pacific. New Caledonia, also in the South Pacific, has a special semiautonomous territorial status. France also administers two uninhabited territories: the *Terres Australes et Antarctiques Françaises* (French Southern and Antarctic Lands) and Clipperton Island.

France is an agricultural powerhouse. It has the most arable land and forested acreage among the EU countries and is strongly attached to its rural heritage. The latter fact is evident in the loving care it bestows on thousands of well-preserved villages, nostalgic representations of peasant life, and vigorous defense of the traditional food and beverage products of its country *terroirs*. However, France is now an overwhelmingly urban nation—a trend that dates back to the 1960s. Nearly 85% of the French population lives in or close to a large or midsized city. Cosmopolitan Paris stands apart from France's other cities as it is the national capital, most populous urban area by far (12 million metro population), undisputed economic and cultural center, transportation hub, and only French city with a truly global stature. Its second and third largest cities, Marseille and Lyon, are major European cultural and economic hubs. France counts nineteen other cities that have official status as *métropoles*, or metropolises. They include both larger cities (metro populations of 500,000 to 1 million) of national stature (Bordeaux, Grenoble, Lille, Montpellier, Nantes, Nice, Rennes, Rouen, Saint-Étienne, Strasbourg, Toulon, and Toulouse) and midsize regional centers (e.g., Clermont-Ferrand, Dijon, and Orléans). Additionally, France counts twenty smaller cities with a population of at least 95,000. France's cities are linked by a well-developed transportation infrastructure. Roads designated by the prefix "A" (for *Autoroute*) form the core of France's national highway system. The extensive system of high-speed TGV trains has shrunk distances between French cities. Charles de Gaulle airport outside Paris is France's most important national and international hub for air travel and the second busiest airport in Europe. France's major ports are Dunkerque, Le Havre, Saint-Nazaire (also a shipbuilding center), Marseille (the nation's busiest), and Toulon (home of a major naval base). The trend toward urbanization notwithstanding, France has relatively low population density—104 inhabitants per square kilometer, compared to 233/km² in Germany and 192/km² in Italy.

The diverse makeup of the French people is both ancient and modern. There is an important continental Celtic substratum (the Gauls) dating back to the ninth century BCE. Basques, Ligurians, Greeks, Romans, insular Celts (Britons/Bretons), Germanic peoples (Franks, Alemanni, Burgundians, and Visigoths), Saracens (Muslim Arabs and Berbers), and Norsemen are also part of the demographic constitution of ancient Gaul and early medieval France. In the nineteenth and twentieth centuries, France became a magnet for immigrants from Europe, its onetime colonies, and beyond. A major wave of immigration occurred between 1945 and 1975. This wave included large numbers of immigrants from Spain, Italy, Portugal, Algeria, Morocco, Tunisia, Turkey, sub-Saharan Africa, Vietnam, China, and Eastern Europe. The "immigrant" population of France (i.e., foreign-born naturalized citizens and noncitizen foreign-born residents) is currently estimated to be between 5.7 and 6 million (9% of the population). Roughly 40% of the population can be considered at least partially the product of immigration (*issu de l'immigration*) going back two generations.

Further Reading
Blatt (2019); Farmer (2020); Fort (2014); Gibbons (2003); Robb (2007); Whalen and Young (2014).

Administrative and Territorial Subdivisions

Heir to a centuries-old tradition of political and administrative centralization and state authority that reaches back to age of the monarchy but is often described as "Jacobin" in reference to the Revolution, the French Fifth Republic is unitary rather than federal. Sovereignty, lawmaking authority, and many public services remain in the hands of the central government. However, beginning in 1982, there has been a concerted push in favor of decentralization that has strengthened regional and local institutions.

There are four levels of territorial and administrative divisions below the national level in France. The first—and, increasingly, the most important—is that of the regions. France's regional structure was created in 1960 as a framework for targeted economic development programs. The regions acquired a legal status with administrative and fiscal prerogatives in 1982 and were subsequently strengthened via subsequent reforms. France's regions were restructured in 2016, with their number reduced from twenty-two to thirteen in continental France: Brittany, Normandy, Hauts-de-France, Île-de-France, Grand Est, Pays de la Loire, Centre-Val de Loire, Bourgogne-Franche-Comté,

Nouvelle-Aquitaine, Auvergne-Rhône-Alpes, Occitanie, Provence-Alpes-Côte d'Azur (Sud), and Corsica. Each region has a regional council and a president elected by the members of the council. The councils are not legislative assemblies, but they may levy some taxes. The presidents preside over council meetings and serve as chief executives of their regions. The regions have authority over education, transportation and infrastructure, economic development, social programs, public health, the environment, tourism, and cultural heritage preservation.

The second level of administrative subdivision is that of the departments. Continental France is comprised of ninety-six departments. Each is assigned a two-digit number (e.g., 75 for Paris) that is part of the postal code for localities in the department and featured on car license plates. Created in 1790, the departments reflect the French revolutionary desire to break with the traditional provinces of the *ancien régime* and to create a practical administrative structure based on reason and natural geography. Departments are relatively small in size—the average area is just over 6,000 km^2—and the vast majority derive their name from local rivers and mountains. For nearly two centuries, the departments were the main administrative subdivisions of France and ultimate authority in each department was vested in its prefect, who was named by the French president and represented the national government. The prefect still has primary authority over law enforcement, public safety, emergency response, and the issuing of government documents. However, since 1982, political power at the departmental level has shifted to the departmental councils, and to the council president. Departments are responsible for the local management of numerous national administrative services and have authority in a number of key areas such as education, infrastructure, social assistance, tourism, and culture. Departments are further divided into *arrondissements* and cantons.

Below the department level is the commune (also created during the Revolution), which corresponds roughly to incorporated municipalities and incorporated towns and their surrounding rural areas. There are over 36,000 local communes in continental France. Each is governed by a municipal council and a mayor, elected by the council. Communes are responsible for important services such as urban planning, primary schools, the organization of elections, public sanitation, municipal police forces, public records, and civil marriages.

"Intercommunal" groupings among communes in the same department have been possible since 1890 but were given fiscal powers only in 1999 and were further strengthened as distinct administrative entities in 2015 (NOTRe reform). The formation of intercommunal cooperative entities (*établissements publics de coopération intercommunale,* or EPCI) of varying sizes and types is beneficial to both small rural communities (often too small and lacking the necessary resources to provide for essential services on their own) and to urban areas (cooperation between central cities and the surrounding suburbs). The twenty-one larger urban areas officially designated as *métropoles,* or metropolises, represent a special category of intercommunality. Created in 2010, and significantly strengthened by the MAPTAM reform of 2014, metropolis status represents the highest degree of intercommunal integration, is designed to promote economic development and greater international visibility for France's larger cities, and involves administrative and policy prerogatives second only to those of the regions below the national level. More balanced regional development and equitable access to services across France are a national priority in France that is promoted by the *Commisariat Général à l'Égalité des Territoires* (National Commission for Territorial Equality), which replaced DATAR (*Délégation à l'Aménagement du Territoire et à l'Action Régionale*) in 2014.

A legacy of French colonialism, France's overseas departments and territories, casually referred to as the "DROM-COMs" (DROM = *département et région d'outre-mer*, COM = *collectivité d'outre-mer*), include both entities with the dual status of department and region (Guadeloupe, Martinique, French Guiana, Réunion, and Mayotte) that are from a legal standpoint fully and equally integrated in the governmental and administrative structure of the French Republic (i.e., like the state of Hawaii in the United States) and less fully integrated overseas "territorial collectivities" (Saint Pierre and Miquelon, Saint Martin, Saint Barthélemy, French Polynesia, and Wallis and Futuna). New Caledonia has a special semiautonomous status under the Nouméa Accord (1998) but has voted against independence in several recent referenda.

See also: Chapter 1: Cities; Overseas France; Regional Identities. Chapter 2: Overview.

Further Reading
Cole (2010); Loughlin (2007); Pasquier (2015).

Cities

It is not surprising that Paris should get the lion's share of attention in any discussion of French cities. It is France's only mega city (population: 2.1 million city, 7.1 million consolidated urban area, 12.5 million greater metropolitan area); its only city with global standing; and the undisputed political, economic, and cultural capital of the French nation. The preponderance of Paris was once a source of concern, exemplified by the geographer Jean-François Gravier's influential essay, *Paris and the French Desert* (1946). In response, an effort was made to elevate France's "regional" cities—one that today includes official designation as a "metropolis," which applies to twenty-one urban areas. Indeed, France's other major cities are vibrant places to live and work. Their historic city centers have been preserved and renovated and are accessible to residents thanks to first-rate public transportation and large pedestrian zones. They have shiny new cultural venues designed by cutting-edge architects and festivals celebrating a wide range of art forms that attract international visitors. Mainland France has numerous midsized cities but relatively few truly big ones aside from Paris—forty municipalities (communes) with populations of 100,000 or more but just six with populations of 300,000 or more. The seven largest metropolitan areas in France—all with a population over one million—are (2016 population order) Paris, Lyon, Marseille, Toulouse, Bordeaux, Lille, and Nice. By comparison, Germany has eleven metropolitan areas with populations of 2 million or more. Another cause for concern for policy makers is France's *banlieues*, a term that applies to all suburban areas but is used especially as shorthand for the socially and economically disadvantaged enclaves that lie on the outskirts of France's major cities. The spectacular riots that took place in the *banlieues* in November 2005 are in fact part of an unbroken chain of urban unrest that began in late 1970s.

Marseille is France's second largest city with a population of 861,000 in the city proper and 1.9 million in the surrounding consolidated urban area. Located in southeastern France on the Mediterranean, it is the seat of Bouches-du-Rhône department and Provence-Alpes-Côte d'Azur (PACA) region. Its key monuments and sites include the picturesque Old Port, the bustling La Canebière (an avenue) through the center of town, the Byzantine-Romanesque revival Notre-Dame de la Garde basilica, Stade Vélodrome (the home stadium of the city's beloved Olympique de Marseille soccer team), and the new Museum of European and Mediterranean Civilizations (MUCEM). Known as the "Phocaean City" for its origins as a Greek trading center (Massalia [romanized as Massilia], 600 BCE) and having a mythical reputation as a seedy center of organized crime, Marseille is a multicultural port city with a distinctly Mediterranean and southern French feel. Like Paris (and Lyon), Marseille is divided into semi-self-governing *arrondissements*.

Lyon is the third largest city in France (population: 513,000 city, 1.4 million consolidated urban area). Located at the confluence of the Rhône and Saône rivers in eastern France, it is the seat of Rhône department and Auvergne-Rhône-Alpes region. Its major monuments and sites include the old city (Vieux Lyon) with its large concentration of Renaissance-era buildings, the classically inspired Place Bellecour (the city's main square), the now gentrified neighborhood of La Croix Rousse (the former hub of the city's once thriving silk industry and its rebellious workers, the Canuts), Notre-Dame de Fourvière basilica on a hilltop overlooking the city, and its renovated Opera House. Lyon (Lugdunum) was the administrative capital and largest city of Roman Gaul. Today, it rivals Paris as the gastronomic capital of France and is a center for the banking, chemical, pharmaceutical, biotechnology, and plastics industries. It is also known for its annual four-day-long Festival of Lights in December. The Lyon urban area officially constitutes a "territorial collectivity," which is the functional equivalent of a metropolis.

France's fourth, fifth, and sixth largest cities are Lille (1.2 million consolidated urban area population), Bordeaux (787,000), and Toulouse (768,000). Known for its Flemish flavor, the northern city of Lille is the capital of the Hauts-de-France region and hub of a conurbation that includes the neighboring French cities of Tourcoing and Roubaix and extends into Belgium. Located in a region of older industries, Lille has made a concerted effort to revitalize. The capital of the Nouvelle-Aquitaine region in southwestern France and, located 50 km (31 mi) from the Atlantic Ocean, Bordeaux owes much of its prosperity to the famous winemaking region of which it is the hub (like Nantes, it was also a center of the Atlantic slave trade). Bordeaux is known for its eighteenth-century Place de la Bourse. Located on the banks of the Garonne River and known as the "Pink City" for the color of its brick buildings and terra-cotta

RURAL LIFE

Rural areas comprise 75% of French territory and are home to 20% of the population. Land used for agricultural purposes takes up roughly 50% of the territory of continental France but only 2.7% (2015) of the working population is involved in agriculture (compared to 8.4% in 1980, and 31% in 1955). In the north—e.g., the vast plains of the Beauce (France's "bread basket")—and parts of the south, there are open fields and large farms that specialize in certain crops. In the hinterlands of the Atlantic seaboard and in north-central France, land use is more diversified and farms tend to be smaller. In highland areas like the Massif Central, traditional forms of rural life persist. *Bocage*—small fields bounded by hedgerows—is still prevalent in parts of the west (Normandy). The rural exodus of the 1960s and 1970s has halted. However, most "neorurals" who have moved back the country live close to cities and larger towns. This has left more isolated rural areas depopulated and economically precarious. French people are strongly attached to the countryside and to idealized images of rural life and the peasants (*paysans*) of old. This attachment is seen in the loving attention given to small towns. In 1981, an association was created to promote the "Most Beautiful Villages of France."

tile roofs, Toulouse is the capital of Occitanie region in southern France. It is today the hub of the European aerospace industry (e.g., Airbus). Its most famous monuments are the Romanesque Basilica of Saint-Sernin and the neoclassical Capitole, which serves as its city hall. Other important cities in France include Nantes (647,000 consolidated urban area population), Nice (545,000), Strasbourg (494,000), and Montpellier (465,000). Nantes is a major port and shipbuilding center. Nice is the unofficial capital of the French Riviera. Known for its Gothic cathedral, Germanic Strasbourg is the capital of Grand Est region and the seat of the European Parliament. Montpellier is a university town and one of the fastest growing cities in France.

See also: Chapter 1: Administrative and Territorial Subdivisions; Paris. Chapter 6: Suburbs. Chapter 12: Contemporary Architecture; Modern Architecture.

Further Reading
Carpenter (2014); Cohen (1998); Cole and John (2001); Hewitt (2019); Newsome (2009); Pain and Ardinat (2011); Scargill (1983).

Climate

Given its favorable geographical situation at the western edge of continental Europe at roughly equal distance from the equator and the North Pole (42°–52° latitude), its four different seafronts (Mediterranean, Atlantic, English Channel, and North Sea), and varied topography of mountains and plains, continental France has a generally temperate climate with four regional variants. The climate in the western half of the country—about two-thirds of its total area—is oceanic or semi-oceanic (further inland, e.g., Paris) with mild winters, cool summers, and frequent light rainfall (30 inches/800 mm annual total). In the southern coastal area, the climate is Mediterranean with warm, sunny, and dry summers (sometimes up to three months without rain); very mild winters; and rainstorms in the spring and fall. There is a semi-continental climate in the northeast that reaches down into the northern part of the Rhône Valley, with warm and periodically stormy summers and cold winters with frequent snow. In this zone, the July–January temperature differential can reach 65°F (18°C). A mountain climate (also referred to as alpine or highland) pervades in areas of higher elevation in the Pyrenees, Alps, and Massif Central (central France) regions. Here, the winters are long and cold and there is heavy rainfall spread throughout the year (80 inches/2,000 mm annual total). The average daily temperature for January is 38°F (3°C) in Paris and 43°F (6°C) in Marseille; the July average is 66°F (19°C) and 73°F (23°C), respectively. Corsica exhibits both Mediterranean (along the coast) and mountain climate types (higher elevations inland). The climate in France's overseas departments and territories (Guadeloupe, Martinique, French Guiana, Réunion, Mayotte, French Polynesia, and New Caledonia) is tropical. Most of continental France is not prone to extreme weather. However, there are landslides in the north, avalanches in the Alps and Jura, and flooding in the southeast. French authorities have taken summer heat waves more seriously since the catastrophic heat wave of 2003, which resulted in 15,000 deaths.

See also: Chapter 1: Natural Resources and Environment; North and South; Overseas France. Chapter 4: Agriculture. Chapter 14: Wine.

Further Reading
"Climate and Weather in France" (n.d.).

Historical Sites

France has forty-three UNESCO World Heritage Sites—the fourth highest total in the world (behind Italy, China, and Spain). They include world-famous monuments (e.g., Pont du Gard Aqueduct, Chartres Cathedral, Mont-Saint-Michel Abbey, Palace of Versailles), larger sites of architectural achievement and cultural heritage (e.g., the Loire Valley châteaux district, the Nord-Pas-de-Calais mining basin, and the rebuilt city center of Le Havre), and sites of great natural beauty that are also distinctive human habitats (e.g., Mont Perdu and its surrounding area in the Pyrenees, the Canal du Midi, and the Climats vineyards of Burgundy). France has over 14,000 "classified monuments" of national interest and close to 30,000 "registered monuments" of regional interest. All of France's Gothic cathedrals and other great historic churches are the property of the state, which maintains them as cultural monuments and makes

> **NATIONAL PARKS**
>
> Created in 1960 and restructured in 2006, France's national park system consists of ten parks—Vanoise, Port-Cros, Pyrénées, Cévennes, Écrins, Mercantour, Guadeloupe, La Réunion, Guyane (Amazonian Park), Calanques, and Forests of Champagne and Burgundy. Together, they cover an area of 54,409 km² (33,808 mi²). Additionally, France has fifty-one regional natural parks (PNR)—covering 15% of the national territory and home to 6% of the population—and six maritime natural parks. The national parks each have a "core zone" where the mission is strict preservation of the natural environment and a peripheral "associated zone" where regulated human activity (tourism, hunting, exploitation of natural resources, etc.) is permitted. The PNR balance conservation and the promotion of environmentally sustainable economic activity that benefits the local population. France has two types of protected nature reserves: national nature reserves (RNN, 167 total) and regional nature reserves (RNR, 172 total). Corsican nature reserves (7 total) are analogous to latter category.

them available to local congregations as places of worship. Launched in 1984, France holds an annual celebration of its architectural and cultural heritage in September called "Les Journées du Patrimoine," the model for the EU's European Heritage Days. Historical sites related to World Wars I and II are of particular importance in France. In the case of World War I, there are the sites of major battles (e.g., Verdun and Douaumont Ossuary) and the monuments honoring local war dead, found in practically every French town. In the case of World War II, there are memorials of heroism (e.g., plaques on the walls of buildings in Paris where members of the Resistance were killed) and reminders of barbarism (e.g., the Vel d'Hiv Memorial in Paris, near the former site of the bicycle racing arena where the French police detained French Jews before their deportation to camps). Led by Pierre Nora, French historians have been instrumental in developing the concept of collective memory as embodied in sites of memory (*lieux de mémoire*).

See also: Chapter 1: Paris. Chapter 2: Overview; Timeline. Chapter 4: Tourism. Chapter 12: Gothic Cathedrals; Loire Valley Châteaux; Versailles.

Further Reading
Bern (2014); Blowen et al. (2000); Carrier (2005); Gordon (2018); Hertzog (2016); UNESCO (2018).

Mountains

France has three regions of older mountains formed mostly by the Hercynian orogeny of the late Paleozoic Era. The largest is the Massif Central, an area of rounded volcanic

Puy de Sancy in the Massif Central highland area of central France (Auvergne). With an elevation of 1,886 m (6,188 ft), it is the highest peak in the rugged Massif Central, an area cherished by outdoors enthusiasts. France's other mountain ranges are the Vosges, Jura, Alps, and Pyrenees. (Rogermechan/Dreamstime.com)

mountains (*puys* in French), highlands, and plateaus covering 90,000 km² (56,000 mi²) in central and southern France. The average elevation is 715 m (2,346 ft) and the highest peak is Puy de Sancy at 1,886 m (6,188 ft). On its eastern edge, the Massif Central is separated from the Alps by the Rhône river furrow. The southern part of the Massif Central features the rugged terrain of the Cévennes, the chalky limestone plateaus known as the Causses (e.g., Larzac), and the deep river gorges that cut through these plateaus (e.g., Gorges du Tarn). The Massif Central is known for its spa towns (e.g., Vichy) and mineral waters but was a relatively isolated region until opened by advances in transportation and infrastructure such as the stunning Millau Viaduct. The second largest of these older upland regions is the Armorican Massif, a hilly plateau covering 70,000 km² (43,500 mi²) in northwestern France. In this massif, the average elevation is only 104 m (341 ft) and the highest elevation is 384 m (1,260 ft). The Vosges are the smallest of the older mountainous regions. This range covers 8,700 km² (5,400 mi²) in northeastern France. It separates the historic regions of Alsace and Lorraine, with steeper slopes overlooking the Alsatian plain. The average elevation is 530 m (1,740 ft) and the highest point is the Ballon de Guebwiller at 1,424 m (4,672 ft). Together with the Palatinate Forest massif in Germany, the Vosges are part of one of the most densely forested regions in Europe. They contain rich pasturelands and world-famous vineyards on their Alsatian slopes.

France's three newer mountain ranges (formed during the Cenozoic Era) are the Jura, the Alps, and the Pyrenees. The Jura—from which the term "Jurassic" is derived—cover an area of 5,840 km² (3,630 mi²) in eastern France and form a natural border between France and Switzerland. The average elevation is 660 m (2,165 ft) and the highest peak is Crêt de la Neige at 1,720 m (5,643 ft). The area is very attractive for lovers of outdoor sports. The Vosges and Jura Basins between the two mountain ranges are a historically important coal-mining region. The Alps cover an area of 35,000 km² (21,750 mi²) in southeastern France and form a natural border between France and both Switzerland and Italy. The average elevation is 1,120 m (3,670 ft) and the highest peak—in all of Europe—is Mont Blanc at 4,808 m (15,777 ft). The French Alps include five summits at over 4,000 m (approx. 13,000 ft) and 300 km² (186 m²) of glaciers. Known for its majestic snow-covered peaks and ski resorts, the region has hosted the Winter Olympic three times: 1924 (Chamonix), 1968 (Grenoble), and 1992 (Albertville). The 11.6 km long (7.2 mi) Mont Blanc Tunnel (1965) linking France and Italy is the most important roadway tunnel in the French Alps. Forming a natural border between France and Spain, the Pyrenees cover an area of 18,000 km² (11,200 mi²) in southern France. The average elevation is 1,088 m (3,570 ft) and the highest peak in the French Pyrenees is Pic Vignemale at 3,298 m (10,820). The terrain is both breathtakingly beautiful and foreboding, and attracts mountain climbers, hikers, and skiers. The Pyrenees mountain stages of the Tour de France bicycle race (esp. at Col de Tourmalet) are famously challenging. The region is culturally and linguistically diverse (Basque, French, Occitan, Spanish, Aragonese, and Catalan are all spoken in parts of it) and rich in rural traditions (e.g., transhumance).

See also: Chapter 1: Natural Resources and Environment; Regional Identities. Chapter 4: Tourism. Chapter 15: Outdoor Pastimes; Tour de France; Vacations.

Further Reading
Beattie (2006); Carr (2018).

Natural Resources and Environment

Continental France's underground natural resources are modest: coal (140 million metric tons in reserves but in deep veins therefore hard to mine), iron ore (near depletion), bauxite, zinc, uranium (mostly in the Massif Central), antimony, arsenic, potash, feldspar, fluorspar, and sodium chloride (mines and coastal salt marshes). Its overseas departments and territories are somewhat better endowed: there are oil and gold deposits in French Guiana, and New Caledonia has 25% of the world's nickel reserves. However, France has rich and well-irrigated land: 18.5 million ha (45.7 million acres) of arable land, covering 33% of its mainland territory—ranking seventeenth in the world and first in the EU. French agricultural wealth has been referred to as *le pétrole* vert ("green oil"). Forests cover another 31% of the national territory with

16 million ha (39.5 million acres) on the mainland and another 7 million ha (17.3 million acres) of tropical forests in its overseas departments and territories. France has 153,000 ha (378,000 acres) of inland waterways. The Rhône River is a major source of hydroelectric power and France has the second highest potential for wind power in Europe. It has 5,500 km (3,400 mi) of coastline and its offshore exclusive economic zone (EEZ) is the second largest in the world. The annual haul of the French fishing industry is 480 billion metric tons (70% coastal, 30% deep sea)—twenty-first in the world, fourth in Europe—with room to grow.

France has not always had a stellar record of protection of the environment and biodiversity, but it has made major strides in recent years and has sought to position itself as a world leader in the fight against climate change. France was ranked second in the world in the 2018 edition of the Yale Environmental Performance Index, behind Switzerland (the United States was twenty-seventh). The French government has had a ministry of environment under different names since 1971. Convened in 2007 by President Nicolas Sarkozy, a series of high-level discussions among national and local government officials, industry leaders, workers' representatives, and delegates from relevant NGOs, known as "Le Grenelle de l'Environnement," led to two broad new laws in 2009–2010 and a set of 268 French national commitments on the environment. The goals pertain to climate change and energy policy, biodiversity and natural resources, environmental health, sustainable modes of production and consumption, ecological democracy, and job creation and competitiveness in a green economy. Specific measures taken in recent years include bans on disposable plastic plates, cups, and cutlery (effective in 2020) and on both fossil fuel–powered cars and fossil fuel production (effective in 2040). In December 2015, France hosted the United Nations Climate Change Conference, also known as COP21, which led to the historic Paris Agreement and its overall goal of limiting global warming to below 2°C by the end of the century. When the U.S. administration led by President Donald Trump withdrew from the agreement, President Macron responded via Twitter with an exhortation to "Make our planet great again" and offered research grants to American climate scientists. France's leading political party focusing on environmental issues is the left-leaning EELV (Europe Écologie–Les Verts). High-profile environmental issues include air pollution; water pollution due to toxic chemicals, urban waste, and nitrate runoffs from agriculture; the creation of more sustainable cities; French and EU opposition to genetically modified organisms (GMOs); the protection of endangered plant and animal species; and the large role nuclear power plays (75% of all electricity generated in France comes from nuclear power, to be reduced to 50% by 2025).

See also: Chapter 1: Climate; Mountains; Rivers. Chapter 4: Agriculture; Energy; Tourism. Chapter 15: Outdoor Pastimes.

Further Reading
Bess (2003); Ford (2016); Garrard et al. (2019); Marrani and Turner (2019); Szarka (2008).

North and South

Like many other nations, France has its north and its south, which differ in language, historical memory, cultural traditions, family structures, land use, food, and voting patterns. Where the north ends and the south, or *Midi*, begins is debatable. One relatively common notion is that of an imaginary dividing line that runs northwest to southeast from Saint-Malo to Geneva. Similarly, some economists and geographers observe different historical patterns of economic development north and south of a line from Caen to Marseille. The Loire River also represents a sort of cultural boundary between the two. Others maintain that the *Midi* lies south of the 45th parallel. However, such distinctions are only approximations and lack context. The most historically relevant criterion for distinguishing between the French north and south pertains to the *langue d'oïl/langue d'oc* distinction. In terms of its linguistic development, France can be divided into a northern zone in which the Vulgar Latin vernacular evolved into the "langue d'oïl" dialects of Gallo-Roman—one of which became modern standard French—and a southern zone in which it developed into the "langue d'oc" dialects of Occitano-Roman. The terminology is based on the word used for "yes": "oïl" (i.e., "oui") in the northern dialects and "oc" in the southern ones. In this distinction, *les pays de langue d'oc*, or Occitania (the *Midi*), reach above the 45th parallel into western and central France but stop well short of the Loire River. The present-day regions of Occitanie and Provence-Alpes-Côte d'Azur (also called Région Sud) constitute France's "Deep South." Two other historical factors are part of the north-south distinction. One is the stronger presence of Roman civilization in the south. The other is the stronger presence of the French monarchy in the north.

A number of historical conflicts may be read partially as north-south clashes. The Albigensian Crusade (1209–1229) was ostensibly a military campaign undertaken by the Capetian French king on behalf of the pope to stamp out the heresy of Catharism in the south. However, it had the added objective forcing the Counts of Toulouse into submission. Similarly, the War of the Camisards (1702–1710) was ostensibly about religion. The Camisards were French Protestants (Huguenots) who had taken refuge in the Cévennes region after King Louis XIV had rescinded the Edict of Nantes. The revolt of the Languedoc winegrowers in 1907, led by Marcelin Albert and Ernest Ferroul, also had a regional dimension. Such dramatic tensions are now a thing of the past. France has achieved a high degree of national cohesion and northern language and culture are dominant. Moreover, large numbers of northerners have moved to the south in search of sunshine and jobs. Increasingly, *le Midi* is a benign fixture of France's cultural diversity, a stereotype typically associated with the iconic southern accent of the actor and singer Fernandel (1903–1971), the novels and films of Marcel Pagnol (1895–1974), orange clay tile roofs (as opposed to grey slate ones in the north), the style of farmhouse known as the *mas provençal*, the lavender fields of Provence, pastis (an anise-flavored aperitif from Marseille), ratatouille and bouillabaisse, and the easygoing lifestyle of the Riviera.

The situation of the Occitan language itself is both complex and endangered (according to UNESCO). French is the dominant everyday language of the *Midi* and there is no single recognized standard form of Occitan in wide usage, but six regional dialects: Limousin, Auvergnat, Vivaro-Alpine, Gascon, Languedocien, and Provençal. Estimates of the number of Occitan speakers vary widely. The most conservative figure is 100,000 fluent and regular speakers of all dialects. However, in 2013, the French Ministry of Culture's Advisory Council on the Promotion of Regional Languages estimated 600,000 self-identified fluent speakers of Languedocien (the most prominent dialect of Occitan) and another 1.6 million people claiming some familiarity with it (numbers for "Franco-Provençal" were 80,000 fluent/heritage speakers and 130,000 with some familiarity). By contrast, there were between 12 and 14 million Occitan speakers in the 1920s—roughly one-third the total population of France.

See also: Chapter 1: Climate; Regional Identities. Chapter 2: Timeline. Chapter 4: Tourism. Chapter 5: Protestantism. Chapter 9: Overview; Regional and Minority Languages, Dialects, and Varieties of French. Chapter 14: Regional Culinary Traditions. Chapter 15: Vacations.

Further Reading

Cleere (2001); Garrett (2006); Gentile and Doorslaer (2019); Hale (2010).

Overseas France

France's overseas departments and territorial collectivities are the remnants of once vast former colonial empires. Saint Pierre and Miquelon are two tiny islands that together make up a self-governing territorial collectivity in the northwest Atlantic Ocean, 25 km (16 mi) off the coast of Newfoundland. The territory has a population of just over 6,300. It is the last vestige of the New France colony in North America. In recent years, overfishing and territorial disputes with Canada (fishing rights and off-shore oil exploration) have been sources of concern in this tiny French outpost. Four islands in the Caribbean are under French sovereignty. Guadeloupe (population approx. 450,000) and Martinique (population approx. 385,000) are both full-fledged French departments and regions. As such, they are also part of the EU and use the Euro as currency. Both are in fact small groups of islands that are part of the Lesser Antilles. The capital of Guadeloupe is Basse-Terre; Point-à-Pitre, its largest city. The capital and largest city of Martinique is Fort-de-France. Both islands had plantation economies supported by slave labor in the colonial era. Slavery was permanently abolished in all French territories in 1848. People of African descent make up the great majority of the population of both island groups. While French is the official language, many people speak Antillean Creole. Tourism, agriculture (sugar, bananas), and rum production are important parts of the economy. However, both islands require financial aid from the French government. There is a large community of people from Guadeloupe and Martinique living in mainland France. Referred to as *Antillais*, many moved there in the 1970s. The islands are known for their contribution to popular music (e.g., Zouk) and for having produced numerous major contemporary writers and intellectuals (e.g., Aimé Césaire, Frantz Fanon, Édouard Glissant, and Patrick Chamoiseau from Martinique; Maryse Condé and Simone Schwarz-Bart from Guadeloupe). France's two other Caribbean island territories are Saint Martin and Saint Bathélemy. Sovereignty over the island of Saint Martin is shared between France and the Netherlands. The northern half (population approx. 37,000) is French. The island suffered severe damage from Hurricane Irma in 2017. Saint Barthélemy (population approx. 9,500) is 35 km (22 mi) southeast of Saint Martin near the top of the Lesser Antilles (Leeward Islands). It has an important tourism industry. French Guiana (area 83,534 km^2/32,253 mi^2, population approx. 280,000, capital Cayenne) is located between the country of Suriname and the Brazilian state of Amapá on the northern coast of South America. It too is a French department and region. French Guiana has a high degree of biodiversity, with close to 92% of its territory covered by rain forests. Between 1852 and 1953, it was home to a system of penal colonies, including the legendary Devil's Island. Today, it is the home of Guiana Space Centre in Kourou, which is the main launch site for the European Space Agency. Over half of the population is of mixed African and French descent, whereas Indigenous groups (e.g., Arawak, Teko, and Wayampi) make up 3%–4% of the population. Famous Guianese include the poet Léon Damas, the politicians Félix Éboué and Christiane Taubira, and the singer Henri Salvador.

France has sovereignty over two island territories in the Indian Ocean near Madagascar—Réunion and Mayotte—both of which are departments and regions of France. Réunion (population approx. 866,000, capital Saint-Denis) was claimed by the French in 1642 and first colonized by the French East India Company. Réunion has no Indigenous population but is racially and ethnically diverse, with large numbers of Africans (many the descendants of slaves), Indians, Europeans, Malagasy, and Chinese. Saint-Denis (population 150,000) is the largest French city outside continental France. Réunion Island is dominated by two volcanos, Piton des Neiges and Piton de la Fournaise. Much smaller, Mayotte (population approx. 267,000, capital Mamoudzou), was acquired by France in 1841 and voted to remain French when the rest of the Comoros (Comoro Islands) gained independence in 1975. Fluency in French among the people is low compared to Shimaore (a Bantu language) and Kibushi (a Malagasy language). Islam is the majority religion of Mayotte.

France's most distant overseas territories are in the Pacific Ocean. Wallis and Futuna (population approx. 12,000) is a tiny island group and overseas collectivity in the South Pacific whose closest neighbors are Vanua Levu island of Fiji to the southwest and Samoa to the northeast. French Polynesia stretches across over 3,000 km (2,000 mi) in the South Pacific and is comprised of 118 islands and atolls, out of which 67 are inhabited. This French overseas collectivity, which is also officially designated an "overseas country" in recognition of its degree of self-rule and cultural distinctiveness, is made up of five main island groups, or archipelagos: the Society Islands, the Tuamotu Archipelago, the Gambier Archipelago, the Marquesas Islands, and the

Austral Islands. The most well-known—and populous—island is Tahiti (Society Islands group, 17°40′ S, 149°25′ W, population 190,000), which is where the capital of French Polynesia, Papeete, is located. With its black sand beaches and clear blue water, it is a major tourist destination. It was also made famous in the paintings of Paul Gauguin, who resided there from 1891 to 1893 and from 1895 to 1901, before moving to the Marquesas. A French protectorate was established over parts of Polynesia in 1842 and confirmed following the Franco-Tahitian War of 1844–1847 (Tahiti was officially annexed in 1880). About 67% of the population of French Polynesia is unmixed Polynesian; about 12% is European, and 19% are mixed. French is the language spoken at home by two-thirds of the population, with most of the remainder speaking Tahitian and other Polynesian languages. New Caledonia (population approx. 278,000, capital Nouméa) is a special status French overseas collectivity and archipelago in the southwest Pacific (Melanesia), located 1,210 km (750 mi) from Australia. Relations between the Kanaks (Indigenous inhabitants, 40% of the population) and the New Caledonians, or Caldoches (people of French and European descent, 27% of the population), have been tense; and the independence demands of the former have led to violence, especially in the 1970s and 1980s. The Nouméa Accord of 1998 contained provisions for greater autonomy and a referendum on independence. Held in November 2018, this referendum resulted in a vote of 56.4% in favor of maintaining the political status quo vs. 43.6% in favor of independence. French is widely spoken in New Caledonia. However, Kanak languages are also spoken and taught in school.

See also: Chapter 1: Administrative and Territorial Subdivisions; Natural Resources and Environment. Chapter 2: Overview; Timeline. Chapter 4: Tourism. Chapter 6: Blacks. Chapter 9: Francophonie; Regional and Minority Languages, Dialects, and Varieties of French.

Further Reading
Bonilla (2015); Britton (2018); Chappell (2013); Childers (2016); Hyles (2017); Lambeck (2018); Médea (2010); Mrgudovic (2012); Mrgudovic (2013); Naepels (2017); Ramsay (2011); Redfield (2000); Wideman (2003).

Paris

Known worldwide as the "City of Lights" and to locals as "Paname," Paris is France's national capital, economic and cultural hub, and largest city by far (its metro population of 12.5 million represents 19% of the national total). It is one of just seven "Alpha +" global cities according to the Globalization and World Cities Research Center (2016). Only London and New York are classified as "Alpha ++." Experts believe that it stands to gain ground on London as a European financial capital in the context of the UK's withdrawal from the EU. While France's other urban centers have found enhanced stature in the past twenty to thirty years, Paris still plays a preponderant

A view of the Paris skyline from the left bank facing northwest. Paris is the national capital as well as France's largest city and economic and cultural hub. The Eiffel Tower is near the horizon; the modern skyscrapers of La Défense (business district) are behind it in the distance. (Vvoevale/Dreamstime.com)

role in the economic life of the French nation. The Paris region accounts for nearly one-third of the national GDP and is home to the headquarters of twenty-nine out of the thirty-one French companies in the Fortune Global 500.

Paris takes its name from the ancient Celtic tribe of the Parisii, which had a settlement on the Île de la Cité, an island in the Seine that runs through the city's heart. This was also the site of an important Gallo-Roman town known as Lutetia, or Lutèce in French. Clovis, the Merovingian king of the Franks, made Paris his capital in 508. Since then, Paris's fortune rose with that of the French monarchy. It grew in population and stature thanks also to the economic prosperity of its surrounding region, which includes rich farmland. By the end of the thirteenth century, its population had reached 200,000, making it the largest city in Europe. At the same time, its university was arguably the most prestigious and its regional architectural style—later known as Gothic—had spread throughout Western Europe. While Louis XIV made Versailles the de facto capital in 1682, Paris regained its role as the center of political life during the French Revolution (1789–1799). Throughout the nineteenth and early twentieth centuries, Paris served as the unofficial capital of the international avant-garde—attracting painters, poets, novelists, intellectuals, composers, and political dissidents from around the world (including many Americans like Gertrude Stein, Janet Flanner, Ernest Hemingway, Man Ray, James Baldwin, and Miles Davis). Liberation from German occupation near the end of World War II (August 1944) marked the beginning of a new era and new concerns. One was that Paris was losing standing to New York and other world cities. Another was the fate of the chaotically sprawling and, in large pockets, socioeconomically disadvantaged suburbs (*la banlieue*) just beyond the city limits. The spectacular presidential building projects of François Mitterrand in the 1980s and early 1990s (e.g., Louvre Pyramid) were one attempt to restore some modernist prestige to the city. The highly ambitious Grand Paris project, launched in 2007, includes integration of the suburbs among the goals of its effort to transform Paris into a sustainable and cutting-edge global metropolis and improve the quality of life throughout the region.

Paris covers an area of 105 km² (41 mi²) in an ovular shape bisected by the Seine River, dividing the city into its Left Bank (southern) and Right Bank (northern) halves. At its city limits, the city is ringed by the Boulevard Périphérique, a highway built during 1958–1973 on the location of former fortifications. Paris is divided into twenty distinct and semi-self-governing *arrondissements*. Prominent modern mayors of Paris include Jacques Chirac (1977–1995), Bertrand Delanoë (2001–2014), and Anne Hidalgo (2014–present). Paris's most famous neighborhoods include the university-rich Latin Quarter and Montparnasse, famous for its cafés, on the Left Bank; and the gentrified Marais, the Bastille district, the Grands Boulevards shopping and business district, and former Bohemian mecca of Montmartre on the Right Bank. Government institutions and foreign embassies are concentrated in the Seventh and Eighth *Arrondissements*. The Sixteenth is one of the wealthiest residential districts. La Défense, just beyond the western outskirts of the city is a business district of glittering skyscrapers. The most visited monuments in Paris include Notre-Dame Cathedral (seriously damaged by fire in 2019), Sacré-Cœur Basilica in Montmartre, the Louvre Museum, the Eiffel Tower, the Centre Georges Pompidou, the ornate Garnier Opera, and the Arc de Triomphe (at the end of the Champs-Élysées). Paris has been selected to host the Summer Olympics in 2024.

See also: Chapter 1: Cities; Historical Sites; North and South; Transportation. Chapter 2: Overview; Timeline; Napoleon III and the Second Empire. Chapter 4: Overview; Luxury Goods; Tourism. Chapter 6: Suburbs. Chapter 12: Contemporary Architecture; Fashion; Modern Architecture; Modern Art and the School of Paris; Versailles. Chapter 13: Chanson.

Further Reading

DeJean (2015); Enright (2016); Evenson (1979); Hazan (2010); Higonnet (2002); Jones (2004); Jonnes (2009); Rearick (2011); Sante (2006).

Population

According to French government statistics (INSEE, 2018), France has a population of 67.2 million (65 million in the continental mainland, 2.2 million in the overseas departments), which makes it the second most populous country in the EU after Germany. France has enjoyed a modest population growth in recent years. The population of continental France increased by 2.07% between 2013 (63.7 million) and 2018, compared to 2.52% between 2008 (62.1 million) and 2013. Between 1946 and 1974 (the French Baby Boom), the nation's population increased by 30.4%. By comparison, over a comparable period beginning in 1990 and ending in 2018, it grew by only 14.9%. France's population density is considerably lower than that of its neighbors: 104 inhabitants per square kilometer—compared to 233/km^2 in Germany and 192/km^2 in Italy. France's projected population in 2040 is 73 million.

A closer look reveals several additional demographic trends. One is that while France continues to enjoy modest rates of population growth, natality (birth rates) is in decline. In 2017, France registered 767,000 live births—the third straight year of decline. The natality rate was 12.9 in 2010, 13.3 in 2000, and 14.8 in 1982. Fertility rates have been relatively stable over the past ten years, following modest increases between 1995 and 2008, and a period of steep decline since the mid-1960s. The French fertility rate for 2017 was 1.88 live births/woman, whereas the EU average in 2016 was 1.60 live births/woman. Like women in other countries, French women are now waiting until they are older to have children. In 2018, the average age among French women for the birth of a first child was 30.6, compared to 28.1 in 2010. One conclusion that can be drawn is that most of France's recent population growth is due to immigration.

Another major trend is that the French population is aging. France now has equal proportions of inhabitants under twenty and over sixty: 24%. By comparison, in 1970, 33% of the population was under twenty and just 18% was over sixty. At present, 9.2% of the French population is seventy-five or older. The average life expectancy in France is 79.5 for men and 85.3 for women. The median age in France now stands at 40.5. By comparison, it was 38.3 in 2008 and 34.9 in 1995. The significant aging of the French population presents a serious challenge for French retirement entitlement programs and raises questions about healthcare, the labor market, and the role of senior citizens in French society.

The contours of family life in France are also changing. The number of single-person households and single-parent families is growing. The former represent 30.8% of all French households and the latter make up 22.5% of all families. Marriage rates are in steady long-term decline. There were 227,000 marriages, 192,000 civil unions, and 128,000 divorces in France in 2016. A very slight increase in marriages in the past few years is thought to be due to a "catching-up" effect in same-sex marriages since their legalization in 2013. The number of divorces has been declining in France since the mid-2000s—in correlation to the even greater decline in marriages. However, the long-term trend is that of a significant increase in divorces. There were just 34,663 divorces in France in 1950, 55,612 in 1975, 100,505 in 1985, and 133,909 in 2010. Presently, 44% of all French marriages end in divorce. The number of civil unions (PACS) has been in steady decline since 2010 following a period of rapid increase since their legalization in France in 1998. The most striking long term trend in the domestic life of couples has been the normalization and widespread growth of cohabitation (*l'union libre*), or domestic partnerships outside of marriage or civil union. In 1975, there were fewer than 450,000 French couples cohabitating; by 2012, the total was 8.5 million.

Presently, there are an estimated 500,000 *union libre* couples/households formed annually—significantly more than marriages and civil unions combined. Overall, approximately, 45% of French couples in committed relationships and forming households are married, 30% are in civil unions, and 25% are freely cohabiting. In 2016, 59.9% of all children in France were born out of wedlock. This figure compares to 48.4% in 2005, and 38.6% in 1995. Around 10% of French children under the age of eighteen live in blended families.

Finally, France's population is becoming increasingly diverse in racial and ethnic terms. According to an old cliché, first spread in nineteenth-century textbooks and later given a humorous new take in the popular Astérix comics, the French have supposedly descended from the ancient Gauls. The Gauls were indeed major contributors to the demographic constitution of the French people. However, there are no "ethnic" Gauls in France today—although "Gaulois" has become a slang term for whites. It would be more accurate to say that French "stock" (a problematic term) is itself the product of centuries of migration, invasions, colonization, regional particularism, and mixing. The "outsiders" who helped to forge the French people from ancient times through the early Middle Ages include Celtic Gauls (from ninth century BCE), Ligurians (eighth century BCE), Ionian Greeks (seventh century BCE), Romans (from late second century BCE), Celtic Britons (fourth and fifth centuries CE), various Germanic peoples (fourth through sixth centuries CE), Umayyad Caliphate Arabs and Berbers (eighth century CE), and Norsemen (tenth century CE). The result was a regionally diverse Gallo-Roman substratum that the French monarchy—originally a Frankish (i.e., Germanic) monarchy—melded into a nation over the course of ten centuries (500–1500).

Arguably more visible today are the effects of modern immigration beginning in the nineteenth century. Belgians, Poles, and Eastern European Jews were among the major immigrant groups in the late nineteenth and early twentieth centuries. Large numbers of Spanish and Italians arrived from the 1920s through the 1960s. In the 1960s and 1970s, Portuguese and Algerian immigrants settled in France in roughly equal numbers. (Algeria was part of France until 1962.) An influx of other Maghrebi (Moroccans and Tunisians) occurred in the 1980s, alongside an influx of sub-Saharan Africans, from France's former colonies, who collectively represent the most important category of immigrants in the 1990s and 2000s. France also has large communities of people of Chinese and Vietnamese descent. France's Roma (Romani) minority (perhaps 400,000 people) includes families established in France for many generations and more recent migrants. Depending on their country of origin and custom, French Roma may identify as *Roms*, *Manouches*, *Tsiganes*, *Gitans*, or *Gens du voyage* ("Travelers"). Finally, one must not overlook immigration from other countries in the EU (i.e., other than Spain, Italy, and Portugal)—made easier by the free circulation of people in the Schengen Area (instituted in 1995). There is much heated discussion regarding "foreigners" and "immigrants" in France, but these terms are used imprecisely and often with xenophobic connotations. *Immigré* is a French term that is used to refer to all foreign-born residents of France: naturalized foreign-born citizens, legal resident aliens, and undocumented migrants. The most recent official estimates count between 5.7 and 6.0 million *immigrés* residing in France—approximately 9% of the total population. Another term used to discuss immigration as a broader reality is *issu de l'immigration*—a modifier that designates someone who is a "product of immigration" and includes both actual immigrants regardless of citizenship or official status and their French-born children and sometimes grandchildren. Going back one generation (one parent), roughly 25% of the French population is the product of an immigration background; going back two generations (one parent or grandparent), the total becomes 40%. In 2017, 262,000 foreign nationals received first-time residency permits. Approximately 100,000 foreign nationals applied for asylum in France in the same year. Reluctant though some may be to embrace the fact, France is a melting pot.

See also: Chapter 2: Timeline. Chapter 6: Arabs; Blacks; Immigration. Chapter 7: Marriage, Divorce, Civil Unions, and Cohabitation Today. Chapter 9: Regional and Minority Languages, Dialects, and Varieties of French.

Further Reading
Diebolt and Perrin (2016); Mazui et al. (2015); Rosental (2018).

Regional Identities

Regional identities are relatively strong in France due to their deep historical roots. France's historical regions include French Flanders, Artois, Île-de-France, and Picardy in the north; Champagne, Lorraine, Alsace, Franche-Comté, and Burgundy in the east; Savoy, Dauphiné, Provence, Languedoc, Roussillon, and Foix in the southeast; Béarn (Navarre), Gascony, Saintonge, and Charente in the southwest; Poitou, Saumurois, Anjou, Maine, Brittany, and Normandy in the west; and Orléanais, Touraine, Berry, Nivernais, Bourbonnais, Lyonnais, Auvergne, Limousin, and Périgord in central France. Most were separate provinces under the monarchy—a status they lost under the French Revolution, which subdivided the national territory into smaller departments. Today, French regional identities are expressed mainly through folk traditions, cuisine, language, musical traditions, and stereotypes conveyed through popular culture—like the hit Danny Boon comedy about life in the North, *Bienvenu chez les Ch'tis* (2008, trans. *Welcome to the Sticks*).

Regional identity is most assertive in France's peripheral regions—particularly where political integration in the national community is more recent and attachment to regional languages is stronger. Official insistence on the French language as an essential component of national unity and democracy itself and a corresponding disparaging of regional languages as archaic vestiges of a primitive past date back to the famous *Report on the Necessity and Means to Eradicate Patois and Universalize the French Language* presented to the National Convention in 1794 by Abbé Grégoire, a progressive cleric. The Deixonne Law of 1951 authorized the teaching of regional languages (e.g., Basque, Breton, Catalan, Occitan, Alsatian, and Corsican) in schools as an elective subject. France signed the European Charter for Regional or Minority Languages in 1999 but has not ratified it.

Located on the Armorican Peninsula and Atlantic coast in western France, Brittany (*Breizh* in the Breton language, population 4.6 million) was an independent duchy brought under French royal control in 1532. Political integration came, rather begrudgingly on the part of Bretons, following the French Revolution. Brittany was (and still is) a strongly Catholic region. As such, resentment of the anticlerical policies of the Revolution was one reason—suppression of Breton privileges and resistance to military conscription were the others—for the high level of opposition there to the national government of the Republic in Paris (e.g., royalist uprising of the Chouans, 1794–1800). Brittany is a region with deep Celtic roots. Bretons are descendants of Britons, who began migrating to the Armorican Peninsula from western Britain in the fourth century CE. Breton is a southwestern Brittonic Celtic language that resembles Cornish. The total number of Breton speakers in the region today is around 200,000.

Brittany is a maritime region that played a key role in French exploration and colonization of New France (Canada) and in World War II. It was seriously affected by the massive oil spill caused by the sinking of the Amoco Cadiz supertanker in 1978. Brittany is known for its commercial fishing industry and as a major agricultural region. Details of Brittany's rich cultural heritage include the great Neolithic stone arrangement at Carnac and its Celtic musical tradition, revived by Alan Stivell in the 1970s.

Located between the Vosges mountains and the Rhine River in northeastern France, Alsace (population 1.8 million) was part of the Holy Roman Empire before most of it became French in 1639 as the result of military conquest. France's control over Alsace was formally recognized in the Treaty of Westphalia (Thirty Years' War) in 1648. Other Alsatian cities and towns came under French control somewhat later (e.g., Strasbourg in 1681). However, even under French rule, the Germanic character (language, culture, trade) of the region remained strong. Political integration progressed more quickly after the French Revolution. France ceded Alsace and part of Lorraine to Germany when it lost the Franco-Prussian War (1870–1871). Between 1871 and 1918, Alsace was part of the German Empire, although over 100,000 Alsatians chose exile and pro-French sentiment remained strong in the region. Alsace returned to France following the German Empire's defeat in World War I (1914–1918). It was occupied by Germany during World War II but not formally annexed. With modernization and economic development during the postwar period (1945–1975), Alsace became progressively more French, but regional pride has remained strong. Alsatian is an Alemannic dialect of Upper German that is similar to Swabian and Swiss German. Use of the dialect is in decline but it is still at higher levels than other regional languages in France. According to a 2012 survey conducted for the Office pour la Langue et les Cultures d'Alsace et de Moselle (OCLA), 43% of the region's residents declared that they spoke Alsatian (but did so primarily in a family context). Age is a key factor in Alsatian language use: 74% of people age 60+ in the region speak Alsatian, compared to 54% of people age 45–59, 24% of people age 30–44, and 12% of people age 18–29. Another distinctive feature of Alsatian culture is its large Protestant

(Lutheran) community. Alsatian cuisine, which includes *Baeckeoffe* (a dough-sealed casserole dish with beef, pork, and mutton) and *Flammekeuche* (a thin flat bread with whipping cream, bacon, and onions), is quite popular in the rest of France.

Located in the Mediterranean Sea—11 km (7 mi) from the Italian island of Sardinia across the Strait of Bonifacio and 233 km (145 mi) from Nice—the island of Corsica (population approx. 320,000) has a particularly strong sense of regional and national identity. Considered part of metropolitan (continental) France, Corsica is an administrative region with a higher degree of self-government due to its additional special status as a territorial collectivity. Formerly a possession of the Republic of Genoa, it declared its independence in 1755. However, the fledging Republic of Corsica, led by Pasquale Paoli (1725–1807), did not have control over the entire island. Genoa sold the island to France in 1767, but the renegade republic resisted French rule. France crushed the rebellion in 1769 and Corsica was incorporated into France as a province. Ethnic Corsicans constitute 56% of the population and French mainlanders 29%. Corsican is part of the Italo-Dalamatian branch of Romance languages, as is Italian. It most closely resembles Tuscan. Today, French is the dominant language in Corsica. According to a 2014 survey conducted for the Territorial Collectivity of Corsica, 28% of Corsicans profess to speak the dialect "well" and an additional 11% "somewhat well." There is a relatively strong nationalist movement in Corsica. Extremists have perpetrated over 10,000 acts of violence since 1975, including bombings of police stations and vacation homes (seen as a form of colonialism). Violent pro-independence groups laid down their arms in 2014 but an electoral alliance (Pè a Corsica) of autonomists (Femu a Corsica) and separatists (Corsica Libera) won a majority in the Territorial Assembly in 2017. This led to calls for making Corsican an official language alongside French and pressure on Paris for a greater autonomy. Corsica is known for the citadels that dot the island and the *paghjella* tradition of polyphonic song, recognized by UNESCO as part of the Intangible Cultural Heritage of Humanity.

French Basque Country, or Northern Basque Country (as opposed to the much larger Southern Basque Country of Spain), is a small region (area 2,967 km²/1,146 mi², population approx. 300,000) in the far southwestern corner of France, near the Pyrenees. In administrative terms, it encompasses an "agglomeration community" of 158 local communes, including the cities of Bayonne and Biarritz. Present-day French Basque Country, which was formerly part of the Kingdom of Navarre, became French when the Protestant king of that small country, Henry de Bourbon, became King Henry IV of France in 1589. However, it enjoyed a large measure of autonomy until the French Revolution. The origins of the Basque people are unclear, and they are unlike any other group in Western Europe. Basques are thought to have arrived in the region over 5,000 years ago and have survived countless invasions over the centuries. The Basque language (Euskara), too, is an anomaly. Some conjecture that its origins are non-Indo-European (due to certain similarities with Northeast Caucasian languages like Chechen). Others suggest a possible connection to Ligurian, spoken by inhabitants of southeastern France in pre-Roman times. Basque is spoken today by roughly 50,000 people in French Basque Country (and 700,000 in Spanish/Southern Basque Country). There are nationalists in the French Basque Country. However, it has not generally known the kind of separatist violence that has plagued Spanish Basque Country. Today, French Basque Country is a relatively prosperous region. Basque culture ranges from mythology (e.g., Mari, the goddess of the Earth) to the popular racket game called *pelote*, or *pelota*.

See also: Chapter 1: Administrative and Territorial Subdivisions; North and South; Overseas France. Chapter 2: Overview; Timeline. Chapter 9: Regional and Minority Languages, Dialects, and Varieties of French. Chapter 13: Folk Music. Chapter 14: Regional Culinary Traditions.

Further Reading

Carrington (2015); Douglass and Zulaika (2007); Fischer (2010); Mewes (2014); Northcutt (1996); Schrijver (2006); Woodworth (2007).

Rivers

France has fifty rivers that empty into the sea (*fleuves*) and many tributaries and smaller streams (*rivières*). France's rivers have played an important role in the nation's history and identity; and have provided the names of most of its ninety-six mainland departments. France's five main rivers are the Seine, the Loire, the Rhône, the Rhine, and the Garonne.

The Seine is 776 km (482 mi) long and flows northwest from its source near Dijon through northern France to its mouth in the English Channel at Le Havre, passing through Troyes, Paris, and Rouen. Its main tributaries are the Aube, Yonne, Marne, Oise, and Eure. It is most famous as the river that runs through the French capital. The Loire is 1,012 km (629 mi) long (the longest river in France) and flows north and then west through central and western France from its source in the southern Massif Central to its mouth in the Bay of Biscay (Atlantic Ocean) at Saint-Nazaire, passing through Nevers, Orléans, Tours, and Nantes. Its main tributaries are the Allier, Cher, Sarthe, Creuse, and Vienne. The original powerbase of the French (Frankish) monarchy was the area from the Seine to the Loire, and the rich hunting grounds of the central Loire Valley was one of the reasons that led to the construction of the magnificent Renaissance châteaux for which the region is world famous. The mighty Rhône is 323 km (200 mi) long in France and flows southwest from its source in the Swiss Alps to its mouth in the Mediterranean Sea in the Camargue delta region (famous for its wild horses), passing through Geneva, Lyon, Valence, Avignon, and Arles. Its main tributaries are the Saône, Ain, Isère, Ardèche, and Durance. The Rhône has been important for commercial traffic since the time of the Greeks and the Romans, who founded colonies on the Mediterranean coast and in Provence. It is an important source of hydroelectric power and is at the heart of a major winemaking region. A 190 km long (118 mi) section of the Rhine flows through northeastern France in Alsace (including the outskirts of Strasbourg). The river forms part of France's borders with

Germany and Switzerland and has had great historical and commercial significance to France. The Garonne is 524 km long (326 mi) in France (91% of its total length) and flows north and northwest through southwestern France from its source in Spanish Pyrenees to its mouth north of Bordeaux, where it joins the Dordogne to form the Gironde (France's largest estuary) and empties into the Bay of Biscay (Atlantic Ocean), passing through Toulouse. Its main tributaries are the Ariège, Tarn, and Lot.

See also: Chapter 1: Mountains; Natural Resources and Environment; Paris. Chapter 12: Loire Valley Châteaux. Chapter 15: Outdoor Pastimes.

Further Reading
Coates (2018); Garrett (2011); Pritchard (2011); Sciolino (2019); White (1996).

Transportation

France has an extensive and modern transportation system that was developed with the help of government agencies like DATAR (Délégation interministérielle à l'Aménagement du Territoire et à l'Attractivité Régionale, 1963–2014). As a matter of both tradition and planning, most of France's transportation networks are radial in structure, with Paris at the center. However, France has attempted to correct the potential shortcomings of this system by creating better connections between regional cities and other major European transportation hubs.

France has over 1 million km (620,000 mi) of paved roads and highways, which represents over 20% of the EU total. The vast majority of all French passenger traffic (80%) and freight traffic (85%) travels overland by road. The top tier of the French highway network is the "Autoroute" system, which is equivalent to the U.S. Interstate system. These numbered roads begin with the prefix "A" (other national highways begin with "N" and departmental highways and roads with "D"). Highways A1–A89 form the core of this intercity system, which is comprised of 11,882 km (7,383 mi) of highways. A6 (Paris to Lyon) and A7 (Lyon to Marseille) are known as "Les Autoroutes du Soleil" ("Highways of Sunshine") because they are the main roads used by summer holiday travelers to reach the Mediterranean beaches. The minimum age for obtaining a driver's license for an automobile in France is eighteen. However, one can obtain a learner's permit at age fifteen. Serious road accidents have been a persistent problem, which authorities have tried to address through educational campaigns and stricter enforcement of traffic laws. In 2017, there were 3,684 traffic fatalities in mainland France.

Approximately 10% of both passenger and freight traffic in France travels by rail. France ranks first in Europe for the volume of rail passenger travel. Intercity rail passenger service in France is provided by the SNCF (Société Nationale des Chemins de Fer Français). Launched in 1981, the TGV (Train à Grande Vitesse) system of high-speed trains is a main reason for the prevalence of rail passenger travel in France. In

2017, 110 million passengers traveled by TGV. With the TGV, Lyon is just two hours from Paris, Marseille three hours. The 50 km (31 mi) Channel Tunnel (Chunnel) under the English Channel between France and England, which opened in 1994, has greatly facilitated train and automobile (via rail shuttle) travel between the European continent and Great Britain. Another key component of French train travel is the regional express trains (TER) system, cooperated by regional councils and used by over 330 million people each year.

France ranks fourth in Europe in volume of passenger air travel. International air travel has increased while domestic air travel has declined somewhat due to competition from the TGV. Low-cost carriers are now authorized to operate domestic air routes, and this is expected to help increase domestic air travel (another new alternative to rail travel is intercity bus service, which was deregulated in 2015). The busiest French airports are Paris-Charles de Gaulle (CDG), Paris-Orly (ORY), Nice (NCE), Lyon-Saint Exupéry (LYS), Marseille (MRS), Toulouse-Blagnac (TLS), Basel-Mulhouse (BSL/MLH), and Bordeaux-Mérignac (BOD). As much as 70% of all French air traffic goes through Paris. Charles de Gaulle is the second busiest airport in Europe (after London-Heathrow) and France's only major international hub.

Activity in French ports is somewhat underperforming given France's miles of coastline and numerous seaports. France ranks fifth in the EU in maritime freight traffic handled (Rotterdam alone handles more than all French ports combined). France's three biggest ports are Marseille (fifth in Europe), Le Havre, and Dunkerque. Rouen is the busiest grain shipping port in Europe.

Public transportation in France is well developed. Six French cities have subways: Paris, Lyon, Marseille, Lille, Toulouse, and Rennes. The Paris Métro is the oldest (1900), most extensive (16 lines, 300 stations), busiest (1.5 billion passengers), and most iconic (e.g., the Art Nouveau station entrances designed by Hector Guimard) subway system in France—and one of the best and busiest in the world (second in Europe after Moscow, tenth in the world). The Grand Paris Express project, an integral part of the Grand Paris urban strategic plan, is expected to greatly improve transport in the Greater Paris area. The project involves four new commuter rail lines (slated to begin operation in 2023) as well as the extension of two existing lines, and is projected to cost €38 billion. Tramway (streetcar) systems have proven extremely popular in France since the 1980s. Twenty-nine French cities have a tram.

See also: Chapter 1: Cities; Paris; Rivers. Chapter 4: Trade.

Further Reading
Augé (2002); Boquet (2017); Meunier (2002); Ovenden (2009); Régnier and Brenac (2019); Simmons (2014).

SELECTED BIBLIOGRAPHY
Augé, Marc. *In the Métro.* Trans. Tom Conley. U Minnesota P, 2002.
Beattie, Andrew. *The Alps: A Cultural History.* Oxford UP, 2006.
Bern, Stéphane. *The Best Loved Villages of France.* English ed. Flammarion, 2014.

Bess, Michael. *The Light-Green Society: Ecology and Technological Modernity in France, 1960–2000*. U Chicago P, 2003.

Blatt, Ari J., and Edward Welch, eds. *France in Flux: Space, Territory and Contemporary Culture*. Liverpool UP, 2019.

Blowen, Sarah, et al., eds. *Recollections of France: Memories, Identities and Heritage in Contemporary France*. Berghahn, 2000.

Bonilla, Yarimar. *Non-Sovereign Futures: French Caribbean Politics in the Wake of Disenchantment*. U Chicago P, 2015.

Boquet, Yves. "The Renaissance of Tramways and Urban Development in France." *Miscellanea Geographica*, vol. 21, no. 1, 2017, pp. 5–18.

Britton, Celia. *Perspectives on Culture and Politics in the French Antilles*. Legenda, 2018.

Carpenter, Juliet, and Roelof Verhage. "Lyon City Profile." *Cities*, vol. 38, 2014, pp. 57–68.

Carr, Matthew. *The Savage Frontier: The Pyrenees in History and the Imagination*. New P, 2018.

Carrier, Peter. *Holocaust Monuments and National Memory Cultures in France and Germany since 1989: The Origins and Political Function of the Vél' D'Hiv' in Paris and the Holocaust Monument in Berlin*. Berghahn, 2005.

Carrington, Dorothy. *Granite Island: Portrait of Corsica*. Penguin, 2015.

Chappell, David A. *The Kanak Awakening: The Rise of Nationalism in New Caledonia*. U Hawai'i P, 2013.

Childers, Kristen Stromberg. *Seeking Imperialism's Embrace: National Identity, Decolonization, and Assimilation in the French Caribbean*. Oxford UP, 2016.

Cleere, Henry. *Southern France: An Oxford Archaeological Guide*. Oxford UP, 2001.

"Climate and Weather in France." n.d. *About France*, https://about-france.com/climate-weather.htm.

Coates, Ben. *The Rhine: Following Europe's Greatest River from Amsterdam to the Alps*. Brealey, 2018; esp. ch. 10 ("Borderlines: Strasbourg and Alsace").

Cohen, William B. *Urban Government and the Rise of the French City: Five Municipalities in the Nineteenth Century*. St. Martin's, 1998.

Cole, Alistair. "France: Between Centralization and Fragmentation." *The Oxford Handbook of Local and Regional Democracy in Europe*, eds. Frank Hendriks et al. Oxford UP, 2010, pp. 307–330.

Cole, Alistair, and Peter John. *Local Governance in England and France*. Routledge, 2001; esp. pp. 122–141 ("Governing French Cities").

Crackenthorpe, David. *Marseille*. Signal, 2012.

DeJean, Joan. *How Paris Became Paris: The Invention of the Modern City*. Bloomsbury, 2015.

Diebolt, Claude, and Faustine Perrin. *Understanding Demographic Transitions. An Overview of French Historical Statistics*. Springer, 2016.

Douglass, William, and Joseph Zulaika. *Basque Culture: Anthropological Perspectives*. Center for Basque Studies, 2007.

Enright, Theresa. *The Making of Grand Paris: Metropolitan Urbanism in the Twenty-First Century*. MIT P, 2016.

Evenson, Norma. *Paris: A Century of Change, 1878–1978*. Yale UP, 1979.

Farmer, Sarah. *Rural Inventions: The French Countryside after 1945*. Oxford UP, 2020.

Fischer, Christopher J. *Alsace to the Alsatians?: Visions and Divisions of Alsatian Regionalism, 1870–1939*. Berghahn, 2010.

Ford, Caroline. *Natural Interests: The Contest Over Environment in Modern France*. Harvard UP, 2016.

Fort, Monique, and Marie-Françoise André. *Landscapes and Landforms of France*. Springer, 2014.

Garrard, Greg, et al. *Climate Change Scepticism: A Transnational Ecocritical Analysis*. Bloomsbury, 2019, pp. 175–206 ("Climato-scepticisme in France").

Garrett, Martin. *The Loire: A Cultural History*. Oxford UP, 2011.

Garrett, Martin. *Provence: A Cultural History*. Oxford UP, 2006.

Gentile, Paola, and Luc van Doorslaer. "Translating the North–South Imagological Feature in a Movie: *Bienvenue chez les Ch'tis* and its Italian Versions." *Perspectives*, vol. 27, no. 6, 2019, pp. 797–814.

Gibbons, Bob. *France: Travellers' Nature Guide*. Oxford UP, 2003.

Gordon, Bertram H. *War Tourism: Second World War France from Defeat and Occupation to the Creation of Heritage*. Cornell UP, 2018.

Hale, Julian. *The French Riviera: A Cultural History*. Oxford UP, 2010.

Hazan, Eric. *The Invention of Paris: A History in Footsteps*. Trans. David Fernbach. Verso, 2010.

Hertzog, Anne. "Cultural Policy and the Promotion of World War I Heritage Sites in France: Emerging Professions and Hybrid Practices." *Cultural Policy, Work and Identity: The Creation, Renewal and Negotiation of Professional Subjectivities*, ed. Jonathan Paquette. Routledge, 2016.

Hewitt, Nicholas. *Wicked City: The Many Cultures of Marseille*. Hurst, 2019.

Higonnet, Patrice. *Paris: Capital of the World*. Trans. Arthur Goldhammer. Belknap-Harvard UP, 2002.

Hyles, Joshua R. *Guiana and the Shadows of Empire: Colonial and Cultural Negotiations at the Edge of the World*. Lexington, 2017.

Jones, Colin. *Paris: The Biography of a City*. Allen Lane, 2004.

Jonnes, Jill. *Eiffel's Tower: The Thrilling Story Behind Paris's Beloved Monument and the Extraordinary World's Fair That Introduced It*. Penguin, 2009.

Lambeck, Michael. *Island in the Stream: An Ethnographic History of Mayotte*. U Toronto P, 2018.

Loughlin, John. *Subnational Government: The French Experience*. Palgrave Macmillan, 2007.

Marrani, David, and Stephen J. Turner. "The French Charter of the Environment and Standards of Environmental Protection." *Environmental Rights: The Development of Standards*, eds. Stephen J. Turner et al. Cambridge UP, 2019, pp. 309–322.

Mazui, Magali, et al. "The Demographic Situation in France: Recent Developments and Trends over the Last 70 Years." *Population*, vol. 70, no. 3, 2015, pp. 393–460.

Médéa, Laurent. *Reunion: An Island in Search of an Identity*. Unisa Press, 2010.

Meunier, Jacob. *On the Fast Track: French Railway Modernization and the Origins of the TGV, 1944–1983*. Praeger, 2002.

Mewes, Wendy. *Brittany: A Cultural History*. Signal, 2014.

Mrgudovic, Nathalie. "The French Overseas Territories in Transition." *The Non-Independent Territories of the Caribbean and Pacific: Continuity and Change*, eds. Peter Clegg and David Killingray. Institute of Commonwealth Studies, 2012, pp. 85–103.

Mrgudovic, Nathalie. "Evolving Approaches to Sovereignty in the French Pacific." *Independence Movements in Subnational Island Jurisdictions*, eds. Godfrey Baldacchino and Eve Hepburn. Routledge, 2013, pp. 62–79.

Naepels, Michel. *War and Other Means: Violence and Power in Houlaïlou (New Caledonia)*. Trans. Rachel Gomme. Australian National UP, 2017.

Newsome, W. Brian. *French Urban Planning, 1940–1968: The Construction and Deconstruction of an Authoritarian System*. Lang, 2009.

Northcutt, M. Wayne. *The Regions of France: A Reference Guide to History and Culture*. Greenwood, 1996.

Ovenden, Mark. *Paris Underground: The Maps, Stations, and Design of the Métro*. Penguin, 2009.

Pain, Kathy, and Gilles Ardinat. "French Cities." *Global Urban Analysis: A Survey of Cities in Globalization*, eds. Peter J. Taylor, et al. Earthscan, 2011, pp. 231–235.

Pasquier, Romain. *Regional Governance and Power in France: The Dynamics of Political Space*. Palgrave Macmillan, 2015.

Piette, Gwenno. *Brittany: A Concise History*. 2nd ed. U Wales P, 2008.

Pritchard, Sarah B. *Confluence: The Nature of Technology and the Remaking of the Rhône*. Harvard UP, 2011.

Ramsay, Raylene, ed. *Nights of Storytelling: A Cultural History of Kanaky*. U Hawai'i P, 2011.

Rearick, Charles. *Paris Dreams, Paris Memories: The City and Its Mystique*. Stanford UP, 2011.

Redfield, Peter. *Space in the Tropics: From Convicts to Rockets in French Guiana*. U California P, 2000.

Régnier, Hélène, and Thierry Brenac. "Safe, Sustainable… but Depoliticized and Uneven: A Critical View of Urban Transport Policies in France." *Transportation Research*, vol. 121, 2019, pp. 218–234.

Robb, Graham. *The Discovery of France: A Historical Geography from the Revolution to the First World War*. Norton, 2007.

Rosental, Paul-André. *Population, the State, and National Grandeur: Demography as Political Science in Modern France*. Lang, 2018.

Sante, Luc. *The Other Paris*. Farrar, Straus, and Giroux, 2015.

Scargill, Ian. *Urban France*. Routledge, 1983.

Schrijver, Frans. *Regionalism after Regionalisation: Spain, France and the United Kingdom*. Amsterdam UP, 2006.

Sciolino, Elaine. *The Seine: The River that Made Paris*. Norton, 2019.

Simmons, Graham. *The Airbus A380: A History*. Pen & Sword, 2014.

Szarka, Joseph. "France: Towards an Alternative Climate Policy Template?" *Turning Down the Heat: The Politics of Climate Policy in Affluent Democracies*, eds. Hugh Compston and Ian Bailey. Palgrave Macmillan, 2008, pp. 125–143.

UNESCO. *World Heritage Sites: A Complete Guide to 1073 UNESCO World Heritage Sites*. Firefly, 2018.

Whalen, Philip, and Patrick Young, eds. *Place and Locality in Modern France*. Bloomsbury, 2014.

White, Freda. *Three Rivers of France: Dordogne, Lot, Tarn*. 1952; Pavilion, 1996.

Wideman, John Edgar. *The Island Martinique*. National Geographic, 2003.

Woodworth, Paddy. *The Basque Country: A Cultural History*. Oxford UP, 2007.

CHAPTER 2

HISTORY

OVERVIEW

When does French history begin? One answer often given is 52 BCE, the year that Julius Caesar led the Roman Legion to victory at the siege of Alesia over Gaulish forces under the command of Vercingetorix. The Romans already had a well-established province along the Mediterranean coast of southern Gaul when they began a military campaign to expand their dominion northward. It is a misconception to think of the Celtic Gauls, who had been established in the coveted territory since 900 BCE, as a single people occupying a unified homeland—a notion popularized in nineteenth-century history textbooks that famously proclaimed the Gauls as the "ancestors" of the French. Still, Alesia is significant because it paved the way for the development of a hybrid and increasingly distinct Gallo-Roman civilization that perdured for five centuries. The Christian religious culture of Roman Gaul and linguistically distinct Romance dialects that developed there based on the Vulgar Latin vernacular—including the ancestor of French—are among the most consequential legacies of this civilization, which is the precursor of French civilization.

Between the third and the fifth centuries of the Common Era, Roman Gaul had to contend with invasions by Germanic tribes. These tribes established power centers in different parts of Gaul during the collapse of Roman imperial military and political power—a situation that not only contributed to the regional diversity of what was to become France but also gave the future country its name, which is derived from that of the Franks, a people established in the north that gradually asserted its dominance throughout Gaul. Thus, another contender for France's point of origin is 496 CE, the year that Clovis, the king of the Franks, converted to Christianity. Like the heroic resistance of Vercingetorix, the "baptism of Clovis" is the stuff of national legend. It nonetheless points to the one of the sources of the strength of the Merovingian Frankish kings: their acceptance of Christianity and other cultural characteristics of the territory over which they ruled. The Merovingians were eventually supplanted by the Carolingians—most notably by Charles Martel, who halted the advance of the Umayyad Muslim armies at Tours in 732, and by Charlemagne, who later ruled over much of Western Europe as Holy Roman Emperor (crowned 800). The Frankish kings were the ancestors of the later French ones. Without them, there would have been no France.

The Carolingian Empire broke up following Charlemagne's death and a new status quo in Europe was finalized by the Treaty of Verdun (843 CE) among his grandsons, with Charles the Bald getting the core of present-day France (West Francia). However, a distinct territory is not necessarily a nation. One could venture that the nation building that produced France began in 987 CE, the date that Hugh Capet became king of the Franks, initiating the Capetian dynasty, which continued via a direct line of succession for three-and-a-half centuries (through 1326)—and via its Valois and Bourbon branches, through the proclamation of the First Republic during the French Revolution (1792). One cannot underestimate the importance of this relative dynastic and political stability. Building on the aggressive nation-building and political consolidation of the early Capetian kings and the prosperity of their power base in the north, France was not only the most "cohesive" nation in medieval Western Europe, but also experienced its first golden age as a nation during the twelfth and thirteenth centuries—coinciding with reigns of three powerful and prestigious kings: Philip II (1180–1223), Louis IX (1226–1270), and Philip IV (1285–1314). During this time, Paris became the most populous, the wealthiest and the most intellectually vibrant city in western Christendom. Gothic architecture is emblematic of this French medieval golden age: from its point of origin in the Île-de-France region, it soon spread to thriving urban centers throughout France and then to points beyond.

The period of the Valois and Bourbon kings is commonly referred to as the ancien régime because it fostered the development of the political, social, and cultural status quo—with varied high and low points—that was violently and permanently disrupted by the Revolution. Under the Valois kings, France faced a series of epic crises in the fourteenth, fifteenth, and sixteenth centuries: the Hundred Years' War (1337–1453) with England, Black Death (bubonic plague, 1348–1352), and the Protestant Reformation and ensuing Wars of Religion (1562–1598). The high points of the Valois era include Joan of Arc's rousing patriotic victory at the Siege of Orleans (1429) and the French phase of the Renaissance, which began under Francis I (1515–1547). The French Renaissance featured important literary works in French (e.g., by Ronsard, Montaigne, and Rabelais), the construction of the great Loire Valley châteaux (e.g., Chenonceau, Chambord), the exploration and early colonization of New France (Cartier, Champlain) in present-day Canada, and the spread of scientific knowledge and humanist thought.

France reached new heights of cultural refinement and power as a nation under the first four Bourbon absolute monarchs: Henri IV (1589–1610); Louis XIII, aided by the ruthless Cardinal Richelieu (1610–1643); the fabled Sun King, Louis XIV (1643–1715); and Louis XV (1715–1744). Louis XIV moved the royal court and seat of government to Versailles (1682), which he transformed into a resplendent expression of the French baroque style.

French civilization during the seventeenth and eighteenth centuries was arguably at its all-time zenith. The seventeenth century was characterized by rationalism and the studied order, moral rectitude, and antique grandiosity of French classicism. Its leading figures included the mathematician-philosopher Descartes, the painter Poussin, the playwrights Racine and Molière, and the landscape architect Le Nôtre.

With its lively salons, nascent café culture, academies, and newspapers, Paris was the epicenter of the Enlightenment in the more progressive eighteenth century—characterized by the political theories of Montesquieu and Rousseau; the literary works of Voltaire; Diderot and d'Alembert's *Encyclopedia*; the work of scientists and mathematicians like Buffon, Fourier, Lavoisier, Lamarck, and Laplace; and the libertine *joie de vivre* found in the paintings of Watteau and Fragonard.

At the same time, trouble was brewing. During the reigns of Louis XIV and Louis XV, the intellectual and cultural brilliance of France stood in stark contrast to the decidedly mixed results of numerous wars with rival European powers like Holland, Spain, Austria, Prussia, and Great Britain. For instance, the Seven Years' War (1756–1763) resulted in France's loss of its North American colonial empire and alarming national debt. These problems only grew worse under Louis XVI (1774–1792), whose involvement in the American War of Independence (1775–1783) was something France could ill afford. Dissent was on the rise and took aim at both royal despotism and the egregious inequalities of vestigial feudalism. Ultimately, the ancien régime could not withstand such challenges, and collapsed.

While France has multiple points of origin, "modern" France has only one: 1789, the start of the French Revolution. Historians may downplay the idea of the Revolution as a paradigmatic rupture by stressing both the gradual pace of social and economic changes that were pulling France into the modern world and examples of continuity that span the revolutionary divide, such as the continued French tradition of concentration of power in a centralized national government. Nevertheless, both as a fixture of French national mythology and as the opening act of a century of exceptional political and social ferment, the Revolution encapsulates France's self-conscious desire to reinvent itself as a nation. Based on the principles of liberty, equality, and fraternity and defined in its current constitution as indivisible, secular, democratic, and social, the French refer to this new and improved nation simply as the Republic.

The revolutionary period can be divided into three phases: a liberal phase (1789–1792), a radical phase (1792–1794), and a conservative phase (1794–1799). The first was characterized by critical reforms like the adoption of the Declaration of the Rights of Man and the Citizen (1789), the abolition of feudal privileges (1789), the beginnings of a constitutional monarchy, and controversial measures designed to limit the wealth and power of the Catholic Church. The second phase was characterized by rising unrest, the proclamation of the First Republic (1792), France's invasion by foreign powers sympathetic to the French king, the execution of Louis XVI (1793), civil war between royalists and the republican government, and the Reign of Terror under Robespierre. The third phase was characterized by the Thermidorian Reaction against Robespierre and other radical leaders, the restoration of order by the Directory (1795–1799), military victory against France's foreign adversaries, and the rise of Napoleon Bonaparte—the main perpetrator of a coup d'état that set up the Consulate (1799–1804) and effectively ended the Revolution. The Revolution reshaped the French state and created a new secular political culture and patriotic national identity based on individual rights and popular sovereignty. However, it also resulted in a bitterly divided nation and left a number of problems unresolved, like, the place of the

Catholic Church and Catholicism in French society and the prospect of social and economic justice for the nascent working classes. One result of the unresolved turmoil was that France would experience several regime changes in the nineteenth century, including three republics, two forms of constitutional monarchy, three further revolutions, and two empires: the First Republic (1792–1804), the First Empire (1804–1814), the Bourbon Restoration (1814–1830), the Revolution of 1830, the July Monarchy (1830–1848), the Revolution of 1848, the Second Republic (1848–1852), the Second Empire (1852–1870), the Paris Commune (1871), and the Third Republic (1870–1940).

Aside from momentarily bringing most of Western Europe under the control of the French Empire before his ultimate defeat at Waterloo (1814), Napoleon Bonaparte (aka Napoleon I) is also known for restoring order while preserving some of the achievements of the Revolution (e.g., the Napoleonic Code of 1804). Following the July Revolution of 1830, Louis-Philippe, of the more liberal Orleans branch of the French royal family, headed a more moderate monarchy that catered to the bourgeoisie and promoted industrialization. During the early years of the Second Republic, social programs that helped the working class were created, slavery was abolished in French colonies, and universal suffrage was instituted (for men). However, its first elected president, Louis-Napoléon Bonaparte (the nephew of Napoleon I) staged a coup rather than leave office at the end of his term and instituted the Second Empire in 1852, taking the name Napoleon III. This regime alternated between an authoritarian and a liberal phase but consistently supported economic development and modernized Paris on a grand scale.

Following France's defeat in the Franco-Prussian War (1871), which also resulted in the Paris Commune uprising, the Third Republic was established as a supposedly temporary solution prior to a planned restoration of the monarchy that never happened. By the end of the decade, moderate republicans—the so-called Opportunists (e.g., Gambetta, Simon, Grévy, and Ferry)—had gained the upper hand and set about establishing a true parliamentary regime and laying the foundations a secular republican political culture and national identity. One of the cornerstones of their approach was primary education, which the Ferry Laws of 1881–1882 made compulsory, free, and secular. The regime faced criticism from traditionalist Catholics on the right and socialists on the left; however, progressives rallied around the core values of republicanism during the Dreyfus Affair (1894–1906). Two constants throughout the nineteenth century were industrialization and colonialism, which began its second French chapter in Algeria in 1830 and expanded greatly from the 1860s through the 1890s under both the Second Empire and Third Republic (esp. in Indochina and sub-Saharan Africa).

The nineteenth and early twentieth centuries in France were also a time of intense artistic and intellectual activity. Nearly every style, movement, and school of thought—romanticism, realism, impressionism, utopian socialism, positivism, symbolism, naturalism, modernism, cubism, and so on—was well represented in France. Paris had a lively Bohemian subculture and attracted avant-garde artists and writers from across Europe and beyond and was the artistic capital of the western world. Key French contributors to an emerging modern sensibility included poets (Hugo,

Baudelaire, Rimbaud, Mallarmé, Apollinaire), novelists (Balzac, Flaubert, Zola, Proust), painters (Delacroix, Courbet, Manet, Monet, Gauguin, Cézanne, Matisse), composers (Berlioz, Debussy, Fauré, Satie, Ravel), and a wide array of philosophers and social theorists (Chateaubriand, Constant, Saint-Simon, Comte, Proudhon, Michelet, Bergson, Durkheim). The period also included a long list of great men and women of mathematics, science, and engineering (Cuvier, Geoffroy Saint-Hilaire, Fourier, Cauchy, Foucault, Pasteur, Eiffel, Pierre and Marie Curie).

France was devastated materially and morally by the two world wars of the twentieth century. During World War I (1914–1918), the Western Front cut through northeastern France, so many of the conflict's bloodiest battles took place there (e.g., Verdun, 1916). The French armed forces suffered staggering casualties, but thanks to strong political (e.g., Clemenceau) and military (e.g., Joffre, Foch) leadership, France stood its ground and was among the victorious Allied powers. The period between the two wars was characterized by cultural ferment, political uncertainty, economic crisis, and social unrest. In the field of art and literature, Dada and Surrealism offered a radical critique of bourgeois institutions and mentalities. The Popular Front government of Léon Blum (1936–1937) briefly brought together a left-wing coalition that offered the French working classes some prized new social reforms. World War II (1939–1945) was the greatest turning point in French history since the Revolution of 1789. Following the quick defeat of French forces by the Nazi German war machine in 1940, part of France faced military occupation (1940–1944) while another part was administered directly the reactionary Vichy regime, led by the elderly World War I hero, Marshal Philippe Pétain. The regime collaborated with Nazi Germany and targeted French Jews with anti-Semitic laws and deportation. While large numbers of French people suffered in silence or adopted a wait-and-see attitude, some supported Vichy and collaborated with the German occupiers while others identified with the call to keep up the fight issued from London in 1940 by a relatively unknown general, Charles de Gaulle, who went on to lead a military command and government-in-exile (Free France). The most patriotic joined the Resistance. Following the D-Day invasion of Normandy (June 6, 1944), Resistance actions intensified, and Paris was liberated. The Liberation of France marks not only the end of the occupation but also France's reintegration into the Allied powers set to defeat Nazi Germany in Europe (1945). The Provisional Government of the French Republic, led by de Gaulle, set about not only reestablishing a parliamentary republic but also refashioning France into a prosperous and modern social democracy.

The years 1945–1975 are known as the Glorious Thirty (les Trente Glorieuses). The most "glorious" thing about them was the unprecedented economic growth that France enjoyed during the period. However, this growth also provided the backdrop for a number of other profound institutional and societal changes in a relatively short period of time, such as the constitutional transition from the weaker Fourth Republic (1946–1958) to the Fifth Republic (1958–present), a presidential regime offering greater stability. During the same period, France lost its sprawling empire through decolonization, which in some instances entailed a relatively peaceful process of negotiation and referenda (Morocco, Tunisia, sub-Saharan Africa), but in others involved intense armed conflict (Vietnam, Algeria). France also experienced large-scale immigration that was to make it a more racially and ethnically diverse country. Whereas much of the country still had a nineteenth-century feel in 1945, a demographic boom (leading to a youth boom in the 1960s and 1970s), urbanization, and fast-paced modernization would propel it into the vanguard of the postindustrial twentieth century. One result was the emergence of a markedly more liberal, individualistic, and consumerist society with a large and prosperous middle class. Finally, France faced the humbling reality that it was a midrange power but sought other ways to attain grandeur and play a larger role on the international stage, as a driving force (with Germany) of the European Community (e.g., Treaty of Rome, 1957), as a NATO member with an independent foreign policy (often at odds with the United States), as an advocate for human rights in the world (and neocolonial power in Africa), as a nuclear power, as a leading industrial nation (the world's fifth largest economy by GDP in 1975), as a technological innovator (e.g., the supersonic Concorde, the high-speed TGV train, the internet precursor Minitel), as a pillar of Francophonie, and as a cultural exception in the age of globalization. France remained culturally relevant throughout the Glorious Thirty and 1980s in the fields of existentialism and the Theatre of the Absurd (Sartre, Beauvoir, Camus, Ionesco, Genet), Nouvelle Vague cinema (Truffaut, Godard, Chabrol, Varda), the New Novel (Robbe-Grillet, Butor, Duras), fashion (Dior, Saint Laurent, Cardin, Gaultier), the vibrant chanson tradition of popular song (Montand, Ferré, Aznavour, Brassens, Barbara), nouvelle cuisine (Bocuse, Troisgros, Vergé), and structuralist/post-structuralist "French Theory" (Barthes, Cixous, Kristeva, Derrida, Foucault, Lyotard, Baudrillard). Since 1945, its researchers have also won over thirty combined Nobel Prizes and Fields Medals.

Contemporary French history is synonymous with the Fifth Republic and is customarily divided into smaller chunks corresponding to the terms in office of its presidents—Charles de Gaulle, Georges Pompidou, Valéry Giscard d'Estaing, François Mitterrand, Jacques Chirac, Nicolas Sarkozy, François Hollande, and Emmanuel Macron. The presidency of de Gaulle (1958–1969) is known for the conclusion of the bloody and divisive Algerian War (1954–1962), decolonization in sub-Saharan Africa, diplomatic reconciliation with Germany, France's withdrawal from the unified military command structure of NATO in 1966, and the legalization of contraception. However, desire for greater individual freedom (particularly on the part of the young), tensions on France's overcrowded university campuses, and worker discontent with capitalism soon exploded into the massive protests of May 1968. The presidencies of Pompidou (1969–1974) and Giscard (1974–1981) continued to focus on economic policy and social reforms even as the growth rate of the French economy began to slow and the nation fell into recession.

The presidency of Mitterrand (1981–1995) is arguably the most historically significant of the Fifth Republic after that of the regime's founder, de Gaulle. A Socialist, Mitterrand led the first left-of-center administration of the Fifth Republic. He pursued a progressive policy agenda in the early years of his administration but shifted to fiscal austerity and market-friendly pragmatism as early as 1983. His objective was not only to save the French economy from a free fall, but also to position France as a leader of enhanced European integration. Hence the most important achievement of Mitterrand's presidency was the ratification of the Maastricht Treaty (1992), which created the EU. Mitterrand's presidency is also known for the series of monumental building projects in Paris (e.g., Louvre Pyramid) he undertook and France's decision to fight in the Persian Gulf War (1990–1991) on the side of the U.S.-led coalition against Iraq. During the Mitterrand years, French society began exhibiting tensions related to its increasing multicultural makeup (e.g., the political rise of Jean-Marie Le Pen and the National Front and the Muslim Headscarf controversy) and economic stagnation (e.g., high rates of unemployment). The presidency of Chirac (1995–2007) is known for the latter's willingness to acknowledge French collective responsibility for crimes of the past (e.g., slavery and Vichy's persecution of French Jews), the crisis election of 2002 (Chirac was reelected after facing Le Pen in the runoff round), vocal French opposition to the U.S.-led war in Iraq, French voters' rejection of a proposed EU constitution (2005), and widespread "rioting" in socially disadvantaged suburbs in 2005.

The one-term presidencies of Sarkozy (2007–2012) and Hollande (2012–2017) focused on institutional and economic reforms, including measures affecting retirements, taxes, higher education, and the labor market. Known for his brash style and media exposure, Sarkozy was also very active on the international scene, furthering rapprochement with the United States (e.g., France's rejoining of the unified military command structure of NATO) and taking the lead in the NATO military intervention in Libya (2011). Hollande defeated Sarkozy in the 2012 election and decided not to stand for reelection in 2017 due to historically low approval ratings. One of the signature reforms of his presidency was the legalization of same-sex marriage (2013). In 2015–2016, France suffered a series of lethal terrorist attacks—a commando-style attack on the Paris editorial offices of the satirical newspaper *Charlie Hebdo* (January 2015); coordinated attacks on a number of targets in Paris, including the national stadium, Bataclan concert hall, and sidewalk cafés (November 2015); and the Bastille Day truck attack on the Promenade des Anglais in Nice (July 2016).

Macron, a thirty-nine-year-old centrist, relative political novice, and former investment banker, decisively beat Marine Le Pen for the presidency in 2017. His new political party also won a majority in the 2017 National Assembly elections. Macron's stated intentions as president were to shake up the political and economic status quo with bolder market-friendly structural reforms and to bring France "back" as a leader and innovator on the international stage. He has had some success in these areas. However, he has also been criticized for his imperious style (one derisive nickname for Macron is "Jupiter") and insensitivity to the challenges of working people. Macron has also faced two unprecedented crises: the Yellow Vests protests of 2018–2020 and the global COVID-19 pandemic of 2020–2022. In the presidential election of 2022, Macron faced a stiff challenge from Le Pen, who again qualified for the runoff; however, he ultimately prevailed, becoming the first French incumbent president in twenty years to be reelected. However, the results also showed a French electorate that was both highly polarized and disenchanted with the status quo and a sizeable portion of Macron's comfortable margin of victory was a vote against Le Pen rather than in favor of him and his policies.

In spite of the challenges it faces, France has reasons to be optimistic when looking toward the future. In 2000, the UN's World Health Organization ranked France's healthcare system the best in the world. As of 2015, it was still the world's sixth largest economy by GDP (but slipped to seventh in 2020). In 2016, it was the world's leading tourist destination. In 2017, it ranked nineteenth among 128 nations in the World Economic Forum's Social Progress Index (third in access to basic knowledge, ninth in access to advanced education). Its reorganized universities are climbing in international rankings. It also boasts a younger generation of artists (JR, Kader Attia), public intellectuals (Thomas Piketty, Rokhaya Diallo), filmmakers (Céline Sciamma, Mia Hansen-Løve, Ladj Ly), writers (Florian Zeller, Leïla Slimani, Édouard Louis), musicians (Soprano, Christine and the Queens, Pomme), and fashion designers (Nicolas Ghesquière, Hedi Slimane) on the rise internationally.

Further Reading

Bancel (2017); Bell (2001); Blanchard (2014); Boucheron (2019); Nora and Kritzman (1996–1998); Norwich (2018); Popkin (2020); Rosanvallon (2007); Sowerine (2018); Stovall (2015); Zeldin (1973–1977).

TIMELINE

15,000 BCE	Cave paintings of Lascaux (southwestern France). Nearly 600 animal paintings, including a scene of a man killed in an encounter with a bison.
3,600 BCE	Fortified village of Chassey-le-Camp (eastern France). The site gives its name to the Chassey civilization of the late Neolithic period (4,500–3,500 BCE).
3,300 BCE	Megalithic civilization. Carnac site featuring nearly 3,000 aligned stone dolmens, tumuli, and menhirs (Brittany).
3,100–2,400 BCE	Copper Age. SOM culture (Seine-Oise-Marne, northern France).
1,200–1,000 BCE	Ligurian migration to southeastern France.
900–450 BCE	Migration of Celtic tribes that the Romans call Galli, or Gauls. Development of La Tène culture (500–50 BCE).
600 BCE	Colony of Massalia (present-day Marseille) is founded by Greek merchants from Phocaea in Asia Minor.
125–121 BCE	Roman occupation and colonization of the coastal region of southern Gaul begins.
58–50 BCE	Gallic Wars. Gauls unite under Vercingetroix, whose defeat at Alesia (52 BCE) leads to Roman dominion over all Transalpine Gaul.
52 BCE	The Roman city of Lutetia (Paris) is founded.
177	The first Christian martyrs of Roman Gaul are put to death in Lyon (Lugdunum). Christianity spreads in the region.
253	First Germanic incursions into Gaul.
406	Massive Germanic invasions of Gaul by groups fleeing the advances of the Huns further to the east, including Salian Franks centered in the north.

451	Attila the Hun defeated near Troyes.
481	Clovis is proclaimed king of the Franks. Following his baptism (496), he consolidates Christianity in Gaul and expands the Frankish kingdom via military conquest. Beginning of the Merovingian dynasty.
732	Charles Martel defeats the Umayyad Muslim armies at the Battle of Tours and becomes de facto ruler of the Frankish kingdom.
751	Pepin the Short is crowned king of the Franks, marking the beginning of the Carolingian dynasty.
800	Charlemagne is crowned emperor of the Romans. Carolingian Renaissance (involving art, architecture, literature, education, religion, jurisprudence).
843	The breakup of the Carolingian empire following the death of Charlemagne's son is made official by the Treaty of Verdun; West Francia is ruled by Charles the Bald.
885–886	Viking siege of Paris. Normandy ceded to the Normans (Norseman).
911	Benedictine abbey of Cluny is founded.
987	Hugh Capet is elected king of the Franks. Beginning of the Capetian dynasty.
989–1033	Peace of God movement attempts to limit the violence associated with private wars among the nobility.
1020	Adalberon, Bishop of Laon, outlines the three orders of feudal society.
1066	William the Conqueror, Duke of Normandy, invades England and is crowned king despite remaining a vassal of the king of France.
1096–1099	First Crusade.
1115	Completion of *The Song of Roland*.
1150	The University of Paris is founded.
1163–1250	Construction of the cathedral of Notre-Dame in Paris, marking the ascendance of the Gothic style of architecture.
1180–1223	Reign of Philip II (Philip Augustus), who fights the English and his own nobility to broaden the authority of the French monarchy.
1209–1229	Albigensian Crusade signals the north's ascendancy over the south.
1214	Battle of Bouvines. Philip Augustus defeats a coalition of Imperial (German), English, and Flemish forces.
1225–1230	First part of the *Roman de la Rose* written by Guillaume de Lorris.
1226–1270	Reign of Louis IX (Saint Louis).
1256–1259	Thomas Aquinas teaches theology at the University of Paris.
1285–1314	Reign of Philip IV. Royal administration is strengthened.
1302	Estates General convene for the first time.
1309–1377	Babylonian Captivity: papacy relocates to Avignon.
1337–1453	Hundred Years' War between England and France. The first phase of the war is disastrous for the French (e.g., Crecy, 1348). Joan of Arc helps to shift momentum in favor of the French (e.g., Orleans, 1429).
1348–1352	Black Death (bubonic plague) pandemic.
1358	Jacquerie uprising of peasants and failed revolution led by Etienne Marcel.
1431	Joan of Arc is tried and burned at the stake.
1461–1483	Reign of Louis XI; war with Charles the Bold, Duke of Burgundy.

1470	Printing press comes to France.
1515–1547	Reign of Francis I, who supports the Renaissance.
1519	Work begins on Chambord château in Loire Valley.
1532–1534	François Rabelais publishes *Pantagruel*, followed by *Gargantua*.
1532	Brittany is joined to France.
1534	First voyage of Jacques Cartier to the New World; eastern Canada claimed for France.
1539	Ordinance of Villiers-Cotterêts makes French the official language of kingdom.
1546–1549	Expansion of the Louvre by architect Pierre Lescot (French classicism).
1547–1559	Reign of Henry II. Alliance with Protestant princes in war against Holy Roman Emperor Charles V and persecution of Protestants in France.
1562–1598	Wars of Religion between French Catholic and Protestant factions.
1572	Saint Bartholomew's Day Massacre of Protestants.
1580	Publication of Michel de Montaigne's *Essays*.
1587–1589	War of the Three Henrys. Henry III, Henry of Guise—leader of the Catholic League and ally of Spain—and Protestant Henry of Navarre vie for power.
1589–1610	Reign of Henry IV (Henry of Navarre). Beginning of Bourbon dynasty.
1598	Edict of Nantes guarantees limited religious freedom for Protestants.
1608	Samuel de Champlain founds Quebec (colonization of New France).
1610–1643	Reign of Louis XIII. Cardinal Richelieu pushes for absolute monarchy and French dominance in Europe.
1618–1648	Thirty Years' War between Bourbon France and the Habsburg Empire.
1627–1628	Siege of La Rochelle. Protestant autonomy in France is dealt a blow.
1635	Académie Française is founded.
1637	René Descartes publishes rationalist *Discourse on the Method*.
1637–1638	Nicolas Poussin paints *The Arcadian Shepherds*, a leading example of French classicism.
1643–1715	Reign of Louis XIV. Royal absolutism and French power and prestige reach their pinnacle under the "Sun King."
1648–1653	The Fronde. Cardinal Mazarin and troops loyal to the crown put down the rebellion against absolute monarchy.
1661	Personal Reign of Louis XIV begins.
1670	Theatrical premières of Jean Racine's *Berenice* (tragedy) and Molière's *The Bourgeois Gentleman* (comedy).
1672–1678	Franco-Dutch War. Louis XIV establishes himself as Europe's preeminent ruler.
1682	French court and government relocate to Versailles. The palace and gardens are transformed (1661–1710).
1685	Edict of Fontainebleau revokes the Edict of Nantes, driving French Protestants into exile and underground.
1689–1697	War of the League of Augsburg. French expansionism is held in check.
1702–1704	War of the Camisards. Protestants in the Cévennes region undertake an armed revolt against the French king.
1715–1774	Reign of Louis XV. France is the epicenter of the Age of Enlightenment.

1717	Jean-Antoine Watteau completes *The Embarkation for Cythera*.
1751	Publication of the first volume of *Encyclopédie* by Diderot and d'Alembert.
1756–1763	Seven Years' War against Great Britain and Prussia. France loses its colonial possessions in North America and India.
1762	Publication of *The Social Contract* by Jean-Jacques Rousseau.
1768	Corsica ceded to France.
1774–1792	Reign of Louis XVI: France supports American Independence; unsuccessful attempts to resolve national debt crisis; chain of events leading to the French Revolution.
1781	Noble Reaction. Measures to strengthen the privileges and revenue sources of the aristocracy provoke resentment.
1789–1799	French Revolution.
1789	May 5. The Estates General meet at Versailles.
	June 20. Tennis Court Oath. National Assembly (Third Estate + allied representatives of the clergy and nobility) make pledge to draft a constitution.
	July 14. Parisian crowd storms the Bastille.
	August 4. Abolition of feudal privileges following a series of peasant revolts known as the Great Fear.
	August 26. The Declaration of the Rights of Man and of the Citizen is adopted by the National Assembly.
	October 5–6. Women's March on Versailles.
	November 2. Nationalization of Church Property.
1791	September 3. Constitution establishes a parliamentary monarchy.
1792	August 10. Storming of the Tuileries Palace in Paris. The king is deposed and charged with treason.
	September 20. French revolutionary army defeats the Prussians at Valmy.
	September 22. National Convention proclaims First Republic.
1793	January 21. Execution of Louis XVI by guillotine.
	England, Holland, and Spain join Austro-Prussian War with revolutionary France. Counterrevolutionary insurgency leads to civil war (e.g., Wars of the Vendée, 1793–1796).
	April 6. The Committee of Public Safety is formed.
1793–1794	Reign of Terror led by Maximilien Robespierre.
1794	The École Polytechnique and the École Normale Supérieure are founded.
	July 27. Thermidorian Reaction. Robespierre is executed.
1795–1799	Moderates and conservatives govern France under five-person Directory: French military victories against foreign foes and domestic insurgents.
1799	18 Brumaire coup against the Directory; Napoleon Bonaparte leads three-person Consulate. Revolution ends.
1801	Concordat with the Holy See in Rome (Pope Pius VII).
1804	Napoleonic Civil Code is adopted.
1804–1814	First Empire. Napoleon Bonaparte becomes Napoleon I.
1805–1806	French fleet defeated at Trafalgar (October 1805) by the British; Napoleon victorious against Russians and Austrians at Austerlitz (December 1805), and Prussians at Jena (October 1806).

1808	Continental Blockade. Napoleon attempts to cripple the British economy by cutting off all trade from the continent.
1812	Napoleon invades Russia. Grande Armée retreats, trapped by Russian winter.
1814	France invaded by coalition forces. Napoleon abdicates, exiled to Elba.
1814–1830	Restoration of the Bourbon monarchy. Louis XVIII (1814–1824); Charles X (1824–1830).
1815	Hundred Days. Napoleon returns from exile and seizes power before being defeated at Waterloo (June 18).
1830	French forces take Algiers; annexation of Algeria (1834) marks the start of the second era of French colonialism.
	July 27–29. July Revolution. Bourgeoisie supports English-style parliamentary monarchy.
	Première of *Symphonie fantastique* of Hector Berlioz (romanticism).
1830–1848	Reign of Louis-Philippe of Orleans (July Monarchy).
1833	Guizot Law expands public primary education for boys.
1848	Revolution (February 22–24) deposes Louis-Philippe.
1848–1852	Second Republic: universal suffrage (for men); social programs for unemployed leads to conservative backlash.
1848	Abolition of slavery in French colonies (Schœlcher Decree).
	Louis-Napoléon Bonaparte, the nephew of Napoleon I, elected president.
1851	Bonaparte stages a coup d'état to remain in power at end of term.
1852–1870	Second Empire: authoritarian phase (1852–1860); liberal phase (1860–1870). Louis-Napoléon Bonaparte reigns as Napoleon III.
1853–1856	Crimean War. France and Britain defeat Russia.
1853–1870	Eugène Haussmann (Prefect of the Seine) oversees a massive rebuilding of Paris.
1857	French colonial expansion in Africa—Dakar (Senegal) is founded.
	Publication of Charles Baudelaire's poetry collection, *The Flowers of Evil*; obscenity trial for Gustave Flaubert's realist novel, *Madame Bovary*.
1859	French colonial expansion in Indochina—Saigon (Vietnam) occupied.
1859–1860	Napoleon III intervenes in the Italian War between Piedmont and Austria. France annexes Nice and Savoy.
1863	Édouard Manet's *Luncheon on the Grass* is rejected by the jury of the Salon and exhibited at the Salon des Refusés.
1864	The right to strike is given legal protection.
1870–1871	Franco-Prussian War. Napoleon III is taken prisoner; France loses Alsace and part of Lorraine.
1870–1940	Third Republic.
1870	Crémieux Decree offers citizenship to Jews living in French Algeria; Muslims are denied citizenship by Decree 137 and their subaltern status will be codified by the Indigenous Code (1875).
1871	Paris Commune. French troops are sent in to crush the socialist urban insurrection.
1873–1879	Ultraconservative "Moral Order" government of Patrice de Mac Mahon.

1874	Claude Monet's *Impression, Sunrise* (1872) inspires the coinage of the term "impressionism."
1875	Constitutional laws are passed setting up a parliamentary regime.
1876	Republicans win a parliamentary majority. "Opportunist" moderates (led by Gambetta, Ferry, Grévy, and Simon) form the dominant bloc.
1877	Constitutional crisis. Mac Mahon dismisses the republican prime minister, Jules Simon, and dissolves the Chamber of Deputies.
1879	President MacMahon resigns, succeeded by Jules Grévy.
1881	French protectorate established in Tunisia.
1881–1882	Ferry Laws: primary instruction is compulsory; public schools are tuition-free and secular.
1883–1884	French conquest of Indochina.
1884	Labor unions are legalized. Divorce is once again legalized.
1884–1905	Large-scale colonial expansion via armed conquest in Africa: French Sudan (now Mali, 1890), Guinea (1891), Dahomey (now Benin, 1894), Madagascar (1896), Upper Volta (now Burkina Faso, 1896), Niger (1900), Chad (1900), Mauritania (1902), Ubangi-Shari (now Central African Republic, 1903).
1885	Successful test of Louis Pasteur's rabies vaccine.
	State funeral for Victor Hugo, romantic poet and author of *Les Misérables* (1862).
1886–1889	Boulanger Affair. The nationalist minister of war gains a cult following but backs down from staging a coup.
1889	Eiffel Tower is erected for the Paris World's Fair.
1894–1906	Dreyfus Affair. Jewish army officer Alfred Dreyfus is falsely convicted of espionage. The case inflames anti-Semitic bigotry and rallies progressives to Dreyfus's cause (e.g., Émile Zola's *J'accuse!*).
1895	Lumière brothers hold the first screenings of motion pictures made with their cinematograph.
1898	Pierre and Marie Curie discover the elements radium and polonium.
	Fashoda Incident. War between France and Britain in the White Nile region of Africa is averted.
1901	Law authorizing nonprofit associations. Émile Combes uses it to suppress religious congregations.
1903	First edition of the Tour de France bicycle race.
1905	The SFIO (Section Française de l'Internationale Ouvrière) is founded. Led by Jean Jaurès, the party advocates democratic socialism.
	Passage of law separating church and state.
1907	Pablo Picasso paints *Les Demoiselles d'Avignon*, precursor of cubism.
1912	Morocco becomes a French protectorate.
1913	Ballets Russes production of *The Rite of Spring* (music by Stravinsky, choreography by Nijinsky).
	Marcel Proust publishes *Swan's Way* (vol. 1 of *In Search of Lost Time*).
1914–1918	World War I. Many major battles on the western front take place in northeastern France.
1914	First Battle of the Marne. French and British forces thwart German plans for a swift victory. Trench warfare ensues.

1916	Battle of Verdun. France beats back a major German offensive.
1917	Marcel Duchamp exhibits "readymade" *Fountain* (upside-down urinal) at the Society of Independent Artists show in New York.
1918	November 11. Armistice between France and defeated Germany.
1919	Treaty of Versailles formally ends World War I. Alsace and Lorraine are returned to France.
1920	Congress of Tours. The SFIO splits into Socialist and Communist factions. The latter forms the French Communist Party (PCF).
1924	André Breton publishes the *Surrealist Manifesto*.
1926	Right-of-center government led by Raymond Poincaré stabilizes French franc in effort to restore confidence and promote economic growth.
1929	Construction begins on the Maginot Line.
1931	French economic crisis worsens.
1934	February 6. Right-wing leagues stage violent demonstrations in Paris.
1936	Victory of Léon Blum-led leftist Popular Front coalition in legislative (parliamentary) elections. Reforms include the forty-hour work week, collective bargaining rights, and two weeks' paid vacation.
1938	Munich Agreement. France and Great Britain allow Hitler-led Germany to annex a German-speaking region of Czechoslovakia.
1939–1944	World War II. France's rapid defeat and subsequent occupation (1940–1944) are national traumas.
1940	May through June. German Blitzkrieg offensive in France.
	June 18. General Charles de Gaulle issues appeal from London urging France to continue fighting and forms government-in-exile (Free France).
	June 22. France signs armistice with Germany, which occupies northern France, including Paris and Atlantic Coast.
	July 10. French legislature votes to give Philippe Pétain emergency powers as head of government. Vichy regime begins.
	October 3. First anti-Jewish laws of reactionary Vichy government.
	April 18. Pierre Laval head of government under Pétain. Vichy collaboration with Germany intensifies.
	October 16–17. Vel d'Hiv roundup of French Jews.
	November 8. American forces invade North Africa, prompting the German occupation of the "Free Zone" in southern France.
	Publication of *The Stranger* by Albert Camus.
1943	May 27. Jean Moulin (Conseil National de la Résistance) unifies eight Resistance movements.
	June 3. Conseil Française de Libération Nationale is created in Algiers to coordinate efforts to liberate France.
1944	April 21. Women obtain the right to vote via CFLN decree.
	June 2. The CFLN transforms itself into the Provisional Government of the French Republic (GPRF).
	June 6. D-Day, the beginning of the Allied invasion of Normandy.
	August 25. Liberation of Paris.

1945	May 9. Unconditional surrender of Germany.
	October 4. Social security administration is set up to provide centralized management of health insurance and retirement pensions.
1946	January 20. De Gaulle resigns as head of the provisional government in opposition to proposed new constitution.
1946–1954	First Indochina War. French defeat at Diên Biên Phu (May 7, 1954) marks the end of colonial rule in Indochina.
1946–1958	Fourth Republic. It proves incapable of dealing effectively with decolonization but lays foundation for vigorous economic growth of the "Glorious Thirty" (1945–1975).
1949	April 4. France is a charter member of NATO.
	Publication of *The Second Sex* by Simone de Beauvoir.
1951	April 18. Treaty of Paris creates the European Coal and Steel Community, based on proposal by Jean Monnet and Robert Schuman.
1953	January 3. Premiere of Samuel Beckett's *Waiting for Godot*, an example of the Theatre of the Absurd.
1954–1962	Algerian War.
1956	Right-wing populism (Poujadism) on the rise.
	Independence of Morocco (March 2) and Tunisia (March 20).
1957	Battle of Algiers: urban guerilla warfare by Algerian National Liberation Front (FLN).
	Treaty of Rome. France is among the six original signers of the treaty creating the European Economic Community (EEC).
	Publication of Roland Barthes's *Mythologies*.
1958	May 13. Algerian Crisis. Military leaders in Algiers foment a pro-French public insurrection in open defiance of national government.
	June 2–3. Charles de Gaulle forms a new government (cabinet) with emergency powers and a mandate to draft a new constitution.
	September 28. Constitution is approved by referendum.
1958–present	Fifth Republic. A bicameral parliamentary regime with a reinforced executive branch headed by a strong president.
1958–1969	Presidency of Charles de Gaulle.
1959	May 4. Theatrical release of *The Four Hundred Blows*, directed by François Truffaut, marks the beginning of French New Wave cinema.
	September 16. De Gaulle supports self-determination in Algeria.
1960	February 13. Successful test of first French atomic bomb.
	Referenda resulting in independence of France's sub-Saharan African colonies.
1961	Organisation de l'Armée Secrète (OAS) undertakes terror campaign to prevent Algeria's independence.
	April 22–25. Failed putsch by rogue generals opposed to Algerian self-determination (Challe, Jouhaud, Salan, Zeller) in Algiers.
	October 17. Algerian protest march in Paris. Brutal police suppression results in numerous deaths.
	December 24. Yves Saint Laurent opens his fashion house in Paris.

1962	March 18. Évian Accords recognize Algeria's right to self-determination and bring an end to the Algerian War. Algerian independence triggers mass exodus of Pieds Noirs (French settler population).
	October 28. Constitutional amendment providing for direct popular election of the president approved by referendum.
1963	France and Germany (Federal Republic) sign treaty of friendship.
1965	Presidential election: Charles de Gaulle defeats François Mitterrand, 55.2% to 44.8% (second round).
1966	De Gaulle orders France's withdrawal from the unified military command of NATO and closing of American bases in France.
1968	May 68 protests. Students fight riot police at barricades in Paris Latin Quarter. Snap parliamentary elections favor de Gaulle.
1969	First flight of Concorde supersonic passenger airliner.
	April 28. President de Gaulle resigns after a failed referendum on his plans for reforms of French regional structure and Senate.
	June 15. Presidential election: Georges Pompidou defeats Alain Poher, 58.2% to 41.8% (second round).
1969–1974	Presidency of Georges Pompidou.
1970	December 2. Michel Foucault (post-structuralism) delivers inaugural lecture at the Collège de France.
1971	March 10. Gay rights activists found Front Homosexuel d'Action Révoltutionnaire (FHAR).
	April 5. "Manifesto of the 343" in favor of abortion rights is published.
	June. Épinay Congress leads to the creation of François Mitterrand-led Socialist Party (PS) and adoption of Common Program political agenda with French Communist Party (PCF).
1972	October 5. Anti-immigrant, right-wing National Front is founded by Jean-Marie Le Pen and others.
1973	October 16–17. Oil price hikes and embargo imposed by OPEC nations cause shortages that exacerbate the economic recession.
1974	April 2. President Pompidou dies in office.
	May 19. Presidential election: Valéry Giscard d'Estaing defeats François Mitterrand, 50.8% to 49.2% (second round).
1974–1981	Presidency of Valéry Giscard d'Estaing.
	November 26, 1974. Passage of the Veil Law legalizing abortions during first ten weeks of pregnancy.
1976	October 26. Parliament approves economic austerity measures proposed by Prime Minister Raymond Barre.
1977	January 31. Inauguration of Centre Georges Pompidou (incl. National Museum of Modern Art).
1979	December 24. European Space Agency's first launch of expendable launch vehicle for satellites, Ariane 1.
1981	May 10. Presidential election: François Mitterrand defeats Valéry Giscard d'Estaing, 51.8% to 48.2% (second round).
1981–1995	Presidency of François Mitterrand.
1981	September 17. Abolition of the death penalty.
	November 9. Law authorizing independent local FM radio stations.

1982	January 28. Defferre Law lays the foundation for decentralization of territorial/public administration.
	February 13. Nationalizations in financial and industrial sectors.
	June 21. Inaugural Fête de la Musique.
1983	March 23. Pressure from financial markets and G7/European partners leads to implementation of fiscal austerity policies.
	October 15. Start of the March for Equality and against Racism (Marche des Beurs).
1984	June 24. Massive protests against Savary Plan for the reorganization of French schools seen as a threat to private schools and to parental choice.
	October 15. Founding of the antiracist organization SOS Racisme.
1985	July 10. The Greenpeace vessel *Rainbow Warrior* sinks in Auckland harbor, New Zealand. The French government is responsible.
	October 17. Claude Simon is awarded the Nobel Prize for Literature.
1986	February 28. Single European Act provides for an integrated market and free trade bloc in the EC. Its architect is Jacques Delors.
1986–1988	First political "cohabitation." Following a conservative victory in parliamentary elections, executive power is shared by a president of the left (Mitterrand) and a prime minister (Jacques Chirac) of the right.
1987	March 16. The publicly owned television channel TF1 is privatized.
1988	March 4. Inauguration of the Louvre Pyramid (arch. I. M. Pei) in Paris.
	May 8. Presidential election: François Mitterrand defeats Jacques Chirac, 54.0% to 46.0% (second round).
	November 6. Referendum on self-determination in New Caledonia. Majority approves the Matignon Accords.
1989	May 15. Publication of *In Praise of Creoleness* by Jean Bernabé, Patrick Chamoiseau, and Raphaël Confiant.
	July 14. Bicentennial of the French Revolution with an international musical parade by advertising filmmaker Jean-Paul Goude.
	September 13. Three female Muslim middle school students are suspended for wearing headscarves at school, starting the Headscarf Affair.
1991	January 16. France enters the Persian Gulf War on side of the U.S.-led coalition.
1992	April 22. Opening of Euro Disney theme park (now Disneyland Paris).
	September 20. French referendum on the Maastricht Treaty creating the EU and Euro currency (51% in favor, 49% opposed).
1993	March 28. Conservatives win a majority in parliamentary elections, leading to a second cohabitation (1993–1995).
1994	May 6. Inauguration of Channel Tunnel between Great Britain and France.
	June 23. Start of French military's Opération Turquoise in Rwanda, later accused of facilitating Hutu genocide of Tutsi.
	August 4. Toubon Law requiring the use of French in government and business (incl. advertising) with quotas of French-language songs in broadcasts.

1995	May 7. Presidential election: Jacques Chirac defeats Lionel Jospin, 52.6% to 47.4% (second round).
1995–2007	Presidency of Jacques Chirac.
1995	May 31. Theatrical release of *La Haine* (dir. Mathieu Kassovitz), iconic film about social resentment and violence in the multicultural suburbs.
	July 16. Chirac acknowledges France's collective responsibility for the persecution of French Jews under the Vichy regime.
	November 15. Juppé Plan (austerity-minded entitlement reforms) met with three weeks of strikes.
1997	June 2. Following left coalition's victory in early parliamentary elections, Lionel Jospin (PS) is named prime minister, starting a long period of left-right cohabitation (1997–2002).
1998	June 13. Aubry Law establishing a thirty-five-hour work week.
	July 12. Led by Zinedine Zidane, France wins the men's soccer World Cup for the first time, at home.
1999	November 15. Law establishing civil unions (PACS), available to same-sex couples.
2000	June 6. Gender Parity Law requiring French political parties to field lists of candidates with (nearly) equal numbers of men and women.
2001	May 21. Taubira Law designating the slave trade and slavery as crimes against humanity.
2002	April 21. First round of the French presidential election results in a political "earthquake": Jean-Marie Le Pen (16.86%) qualifies for the runoff.
	May 5. Presidential election: Jacques Chirac defeats Jean-Marie Le Pen, 82.2% to 17.8% (second round).
2003	March 10. Chirac reaffirms French opposition to the U.S.-led push for war against Iraq.
	August 21. Reform of the French retirement system. Benefits of public employees aligned with private sector.
2004	March 15. Law prohibiting "ostensible signs" of religious affiliation in public schools (i.e., Muslim headscarf ban).
2005	May 29. French voters reject ratification of the Rome Treaty (Treaty Establishing a Constitution for Europe, or TCE).
	October 27. Beginning of three weeks of rioting and unrest in French suburbs following the deaths of two teenagers in Clichy-sous-Bois.
2006	April 21. First Employment Contract (CPE) reform making it easier to dismiss employees under the age of twenty-six is repealed after massive protests.
2007	May 6. Presidential election: Nicolas Sarkozy defeats Ségolène Royal, 53.1% to 46.9% (second round). Royal (PS) is the first woman to qualify for the runoff.
2007–2012	Presidency of Nicolas Sarkozy.
2007	June 26. Sarkozy announces the Grand Paris regional urban initiative.
	July 6. Grenelle Environment Round Table starts—multiparty talks on climate change, sustainability, biodiversity, and natural resources.
	August 11. LRU (Pécresse) reform gives French universities greater autonomy.

October 25. First commercial flight of the Airbus A380.

November 20. Immigration law regulating family reunification-based entries. Measures include proof of linguistic competency in French.

2008   February 8. Joint session of the French Parliament ratifies the Lisbon Treaty on the institutions of the European Union.

October 9. J. M. G. Le Clézio is awarded the Nobel Prize for Literature.

2009   March 11. Sarkozy announces France's return to the unified military command structure of NATO.

2010   October 10. Law prohibiting the dissimulation of one's face in public. Its main effect is to ban the wearing of niqabs by Muslim women.

November 10. Minimum retirement age is raised to sixty-two (from 60).

2011   French Air Force takes the lead in the NATO military intervention against the Gaddafi regime in Libya.

2012   March 11, 12, and 19. Terror attacks in Toulouse and Montaubon targeting French soldiers and a Jewish school.

May 6. Presidential election: François Hollande defeats Nicolas Sarkozy, 53.1% to 46.9% (second round).

2012–2017   Presidency of François Hollande.

2012   December 20. Taxation of highest income bracket at 75%. The government repeals measure in January 2015.

2013   January 11. French military intervention in Mali.

April 23. Passage of the Taubira Law authorizing same-sex marriage.

October–November. Red Cap protests in Brittany against new ecotax on highway truck traffic.

December 5. Military intervention in the Central African Republic.

2014   April 16. Prime Minister Manuel Valls announces €50 billion austerity package.

August 1. Opération Barkhane, French military intervention in the Sahel region of Africa to combat armed jihadi groups.

September 20. France joins military operations against the Islamic State (ISIL) in Iraq and Syria.

October 9. Patrick Modiano is awarded the Nobel Prize for Literature.

December 31. Withdrawal of French forces from Afghanistan.

2015   January. Terror attack at the editorial offices of the satirical newspaper *Charlie Hebdo* in Paris leaves twelve dead. (Jan. 7); hostages taken and murdered at a kosher supermarket (Hypercacher) in Paris (Jan. 9); nationwide Republican Rally of National Unity is held (Jan. 11); "Je suis Charlie" ("I am Charlie") becomes rallying cry.

July 24. Law on domestic surveillance and intelligence gathering authorizes telephone and e-mail taps without usual judicial permission.

August 6. Macron Law modernizing labor law and economic regulations.

November 13. Coordinated terror attacks in Paris (130 deaths). The government declares a state of emergency that will last through October 2017.

November 30–December 12. Paris Climate Conference leads to an international agreement on measures to limit global warming.

2016	March 31. Nuit Debout movement begins voicing discontent with economic inequality and government policies favoring big business.
	April 6. Emmanuel Macron founds a centrist/liberal political party subsequently known as La République en Marche (LREM—The Republic on the Move).
	July 14. Terror attack in Nice. A truck is driven onto the Promenade des Anglais during Bastille Day festivities, killing eighty-six people.
	August 8. El Khomri Law implements further labor reforms, including changes to the collective bargaining process.
	December 1. Hollande announces that he will not seek reelection.
2017	January 24. Plan to reduce the share of electricity production of France from nuclear power from 75% to 50%.
	March 20. Start of social unrest and protests in French Guiana.
	April 23. First round of the French presidential election. Centrist Macron (24.01%) and right-wing populist Marine Le Pen (21.30%) qualify for the runoff. Nine other candidates are eliminated, including mainstream conservative François Fillon (20.01%), leftist populist Jean-Luc Mélenchon (19.58%), and Socialist Benoît Hamon (6.35%).
	May 7. Presidential election: Emmanuel Macron defeats Marine Le Pen, 66.1% to 33.9% (second round).
2017–	Presidency of Emmanuel Macron (first term, 2017–2022).
	June 11, 18. Parliamentary elections. Macron's party (LREM) wins an absolute majority in National Assembly (314 out of 577 seats, 54.22%).
	September 6, 19. Hurricanes Irma and Maria strike the French Antilles.
	September 23. Major reform of French labor law, completing the overhaul started by the El Khomri Law.
	September 24. Strong showing by Les Républicains in partial senatorial elections allows conservatives to keep their Senate majority.
	October 30. Counterterrorism law incorporating measures previously available only under a state of emergency.
	December 6. Death of popular music icon Johnny Hallyday.
2018	February 20. Start of general strike in Mayotte to protest against violent crime, poverty, Comorian immigration, and the state of public services.
	March 23–24. Trèbes terrorist hostage crisis. Lt. Col. Arnaud Beltrame (Gendarmes) murdered after taking the place of one of the hostages.
	April 3. Beginning of a three-month long strike of French railway workers to protest the proposed loss of their civil service status.
	July 15. French men's national team beats Croatia 4–2 to win second FIFA soccer World Cup.
	August 5. Anti-sexual harassment law takes effect.
	November 4. Voters in New Caledonia reject independence.
	November 17. Start of Yellow Vests protest movement that continues through 2020. The original cause is an unpopular ecotax on gasoline and diesel. The scope broadens to include issues of economic injustice, democratic governance and political institutions, neoliberal economic policies, and the legitimacy of Macron's presidency.
	December 11. Suspected Islamist extremist kills five people in an attack on the Strasbourg Christmas Market.

2019	February 28. Académie Française approves a report favoring the feminization of masculine names of occupations and professions.
	April 15. Notre-Dame Cathedral in Paris is severely damaged by a fire that starts in the roof. Macron vows to rebuild the monument in five years.
	April 25. Macron announces measures in response to Yellow Vests protests, including reduced number of MPs, lower threshold for citizen-initiated referenda, elimination of tax shelters for the rich, and convention on equitable measures for shift away from nonrenewable of energy.
	May 26. European Parliament elections in France are a setback for Macron's party and allies.
	December 5. Beginning of strikes and protests against planned overhaul of retirement regimes.
2020	France reports first COVID-19 case in Europe. After a series of limited social distancing measures and closures, a national lockdown begins on March 16, to be gradually lifted beginning on May 11.
	June 28. "Green Wave" in pandemic-delayed second round of French municipal elections with a strong showing by EELV and PS with Green mayors elected in Lyon, Marseille, and other cities.
	July 3. Jean Castex replaces Édouard Philippe as PM.
	October 16. Middle school teacher Samuel Paty is beheaded in the Paris suburb of Conflans-Sainte-Honorine. President Macron announces measures designed to reform the practice of Islam in France and combat Islamist extremism.
	November 21. Police beating of Black music producer Michel Zecler sparks unrest.
	October 30. Second nationwide lockdown begins in effort to contain the COVID-19 pandemic after a notable spike in cases since August. The new restrictions are eased at the end of November ahead of the Christmas and New Year's holidays.
2021	January 16. Nationwide COVID-19 curfew implemented.
	April 3. Third nationwide COVID-19 lockdown begins (through May).
	April 24. Law "reinforcing the respect of the principles of the Republic" (aka anti-religious separatism law). Provisions include protections for civil servants (incl. teachers) and the religious neutrality of public services, new penalties for online extremist and hate speech, and stricter controls of civic and religious associations (incl. monitoring of foreign funding, grounds for dissolution, local charters outlining contractual obligation to respect republican values, and secularism on the part of associations receiving public funding).
	June 9. Implementation of COVID-19 "health passes" for access to certain public venues and business; August 9 expansion of the passes (incl. restaurants, cafés, and transport) prompts protests.
	June 20–27. Regional elections: incumbents do well, National Rally underperforms, LREM fails to win a region.
	June 26. Medically assisted procreation procedures authorized for single women and lesbian couples.
	October. *Le Robert* dictionary adds nonbinary pronoun "iel" to its online edition.

November 30. Remains of Josephine Baker reinterred at Panthéon.

December 31. French death toll since beginning of the COVID-19 pandemic: 123,000; total infections: 12 million; 75% of population fully vaccinated.

2022
April 10, First round of the French presidential election. Emmanuel Macron (LREM/centrist, 27.85%) and Marine Le Pen (RN/far right, 23.15%) qualify for the runoff. Ten other candidates are eliminated, including Jean-Luc Mélenchon (LFI/far-left, 21.95%), Éric Zemmour (R/far-right, 7.07%), Valérie Pécresse (LR/center-right, 4.78%), and Dominique Jadot (EELV/ecologist, 4.6%).

April 24: Second round (runoff) of the French presidential election. Emmanuel Macron wins reelection (five-year term), defeating Marine Le Pen, 58.55%–41.45%.

May. In preparation for the June legislative elections, parties of the mainstream center-left and populist far left form a coalition (the New People's Ecological and Social Union, or Nupes) in an effort to deprive Macron of a favorable majority in the National Assembly. Maron's centrist party (LREM) rebrands itself as "Renaissance." Macron starts his second term (2022–2027) by naming Élisabeth Borne prime minister and tasking her to form a new cabinet.

June. Macron (Renaissance and allied centrist parties in Ensemble coalition) fails to win an absolute majority in the National Assembly, Nupes coalition emerges as a potent opposition bloc, and far-right National Rally wins record number of seats in legislative elections.

Charlemagne and the Carolingian Dynasty

Charlemagne (742–814), also known as Carolus Magnus and Charles the Great, is considered the "Father of Europe" because he was crowned emperor of the Romans by Pope Leo III in 800 and he ruled over virtually all of Western Europe—the first time much of the continent had been united since the fall of the Roman Empire. He began as king of the Franks (768), like his father, Pepin the Short (714–768), the founder of the Carolingian dynasty. The family had effectively ruled the Frankish kingdom since the days of Charlemagne's grandfather, Charles Martel (686–741), mayor of the palace of Austrasia and Neustria, who defeated Muslim armies at the Battle of Tours in 732. Endowed with a strong will, natural intelligence, and a forceful presence, Charlemagne was a brilliant military commander who expanded the Frankish kingdom through conquest, taking over Saxony, the Lombard kingdom in northern Italy, the territory of the Avars (Danube river region), and a sliver of northern Spain. Following his invasion of the Iberian Peninsula, his army was ambushed by Basque forces at Roncevaux Pass in the Pyrenees Mountains—a battle later immortalized in the epic poem *The Song of Roland* (composed 1040–1115), which is considered the first masterpiece of French literature. Charlemagne strengthened the Frankish kingdom's ties to the church, giving rise to an early version of divine right monarchy, and his imperial title was in part compensation for crushing a rebellion against the pope. He laid the foundations for a more centralized form of rule, sending *missi dominici* to make sure that his orders were carried out throughout the realm and to check up on the 300 counts appointed as his representatives in different districts. He restructured and expanded the imperial bureaucracy and encouraged the development of a loyal and close-knit circle of aristocratic families at court as well as a wider network of vassals—one of the foundations of the feudal social structure of the Middle Ages. His reign is associated with the Carolingian Renaissance, a great flowering of art, learning, and renewed interest in classical civilization. One of its leading figures was the clergyman Alcuin of York (735–804), who led an educational reform focused on the teaching of the seven liberal arts—divided into the trivium (grammar, logic, and rhetoric) and the quadrivium (arithmetic, geometry, music, and astronomy). Although his empire extended far beyond France and had its capital in present-day Germany (Aachen, or Aix-la-Chapelle), the French consider Charlemagne one of the greatest figures in French history. He served as a model of strong leadership for future rulers like the Capetians kings and Napoleon. However, the Carolingian empire did not survive for long after the death of its founder. Indeed, its three-way partition among Charlemagne's grandsons (Charles the Bald, Louis the German, and Lothair) in 843 was decisive for the future national borders of Europe. Charles received West Francia (formerly Gaul, then Neustria)—the core of present-day France.

See also: Chapter 2: Timeline; Clovis and the Merovingian Dynasty; Louis IX and the Capetian Dynasty.

Further Reading
Costambeys et al. (2011); Dunbabin (2000); Nelson (2019); Riché (1993).

Clemenceau (Georges) and World War I

Georges Clemenceau (1841–1929) was a towering political figure of the Third Republic era. Prime minister as well as minster of war during the final years of World War I and first years of the postwar period (1917–1920), he helped rally France and its allies to victory over Germany thanks to his strong leadership and tenacious commitment to the war effort. Along with the prime ministers of Italy and Great Britain and U.S. president Woodrow Wilson, he was part of the "Big Four" group of framers of the Treaty of Versailles (1919) at the Paris Peace Conference, at which he advocated forcefully for a harder line against Germany, including heavy reparations and disarmament. Clemenceau was from the Catholic and conservative region of Vendée but came from a staunchly republican family. His father was a rationalist freethinker in the Voltairean tradition and an admirer of the French Revolution. Although Clemenceau went to medical school and practiced medicine intermittently, the bulk of his adult life was devoted to journalism and politics. He wrote for and founded numerous newspapers, and was given the nickname "The Tiger" for his fierce commentaries on public issues. He held a range of political offices throughout his career: member of the

Legislative Assembly during the Second Empire, mayor of the Montmartre district of Paris during the Paris Commune of 1871, member of the Chamber of Deputies of the Third Republic (leader of the Radical Republicans and a forceful opponent of Ferry's policy of colonial expansion), an earlier term as prime minister from 1906 to 1909 (taking a hard line against striking miners and implementing the 1905 law of separation of church and state), and senator (1909–1920). He retired from politics after a losing bid for the presidency in 1920. Not surprisingly, he made many enemies in politics. He was falsely implicated in the Panama Scandal and temporarily retired from political life in 1892. His political comeback owed much to his principled stand in defense of Captain Alfred Dreyfus during the Dreyfus Affair (1894–1906). He helped to rally many intellectuals to the pro-Dreyfus (Dreyfusard) position and his newspaper, *L'Aurore*, published novelist Émile Zola's famous open letter to the president of the French Republic, "J'accuse!," accusing the government of anti-Semitism and willfully perpetrating a miscarriage of justice. A man of erudition and culture, Clemenceau was a friend to painters and writers and was a passionate supporter of the work of Claude Monet (1840–1926). When he took over France's wartime government in 1917, an allied victory seemed far from likely. The Americans were not yet fully involved in the war, French public opinion had grown weary, and some French politicians believed that France should either surrender or negotiate a peace agreement with Germany. However, Clemenceau continued to advocate total war until the end and pushed for the appointment of Ferdinand Foch (1851–1929) as the Supreme Allied Commander. The Allies beat back the German Spring Offensive of 1918 and launched an effective counteroffensive that paved the way for an Allied victory. The armistice ending the war was signed on November 11, 1918. Clemenceau felt that Wilson was too much of an idealist. A hardened realist with deep-seated animosity toward Germany, Clemenceau was instrumental in obtaining the harsher terms of the Treaty of Versailles. Retired from political life, Clemenceau toured the United States in 1922 (stops included Lincoln's tomb and Arlington National Cemetery) in an attempt to rally American public opinion against isolationism (he had previously lived in the United States during Reconstruction and been married to an American woman).

See also: Chapter 2: Timeline; de Gaulle (Charles), World War II, and the Fifth Republic; Ferry (Jules) and the Third Republic.

Further Reading
Bredin (1986); Dallas (1993); Greenhalgh (2014); Smith et al. (2003).

Clovis and the Merovingian Dynasty

Clovis (466–511), also known as Chlodovech, was the king of the Franks and founder of the Merovingian dynasty, which ruled much of Gaul for over 200 years. France gets its name from the Franks and the Merovingian dynasty is customarily considered

GAULS

The Gauls were a Celtic people from Central Europe established throughout the territory of present-day France since the fifth century BCE. Many French people have some Gaulish stock in their bloodlines; however, the notion that the Gauls are the common "ancestors" of the French is a myth popularized by the primary school textbooks of the Third Republic era. In fact, there were scores of Gaulish tribes with different dialects and customs; and Gaul was never unified under a single government until it was conquered by the Romans. During the latter part of the nineteenth century, the Gauls made for a good fixture of French popular history and cultural identity because the reference suggested both a nation of astute and hardworking country folk and a tradition of resistance to tyranny. Indeed, France's first national hero was Vercingetorix, an Arverni chieftain who led a coalition of Gaulish forces—valiantly but unsuccessfully—against the Romans at Alesia in 52 BCE. The national myth of France's proud Gaulish ancestry has survived in popular culture (with much ironic self-mockery) in the Astérix series of comics (created by Goscinny and Uderzo in 1959)—named for its feisty protagonist with a moustache like Vercingetorix's.

France's first "national" dynasty. Son of Childeric, Clovis was elected his father's successor in 481 CE and began to consolidate power. Prior to his rise, the multiple Frankish tribes had different rulers and kingship was not necessarily hereditary. The Franks were one of several Germanic peoples who had begun making incursions into Roman Gaul in the third century CE and, fleeing the advances of the Huns further to the east, had launched a massive invasion of Gaul in the early fifth century. Taking advantage of the weakness of the western Roman Empire, the Franks and other Germanic peoples established powerbases in separate regions of Gaul. The Franks were originally based in the north. Clovis defeated Syagrius—the ruler of a small Roman rump state—in 486 CE, the Alemanni in 496, the Burgundians in 500, and the Visigoths in 507. His conversion to Christianity and baptism by Saint Remigius (Remi) in Reims in 496 (traditional date) are the stuff of national legends, which purport that Clovis adopted the faith of his wife, Clotilde, because her deity had brought him victory over the Alemanni at the Battle of Tolbiac. Others have interpreted his baptism as confirming France's identity as a Christian nation and establishing the Franks as the protectors of Catholicism. This traditional view was first articulated by Saint Gregory of Tours (539–594) in his *History of the Franks* and was echoed more recently by Pope John Paul II, who referred to France as the "eldest daughter of the church" when he visited France to celebrate the 500th anniversary of the baptism in 1996. Aside from Frankish territorial expansion and consolidation of Catholic Christianity in post-Roman Western Europe, the reign of Clovis is also known for the compilation of a written legal code known as *The Laws of the Salian Franks*, which combined Roman law, Christian principles, Frankish customs, and royal edicts. Following Frankish rules of inheritance, Clovis's kingdom was split up among his sons after his death.

See also: Chapter 1: Regional Identities. Chapter 2: Timeline; Charlemagne and the Carolingian Dynasty. Chapter 5: Catholicism. Chapter 9: Regional and Minority Languages, Dialects, and Varieties of French.

Further Reading
Geary (1988); James (1988); Terrio (1999); Wood (1994).

De Gaulle (Charles), World War II, and the Fifth Republic

Charles de Gaulle (1890–1970) influenced the destiny of France more than any other French leader since Napoleon and ranks as the towering figure of the twentieth century. His refusal to accept neither France's defeat nor the legitimacy of the Vichy regime in 1940 and quick organization of a government-in-exile helped France emerge from World War II on the side of the victorious Allies. His leadership of the Provisional Government of the French Republic during the final phase of the conflict and early postwar years (1944–1946) helped lay the foundation for the thirty-year period of prosperity known as the Glorious Thirty (1945–1975). His return to political life in 1958 coincided with the creation of a new republic that ultimately proved to be the most stable regime since the Revolution. His presidency (1958–1969)—while not without missteps—was marked by the end of the Algerian War (1954–1962), decolonization in sub-Saharan Africa, and a pivotal role in the European Community.

De Gaulle was born in Lille to a conservative Catholic family. As a young army officer, de Gaulle excelled as a military theorist (*The Army of the Future*, 1934). After the outbreak of war with Germany (January 1940), he commanded an armored division as a temporary brigadier general (the highest rank he ever attained) and later served as undersecretary of state for national defense and war. He left for London when Marshal Philippe Pétain, his former mentor, took the reins of government with plans to seek an armistice with Germany, and delivered the famous radio speech (June 18, 1940) in which he appealed to his countrymen to continue the fight. From London, de Gaulle rallied Free French Forces to continue military operations against Germany and its Axis allies. De Gaulle's organization became the French Committee of National Liberation (CFLN), a de facto government-in-exile. His gambit was audacious because he was an obscure figure without official standing. The British were wary of him; the Americans lobbied for a replacement. One of de Gaulle's most significant achievements during the war was to successfully coordinate with different factions that were part of the Resistance in France with the help of his emissary, Jean Moulin (1889–1943). After the liberation of Paris (August 1944), he marched triumphantly up the Champs-Élysées and installed the Provisional Government of the French Republic (GPRF) in the French capital.

Under de Gaulle, the provisional government introduced major reforms, including women's suffrage and a unified social security system. Irritated by the increasingly partisan nature of the GPRF, de Gaulle resigned. However, he continued to lobby vigorously for a government with a strong executive (e.g., Bayeux Address). The Fourth Republic (November 1946) was virtually the opposite of what de Gaulle wanted. He retired from public life and worked on his memoirs at his home in Colombey-les-Deux-Églises. The Fourth Republic proved ill-equipped to deal with the Algerian conflict. When French generals in Algiers fomented an insurrection of the city's French population on May 13, 1958, the Fourth Republic teetered on the brink of collapse and civil war. Coming out of retirement to assume the duties of prime minister, de Gaulle was given emergency powers to deal with the Algerian crisis and a mandate to help draft a new constitution. The result was the Fifth Republic, a regime with a strengthened executive branch (October 1958), led by de Gaulle himself as president. The French Algerian hardliners were at first delighted by de Gaulle's return to power (for this reason, many on the left likened it and France's regime change to a coup). However, de Gaulle did not see Algeria and France's far-flung empire as essential components of the modern type of French greatness he envisioned. He thwarted an attempted putsch by military

Portrait of Charles de Gaulle (1890–1970) by the French painter Bernard Buffet (1928–1999) for a January 1959 issue of *Time* naming de Gaulle the magazine's 1958 person of the year. A relatively unknown army officer at the beginning of World War II, General de Gaulle seized the moment of France's military defeat by Nazi Germany (June 1940) to create an alternative government in exile (Free France), which later coordinated with the French Resistance and Allied forces to play a pivotal role in the Liberation of France (1944). De Gaulle was also the founder and first president (1958–1969) of the French Fifth Republic—remembered for ending the Algerian War (1954–1962), facilitating decolonization in Africa, promoting economic and social modernization, defending French independence and grandeur on the international stage, and the massive student protests of May 1968. *(Time* magazine)

commanders in Algiers (April 1961) and negotiated the Évian Accords (1962), which ended the atrocious war and paved the way for Algerian independence.

Gaullism involved three key principles: the assertion of France's destiny as a major world power with an independent role on the international stage; a centralized state that would serve as the guiding force behind economic development within a framework of capitalism tempered by an adequate social safety net; and firm anticommunism without subservience to American power. De Gaulle was reelected for a second seven-year term as president in 1965. However, he initially mishandled the massive student protests and worker strikes of May 1968, which reflected a broader desire for greater individual liberty and a less rigid, paternalistic, and conservative society. "The General" survived May 68 but had lost his commanding aura. After voters rejected his proposed reforms of the French Senate and regions in a 1969 referendum, he resigned and died the following year. Today, Gaullism still resonates, and de Gaulle is revered across the political spectrum in France.

See also: Chapter 2: Timeline; Clemenceau (Georges) and World War I; Ferry (Jules) and the Third Republic; Mitterrand (François) and France in the 1980s and 90s. Chapter 3: Overview; Presidency and Executive Branch; Republic; Right.

Further Reading

Berstein (1993); Chafer (2002); Chapman (2018); Cooper (2014); Evans (2012); Feenberg and Freedman (2001); Gildea (2015); Hazareesingh (2012); Jackson (2001); Jackson (2018); Naylor (2000); Nester (2014); Nord (2015); Ross (1995); Shennan (1989); Shepard (2006).

VICHY FRANCE

Vichy France refers to the French regime (1940–1944) established in the wake of France's surrender to Nazi Germany at the beginning of World War II—so named because it was based in the resort town of Vichy in central France. The regime was led by the elderly World War I military hero, Philippe Pétain (1856–1951). It legally represented the French state throughout the country, although its authority was less encumbered by the Germans in the unoccupied "Free Zone" in central and southern France. While some average Frenchmen believed that the conservative regime, on reasonably good terms with Germany, might help alleviate French suffering during the ongoing war in Europe and continued German occupation of half of France, French reactionaries and authoritarians saw it as an opportunity to scuttle the despised liberal Republic. Under Pétain, the Vichy regime actively collaborated with Nazi Germany, proactively implemented policies that deprived French Jews of their civil rights, rounded up and deported Jews (using the French police) without German coercion, carried out a wide range of policies that were resolutely antidemocratic and antimodern in nature, and actively fought against the French Resistance. The regime's master plan was a traditionalist "National Revolution," symbolized in its motto, "Work, Family, Homeland," which took the place of the Republic's "Liberty, Equality, Fraternity." Pétain maintained cordial relations with American diplomats (who were suspicious of Charles de Gaulle) and practiced a wait-and-see attitude in his later relations with the Germans, after momentum had shifted in favor of the Allied powers. He was convicted of treason after the war. However, the provisional government of France, led by de Gaulle, commuted his death sentence to life imprisonment. The legacy of Vichy remains a complicated and sensitive topic in France (e.g., historian Henry Rousso's concept of the "Vichy Syndrome"). The consensus view is now that the regime was guilty of crimes against humanity and is emblematic of the French nation's collective moral failings during the war years. The first French leader to formally acknowledge France's collective responsibility for the persecution of French Jews and other crimes committed by the Vichy regime was Jacques Chirac, in 1995. However, Vichy was one of the topics raised in the 2017 presidential debate between Emmanuel Macron and Marine Le Pen, who took issue with the consensus.

Ferry (Jules) and the Third Republic

Jules Ferry (1832–1893) was one of the most prominent political leaders of the early decades of the Third Republic (1870–1940). He is remembered chiefly as the "father of the republican school" for his secularist reforms of public education and as one of the architects of the major expansion of the French colonial empire at the end of the nineteenth century. Originally from the Vosges department in northeastern France and a lawyer by training, he was an opposition member of Parliament during the final years of the Bonapartist regime before holding several high-level offices under the Third Republic—mayor of Paris, member of the Chamber of Deputies (National Legislative Assembly), minister of public instruction (education), president of the Council of Ministers (prime minster), minister of foreign affairs, senator, and president of the French Senate. He was shot by a mentally imbalanced assassin and died in 1893. The Republic established in the wake of France's defeat in the Franco-Prussian War (1870) was originally intended as a temporary arrangement and did not get a full set of constitutional laws until 1875. However, a series of events allowed it to develop into a truly democratic parliamentary regime—the first stable and broadly supported regime of its type in French history. These events included a failed attempt to restore the monarchy in 1873 and a constitutional crisis in 1877 that was ultimately decided in the Republicans' favor—caused by the archconservative, authoritarian president, Patrice de MacMahon's (1808–1893) refusal to accept republican victories in parliamentary elections. Ferry was part of a group of moderate republicans known as the Opportunists, who believed that a "republican" republic could be established within the existing institutional framework and political circumstances and did not require another revolution. The Opportunists—whose leaders also included Léon Gambetta (1838–1882), Jules Grévy, and Jules Simon—appealed to rural voters by stressing order, education, and gradual progress. They were socially conservative (i.e., not overly sympathetic to the workers' movement), politically moderate, and culturally progressive (defenders of individual rights and staunch opponents of ecclesiastical influence). Ferry's crowning achievement was a series of laws in 1881–1882 by which education was made free, compulsory, and secular. The last point (*Laïcité*) proved controversial since it essentially involved a forcible separation of church and school. The Ferry Laws exacerbated the domestic cold war between conservative and traditionalist Catholics, who tended to favor a restoration of the monarchy and could not conceive of French identity without the Catholic faith at its core, and republicans, who understood that public education could play a major role in building a moderate republican consensus. This Franco-French culture war took generations to subside and is not completely forgotten even today. For the French left, Ferry has been generally viewed as a hero and a founding father. However, his support for aggressive expansion of the French colonial empire (e.g., Tunisia, the Tonkin and Annam regions of central Vietnam, Madagascar, and the French Congo), which did not enjoy broad popular support at the time, has complicated his legacy.

See also: Chapter 2: Timeline; Clemenceau (Georges) and World War I; de Gaulle (Charles), World War II, and the Fifth Republic; Napoleon III and the Second Empire. Chapter 3: Left; Republic. Chapter 5: Laïcité. Chapter 8: Republicanism and Public Schools.

Further Reading

Aldrich (1996); Brocheux (2009); Chafer and Sackur (2001); Conklin (1997); Hazareesingh (2002); Mayeur and Rebérioux (1984); Nord (1995); Singer (1975); Thomas (2011); Weber (1976).

FRENCH COLONIAL EMPIRE AND DECOLONIZATION

France's first colonial empire—from the sixteenth through the eighteenth centuries—centered on North America (Eastern Canada, or New France), the West Indies (Martinique, Guadeloupe, Haiti), slave trade ports on the Atlantic coast of Africa (Dakar), and the Indian Ocean (Pondicherry, Reunion, Mauritius). New France was lost at the end of the Seven Years' War against Great Britain (1763). The second French colonial empire—built in the nineteenth century and consolidated in the twentieth—focused on Africa (Maghreb, French West Africa, French Equatorial Africa), Indochina (Vietnam, Cambodia, Laos), the South Pacific (French Polynesia, New Caledonia), and mandates in Lebanon and Syria. At its peak, the empire encompassed 68.7 million colonized people and 12.3 million km² of territory (incl. one-third of the African continent). Decolonization took place in the 1950s and 1960s as the result of wars for independence (Indochina, 1946–1954; Algeria, 1954–1962), negotiated settlements (Morocco and Tunisia, 1956), and referenda on national sovereignty (sub-Saharan Africa, 1960). The history of French colonialism is still a contentious issue due to its egregious violation of French republican principles of liberty and national self-determination, France's ongoing neocolonial sphere of influence in Africa (referred to as "Françafrique"), and the demographic and social impact of postcolonial immigration to France (e.g., the militant postcolonial rhetoric in favor of minority rights employed by the Indigènes de la République).

Francis I and the Renaissance

A king of the Valois dynasty (Angoulême branch), Francis I (1494–1547, reign beginning in 1515) is associated with the development of the Renaissance in France. He was an intelligent and charming man and carried out his official duties with panache, which helped to reinvigorate the monarchy. However, he was not a gifted politician. While on a military campaign in Italy (1515–1516), he was impressed with the art of the Italian Renaissance. One result was that he brought Italian artists and architects to France to transform his royal châteaux (e.g., Fontainebleau) into sumptuous showcases of Renaissance classicism. Among them was Leonardo da Vinci (1452–1519), who is buried at Amboise. While the Louvre remained the official royal palace and was given a grand, classically inspired expansion (1546–1549) by the architect Pierre Lescot, the epicenter of the royal court was in the Loire Valley (one of the oldest parts of the royal domain), where it traveled with the king from château to château. The largest was Chambord—built (1519–1547) in a French style that combined medieval touches and classicism. While the court was dominated by high-level royal officials and the cream of the nobility, it also included men of letters. One of the most important was the humanist Guillaume Budé, who persuaded Francis to found a royal college (1530, later renamed Collège de France) in Paris dedicated to subjects such as Hebrew, Ancient Greek, and mathematics, which were not part of the traditional curriculum of the conservative Sorbonne. The assertion of a national artistic and literary identity was one of the preoccupations of the period. One example was *Defense and Illustration of the French Language* (1549), published two years after Francis's death, in which Joachim du Bellay, a member of a group of poets known as La Péliade, asserted that French was a literary language equal to Greek and Latin. Francis also encouraged the exploration of the new world (e.g., first voyage of Jacques Cartier, 1534). Two of the greatest challenges that he had to contend with were the rise of Emperor Charles V (1500–1558) of the House of Habsburg—who ruled over vast territories that included the German lands of the Holy Roman Empire, Spain, the Netherlands, and Burgundy—and the spread of Protestantism (esp. Calvinism). Francis went to war with his bitter rival, Charles V, and suffered a humiliating defeat at the Battle of Pavia (1525). Captured on the battlefield and imprisoned in Madrid, his release required significant territorial concessions, but Francis later repudiated the terms of the Treaty of Madrid (1526), leading to more war. France remained a majority Catholic country through the Reformation, but it had an important Protestant minority. The existence of this minority and the resonance of Reformation theology and ideas (e.g., the Francis's intellectual sister and great patron of the arts, Marguerite de Navarre, was interested in protestant ideas and supported reform of the church) called into question the French monarchy's long-standing special relationship with the Catholic Church—it was the church's (and the papacy's) protector and exercised considerable authority over religious affairs in the kingdom via the doctrine of Gallicanism—and posed a broader threat to the unity of the kingdom. After the Affair of the Placards (1534), in which anti-Catholic posters were put up in Paris and elsewhere (including one tacked on the door of the king's bedroom at Amboise), Francis could no longer ignore its implications. The persecution of Protestants became the law of the land in 1540 (Edict of Fontainebleau). Religious dissenters were burned at the stake (Étienne Dolet) and exiled (Jean Calvin). However, the situation spiraled out of control after Francis's death, leading to the civil war known as the French Wars of Religion (1562–1598). The latter came to an end only when Henry de Bourbon (1553–1610), the Protestant king of Navarre, ascended to the French throne (1589), reconverted to Catholicism, and offered limited rights and protection to Protestants (Edict of Nantes, 1598).

See also: Chapter 2: Timeline; Louis IX and the Capetian Dynasty; Louis XIV and the Absolute Monarchy. Chapter 5: Catholicism; Protestantism. Chapter 9: Language Laws and Policies. Chapter 12: Loire Valley Châteaux.

Further Reading
Eccles (1998); Frieda (2018); Holt (2002); Knecht (2002); Knecht (2005); Knecht (2017).

Joan of Arc and the Hundred Years' War

Joan of Arc (1412–1431) was one of France's oldest national heroes as well as one of the most legendary and studied figures of world history. She was associated with the long, multistage military conflict between France and England known as the Hundred Years' War (1337–1453), which had a complex array of economic and geopolitical stakes but initially involved a dynastic dispute between the Plantagenet kings of England and the Valois kings of France—namely, the king of England's claim to be the rightful heir to the French throne. Joan was born to a family of modest tenant farmers in the town of Domrémy (Lorraine). At the time of her involvement in the war, things were not going well for France. The English (led by King Henry VI of Lancaster, 1421–1471) and their allies, the Burgundians (led by Philip the Good, Duke of Burgundy, 1396–1467), controlled most of northern France and idle soldiers terrorized the countryside. The French throne was technically vacant because the Dauphin Charles (future King Charles VII, 1403–1461) had still not been consecrated (i.e., crowned) and was reluctant to fight the English. Still a teenager at the time, but as courageous and patriotic as she was religiously devout and of a mystic disposition, Joan claimed to have heard voices (Saints Michael, Catherine of Alexandria, and Margaret of Antioch) commanding her, in the name of God, to rid France of the English and restore the French throne to Charles. In 1428 and 1429, the sixteen-year-old twice visited a local French-held fortress to tell of her visions and convince the French military commander, Robert de Baudricourt, to allow her to go see the Dauphin. Baudricourt at first suggested that the young woman might be either insane or a witch, but eventually gave his consent. The meeting took place on March 8, 1429, after Joan identified the Dauphin hidden among his courtiers. Charles offered somewhat reluctant support. Dressed in men's clothes, Joan took command of an army and marched on Orleans, which had been under siege for a year. She won an improbable, astounding victory there, liberating the city on April 29, 1429—an exploit for which she earned the nickname the Maid of Orleans. This gave the French momentum and made her a living legend. Following additional military successes in which Joan was aided by the Duke of Alençon, Charles VII was crowned at Reims on July 17, 1429 with Joan in attendance. In 1430, she was taken prisoner by the Burgundians while trying to relieve the besieged city of Compiègne. The theology faculty of the pro-English University of Paris suspected Joan of heresy and asked her to be handed over for trial by the Inquisition. Her trial, over which the bishop of Beauvais (Cauchon) and the vice inquisitor of France (Lemaître) presided, began in January 1431. In prison, Joan was threatened with torture and interrogated on a range of potential offenses, including blasphemy, sorcery, demonic possession, insubordination to church authority, heresy, attempted suicide, and wearing men's clothes. Following her conviction, she signed a letter of abjuration under duress but later recanted. Joan of Arc was burned at the stake in Rouen on May 30, 1431. Her guilty verdict was subsequently annulled in 1456 and she was canonized (made a saint of the Catholic Church) by Pope Benedict XV in 1920. Joan's universal appeal was one reason why the date of her death (and future feast day), May 30, was once under consideration as a possible date for France's national holiday, and why the second Sunday in May—in commemoration of the liberation of Orleans—is still an official national holiday in France celebrating "Joan of Arc and Patriotism." Nonetheless, different ideological factions have celebrated Joan for different reasons. For conservative Catholics, she represented purity, piety, obedience, and the royalist tradition; for republicans, she was a patriotic hero who came from the ranks of the common people to defend French liberty and independence; for the radical left, her story was a cautionary tale about ecclesiastical power and the fecklessness of the monarchy; and for right-wing ethno-nationalists, she was said to have fought to save the authentic French nation from foreign subjugation. While these divergent interpretations have subsided somewhat in recent times, controversial traces still persist. For example, the National Rally holds a massive gathering in Joan's honor in Paris every year on May 1 as an alternative to traditional (and left-leaning) French Labor Day observances.

See also: Chapter 2: Timeline; Francis I and the Renaissance; Louis IX and the Capetian Dynasty. Chapter 5: Catholicism.

Further Reading
Allmand (1988); Castor (2014); Fraioli (2005); Warner (2013).

Louis IX and the Capetian Dynasty

Louis IX (1214–1270) is one of the most revered kings in French history. Known for his piety and sense of justice (he regularly heard cases personally, sometimes at the foot of a great oak tree on the grounds of Vincennes Castle), Louis enhanced the moral authority and prestige of the French monarchy. He was part of a long line of kings of the Capetian dynasty, which began in 987 with the election of Hugh Capet and lasted for over three-and-a-half centuries. Cadet branches of the family line—the Valois beginning in 1326 and the Bourbon after 1598—helped to extend the dynasty's reign through the French Revolution. This dynastic continuity was crucial to the sustained prosperity, relative political coherence, and emergent sense of national identity in the Kingdom of France in the Middle Ages. The Capetians succeeded in their project of nation building by increasing the size of the royal domain (i.e., the territory over which they exercised direct local authority), successfully fighting disobedient vassals, encouraging commerce and the growth of towns (to which they granted a modicum of independence), restructuring and strengthening the royal administration and judiciary, and cultivating the monarchy's historically close ties to the Catholic Church. The other prominent Capetian kings of the era were Louis IX's grandfather and grandson—Philip II (1165–1223, reign beginning in 1180), also known as Philip Augustus; and Philip IV (1268–1314, reign beginning in 1285), also known as Philip the Fair. The Capetian era saw a great development of monastic life and urban Christianity, exemplified by the spread of Gothic art and architecture, which originated as a royal style in the Paris region. During Louis IX's reign (1226–1270), students and professors from all over Europe came to the University of Paris (founded in 1150), which had the most prestigious faculty of theology in all of western Christendom. Notre-Dame Cathedral in Paris (1163–1250), a rigorous example of the Gothic style (then known as the "French style"), was nearing completion; and Louis IX ordered the construction of the Sainte-Chapelle (1242–1248)—known for its magnificent stained glass windows—as part of the royal palace complex on the Île-de-la-Cité in Paris. Louis also faced challenges as king. One was the threat from the counts of Toulouse, who ruled over vast territories as quasi-sovereigns. While Louis was still a boy, their revolt was put down with help of ruthless military commanders like Simon de Montfort and the strong leadership of the young king's mother, Blanche of Castile. The treaty imposed on Count Raymond VII at the end of the conflict (1229) included provisions for the eventual annexation of the former's territories into the French royal domain. Because the counts adhered to Catharism, also known as the Albigensian heresy, the war is also referred to as the Albigensian Crusade. The monarchy's victory also signaled the north's inexorable ascendancy over the south. Another great threat was posed by the ongoing conflict with the kings of England. The Plantagenet dynasty in England possessed vast territories in France, which theoretically made the English king a vassal of the French one. According to the terms of a negotiated settlement in 1258, King Henry III of England recognized Louis IX of France as his suzerain but was allowed to keep the province of Aquitaine. The peace with England fell apart in the next century when the English king laid claim to throne of France as well, leading to the Hundred Years' War (1337–1453). In spite of the undeniable religious fervor to which it attested, Louis IX's involvement in the Crusades was less than triumphant. During the Seventh (1248–1254), which he led, he not only failed to free Jerusalem from the hands of its Muslim rulers but was also captured and held for ransom in Egypt. He died of disease outside Tunis at the start of the Eighth Crusade. Louis was made a saint in the Catholic Church in 1297.

See also: Chapter 2: Timeline; Francis I and the Renaissance; Joan of Arc and the Hundred Years War. Chapter 5: Catholicism; Chapter 12: Gothic Cathedrals.

Further Reading
Bradbury (2007); Le Goff (2009); Tyerman (2006).

Louis XIV and the Absolute Monarchy

Louis XIV (1638–1715) is often considered the greatest king of France. He is unquestionably the one who attained the most glorious reputation and did so by design. His reign of seventy-two years (1643–1715) was the longest in French history and coincided with the height of French power and cultural preeminence. Known as the Sun King because he compared himself to the Greek god Apollo and positioned himself symbolically as the radiant center of all things, Louis XIV was a consummate practitioner of royal absolutism. Developed under his two predecessors—Henry IV and Louis XIII, who was aided by the able and ruthless Cardinal Richelieu—the doctrine of absolutism holds that the king's power is supreme and therefore not limited by custom, written laws (i.e., a constitution), or parliamentary review. As a boy, when the affairs of state were in the hands of his mother, Anne of Austria, and Cardinal Mazarin, Louis was horrified by the Fronde (1648–1653), during which powerful nobles, the Paris Parlement (supreme court), and the people of Paris all rose up against the crown. One result was the advent of his "personal reign," beginning in 1661, when he chose not to name a prime minister and assumed direct responsibility for the affairs of state. Another result was his decision in 1682 to move the seat of government to Versailles, 22 km outside Paris. Between 1661 and 1710, he transformed a modest castle that had once been used primarily for royal hunting junkets into the most grandiose royal palace in all of Europe.

Everything at Versailles—from the history paintings on the ceiling of the Hall of Mirrors and the arcane ritual surrounding the king's rising from bed in the morning to the seemingly infinite perspectives of the gardens and the magnificent outdoor spectacles that incorporated plays by Molière and opera-ballets by Lully—served one purpose: the highly disciplined exultation of the king. Although Versailles put a large hole in the royal finances, it served Louis well on two levels: it insulated the king and monarchy from the humors of the Parisian populace and kept the nobility preoccupied with prestige, privilege, luxury, and spectacle rather than the pursuit of power. The reign of Louis XIV was also marked by an endless string of wars with France's European rivals. These included the final years of the Thirty Years' War (1618–1648), the War of Devolution (1667–1668), the Franco-Dutch War (1672–1678), the War of the League of Augsburg (1689–1697), and the War of Spanish Succession (1701–1713). France made modest territorial gains and imposed itself as a military power to be reckoned with (and contained), but the net result was hardly brilliant. It made the monarchy unpopular and compounded its financial difficulties. Toward the end of Louis XIV's reign, the French people were not doing well, opposition was on the rise, and the king's decision to revoke Edict of Nantes and religious rights for Protestants sparked an exodus of Huguenots and a Protestant insurgency in the Cévennes region of southern France (War of the Camisards, 1702–1704). There was a brief interval of liberalism and relaxed, elegant living immediately following Louis's death: the Regency (1715–1723). However, reform proved elusive as the wars and financial problems continued. France lost most of its North American colonial empire in 1763 in the Seven Years' War, and the proud edifice of the French absolute monarchy, so resplendent under the Sun King, was ultimately swept away by the Revolution (1789–1799).

See also: Chapter 2: Timeline; Francis I and the Renaissance; Louis XVI and the End of the Ancien Régime. Chapter 6: Nobility. Chapter 9: Académie Française. Chapter 11: Seventeenth-Century Theatre. Chapter 12: Versailles. Chapter 13: Classical Music; Dance; Opera.

Further Reading

Beik (2000); Burke (1992); Cowart (2008); Doyle (2001); Elias (2005); Hogg (2019); Mansel (2019); Shennan (2007).

Louis XVI and the End of the Ancien Régime

Louis XVI (1754–1793, reign 1774–1792) succeeded his grandfather, Louis XV, as king. He is best known for his marriage to the young Archduchess Marie Antoinette of Austria (1755–1793) and for being king when the French monarchy was toppled during the French Revolution (1789–1799). Louis XVI cared for his people and remained relatively popular up until the start of the Revolution. However, he was not a strong leader. He devoted considerable time to his hobbies, which included locksmithing, cartography, and model ships. There were multiple causes for the political crisis that was to become a revolution. The most pressing one was the monarchy's debt problem. The already grave financial situation of the crown was exacerbated by France's costly involvement in American War of Independence (1775–1783) on the side of the American insurgents, which also helped spread democratic and constitutional ideals in France. Several royal ministers (e.g., Turgot, Necker, and Calonne) had attempted fiscal and institutional reforms, but these measures faced stiff opposition due to their reliance on new taxes and to the threat they posed to the traditional privileges of the elites. The regime's financial crisis thus played out against a backdrop of broader political and social discontent. The magistrates of the Paris Parlement saw themselves as checks on the absolute power of the monarchy and frequently opposed forceful royal initiatives. The aristocracy hoped to gain back some of the power that it had lost during the consolidation of royal power in the seventeenth and eighteenth centuries. The rising bourgeoisie objected to the archaic social hierarchy that still favored the aristocracy and pressed for equal rights and other political and structural reforms. The people in cities and towns faced a sluggish economy, shortages, and high prices for basic staples while the peasants faced feudal oppression, harsh winters, bad harvests, and occasional famines. Finally, the reform-minded political ideas that had flourished during the Enlightenment—Locke's and Condorcet's ideas concerning natural rights, Montesquieu's on the separation of powers, Rousseau's on the social contract, and Voltaire's on despotism and clericalism—were having an impact on public opinion thanks to newspapers, coffee houses, and other means of dissemination.

In order to resolve the financial and political impasse, Louis XVI convened a meeting of the Estates General in 1788. When this consultative assembly, comprised of separate delegations representing each of the three traditional tiers of feudal society (clergy, aristocracy, commoners), began meeting at Versailles in 1789, discord and trouble were in the air (one obstacle was the rule giving each delegation one vote). At the urging of the progressive cleric and political theorist Sieyès (1748–1836), the

REVEIL DU TIERS ETAT.

A French political cartoon from 1789, at the beginning of the French Revolution (1789–1799). It depicts "The Awakening of the Third Estate": a figure representing the Third Estate (commoners) awakens from a nightmare of oppression, shakes off his shackles, grabs a musket, and causes the figures representing the privileged orders of society—the aristocracy and the clergy—to recoil with fear. The Revolution began when the representatives of the Third Estate in the Estates General (convened by the king to discuss urgent fiscal and political reforms) declared themselves a constitutional assembly; it achieved some early progress (e.g., the Declaration of the Rights of Man) before turning violent and spiraling out of control (e.g., widespread social unrest, foreign invasion, civil war, regicide, Reign of Terror, and multiple coups d'État). (Library of Congress) delegation representing the Third Estate (commoners), dominated by the bourgeoisie, proclaimed itself the National Assembly—prompting liberal delegates from the clergy and aristocracy to join them—and vowed to write a constitution for the kingdom (Tennis Court Oath, June 20). Fearing that the assembly might be prevented from doing its work, the Parisian crowd, looking for weapons, stormed the Bastille prison (July 14), a hated symbol of the regime's tyrannical excesses. Notable progress was made in 1789—feudal privileges were abolished on August 4 and the Declaration of the Rights of Man and the Citizen was issued on August 26. A peaceful transition to a constitutional monarchy might have been possible with the king's cooperation. However, Louis XVI balked. First, he attempted to lock out the National Assembly. In October 1789, another Parisian mob, led by women, marched to Versailles and forced the king to return to Paris. Louis felt that it was an affront to royal dignity to compromise with the upstart assembly and he was also troubled by measures targeting the Catholic Church, including the nationalization of ecclesiastical property (November 1789) and the Civil Constitution of the Clergy (July 1790). Joined by the royal family, Louis fled Paris in June 1791 in an attempt to join up with royalist troops preparing a counterrevolutionary offensive with the help foreign powers but was arrested in the town of Varennes and brought back to Paris. This tense situation escalated further following the Austro-Prussian invasion of France in 1792. The Tuileries Palace was stormed by elements of the National Guard and Parisian radicals on August 10, 1792, following which Louis was suspended as king and formally charged with treason. After the French revolutionary army defeated the Prussians at the Battle of Valmy, the monarchy was officially abolished and the First Republic was proclaimed (June 22, 1792). Louis was executed by guillotine on January 21, 1793, followed shortly by Marie Antoinette. Revolutionary France descended into war, chaos, and dictatorship. The regicide is one of the factors that will make the legacy of the French Revolution a source of bitter division in France for generations to come.

See also: Chapter 2: Timeline; Louis XIV and the Absolute Monarchy; Napoleon Bonaparte (Napoleon I) and the First Empire; Robespierre (Maximilien) and the French Revolution. Chapter 6: Nobility. Chapter 11: Eighteenth-Century Literature. Chapter 12: Versailles.

Further Reading

Blackman (2019); Caiani (2012); Chartier (1991); Dunn (1994); Hardman (2016); Hardman (2019); Kaiser (2011); Lüsebrink and Reichardt (1997).

DECLARATION OF THE RIGHTS OF MAN AND THE CITIZEN

If the storming of the Bastille on July 14, 1789 is the decisive symbolic gesture of the French Revolution, the Declaration of the Rights of Man and the Citizen is its enduring foundational text. Imbued with the thinking of the Enlightenment, the declaration (drafted by Abbé Sieyès and the Marquis de Lafayette) was issued by the National Constituent Assembly on August 26, 1789. It begins with the immortal assertion: "Men are born and remain free and equal in rights. Social distinctions may be based only on considerations of the common good" (Art. 1). It establishes liberty, property, safety, and resistance to oppression as inalienable rights (Art. 2), and the nation (popular sovereignty) as the sole source of political authority (Art. 3). Later articles offer specific guarantees of due process and the rule of law (Arts 7–9), freedom of opinion (incl. in matters of religion) and of speech (Arts 10–11), and the accountability of public officials (Art. 15). The Declaration of 1789 is one of the sources of the Universal Declaration of Human Rights of 1948 (United Nations) and is recognized in the preamble of the Constitution of the Fifth Republic (1958) as a supreme norm of French constitutional law.

Macron (Emmanuel) and the New Political Landscape of France

On May 14, 2017, Emmanuel Macron (born 1977) became the ninth president of the Fifth Republic—making the relative political novice the youngest French head of state since Napoleon Bonaparte. He had never before held, or even run for, an elected office and was known to the public primarily for his brief stint as economy minister under President François Hollande. Prior to that, he had a background in investment banking. His party, La République en Marche (The Republic on the Move, abbreviated LREM in French), which won a majority in the June 2017 elections to the National Assembly, had been founded just a year before his presidential run. Although formerly a member of the Socialist Party (PS), Macron is best described as a liberal centrist—a political outlook that has traditionally been electorally precarious in a country with strong left-right polarization. Macron is moderately liberal on most political and social issues but a strong advocate of a free market economy, the EU, and a global economy driven by innovation and competitiveness. The best recent historical precedent for Macron's political philosophy is Jacques Delors (b. 1925), finance minister under François Mitterrand and later president of the European Commission (1985–1995)—a market-friendly Socialist who mentored the young Macron. Another comparison would be President Valéry Giscard d'Estaing (1926–2020, in office 1974–1981), although Giscard came to centrist liberalism from the right.

Macron was born in the northern city of Amiens. He holds a diploma in piano performance from the Amiens Conservatory and worked as graduate assistant for the influential philosopher Paul Ricœur while studying philosophy at Nanterre University (Paris). He also holds advanced degrees from Sciences Po (Paris) and France's École Nationale d'Administration. In 2007, he married his former high school French teacher, Brigitte Auzière (née Trogneux). Macron's meteoric rise to the French presidency and the subsequent success of LREM in the 2017 legislative elections were interpreted as the harbingers of a significant reordering of the French political landscape, characterized by an ascendant center, a marginalized and weakened Socialist Party, and conventional conservatives (i.e., Les Républicains) at risk of being outflanked by the populist far right (i.e., Marine Le Pen and the National Rally). In the first round of the 2017 presidential election, Macron (24%) came out on top, followed by Le Pen (21%). Nine other candidates were eliminated, including Fillon (Les Républicains, 20%), populist leftist candidate Jean-Luc Mélenchon (La France Insoumise, 19%), and Hamon (PS, 6%). The runoff round between Macron and Le Pen was a showdown between two radically different visions of France—with Le Pen advocating a French withdrawal from the EU (a position subsequently diluted), economic protectionism, populist critiques of the elites, an emphasis on law and order, and a thinly disguised nativist view of French national identity that underpinned a hard line on immigration and rejection of multiculturalism. Macron won by a landslide, 66% to 34%. Once in office, he chose Nantes mayor Édouard Philippe as his first prime minister (Philippe was replaced by Jean Castex in July 2020). The earliest major initiatives of Macron's presidency included a reiteration of French support for the EU, a Bastille Day state visit by U.S. president Donald Trump, research grants for U.S. climate scientists at odds with the Trump administration's skepticism on climate change, businessfriendly reforms of French labor laws, and the passage of tough new counterterrorism legislation.

Macron also suffered setbacks, including the massive, protracted, and unruly Yellow Vest protests of 2018–2020; his party's lackluster showing in European parliamentary (2018) and French municipal (2020) elections; and a new wave of opposition to a major retirement pension reform (2019). Known as "Jupiter" for his imperious self-confidence, Macron's approval rating dropped to 34% (BVA) in December 2019. Beginning in January 2020, Macron led France through the COVID-19 pandemic and its major economic repercussions. His record on pandemic response was mixed, but adequate. The *Foreign Policy* Analytics COVID-19 Global Response Index gave France a score of 72.0 points out of 100 for its overall pandemic response as of October 1, 2020. By December 2020, Macron's approval rating had improved to 44% (BVA).

In the early months of the presidential election year of 2022, Macron's prospects for reelection were unclear. The French economy had rebounded from the shock of the pandemic better than most (7% growth in 2021 and the lowest French unemployment rate in thirteen years at 7.4% in the fourth quarter of 2021). Macron was also given high marks for his handling of Russia's 2022 invasion of Ukraine, rallying EU and NATO allies in favor of sanctions against Russia and military aid for Ukraine while maintaining open lines of communication with Russian president Vladimir Putin and cautioning against escalation. However, there was considerable French anxiety over the high cost of living at home and Macron was perceived as arrogant, governing primarily for the benefit of the rich, and insensitive to the travails of ordinary French people. At first, it appeared that Valérie Pécresse, the nominee of the Les Républicains (LR), would be a strong challenger to Macron and that Marine Le Pen's chances might be imperiled by stiff competition on the far right from ultranationalist Éric Zemmour, a political commentator and media personality known for his incendiary rhetoric. However, neither scenario came to pass. Pécresse conducted a lackluster campaign and Le Pen broadened her appeal by softening her rhetoric and emphasizing so-called bread-and-butter issues. The top five vote getters in the first round (April 10), were Marcron (27.84%), Le Pen (23.15%), Mélenchon (21.95%), Zemmour (7.07%), and Pécresse (4.78%). Significant voting trends from the presidential first round of 2022 included an elevated abstention rate of 26%, a shockingly low combined total of just 6.53% for the candidates of the two parties that had dominated French politics for a half century (LR's Pécresse and the PS's Anne Hidalgo, who received just 1.75%), the emergence of three highly polarized and relatively equal voting blocs (the Macron, Le Pen, and Mélenchon electorates), and the total of close to 58% of the vote going to nonmainstream candidates (including 32% for candidates representing the far right). These trends suggested broad discontent with politics as usual, continued reshaping of the French political landscape in favor of Macronist centrism and populist opposition on both the far right and the far left to the detriment of the traditional and once dominant center-right and center-left, and the very real possibility that Le Pen might win the presidency in the second round. Ultimately, the razor-thin gap initially separating the two finalists, according to some early polls, widened, and Macron prevailed comfortably over Le Pen in the runoff (April 24), 58.55%–41.45%—becoming the first French incumbent president to win reelection in twenty years. Macron's victory reassured the financial markets and France's allies; however, his mandate to govern effectively during his second term was significantly attenuated by his failure to win an absolute majority in the June 2022 legislative elections, despite the fact that the pro-Macron centrist alliance—Ensemble (Together), made up of LREM (rebranded as "Renaissance" after the presidential election) and three smaller parties—won the most seats in the new National Assembly. In these most recent parliamentary elections, a newly formed coalition of center-left and far-left parties that had christened itself the New People's Ecologist and Social Union (Nouvelle Union Populaire Écologiste et Sociale, or Nupes), anchored by Mélenchon's La France Insoumise party, emerged as a strong opposition force in the National Assembly, and the far-right National Rally won an unprecedented number of seats in the chamber—an achievement as historically significant as its continued progress in presidential elections over the past twenty years: from 17.8% in the second round of the presidential election of 2002, to 33.9% in 2017, to 41.5% in 2022. The way the 2022 presidential election played out also hinted that the 2027 edition, when Macron would be barred from running again but French voters nevertheless might want to break with ten years of "Macronism," could be even more unpredictable.

See also: Chapter 2: Timeline; Sarkozy (Nicolas) and the Hyper Presidency. Chapter 3: Center; Elections; Presidency and Executive Branch; Protests. Chapter 4: Innovation and Startups; Labor Relations; Social Security and Healthcare; Unemployment.

Further Reading

Cauchemez (2020); Cohen (2019); Cole (2019); Donadio (2020); Drozdiak (2020); Evans and Ivaldi (2018); "France's Napoleonic Approach" (2020); "France's Response" (2020); Macron (2017); Marlière (2022); Palombarin and Amable (2021); Salje (2020); Ward (2020).

Mitterrand (François) and France in the 1980s and 1990s

After Charles de Gaulle, François Mitterrand (1916–1996) is the second most prominent French political figure since the end of World War II. He served two full seven-year terms as president from 1981 to 1995. Mitterrand was instrumental in making the Socialist Party (PS, founded 1971) a more moderate left-of-center force capable of appealing to the middle class and winning elections. His election to the presidency signaled the beginning of an era in which electoral shifts in power between the left and right became a normal occurrence. Born into a devout Catholic middle-class family and trained as a lawyer, Mitterrand was a conservative nationalist in his youth, drifted first toward the center and then toward the left, before governing mostly as a pragmatic progressive. During World War II, he served in the French army and was taken prisoner by the Germans in 1940, escaping in 1941. He worked briefly as an official of the Vichy regime before joining the Resistance in 1943. Mitterrand held several high-level positions in the governments of the Fourth Republic. During the presidency of Charles de Gaulle, he was a leading voice of the opposition and forced de Gaulle into a runoff round in the presidential election of 1965. He also narrowly lost the presidential election of 1974 to center-right candidate Valéry Giscard d'Estaing, but won his rematch with Giscard in 1981. The early years of his administration included Communist ministers and were marked by several signature progressive policy initiatives, including the abolition of the death penalty and nationalization of key financial and industrial companies. However, a shift to more moderate and pragmatic policies (e.g., austerity measures) took place in 1982–1983. The shift was a response to pressures from financial markets and France's allies during a period of growing ascendancy of free market economic theories. Additionally, Mitterrand did not wish to compromise efforts to create a stronger economic and political union in Europe—an objective that took on added significance in the wake of German reunification in 1990. The ratification of the Maastricht Treaty (1992–1993) creating the EU can be considered one of the greatest achievements of his presidency. Mitterrand endured two periods of "cohabitation" with prime ministers and cabinets of the right following conservative victories in parliamentary elections: sharing power first with Jacques Chirac (1985–1988), whom he ultimately defeated in the presidential election of 1988, and later with Édouard Balladur (1993–1995). Mitterrand was a strong proponent of government support for art, architecture, and culture—as is reflected in the projects undertaken by his popular minister of culture, Jack Lang (e.g., the annual Fête de la Musique and the ambitious program of major presidential building projects in Paris, e.g., the Louvre Pyramid). In the area of foreign affairs, Mitterrand's France participated in the U.S.-led coalition that went to war against Iraq in the Gulf War (1990–1991) and was a supporter of the Hutu regime of President Juvénal Habyarimana of Rwanda, whose 1994 assassination helped spark the Rwandan genocide. The subsequent French military intervention in the country under UN Resolution 929 (Opération Turquoise) has been widely criticized for failing to stop the mass killings. Under Mitterrand, French society became increasingly fractured along economic, racial, and religious lines. Unemployment was high and calls from immigrants and minorities for equal rights and inclusion (e.g., the 1983 March for Equality and against Racism) were met by the rise of the xenophobic Front National (founded by Jean-Marie Le Pen in 1972). Nonetheless, Mitterrand enjoyed a fair degree of personal popularity throughout much of his presidency, including among the more liberal young, who called him "Tonton" (French for "uncle") and who were in turn christened the "Mitterrand Generation" in a famous series of ads for his reelection campaign.

See also: Chapter 2: Timeline; de Gaulle (Charles), World War II, and the Fifth Republic; Sarkozy (Nicolas) and the Hyper Presidency. Chapter 3: European Union; Left; Presidency and Executive Branch. Chapter 12: Contemporary Architecture; Ministry of Culture. Chapter 13: Fête de la Musique.

Further Reading
Bell (2005); Friend (1998); Maclean (1998); Short (2014).

Napoleon Bonaparte (Napoleon I) and the First Empire

Napoleon Bonaparte (1769–1821) was a French military commander of Corsican origin who rose rapidly through the ranks of the French army during the wars of the French Revolution, seized political power in France in a 1799 coup that made him the dominant member of the new ruling Consulate, founded the First French Empire in 1804, and went on to conquer or otherwise control most of Europe during the Napoleonic Wars (1803–1815) before being twice defeated by European coalition forces—definitively so at the Battle of Waterloo in 1815. As a political leader, Napoleon effectively ended the French Revolution. He preserved key elements of republican culture and social reforms (e.g., a minimal degree of civil equality written into law, largely secular government, reliance on the patriotic sentiment of the French people) while leading an authoritarian and conservative government capable of maintaining order. He modernized and centralized France's government and public administration (e.g., state-appointed prefects in each department), instituted key economic and educational reforms (e.g., Bank of France, French Franc, Imperial University, *lycée* system), and struck a deal with the Holy See in Rome (Concordat, 1801) that restored some of the Catholic Church's former privileges and influence in France while also formally recognizing other faiths (e.g., Protestantism, Judaism). Finally, he sponsored the creation of a unified written Civil Code (Napoleonic Code, 1804) that influenced the legal systems of many other countries and remains in effect today, in updated form. As a military leader, he was forward-thinking and arguably brilliant, but also overly ambitious and sometimes reckless. His success in waging war was based on a range of factors, including the effective use of conscription, charismatic leadership, and a loyal officer corps recruited and promoted on the basis of merit; significant improvements in training, logistics, and arms production; and tactical reliance on artillery and deep lines. While he ultimately failed to unite Europe under French control and hegemony, the threat posed by his military expansionism was the chief impetus behind the Congress of Vienna (November 1814 to June 1815), which sought to limit the disruptive forces of revolution and nationalism and established a geopolitical framework and balance of power for Europe that held together until World War I. Napoleon left an indelible mark on French national identity (e.g., a centralized and unitary notion of nation, an obsession with greatness on the international stage, the paradigm of the "providential leader" who saves the nation in a time of crisis) and regularly ranks as one of the most significant figures of world history—second only to Jesus Christ in several classifications.

Napoleon was born to a family of the minor Corsican nobility just a year after the island had been acquired by France from the city-state of Genoa. The French Revolution provided opportunities for advancement for an ambitious young officer like Napoleon given that many of the highest-ranking officers, all aristocrats, sided with the king and joined the ranks of the royalist Émigrés. Napoleon proved himself by commanding troops that suppressed a royalist insurrection in 1795 and was promoted to the rank of major general. He then achieved greater success by leading the armies of the French Republic to a string of impressive victories against the Austrians in Italy. Napoleon left his army in the Middle East in the middle of a lackluster campaign in Egypt and Syria (1798–1801) to take part in the "18 Brumaire" coup against the weakened Directory (November 1799). He emerged as the dominant member of the new regime (Consulate) and was given the title of First Consul. He decisively defeated the Austrians once again at the Battle of Marengo in 1801 and orchestrated the sale of France's American territory to the United States in 1803 (Louisiana Purchase) in part to raise money for France's war effort. On the strength of his military success, he crowned himself emperor of the French in a spectacular ceremony at Notre-Dame Cathedral in Paris in 1804. The following year, 1805, was marked by both defeat and triumph. Napoleon's fleet was crushed by Great Britain's at Battle of Trafalgar (October). However, his army won one of its greatest victories at the Battle of Austerlitz (December), over the Austrians and Russians. This resulted in the establishment of the Confederation of the Rhine, an assemblage of client states loyal to Napoleon that created a buffer between the French Empire to the west—130 departments stretching from Hamburg to Rome—and Prussia and Austria to the east and south. With his position on the continent strengthened, Napoleon turned to economic warfare against Great Britain, creating the Continental System, or Blockade, in 1806. Two years after Russia withdrew from the Continental System (1810), Napoleon retaliated by invading

Russia (1812), an ill-conceived campaign that ultimately proved to be the turning point of the Napoleonic Wars as his troops were drawn deeper and deeper into Russian territory by Russian forces in tactical retreat. Although Napoleon took Moscow, his troops were ill prepared for the harsh Russian winter of 1812 and were mercilessly harassed when they attempted a withdrawal of their own. The emperor was no longer invincible. He suffered another decisive defeat at the Battle of Leipzig in 1813, and coalition forces captured Paris in 1814. Napoleon abdicated and was exiled to the island of Elba. The French (Bourbon) monarchy was restored with Louis XVIII (1755–1824), the brother of Louis XVI, on the throne. Napoleon attempted a comeback with his Hundred Days campaign (March through July 1815), but was defeated a second time, by mostly British and Prussian forces, at the Battle of Waterloo (July 15). He once again abdicated (June 22), surrendered (July 15), and was exiled to island of Saint Helena, where he died. Despite defeat, Napoleon's legend loomed large over France, where his remains returned in 1840. They were eventually interred in a grandiose tomb at the Hôtel des Invalides in Paris.

See also: Chapter 2: Timeline; Louis XVI and the End of the Ancien Régime; Napoleon III and the Second Empire; Robespierre (Maximilien) and the French Revolution. Chapter 3: Judicial System; Military; Right. Chapter 5: Catholicism; Laïcité.

Further Reading
Bell (2007); Bell (2015); Ellis (2003); Hazareesingh (2005); Horne (2004); Jordan (2012).

Napoleon III and the Second Empire

Charles-Louis-Napoléon Bonaparte (1808–1873), more commonly referred to as Louis-Napoléon Bonaparte, was the nephew of Napoleon I—the son of the former's younger brother, Louis (king of Holland, 1806–1810), and Hortense de Beauharnais (Napoleon I's stepdaughter via his first wife, Empress Josephine). He spent his childhood, youth, and early adulthood in exile in a number of European countries, where he developed liberal and romantic leanings, a particular interest in the cause of Italian national independence (much of Italy was then under Austrian and papal control), and a strong affinity for the legend and ideals of his famous uncle. He was involved in a number of French political plots—including a failed coup attempt against King Louis-Philippe, for which he was exiled to the United States—and developed the political ideology of Bonapartism in his writings. These works asserted that France could achieve due greatness (including industrial might and social progress) and true political liberty (i.e., compatible with order) only under a strong and providential leader (i.e., visionary and called by destiny) such as an emperor. His calls for wiping out poverty won him the support of some on the left. He got his chance to provide such leadership when he was elected to a four-year term as president of the Second Republic (1848–1852). The Republic, founded after the Revolution of February 1848 toppled the increasingly unpopular Orleans monarchy of Louis-Philippe. At first, there was optimism that the new experiment in republicanism would be more inclusive and democratic: the politically moderate romantic poet Alphonse de Lamartine (1790–1869) and the socialist Louis Blanc (1811–1882) were both members of the provisional government, universal suffrage (for men) was established, and the National Workshops were created for unemployed workers. However, tensions deepened after rural and provincial voters elected a conservative National Assembly. Paris rose in insurrection again in June 1848 and the rebellion was crushed by troops under the command of General Louis-Eugène Cavaignac. It was against this backdrop that France held its first-ever popular election of its first president in December 1848, which Louis-Napoléon Bonaparte won handily thanks to his name recognition, the popularity of his illustrious uncle, and the support of the monarchist and archconservative Party of Order, led by Adolphe Thiers (1797–1877). As his nonrenewable four-year term approached its end in 1852, he followed his uncle's example and staged a coup, soon followed by the establishment of the Second Empire (1852–1870). He took the name of Napoleon III in deference to Napoleon I's son, the Duke of Reichstadt (1811–1832), who was titular emperor for a short time after his father's abdication but never reigned. Napoleon III ruled France for eighteen more years, during which industrialization progressed and the country was prosperous. Paris was modernized and given its luxurious grand boulevards under the supervision of Baron Eugène Haussmann, Napoleon III's prefect of the Seine department (i.e., Paris). This urban transformation and the accompanying expansion of the middle class and leisure were depicted in the poems of Charles Baudelaire and the works of the impressionist painters (e.g., Manet, Pissarro, Monet, Renoir, Caillebotte, and Degas). French colonial expansion (Algeria, Senegal, Indochina) and intervention in European wars (Crimean War, Italian War) also continued. After its initial "authoritarian" phase (1852–1860), the Second Empire entered a "liberal" phase (1860–1870), characterized by a rapprochement with liberals and workers and a greater degree of parliamentarianism. However, Napoleon's armies and his own prowess as a commander were no match for a rising Prussia-dominated Germany, which quickly defeated the French in the Franco-Prussian War (1870–1871). France's crushing military defeat led to the collapse of the Second Empire and the establishment of the Third Republic (1870–1940), dashed hopes for yet another restoration of the French monarchy, resulted in the annexation of Alsace and part of Lorraine by the victorious and newly unified Germany, and led to the radical uprising known as the Paris Commune (1871) brutally suppressed by French troops. Napoleon III died in exile in England.

See also: Chapter 1: Paris. Chapter 2: Timeline; Ferry (Jules) and the Third Republic; Napoleon Bonaparte (Napoleon I) and the First Empire. Chapter 3: Right. Chapter 6: Bourgeoisie and Middle Class. Chapter 11: Novel in the Nineteenth Century. Chapter 12: Impressionism; Modern Architecture.

Further Reading
Agulhon (1983); Baguley (2000); Hazareesingh (1998); Kirkland (2013); Strauss-Schom (2018).

Robespierre (Maximilien) and the French Revolution

Robespierre (1758–1794) was one of the most influential, powerful, and controversial figures of the French Revolution (1789–1799). He had received training as a lawyer in Paris and practiced law in his hometown of Arras, in northern France. He was influenced by the political ideas of Jean-Jacques Rousseau and as a journalist wrote articles in favor of democratic reforms of the monarchy and in defense of the interests of the common people and the poor. He was a member of both the Estates General and National Constituent Assembly in the early stages of the Revolution before being elected to the National Convention in 1792 as a deputy representing Paris (he became the chamber's president in 1794). By that time, he had risen to prominence as president of the Jacobin Club, a political organization advocating more radical political and social policies. His single-minded devotion to the Revolution and reputed moral rectitude were the reason for his nickname, "The Incorruptible." Following the execution of King Louis XVI (1793), Robespierre became the leader of the left-wing Montagnard faction of the chamber. Forming an alliance with the volatile Sans-culottes, militant revolutionaries from the lower rungs of Parisian society, the Montagnards supplanted the more moderate ruling Girondins in June 1793. The new leadership faced a dire situation: Revolutionary France was still at war with its neighbors, a bloody civil war was unfolding in the Vendée region of western France between government forces and ultraroyalist insurgents, and the people were upset about high prices and shortages and increasingly skeptical of the benefits of the Revolution. Formed by Georges Danton in April 1793, the Committee of Public Safety was tasked with turning the situation around. Robespierre took a seat on the committee in July 1793 and became its dominant member, turning it into an instrument of dictatorial government. The repressive methods (e.g., revolutionary tribunals and summary executions) that the committee used against those considered enemies of the Revolution—priests, hoarders, war profiteers, nobles, federalists, and more extremist revolutionary groups like the Hébertistes—with the backing of the Convention and the help of vigilantes gave rise to the Reign of Terror (September 5, 1793 to July 27, 1794). In August 1793, the convention also enacted massive conscription to shore up the war effort. The internal and national security situations improved but the Reign of Terror continued, becoming increasingly directed at anyone who posed a threat to Robespierre, the committee, and the Jacobins. The Terror's final toll is a matter of debate but includes an estimated 300,000 arrests, 10,000 political prisoner deaths, and 17,000 officially acknowledged executions. Well-known victims of the Terror include Paris's first mayor Jean-Sylvain Bailly, Philippe Égalité (i.e., Louis XVI's liberal cousin and the former Duke of Orleans), the women's rights advocate Olympe de Gouges, the mathematician and philosopher Condorcet, the chemist and tax collector Lavoisier, Danton, and the journalist Camille Desmoulins. The radicalization of the Revolution, which Robespierre supported, also included ambitious attempts to reshape French society and culture in a republican mold. One example was the creation of the ten-month republican calendar (in use 1793–1805). Another was the Cult of the Supreme Being, a civil religion established by Robespierre as a more rational alternative to Catholicism. The autocratic rule of Robespierre was untenable. Increasingly unpopular, Robespierre and his associates were ousted in a parliamentary coup on July 27, 1794, known as the Thermidorian Reaction. Robespierre was guillotined on July 28. This put an end to the Reign of Terror and gave rise to a more conservative regime called the Directory (1794–1799). Robespierre was not always the historical persona non grata that he has become today (radical republicans and revolutionary socialists tended to view him as a tough leader devoted to the revolutionary cause). More recently, the Reign of Terror has come to be seen by some as a harbinger of modern totalitarianism, an assertion challenged by others.

See also: Chapter 2: Timeline; Louis XVI and the End of the Ancien Régime; Napoleon Bonaparte (Napoleon I) and the First Empire. Chapter 3: Left; Republic. Chapter 5: Catholicism; Rationalism and Universalism.

Further Reading

Andress (2006); Andress (2015); Edelstein (2010); Furet and Ozouf (1989); Higonnet (1998); Kaplan (1995); Popkin (2019); Schama (1989); Scurr (2006); Wahnich (2012).

Sarkozy (Nicolas) and the Hyper Presidency

Nicolas Sarkozy (b. 1955) was president of the French Republic for a single five-year term from 2007 to 2012. His long political résumé includes terms as mayor of the Paris suburb of Neuilly (1983–2002), minister of budget (1993–1995), minister of the interior (2002–2004, 2005–2007), and minister of finance (2004). Sarkozy's family background—Hungarian on his father's side, French and Greek Jewish on his mother's—is the most diverse of any modern French head of state. A lawyer by profession, he is known for his brash style and emphasis on media exposure. As minister of the interior during the second term of President Jacques Chirac (1932–2019), Sarkozy sparked controversy while on a tour of the Paris suburb of Aubervilliers in 2005 by using the term "racaille" (French for "riff-raff" or "scum") in reference to allegedly delinquent minority youths. Following his election as president, Sarkozy was known for his ostentatious display of luxurious taste and associations with the rich and famous; and he became a fixture of the tabloid press following his divorce from his second wife, Cécelia, and subsequent remarriage to the singer-songwriter and one-time model Carla Bruni. Though these proclivities contributed to Sarkozy's unpopularity, others were drawn to his willingness to break with political conventions. When he ran for president in 2007, Sarkozy successfully positioned himself as an outsider (in spite of his extensive political résumé) and a force for change by distancing himself from the incumbent president and proposing a bold program of action that he vowed would strengthen France economically by emphasizing hard work and individual wealth, while getting tough on crime, illegal immigration, and abuses of the social welfare system. He defeated his Socialist rival Ségolène Royal (b. 1953), the first woman to become the presidential candidate of a major party and qualify for the run-off, 53% to 47%. In office, Sarkozy launched an ambitious series of reforms involving the criminal justice system, the environment, taxes, employment, deficits, immigration, urbanism, government institutions, and education. He also dealt with the negative effects of the economic crisis of 2008. In the area of foreign policy, Sarkozy pursued closer ties to the United States (e.g., France's reincorporation into the unified command structure of NATO, 2009) and had France take the lead in the NATO military intervention against the Gaddafi regime in Libya (2011). He lost his bid for reelection in 2012—losing to the more sedate Socialist candidate François Hollande, 48% to 52%. The contrast between the two men was evident in the derisive nicknames used for each. Sarkozy was referred to as "Sarko the American" (a moniker he found flattering) and "President Bling-Bling." Hollande was called "Mister Normal" or, more negatively, "Flamby," in reference to a brand of custard. Personal unpopularity, a record of volatility and inconsistency in the area of domestic reforms, a poor economy, and a strategy that relied on siphoning off potential National Front (far-right) voters all contributed to Sarkozy's defeat. Sarkozy attempted a comeback in 2012 but was eliminated in the presidential primary phase. In 2021, Sarkozy was found guilty of corruption related to the attempted bribing of a judge in exchange for information about an investigation into alleged campaign finance violations.

Hollande went on to become the least popular president (2012–2017) in the history of the Fifth Republic during a term that was marred by a series of unprecedented terror attacks in France: the attack on the editorial offices of the controversial satirical newspaper *Charlie Hebdo* in January 2015, the November 2015 attacks in Paris, and the Nice truck attack on Bastille Day in 2016.

See also: Chapter 1: Natural Resources and Environment; Paris. Chapter 2: Timeline; de Gaulle (Charles), World War II, and the Fifth Republic; Macron (Emmanuel) and the New Political Landscape of France; Mitterrand (François) and France in the 1980s and 90s. Chapter 3: Presidency and Executive Branch; Right. Chapter 6: Suburbs. Chapter 7: Universities and Higher Education.

Further Reading

Gaffney (2015); Hewlett (2011); Raymond (2013); Reza (2008); Sarkozy (2007).

SELECTED BIBLIOGRAPHY

Achille, Etienne, et al., eds. *Postcolonial Realms of Memory: Sites and Symbols in Modern France*. Liverpool UP, 2020.

Agulhon, Maurice. *The Republican Experiment, 1848–1852*. Trans. Janet Lloyd. Cambridge UP, 1983.

Aldrich, Robert. *The French Presence in the South Pacific, 1842–1940*. Macmillan, 1990.

Aldrich, Robert. *Greater France: A History of French Overseas Expansion*. Macmillan, 1996.

Allmand, Christopher Thomas. *The Hundred Years War: England and France at War, c. 1300–c. 1450*. Cambridge UP, 1988.

Andress, David, ed. *The Oxford Handbook of the French Revolution*. Oxford UP, 2015.

Andress, David. *The Terror: The Merciless War for Freedom in Revolutionary France*. Farrar, Straus, and Giroux, 2006.

Baguley, David. *Napoleon III and His Regime: An Extravaganza*. LSU P, 2000.

Bancel, Nicolas, et al., eds. *The Colonial Legacy in France: Fracture, Rupture, and Apartheid*. Trans. Alexis Pernsteiner. Indiana UP, 2017.

Beik, William. *Louis XIV and Absolutism: A Brief Study with Documents*. Palgrave Macmillan, 2000.

Bell, David A. *The Cult of the Nation in France, Inventing Nationalism, 1685–1800*. Harvard UP, 2001.

Bell, David A. *The First Total War: Napoleon's Europe and the Birth of Warfare as We Know It*. Houghton Mifflin, 2007.

Bell, David A. *Napoleon: A Concise Biography*. Oxford UP, 2015.

Bell, David S. *Francois Mitterrand: A Political Biography*. Polity, 2005.

Berstein, Serge. *The Republic of De Gaulle, 1958–1969*. Trans. Peter Morris. Cambridge UP, 1993.

Birnbaum, Pierre. *Léon Blum: Prime Minister, Socialist, Zionist*. Trans. Arthur Goldhammer. Yale UP, 2015.

Blackman, Robert H. *1789: The French Revolution Begins*. Cambridge UP, 2019.

Blanchard, Jean-Vincent. *Eminence: Cardinal Richelieu and the Rise of France*. Bloomsbury, 2011.

Blanchard, Pascal, et al., eds. *Colonial Culture in France since the Revolution*. Trans. Alexis Pernsteiner. Indiana UP, 2014.

Boucheron, Patrick, and Stephane Gerson. *France in the World: A New Global History*. Other P, 2019.

Bradbury, Jim. *Capetians: Kings of France, 987–1328*. Hambledon Continuum, 2007.

Bredin, Jean-Denis. *The Affair: The Case of Alfred Dreyfus*. Trans. Jeffrey Mehlman. Braziller, 1986.

Brocheux, Pierre, and Daniel Hémery. *Indochina: An Ambiguous Colonization, 1858–1954*. U California P, 2009.

Burke, Peter. *The Fabrication of Louis XIV*. Yale UP, 1992.

Caiani, Ambrogio A. *Louis XVI and the French Revolution, 1789–1792*. Cambridge UP, 2012.

Castor, Helen. *Joan of Arc: A History*. Faber and Faber, 2014.

Chafer, Tony. *The End of Empire in French West Africa, 1936–60: France's Successful Decolonization?* Berg, 2002.

Chafer, Tony, and Amanda Sackur, eds. *Promoting the Colonial Idea: Propaganda and Visions of Empire in France*. Palgrave Macmillan, 2001.

Chapman, Herrick. *France's Long Reconstruction: In Search of the Modern Republic*. Harvard UP, 2018.

Charle, Christophe. *A Social History of France in the 19th Century*. Berg, 1994.

Chartier, Roger. *The Cultural Origins of the French Revolution*. Trans. Lydia G. Cochrane. Duke UP, 1991.

Cauchemez, Simon, et al. "Lockdown Impact on COVID-19 Epidemics in Regions across France." *The Lancet*, vol. 396, no. 10257, 2020, pp. 1068–1069.

Chirac, Jacques. *My Life in Politics*. Trans. Catherine Spencer. Palgrave Macmillan, 2012.

Cohen, Paul. "France's Philosopher Presidents." *Dissent*, 29 Mar. 2019, https://www .dissentmagazine.org/online_articles/frances-philosopher-presidents.

Cole, Alistair. *Emmanuel Macron and the Two Years that Changed France*. Manchester UP, 2019.

Conklin, Alice. *A Mission to Civilize: The Republican Idea of Empire in France and West Africa, 1895–1930*. Stanford UP, 1997.

Cooper, Frederick. *Citizenship between Empire and Nation: Remaking France and French Africa, 1945–1960*. Princeton UP, 2014.

Costambeys, Marios, et al. *The Carolingian World*. Cambridge UP, 2011.

Cowart, Georgia. *The Triumph of Pleasure: Louis XIV and the Politics of Spectacle*. U Chicago P, 2008.

Daileader, Philip, and Philip Whalen. *French Historians 1900–2000: New Historical Writing in Twentieth-century France*. Wiley, 2010.

Dallas, Gregor. *At the Heart of a Tiger: Clemenceau and His World*. Macmillan, 1993.

Dewhurst Lewis, Mary. *Divided Rule: Sovereignty and Empire in French Tunisia, 1881–1938*. U California P, 2013.

Donadio, Rachel. "France: After Lockdown, the Street." *The New York Review of Books*, 23 Jul. 2020, https://www.nybooks.com/articles/2020/07/23/france-after-covid-19-lockdown/.

Dorigny, Marcel, ed. *The Abolitions of Slavery: From L.F. Sonthonax to Victor Schoelcher, 1793, 1794, 1848*. Berghahn, 2003.

Doyle, William, ed. *Old Regime France, 1648–1788*. Oxford UP, 2001.

Drozdiak, William. *The Last President of Europe: Emmanuel Macron's Race to Revive France and Save the World*. PublicAffairs, 2020.

Dueck, Jennifer. *The Claims of Culture at Empire's End: Syria and Lebanon under French Rule*. Oxford UP, 2010.

Dunbabin, Jean. *France in the Making, 843–1180*. 2nd ed. Oxford UP, 2000.

Dunn, Susan. *The Deaths of Louis XVI: Regicide and the French Political Imagination*. Princeton UP, 1994.

Eccles, W. J. *The French in North America, 1500–1763*. Michigan State UP, 1998.

Edelstein, Dan. *The Terror of Natural Right: Republicanism, the Cult of Nature, and the French Revolution*. U Chicago P, 2010.

Elias, Norbert. *The Court Society*. Collected Works of Norbert Elias, vol. 2; ed. Stephen Mennell, trans. Edmond Jephcott. University College Dublin P, 2005.

Ellis, Geoffrey. *The Napoleonic Empire*. Palgrave Macmillan, 2003.

Evans, Jocelyn, and Gilles Ivaldi. *The 2017 French Presidential Elections: A Political Reformation?* Palgrave Macmillan, 2018.

Evans, Martin. *Algeria: France's Undeclared War.* Oxford UP, 2012.

Feenberg, Andrew, and Jim Freedman. *When Poetry Ruled the Streets: The French May Events of 1968.* SUNY P, 2001.

Fraioli, Deborah A. *Joan of Arc and the Hundred Years War.* Greenwood, 2005.

"France's Napoleonic Approach to Covid-19." *The Economist,* 4 Apr. 2020, https://www.economist.com/europe/2020/04/04/frances-napoleonic-approach-to-covid-19.

"France's Response to COVID-19." *Strategic Comments,* vol. 26, no. 5, 2020, pp. iv–vi.

Frieda, Leonie. *Francis I: The Maker of Modern France.* Harper, 2018.

Friend, Julius W. *The Long Presidency: France in the Mitterrand Years, 1981–1995.* Westview, 1998.

Furet, François, and Mona Ozouf, eds. *Critical Dictionary of the French Revolution.* Trans. Arthur Goldhammer. Belknap-Harvard UP, 1989.

Gaffney, John. *France in the Hollande Presidency: The Unhappy Republic.* Palgrave Macmillan, 2015.

Geary, Patrick J. *Before France and Germany: The Creation and Transformation of the Merovingian World.* Oxford UP, 1988.

Gershovich, Moshe. *French Military Rule in Morocco: Colonialism and Its Consequences.* Cass, 2000.

Gildea, Robert. *Fighters in the Shadows: A New History of the French Resistance.* Belknap-Harvard UP, 2015.

Gluckstein, Donny. *The Paris Commune: A Revolution in Democracy.* Bookmarks, 2006; Haymarket, 2011.

Greenhalgh, Elizabeth. *The French Army and the First World War.* Cambridge UP, 2014.

Hardman, John. *The Life of Louis XVI.* Yale UP, 2016.

Hardman, John. *Marie-Antoinette: The Making of a French Queen.* Yale UP, 2019.

Harris, Ruth. *Dreyfus: Politics, Emotion, and the Scandal of the Century.* Holt, 2010.

Hazareesingh, Sudhir. *From Subject to Citizen: The Second Empire and the Emergence of Modern French Democracy.* Princeton UP, 1998.

Hazareesingh, Sudhir. *In the Shadow of the General: Modern France and the Myth of De Gaulle.* Oxford UP, 2012.

Hazareesingh, Sudhir. *Intellectual Founders of the Republic: Five Studies in Nineteenth-Century French Republican Political Thought.* Oxford UP, 2002.

Hazareesingh, Sudhir. *The Legend of Napoleon.* Granta, 2005.

Hewlett, Nick. *The Sarkozy Phenomenon.* Societas, 2011.

Higonnet, Patrice. *Goodness beyond Virtue: Jacobins during the French Revolution.* Harvard UP, 1998.

Hogg, Chloé. *Absolutist Attachments: Emotion, Media, and Absolutism in Seventeenth-century France.* Northwestern UP, 2019.

Holt, Mack, ed. *Renaissance and Reformation France.* Oxford UP, 2002.

Horne, Alistair. *The Age of Napoleon.* Modern Library, 2004.

Hunt, Lynn. *Politics, Culture and Class in the French Revolution.* U California P, 1985.

Jackson, Julian. *De Gaulle*. Belknap-Harvard UP, 2018.

Jackson, Julian. *France: The Dark Years, 1940–1944*. Oxford UP, 2001.

Jackson, Julian. *The Popular Front in France: Defending Democracy, 1934–38*. Cambridge UP, 1988.

Jackson, Julian, et al., eds. *May 68: Rethinking France's Last Revolution*. Palgrave Macmillan, 2011.

James, Edward. *The Franks*. Blackwell, 1988.

Jordan, David P. *Napoleon and the Revolution*. Palgrave Macmillan, 2012.

Kaiser, Thomas E., and Dale K. Van Kley, eds. *From Deficit to Deluge: The Origins of the French Revolution*. Stanford UP, 2011.

Kaplan, Stephen Laurence. *Farewell, Revolution: Disputed Legacies, France, 1789/1989*. Cornell UP, 1995.

Kirkland, Stephane. *Paris Reborn: Napoléon III, Baron Haussmann, and the Quest to Build a Modern City*. St. Martin's, 2013.

Knecht, R. J. *The French Wars of Religion, 1559–1598*. 3rd ed. Routledge, 2017.

Knecht, R. J. *The Rise and Fall of Renaissance France, 1483–1610*. 2nd ed. Wiley-Blackwell, 2002.

Knecht, R. J. *The Valois: Kings of France 1328–1589*. Hambledon Continuum, 2005.

Kurtz, Geoffrey. *Jean Jaurès: The Inner Life of Social Democracy*. Penn State UP, 2014.

Lackerstein, Debbie. *National Regeneration in Vichy France: Ideas and Policies, 1930–1944*. Routledge, 2012.

Landes, Joan B. *Women and the Public Sphere in the Age of the French Revolution*. Cornell UP, 1988.

Lawrence, Mark Atwood, and Fredrik Logevall, eds. *The First Vietnam War: Colonial Conflict and Cold War Crisis*. Harvard UP, 2007.

Le Goff, Jacques. *Saint Louis*. Trans. Evan Gollrad. U Notre Dame P, 2009.

Lorcin, Patricia M. E., ed. *Algeria & France, 1800–2000: Identity, Memory, Nostalgia*. Syracuse UP, 2006.

Lüsebrink, Hans-Jürgen, and Rolf Reichardt. *The Bastille: A History of a Symbol of Despotism*. Trans. Norbert Schürer, Duke UP, 1997.

Maclean, Mairi, ed. *The Mitterrand Years: Legacy and Evaluation*. Macmillan, 1998.

Macron, Emmanuel. *Revolution*. Trans. Jonathan Goldberg and Juliette Scott. Scribe, 2017.

Manning, Patrick. *Francophone Sub-Saharan Africa 1880–1985*. Cambridge UP, 1988.

Mansel, Philip. *King of the World: The Life of Louis XIV*. Allen Lane, 2019.

Marlière, Philippe. "France Is Still in Trouble." *New York Times*, 26 Apr. 2022, https://www.nytimes.com/2022/04/26/opinion/macron-france-le-pen.html.

Marrus, Michael R., and Robert O. Paxton. *Vichy France and the Jews*. Basic, 1981.

Mayeur, Jean Marie, and Madeleine Rebérioux. *The Third Republic from Its Origins to the Great War, 1871–1914*. Trans. J. R. Foster. Cambridge UP, 1984.

McKenzie, Brian Angus. *Remaking France: Americanization, Public Diplomacy, and the Marshall Plan*. Berghahn, 2005.

Naylor, Phillip C. *France and Algeria: A History of Decolonization and Transformation.* UP Florida, 2000.

Nelson, Janet L. *King and Emperor: A New Life of Charlemagne.* U California P, 2019.

Nester, William R. *De Gaulle's Legacy: The Art of Power in France's Fifth Republic.* Palgrave Macmillan, 2014.

Nora, Pierre, and Lawrence Kritzman, eds. *Realms of Memory: The Construction of the French Past.* Trans. Arthur Goldhammer. Columbia UP, 1996–1998. 3 vols.

Nord, Philip. *France's New Deal: From the Thirties to the Postwar Era.* Princeton UP, 2015.

Nord, Philip. *The Republican Moment: Struggles for Democracy in Nineteenth-century France.* Harvard UP, 1995.

Norwich, John Julius. *A History of France.* Atlantic Monthly P, 2018.

Palombarin, Stefano, and Bruno Amable. *The Last Neoliberal: Macron and the Origins of France's Political Crisis.* Verso, 2021.

Paxton, Robert O. *Vichy France: Old Guard and New Order, 1940–1944.* Rev. ed. Columbia UP, 2001.

Pedder, Sophie. *Revolution Française: Emmanuel Macron and the Quest to Reinvent a Nation.* Bloomsbury, 2018.

Pilbeam, Pamela M. *The Constitutional Monarchy in France, 1814–1848.* Routledge, 1999.

Popkin, Jeremy D. *A History of Modern France.* 5th ed. Routledge, 2020.

Popkin, Jeremy D. *A New World Begins: The History of the French Revolution.* Basic, 2019.

Price, Munro. *The Perilous Crown: France Between Revolutions 1814–1848.* Macmillan, 2007.

Raymond, Gino. *The Sarkozy Presidency: Breaking the Mould?* Palgrave Macmillan, 2013.

Reza, Yasmina. *Dawn, Dusk, or Night: A Year with Nicolas Sarkozy.* Trans. Yasmina Reza and Pierre Guglielmina. Random House, 2008.

Riché, Pierre. *The Carolingians: A Family Who Forged Europe.* Trans. Michael Idomir Allen. U Pennsylvania P, 1993.

Rosanvallon, Pierre. *Demands of Liberty: Civil Society in France since the Revolution.* Trans. Arthur Goldhammer. Harvard UP, 2007.

Ross, Kristin. *Fast Cars, Clean Bodies: Decolonization and the Reordering of French Culture.* MIT P, 1995.

Ross, Kristin. *May '68 and Its Afterlives.* U Chicago P, 2002.

Rousso, Henry. *The Vichy Syndrome: History and Memory in France since 1944.* Trans. Arthur Goldhammer. 2nd ed. Harvard UP, 1994.

Salje, Henrik, et al. "Estimating the Burden of SARS-CoV-2 in France." *Science*, vol. 368, no. 6500, 2020, pp. 208–211.

Sarkozy, Nicolas. *Testimony: France in the Twenty-first Century.* Trans. Philip H. Gordon. Pantheon, 2007.

Schama, Simon. *Citizens: A Chronicle of the French Revolution.* Knopf, 1989.

Scurr, Ruth. *Fatal Purity: Robespierre and the French Revolution.* Holt, 2006.

Shennan, Andrew. *Rethinking France: Plans for Renewal, 1940–46.* Oxford UP, 1989.

Shennan, J. H. *The Bourbons: A History of a Dynasty.* Bloomsbury, 2007.

Shepard, Todd. *The Invention of Decolonization: The Algerian War and the Remaking of France*. Cornell UP, 2006.

Short, Philip. *A Taste for Intrigue: The Multiple Lives of François Mitterrand*. Holt, 2014.

Singer, Barnett B. "Jules Ferry and the Laic Revolution in French Primary Education." *Paedagogica Historica: International Journal of the History of Education*, vol. 15, no. 2, 1975, pp. 406–425.

Smith, Leonard V., et al. *France and the Great War, 1914–1918*. Cambridge UP, 2003.

Sowerine, Charles. *France since 1870: Culture, Politics and Society*. 3rd ed. Red Globe P, 2018.

Stovall, Tyler. *Transnational France: The Modern History of a Universal Nation*. Westview P, 2015.

Strauss-Schom, Alan. *The Shadow Emperor: A Biography of Napoleon III*. St. Martin's, 2018.

Terrio, Susan J. "Crucible of the Millennium?: The Clovis Affair in Contemporary France." *Comparative Studies in Society and History*, vol. 41, no. 3, 1999, pp. 438–457.

Thomas, Martin, ed. *The French Colonial Mind*. U Nebraska P, 2011. 2 vols.

Tyerman, Christopher. *God's War: A New History of the Crusades*. Belknap-Harvard UP, 2006.

Wahnich, Sophie. *In Defence of the Terror: Liberty or Death in the French Revolution*. Trans. David Fernbach. Verso, 2012.

Wall, Irwin M. *The United States and the Making of Postwar France, 1945–1954*. Cambridge UP, 1991.

Ward, Alex. "Why France Has 4 Times as Many Coronavirus Deaths as Germany." *Vox*, 17 Apr. 2020, https://www.vox.com/2020/4/17/21223915/coronavirus-germany-france-cases -death-rate.

Warner, Marina. *Joan of Arc: The Image of Female Heroism*. New ed. Oxford UP, 2013.

Watson, William E. *The Tricolor and the Crescent: France and the Islamic World*. Praeger, 2003.

Watts, Jonathan. "Bruno Latour: 'This Is a Global Catastrophe That Has Come from Within.'" *The Guardian*, 6 Jun. 2020, https://www.theguardian.com/world/2020/jun /06/bruno-latour-coronavirus-gaia-hypothesis-climate-crisis.

Weber, Eugen. *Peasants into Frenchmen: The Modernization of Rural France, 1870–1914*. Stanford UP, 1976.

Williams, Charles. *Petain: How the Hero of France Became a Convicted Traitor and Changed the Course of History*. Palgrave Macmillan, 2005.

Wood, Ian. *The Merovingian Kingdoms, 450–751*. Longman, 1994.

Zeldin, Theodore. *History of French Passions, 1848–1945*. Clarendon P, 1973–1977. 5 vols.

CHAPTER 3

GOVERNMENT AND POLITICS

OVERVIEW

Modern French political life traces its origins back to the French Revolution (1789–1799) and the Napoleonic period (1799–1815) that followed. This tumultuous era left many issues unresolved (e.g., the type of regime that best suited France, reconciliation of democracy and order, church-state relations, and social justice/security in the industrial era). However, it also introduced new paradigms that were to remain permanent fixtures of French political culture, such as the inalienable rights and fundamental equality of citizens in the eyes of the law, the people as the ultimate source of sovereignty, vigorous political debate (and dissent) marked by intense left-right polarization, and the enduring presence of a well-organized and centralized state with considerable means of influence over economic and social life. After several instances of regime change in the wake of coups, revolutions, and military defeats, the republican form of government had established itself as a generally accepted norm in France by the end of the nineteenth century. But the French understanding of "The Republic" traditionally entails more than just a constitutional democracy without a monarch. It is the embodiment of a universalistic philosophical ideal and a specific iteration of French national identity. In addition to "Liberty, Equality, Fraternity," the republican model is founded on the Enlightenment's faith in reason and progress and strict secularism of public life. Once controversial (reviled by some, venerated by others), this broader understanding of the Republic is now the object of a fairly broad consensus and is set down in the preamble of the current French Constitution, which prescribes, "France shall be an indivisible, secular, democratic and social Republic."

France's current regime is known as the Fifth Republic because it was preceded by four others dating back to the Revolution. It was founded in 1958 in the challenging context of the Algerian War of Independence (1954–1962). Charles de Gaulle was its principal founder and first president. The Fifth Republic is not perfect (e.g., some complain that it concentrates too much power in the hands of the "monarchical" president or that it stifles civil society), but it is arguably the most successful, resilient, and popular republican regime in French history. The Fifth Republic combines elements of the presidential and parliamentary systems of government. The constitution and traditional practice favor the executive branch over the legislative branch. The former is two-headed—with a president (head of state) directly elected by voters every five years and a prime minister (head of government), who is named by the president but must have the confidence of a majority in the lower house of parliament (National Assembly). The possibility for a divided executive (cohabitation) still exists if the president's party or coalition partners should lose or fail to obtain (or maintain) a majority in the lower house. However, recent constitutional tweaks have reinforced the likelihood of united government behind the president. In such cases, the president sets the broad legislative and policy objectives of the government and takes the lead in matters pertaining to foreign affairs and national security, while the day-to-day operations of the administration and primary responsibility for domestic affairs are left to the prime minister and their cabinet. France has a bicameral legislature (parliament) comprised of a National Assembly and a Senate. Although the National Assembly is the lower house, it has more power (e.g., it may vote to overturn the prime minister's government) and enhanced legitimacy because its members are chosen by direct popular vote in legislative elections held once every five years. Senators are elected indirectly for six-year terms. The president has the power to dissolve the National Assembly and hold new legislative elections, but not the Senate.

France's politically independent judicial system includes different types of courts for civil and criminal cases. It is topped by three tribunals that share the prerogatives of a supreme court: the Cour de Cassation (civil and criminal appeals), the Conseil d'État (administrative rulings), and the Conseil Constitutionnel (elections oversight and constitutionality of legislation). As a unitary state with a historical aversion to federalism, power is concentrated in the national government. France is organized into three main levels of "territorial collectivities" at the subnational level: 18 regions, 101 departments, and over 35,000 local communes. Since 1982, France's territorial collectivities—in particular, its regions—have been given increased responsibilities. However, they do not legislate. Each type of territorial collectivity has its own type of popularly elected governing council. France has been a driving force behind the project of a united Europe since the creation of the European Coal and Steel Community (ECSC) in 1951 and the European Economic Community (EEC) in 1957 and is a charter member of the EU. It is an active member of numerous other international organizations, including the United Nations (it has a permanent seat and veto power on the UN Security Council) and the North Atlantic Treaty Organization (NATO). It seeks to play a prominent role in international affairs—an aspiration that relies in part on its military might, including its independent nuclear arsenal.

Democratic elections are the foundation of political life in France; however, public protests are an important means of direct political expression, and large demonstrations against unpopular policies are a French tradition. The two-round presidential election is the main event of French politics. The 2017 and 2022 French presidential elections have conceivably reshaped the French political landscape. Since the 1980s, two main forces have dominated electoral politics and taken turns in governing France: the center-left Socialist Party (PS, social democrats and progressives) and the center-right party now known as The Republicans (LR, traditional conservatives and neo-Gaullists). However, neither party's presidential candidate made it to the second-round runoff in either 2017 or 2022 (in 2022, their two candidates' combined share of the first-round vote was just 6.5%). The finalists in both of the most recent presidential elections were the centrist Emmanuel Macron (b. 1977)—a relative political new-comer whose party, the Republic on the Move (LREM, renamed Renaissance in May 2022), was less than a year old in 2017—and the far-right populist Marine Le Pen (b. 1968) of the National Rally (RN, formerly the National Front). Macron prevailed in a 66%–34% second-round landslide in 2017, and LREM went on to win a majority in the National Assembly. In 2022, the result was much closer, with Macron defeating Le Pen 58.55%–41.45% in the second round. Macron's still comfortable margin of victory in 2022 (seventeen points) was mitigated by his centrist coalition's (Ensemble, comprised of Renaissance and allied parties) failure to win a majority in the National Assembly in the June 2022 legislative elections. Furthermore, in both 2017 and 2022, far-left populist Jean-Luc Mélenchon—the leader of La France Insoumise (LFI)—did well: a fourth-place finish in the first round of 2017 at 19.6% and a third-place finish in the first round of 2022 at 22%, a little more than one point shy of qualification for the runoff. It is too early to tell which parties or formations will dominate France's shifting political landscape in the future. The Macron, Le Pen, and Mélenchon electorates were roughly equal in the presidential first round of 2022. The June 2022 National Assembly elections were not only a setback for Macron and Renaissance. They also resulted in the relative success of the Nouvelle Union Populaire Écologiste et Sociale (i.e., New People's Ecologist and Social Union), or Nupes, a newly formed coalition of left-of-center parties anchored by LFI, which emerged as a potent opposition force in the new National Assembly; and in the astonishing record number of seats in the chamber won by RN. While Renaissance's historic two presidential victories and one outright absolute majority in the National Assembly (2017) arguably make it the pre-eminent French political party of the moment, there is uncertainty about an already diminished Renaissance's future without Macron at the helm in 2027 and beyond. Moreover, French political culture remains, as in the past, highly polarized along left-right lines notwithstanding the currently ascendant center, although this polarization has most recently benefited the populist extremes on both the right and the left. RN's appeal has grown continuously alongside discontent with the political establishment (its share of the second-round presidential vote has steadily increased from 18% in 2002, to 34% in 2017, to 41.5% in 2022). A presidential victory by RN in 2027 would change everything in French politics.

The future of French electoral politics depends on several unknowns. One is the long-term viability of Renaissance (and of the autonomous political center built around it) after the end of Macron's second term in office (2022–2027). A second is the ability of RN not only to pull off a presidential election "upset" in 2027 (or 2032) but also to continue making significant gains at other levels (parliamentary, regional, and local). A third is whether the once-dominant legacy parties of center-right and center-left, LR and the PS, will persevere in staking out independent paths (perhaps hoping to benefit from a collapse of the Macronist center that had cannibalized large swaths of their electorates) at the risk of completing their slide into oblivion or opt for rapprochement with their respective populist rivals, RN and LFI. The relative success of the Nupes coalition (LFI, the PS, Europe Ecology-The Greens [EELV], the French Communist Party [PCF], and several smaller parties) in the 2022 National Assembly elections could be the harbinger of further restructuring and consolidation on the French left. Rapprochement between LR (and the broader mainstream right) and RN is a more complicated proposition given the stigma that still surrounds the latter in much of the French political establishment. In addition to the major parties already mentioned (i.e., ones that have governed in the past and/or have tallied impressive vote totals in recent elections), there are numerous smaller ones spread across the ideological spectrum, such as Reconquête (far right), La France Debout (far right), Mouvement Démocrate (center), Horizons (center), Génération.s (left), and Le Nouveau Parti Anticapitaliste (far left). The current political mood in France is tense, wary, disaffected, and potentially volatile (e.g., the Yellow Vests protests of 2018–2020). Major issues include employment, the cost of living, economic inequality and precariousness, education, France's competitiveness in the global economy, the future of the European Union, crime, terrorism, immigration, secularism and French identity in a more religiously and racially diverse society, social entitlements reforms (esp. retirements), health care, climate change and the environment, and the reinvigoration of democratic institutions.

Further Reading
Boyron (2012); Brouard et al. (2009); Chabal (2020); Cole (2017); Cole and Raymond (2006); Cole et al. (2008); Cole et al. (2013); Culpepper et al. (2006); Drake et al. (2020); Elgie et al. (2016); Gabriel et al. (2013); Gordon and Meunier (2001); Hazareesingh (1994); Knapp and Wright (2006); Maclean and Szarka (2009); Rieker (2017); Safran (2009); Safran (2019); Sauger (2010); Waters (2012).

Center

The modern French political landscape has always had a center. Historical examples include moderate factions and leaders in the French Revolution like the Girondins and the Marquis de Lafayette, liberal political thinkers like Germaine de Staël and Benjamin Constant, the more liberal Orleanists (e.g., King Louis-Philippe's prime minister François Guizot), the pragmatic and moderate Opportunist Republicans in the early decades of the Third Republic (1870–1900), the Christian Democrats (e.g., Georges Bidault, Robert Schuman) of the Popular Republican Movement (MRP, 1944–1967) during the Fourth Republic, and figures affiliated with the Fondation Saint-Simon (a think tank founded by historian François Furet) in the 1980s and 1990s. However, given the marked left-right polarization of French politics, a legacy of the French Revolution (1789–1799) reinforced by Fifth Republic presidentialism, centrists have formerly not been left with much room to develop as an independent force. Hence, most politicians who identified as "centrists" (or were classified as such) since the 1960s were associated with the most moderate faction of the right, the most prominent example being President Valéry Giscard d'Estaing (1974–1981) and politicians affiliated with his center-right Union for French Democracy (UDF, coalition 1978–1997, party 1997–2007).

President Emmanuel Macron with President Xi Jinping of China and Chancellor Angela Merkel of Germany at the Élysée Palace (French president's official residence) in Paris during Xi's state visit to France in 2018. When he was elected president in 2017, Macron (b. 1977) became the youngest leader of France since Napoleon Bonaparte. He has pursued economic and social entitlements reforms, sought to raise France's international profile, and dealt with both the Yellow Vest protests and COVID-19 pandemic. (Frédéric Legrand/Dreamstime.com)

Emmanuel Macron's meteoric political rise in 2016–2017, which culminated in his election as president in 2017 and reelection in 2022, has the potential to significantly alter the place, identity, and electoral appeal of French centrism for three reasons. The first is that while Macron himself came from the moderate and liberal (free market-friendly) wing of the Socialist Party—his role model is the former Socialist finance minister (1981–1984) and European Commission president (1985–1995) Jacques Delors—he has built a political movement that has pulled in both voters and politicians (e.g., his first two prime ministers, Édouard Philippe and Jean Castex) from the center-right. Furthermore, Macron's young The Republic on the Move (LREM) party—renamed Renaissance in May 2022 (a change intended to underscore its emphasis on innovation and reasonable solutions, reiterate its Europeanist policies, and appeal to a wider range of the elctorate)—won an outright majority in the June 2017 National Assembly elections, which provided a solid foundation for the party's future at the national level and suggests that its reach extends beyond presidential politics. Finally, LREM/Renaissance may benefit from the fact that the legacy parties of the mainstream left and right (Socialist Party and The Republicans) are under intense pressure from more radical forces on both ends of the political and ideological spectrum, which has alienated some of the moderate middle-class electorate of each party. France's other centrist parties include Mouvement Démocrate (more commonly known as MoDem), Horizons, the Radical Party, the Union for Democrats and Independents (UDI), The Centrists, and Centrist Alliance. MoDem has maintained close ties to Macron and LREM/Renaissance and was part of the Ensemble (Together) alliance—as was Philippe's boutique party, Horizons—that backed Macron's 2022 presidential reelection candidacy and operated as a coalition for the 2022 National Assembly elections, which ultimately produced an unsatisfactory outcome for Ensemble, which failed to secure an absolute majority in support of the reelected president.

A good synopsis of centrist thinking and policy priorities, Macron's declaration of principles (*profession de foi*) for the second round of the 2017 presidential election highlighted objectives in six broad "work zones":

1. Reinforcing the security of the nation by maintaining peace and fighting Islamist terrorism internationally, investing in domestic law enforcement, and restoring the authority of state and respect for its secular norms;
2. Placing proficiency in basic skills and the general knowledge of nation's culture and values at the core of educational policy;
3. Creating jobs by simplifying labor laws while also making major investments in training and continuing education;
4. Modernizing the economy by stressing economic mobility, the digital economy, research, innovation, and entrepreneurship freed of rigid regulations while maintaining a safety net for the most vulnerable members of society;
5. Fostering a democratic renewal in the nation's political life by holding elected officials and public servants to higher ethical standards, reducing the number of members of parliament so that representation of the public interest is simpler, and promoting candidates from outside the milieu of career politicians; and
6. Conducting a foreign policy that defends the nation's interests, promotes an ambitious and democratically vigorous vision of Europe, and implements a new policy in Africa emphasizing peace and free enterprise.

See also: Chapter 2: Timeline; Macron (Emmanuel) and the New Political Landscape of France. Chapter 3: Left; Right. Chapter 6: Bourgeoisie and Middle Class.

Further Reading
Craiutu (2012); Elgie (2018); Le Béguec (2015); Todd (2015); Zaretsky (2017).

Constitutional Council

France's supreme court on matters of constitutional law is the Constitutional Council (Conseil Constitutionnel), created in 1958. It also oversees French elections and referenda and must be consulted by the legislative and executive branches in moments of constitutional crisis or when the president invokes Article 16 of the French constitution (emergency powers). The council is comprised of nine members who serve a nonrenewable term of nine years and who are chosen in equal numbers by the president of the Republic, the president of the National Assembly, and the president of the Senate. Former presidents are ex officio lifetime voting members of the council. The council's current president is Laurent Fabius, named by President François Hollande in 2016.

Originally, only four officials could request that the constitutionality of a law (or treaty) be reviewed by the council: the presidents of the Republic, National Assembly, the Senate, and the prime minister—and the review had to take place before the law was passed and promulgated. Two changes in the 1970s increased the council's authority. A 1971 decision by the council stipulated that the rights enumerated in the 1789 Declaration of the Rights of Man and the Citizen were higher norms of French constitutional law. This not only broadened the grounds on which the constitutionality of laws could be assessed, but also turned the council itself into a guardian of civil liberties. In 1974, a constitutional amendment extended the right to trigger the review of a law or treaty—still prior to promulgation—to a petition supported by sixty parliamentarians of either chamber. This change enhanced the rights of political minorities to prevent majorities from forcing through a questionable law. A more far-reaching change in the council's prerogatives occurred in 2008 when a new constitutional amendment gave parties to civil, criminal, or administrative proceedings the right to appeal a lower court's or tribunal's decision on constitutional grounds, provided that either the High Court of Judicial Appeals (Cour de Cassation) or the Council of State (Conseil d'État) agreed to refer the matter to the Constitutional Council—that is, individual citizens now had the right to question the constitutionality of laws already on the books. However, this significant change was unlikely to usher in an era of widespread a posteriori constitutional challenges to unpopular or controversial laws as a work-around to the political and legislative process due to the long-standing French traditions of deference to the legislative branch and supremacy of written law over precedent.

See also: Chapter 3: Judicial System; Parliament; Presidency and Executive Branch.

Further Reading
Dyevre (2017); Latour (2009); Rogoff (2014).

Counterterrorism

The threat of terrorism targeting civilians in France is not a new problem. Since the 1950s, a range of causes and conflicts has served as a rationale for terrorist attacks in Paris and elsewhere. Until 2015, the deadliest such attack on French soil was a 1958 passenger train bombing that killed twenty-eight people, committed by the OAS, a right-wing group opposed to Algerian independence. Other attacks that have marked the French collective memory include ones attributed to the Venezuelan leftist and pro-Palestinian terrorist known as "Carlos the Jackal" (Ilich Ramírez Sánchez) in the 1970s, the 1982 attack on Goldenberg's Delicatessen in a Jewish neighborhood of Paris, and the 1995 bombing of the Saint-Michel commuter rail station in Paris during the Algerian Civil War (1991–2002). Since 2012, however, a series of attacks involving operatives or "lone-wolf" sympathizers of Islamist terror groups like Al-Qaeda in the Arabian Peninsula and the Islamic State of Iraq and the Levant (ISIL)—many of them French citizens or legal residents of France—has shaken France to its core. The three most infamous and deadly episodes all took place within an eighteen-month span in 2015–2016: the raid on the editorial offices of the satirical newspaper *Charlie Hebdo* (12 dead) and related hostage-taking at a kosher supermarket (4 dead), both in Paris, in January 2015; the coordinated attacks on multiple sites in Paris (Stade de France, Bataclan concert hall, sidewalk cafés) in November 2015 (130 dead); and the truck attack on the Promenade des Anglais in Nice, on Bastille Day, in July 2016 (86 dead).

In response, France has strengthened its counterterrorism laws and policies in various ways—more vigorous police tracking of individuals who represent a security risk (flagged in national databases with a *Fiche S*, or "S Card"), stepped-up prosecutions for "conspiratorial associations" related to a terrorist enterprise, expanded warrantless searches under certain conditions, more sophisticated means of video and cyber surveillance, pre-charge detentions, freezing the financial assets of individuals and entities believed to support terrorism, and the confiscation of passports of individuals who have traveled abroad to fight with jihadi groups. Launched in 1978 and modified several times since then, Vigipirate is France's nationwide alert system for terrorist and other national security threats.

After the 2015–2016 attacks, some experts argued that France already had all the tools it needed to fight terrorism. Nonetheless, a state of emergency was declared in 2015 and extended multiple times through November 1, 2017, when a sweeping new homeland security and counterterrorism law was passed under President Macron that made permanent many of the exceptional measures permitted under the state of emergency—the power to order the temporary closure of mosques or other places of worship where preachers have glorified terrorism or support for terrorism is known among the faithful, the authority to place individuals suspected of having terrorist ties but not formally charged with a crime under a form of limited house arrest, and the use of sophisticated algorithms to cull phone and e-mail communications for signs of suspicious activity. Proponents of the law maintained that it gave authorities more effective and modern means to prevent future attacks. Critics worried that it represented a threat to civil liberties, unfairly targeted French Muslims, and did not address the root causes of domestic terrorism.

See also: Chapter 2: Timeline; Macron (Emmanuel) and the New Political Landscape of France; Sarkozy (Nicolas) and the Hyper Presidency. Chapter 3: Military. Chapter 5: Islam.

Further Reading

Chowanietz (2016); D'Amato (2019); Foley (2013); Kepel (2017); Lançon (2020); Onishi and Méheut (2020); Titley (2017); Truc (2018); Vargo (2020).

Elections

French elections are held on Sundays so as not to conflict with voters' work obligations and to favor higher voter turnout. There is currently no early, electronic, or absentee voting. Voters who are unable to vote on election day in the locality where they are registered may authorize another registered voter to vote on their behalf by proxy. At their designated polling places, voters vote by inserting a paper ballot into a ballot box, which is still called an "urn." The legal voting age in France is eighteen. The direct popular election of the president, which takes place every five years in two rounds, is the most important national election. It receives massive media attention and structures political life in France to a preponderant extent. In the first round (mid-April), there are typically around ten candidates representing all the major parties and key minor parties, as well as some independent candidates. With or without a party's nomination, a presidential candidate qualifies for the ballot in the first round by securing the endorsements (*parrainages*) of 500 elected officials from thirty different departments. Unless a candidate wins the presidency in the first round by receiving a majority of votes cast, the top two vote getters in the first round face-off in the second-round runoff (late April–early May). Whoever receives the most votes in the second round is elected president and takes office within ten days. Since 1974, there has traditionally been a single nationally televised debate between the two finalists. To win the second round of the presidential election, a candidate must put together a broad presidential majority that reaches far beyond their own party. The French presidential election displays other unique characteristics. The campaign calendar is relatively short. Party primaries and nominating congresses typically feature two rounds of voting and take place in the late fall or early winter before the election year. The official list of candidates is announced by the Constitutional Council in March. From this point on, all candidates are to be given equal time and coverage in the media. An official campaign begins on the second Sunday preceding the first-round vote. There is an abbreviated official campaign that begins on the second Friday prior to the second round of voting. The main feature of the official campaign is a series of nationally broadcast candidate video clips that are publicly financed, bundled together at specific times, equal in total time, and adhere to certain format and content guidelines (personal "attack ads" are prohibited). There is no private purchasing of time for the airing of campaign ads in presidential elections (or any other type of election). There are strict campaign finance laws in France: spending is capped, only physical persons and parties are allowed to make contributions (which must be disclosed), and all official candidates in a presidential election are entitled to some degree of public funding. French campaign regulations are designed to treat all official candidates equally and thereby give voters an even playing field on which to compare candidates and make an informed choice.

Legislative (i.e., parliamentary) elections, in which all delegates (*députés*) to the National Assembly are selected, are the second most important type of elections held in France. Unless early elections are held following a presidential dissolution of the assembly, legislative elections are regularly scheduled to take place every five years shortly after the presidential election (i.e., in June). The format is similar to that of a presidential election insofar as there two rounds of voting. However, "triangular" runoffs between three finalists are not uncommon. Senatorial elections are held every three years to fill half of the seats in the chamber. Senators are not elected directly by voters but by 150,000 designated electors made up of elected officials. The election format—two-round or one-round proportional—depends on the number of seats allotted to each department. Regional, departmental, and municipal council elections are held every six years. Elections to the European Parliament are held every five years. Departmental elections are in two rounds and are contested by two-person tickets, with one male and one female candidate. This is one example of the implementation of a 1999 constitutional amendment mandating gender parity in elections. Parties are also required to field relatively equal numbers of male and female candidates and to list male and female candidates in alternate order in slate elections.

See also: Chapter 1: Administrative and Territorial Subdivisions. Chapter 2: Time-line; Macron (Emmanuel) and the New Political Landscape of France. Chapter 3: European Union; Parliament; Presidency and Executive Branch.

Further Reading
Evans and Ivaldi (2018); Lewis-Beck et al. (2011); Opella (2005); Wall (2014).

European Union

France has been involved in every phase of the construction of a united Europe since the creation of the six-member European Coal and Steel Community (ECSC) in 1951—a precursor of the European Economic Community (EEC, Treaty of Rome, 1957)—through the current twenty-seven-member EU, established by the Maastricht Treaty (1992). It was part of the first group of EU member nations to qualify for the use of the European common currency, the Euro. As such, it is a part of the nineteen-member Euro area, more commonly called the Eurozone, in which the European Central Bank (ECB), headquartered in Frankfurt, Germany, sets monetary policy for the member countries. France was also among the original members of the Schengen Area (established in 1995), within which there is free circulation of individuals from member countries. France is a member of the Erasmus student exchange program (created in 1987), the European Atomic Energy Community (EAEC, or Euratom, 1957), and every major European structure for defense cooperation and integration, including the European Defense Force (EDF). Several important European institutions are headquartered in France, including the European Parliament (Strasbourg), the European Court of Human Rights (Strasbourg), the Council of Europe (Strasbourg), and the European Space Agency (Paris).

From the French perspective, the EU is not only a foundation for sustainable peace, prosperity, free trade, and liberal democracy on the continent, it is also a means by which France can wield more power and influence internationally. The cultivation of close relations with Germany and the conviction that the Franco-German tandem is the "engine" of European unity have been a major component of France's European policy from the era of President Charles de Gaulle and Chancellor Konrad Adenauer. Several French officials have made important contributions to European unity. Foreign minister Robert Schuman (1886–1963) and government economic planner Jean Monnet (1888–1979) were among the architects of the ECSC and the Treaty of Rome creating the EEC. Jacques Delors (b. 1925) was president of the European Commission from 1985 to 1995 and played an instrumental role in the creation of the Single Market (Single European Act, 1986) and preparation for and implementation of the Maastricht Treaty. During his post-presidency, Valéry Giscard d'Estaing (1926–2020) served as president of the Convention on the Future of Europe, which drafted a detailed proposal for a European constitution. While the constitution itself was ultimately not fully ratified, many of its provisions were later incorporated in the Treaty of Lisbon, the current governing document of the EU (signed 2007, implemented 2009). French voters' rejection of the proposed EU constitution and the razor-thin margin by which they approved the Maastricht Treaty are indications of creeping Euroscepticism in French public opinion, which contrasts with the generally strong support for the EU among leaders, including French president Emmanuel Macron. The current and former governing parties are all officially pro-EU (despite some dissenters in the ranks), but this consensus does not apply to parties farther to the left and the right, like the left-wing France Unbowed (LFI), and the right-wing National Rally (RN), although both currently stop short of advocating a hard French version of "Brexit." Concerns often raised about the EU include an alleged lack of transparency and democracy in EU institutions, fear that the Euro may ultimately prove unsustainable without effective political union, EU integration's apparent failure to bring down unemployment rates, and overemphasis on fiscal austerity (and pleasing big business interests and the financial markets) at the expense of social welfare and economic stimulus. Sovereignists complain that membership in the EU forces France to give up too much of its national sovereignty. Counterarguments on the part of the pro-EU camp center on reminders of all the ways in which France has benefited from the EU and the havoc that its disintegration would wreak on the economies of its member states.

See also: Chapter 2: Timeline; de Gaulle (Charles), World War II, and the Fifth Republic; Macron (Emmanuel) and the New Political Landscape of France; Mitterrand (François) and France in the 1980s and 90s. Chapter 4: Overview; Agriculture; Trade. Chapter 8: Erasmus and International Educational Exchange in France.

Further Reading
Brinkley and Hackett (1991); Caton (2015); Dinan et al. (2017); Grossman (2019); Krotz and Schild (2013); Likaj et al. (2020), Pinder and Usherwood (2018).

Far Right

France has several political parties and numerous militant groups that can be situated on the far right. Common themes include disdain for globalization, multiculturalism, liberalism, and the nation's elites; and emphasis on law and order, forceful leadership, (European) cultural heritage, and putting France first. Many on the far right espouse some variation on the theme of a great divide between the "real nation" (the native French and their ancestral traditions and people who have fully assimilated those traditions) and the "legal nation" (currently functioning as a liberal and pluralistic democracy)—a distinction first made by Charles Maurras (1868–1952), the leader of the right-wing Catholic and royalist Action Française movement (founded in 1899) and theorist of "integral nationalism."

Since it was founded by Jean-Marie Le Pen in 1972, the National Front (Front National—FN), which changed its name to the National Rally (Rassemblement National—RN) in 2018, has been the leading political force of the French far right. A veteran of French colonial wars in Indochina and Algeria, Le Pen was first elected to the National Assembly in 1956 as a candidate of Pierre Poujade's populist UDCA (Union for the Defense of Shopkeepers and Craftsmen). The FN started gaining traction in the 1980s by adopting a hard line on immigration that stressed the allegedly unassimilable nature of Muslim immigrants from France's former North African and sub-Saharan African territories, advocating a get-tough approach in response to rising crime rates, condemning France's ruling political elite as feckless and corrupt, and appealing to the sense of economic disenfranchisement felt by the white working-class and lower middle-class people in a time of high unemployment and economic globalization. With increasing reliance on economic populism, the FN attempted to position itself as "neither left nor right." The strategy proved moderately successful as many working-class voters abandoned the French Communist Party in favor of the FN. In the 2002 presidential election, Le Pen produced what has been likened to a "political earthquake" when he qualified for the second-round runoff against the incumbent, Jacques Chirac. A measure of the relative strength of the FN's appeal was that its candidate averaged 15% in the first round of the five presidential elections held between 1988 and 2012.

The party presidency was taken over by Marine Le Pen, Jean-Marie's daughter, in 2011. Under her leadership, its positions still reflect the party's traditional core values. However, she has attempted to "de-demonize" the party by softening some of its positions and rhetoric, focusing on bread-and-butter economic issues like the high cost of living that adversely affects ordinary French people and families, stressing her self-styled image as an independent woman, identifying more closely with the Republic (esp. republican secularism), and purging the party of overt racism and anti-Semitism. These efforts led to the 2015 expulsion of her father. Marine Le Pen was the party's nominee for president in 2012, 2017, and 2022. In 2012, she failed to qualify for the second-round runoff. In 2017, she won 21.3% in the first round and 33.9% in the second round. The rebranded RN was the top vote getter in the 2019 European Parliament elections in France (23%) but underperformed in the 2021 regional elections. In the presidential election of 2022, Le Pen faced early stiff competition for votes from

Éric Zemmour, a provocative right-wing commentator. The latter's incendiary and divisive campaign rhetoric may have ended up helping Le Pen by allowing her to project a comparatively more sedate and inclusive form of nationalist populism. Le Pen received a 23% share of the vote in the 2022 first round and was defeated by Macron in the runoff, 41.5% to Macron's 58.5%. Not only were her vote shares record highs for the RN (and placed Le Pen closer to the French presidency than ever), but the three far-right candidates had a combined first-round vote share of 32% in 2022—a clear sign that right-wing populism/nationalism is on the rise in France. Furthermore, RN obtained a result of "seismic" proportions in the June 2022 legislative elections by winning a historically unprecedented eighty-nine seats in the new National Assembly. Smaller right-wing nationalist parties include Zemmour's Reconquest (Reconquête!), Rise Up France (Debout La France), and The Patriots. There are also numerous far-right fringe groups, such as the neofascist and white nationalist Generation Identity (Génération Identitaire), banned in 2021.

Le Pen conducted her 2017 presidential campaign under the generic heading "Marine, Présidente." Her declaration of principles for the second round centered on five main policy objectives that sought to appeal to a broad spectrum of the electorate:

1. Lower taxes to boost purchasing power without sacrificing the basic forms of national solidarity that help the needy and elderly;
2. Stimulate economic growth by rewarding hard work and create jobs by giving preferential treatment to French businesses;
3. Restore the integrity of democracy by giving the people a more direct say on major issues (e.g., through referenda and renegotiation of EU treaties);
4. Ensure domestic law and order and internal security by reestablishing border controls, beefing up law enforcement and the military, and adopting zero-tolerance policies; and
5. Eradicate the "Islamist menace" that threatens France by strict enforcement of secular norms, expulsion of suspected radicals, and shutting down of fundamentalist organizations and mosques.

See also: Chapter 2: Timeline; Macron (Emmanuel) and the New Political Landscape of France. Chapter 3: European Union; Right. Chapter 5: Islam; Judaism. Chapter 6: Arabs; Blacks; Immigration; Working Class.

Further Reading
Bar-On (2013); Eltchaninoff (2018); Lilla (2018); Marcus (1995); Marthaler (2020); Mounck (2022); Shields (2007); Stockemer (2017).

Judicial System

France has an independent judiciary comprised of several different types of courts and tribunals. Disputes between individuals and public institutions and administrative services of the state or regional and local authorities are handled by a *tribunal administrative* (administrative tribunal), which is not a judicial court. Civil cases are heard in either a local *tribunal de proximité* (<€10,000 at stake) or district *tribunal judiciaire*. This type of court also has jurisdiction over torts, probate cases, and contract disputes. In major cases (≥€10,000 at stake), both the plaintiff and defendant are represented by counsel and the case is heard by a three-judge panel without a jury in a *tribunal de grande instance* (TGI)—i.e., superior court. Family affairs courts (a single judge presiding over closed proceedings) are a subcategory of the *tribunal de grande instance*. France has several specialized civil courts. A *conseil des prud'hommes* (labor court) hears cases involving disputes between employees and employers. A *tribunal de commerce* hears cases pertaining to acts of commerce, including business-to-business disputes and bankruptcies. Its judges are not professional magistrates but businesspeople elected by other businesspeople.

Four types of courts deal with criminal cases. Cases involving minor infractions (*contraventions*) that are punishable by fines, community service, or the suspension of privileges (e.g., a driver's license) are heard in a *tribunal de police* (police tribunal). A single judge presides over the case. The state is represented by the public prosecutor, their deputy, or a police captain. Cases involving criminal offenses that are officially considered misdemeanors (*délits*), including some that may be classified as lower-class felonies in other countries, are tried in a *tribunal correctionnel* (a section of the TGI). This type of court has jurisdiction over property crimes such as theft, embezzlement, and fraud; crimes against persons such as assaults, child abuse, and procuring (prostitution); and crimes against society such as the use of counterfeit documents, violence against a public official, and usurpation of a professional title without proper accreditation. A case may be tried by a single judge or a three-judge panel—in either case without a jury. Cases involving major criminal offenses (punishable by 20+ years in prison) such as murder, armed robbery, and terrorism are tried in a *cour d'assises* (assize court). There is one such court in every department. A three-judge panel (a president and two assessors) hears the case, which is decided by the judges in consultation with a six-person citizen jury. In addition to the prosecutor (who represents the people as an agent of *le ministère public*) and the attorney for the defense, there may also be an attorney who represents the victim (in French legal terminology, *la partie civile*). Beginning in 2023, following a test period, felonies punishable by 15–20 years in prison (e.g., rape and involuntary homicide involving non-repeat offenders) will be tried before a five-magistrate panel (no jury) in a *cour criminelle*. There are special courts in France for minors: the *juge pour enfants* (judge for children), *tribunal pour enfants* (tribunal for children) and *cour d'assises des mineurs* (assize court for minors).

Criminal investigations in France take place in two phases: a preliminary police investigation under the supervision of the public prosecutor's office after a criminal complaint filed by a victim or a law enforcement official in order to determine if a crime has been committed and to identify a suspect, followed by an in-depth investigation under the supervision of *a juge d'instruction* (an investigating magistrate), who determines if a case for prosecution of the suspect can be built. The evidence is initially presented at a pretrial hearing that is similar to a grand jury hearing.

Appeals in civil cases, lesser criminal cases, and cases involving special jurisdictions are heard in *cours d'appel* (courts of appeals), which have separate chambers for dealing with different types of cases (there are 35 district courts of appeals nationwide). Appeals in cases first tried in an assize court (major criminal cases) are heard by a differently composed assize court. Any of the above-mentioned cases may be further appealed to the national *Cour de Cassation*, a high court of judicial review, which does not pass judgment on the substance of a case but only on its procedural regularity and uniform application of the law. Appeals in most cases first heard in an administrative tribunal are heard by one of the seven regional *cours administratives d'appel* (administrative courts of appeals). Final review (cassation) of administrative law cases on procedural grounds are heard by the Conseil d'État (Council of State). This venerable national institution has a hybrid role. While it has the final say on matters of administrative justice, it also hears some appeals directly and may be asked to nullify certain ministerial decrees alleged to be improper. It also advises the government on the language of proposed laws and decrees and on the interpretation of existing decrees. Since 2008, an individual (or corporate entity) involved in a civil, criminal, or administrative proceeding who believes that they have been subjected to a law or other official text that is unconstitutional, may ask the Conseil Constitutionnel (Constitutional Council) to review the constitutionality of that law or text. A constitutional appeal of this nature (*question prioritaire de constitutionnalité*) is not made directly by the plaintiff but upon referral by the Cour de Cassation or Conseil d'État.

LAW ENFORCEMENT

Police power in France is centralized under the authority of the Ministry of the Interior. The National Police has responsibility for law enforcement and public safety in urban areas, whereas the National Gendarmerie has responsibility in smaller towns and rural areas. The latter is also responsible for security on highways and at airports. It is considered a branch of the French armed forces. Both organizations have special forces units. The Gendarmerie's special forces include the GIGN, an elite unit used in counterterrorism and hostage rescue operations. The CRS (Republican Security Companies), a branch of the National Police, are mobile reserve units known for providing security at major public events and sensitive sites. The DCPJ (Central Directorate of the Judicial Police), the equivalent of the U.S. FBI, investigates major crimes nationwide, including organized crime and cybercrime. It works closely with the DGSI (General Directorate for Internal Security) on counterterrorism. The latter's counterpart in foreign intelligence gathering is the DGSE (General Directorate for External Security), France's equivalent of the CIA. Local police forces (*police municipale*) are maintained in many French cities and towns under the authority of the mayor. The Paris Prefecture of Police is a special branch of the Ministry of the Interior that oversees the National Police and other emergency services (as well as the delivery of residency cards to foreigners) in Paris and surrounding suburban departments.

See also: Chapter 2: Napoleon Bonaparte (Napoleon I) and the First Empire. Chapter 3: Constitutional Council; Counterterrorism. Chapter 7: Gender Equality and Sexual Harassment.

Further Reading
de Maillard and Skogan (2020); Elliott (2006); Steiner (2018); Terrill (2012).

Left

Historically, the French left is defined in terms of a strong attachment to the legacy of the French Revolution (liberty, equality, fraternity, and the power of the people over tyranny and privilege) and the values of the Republic (secularism, education, democracy, the indivisibility of the nation, non-chauvinistic patriotism, justice, and the rule of law). It sees itself as on the side of progress, individual emancipation, freedom of conscience, and social justice, and defends the ideal of a pluralistic and open society in which civil and political rights are broadly protected and racism is anathema. It positions itself as an advocate of working people, is suspicious of big business, and supports a generous social safety net and broad array of egalitarian public goods and services. It espouses an internationalist outlook that is sympathetic to the developing world, oppressed peoples, and minorities, and is wary of militarism. In recent times, it has staked out increasingly environmentalist positions. In the pantheon of heroes of the left, one finds Voltaire, Jean-Jacques Rousseau, Abbé Sieyès, Georges Danton, Jean-Paul Marat, Louis Blanc, Victor Hugo, the Communards, Jules Ferry, Émile Zola, Jean Jaurès, Georges Clemenceau, Léon Blum, Jean-Paul Sartre, Aimé Césaire, the student protesters of May 68, the signers of the Manifesto of the 343 (in favor of abortion rights), François Mitterrand, and the *Charlie Hebdo* martyrs.

In terms of the political landscape today, the French left is divided into three factions. Moderates and pragmatists (the center-left) were formerly the dominant faction—social democrats who have made their peace with the market economy and support the EU in its current form but still favor a bigger role for the state in economic life and as a guarantor of social solidarity. For close to fifty years, the Socialist Party (PS) embodied the French center-left. The party came into existence as the result of efforts in the 1960s to unite the non-Communist left but traces its roots back to the democratic socialist SFIO (Section Française de l'Internationale Ouvrière), founded in 1905. Following the Épinay Congress of 1971, the newly created PS was led by François Mitterrand, who concluded an electoral alliance with the French Communist Party (PCF) known as the Programme Commun (1972) and won the presidency in 1981. Reelected in 1988, Mitterrand remained president until 1995. The PS has been in power two other times—during the cohabitation premiership of Lionel Jospin (1997–2002) and during the presidency of François Hollande (2012–2017). During these periods, the Socialists and their allies championed progressive social reforms such as the abolition of the death penalty (1981), minimum income for the poor (1988), the thirty-five-hour workweek (2000), and marriage equality for same-sex couples (2013).

However, the Socialists lost considerable support due to their embrace of fiscal austerity and rapprochement with global big business. Hollande recorded the lowest presidential approval ratings in history and the party went on to historically poor results in the 2017 presidential and legislative elections: its presidential candidate, Benoît Hamon, finished a distant fourth in the first round with 6.4% of the vote and the PS won just thirty seats in the National Assembly. The PS candidate in the 2022 presidential election, Paris mayor Anne Hildalgo, did even worse, garnering a paltry 1.75% share of the first-round vote. While the PS remains for the time being somewhat more competitive at the regional and local levels, its disastrous result in 2022, following its poor one in 2017, suggest that the PS could be a spent force in national politics, if not on the verge of extinction. Created via a merger in 2010, Europe Ecology–The Greens (EELV), is a pro-EU and progressive ecologist party that has often formed alliances with the PS. EELV and its antecedents (the French Green Party dates back to 1984) have done better in European parliamentary elections, including a 16.3% vote share in 2009. Its highest share in a national election came in the legislative elections of 1997 (6.8%). The party did relatively well in the 2020 municipal elections, prompting talk of a mini "green wave." Its 2022 presidential candidate, Dominique Jadot, received a 4.6% share of the vote in the first round—disappointing but still better than the PS candidate. In the wake of the 2017 election cycle, many moderates left the PS to join President Macron's liberal centrist party (LREM, now called Renaissance). Hamon formed his own boutique party, Génération.s, in 2017, with the goal of sparking a rebirth of the progressive, non-populist left. The poor 2022 presidential election results for both the PS and EELV have increased pressure on these parties to make common cause with the ascendant populist left. Another smaller (but less moderate) party of the traditional left is the Republican and Socialist Left (Gauche Républicaine et Socialiste, or GRS), which traces its roots back to the Mouvement des Citoyens (Citizens' Movement), founded by dissident former PS members Jean-Pierre Chevènement and Max Gallo in 1993.

The second faction is the "left of the left," which includes leftist populists, proponents of alter-globalization, Eurosceptical democratic socialists, and radical eco-socialists. One of the main driving forces of this faction is Jean-Luc Mélenchon, who left the PS in 2008 to form the Left Party (Parti de Gauche). In 2016, Mélenchon formed a new party with a distinctly populist character called La France Insoumise (LFI), which can be translated into English as "Unsubmissive France" or "France Unbowed." He was the party's nominee in the presidential election of 2017 and finished fourth in the first round, with a 19.6% share of the vote—just two points away from qualification for the runoff. Once again a candidate for the presidency in 2022, Mélenchon improved on his 2017 result, receiving just shy of 22% of the first-round vote—a third-place finish a little more than one point from Marine Le Pen and qualification for the runoff. Key points of LFI's 2017 program ("The Future in Common") were a constitutional convention to create the Sixth Republic, the possibility of recall elections for French elected officials, France's withdrawal from NATO, democratic restructuring of the EU through major changes to existing treaties, working toward the use of 100% renewable energy by 2050, an increase in the minimum wage, and stringent banking regulations separating investment banks from savings banks.

Founded at the Congress of Tours in 1920, the French Communist Party (PCF) was once the largest opposition party in France—regularly receiving a 20% share of the vote in the first round of legislative elections between 1946 and 1978. However, the PCF hemorrhaged support in 1970s, 1980s, and 1990s due to the electoral dominance of the PS, the negative image of communism in general, and its loss of a significant share of the working-class vote to the right-wing National Front (now called the National Rally). In the 2017 legislative elections, the PCF received just a 2.7% share of the vote. Its 2022 presidential candidate (Fabien Roussel) received 2.3% of the first-round vote (a figure that might have put Mélenchon into the second round had the PCF not fielded its own candidate). While the PCF can now be considered a minor party, it still has a relatively large membership (70,000), historic ties to a major labor union (CGT), and an ownership share of a still influential daily newspaper, *L'Humanité*. Its anti-capitalist rhetoric and many of its policy positions are compatible with those advocated by Unbowed France. A question that looms large over the future of the left is whether factional division will continue to be the norm or a "big tent" alliance spanning the center-left and left of the left will be formed for major elections to offset the shrinking stature of the once dominant PS. Indeed, for the June 2022 National Assembly elections, the PS, EELV, the PCF, and Générations formed a provisional coalition, the New People's Ecologist and Social Union (Nupes)—a name based on that of the smaller Union Populaire (People's Union) coalition that backed Mélenchon's 2022 presidential candidacy. The four main points of the Nupes platform were "Earn more to live better" (e.g., price freezes on basic necessities), "An economy for the people and the planet" (e.g., transition to green agriculture), "Social and human progress" (e.g., retirement at age 60, Sixth Republic, citizen referenda, 1% of the GDP for culture), and "Fiscal justice" (e.g., taxes on multinational corporations). While Nupes fell short of its stated objective of winning a majority in the National Assembly and forcing Macron into a power-sharing arrangement (cohabitation) with Mélenchon as prime minister, it emerged as a potent opposition force in the chamber—an outcome that could facilitate continued collaboration and consolidation among the parties of the French left.

The parties that make up the third faction of the French left, the "ultra-left," are more interested in dissent and ideas than in electoral success. The best known of these parties are Workers' Struggle (Lutte Ouvrière, or LO, founded in 1956) and the New Anticapitalist Party (NPA, founded in 2009). Both have Trotskyist roots and regularly run candidates in presidential elections.

See also: Chapter 2: Timeline; Ferry (Jules) and the Third Republic; Macron (Emmanuel) and the New Political Landscape of France; Mitterrand (François) and France in the 1980s and 90s; Robespierre (Maximilien) and the French Revolution; Sarkozy (Nicolas) and the Hyper Presidency. Chapter 3: Center; Protests; Republic; Right. Chapter 4: Social Security and Health Care. Chapter 5: Laïcité. Chapter 6: Income Distribution and Inequality; Working Class. Chapter 8: Republicanism and Public Schools.

Further Reading

Bell and Criddle (2014); Clift (2017); Davey (2015); Di Francesco-Mayot (2017); Judt (1986); Kaplan (2002); Marlière (2019); Raymond (2005); Serfaty (2019), Stangler (2020); van Haute (2016).

Military

France is a world military power situated in a tier just below that of the three superpowers: United States, Russia, and China. It has the sixth largest defense budget in the world. The 2018 national budget allotted €42.5 billion to defense. This figure represents 9.5% of the total general budget. French defense spending in 2017 was equivalent to 2.2% of the GDP according the World Bank. A plan announced in 2018 calls for a 40% increase in defense spending by 2025. France is ranked fifth in the world in overall military strength according to Global Firepower's "2018 Military Strength Ranking." It has the largest active duty military force in Europe (not counting Russia), with over 200,000 active duty personnel. Its army has more than 400 combat tanks and 6,300 armored fighting vehicles. Its air force has more than 1,200 total aircraft, including 280 fighter/attack planes (counting naval aviation). Its navy has close to 120 large ships, including four aircraft carriers, twelve destroyers, and ten nuclear-powered submarines. France has a potent, independent, and primarily sea-based nuclear deterrent. It successfully tested its first atomic weapon in 1960, becoming the fourth nation to join the "nuclear club." It currently has the third largest stockpile of nuclear weapons in the world (300 nuclear warheads).

France has a proud military tradition dating back to the days of the monarchy. It was the greatest military power in the world under Napoleon (1799–1815) and showed strength and resilience in World War I (1914–1918). During the presidency of Charles de Gaulle (1958–1969), France charted an independent course in matters of national defense and foreign policy with respect to the United States while remaining a U.S. ally. France is a charter member of NATO (1949), but it withdrew from NATO's unified military command structure in 1966. Military rapprochement with the United States and NATO began with participation in the U.S.-led coalition in the 1990–1991 Gulf War. France sent forces to Afghanistan in 2001 and withdrew most of them in 2012. A new rift between France and the United States opened with France's vocal opposition to the U.S.-led invasion of Iraq in 2003; however, France rejoined the integrated NATO command structure in 2009 under President Nicolas Sarkozy. In recent years, the military has been active in international military missions in a range of locations in Africa (where it was once a leading colonial power), including Ivory Coast, Chad, Libya, Somalia, Mali, and the Central African Republic. France derives additional influence over global military and foreign affairs via its permanent seat and veto power on the UN Security Council. It has an all-volunteer, professional military (mandatory conscription ended in 2001) that includes the French Foreign Legion, an elite infantry corps that was founded in 1831 and is open to both French citizens and foreign nationals. The president of the Republic is the commander-in-chief of French armed forces. Civilian control is further guaranteed through the Ministry of Armed Forces (formerly, Ministry of Defense). The top military officer is the chief of the general staff of the armies. One of France's most honored patriotic and military traditions is the annual military parade on the Champs-Élysées on July 14 (Bastille Day).

See also: Chapter 2: Timeline; Clemenceau (Georges) and World War I; de Gaulle (Charles), World War II, and the Fifth Republic; Napoleon Bonaparte (Napoleon I) and the First Empire. Chapter 3: Counterterrorism; Presidency and Executive Branch.

Further Reading

Charbonneau (2008); Chuter (1997); Gordon (1993); Gordon (1995); Hopkins and Hu (1994); Laird (2019); Osterman (2018); Stöhs (2018).

Parliament

France has a bicameral legislature. The lower house, the National Assembly, consists of 577 delegates (*deputés*) who serve five-year terms. The National Assembly meets in the Palais Bourbon, on the left bank of the Seine in Paris. The upper house, the Senate, consists of 384 senators who are elected as representatives of France's departments. Senators serve six-year terms and are elected indirectly by a body of 150,000 electors made up of other elected officials. The Senate meets in the Palais de Luxembourg. The National Assembly has greater authority and standing than the Senate because its members are chosen by direct popular election. The prime minister's government requires the support of the National Assembly and may be ousted by a vote of no confidence or a motion of censure in the chamber. However, the president has the power to dissolve the National Assembly and call for new legislative elections. The Senate was designed to be more isolated from political whims, and carefully deliberative. This is the reason for its indirect mode of election and its indissoluble nature. Members of both chambers normally join caucuses, which may be limited to members of a single party or include members from several parties with compatible political views.

Legislation may originate in either chamber with a few notable exceptions (e.g., finance bills must start in the National Assembly). If the proposed legislation comes from the executive branch (the prime minister's government can propose legislation, but not the president, who may "legislate" via referendum), its consideration may begin in either chamber. The legislative process resembles that in other parliamentary democracies. A bill is first considered by the relevant committee and then, if approved by the committee, examined, debated, and voted on the floor of the chamber in which it originated. Back-and-forth consideration and negotiation between the two chambers is called the "parliamentary shuttle." Passage by both chambers is required for a bill to become law. However, there are special procedures that authorize the executive to legislate by decree. Most laws are passed by a simple majority of the members voting (there is no parliamentary maneuver equivalent to the U.S. Senate's tradition of the filibuster). Constitutional amendments must be passed by a three-fifths majority at a joint session of parliament, which is called the Congress and convenes at Versailles (they may also be approved by referendum). Some experts feel that the French system of government is too heavily weighted in favor of the executive (esp. the president) and several recent reforms have been implemented to enhance the role of parliament.

France has a third constitutionally designated representative assembly, but it does not legislate—the Economic, Social, and Environmental Council—a 233-member advisory body that meets at the Palais d'Iéna. Most (70%) of its members are elected by organizations that represent specific interests (unions, professional groups, non-profit organizations, etc.). The government (executive) names the remaining (30%) members, who may include experts and representatives of stakeholder groups not covered by the officially recognized nominating organizations. The council represents civil society and is consulted by the government on major issues and potential legislation that impacts the economy, society, or the environment.

See also: Chapter 2: Timeline; Macron (Emmanuel) and the New Political Landscape of France. Chapter 3: Elections; Presidency and Executive Branch; Republic.

Further Reading
Costa (2014); Gabriel et al. (2018); Rozenberg (2020); Smith (2009).

Presidency and Executive Branch

The French Fifth Republic is a semi-presidential regime. It displays certain features of a presidential regime insofar as the president of the Republic is not a ceremonial figure but has actual executive power, derives considerable political legitimacy and capital from being popularly elected, and is not responsible to the parliament. However, it also has features of a parliamentary regime insofar as the "government" (the prime minister and ministers who make up the cabinet) needs the backing of a majority in the National Assembly. The French system thus has the unusual feature of a two-headed executive with both a president (the head of state) and a prime minister (the head of government). By design and by tradition, the Fifth Republic gives greater weight to the executive branch than to the legislative branch, and to the president within the executive branch. Under normal circumstances, the presidential and National Assembly (the lower but more important chamber of parliament) majorities coincide and the system functions like a "republican monarchy." The president determines the major policy initiatives and handles the most important affairs of state and the prime minister, with the help of the other ministers, looks after domestic affairs and the day-to-day operations of the executive branch of government, and develops proposed major new legislation to be considered by parliament.

"Cohabitation" was an intermittent problem under the Fifth Republic before the passage of the constitutional amendments and other fixes designed to make it unlikely (though still possible). Under cohabitation, the president must name and share executive power with a prime minister who represents a parliamentary majority not aligned with the president following a National Assembly election loss by the president's party or coalition or the breakup of that coalition. In such cases, the balance of executive power shifts to the prime minister even though the president retains preeminence in foreign affairs and national security. Even under normal circumstances, the exact nature of the working relationship between the president and the prime minister varies, but the latter is typically subservient to the former, notwithstanding the prime minister's own constitutionally prescribed powers. In certain cases (e.g., a major policy setback, poor results in a key off-year election, declining approval ratings, or preparation for upcoming legislative elections), the president may signal a new direction by naming a new prime minister, who then shuffles the cabinet. Cohabitation occurred twice during the presidency of François Mitterrand, and once under President Chirac.

The president's role in the business of governance is largely unspecified in the constitution, but their constitutional powers give them the tools to have a significant impact on the political direction of the country. Moreover, the French people clearly view the president as the nation's leader and head of the executive branch. The president names the prime minister and is consulted by the latter on the composition of the government (cabinet). The president may ask for the resignation of the prime minister and their government. The president, not the prime minister, conducts meetings of the council of ministers (cabinet), signs executive decrees, and directly makes a number of high-level military and civilian appointments. The president has the power to dissolve the National Assembly and call for new legislative elections and may also call for a referendum on a proposed change to the constitution or some other major legislative initiative. The president is the commander-in-chief of French armed forces and has a special role in international diplomacy and the negotiation and signing of treaties. Pursuant to Article 16 of the French constitution, the president may assume emergency powers for a limited time in circumstances of grave danger to the Republic. The president takes office eight to thirteen days following their election, or reelection, in a ceremony at the Élysée Palace (the president's official residence) that includes an address to the nation, but no oath. When the president is elected to a first term, this is followed by a motorcade up the Champs-Élysées and the relighting of the flame at the tomb of the unknown soldier at the base of the Arc de Triomphe, tributes to historical figures of special importance to the president, and a reception at Paris city hall (second-term inaugurations tend to be more scaled-back affairs). Presidents are limited to two consecutive terms but may run again for a nonconsecutive term. If a president dies in office, resigns, is removed from office, or prevented from performing their duties due to illness, the president of the Senate serves as interim president until the titular president is able to resume their duties or a new presidential election is held (within thirty-five days).

According to the constitution, it is the prime minister, assisted by the members of the government (cabinet ministers), who is responsible for conducting the political business of the nation, executing laws, ensuring the national defense, and heading the public administration. The prime minister may submit a legislative proposal to the parliament or also ask for its approval to legislate by ordinance (decree), a method typically used for technically complex or politically sensitive measures. The prime minister and other ministers do not need to be confirmed by parliament, but they are responsible to the parliament and appear before the National Assembly on a regular basis to answer lawmakers' questions and defend their actions. They must have the support of a majority in the National Assembly. The prime minister's government may be ousted if it loses a vote of confidence or motion of censure in the chamber. The structure and nomenclature in each government (the ministers who make up the cabinet and their respective ministries) vary and a clear hierarchy among ministers is manifest in both their official titles (minsters of state have the highest status) and the order in which they are named. The prime minister's official residence is Hôtel de Matignon. Journalists use "Matignon" as shorthand to refer to the office of the prime minister just as they use "L'Élysée" to refer to the office of the president. Certain key ministries are also commonly referred to by their Paris location. Foreign Affairs is "Le Quai d'Orsay," Economy and Finance is "Bercy," Justice is "La Place Vendôme," Interior is "La Place Beauvau," Culture is "La Rue de Valois," and Education is "La Rue de Grenelle." Many top positions in ministries and other administrative agencies are filled from the ranks of *les grands corps de l'État*—elite corps of public servants who have studied at specific *grandes écoles* and have a lifetime tenure in a specific corps of experts.

See also: Chapter 2: Timeline; de Gaulle (Charles), World War II, and the Fifth Republic; Macron (Emmanuel) and the New Political Landscape of France; Mitterrand (François) and France in the 1980s and 90s; Sarkozy (Nicolas) and the Hyper Presidency. Chapter 3: Elections; Parliament. Chapter 12: Ministry of Culture.

Further Reading
Bell (2000); D. S. Bell and Gaffney (2013); Gaffney and Milne (1997); Genieys (2010).

Protests

Public protest—especially large street demonstrations (*manifestations*, or *manifs*)—is an important form of political expression and check on government power and overreach. For many French people, it is a rite of passage of one's youth that often leads to other forms of political engagement later in life. Major protests are national in scope, but most include a Parisian component because political power is still concentrated in Paris. Bringing tens of thousands of people—and sometimes a million or more people—into the streets of the capital can have a powerful impact on the country's political decision-making. Progressive and left-wing protests tend to take place around Place de la République and the Place de la Bastille in eastern Paris, whereas

A Yellow Vest protest in the city of Bordeaux (Gironde department, southwestern France) in 2018. The movement's name derives from the fluorescent yellow safety vests that all French motorists are required to keep in their vehicles. It began as a protest of an ecotax on diesel and gasoline, but developed into a wide-ranging indictment of neoliberalism, government austerity measures, insufficient democracy, and the leadership style and policies of President Emmanuel Macron. (Chelsdo/Dreamstime.com)

conservative and right-wing ones tend to take place in western locations in the city, like Champ de Mars and Place de la Concorde. The Champs-Élysées is another prominent locus of protest, especially when the issue mobilizes people across the political spectrum. Student protests of all persuasions often involve the Latin Quarter (university district) of Paris and its main thoroughfare, Boulevard Saint-Michel.

Recent French history is full of noteworthy examples of massive protests. In May–June of 1968, student protesters, supported by striking workers, nearly brought down the government and ushered in a new era of liberal social change. In 1984, 850,000 to 2 million conservative protesters nationwide forced the Socialist government to abandon a plan to merge public and private schools. In November 1995, left-leaning protesters and striking workers staged a month-long protest that forced a conservative government to abandon austerity-minded reforms of the retirement system. In 2002, close to a million people nationwide protested xenophobic right-wing candidate Jean-Marie Le Pen's qualification for the presidential runoff. In 2005, weeks of protests and rioting on the outskirts of French cities came in response to yet another fatal encounter between minority youths and the police. In 2013, both supporters and opponents of the Hollande administration's proposed law to extend marriage rights to same-sex couples staged massive rallies. On January 11, 2015, an estimated 3.7 million people nationwide took part in "republican marches" in support of free speech, secularism, and tolerance in reaction to the terrorist attack on the editorial offices of the satirical newspaper *Charlie Hebdo*—many of them brandishing signs proclaiming "Je suis Charlie." In 2017, business-friendly labor law reforms led to the Nuit Debout ("Up All Night") movement.

The most striking example of protest during the presidency of Emmanuel Macron was the Yellow Vest movement of 2018–2020. Named for the fluorescent yellow safety vests that French motorists are required to carry in their vehicles for roadside emergencies, the movement began in May 2018 with an online petition against a new ecotax on gasoline and diesel. Weekly grassroots "Acts" featured people wearing the vests occupying roundabouts, major avenues and public spaces, highway interchanges, and toll plazas. Officials estimate that 1.3 million took part in the movement's Act I (November 17, 2018). In November–December 2018, the protests took on an insurrectional quality with violent encounters between protesters and the police and acts of vandalism on the Champs-Élysées and elsewhere. For the Yellow Vests, the ecotax on fuel was emblematic of the disproportionate burden of sacrifice and austerity that market-oriented government policies placed on ordinary people. Broader demands ranged from inflation-indexed household revenues and massive reinvestment in public services, to citizen-initiated referenda (RIC) and recall elections and the president's resignation. Macron addressed the nation in December and organized a nationwide consultation ("Le Grand Débat") in 2019 on four sets of issues: taxes and public spending, democracy and citizenship, government structures and public services, and ecological transition. He announced a limited array of conciliatory reforms in April 2019.

See also: Chapter 2: Timeline; de Gaulle (Charles), World War II, and the Fifth Republic; Macron (Emmanuel) and the New Political Landscape of France. Chapter 3: Left; Republic. Chapter 4: Labor Relations. Chapter 6: Income Distribution and Inequality; Suburbs; Working Class. Chapter 7: Feminism and Women's Rights; LGBTQ+ Community. Chapter 8: Universities and Higher Education.

Further Reading
Baumgartner (1994); Grossman (2019); Lem (2020); Vassallo (2010); Wilson (1994).

Republic

After a preamble affirming the French people's profound attachment to the inalienable political and civil rights and principle of national sovereignty set down in the Declaration of the Rights of Man and the Citizen of 1789, the first article of the French constitution (i.e., the constitution of 1958 establishing the Fifth Republic) begins as follows: "France shall be an indivisible, secular, democratic and social Republic. It shall ensure the equality of all citizens before the law, without distinction of origin, race or religion." These words are more than boilerplate language stating the obvious—namely, that the structures and rules of the regime are those of a democratic republic that treats its citizens equally and respects their liberty. They offer a particular definition of France's national identity as shaped over nearly 170 years by the legacy of the Revolution, previous republics, and Liberation at the end of World War II. They furthermore affirm that France's identity as a Republic depends on its dedication to certain modern values that go beyond the democratic quality of its political institutions. "Indivisible" means that France can never be federalist, that it requires a high degree of national cohesion lest it come apart at the seams, and that its cherished fraternity precludes "particularism" of any kind (i.e., one must consider oneself a citizen of the Republic first rather than the member of a race, religion, social class, ethnic or cultural community, or region). "Secular" involves more than the institutional separation of church and state as spelled out in the law of 1905. It implies each person's civic duty to keep their religion (if any) and subjective moral norms—private matters—separate from their public life as a citizen and to use rational criteria of judgment—seen as both liberating and common to all people—in their deliberations on political matters. "Social" means that France assents to a significant public investment in social solidarity. Private property and enterprise are protected. However, there are also protections for working people, a comprehensive social safety, and accessible public goods and services that benefit all. France's democratic institutions are only part of its aspirational identity as "La République," which is indicative of a universalistic civilization based on progressive and humanist ideals. Régis Debray, a political philosopher and staunch defender of *Laicité* (secularism), put things even more succinctly when making a distinction between French republicanism and American liberal democracy: French Republic = Democracy + Enlightenment.

MARIANNE

"Marianne" is the name given to the female personification of the French Republic. The figure traces her roots back to classically inspired representations of Liberty, Reason, and the Nation during the French Revolution featuring a young woman in Roman attire with various allegorical accoutrements such as a red Phrygian cap (liberty), a fasces (power/authority), a level and plumb line (equality), an urn (suffrage), a pike, and/or a plough. The name is derived from a popular French women's name in the nineteenth century but is sometimes construed as a secular republican answer to Catholic devotion to the Virgin Mary. Marianne could be given a bellicose and revolutionary interpretation (as in Eugène Delacroix's 1830 painting of *Liberty Leading the People*) or a more serenely magisterial and matronly interpretation (as in the monumental statue by Charles and Léopold Morice that stands at Place de la République in Paris and the "Marianne the Sower" figure used on French stamps and coins throughout the twentieth century). A bust of Marianne is a feature of every French town hall. In recent times, famous celebrities (e.g., Brigitte Bardot, Mireille Mathieu, Catherine Deneuve, Laetitia Casta) have lent their traits to such busts.

France has known five iterations of the Republic since the Revolution; each made significant contributions to France's political culture and institutions even as the French polity was riven by a political and cultural civil (cold) war between pro- and anti-republican camps through the middle of the twentieth century (e.g., two restorations of monarchy, Sacré Cœur Basilica vs. the Eiffel Tower, the Dreyfus Affair, and Vichy period). The legacy of the First Republic (1792–1804) includes the break with absolute monarchy and feudalism, popular sovereignty, constitutional government, the rights of man, and republican patriotism. The legacy of the Second Republic (1848–1852) includes universal suffrage for men and the abolition of slavery. The legacy of the Third Republic (1870–1940) includes public education, republican civic culture, parliamentary democracy, and the separation of church and state. The legacy of the Fourth Republic (1946–1958) includes planned economic growth, social welfare, and membership in the European Community. The legacy of the Fifth Republic (1958–present) includes political stability behind a strong executive, decolonization, a more open society, and the decentralization of public and territorial administration. The French do not generally revere

Detail of the *Monument to Republic* that stands at Place de la République in eastern Paris—a traditional focus of political demonstrations (esp. by the left). The statue by Léopold Maurice (final version inaugurated in 1883) depicts Marianne, the traditional patriotic personification of the French Republic. She holds aloft an olive branch (symbol of peace), wears a Phrygian cap (a Roman symbol of liberty popularized during the French Revolution), and rests her hand on a tablet representing the Declaration of the Rights of Man and the Citizen of 1789; the word "Égalité" (Equality) can be seen on the pedestal—one part of the French Republic's motto of Liberty, Equality, Fraternity. (Rene Drouyer/Dreamstime.com)

their constitution (it is amended on a regular basis), political institutions, and revolutionary and republican founding fathers (following the nineteenth-century historian Jules Michelet, the people are considered the true heroes of the French Revolution). Compared to the United States, monuments honoring former presidents are both fewer in number and less hagiographic (Charles de Gaulle is an exception). However, "La République" itself basks in the sacred aura of civil religion and the patriotic pride of French exceptionalism.

See also: Chapter 1: Administrative and Territorial Subdivisions. Chapter 2: Timeline; de Gaulle (Charles), World War II, and the Fifth Republic; Ferry (Jules) and the Third Republic; Robespierre (Maximilien) and the French Revolution. Chapter 3: Parliament; Presidency and Executive Branch; Protests. Chapter 3: Public Sector and Privatization; Social Security and Health Care. Chapter 5: Laïcité; Rationalism and Universalism. Chapter 8: Republicanism and Public Schools.

Further Reading
Agulhon (1981); Berenson (2011); Chabal (2015); Leruth (1998).

Right

According to René Rémond, the modern French right is divided into three ideological families originally made up of the supporters of the three regimes that represented different conservative alternatives to the Revolution and the Republic in the nineteenth century. *Legitimists* were authoritarian reactionaries and ultraconservative Catholics who thought that the Revolution and Republic were abominations and supported the restauration of the Bourbon line of divine right kings (1814–1830). *Orléanists* were moderates on issues of religion and politics who accepted the early reforms of the Revolution and favored the constitutional monarchy of Louis-Philippe (1830–1848), an ally of the bourgeoisie and proponent of industrial development. *Bonapartists* were supporters of the First (1804–1814/1815) and Second (1852–1870) Empires who espoused an amalgam of patriotism, populism, progress, militarism, statism, and capitalism and believed that only a providential leader could unite the fractious country, modernize society, and restore France to its rightful greatness. Faint echoes of Rémond's political taxonomy can still be found in the contemporary (i.e., post-WWII) French right. Rémond viewed Gaullism—the ideology associated with Free France leader and Fifth Republic founder Charles de Gaulle—as an offshoot of Bonapartism because of its mythology of the military man who saves the nation in a time of crisis, its belief in French greatness, and its dual emphasis on order and reform. However, perhaps the most enduring legacy of de Gaulle and Gaullism was to reconcile the right to republicanism. Furthermore, the contemporary center-right has always had a moderate and liberal faction that can trace its roots back to Orleanism (e.g., Valéry Giscard d'Estaing, president from 1974 to 1981). However, Emmanuel Macron's presidential victories in 2017 and 2022 have at least temporarily pulled part of the center-right—e.g., MoDem (the political descendant of Giscard's UDF party), Horizons (a boutique party founded by former LR member and Macron prime minister Édouard Philippe), and Agir (a moderate and reformist micro-party)—into an independent bloc that spans the traditional French left-right divide. Finally, the National Rally (RN) party of Marine (and Jean-Marie) Le Pen has the support of many ultraconservatives who once might have been Legitimists (or supporters of the Vichy regime, 1940–1944)—although the RN is vociferously populist, more or less secular, and claims allegiance to the Republic.

The dominant party of the mainstream right today (there are also several smaller ones) is The Republicans (LR). It traces its roots back to the neo-Gaullist Rally for the Republic (RPR), founded by Jacques Chirac in 1976. Following Chirac's lopsided reelection as president in 2002 (vs. J. M. Le Pen), the RPR merged with other parties into the Union for a Presidential Majority (UMP) and was subsequently rechristened the Union for a Popular Majority. It held a majority in the National Assembly between 2002 and 2012—the longest such streak in the history of the Fifth Republic. It lost that majority after Nicolas Sarkozy lost his presidential reelection bid in 2012. The adoption of its current name in 2015 is an affirmation of the party's desire to function as a "big tent" and of its attachment to French republican values. The party is divided into three strands: a centrist wing of *economic and social moderates* (pro-business and EU, pluralistic view of French society, support for a comprehensive social safety net and environmental protections), a core group of *classic conservatives* (staunchly pro-business and guardedly pro-EU, more conservative stances on social issues like law enforcement, immigration, marriage equality, and entitlement reforms), and a *populist and sovereignist* fringe (positions on a range of issues that reflect fear that French independence and identity are undermined by globalization and multiculturalism).

The 2017 presidential and legislative election cycle was a disappointment for LR, whose presidential candidate, François Fillon (a classic French conservative), had been the presumptive frontrunner but failed to qualify for the second round. Fillon's platform read like a synthesis of the positions of LR's different strands: "liberate employment and growth" (e.g., reduce public debt, social assistance reform), improve the "purchasing power" of French households, "protect the French people" (e.g., zero-tolerance criminal justice), "defeat Islamic totalitarianism," "defend rural life" and traditions, "strengthen national solidarity" (e.g., school uniforms and pro-family policies), "jump-start" the European project (e.g., with renewed emphasis on its more limited original priorities), and "prepare the future" (e.g., curbs on immigration, carbon-neutral economy, 5G). LR faces a number of challenges as a party, the most important of which is the prospect of being doubly outflanked by the unapologetically liberal and centrist Renaissance (Macron's party) to its left and the unapologetically populist and nationalist RN on the far right. This particular challenge took on a more urgent tone in light of the surprisingly weak performance of LR's candidate in the 2022 presidential election, Île-de-France region president and former cabinet minister (budget, higher education) Valérie Pécresse, who received a historically low (for her party) 4.78% share of the vote in the first round (the second time in a row that the party's candidate failed to qualify for the two-person runoff). While commentators faulted the initially high-polling candidate for running a lackluster campaign, they also suggested that many of the voters that make up the party's base cast "useful ballots" (i.e., votes for candidates perceived as having a real chance of winning) in the first round:

for either Emmanuel Macron or Marine Le Pen depending on their ideological affinities. The June 2022 legislative elections offered additional evidence of the daunting challenges faced by a waning LR party squeezed between ascendant centrists and a surging far right. Its candidates received slightly less than 7% of the second-round vote, resulting in just sixty-one seats in the new National Assembly—enough to give it residual clout in a fragmented chamber without an absolute majority backing Macron but still twenty-eight fewer than Le Pen's RN.

See also: Chapter 2: Timeline; de Gaulle (Charles), World War II, and the Fifth Republic; Napoleon Bonaparte (Napoleon I) and the First Empire; Napoleon III and the Second Empire; Pétain (Philippe) and Vichy France; Sarkozy (Nicolas) and the Hyper Presidency. Chapter 3: Center; Far Right; Chapter 4: Public Sector and Privatization. Chapter 5: Catholicism. Chapter 6: Bourgeoisie and Middle Class.

Further Reading
Ahearne (2014); Knapp (1994); Knapp (2003); Lees (2017); Rémond (1966); Rispin (2019).

SELECTED BIBLIOGRAPHY

Agulhon, Maurice. *Marianne into Battle: Republican Imagery and Symbolism in France, 1789–1880.* Trans. Janet Lloyd. Cambridge UP, 1981.

Ahearne, Jeremy. *Government through Culture and the Contemporary French Right.* Palgrave Macmillan, 2014.

Bar-On, Tamir. *Rethinking the French New Right: Alternatives to Modernity.* Routledge, 2013.

Baumgartner, Frank R. "The Politics of Protest and Mass Mobilization in France." *French Politics and Society*, vol. 12, no. 2/3, 1994, pp. 84–96.

Bell, David S. *Presidential Power in Fifth Republic France.* Berg, 2000.

Bell, David S., and Byron Criddle. *Exceptional Socialists: The Case of the French Socialist Party.* Palgrave Macmillan, 2014.

Bell, David S., and John Gaffney. *The Presidents of the French Fifth Republic.* Palgrave Macmillan, 2013.

Berenson, Edward G. *The French Republic: History, Values, Debates.* Cornell UP, 2011.

Body-Gendrot, Sophie, and Catherine Wihtol de Wenden. *Policing the Inner City in France, Britain, and the US.* Palgrave Macmillan, 2014.

Boyron, Sophie. *The Constitution of France: A Contextual Analysis.* Bloomsbury, 2012.

Brinkley, Douglas, and Clifford Hackett. *Jean Monnet: The Path to European Unity.* St. Martin's, 1991.

Brouard, Sylvain, et al., eds. *The French Fifth Republic at Fifty: Beyond Stereotypes.* Palgrave Macmillan, 2009.

Caton, Valerie. *France and the Politics of European Economic and Monetary Union.* Palgrave Macmillan, 2015.

Chabal, Emile. *A Divided Republic: Nation, State and Citizenship in Contemporary France.* Cambridge UP, 2015; esp. pp. 55–79.

Chabal, Emile. *France*. Polity, 2020.

Charbonneau, Bruno. *France and the New Imperialism: Security Policy in Sub-Saharan Africa*. Ashgate, 2008.

Chowanietz, Christophe. *Bombs, Bullets, and Politicians: France's Response to Terrorism*. McGill-Queen's UP, 2016.

Chuter, David. *Humanity's Soldier: France and International Security, 1919–2001*. Berghahn, 1997.

Clift, Ben, and Sean McDaniel. "Is This Crisis of French Socialism Different?: Hollande, the Rise of Macron, and the Reconfiguration of the Left in the 2017 Presidential and Parliamentary Elections." *Modern & Contemporary France*, vol. 25, no. 4, 2017, pp. 403–415.

Cole, Alistair. *Franco-German Relations*. Routledge, 2001.

Cole, Alistair. *French Politics and Society*. 3rd ed. Routledge, 2017.

Cole, Alistair, and Gino Raymond, eds. *Redefining the French Republic*. Manchester UP, 2006.

Cole, Alistair, et al., eds. *Developments in French Politics 4*. Palgrave Macmillan, 2008.

Cole, Alistair, et al., eds. *Developments in French Politics 5*. Red Globe P, 2013.

Costa, Olivier, ed. *Parliamentary Representation in France*. Routledge, 2014.

Craiutu, Aurelian. *A Virtue for Courageous Minds: Moderation in French Political Thought, 1748–1830*. Princeton UP, 2012.

Culpepper, Pepper D., et al., eds. *Changing France: The Politics that Markets Make*. Palgrave Macmillan, 2006.

D'Amato, Silvia. *Cultures of Counterterrorism: French and Italian Responses to Terrorism after 9/11*. Routledge, 2019.

Davey, Eleanor. *Idealism beyond Borders: The French Revolutionary Left and the Rise of Humanitarianism, 1954–1988*. Cambridge UP, 2015.

de Maillard, Jacques, and Wesley G. Skogan. *Policing in France*. Routledge, 2020.

Di Francesco-Mayot, Sophie. "The French Parti socialiste (2010–16): From Office to Crisis." *Why the Left Loses: The Decline of the Centre-Left in Comparative Perspective*, eds. Rob Manwaring and Paul Kennedy. Policy P, 2017, ch. 10.

Dinan, Desmond, et al., eds. *The European Union in Crisis*. Palgrave Macmillan, 2017.

Drake, Helen, et al., eds. *Developments in French Politics 6*. Red Globe P, 2020.

Dyevre, Arthur. "The French Constitutional Council." *Comparative Constitutional Reasoning*, eds. András Jakab, et al. Cambridge UP, 2017, pp. 323–355.

Elgie, Robert. "The Election of Emmanuel Macron and the New French Party System: A Return to the *éternel marais*?" *Modern & Contemporary France*, vol. 26, no. 1, 2018, pp. 15–29.

Elgie, Robert, et al., eds. *The Oxford Handbook of French Politics*. Oxford UP, 2016.

Elliott, Catherine. *French Legal System*. 2nd ed. Pearson Longman, 2006.

Eltchaninoff, Michel. *Inside the Mind of Marine Le Pen*. Trans. James Ferguson. Hurst, 2018.

Evans, Jocelyn, and Gilles Ivaldi. *The 2017 French Presidential Elections: A Political Reformation?* Palgrave Macmillan, 2018.

Foley, Frank. *Countering Terrorism in Britain and France.* Cambridge UP, 2013.

Gabriel, Oscar W., et al., eds. *Political Participation in France and Germany.* ECPR P, 2013.

Gabriel, Oscar, W., et al., eds. *Political Representation in France and Germany: Attitudes and Activities of Citizens and MPs.* Palgrave Macmillan, 2018.

Gaffney, John, and Lorna Milne, eds. *French Presidentialism and the Election of 1995.* Ashgate, 1997; esp. 5–22 (Peter Morris, "Presidentialism in France: A Historical Overview") and 23–42 (Lorna Milne, "The Myth of the President in French Political Culture").

Genieys, William. *The New Custodians of the State: Programmatic Elites in French Society.* Transaction, 2010.

Gordon, Philip H. *A Certain Idea of France: French Security Policy and the Gaullist Legacy.* Princeton UP, 1993.

Gordon, Philip H. *France, Germany, and the Western Alliance.* Westview, 1995.

Gordon, Philip H., and Sophie Meunier. *The French Challenge: Adapting to Globalization.* Brookings Institution, 2001.

Grossman, Emiliano, ed. *France and the European Union: After the Referendum on the European Constitution.* Routledge, 2019.

Grossman, Emiliano. "France's Yellow Vests: Symptom of a Chronic Disease." *Political Insight*, vol. 10, no. 1, 2019, pp. 30–34.

Halimi, Serge, and Pierre Rimbert, "France's Class Wars: Gilets Jaunes Take on Government and Politicians." Trans. George Miller. *Le Monde Diplomatique.* February 2019, https://mondediplo.com/2019/02/02gilets-jaunes-class-war.

Hazareesingh, Sudhir. *Political Traditions in Modern France.* Oxford UP, 1994.

Hopkins, John C., and Weixing Hu. *Strategic Views from the Second Tier: The Nuclear Weapons Policies of France, Britain, and China.* Transaction, 1994.

Ivaldi, Gilles. "Populism in France." *Populism around the World*, ed. David Stockemer. Springer, 2018, pp. 27–47.

Judt, Tony. *Marxism and the French Left: Studies on Labour and Politics in France, 1830–1981.* Oxford UP, 1986.

Kaplan, Roger F. S. *Conservative Socialism: The Decline of Radicalism and the Triumph of the Left in France.* Transaction, 2002.

Kepel, Gilles. *Terror in France: The Rise of Jihad in the West.* Trans. Antoine Jardin. Princeton UP, 2017.

Knapp, Andrew. "From the Gaullist Movement to the President's Party." *The French Party System*, ed. Jocelyn A. J. Evans. Manchester UP, 2003, pp. 121–136.

Knapp, Andrew. *Gaullism since de Gaulle.* Dartmouth, 1994.

Knapp, Andrew, and Vincent Wright, eds. *The Government and Politics of France.* 5th ed. Routledge, 2006.

Krotz, Ulrich, and Joachim Schild. *Shaping Europe: France, Germany, and Embedded Bilateralism from the Elysée Treaty to Twenty-First Century Politics.* Oxford UP, 2013.

Laird, Robbin F., ed. *French Security Policy: From Independence to Interdependence*. Routledge, 2019.

Lançon, Philippe. *Disturbance: Surviving* Charlie Hebdo. Trans. Steven Rendall. Europa, 2020.

Lane, Philippe. *French Scientific and Cultural Diplomacy*. Liverpool UP, 2013.

Latour, Bruno. *The Making of Law: An Ethnography of the Conseil d'Etat*. Trans. Marina Brilman and Alain Pottage. Polity, 2009.

Le Béguec ; Gilles. "In Search of the Center." *France after 2012*, eds. Gabriel Godliffe and Ricardo Brizzi. Beghahn, 2015, pp. 42–60.

Lees, David. "A Controversial Campaign: François Fillon and the Decline of the Centre-Right in the 2017 Presidential Elections." *Modern & Contemporary France*, vol. 2, no. 4, 2017, pp. 391–402.

Lem, Winnie. "Notes on Militant Populism in Contemporary France: Contextualizing the Gilets Jaunes." *Dialectical Anthropology*, 2020, https://doi.org/10.1007/s10624-020-09595-1.

Leruth, Michael. "The Neorepublican Discourse on French National Identity." *French Politics and Society*, vol. 16, no. 4, 1998, pp. 46–61.

Lewis-Beck, Michael S., et al., eds. *French Presidential Elections*. Palgrave Macmillan, 2011.

Likaj, Xhulia, et al. "Euroscepticism in France: An Analysis of Actors and Causes." Institute for International Political Economy, Hochschule für Wirtschaft und Recht Berlin, working paper no. 132, 2020.

Lilla, Mark. "Two Roads for the New French Right." *The New York Review of Books*, 20 Dec. 2018, pp. 42–46.

Maclean, Mairi, and Joseph Szarka, eds. *France on the World Stage: Nation State Strategies in the Global Era*. Palgrave Macmillan, 2009.

Marcus, Jonathan, ed. *The National Front and French Politics: The Resistible Rise of Jean-Marie Le Pen*. NYU P, 1995.

Marlière, Philippe. "Jean-Luc Mélenchon and *France Insoumise*: The Manufacturing of Populism." *The Populist Radical Left in Europe*, eds. Giorgos Katsambekis and Alexandros Kioupkiolis. Routledge, 2019, pp. 93–112.

Marthaler, Sally. *Partisan Dealignment and the Blue-Collar Electorate in France*. Palgrave Macmillan, 2020.

Mounck, Yascha. "Why Marine Le Pen Is So Close to Power." *The Atlantic*, Apr. 21, 2022, https://www.theatlantic.com/ideas/archive/2022/04/marine-le-pen-french-presidential-election-2022/629615/.

Onishi, Norimitsu, and Constant Méheut. "Once a Slogan of Unity, 'Je suis Charlie' Now Divides France." *The New York Times*, 19 Dec. 2020, https://nyti.ms/3rb1ucz.

Opella, Katherine A. R. *Gender Quotas, Parity Reform, and Political Parties in France*. Lexington, 2005.

Ostermann, Falk. *Security, Defense Discourse and Identity in NATO and Europe: How France Changed Foreign Policy*. Routledge, 2018.

O'Sullivan, Feargus. "'Green Tsunami' Washes over France's City Halls." *Bloomberg CityLab*, 1 Jul. 2020, https://www.bloomberg.com/news/articles/2020-07-01/-green-tsunami-sweeps-climate-focused-french-mayors-into-power.

Pinder, John, and Simon Usherwood. *The European Union: A Very Short Introduction*. 4th ed. Oxford UP, 2018.

Raymond, Gino. *The French Communist Party during the Fifth Republic: A Crisis of Leadership and Ideology*. Palgrave Macmillan, 2005.

Rémond, René. *The Right Wing in France: From 1815 to de Gaulle*. 2nd ed. Trans. James M. Laux. U Pennsylvania P, 1966.

Rieker, Pernille. *French Foreign Policy in a Changing World: Practising Grandeur*. Springer, 2017.

Rispin, William. "Division within the French Centre Right during the Hollande Presidency: The Case of Cultural Insecurity." *Modern & Contemporary France*, vol. 27, no. 3, 2019, pp. 381–396.

Rogoff, Martin A. *French Constitutional Law: Cases and Materials*. 2nd ed. Carolina Academic P, 2014.

Rozenberg, Olivier. *The French Parliament and the European Union: Backbenchers Blues*. Palgrave Macmillan, 2020.

Safran, William. *The French Polity*. 7th ed. Pearson Longman, 2009.

Safran, William, and Michelle Hale Williams. "France." *Politics in Europe*. 7th ed. Ed. M. Donald Hancock. CQ-Sage, 2019, pp. 97–214.

Sauger, Nicolas, ed. *France's Political Institutions at 50*. Routledge, 2010.

Serfaty, Simon. *The Foreign Policies of the French Left*. Routledge, 2019.

Shields, James. *The Extreme Right in France: From Pétain to Le Pen*. Routledge, 2007.

Simmons, Harvey G. *The French National Front: The Extremist Challenge to Democracy*. Routledge, 2019.

Smith, Paul. *The Senate of the Fifth French Republic*. Palgrave Macmillan, 2009.

Sörenson, Karl. *Beyond Françafrique: The Foundation, Reorientation and Reorganisation of France's Africa Politics*. FOI-Swedish Defense Research Agency, 2008.

Stangler, Cole. "Is France's Socialist Party Back from the Dead?" *Foreign Policy*, 20 Jul. 2020, https://foreignpolicy.com/2020/07/20/france-socialist-party-back-from-dead-local-elections-emmanuel-macron-anne-hidalgo-olivier-faure/.

Steiner, Eva. *French Law: A Comparative Approach*. Oxford UP, 2018.

Stockemer, Daniel. *The Front National in France: Continuity and Change under Jean-Marie Le Pen and Marine Le Pen*. Springer, 2017.

Stöhs, Jeremy. *The Decline of European Naval Forces: Challenges to Sea Power in an Age of Fiscal Austerity and Political Uncertainty*. Naval Institute P, 2018; esp. ch. 5, "France: Stretched, but Willing—Europe's Most Capable Naval Force?"

Terrill, Richard J. *World Criminal Justice Systems: A Comparative Survey*. 9th ed. Routledge, 2012, pp. 131–214 ("France").

Titley, Gavan, et al., eds. *After Charlie Hebdo: Terror, Racism and Free Speech*. Zed, 2017.

Todd, Emmanuel. *Who Is Charlie?: Xenophobia and the New Middle Class*. Trans. Andrew Brown. Polity, 2015.

Truc, Gérôme. *Shell Shocked: The Social Response to Terrorist Attacks*. Trans. Andrew Brown. Polity, 2018.

van Haute, Emilie, ed. *Green Parties in Europe*. Routledge, 2016; esp. pp. 92–111 (Bruno Villalba, "From the Greens to Europe Ecologie – The Greens: Renaissance or More of the Same?") and pp. 280–297 (Gareth Price-Thomas, "Green Party Ideology Today: Divergences and Continuities in Germany, France, and Britain").

Vargo, Marc E. *The French Terror Wave, 2015–2016: Al-Qaeda and Isis Attacks from Charlie Hebdo to the Bataclan Theatre*. McFarland, 2020.

Vassallo, Francesca. *France, Social Capital and Political Activism*. Palgrave Macmillan, 2010.

Wall, Irwin. *France Votes: The Election of François Hollande*. Palgrave Macmillan, 2014.

Waters, Sarah. *Between Republic and Market: Globalization and Identity in Contemporary France*. Continuum, 2012.

Wilson, Frank L. "Political Demonstrations in France: Protest Politics or Politics of Ritual?" *French Politics and Society*, vol. 12, no. 2/3, 1994, pp. 23–40.

Zagato, Alessandro, ed. *The Event of Charlie Hebdo: Imaginaries of Freedom and Control*. Berghahn, 2015.

Zaretsky, Robert. "The Radical Centrism of Emmanuel Macron." *Foreign Policy*, 24 Apr. 2017, https://foreignpolicy.com/2017/04/24/the-radical-centrism-of-emmanuel-macron/.

CHAPTER 4

ECONOMY

OVERVIEW

In 2019 (the last year unaffected by the COVID-19 pandemic), France slipped to seventh place among largest economies in the world in terms of Gross Domestic Product (GDP)—behind the United States, China, Japan, Germany, the United Kingdom, and India. It remains in seventh place as of 2022 (projection). Forecasts suggest that it will be the eleventh largest economy in the world in 2060, by which time China will be the largest, India the second largest, and Indonesia, Mexico, Brazil, and Russia are all likely to have joined the top ten. France's GDP (World Bank) in 2018 was USD $2.79 trillion (€2.353 trillion according to official French government figures). Its GDP (World Bank, USD) in 2019 and 2020 was $2.73 trillion and $2.63 trillion, respectively. Its per capita GDP (OECD) in 2018 was USD $41,500. France's GDP grew by +1.7% in 2018, compared to +2.3% in 2017, and to +1.1% in 2016. The year 2017 was therefore France's best growth year since the Great Recession of 2008 (France's GDP shrank by −0.3% in 2008 and by −2.9% in 2009). A total of 691,000 new businesses were started in France in 2018—the highest level of business creation since 2010. Economists project that the French economy will register 7.0% growth in 2021 (bringing the GDP back to USD $2.69 trillion for the year). This represents the highest growth rate in over fifty years and a faster than expected recovery from the economic shock of the COVID pandemic. In a broader context, France enjoyed transformative economic growth during the thirty years following the end of World War II (1945–1975), a period famously known as "Les Trente Glorieuses," or "Thirty Glorious" (a term coined by the economist Jean Fourastié). GDP growth was +8.6% in 1950, +8.0% in 1960, and +5.0% or more during most of the period. The "glorious" years came to an end when the country entered a recession in 1975—brought on by the 1973 oil crisis and other factors. Aside from short spurts of more vigorous growth in the late 1980s (+4.7% in 1988) and late 1990s (+3.9% in 2000) and recessions that reached their low points in 1993 and 2009, the French economy has been relatively sluggish since the mid-1970s, a fact that prompted Nicolas Bavarez to christen the period from 1975 to 2005 as "Les Trente Piteuses," or "Thirty Pitiful."

France's leading economic challenges are chronic high unemployment (at or above 10% in 2016 and 2017, still at 8.6% for the third quarter of 2019, but down to a thirteen-year record low of 7.4% for the fourth quarter of 2021), high levels of public spending and debt (government spending at 57% of the annual GDP, spending on social programs at 32% of the GDP [compared to 19% in the United States], and total national public debt equal to 97% of the GDP [pre-COVID pandemic]), the pursuit of politically delicate reforms of entitlement programs and complex labor laws (often cited as "social" deterrents to job creation), and continued adaptation to a changing and highly competitive global economy. While there is a consensus among experts and government officials that France needs to intensify its efforts to be both fiscally responsible and business-friendly, there is a strong attachment to the French "social model" based on equality, national cohesion, high-quality and accessible public goods and services, a generous social safety net, and a proper role for government as a regulator and counterweight to private interests. The French are justifiably proud of the high quality and accessibility of healthcare in France, the affordable educational opportunities offered by their public universities, their highly developed public transportation system, generous retirement benefits, and the many social programs that benefit working families and the less fortunate. The idea that the "French social model" is a national treasure that merits preservation is the object of a broad consensus that covers virtually the entire political spectrum, although France's major parties have different notions of what the model's preservation (and reform) should entail. Since French law guarantees five weeks' paid vacation to salaried employees and establishes a thirty-five-hour maximum workweek, the French are sometimes maligned as not having a culture of hard work. This is false. The average French worker does not work as many total hours in a year as their American counterpart (1,500 total hours [France] in 2017 according to the OECD, compared to 1,800 [United States]), but they are slightly more productive on an hourly basis (an average of USD $105 GDP [France] per hour worked per person in 2017, compared to $102 [United States]). France's overall per capita GDP is still considerably lower than that of the United States ($62,600 in 2018 for the United States). However, it is somewhat higher than both the OECD and EU averages. The French workforce is highly skilled.

France's comprehensive Social Security system (commonly referred to in French as "La Sécu") dates from 1945 (with older precursors) and includes five separate branches that deal with different types of risks and needs:

1. Healthcare, maternity, paternity, disability, and death;
2. Compensation for workplace accidents and occupational health hazards;
3. Retirement benefits;
4. Family allowances disbursements; and
5. Personal autonomy assistance for the disabled and elderly.

Unemployment insurance is an auxiliary branch of Social Security although its funding and management schemes are different than in the other branches. Healthcare coverage is universal. Due to its combined accessibility, controlled costs, universal coverage, and generally high quality, the French healthcare system is widely considered to be among the best in the world. France's dual commitment to economic growth in a free market environment and to social solidarity is something that it shares with its partners in the EU, a free trade zone comprised of twenty-seven countries whose combined GDP is equivalent to the second largest economy in the world—for the time being, considerably bigger than China's. France is one of the nineteen EU member countries that use the common European currency, the Euro. Inclusion in the Euro Area, or Eurozone, entails meeting strict economic convergence criteria and ceding authority over monetary policy to the European Central Bank.

Economic activity is concentrated in and around France's cities. Paris is still the undisputed economic and financial capital but regional metropolises such as Lyon, Marseille, Toulouse, Lille, Nantes, Nice, Bordeaux, Strasbourg, Rennes, Montpellier, and Grenoble also play a prominent role. Along with Greater Paris, the south (esp. along the Mediterranean coast) and west (Atlantic coast region) are experiencing strong growth, whereas the northeast (an area of older heavy industries) is lagging behind. Like the factory towns of the northeast, France's more isolated rural areas, underprivileged suburbs, and overseas departments are economically disadvantaged.

France's major agricultural, industrial, and service products include wheat and other cereals, sugar beets, oleaginous plants, wine grapes, wine, beef, dairy products (incl. cheese), other foods and beverages, electrical power (nuclear), automobiles, aircraft, rail transportation equipment, iron and steel, industrial machinery, electronics, telecommunications, textiles, pharmaceuticals, plastics, chemicals, cosmetics and beauty products (incl. perfume), luxury goods, financial and insurance products, science and technology research, technical and administrative services, and tourism. General manufacturing and heavy industries have lost ground while technologically advanced and high value-added industries have gained importance. France is the leading exporter in the world of aircraft, wine, beauty products and cosmetics, and luxury goods. Approximately 30% of France's GDP comes from exports and 60% of France's exports go to other European countries. Its leading non-EU trading partners include the United States, China, and Francophone Africa. In 2018, France recorded a small trade deficit of €58.9 billion, compared to €57.9 billion in 2017 and €44.8 billion in 2016. Its reliance on nuclear power for 77% of its electricity has increased its energy independence. However, its need to import virtually all fossil fuels is a leading contributor to its trade deficit. Tourism helps to narrow the gap. France is the top nation in the world for attracting international tourists and ranks fifth in revenue from foreign tourists. While most people know that France is a leading wine and cheese producing country, few realize that it is also the overall leading agricultural nation in the EU by a considerable margin—it has the most arable land and leads production in both plant and animal products. The fertile plains of the Parisian Basin region make up one of Europe's and the world's major breadbaskets. Defined broadly, industry now accounts for approximately 20% of France's GDP (12% from manufacturing, extraction of raw materials, and energy-production; 8% from construction); agriculture for a little over 2%; and tertiary activities (both commercial and noncommercial) nearly 78%. Percentages for the share of employment by sector are similar. One distinctive feature of the French economy is its large public sector. Nearly 20% of the French workforce is made up of public employees: 5.5 million total, out of which close to 4 million are functionaries with tenure. They are known to exercise their political clout through strikes and other means of exerting pressure on the government.

France's main unions are the CFDT (moderate), the CGT (France's oldest union, close to the French Communist Party through much of the twentieth century), Force Ouvrière (militant), CFE–CGC (for managers and executives), and the CFTC (inspired by Christian social teaching). The most influential group that represents business interests and negotiates on behalf of employers is MEDEF. France is home to quite a few corporations that figure among the largest in the world. Most of them are headquartered in Paris and its environs. Paris is a global business and financial capital and hopes to gain in stature by attracting businesses (incl. banks) that may leave London following the United Kingdom's withdrawal from the EU. The Paris Bourse (stock exchange) was one of the founding members of the combined Euronext Exchange—the sixth largest in the world. French companies in the Fortune Global 500 include such well-known names as Axa (insurance), Total (oil), BNP Paribas (banking), Carrefour (supermarkets), Crédit Agricole (banking), EDF (electricity), Engie (energy), Peugeot-Citroën (automobiles), Société Générale (banking), Renault (automobiles), Christian Dior (luxury goods), Vinci (construction), Saint-Gobain (building materials), Sanofi (pharmaceuticals), L'Oréal (beauty products), Danone (food), and Michelin (tires). Airbus is registered in the Netherlands but based in Toulouse.

The French state has traditionally played a directive role in the economic life of the nation, which is nonetheless firmly capitalistic. While French *dirigisme* has roots that stretch back to the seventeenth century, its modern form developed in the post–World War II period, when leaders like Charles de Gaulle mistrusted the business elite and government planning proved essential to the rebuilding and modernization of the economy. Beginning in the 1980s, the government's role in the economy changed. Most publicly held companies were privatized (although the state remains a shareholder in several of the privatized companies). Globalization and the free market orientation of the EU have nudged France in the direction of more business-friendly policies. The government now positions itself as a strategic partner of private enterprise, not its impresario. This is particularly true of President Emmanuel Macron, a former investment banker who was briefly economy minister under François Hollande. Major market-oriented reforms—a frequent source of protest—accelerated during his presidency. Strong emphasis was placed on high-tech innovation and start-ups. It is uncertain that "France is back," as Macron is fond of saying, but there were some encouraging signs in France's economic outlook both before and since the coronavirus (COVID-19) pandemic of 2020–2021. France and the EU took strong measures to mitigate the immediate economic impact of the unprecedented public health crisis, which resulted in shutdowns, significantly reduced production, lost wages and jobs, falling demand, a major decline in tourism, ballooning healthcare expenditures, rising public debt, and a 7.9% contraction of the French economy in 2020. While the long-term impact of the pandemic on the French economy is unknown, the vigorous rebound in 2021 is good news.

Further Reading

Barsoux (1997); Clift (2012); Djelic (1998); Dormois (2004); Global Investment Center (2015); Lafrance (2019); Levy (2008); Levy (2017); Maclean et al. (2006); Maillet et al. (2020); Organisation for Economic Co-operation and Development (2019); Schmidt (1996); Schmidt (1997); Schmidt (2003); Smith (2006); Tiberghien (2018).

Agriculture

At the end of World War II, France was still a predominantly rural nation. During the period known as the "Glorious Thirty" (1945–1975), both the overall rural character of French society and the nature of French agriculture changed radically (e.g., the trend away from small family-farms practicing polyculture and toward larger and more specialized ones). Presently, 2.8% of the French workforce is employed in the agricultural sector—it was 32.0% in 1950 and 8.4% in 1980—and agriculture accounts for just 1.5% of France's GDP. However, France remains the leading agricultural power of the EU. It has the largest area of arable land in the EU (69 million acres, 51% of the surface area of mainland France) and leads the EU in both crop (€40 billion in 2016) and animal production (€25 billion). It is the sixth largest producer and fifth largest exporter of agricultural products in the world.

France's major areas of agricultural production include beef, pork, poultry and eggs, dairy products, wine grapes and wine, wheat and other grains, sugar beets, potatoes, forage, fruits and vegetables, oleaginous plants, and fish and other types of seafood. In terms of sales, its four most lucrative production categories in 2017 were livestock (€11.3 billion), wine (€10.4 billion), dairy and other animal derivative products (€10.2 billion), and grain (€9.7 billion). France is the fourth largest source of seafood in the EU (behind Spain, the United Kingdom [sic], and Denmark). Ocean caught fish is the leading category, followed by freshwater fish and amphibiotic species, crustaceans (lobster, crab, shrimp), and shellfish (oysters, clams, scallops, mussels). While modern industrial farming has come to dominate agriculture, sustainable agriculture, organic products, traditional local products (*les produits de terroir*), and farm-to-table "slow food" all represent major trends in production and consumption. In 2017, organic agriculture (in French, *biologique*) involved over 36,000 producers on 4 million acres of land. Sales of organic products reached €8 billion.

Agricultural policy in France is crafted and carried out by the Ministry of Agriculture in the framework of the EU Common Agricultural Policy (CAP), which was set up in 1962 and is responsible for the distribution of large sums of subsidies to farmers. CAP-related spending represents 40% of the EU budget; its share was around 70% in the mid-1980s. While the CAP has been quite beneficial to French farmers overall, "Brussels" is as much the target of their episodic discontent as "Paris." Changes to agricultural policy often produce spectacular (and sometimes violent) protests on the part of farmers. France's largest and most influential farm organization is FNSEA (National

A French farmer harvesting grapes for the winemaking industry. France is an agricultural powerhouse in Europe in terms of cultivatable land, overall production, exports (it is a world leader in wine exports and its wines have a well-deserved reputation for quality), and the power of its agricultural lobby. While much of French agriculture is industrialized and makes use of the latest agronomic research and new technology, there is also strong emphasis in France on organic and sustainable farming, traditional methods and terroir-specific products, and resistance to genetically modified organisms (GMOs). (Prochasson Frederic/Dreamstime.com)

Federation of Unions of Agricultural Producers), which was founded in 1946 and brings together 200,000 total members. The largest agricultural event of the year is the Paris International Agriculture Show (Salon International de l'Agriculture de Paris), which takes place in late February or early March and attracts over 800,000 visitors.

See also: Chapter 1: Natural Resources and Environment. Chapter 3: European Union. Chapter 4: Trade. Chapter 14: Cheese; Food Quality, Organic Products, and GMO Resistance; Wine.

Further Reading
Bivar (2018); Blanc (2002); Bureau et al. (2015); Heller (2013); Knudson (2009).

Budget, Debt, and Taxes

Fiscal and economic responsibility—limiting government spending, reducing the national debt, and savings-minded reforms of entitlement programs—has been a stated policy priority of every French government for the past thirty-five years. It is a main objective of the presidential administration of Emmanuel Macron (2017–present)—for instance, the "Plan Action Publique 2022" to reduce public expenditures by a 3% share of the French GDP by the end of the president's five-year term. France's obligations as a Eurozone country and the need to create a long-term growth-friendly economic environment are the main reasons for this emphasis. While France has had some success in this respect, its levels of spending (esp. on social programs), debt, and taxation are still among the highest in the Eurozone and among developed nations in general. Reluctance to make the kind of structural changes that would result in more significant savings has much to do with public attachment to the egalitarian "French social model" and to the high political cost of sweeping reforms and strict austerity measures. According to statistics compiled by the government and the OECD (2016), taxes (incl. mandatory contributions to social programs) represent a 46% share of the French GDP. By contrast, the GDP share was 43% for Italy, 38% for Germany, and 26% for the United States. Government expenses in France represent a 57% share of the GDP—compared to 50% in Italy, 44% in Germany, and 38% in the United States. Social spending in France (2016) represents a 32% share of all public spending—compared to 29% in Italy, 25% in Germany, and 19% in the United States. In 2016, the government's budget deficit represented 3.4% of the GDP. France's total public debt stood at €2.15 trillion in 2016—96% of the GDP—compared to 181% in Greece, 132% in Italy, 99% in Spain, 88% in the United Kingdom, 74% in the United States, 68% in Germany, and 42% in Sweden. As a historical comparison, French public debt represented a 55% share of the GDP in 1995 and 80% in 2010. The COVID-19 pandemic of 2020–2021 has put an additional strain on France's finances given the unprecedented government spending to respond the public health crisis and alleviate its economic impact on the French people. France's public deficit in 2021 was projected to be equal to 9% of its GDP for the year according to the French finance ministry. Furthermore, the Cour des Comptes, the government body in charge of auditing the nation's books, issued a warning about the total increase in the national debt over the pandemic period: an estimated total increase of USD $640 billion (€560 billion) from the end of 2019 through the end of 2022—most of it due to pandemic-related spending. The increase would bring the total national debt to 113% of France's GDP.

The 2018 French national government's budget included €446.2 billion in total expenses, including €120 billion given back to taxpayers in the form of refunds and tax breaks. Expenses on the thirty-two government "missions" was €329.6 billion, resulting in a projected deficit of €86.7 billion. The six main general categories of expenses in the 2018 budget were education and research (€99.3 billion, 30% of all programmatic expenses), defense and security (€62.4 billion, 19%), social programs (€52.3 billion, 16%), service of the national debt (€41.2 billion, 12%), ecology and sustainable development (€11.3 billion), and justice (€8.7 billion). A sum of €3.4 billion was allocated for agricultural and rural affairs, €3.0 billion for international affairs, €2.9 billion for culture (close to 1% of the total national budget), €2.1 billion for overseas territories, and €1.7 billion for development aid. One must keep in mind that 39% of the budget across programs and categories is spent on personnel (i.e., salaries), and 15% on operational costs. French spending on defense and security is sixth or seventh depending on the criteria used.

The widespread perception that French taxes are high is essentially true. Its level of taxation as a share of the GDP is often the highest or nearly the highest in the EU (in some years, it is topped by Denmark), consistently 10–12 points above the OECD average. More infamously, President François Hollande (2012–2017) caused a stir when he fulfilled a campaign promise by imposing a tax rate of 75% on incomes above €1 million. The rate was phased out in 2015, but not before prompting a tax "exodus" of wealthy citizens. Presently (2018), the rate on the top bracket (above €153,783/year) is 45%. However, how France gets tax income is also distinctive. Compared to OECD averages, France collects proportionately more tax revenue from social security taxes (37% vs. 26% OECD), payroll taxes (3.5% vs. 1% OECD), and property taxes (9% vs. 6% OECD); and proportionately less tax revenue from personal income taxes (19% vs. 24% OECD), corporate income taxes (5% vs. 9% OECD), and taxes on goods and services (24% vs. 33% OECD). Pro-market experts suggest France spends too much on social entitlements, that there should be greater reliance on progressive income tax, that the corporate income tax rate is still too high but not enough corporate income tax is actually collected due to various tax breaks, and that discounted value-added tax (VAT) rates are applied to too many categories. Under a current government plan, the standard (2018) corporate income tax rate of 33% will be reduced to 28% in 2020 and to 25% in 2022.

See also: Chapter 2: Louis XVI and the End of the Ancien Régime; Macron (Emmanuel) and the New Political Landscape of France; Sarkozy (Nicolas) and the Hyper Presidency. Chapter 3: European Union. Chapter 4: Social Security and Healthcare.

Further Reading

Chorafas (2014); Creel et al. (2014).

Energy

France does not possess significant natural resources in the energy field. Since the oil crisis of the 1970s, satisfaction of its energy needs has evolved considerably. Oil's share in primary consumption has declined dramatically, from close to 70% to 30%. Conversely, electricity's share, spurred by France's reliance on nuclear power, has increased even more dramatically, from 5% to over 40%. Reliance on natural gas has increased moderately, while reliance on coal has declined steadily. Since 2010, there has been a slight but significant increase in renewable energy's share in the satisfaction of France's primary energy consumption needs. In 2015, primary energy consumption in France was as follows: 42.5% from nonrenewable sources of electricity, 30.1% from oil, 14.2% from natural gas, 9.4% from renewable sources, and 3.3% from coal. Fossil fuels still account for close to 50% of France's energy needs. For reasons of energy independence (France imports virtually all of its fossil fuels) and the threats posed by pollution and climate change caused by the emission of greenhouse gases, this reliance on fossil fuels has been a source of great concern for policy makers, energy industry leaders, environmentalists, and public opinion. Overall, 55% of the French national energy supply is national in origin and 45% foreign. France's leading sources of imported oil in 2015 were Saudi Arabia, Kazakhstan, and Nigeria. It gets most of its natural gas from Norway, Russia, the Netherlands, and Algeria. France has important shale gas deposits; however, they are not exploited (fracking is prohibited by law). Perhaps the most unique aspect of France's energy picture is that 77% of French electricity is provided by nuclear power (fifty-five plants nationwide)—higher than any other country in the world. The reliance on nuclear power is a source of public concern and is opposed by activists. However, French nuclear power is considered a success story by the government since it has increased French energy independence and made electricity an important French export for over thirty years. The leading sources of renewable energy (in order of importance) are wood, hydroelectric, biofuel, and wind. France's per capita energy consumption is slightly below the OECD average but well below per capita consumption in the United States. Transportation accounted for 33% of energy consumption in France in 2015; residential use, 30%; industry, 19%; the service economy, 15%; and agriculture, 3%. France ranked nineteenth in the world in 2015 in terms of total CO_2 emissions. Planned bans on domestic oil and gas production and on gasoline and diesel-powered cars, both of which are to take place in 2040, are among the French initiatives designed to reduce CO_2 emissions. Led by giant corporations like Total, Électricité de France, and Engie, the energy industry accounts for 2.0% of the French GDP (2015) and close to 140,000 jobs.

See also: Chapter 1: Natural Resources and Environment; Transportation. Chapter 4: Major Industries.

Further Reading
Belaïd (2016); Chick (2007); Hecht (2009); Ribera and Rüdinger (2014).

Financial Sector

France has a thriving and diverse financial sector that accounts for 9% of the nation's GDP. As in other countries, changes in regulations have broken down barriers between traditional banking, investment banking, and insurance. Now, major banks also have investment banking divisions and may offer insurance products, while some of the largest insurance companies also offer banking services. There has also been a considerable amount of consolidation so that institutions have the kind of scale that allows them to compete in the European and global marketplaces. France's largest banks (in order of total assets) are BNP Paribas, Crédit Agricole (incl. the LCL/Crédit Lyonnais subsidiary), Société Générale, Groupe BPCE (formed by a merger of Banque Populaire and Caisse d'Épargne), Crédit Mutuel (incl. Crédit Industriel et Commercial), and La Banque Postale (a branch of the French postal service). All six are among the 100 biggest banks in the world. BNP Paribas (the eighth largest bank in the world), Crédit Agricole, Société Générale, and BPCE are in the top twenty. BNP Paribas, Crédit Agricole, and Société Générale were on the Financial Stability Board's 2017 list of global systemic banks (G-SIB), commonly called the "too big to fail" list. BPCE was on the 2016 list. Corporate and investment banking has developed along with globalization and the perception that France now has a business-friendly climate and is a good place to invest. The field is diverse and includes all the major international houses, including the "bulge bracket banks" (Goldman Sachs, Credit Suisse, Deutsche Bank, JPMorgan Chase, et al.), which tend to be involved in the biggest French deals. All of France's major banks also have large and active investment banking divisions. Rothschild et Compagnie, the French branch of the international Rothschild and Company group is the former employer of President Emmanuel Macron. President Georges Pompidou was the general manager for a prestigious independent corporate and investment bank. Newer French actors in the CIB field include Bucéphale Finance, Messier Maris & Associés, and ODDO BHF (formerly Oddo et Compagnie). The French government is also involved in the field via the Caisse des Dépôts (CDC, founded in 1815). It makes long-term institutional investments deemed in the public interest (e.g., urban development and universities) and manages pension funds. Jointly owned by the CDC and the state, Bpifrance is a public investment bank specializing in regional initiatives, small and midsized companies, companies with high export potential, and innovative startups.

Since 2000, the Paris Stock Exchange, or Bourse, is part of the consolidated Euronext Exchange (six markets, including Amsterdam and Brussels) and is known as Euronext Paris. Euronext is presently largest exchange in Europe in terms of market capitalization—essentially tied with London SE Group (incl. Milan)—and is the sixth largest in the world after New York (NYSE), Nasdaq, Japan (Tokyo), and Shanghai. Euronext Paris's futures exchange is MATIF, which is among the leading grain futures exchanges in the world. Euronext Paris offers several stock indexes, including the CAC 40 (major French companies), which is followed daily like the Dow Jones Industrial Average, the S&P 500, the Nasdaq Composite, the FTSE 100, the DAX, and the Hang Seng as a leading indicator of the state of global financial markets. French-based Axa and CNP, and reinsurance specialist SCOR, are among the largest insurance companies in the world. Other major French insurance groups include Groupama (incl. Gan), AG2R La Mondiale, Covéa (incl. MMA, MAAF, and GMF), Euresa (incl. MAIF, MACIF, and Matmut), and Aréas. The two main financial regulatory bodies in

France are the AMF (the Autorité des Marchés, formed via the merger of three agencies in 2003), which has oversight over financial markets equivalent to that of the SEC in the United States; and the ACPR (the Agence de Contrôle Prudentiel et de Résolution, a branch of the Banque de France created in 2010, again through the merger of existing agencies), which protects consumers and regulates banks, lenders, and insurance companies. The Banque de France is France's central bank. Its status changed because of the Maastricht Treaty (1992) and the creation of the Eurozone (1999) uniting nineteen EU member countries. In matters of monetary policy and systemic economic and financial stability, it now follows the directives of the European Central Bank (ECB, headquartered in Frankfurt), which has jurisdiction over the Eurozone. It coordinates closely with the ECB and is also part of the European System of Central Banks (ESCB), which extends coordination to non-Eurozone members. The current governor of the Banque de France, named to the position in 2015, is François Villeroy de Galhau. The current president of the ECB is Christine Lagarde of France, who began her eight-year term in November 2019. Lagarde (b. 1956) was formerly France's economy minister (2007–2011) as well as the managing director of the International Monetary Fund (2011–2019).

See also: Chapter 1: Paris. Chapter 3: European Union. Chapter 4: Budget, Debt, and Taxes; Innovation and Startups.

Further Reading
Callahan and Lagneau-Ymonet (2012); Howarth (2013); Lepetit et al. (2016); Massoc (2018).

EUROZONE

France is one of the nineteen (out of twenty-seven) EU member countries in the Euro area, commonly called the Eurozone. Eurozone countries use the common European currency, the Euro (€); their monetary policy is controlled by the independent European Central Bank (ECB), headquartered in Frankfurt, Germany; and they have a higher degree of economic integration. The common currency provision of the Maastricht Treaty (1992) took effect as a locked-in exchange mechanism in 1999; and the full transition to the use of Euro paper money and coins took place in 2002. Qualification for the Eurozone is contingent on five convergence criteria: price stability, sound public finances, sustainable levels of public debt, interest rate convergence, and exchange rate stability prior to admission. The nineteen countries of the Eurozone have a combined population of 340 million and a combined GDP of $12.6 trillion (USD) in 2017. Euro bills feature designs with common historical architectural motifs on both sides; coins have a common reverse side featuring a map of Europe and an obverse side specific to the issuing country. France's €1 and €2 domination coins feature a stylized liberty tree and the letters "RF" for "République Française." The smaller domination coins (cents) feature Marianne, the feminine personification of the Republic.

Innovation and Startups

France was once seen as a country that did not foster entrepreneurship: government regulations were too complex and cumbersome, taxes were too high, and greater emphasis was placed on maintaining social equality (and civil service jobs) than on generating wealth. France was also slower than other developed countries to embrace the internet—out of attachment to its own Minitel system linking teletex terminals through the telephone network, concern about online privacy, and perhaps also wariness of American and Anglophone hegemony on the internet. Given these negative associations, the notion that France could be a haven for tech startups did not seem plausible twenty years ago. However, these characterizations are now out of date. Recent legislation—enabling simplified incorporation as *une société par actions simplifiée* (SAS), creating a new category of very small businesses called "microenterprises," and making it easier to hire and dismiss employees—has made it easier to start a business in France; and the government has realized that tech startups could be an effective means of both stimulating growth and reducing chronically high unemployment. The cultural shift intensified under President Emmanuel Macron, a political centrist with a background in investment banking who is unabashedly pro-business, who vowed to make France a "startup nation" and unveiled a number of ambitious funding programs for technological innovation. In 2017, 591,000 new businesses were started in France—a 7% increase over the previous year and the highest level of new business creation since 2010. Microenterprises formed 40% of the businesses, and 60% were of the SAS type. About 37% of the creators or heads of the new businesses were under thirty, of which 40% were women. The sector in which the most businesses were created was "activity of a specialized, scientific, or technical nature" (103,000 new businesses)—followed by commerce (98,000), construction, healthcare and social services, and transport and warehousing. Building on the new entrepreneur-friendly environment as well as its world-class culture, a large population of highly educated young people, its status as a financial capital, and attractiveness as an alternative to London in the uncertain context of the United Kingdom's withdrawal from the EU, Paris has indeed become a dynamic hub for startups, particularly in the tech field. In 2016, Paris was second to London among European cities in terms of the total number of startups (6,400) and the total sum of venture capital invested (€2.8 billion).

Several French government initiatives have played a part in fostering an environment in which technological innovation and entrepreneurship can thrive. Launched in 2013 and run by the French Digital Agency (under the national economy and finance ministry), "La French Tech" is a multifaceted "ecosystem-building" program designed to give both practical (incl. financial) support and a visible branded identity to French Tech entrepreneurship. Program components include the €200 million French Tech Acceleration Fund to help existing startups expand and innovate, the French Tech Grant program to assist new startups, the creation and funding of French Tech hubs in other countries (e.g., New York, Montreal, and San Francisco), the French Tech Ticket program designed to lure foreign tech and French expatriate startup entrepreneurs to relocate to France, and the French Tech Visa program.

Another program coordinated by the French Digital Agency is the comprehensive French High-Speed Broadband Plan, a public-private partnership involving a €20 billion investment designed to bring fiber optic cable-based high-speed broadband internet to all of France by 2020. In 2017, Macron fulfilled a campaign promise by announcing the creation of a special €10 billion government fund to help bring French-made "disruptive innovation" to the market in the technology field. In 2018, Macron announced the creation of an additional €1.5 billion program to stimulate artificial intelligence research and development. The plan emphasizes ethical use of AI and open source models and leverages vast troves of data collected by agencies of the French government. The government's tech policy priorities are guided by the provisions of 2016 "Digital Republic" law, which focuses on three main priorities: free circulation of data and knowledge, protection of individuals and their privacy, and universal access. Specific provisions concern the classification of certain types and stores of data as public goods, net neutrality, helping small- and medium-sized businesses go digital, helping the expansion of internet access and the digital economy in developing countries, ensuring a "right to be forgotten" online, a digital master plan for public education, and the creation of an online Employment Store for job seekers.

There are also a number of promising private initiatives that have been set up to stimulate and shake up the tech field. Two of them are funded by the French telecom billionaire Xavier Niel. One is École 42, a revolutionary type of coding and computer programming school in Paris that is free for all admitted students, actively recruits students from disadvantaged backgrounds, is open twenty-four hours a day, and uses a peer-to-peer individual project-based curriculum. Another Niel project is Station F, which opened in 2017: a Silicon Valley-inspired incubator located in a renovated nineteenth-century rail depot in Paris that is billed as the world's largest startup site and hosts a "Fighter's Program" for entrepreneurs from nontraditional backgrounds.

E-commerce is developing rapidly in France. With yearly sales increases of 12%–14%, over 200,000 e-commerce websites, and 37.5 million online shoppers in 2017, France is the second largest e-commerce market in the EU and the sixth largest in the world. Over 80% of all internet users in France shop online. E-commerce through mobile devices is on the rise, as are click-and-collect services and online participation in the sharing economy. The biggest product and service areas in terms of sales are tourism and travel (one-third of total sales), clothing, home appliances, and click-and-collect groceries. Cultural products (books, music downloads, event tickets, etc.) and high-tech products are prominent among high-frequency online shoppers. French e-commerce is also increasingly international: in 2016, 41% of all French online shoppers made purchases from foreign e-commerce merchants and 50% of French e-merchants reported sales to customers abroad. Leading French online retailers include Cdiscount, SNCF Connect (rail passenger travel), Fnac (cultural products and electronics), Vente-privée (a members-only discount site), Carrefour (groceries and other products), and E.Leclerc (groceries and other products).

See also: Chapter 2: Macron (Emmanuel) and the New Political Landscape of France. Chapter 3: Financial Sector; Major Industries. Chapter 16: Internet, Social Media, and Video Games.

Further Reading

Alijani (2009); Heller et al. (2019); Organisation for Economic Co-operation and Development (2014); Trumbull (2004); van Uden (2018–2019).

ARTISANS

France has a strong attachment to artisans and to their role in the economy and culture. It is famous for its traditional neighborhood specialty food merchants (butchers, charcutiers, bakers, etc.) and skilled artistic craftsmen (e.g., jewelers, dressmakers, ceramists, luthiers, and art restorers). However, the category is much wider. In fact, there are hundreds of officially designated artisan trades and subfields that are described in the official French Nomenclature of Artisan Trades (NAFA). Other examples include salt production, ice cream and sorbet making, bookbinding, soap and detergent making, solar energy cell production, scientific instrument making, extermination (pest control), taxi driving, poster gluing, knife sharpening, animal grooming, and puppeteering. According to the government, which actively promotes artisan trades as remedy for unemployment, artisan small businesses employ 12% of the working population and account for 20% of the GDP. About 39% are in the building trades, of which 26% are headed by women.

Labor Relations

The history of labor relations in France has been highly contentious and imbued with a strong undercurrent of class conflict pitting the workers against their bosses, the government allies of the latter, and the capitalist system. The right to strike was officially recognized in 1864, but prohibitions on the formation of labor unions were not lifted until 1884. Strikes during the so-called Belle Époque (1871–1914) were often violent affairs. For instance, when workers in the northern factory town of Fourmies staged a general strike in 1891, troops called in to maintain order opened fire on strikers, gunning down nine workers in less than a minute. While animosity and mistrust between workers and bosses remained high well into the twentieth century, the Front Populaire (1936–1938) marked the beginning of an era of negotiated settlements and social reforms. Following the victory of the Popular Front coalition of republican progressives, democratic socialists, and communists in legislative elections, workers staged a general strike to press their advantage. However, instead of violence, the pressure led to pro-labor concessions granted in the Matignon Agreements (1936)—including collective bargaining rights, stronger legal protection of the right to strike, a forty-hour work week, overtime pay, and paid vacations (two weeks). The pattern of effective pressure and negotiated *acquis sociaux* (social rights "won" by working people), with the government playing the role of deal broker, continued after World War II. The provisional post-Liberation government led by Charles de Gaulle, which included the communist union leader Ambroise Croizat (1901–1951) as labor minister, laid the foundation for the current Social Security system in 1945. After striking workers joined student demonstrators in May 1968, they again won major concessions in government-mediated talks, including wage hikes.

A lot has changed since 1968. Economic growth has slowed considerably, shifting the focus to employment and the preservation of jobs. Globalization and competition from cheaper labor in overseas countries have led to a smaller role for heavy industries and manufacturing in the French economy and to fewer traditional factories—once the stronghold of the labor movement. Political life in France may seem as polarized as ever, but most governments—left, right, and center—have adopted a similar approach to the economy even though their rhetoric may differ: emphasis on European convergence and free trade, enhancement of competitiveness in the global market environment, fiscal responsibility, labor market flexibility, job creation, and the fostering of an environment in which entrepreneurship might flourish. A series of recent economic and labor reforms has tilted the playing field markedly to the advantage of business. Finally, trade union membership has declined considerably. Presently, only about 11% of French workers belong to a union—a figure that is roughly equivalent to the rate of unionization in the United States, but only about half the EU average. It is worth noting that French workers do not need to belong to a union in order to be protected and represented by unions since French labor laws give unions an official representative role in collective bargaining on behalf of all workers in a given sector. Hence, one's wages, job security, and rights are the result of union efforts even if one does not belong to one. It is also worth noting that unionization rates vary widely from one sector to another. For example, union membership is at 18% among transport workers, 20% among all public employees (*fonctionnaires*), and above 40% among teachers, healthcare workers, and social services employees. It is therefore not surprising that these categories of workers are the most likely to strike or that their propensity to do so comes with considerable clout given the critical importance of the work they do. This remains true despite a 2007 law that requires public service workers and providers, particularly in public transport, to maintain a minimum level of service during strikes. Strikes are still common in France, but they are diminishing in frequency and duration. There were 712 strikes in 2017, compared to 801 in 2016 and 966 in 2015. Most strikes are local, short, and usually focused on the grievances of workers at a particular site. The more spectacular strikes and "social movements" now tend to occur outside the private sector (where differences are sorted out at the bargaining table) and are more likely designed to put pressure on the government—often to force it to abandon unpopular economic and social reforms—than on employers (except when government *is* the employer). Two of the most noteworthy new *acquis sociaux* in recent years were not a direct result of the workers' movement but were voluntary actions on the part of reformist governments—the thirty-five-hour work week, which was the main feature of the Aubry Law (2000) under the government of Prime Minister Lionel Jospin (a rule very unpopular in the business community that has since been modified several times to allow for greater flexibility); and the provision of a 2016 law recognizing an employee's "right to disconnect" from work-related communication platforms, including emails outside of working hours.

Based on the results of the 2017 professional elections, in which workers voted for the union that they wanted to represent them in collective bargaining talks and other workplace matters, there are five major labor unions that are officially accredited by the government as negotiating partners. The top vote getter was the Democratic Confederation of Labor (CFDT, founded in 1964), formerly close to the Socialist Party. It was followed by the General Confederation of Labor (CGT, founded in 1895)—the nation's oldest and once most powerful union, formerly closely associated with the French Communist Party. After these two giants and rivals came Workers' Force (FO, founded in 1948), the French Confederation of Management–General Confederation of Executives (CFE–CGC, founded in 1944), and the French Confederation of Christian Workers (CFTC, founded in 1919). The CFDT and CFTC are part of the reformist bloc of organized labor. They are generally more willing to work toward compromises with employers and less prone to resist government reforms. The CGT and FO are part of the militant bloc, considered more confrontational and prone to view employer demands and government reforms through the lens of class struggle. The CFE–CGC is officially nonaligned. Similarly, three organizations are accredited to represent the interest of employers and businesses in negotiations. The most influential of the three is the Movement of French Enterprises (MEDEF, founded in 1998 as a successor to the CNPF). While the MEDEF's membership is diverse, it is usually considered the voice of big business and has the ear of policy makers. The other two management unions are the broad-based Confederation of Small and Midsized Businesses (CMPE, founded in 1944) and the Union of Local Businesses (U2P, founded through a merger in 2016), which represents neighborhood and artisan businesses.

French labor law is compiled in the Code du Travail, or Labor Code, a now 3,400-page tome that was first issued in 1896 and is so detailed and complex, as well as hopelessly abstruse in parts, that employers are loath to open it and even labor law specialists find it difficult to interpret. Rooted in the ideas of social democracy, it aims to offset employer power with worker rights, and it assumes adversarial relations between workers and employees. Thus, it codifies every aspect of the relationship between workers and employers in the workplace and labor market—170 pages on firings, and so on. Business owners and numerous economists and policy experts have long accused it of hindering job creation, making the workplace a bureaucratic minefield, and being skewed in favor of workers—most notably, by making them hard to get rid of once they have been given open-ended contracts. Reforming the Labor Code was once considered a "third rail" of French politics. However, two major reforms, the El Khomri Labor Law under President Hollande in 2016 and the Pénicaud reforms under President Macron in 2017 have fundamentally altered labor law in France. Building on the foundation of the El Khomri Law, the latter instituted changes that Macron sold as bringing Scandinavian-style "flexible security" to France. The most important provision allows employers to negotiate layoffs and restructuring plans with labor representatives company by company rather than through sector-wide collective bargaining agreements. Another provision makes it easier for companies to justify layoffs by no longer having to demonstrate the dire nature of the company's situation or consider circumstances outside France in the case of multinational companies. Other provisions streamline proceedings in the French labor courts (Conseils de Prud'hommes) and cap employer penalties for unjust termination of an employee. Both reforms were highly controversial and led to widespread strikes and protests.

See also: Chapter 2: Timeline; Macron (Emmanuel) and the New Political Landscape of France. Chapter 3: Left; Protests. Chapter 6: Major Industries; Public Sector and Privatization; Unemployment. Chapter 6: Working Class.

Further Reading

Chapman (1998); Despax (2017); Johnson (1996); Moss (1976); Parsons (2005); Pernot (2018).

Luxury Goods

France is a leading center of the fashion and luxury goods industries, a sector that encompasses mass fashion, *prêt-à-porter*, *haute couture*, leather goods, jewelry, watches, eyeglasses frames, perfumes, other designer accessories and personal items, and fine wines and spirits. The sector is important both in terms of real economic impact and as a global conduit of French prestige, artistry, elegance, and style. Economically, it represents over 1 million jobs, annual sales of €150 billion, and exports totaling €34 billion. Ten French companies appeared in the 2018 edition of the Deloitte Global Powers of Luxury Goods Top 100 rankings, which also included makers of cosmetics and beauty products. They included the French "big five"—LVMH (Louis Vuitton Moët Hennessy, ranked first in the world), Kering (the parent company of Boucheron, Gucci, Saint Laurent, and other prestige brands; ranked fifth), L'Oréal (sixth), Hermès (eleventh), and Christian Dior (twenty-sixth). The luxury goods industry relies heavily on brand identity and many of France's iconic fashion and luxury brands trace their roots back to visionary founders like master perfumers Pierre-François (1798–1864), Aimé (1834–1910), and Jacques Guerlain (1874–1963); jeweler Louis-François Cartier (1819–1904); trunk maker Louis Vuitton (1821–1892); and designers Coco Chanel (1883–1971), Christian Dior (1905–1957), and Yves Saint Laurent (1936–2008). The aura of such illustrious names is evident in the number (21) of luxury brands included in the 2018 edition of the BrandZ Top 50 Most Valuable French Brands rankings, compiled by the Kantar Millward Brown division of WPP. The brands listed in the top twenty-five were Louis Vuitton (first), Hermès (second), L'Oréal (third), Chanel (fifth), Lancôme (seventh), Cartier (eighth), Garnier (eleventh), Hennessy (seventeenth), Dior (twentieth), Saint Laurent (twenty-first), and Moët et Chandon (twenty-second). The other luxury brands in the top fifty were Sephora, Veuve Clicquot, Rémy Martin, Givenchy, La Roche-Posay, Clarins, L'Occitane, Avène, Martell, and Guerlain. Often used loosely to refer to "high fashion," "haute couture" is a term defined by French law since 1945 and regulated by the Chambre Syndicale de la Haute Couture de Paris—an exclusive trade organization founded in 1868—and

A Louis Vuitton boutique in Hong Kong. Louis Vuitton founded the legendary house in 1854 as a maker of trunks for travelers; it now makes leather goods like the exquisite women's handbag held by the model in the advertisement, high fashion (*couture*), shoes, watches, jewelry, and a range of high-end accessories. It is part of the LVMH Moët Hennessy Louis Vuitton global conglomerate. France is a world leader in the design and production of luxury goods, which have a significant economic impact in the country. (Tea/Dreamstime.com)

the Fédération Française de la Couture, du prêt-à-porter, des Couturiers et des Créateurs de Mode (1973). To use the term, a fashion house must meet certain criteria—like, design made-to-order clothes for private clients and involving one or more fittings, maintain a workshop in Paris with at least twenty full-time permanent staff members, and publicly present full collections (fifty original designs) including both day and evening wear twice a year, once for spring/summer and again for fall/winter.

See also: Chapter 4: Major Industries; Trade. Chapter 12: Fashion. Chapter 13: Wine.

Further Reading
Burr (2008); Donzé (2017); Mensitieri (2020); Pasols (2012); Tungate (2009).

Major Industries

Like other "advanced" or "older" industrialized nations, the share of industry in France's economy has diminished over the course of the past forty years. The industrial sector—including manufacturing, extraction of natural resources, energy, waste management, and treatment of pollutants—now accounts for 12.6% of the French GDP (2017). If one adds construction to the total, the share is 20.1%. Manufacturing now accounts for just 10.2% of the GDP, compared to over 16% in 2000 and 22% in 1970. By comparison, it still accounts for 20% of Germany's GDP. Representing 77.9% of the GDP, services (tertiary activities) dominate the French economy to a greater extent than in most neighboring EU countries. Competition from foreign producers and overseas outsourcing by French companies have played a big part in the relative decline of manufacturing. It is also true that while French industrial output has grown significantly over time (close to a nine-fold increase in value added through manufacturing since 1970), other sectors of the economy have simply grown a lot more. Manufacturing is still an important part of the French economy. It employs 2.8 million salaried employees (2017), which represent 11.1% of the French workforce; and it involves over 213,000 companies—including many that are classified as small or midsized businesses (PME) or "microenterprises."

French industry is diversified. Major branches include aircraft, automobiles, chemicals, cosmetics, electronics, electrical equipment, energy, food processing, luxury goods, machinery, metallurgy, pharmaceuticals, plastics, technology, textiles, and transportation equipment. The eight largest sectors in terms of revenue are food processing, automobiles, metallurgy, chemicals, plastics and other nonmetallic materials, transportation equipment (other than automobiles and aircraft), miscellaneous manufacturing, and equipment and machinery. Industries in which France has a positive balance of trade are aeronautics, chemicals, food processing, pharmaceuticals, and transportation equipment (e.g., rail and shipbuilding). There were twenty-nine French-based companies in the 2018 edition of the *Fortune* magazine list of the 500 largest companies in the world in terms of revenue. Fifteen have something to do with industrial activity. Among them, one finds Christian Dior, Vinci, Saint-Gobain, Sanofi, Bouygues, L'Oréal, Veolia, Schneider, Danone, and Michelin. The twelve biggest French companies were: (1) Axa (insurance, twenty-seventh in the world), (2) Total (oil, twenty-eighth), (3) BNP Paribas (banking, forty-fourth), (4) Carrefour (supermarkets, sixty-eighth), (5) Crédit Agricole (banking, eighty-second), (6) EDF (electricity, ninety-fourth), (7) Engie (energy, 104th), (8) Peugeot (automobiles, 108th), (9) Société Générale (banking, 121st), (10) Renault (automobiles, 134th), (11) Groupe BPCE (banking, 151st), and (12) Auchun Holdings (supermarkets, 156th).

The 105th largest company in the world, Airbus SE, formed as a European consortium in 1970 and registered in the Netherlands, can be added to the listed since it is actually headquartered and maintains major production and research facilities in Toulouse. A maker of commercial aircraft with helicopter, defense, and aerospace divisions, it reported revenue of €67 billion in 2017. It has been quite successful in the market for large capacity passenger airliners—including the A380, the world's largest with a capacity of 853 passengers in an all economy class configuration—surpassing its American rival, Boeing, for the number of orders received over the latest ten-year period. Led by three iconic brands (Renault, Peugeot, and Citroën), the French automobile industry has survived in a highly competitive global environment through mergers and strategic partnerships, increased focus on certain types of vehicles (e.g., SUVs, smaller commercial-use vans, electric and hybrid vehicles), and a strategic approach to global expansion with an emphasis on emerging markets. Renault (est. 1899) is the lead company in the Renault-Nissan-Mitsubishi Alliance, a strategic partnership (formed in 1999) in which each company maintains its distinct corporate identity—currently, the second largest automobile group in the world (behind Volkswagen and ahead of Toyota). Peugeot (est. 1810 as a bicycle maker) and Citroën (est. 1919) are part of Groupe PSA (now also including Opel), which was formed after Peugeot acquired controlling interest in Citroën in 1976, and currently ranks as the ninth largest automobile group in the world. While both groups have had good results in recent years, sales remain concentrated in the EU (56.7% of Renault global sales in 2016, 60.5% of PSA sales), while most of their production is now overseas. The French automotive industry represents 7% of the French workforce and 18% of French manufacturing revenue.

See also: Chapter 1: Transportation. Chapter 4: Agriculture; Energy; Financial Sector; Innovation and Startups; Labor Relations; Luxury Goods; Tourism; Trade; Unemployment.

Further Reading

Cohen (2007); Comité des Constructeurs Français d'Automobiles (2019); Ministère de l'Économie et de la Finance (2015); Ministère du Redressement Productif (2013); Newhouse (2007).

Public Sector and Privatization

The public sector in France is very big. Currently, 20% of all gainfully employed French people work for the government in some capacity. In 2015, there were close to 5.5 million government employees in France, out of which 3.8 million were *fonctionnaires* in the strict sense, that is, civil servants with tenure. The remainder included contract employees (almost 1 million), military personnel (300,000), or those belonging to special categories (like private school teachers whose salaries are paid by the government but who do not have civil service status). Not counting active duty military personnel, France has an average of 72 government employees for every 1,000 inhabitants. Employees of the national government make up the largest category of government employees—44%. Another 35% work for regional and local government. The remaining 21% work for the public hospital system. The largest single group is made up of the nearly 900,000 teachers in the public schools.

Civil servants and government employees form a powerful interest group and have high rates of union membership. They are quick to protest whenever government policies and reforms threaten to affect their job security, working conditions, pay, institutional funding, or retirement plans. The retirements of employees of the SNCF (railroad) or EDF (electric utility) are generally considered more generous—a source of both financial problems for the government and concerns about fairness. One of the long-term goals of government reformers has been to bring public sector retirements in line with private sector ones, but this has proven very difficult, even volatile (e.g., the massive wave of strikes and profits that greeted a plan in 2019 to consolidate the myriad special retirement regimes that apply to categories of public employees). In 2018, the French government also announced a sweeping plan to reduce the number of civil servants by 120,000 by 2020. The cuts are part of a broader plan (Public Action 2020) to overhaul public administration by the end of Macron's first term and is also designed to achieve the goal of reducing public expenses by 3% of the GDP by the same date. Another cost-saving strategy involves making all basic government administrative procedures available online using a single logon, "FranceConnect."

In spite of public antipathy for government bureaucracy and the "special treatment" and "privileges" of certain public sector employees, the French remain strongly attached to the notion of public goods and services, which are thought to reflect and concretize the Republic's values of indivisibility, equality, and fraternity. Equality encompasses equal access to certain basic goods and services (education, healthcare, transport, information) that are seen as essential to being a full and contributing member of a society of citizens and therefore cannot be left entirely up to the marketplace law of supply and demand. The more nebulous of the three terms in the motto of the Republic ("Liberty, Equality, Fraternity"), fraternity enters into the equation of public goods and services in the form of mutualist solidarity (c.f. the theory of Solidarism as formulated by Léon Bourgeois, 1855–1925, and his followers) and national cohesion. The challenge today is to reconcile the higher civic and social mission served by public goods, services, and servants with other practical imperatives like fiscal responsibility, economic vitality, efficiency, openness to competition, and freedom of choice. In an effort to both simplify and widen access to a range of public services with emphasis on underserved rural and urban areas, the French government created France Services in 2019 (motivated in part by the demands of the Yellow Vests protest movement): a network of one-stop physical locations where citizens can obtain personalized help with a range of basic government and public services (postal, employment, health insurance, family subsidies, rural social services, justice, etc.). The program was based on and took over from the existing network of "Houses of Public Services" (MSAP). As of January 2021, there were 1,123 France Service outlets throughout France; the announced goal was to have 2,000 by 2022 (i.e., one outlet no more than thirty minutes away from the place of residence of every citizen).

One of the most striking stories in French political and economic history of the past four decades is the wave of privatizations of state-owned companies. In some cases, privatization has been total. In others, the government has maintained a sizable stake in the companies. Some of the privatized companies were strategic assets while others fulfilled a public service or utility function, which has been partially preserved through regulation and oversight. The long list of public companies that have been privatized since the 1980s includes Saint-Gobain (building materials, 1986), Paribas (banking, 1987, now part of BNP Paribas), Société Générale (banking, 1987), TF1 (television channel, 1987), Havas (advertising, 1987), Matra (aeronautics and defense, 1988, now part of Lagardère), Union des Assurances de Paris (insurance, 1994, now Axa), Elf Aquitaine (oil, 1994, now part of Total), SEITA (tobacco, 1995, now part of Altadis), Usinor (steel, 1995, now part of ArcelorMittal), Péchiney (aluminum, 1995, now part of Rio Tinto Alcan), Renault (automobiles, 1996), France Télécom (telecommunications, 1998, now Orange), CNP Assurances (insurance, 1998), Crédit Industriel et Commercial (banking, 1998, now a subsidiary of Crédit Mutuel), Crédit Lyonnais (banking, 1999, now a subsidiary of Crédit Agricole), Thomson-CSF (electrical systems and defense, 1999, now Thales), Air France (airline, 1999/2004, now part of Air France-KLM), Électricité de France (electricity, partially privatized in 2004), Gaz de France (natural gas, 2005, now part of Engie), and Snecma (aircraft engines, 2004, now Safran). The French government still owns shares in eighty-one companies, including giants like Engie, Renalt, EDF, and Safran. President Macron sold off some of France's stake in certain companies early in his term and is expected to sell off more. One likely candidate is Paris Aéroport (formerly Aéroports de Paris), in which the government is still the majority shareholder.

See also: Chapter 3: Republic; Right. Chapter 4: Financial Sector; Major Industries; Social Security and Healthcare. Chapter 8: Private Schools. Chapter 16: Radio; Television.

Further Reading
Archambault et al. (1999); Berne and Pogorel (2006); Bezes and Gillet (2011); Cole (2010); Elgie (2003); Tirard (2008); Zahariadis (1995).

Social Security and Healthcare

France's Social Security system—more commonly known as "La Sécu" in French—is not the bloated and monolithic welfare state that one might think it is. It is a legal, administrative, and fiscal framework for a hybrid system of social insurance and benefits programs managed by a wide array of institutions at the national, regional, and local level—including many private entities that serve the public interest and are subject to ordinary civil law. It traces its roots back to nineteenth-century mutualist insurance and social assistance collectives formed within various occupational categories, which continued to exist as government-legislated social benefits and private insurance plans developed through the early twentieth century. The current national Social Security framework came into existence in 1945—in the immediate aftermath of the Liberation of France and the end of World War II—through decrees issued by the Provisional Government of the French Republic under Charles de Gaulle. The framework was based on plans drawn up during the war by the National Council of the French Resistance and the proposals contained in the 1942 Beveridge Report. In the decrees establishing the framework in 1945, social security is defined as a basic right, that is, "the guarantee given to everyone in all circumstances that he shall have the necessary means to support himself and his family in decent conditions." The French Social Security system played a key role achieving a relatively broad-based high standard of living in France during the country's period of accelerated economic development from 1945 to 1975. The underlying principle of French Social Security is solidarity, which has both a collective and intergenerational redistributive component. However, close to 60% of the funding of Social Security comes from employer and employee contributions. These payroll deductions and other contributions are mandated by law and include compulsory coverage in many areas. A little over 20% of the funding comes from a special tax called the General Social Contribution (CSG). There is also a special tax (the CRDS) dedicated to paying down the national Social Security debt. Since 1996, over half of the accumulated debt of the Social Security system has been paid off. At the end of 2017, the remaining accumulated debt—commonly called "le trou (hole) de la Sécu"—was €121 billion. French Social Security expenditure in 2019 is projected to be at around €400 billion, 85% of which goes to healthcare and retirement pensions and other old-age benefits (the Social Security budget is approved by the parliament separately from the general national budget). For the first time since 2001, a modest surplus was projected in 2019.

There are three separate main Social Security coverage schemes in France—the "general" scheme (*le régime general*) covering about 80% of the population (including private sector employees and nonworking people, and their dependents), a second one for farmers and farm workers, and a third one covering independent workers (e.g., shopkeepers, artisans, and the "intellectual" professions for certain risks). There are also several special schemes, or regimes, covering specific sectors, especially in the public services and quasi-public services. The trend in Social Security reforms is to align the special schemes with the general one, but such reforms are politically sensitive and often met with strikes and protests. Across the different schemes, there is an array of funds (*caisses*) to handle claims in five separate branches of Social Security: (1) healthcare, maternity, paternity, disability, and death; (2) workmen's compensation for accidents and occupational health hazards; (3) retirements; (4) family benefits; and (5) personal autonomy (esp. assistance to the elderly and the disabled). ACOSS (Central Agency of Social Security Organizations) coordinates the collection and distribution of contributions from employers via URSSAF agencies.

In 2016, France transitioned to a new universal health insurance system (PUMa) that guarantees basic coverage for all citizens and residents across various work statuses. It replaced the CMU universal coverage system in place since 1999, which focused on covering healthcare expenses for individuals not belonging to a compulsory health insurance program through their place of work. One of the key features of the new system is the requirement that each insured person pick a primary care physician who oversees the person's general healthcare and makes referrals to most types of specialists. The insured are responsible for small co-payments and token flat fees for many services. Social Security sets standard fees for treatment and prescription medications that it is willing to reimburse. As a result, these costs are quite low when compared to private healthcare costs in a country like the United States. Many individuals have supplemental insurance plans offered through their place of employment or privately purchased insurance to cover additional costs not reimbursed by Social Security health insurance. A remnant of the CMU system offers supplemental coverage to people whose income is below a given ceiling—resulting in 100% coverage for their medical expenses free of co-payments. Every insured person over the age of sixteen carries an individual chip-embedded health insurance card called "La Carte Vitale," which contains information about that person's coverage and facilitates third-party payer handling of all covered expenses. Another key benefit of the Social Security system is its generous paid maternity, paternity, and adoptive parental leave programs. An expecting mother with fewer than two children already at home is entitled to six weeks' prenatal leave and ten weeks' postnatal leave; fathers of newborns are entitled to eleven consecutive days; the adoption leave for a single adoption is ten weeks, which may be shared by the two adoptive parents.

Retirements and family allocations are the most discussed branches of French Social Security after healthcare. In the "general scheme" that covers most French workers, the legal minimum age of retirement was recently raised to sixty-two (it was formerly sixty; Macron has plans to raise it again, to sixty-five). However, to collect full benefits, the retirement age is sixty-seven (i.e., in 2023, after a series of incremental increases), although exceptions are made for people who have had dangerous or physically taxing occupations, have already worked full time for the requisite number of years, or have worked while raising a large family. Both the early and full retirement ages are lower in many of the public sector "special schemes." The Allocation de Solidarité aux Personnes Agées (ASPA, Solidarity Allowance for the Aged) is a supplemental government pension for people on low incomes. It replaced the Old-Age Minimum Income in 2006. France's system of family allocations is a demonstration of the French state's support for families and is nominally also designed to foster higher birth rates by making it easier for working families to have more children. Families with dependent children and their members may qualify for a wide array of allowances depending on their financial resources, number of children, and other qualifying circumstances. Examples include the child benefit (paid to all families beginning with the second child, regardless of income, but at rates based on income), the family income supplement (for qualified families with three or more children), the shared child-rearing benefit and supplement allowing a parent to stop working or work less in order to look after a child, the disabled child education allowance, the back-to-school allowance (to help qualified families with school supplies, clothing purchases, and other educational expenses), and the family housing allowance. Most of these allowances are managed and disbursed by local offices of the Family Allocations Fund (CAF).

Unemployment insurance is another key component of the Social Security system. It is different from the other branches insofar as it is a result of a collective bargaining agreement between labor and management. Since 2009, unemployment insurance benefits and employment services for jobseekers are centralized in a single agency, Pôle Emploi (Employment Hub). "La Sécu" is not only a familiar part of everyday life for all French people (and therefore a common object of complaints about bureaucratic red tape, unfair treatment, and wastefulness); it is also a source of national pride as part of the "unique" solidarity-based French "republican model" of society.

In its *World Health Report* published in 2000, the World Health Organization found that France had the best overall healthcare system in the world. In some more recent studies using different criteria, it has not ranked as highly. For example, an analysis published in *The Lancet* in 2018 based on data from the Global Burden of Diseases, Injuries, and Risk Factors Study (2016), it ranked it twentieth in the world—Iceland was first, Norway second, Canada fourteenth, Germany eighteenth, the United Kingdom twenty-third, and the United States twenty-ninth. Whatever the ranking, France is widely considered a model for combining high-quality medical care with broad access and affordability. France spends a lot on healthcare annually—11.5% of the GDP in 2017 according to the OECD (the third highest percentage among OECD countries), $4,902 (USD) per capita (the eleventh highest OECD country total). By contrast, the per capita totals for Germany and the United States were $5,728 and $10,209, respectively (the U.S. healthcare expenses share of GDP was 17.1%). As much as 83% of healthcare expenses in France are covered by national health insurance or government programs.

France has an advanced approach to public health that includes traditionally strong occupational and school-based health services; strict anti-smoking laws (a law enacted in 2007 bans smoking in all enclosed public spaces), public interest campaigns on healthy living and sexual and reproductive health; and regulations on the sale of tobacco products, alcoholic beverages, junk food, and food that is high in sugar content. Pharmacies, with their characteristic green cross signs, are a fixture of many shopping districts and neighborhoods and are the only place where one can obtain common over-the-counter medications (e.g., pain relievers and cold and allergy medicine). France's medical schools and university teaching hospitals have a generally very good reputation. Child mortality rates are low. The ten leading major health problems in France in 2016 were back and neck pain, heart disease, lung cancer, skin diseases, sense organ diseases, Alzheimer's disease, cerebrovascular disease, depressive disorders, migraines, and falls. The leading forms of cancer causing premature deaths in 2016 were lung, colorectal, breast, and pancreatic cancer. While France prides itself on its tradition of good food and healthy eating, obesity is on the rise. According to the OECD (2017), 49% of the French population is at least minimally obese. By contrast, the obesity rate is 50.7% in Germany, 61.4% in the United Kingdom, and 71.0% in the United States.

See also: Chapter 2: de Gaulle (Charles), World War II, and the Fifth Republic. Chapter 3: Protests; Republic. Chapter 4: Budget, Debt, and Taxes; Unemployment. Chapter 6: Income Distribution and Inequality; Senior Citizens and Elderly.

Further Reading
Chevreul (2015); Dutton (2002); Dutton (2007); Ewald (2020); Leruth (2017); Nadal (2005); Reid (2009).

Tourism

Tourism is big business in France. In 2016, it involved total revenue of €158.9 billion, 7.1% of the GDP, 82.6 million foreign visitors (one-third of the total number of tourists and vacationers), and a balance of payments surplus of €1.8 billion—a good record in a year that was part of an unusual down cycle in foreign tourism negatively impacted by a string of high-profile terrorist attacks in 2015 and 2016 (the positive balance of payments in tourism was €7.1 billion in 2014). In the first quarter of 2018, hotel occupancy was up 7.4% compared to the previous year—a clear sign of recovery. There are over 300,000 tourism related businesses in France that provide the equivalent of 1 million full-time jobs. France currently ranks as the top tourist destination in the world in terms of the number of visitors—ahead of the United States, Spain, and China. It ranks fifth in terms of revenue—behind the United States, Spain, Thailand, and China. The top five sources of foreign tourists are the United Kingdom, the Netherlands, Germany, Belgium, and the United States. Tourism is the only industry that involves the entire national territory, including the overseas departments and communities. It is a major source of jobs and income in the Paris region (Paris is the third most visited city in the world behind London and Bangkok), the beaches and coastal areas of the Mediterranean and the Atlantic, France's mountain regions (Alps, Jura, Pyrenees, Massif Central, and Vosges), the heartland (camping, rural *gîtes*, and other forms of green tourism), and major historical and cultural sites throughout the country (cathedrals and monasteries, Loire Valley châteaux, villages in Provence, wine making regions, locations of World War I and II historical sites, and festival host cities). The ten most visited monuments, cultural sites, recreation areas, and tourist attractions in France in 2016 were Disneyland Paris (13.4 million visitors), the Louvre (7.0 million), Versailles (6.7), the Eiffel Tower (5.9), Centre Pompidou (3.3), Musée d'Orsay (3.0), Mont-Saint-Michel (2.3), City of Sciences in Parc de La Villette (2.2), and Puy du Fou (2.15). The development and promotion of tourism is a high priority of the French government, which sometimes but not always includes a cabinet-level official whose portfolio explicitly includes tourism. A coordinated approach that involves several ministries (e.g., Foreign Affairs, Economy and Finance, Culture) has been sought. The government has several programs that allow a tourist site or business to receive an official label, such as "Qualité Tourisme" for high-quality service and "Destination pour tous" for sites that are exceptionally inclusive of visitors with disabilities.

See also: Chapter 1: Cities; Historical Sites; Mountains; Overseas France; Paris; Transportation. Chapter 12: Gothic Cathedrals; Loire Valley Châteaux; Versailles. Chapter 14: Gastronomy; Regional Culinary Traditions; Wine. Chapter 15: Museums; Outdoor Pastimes; Vacations.

Further Reading

Baranowski and Furlough (2001); Bauer (1996); Dissart et al. (2015); Endy (2004); Gay (2012); Levenstein (2004); Organisation for Economic Co-operation and Development (2020); van Westering and Niel (2013); Vlès et al. (2014).

Trade

In 2016, France exported a total of €652.2 billion in goods and services and imported €695.6 billion—a relatively small trade deficit of €43.4 billion, which is equivalent 2% of its 2016 GDP. In the same year, France was the sixth leading exporting nation in the world after China (excl. Hong Kong), the United States, Germany, Japan, and South Korea. Exports represented 30% of its total GDP and imports were equivalent to 31% of its GDP. About 9.3% of all French businesses are involved in the export economy. France's international trade is heavily focused on the EU and Eurozone. In 2016, 44% of all French exports went to other Eurozone countries, 14% to EU countries outside the Eurozone—for an EU total share of 58% of French exports—and 42% to other countries. The percentages for imports in the same year were similar. Among EU countries, the largest share of French exports went to Germany (15%), Spain (7.5%), Italy (7.5%), and the United Kingdom (7%) [sic]. Outside Europe, its two biggest trading partners in 2016 were United States (7% of French exports) and China (5%). Approximately 6% of its exports went to Africa, where it maintains special relationships with its former colonies on the continent (e.g., Algeria, Morocco, Tunisia, Niger, Mali, Ivory Coast, Cameroon, Congo-Brazaville).

In 2016, France's agricultural products made up 2% of French exports in terms of revenue, industrial products made up 69%, and commercial services made up 22%. The leading export categories were miscellaneous manufactured products; transportation equipment, including automobiles and aircraft; electrical equipment, electronics, computers, and machinery; scientific, technical, and administrative services; and food, beverages, and tobacco products. Its largest trade surpluses were in transportation equipment and food and beverage products. Its largest trade deficits were in the areas of miscellaneous manufactured products and energy (mostly due to fossil fuel imports and to a slight downturn in nuclear-generated electricity exports). In terms of specific products, leading exports included wheat and other cereals, sugar beets, wine grapes, wine, beef, dairy products (incl. cheese), processed foods, electrical energy, automobiles, aircraft, rail transportation equipment, iron and steel, industrial machinery, electronics, telecommunications, textiles, plastics, chemicals, pharmaceuticals, financial and insurance products, beauty products, and luxury goods. France is the leading exporter in the world of aircraft, wine, beauty products, and luxury goods. A number of French governmental and nongovernmental agencies are active in attracting foreign companies to France, promoting French exports abroad, and encouraging investment in France, including French embassies, the General Directorate of Businesses, French regional authorities, and Business France. The latter is an independent government agency created in 2015 through the merger of Ubifrance (export promotion) and InvestInFrance. Both the Ministry of Foreign Affairs and the Ministry of Economy and Finance have oversight over Business France, which has twenty-five regional partners in France and eighty-five offices and correspondents abroad.

See also: Chapter 1: Transportation. Chapter 3: European Union. Chapter 4: Agriculture; Luxury Goods; Major Industries; Tourism. Chapter 14: Cheese; Wine.

Further Reading
Béraud-Sudreau (2020); Eaton et al. (2011); Messerlin (1996); Salva (2020).

Unemployment

Chronic high unemployment is perhaps the biggest economic challenge France faces. Unemployment was below 4% in 1975, the year that marked the end of the "Glorious Thirty" period of postwar growth. It then climbed steeply through the mid-1980s and has consistently remained above 8% ever since then—periodically topping 9% and even 10%. It went down during an economic growth spurt in the latter half of the 1990s but began a steady climb between 2000 and 2010. It was at or above 10.0% throughout 2015 and 2016 and averaged 9.7% in 2017 before dipping to 9.2% in the first quarter of 2018. Average Eurozone unemployment for the same period was also relatively high at 8.6% (it was 11.0% in Italy). However, the EU average was 7.1% and the OECD average, 5.4%. Unemployment in the United States in Q1 of 2018 stood at 3.9%, and at 3.4% in Germany, the Eurozone exception. In Q3 of 2019, French unemployment was still at 8.6%. Not surprisingly, the unemployment numbers improve with education and age. However, for France it remains high compared to peer nations when these factors are taken into consideration. According to the OECD, unemployment among people without a high school (HS)-level diploma or certificate was at 15.9% in France in 2016; by comparison, the OECD average was 11.7% (the U.S. average was 8.1%). The unemployment rate that same year for people with a HS diploma but no postsecondary education was 9.0% in France; the OECD average was 6.8% (the U.S. average was 5.7%). France approaches the OECD average only for people with a university degree or other tertiary diploma. At this level of education, unemployment in 2016 was at 5.1% in France; the OECD average was 4.6% (the U.S. average was 2.7%). Youth unemployment is a particular problem in France. In the fifteen to twenty-four age bracket, unemployment in France in 2017 was 22.3%; the Eurozone average was 18.8% (in Italy and Germany, the rate was 34.8% and 6.8%, respectively); the OECD average, 11.9% (the U.S. average was 9.2%). The long-term jobless rate (i.e., people unemployed for twelve months or more but still seeking employment) is similarly high. In 2017, 44% of unemployed people in France met the long-term criterion; the OECD average was 31.0% (the U.S. average was 15.1%). In France's disadvantaged *banlieues* (suburbs), unemployment is particularly high—especially among the young and minorities—even though some improvement has occurred here, too, in recent years. According to the 2017 report of the National Observatory of Urban Policy (ONPV), the overall unemployment rate in 2016 was 25.3% in suburban districts classified as high-priority areas for urban policy (1,500 "QPV" throughout France). For people between the ages of fifteen and twenty-nine living in QPV, it was 34.3%; for people without a HS-level diploma, 32.0%; and for the descendants of immigrants, 31.5%. Furthermore, the inactivity rate in the QPV, which refers to working-age people who are neither employed, unemployed (but still seeking employment), or students—essentially, people who have either given up on looking for work or have chosen to not enter the workforce—was 40%.

The causes of these persistently high rates of unemployment in France are multiple and complex. Certainly, mechanization and the loss of industrial jobs to low-wage countries in the context of globalization have played a part. So, too, has job discrimination against minorities, descendants of immigrants, and young people from the suburbs (certain types of surnames and postal codes on résumés are sometimes problematic). The lack of opportunities in small towns and rural areas is also a serious factor. Many observers argue that France's education system is ill adjusted to boosting employment—it is too focused on funneling young people into higher education and selecting a highly educated elite, leaves too many young people without any kind of professional qualification, sorts students into different tracks too quickly, and does a poor job of offering (or publicizing) vocational and technical training options that are geared to the demands of the job market (e.g., apprenticeships). Others say that France is over-reliant on public sector jobs that are out of sync with marketplace reality. Another significant deterrent to higher employment may be the high social cost of jobs, the added-on cost of social entitlement funding, and lack of flexibility in French labor law when it comes to hiring and firing workers. There are two main types of employment contracts in France: limited-duration contracts (*contrats de durée déterminée*, or CDD), which are inherently more flexible (and precarious); and open-ended renewable contracts (*contrats de durée indéterminée*, or CDI), which offer a high degree of employment stability and make it hard for an employer to dismiss employees. Private sector employers protect their interests by offering more short-term CDD positions than long-term CDI positions, and the CDD-to-CDI conversion rate is relatively low. Similarly, the government's approach to unemployment has focused on limited-duration contracts through a plethora of "assisted employment" schemes, offering incentives or subsidies for certain types of fixed-term positions—TUC, CES, CEC, CEV, *Emploi jeune*, CAE, CAv, CUI-CAE, *Emploi d'avenir*, CRE, CIE, *conventions de cooperation*, *contrat de génération*, and so on. Recent labor law reforms have sought to make a shift to a more market-oriented and business-friendly approach by making CDD contracts more flexible and collective bargaining rules more company-specific (as opposed to sector-wide). Welcomed by the business community and the financial markets, these measures are controversial and are still too recent to have had demonstrable and sustained impact on the employment picture. The COVID-19 pandemic wreaked havoc on work in France; however, the country has rebounded more quickly than expected and may be heading into a new period in which the overall employment picture is brighter. The unemployment rate for Q4 of 2021 was 7.4% (down from 8.0% in Q3 of the same year)—the lowest level of unemployment since 2008.

See also: Chapter 2: Macron (Emmanuel) and the New Political Landscape in France; Sarkozy (Nicolas) and the Hyper Presidency. Chapter 3: Labor Relations; Major Industries. Chapter 6: Income Distribution and Inequality; Poverty and Homelessness; Working Class.

Further Reading

Askenazy (2015); Barbier and Knuth (2011); Clegg (2013); Gautie and Caroli (2008); Murphy (2017).

SELECTED BIBLIOGRAPHY

Alijani, Sharam. "Pathways to Innovation: Evidence form Competitiveness Clusters in France." *Emerging Issues and Challenges in Business & Economics: Selected Contributions from the 8th Global Conference*, ed. Francesco Ciampi. Firenze UP, 2009, 163–178.

Archambault, Edith, et al. "France: From Jacobin Tradition to Decentralization." *Global Civil Society: Dimensions of the Nonprofit Sector*, eds. Lester M. Salamon, et al. Johns Hopkins Center for Civil Society Studies, 1999, halshs-02397036.

Askenazy, Philippe. *The Blind Decades: Employment and Growth in France, 1974–2014.* Trans. Susan Emanuel. U California P, 2015.

Baranowski, Shelley, and Ellen Furlough, eds. *Being Elsewhere: Tourism, Consumer Culture, and Identity in Modern Europe and North America.* U Michigan P, 2001.

Barbier, Jean-Claude, and Matthias Knuth. "Activating Social Protection against Unemployment: France and Germany Compared." *Sozialer Fortschritt*, vol. 60, no. 1/2, 2011, pp. 15–24.

Barsoux, Jean-Louis, and Peter Lawrence. *French Management: Elitism in Action.* Taylor & Francis, 1997.

Bauer, M. "Cultural Tourism in France." *Cultural Tourism in Europe*, ed. Greg Richards. CAB International, 1996, 147–164.

Belaïd, Fateh. "Understanding the Spectrum of Domestic Energy Consumption: Empirical Evidence from France." *Energy Policy*, vol. 92, 2016, pp. 220–233.

Béraud-Sudreau, Lucie. *French Arms Exports: The Business of Sovereignty.* Routledge, 2020.

Berne, Michel, and Gérard Pogorel. "Privatization Experiences in France." *Privatization Experiences in the European Union*, eds. Marko Köthenbürger, et al. MIT P, 2006, pp. 162–198.

Bezes, Philippe, and Jeannot Gillet. "The Development and Current Features of the French Civil Service System." *Civil Service Systems in Western Europe*. 2nd ed. ed. Frits M. Meer. Elgar, 2011, pp. 185–216.

Bivar, Venus. *Organic Resistance: The Struggle over Industrial Farming in Postwar France.* U North Carolina P, 2018.

Blanc, Christophe. "Thirty-five Years of Common Agriculture Policy: Consequences on French Agriculture." *Agriculture and The World Trade Organisation: Indian and French Perspectives*, eds. Gurdarshan Singh Balla, et al. Maison des Sciences de l'Homme, 2002, pp. 45–68.

Bureau, Jean-Christophe, et al. "Time to Decide on French Agriculture." *Notes du conseil d'analyse économique*, vol. 27, no. 8, 2015, pp. 1–12.

Burr, Chandler. *The Perfect Scent: A Year Inside the Perfume Industry in Paris and New York.* Holt, 2008.

Callahan, Helen, and Paul Lagneau-Ymonet. "The Phantom of Palais Brongniart: Economic Patriotism and the Paris Stock Exchange." *Journal of European Public Policy*, vol. 9, no. 3, 2012, pp. 388–404.

Chapman, Herrick, et al. *A Century of Organized Labor in France: A Union Movement for the Twenty-first Century?* Palgrave Macmillan, 1998.

Chevreul, Karine. "France: Health System Review." *Health Systems in Transition*, vol. 17, no. 3, 2015, pp. 1–218, xvii.

Chick, Martin. *Electricity and Energy Policy in Britain, France and the United States since 1945.* Elgar, 2007.

Chorafas, Dimitris N. *Public Debt Dynamics of Europe and the U.S.* Elsevier, 2014; esp. pp. 193–215 ("France Is Not Italy. True or False?").

Clegg, Daniel. "France: Integration versus Dualization." *Regulating the Risk of Unemployment: National Adaptations to Post-Industrial Labour Markets in Europe*, eds. Jochen Clasen and Daniel Clegg. Oxford UP, 2013, pp. 34–54.

Clift, Ben. "French Responses to the Global Economic Crisis: The Political Economy of 'Post-Dirigisme' and New State Activism." *The Consequences of the Global Financial Crisis: The Rhetoric of Reform and Regulation*, eds. Wyn Grant and Graham K. Wilson. Oxford UP, 2012, pp. 206–225.

Cohen, Elie. "Industrial Policies in France: The Old and the New." *Journal of Industry, Competition, and Trade*, vol. 7, 2007, pp. 213–227.

Cole, Alistair. "State Reform in France: From Public Service to Public Management?" *Perspectives on European Politics and Society*, vol. 11, no. 4, 2010, pp. 343–357.

Comité des Constructeurs Français d'Automobiles. *The French Automotive Industry: Analyses & Statistics 2019.* CFCA, 2019.

Creel, Jérôme, et al. "Assessing the Future Sustainability of French Public Finances." *Fiscal and Debt Policies for the Future*, eds. Paul Arestis and Malcolm C. Sawyer. Palgrave Macmillan, 2014, pp. 155–194.

Despax, Michel. *Labour Law in France.* 2nd ed. Kluwer, 2017.

Dissart, Jean-Christophe, et al., eds. *Tourism, Recreation and Regional Development: Perspectives from France and Abroad.* Ashgate, 2015.

Djelic, Marie-Laure. *Exporting the American Model: The Post-war Transformation of European Business.* Oxford UP, 1998.

Donzé, Pierre-Yves. "The Birth of Luxury Big Business: LVMH, Richemont and Kering." *Global Luxury: Organizational Change and Emerging Markets since the 1970s*, eds. Pierre-Yves Donzé and Rika Fujioka. Palgrave, 2017, pp. 19–38.

Dormois, Jean-Pierre. *The French Economy in the Twentieth Century.* Cambridge UP, 2004.

Dutton, Paul V. *Differential Diagnoses: A Comparative History of Health Care Problems and Solutions in the United States and France.* Cornell UP, 2007.

Dutton, Paul V. *Origins of the French Welfare State: The Struggle for Social Reform in France, 1914–1947.* Cambridge UP, 2002.

Eaton, Jonathan, et al. "An Anatomy of International Trade: Evidence from French Firms." *Econometrica*, vol. 79, no. 5, 2011, pp. 1453–1498.

Elgie, Robert. "Governance Traditions and Narratives of Public Sector Reform in Contemporary France." *Public Administration*, vol. 81, no. 1, 2003, pp. 141–162.

Endy, Christopher. *Cold War Holidays: American Tourism in France.* U North Carolina P, 2004.

Ewald, François. *The Birth of Solidarity: The History of the French Welfare State.* Trans. Timothy Scott Johnson. Duke UP, 2020.

Gautie, Jérôme, and Eve Caroli. *Low-Wage Work in France.* Russell Sage Foundation, 2008.

Gay, Jean-Christophe. "Why Is Tourism Doing Poorly in Overseas France?" *Annals of Tourism Research*, vol. 39, no. 3, 2012, pp. 1634–1652.

Global Investment Center. *France Investment and Business Guide: Strategic and Practical Information.* International Business Publications, 2015.

Hecht, Gabrielle. *The Radiance of France: Nuclear Power and National Identity after World War II.* New ed. MIT P, 2009.

Heller, Chaia. *Food, Farms, and Solidarity: French Farmers Challenge Industrial Agriculture and Genetically Modified Crops.* Duke UP, 2013.

Heller, David, et al. *The Emergence of Start-ups.* Wiley, 2019.

Hervé-Gruyer, Perrine, and Charles Hervé-Gruyer. *Miraculous Abundance: One Quarter Acre, Two French Farmers, and Enough Food to Feed the World.* Trans. John F. Reynolds. Green, 2016.

Howarth, David. "State Intervention and Market-Based Banking in France." *Market-Based Banking and the International Financial Crisis*, eds. Iain Hardie and David Howarth. Oxford UP, 2013, 128–150.

Johnson, Michael. *French Resistance: Individuals Versus the Company in French Corporate Life.* Cassell, 1996.

Jones, Geoff. *Air France.* Midland, 2008.

Knudson, Ann-Christina L. *Farmers on Welfare: The Making of Europe's Common Agricultural Policy.* Cornell UP, 2009.

Lafrance, Xavier. *The Making of Capitalism in France: Class Structures, Economic Development, the State and the Formation of the French Working Class, 1750–1914.* Brill, 2019.

Lepetit, Laetitia, et al. "Banking in France." *The Palgrave Handbook of European Banking*, eds. Thorsten Beck and Barbara Casu. Palgrave Macmillan, 2016, pp. 603–622.

Leruth, Benjamin. "France at a Crossroads: Societal Challenges to the Welfare State during Nicolas Sarkozy's and François Hollande's Presidential Terms." *After Austerity: Welfare State Transformation in Europe after the Great Recession.* Eds. Peter Taylor-Gooby, et al. Oxford UP, 2017, pp. 67–88.

Levenstein, Harvey. *We'll Always Have Paris: American Tourists in France since 1930.* U Chicago P, 2004.

Levy, Jonah D. "From the *Dirigiste* State to the Social Anaesthesia State: French Economic Policy in the Longue Durée." *Modern & Contemporary France*, vol. 16, no. 4, 2008, pp. 417–435.

Levy, Jonah D. "The Return of the State?: France's Response to the Financial and Economic Crisis." *Comparative European Politics*, vol. 15, no. 4, 2017, pp. 604–627.

Maclean, Mairi, et al. *Business Elites and Corporate Governance in France and the UK.* Palgrave Macmillan, 2006.

Maillet, Paul, et al. "Assessing Short-Term and Long-Term Economic and Environmental Effects of the COVID-19 Crisis in France." *Environmental and Resource Economics*, no. 75, 2020, pp. 867–883.

Massoc, Elsa Clara. *Banking on States?: The Divergent Trajectories of European Finance after the Crisis*. 2018. University of California, Berkeley, Ph.D. dissertation.

Mensitieri, Giulia. *The Most Beautiful Job in the World: Lifting the Veil on the Fashion Industry*. Bloomsbury, 2020.

Messerlin, Patrick A. "France and Trade Policy: Is the 'French Exception' Passée?" *International Affairs*, vol. 72, no. 2, 1996, pp. 293–309.

Ministère de l'Économie et de la Finance. *Industry of the Future: Rallying the New Face of Industry in France*. Publication of the French Government, 2015.

Ministère du Redressement Productif. *The New Face of Industry in France*. Publication of the French Government, 2013.

Moss, Bernard H. *The Origins of the French Labor Movement, 1830–1914: The Socialism of Skilled Workers*. U California P, 1976.

Murphy, John P. *Yearning to Labor: Youth, Unemployment, and Social Destiny in Urban France*. U Nebraska P, 2017.

Nadal, Sophie. "The Welfare State System in France." *Welfare States and the Future*, eds. B. Vivekanandan and Nimmi Kurian. Palgrave Macmillan, 2005, pp. 97–112.

Newhouse, John. *Boeing Versus Airbus: The Inside Story of the Greatest International Competition in Business*. Knopf, 2007.

Organisation for Economic Co-Operation and Development. *OECD Economic Surveys: France 2019*. OECD, 2019.

Organisation for Economic Co-Operation and Development. *OECD Reviews of Innovation Policies: France 2014*. OECD, 2014.

Organisation for Economic Co-Operation and Development. *OECD Tourism Trends and Policies 2020*. OECD, 2020; esp. pp. 171–175 ("France").

Parsons, Nick. *French Industrial Relations in the New World Economy*. Routledge, 2005.

Pasols, Paul-Gerard, and Pierre Leonforte. *Louis Vuitton: The Birth of Modern Luxury*. New ed. Abrams, 2012.

Pernot, Jean-Marie. "France's Trade Unions in the Aftermath of the Crisis." *Rough Waters: European Trade Unions in a Time of Crises*, eds. Steffen Lehndorff, et al. European Trade Union Institute, 2018, pp. 39–64.

Reid, T. R. *The Healing of America: A Global Quest for Better Cheaper and Fairer Health Care*. Penguin, 2009; esp. pp. 46–65 ("France: Vital Card").

Ribera, Teresa, and Andreas Rüdinger. "The Energy Transition in France: A Shift Towards a New Energy Model?" *Intereconomics*, vol. 49, no. 5, 2014, pp. 251–256.

Salva, Jean-Marie. "International Trade in Goods and Services in France: Overview." *Practical Law*, Thomson Reuters, Mar. 2020, https://uk.practicallaw.thomsonreuters.com/w-017-4715.

Schmidt, Vivien. "French Capitalism—Transformed, Yet Still a Third Variety of Capitalism." *Economy and Society*, vol. 32, no. 4, 2003, pp. 526–554.

Schmidt, Vivien. *From State to Market?: The Transformation of French Business and Government*. Cambridge UP, 1996.

Schmidt, Vivien. "Running on Empty: The End of *Dirigisme* in French Economic Leadership." *Modern & Contemporary France*, vol. 5, no. 2, 1997, pp. 229–241.

Smith, Michael Stephen. *The Emergence of Modern Business Enterprise in France, 1800–1930*. Harvard UP, 2006.

Tiberghien, Yves. *Entrepreneurial States: Reforming Corporate Governance in France, Japan, and Korea*. Cornell UP, 2018.

Tirard, Manuel. "Privatization and Public Law Values: A View from France." *Indiana Journal of Global Legal Studies*, vol. 15, no. 1, 2008, pp. 285–304.

Trumbull, Gunnar. *Silicon and the State: French Innovation Policy in the Internet Age*. Brookings Institution, 2004.

Tungate, Mark. *Luxury World: The Past, Present and Future of Luxury Brands*. Kogan Page, 2009.

van Uden, Jenna, ed. *Startup Guide Paris: The Entrepreneur's Handbook*. Startup Guide World IVS, 2018–2019. 2 vols.

van Westering, Jetske, and Emmanuelle Niel. "The Organization of Wine Tourism in France: The Involvement of the French Public Sector." *Wine, Food, and Tourism Marketing*, ed. C. Michael Hall. Routledge, 2013, pp. 35–47.

Vlès, Vincent, et al. "Strengths and Paradoxes of French Tourism Planning." *European Tourism Planning and Organisation Systems: The EU Member States*, eds. Carlos Costa, et al. Channel View, 2014, pp. 418–431.

Zahariadis, Nikolaos. *Markets, States, and Public Policy: Privatization in Britain and France*. U Michigan P, 1995.

CHAPTER 5

RELIGION AND THOUGHT

OVERVIEW

The religious profile of France is very diverse. The largest religious denominations are Roman Catholicism (61% of the population identify as Catholic, equal to 39.6 million people), Islam (7.5% of the population, 4.7 million people), Protestantism (3% of the population, 2.0 million people), Buddhism (0.92% of the population, 600,000 people), and Judaism (0.85% of the population, 550,000 people). Official collection of statistics on religious affiliation is prohibited by law in France. Unofficial polling data is therefore highly approximative and varies widely according to methodology. Some recent polling reports much lower percentages for each of the aforementioned groups. France has the largest Muslim and Jewish communities in Europe. Catholicism is historically the majority religion in France and was the state religion up to the Revolution. On account of both the ancientness of its Christian community, which dates to the era of Roman Gaul, and the dynamism of Catholic Christian culture there in the Middle Ages, France is often referred to as the "eldest daughter of the Church in Europe." The French landscape is still profoundly marked by Catholicism—Romanesque monasteries, Gothic cathedrals, village parish churches, pilgrimage sites (e.g., Lourdes), a national network of Catholic private schools, and a handful of Catholic institutions of higher education. However, one of the most striking trends of French religious history is the steep decline of Catholicism in the modern and contemporary eras. In 1972, 87% of the population of France still identified as Catholic and now only 5% of the much smaller number of self-identifying Catholics report regular attendance at Sunday mass. On the other hand, the growth of Islam and, to a lesser extent, Buddhism has been quite impressive. Islam was not among the religions (Roman Catholicism, Lutheran and Calvinist Protestantism, and Judaism) officially recognized by Napoleon Bonaparte in the early years of the nineteenth century, so its recent rapid rise to become the second leading religion of France has generated a fair amount of debate—for instance, about the construction of mosques, accommodations for halal dietary restrictions, headscarves and veils (laws restricting the practice were passed in 2004 and 2010), fundamentalist theologies, the training of imams, national organizational structures, Islamist-inspired domestic terrorism, and Islamophobia. The Jewish community in France is well established although the majority of French Jews are Sephardi whose families settled in France in the wake of decolonization in French North Africa. French Jews have endured persecution and anti-Semitism since the Middle Ages; however, the Jewish population of France was the first in Europe to be fully emancipated and granted equal rights (1791). Persecution dating back to the Wars of Religion in the sixteenth century and the royal revocation of religious rights and protections for Protestants in 1685 also occupies an important place in the collective memory and identity of the French Protestant community—albeit less so for the growing number of French people who identify as "Evangelical Christians" (now over 25% of all French Protestants).

In counterpoint to this religious diversity, France also ranks as one of the most secular nations in the world. In one recent poll, 29% of French people surveyed described themselves as "atheists" (one of the highest totals in the world) and another 34% described themselves as "not religious." Moreover, a large majority of French people who identify with a particular religion are nonpracticing—three-fourths of Catholics and two-thirds of Muslims. Slightly higher percentages of French Protestants and Jews consider themselves practicing. However, three-fourths of the former and nine-tenths of the latter do not practice regularly. There are many reasons for this deep-seated and broad secularism, including traditions of freethinking and anticlericalism dating back to the eighteenth-century *philosophes*, if not before. Another major factor is the strong legal, political, and social norm of *Laïcité*, or secularism. Full institutional separation of church and state became the law of the land in France only in 1905. However, French *Laïcité* involves more than statutory separation of church and state and its corollaries, guarantees of religious liberty (e.g., in the Declaration of the Rights of Man and of the Citizen of 1789) coupled with a societal imperative of tolerance and pluralism, and government neutrality on matters of religion. It also evokes a century-long campaign dating back to the Revolution that sought to confine religion in general, and the Catholic Church in particular, to the private sphere of life and thereby rid the public sphere of clerical interest. It also has been construed as entailing the individual citizen's civic, moral, and intellectual obligation to keep what is essentially private (esp. religion) and public (esp. politics) separate. While many see *Laïcité* as something quasi-sacred and back stricter applications of the norm, others worry that it has become too rigid and may represent an obstacle to a more pluralistic society.

While some French thinkers and scholars (e.g., Marcel Gauchet) consider France's "exit from religion" irreversible, others (e.g., Danièle Hervieu-Léger and Frédéric Lenoir) see a more nuanced picture. Lenoir points to an intense interest in spirituality that manifests itself in diverse ways—astrology, Eastern religions (e.g., according to one estimate, 5,000,000 people in France claim a spiritual affinity for Buddhism), religious *bricolage* (idiosyncratic constructs that mix elements from different traditions), yoga, meditation, the renewed popularity of pilgrimage, conversions to faiths outside one's family background, and involvement in sects that authorities consider cults. Hervieu-Léger describes different modes of partial "return to religion." Whereas traditional religious identity integrates four poles of religious experience—emotional, ethical, communitarian, and cultural—within a well-defined tradition and community, Hervieu-Léger identifies six styles of neo-religious identity based on the combination of just two poles—*affective* (emotional + communitarian), *patrimonial* (communitarian + cultural), *humanitarian* (emotional + ethical), *political* (communitarian + ethical), *humanist* (ethical + cultural), and *esthetic* (emotional + cultural).

Philosophical thought is highly developed and respected in France. Each year, hundreds of thousands of young people taking the high school baccalaureate exams face the formidable challenge of the philosophy exam—four hours in which to write an essay answering a single broad question such as "Does power exist without violence?" or "Is desire a sign of our imperfection?" The students have plenty of material to draw on in France's rich philosophical tradition. Major French thinkers through the ages include Abelard, Montaigne, Descartes, Pascal, Montesquieu, Rousseau, Voltaire, Diderot, de Staël, Constant, Tocqueville, Comte, Bergson, Bachelard, Merleau-Ponty, Sartre, Beauvoir, Barthes, Lacan, Foucault, Derrida, Deleuze, Cixous, Irigaray, Lyotard, Baudrillard, Virilio, Balibar, Rancière, and Latour. The diverse generation of French philosophers who published their major works between the mid-1940s through the mid-1990s—including thinkers associated with existentialism, structuralism, and post-structuralism (sometimes known as "French Theory" in the anglophone world)—have been particularly influential. French thinkers have focused extensively on questions of rationalism, science, epistemology, progress, liberty, government, social and political power, religion, esthetics, the individual subject, universalism, difference, and language. The great respect for intellectual life in France has also given a prominent voice to public intellectuals on the major political, social, and cultural issues of the day—especially in the twentieth century.

Further Reading

Bourg (2004); Bréchon and Boutaud (2019); Cloots (2015); Davie (1999); Drake (2002); Drake (2005); Garay (2018); Hazareesingh (2015); Hervieu-Léger (2000); Houtman and Aupers (2007); Long (2006); McCaffrey (2009); Meunier (2006); Moriarty (2019); Palmer (2011); Sand (2018); Tallett and Atkin (2003).

Catholicism

Roman Catholicism, the traditional majority religion of France, has had a great impact on the nation. The earliest written records of the presence of Christians in France date from the second century CE and pertain to the persecution and martyrdom of Christians in Lugdunum (Lyon), the most important city in Roman Gaul. Due to the ancientness of its Christian community, France is sometimes called the "eldest daughter of the Church in Europe." Furthermore, many consider the 496 conversion and baptism of the Frankish king Clovis a foundational moment of the French monarchy and nation because it helped underpin continuous Frankish rule over a large part of formerly Roman territory—the core of the future Kingdom of France—in which Christianity was widespread and had been the official religion for over a century and a half. France was a cultural center of western Christendom in the Middle Ages. Its great Benedictine monasteries (e.g., Cluny, Cîteaux, Clairvaux, and Vézelay) played a key role in the development of monastic life. The Gothic style of architecture, which originated in the Paris region, is exemplified in many great cathedrals in France (e.g., Paris, Chartres, Amiens, and Reims) and spread throughout Europe in the twelfth and thirteenth centuries. During the same period, the faculty of theology of the University of Paris was arguably the most illustrious in the western world. The French monarchy had particularly close ties to the church and the papacy. King Louis IX (Saint Louis, 1214–1270) led the Seventh Crusade to the Holy Land and died in Tunisia after having embarked on the Eighth. This close relationship was at other times fraught with tension. From 1309 to 1376, the papacy relocated to Avignon, where it was under French royal protection and hegemony. The Protestant Reformation and its political repercussions led to a series of bloody civil wars between Catholics and Protestants, known as the Wars of Religion, in the sixteenth century (1562–1598). In 1685, Louis XIV reaffirmed Catholicism's position as the sole legal form of Christianity in France by revoking the 1685 Edict of Nantes (promulgated by his Protestant grandfather, Henry IV), which offered French Protestants limited rights and protections. The Revolution had grave consequences for the Catholic Church, which some anticlerical revolutionaries considered as an enemy of the people on par with the divine right absolute monarchy and the aristocracy. Church property was nationalized, and clergymen were required to take an oath of loyalty to the new regime. Some priests and nuns were arrested and killed, and churches were vandalized.

The church rebounded in the nineteenth century. However, devout Catholics, who tended to be more conservative politically, and secularist Republicans were at odds for decades over issues like the secularization of public education (1882), the Dreyfus Affair (1894–1906), and the Law of Separation of Churches and State (1905). During World War II and the German occupation of France (1940–1944), many ultraconservative Catholics sided with the Vichy regime. However, there was also a strong Catholic contingent in the French Resistance. After the war—especially after the Second Vatican Council (1962–1965), which significantly modernized church doctrine and practice—tensions eased. The church accepted to operate within the limits imposed by public secularism (Laïcité), focused on the spiritual and pastoral needs of the faithful, continued to speak out on moral and social issues (e.g., abortion, in vitro fertilization, same-sex marriage, racism, the environment, and the treatment of undocumented immigrants and asylum seekers) in application of church teachings but as one voice among many, and maintained an active role in charitable endeavors and education. However, religious observance among Catholics (and members of other faiths) declined dramatically during the 1960s, 1970s, and 1980s in the face of secularism, individualism, liberalism, and materialism.

The number of French people who identify as Catholics today is low in comparison to the past. In 1972, 87% of the population still considered itself Catholic. That figure dropped to 75% by the early 1980s, and to 61% in 2011 according to a poll conducted by IFOP for Le Journal du Dimanche. The latter figure likely includes many people who identify as Catholic by cultural tradition or family background (some of whom may no longer be believers at all), since only 25% of Catholics in the same 2011 poll—the equivalent of just 15% of the French total population—described themselves as "practicing."

That descriptor is itself vague since it is estimated that as few as 5% of French Catholics attend Sunday mass regularly. More recent polls report much lower percentages of self-identifying Catholics (47% according to Pew Global Attitudes Survey 2017 and 41% according to Eurobarometer 2019). There are approximately 15,000 Catholic priests in France today, out of which just a little over half are under the age of seventy-five. France ordains on average fewer than 100 priests per year. This crisis of religious vocations is partially addressed by reliance on foreign priests, including many from Francophone Africa. There are an additional 30,000 religious people (nuns and brothers who have taken vows) living in France. France counts 13,000 Catholic parishes and 98 dioceses. The Bishop's Conference of France (CEF) is the official voice of the French Church. There are 45,000 Catholic churches and chapels across France (indeed, many villages are still dominated visually by the steeples of their old parish churches on the public square). Given its historical ties to the church and the Catholic background of a large number of its citizens, and in spite of official secularism, several Catholic holy days are public holidays in France: Easter Monday (in March or April), the Feast of the Ascension (39 days after Easter), Pentecost Monday (the Monday following the seventh Sunday after Easter), the Feast of the Assumption of Mary (August 15), All Saints' Day (November 1), and Christmas (December 25). Many Catholic saints are well known to Catholics and non-Catholics alike. Examples include Saint Geneviève (patroness of Paris), Saint Joan of Arc (the hero of the Hundred Years War), Saint Vincent de Paul (the helper of the poor), Saint Bernadette Soubirous (the young girl who experienced apparitions of the Virgin Mary in Lourdes), and Saint Thérèse of Lisieux (a young nun known for her piety). It is still common in France to wish people with Christian first names a happy feast day on the day of the saint with whom they share a name.

See also: Chapter 2: Overview; Timeline; Charlemagne and the Carolingian Dynasty; Clovis and the Merovingian Dynasty; Ferry (Jules) and the Third Republic; Joan of Arc and the Hundred Years War; Robespierre (Maximilien) and the French Revolution. Chapter 3: Republic. Chapter 5: Laïcité; Philosophy (Tradition); Protestantism. Chapter 8: Private Schools. Chapter 12: Gothic Cathedrals. Chapter 15: Holidays.

Further Reading
Byrnes (2005); Chadwick (2000); Dargent (2019); Gadille (1983); Harrison (2014); Kaufman (2005); McMillan (2003); Price (2017); Tallett and Atkin (1996); Tippett-Spirtou (2000).

Islam

At the Battle of Tours in 732, Frankish and Burgundian armies under the command of Charles Martel (the founder of the Carolingian dynasty) defeated the army of the Muslim Umayyad Caliphate, which had invaded Gaul from Spain. Many consider that the religious identity of France and Western Europe would have been different had the battle gone the other way. Aside from the Crusades, contact between western Christendom and the Muslim world continued through the Middle Ages (e.g., trade and the intellectual influence of Islamic philosophers) and into the early modern era (Francis I's strategic alliance with Sultan Suleiman the Magnificent, the ruler of the Ottoman Empire). The presence of Muslims in France in the modern era dates to the second age of French colonialism, which began with the taking of Algiers in 1830 and the subsequent conquest of the rest of Algeria. In French Algeria, a form of political and social apartheid was practiced (it was formalized in a set of laws known as the Indigenous Code, enacted in 1881), under which Muslim Algerians were French subjects but were ineligible for French citizenship unless they renounced Islam (this stipulation was removed when full citizenship rights were extended to all Algerians in 1946). Muslims were among the colonial troops who fought for France on French soil during World Wars I and II (there are Muslim sections in French military cemeteries, and the Grand Mosque of Paris, inaugurated in 1926, was built as a tribute to these fallen Muslim heroes). However, the Muslim community in France was still relatively small until the major wave of immigration from Algeria and France's other former African colonies from 1945 to 1975.

Islam is presently the second largest religion in France. Estimates vary on the total number of French Muslims. According to polling to conducted by IFOP, there were 4.7 million people who identified as or could be considered Muslim in France in

Muslims praying outside the Grand Mosque of Paris on Eid al-Fitr, the holiday marking the end of Ramadan. Islam is now the second largest religion in France after Catholicism. The French Muslim community has faced numerous challenges including the need for more local mosques and imams, secularist laws that prohibit the wearing of hijabs in public schools and face-covering veils and niqabs in public places, anti-immigrant sentiment, Islamophobic bigotry following recent incidents of terrorism, and policies pursued by President Emmanuel Macron aimed at clamping down on radical Islamism. (Pascal Deloche/Dreamstime.com)

2010—7.5% of the total national population. Of the total number of Muslims in the same survey, 35% were between the ages of fifteen and twenty-four; and 28% were between twenty-five and thirty-four—a relatively young population. As with French Catholics and people who identify with other religious groups, these figures likely contain many people who consider themselves Muslim due to family background or for cultural reasons. More recent polling (Pew 2017 and Eurobarometer 2019) reports the percentage of self-identifying Muslims in the French population at 5%. However, even in the older IFOP poll, just 33% of self-identifying Muslims described themselves as "practicing believers" (a number equivalent to 2.5% of the total population of France); other polls report this category closer to 40%; 70% reported fasting during the holy month of Ramadan; 23% reported attendance at Friday prayer services. It is unclear whether the number of practicing Muslims is rising or falling (some suggest it is destined to decline over time as with other religious groups in the markedly secular French environment). However, certain forms of practice are moderately rising. One reason is that younger Muslims are rediscovering their familial religion or taking certain forms of practice more seriously. Some younger Muslims (including inhabitants of France's socioeconomically disadvantaged suburbs) have responded to the Tablighi Jamaat missionary movement within Sunni Islam, which urges stricter observance of Islamic norms and customs. Although the demographic figures and criteria used to determine who qualifies as Muslim vary from one source to another, France is generally thought to have the largest Muslim population (between 3.5 and 5.5 million) in Western Europe—with Germany and the United Kingdom close behind.

According to the French Ministry of Interior, which has jurisdiction over religious affairs, there were 2,500 mosques and other Muslim places of worship in France in 2015 (incl. overseas departments) compared to 1,600 in 2004 (and just 100 in 1970, during the period of so-called Basement Islam, which derives its name from the large number of makeshift places of worship in apartment building basements)—a number that can be seen as an improvement but may still be insufficient to meet the needs of the French Muslim population at its current size. While the construction of new mosques can still generate controversy and reluctance, Islam is becoming more and more a part of mainstream French culture. Other examples include the greater availability of halal food in specialty shops, supermarkets, and restaurants; major local celebrations of the Eid al-Fitr holiday (at the end of Ramadan), which now include festivities which non-Muslims are invited to attend; and the development of stronger Muslim organizations. The most important of the latter is French Council of the Muslim Faith (CFCM), a national elected body set up in 2003 with the backing of the French government as a national regulatory authority for Muslim religious affairs and official voice of the community in dealings with the government and broader public. French Muslims (formerly known as the Union of Islamic Organizations of France, founded in 1981), is a more conservative umbrella organization with ties to the Muslim Brotherhood that was part of the CFCM until 2013. The Collective Against Islamophobia in France (CCIF, founded in 2013) had been the most prominent of several active national organizations that track and fight Islamophobia and other types of discrimination against French Muslims. It was dissolved by the French government in 2020 for allegedly promoting religious separatism and having ties with Islamist radicals—a decision that drew widespread international criticism. The organization reformed in 2021 as the Collective Against Islamophobia in Europe (CCIE) and is now based in Brussels, Belgium.

French Muslims meet with considerable prejudice and discrimination. Some of this is due to deeply engrained cultural stereotypes. However, political discourse about Islam's alleged incompatibility with Western traditions and values (e.g., the right-wing populist National Rally) and concerns about radicalization and terrorism have played a part as well. Many French Muslims are also critical of French government laws that they say target them unfairly, including recent laws that limit the right of Muslim women and girls to wear different types of headscarves and veils in different contexts (e.g., the 2004 law banning hijabs and other so-called ostensible signs of religious identity in public schools and the 2010 "burka ban" law that prohibited the wearing of face-covering clothing of all types in public in the name of security). Such laws are popular in French public opinion and are widely interpreted as part of a necessary reinforcement of the French norm of secularism (*Laïcité*). However, in addition to their allegedly discriminatory nature, critics maintain that they may have an effect that is opposite to what was intended, by contributing to communitarian resentment rather than integration. In 2016, several municipal ordinances banning (on public beaches) a body-covering type of swimwear popular among Muslim women commonly called the "burkini" were struck down by France's administrative supreme court, the Council of State. In 2019, public pressure forced the French sports megastore chain to halt in-store sales of women's sportswear with incorporated hijabs.

See also: Chapter 2: Timeline. Chapter 3: Far Right. Chapter 5: Judaism; Laïcité. Chapter 6: Arabs; Blacks; Immigration; Suburbs. Chapter 8: Republicanism and Public Schools.

Further Reading

Bergeaud-Becker (2013); Bowen (2006); Bowen (2010); Césari (2014); Downing (2019); Gemie (2010); Keaton (2006); Khosrokhavar (2009); Laurence and Vaisse (2006); Plenel (2016); Roy (2007); Scott (2007); Wolfreys (2017); Wright and Annes (2013).

Judaism

Judaism is the fifth largest religion in France after Catholicism, Islam, Protestantism, and Buddhism. As with the other religions, determining the number of people who adhere to Judaism or who identify as Jewish is difficult to do because there are no official statistics and the definition of "Jewish" used in different measures varies. One common estimate is that the Jewish population of France is about 550,000, which is less than 1% of the total population of France. According to a poll conducted in 2015 by IFOP for the Fondation Jean-Jaurès, 64% of French Jews surveyed described themselves as nonpracticing—42% said that they never practiced their faith and 22% said that they did so only rarely. Among the practicing Jews, 26% said that they practiced their faith somewhat frequently and only 10% said that they did so very frequently. While these statistics reflect the highly secular nature of French society in general and are comparable to levels of practice in other religions, younger French Jews tend to practice their faith more regularly than older ones. The age group with the highest share of respondents who described themselves as nonpracticing was French Jews age sixty-five and above (82%). The age group with the highest share who described themselves as practicing were those under thirty-five (53%). According to the same poll, 41% of French Jews identified as Sephardi, 26% as Ashkenazi, and 14% as mixed (19% of respondents did not specify their origin). The families of most French Sephardi Jews came to France from French North Africa (Morocco, Algeria, and Tunisia) in the 1950s and 1960s in the wake of decolonization. The Sephardi community tends to be both more practicing and conservative, and has a stronger sense of attachment to their cultural and religious traditions. Most of France's Ashkenazi Jews are the descendants of people who emigrated to France from Central and Eastern Europe in the early part of the twentieth century (esp. the 1920s and 1930s), but there are also a number of older Ashkenazi Jewish families—usually very secular—who have been in France for two or more centuries.

Most French Jews practice Orthodox Judaism—perhaps 80%. Accordingly, France's national Jewish religious organization, the Union of Jewish Congregations of France, whose executive body is called the Central Consistory and names the chief rabbi of France, is predominantly orthodox. However, there is a small but active community that adheres to Liberal Judaism, which incorporates both Progressive and Reform Judaism—perhaps 20% of French Jews. The appeal of Liberal Judaism is growing in France, but so too is that of the Chabad movement (Lubavitch Hasidism) of ultra-Orthodox Judaism. There are 300 synagogues and other Jewish places of worship in France (200 in the Paris region); and 250–300 Jewish private schools.

The Jewish community of France has seen both persecution (expulsions in the Middle Ages, virulent anti-Semitism at the time of the Dreyfus Affair, and deportations to the death camps during World War II with the complicity of the Vichy regime and the French police) and acceptance (emancipation during the French Revolution, official recognition by Napoleon, and decades of integration into the mainstream of French society). However, a recent upsurge in anti-Semitism and terrorist acts targeting Jews in France has worried the community considerably. Of respondents in the IFOP poll, 43% reported that they had been the targets of anti-Semitic behaviors or acts of aggression, and there has been a small but steady trend of French Jewish immigration to Israel (Aliyah): 13,000 between 2000 and 2009 and 6,628 in 2015 alone but down again somewhat 3,157 in 2017.

See also: Chapter 2: Ferry (Jules) and the Third Republic. Chapter 4: Catholicism; Islam; Laïcité. Chapter 6: Immigration.

Further Reading
Arkin (2013); Benbassa (2001); Berkovitz (2004); Cohen (2011); Katz (2015); Malinovich (2008); Mandel (2014); Samuels (2016); Schnapper et al. (2010); Sémelin (2017); Weitzmann (2019); Wieviorka (2007); Wolf (2003); Zuccotti (1993).

Laïcité

Usually rendered in English as "secularism," but more exactly translated by the cognates "laicism" and "laicity," *Laïcité* is a fundamental component of France's political and cultural identity as a democratic republic. In fact, Article 1 of the present French constitution, adopted in 1958, specifies, "La France est une République indivisible, *laïque*, démocratique et sociale." ("France shall be an indivisible, *secular*, democratic and social Republic.") French republican laicism has four related meanings. It is first *a legal and constitutional norm* requiring strict separation of church and state. The relevant French law dates from 1905 and is known as the "Law of Separation of Churches and State." Enacted in an era of intense animosity between Catholic conservatives (many of them also monarchists) on the right and secularist republicans (some of them vehemently anticlerical) on the left, the law of 1905 was preceded by the 1882 "Ferry Law" that secularized public education in France. The 1905 law replaced hundred year-old legal arrangements dating back to the reign of Napoleon Bonaparte, whereby the state remained essentially secular but certain religions (Catholicism, Protestantism, and Judaism), which Napoleon deemed useful for maintaining order and morality in society, were officially recognized and subsidized by the state (e.g., the state paid clergy salaries and funded the construction and upkeep of houses of worship). The most famous of such arrangements was the 1801 Concordat with the Holy See (Vatican). The Napoleonic system can be seen as a sort of compromise between the anticlerical extremism and dechristianization movement of the French Revolution and the ancien régime status quo, in which Catholicism had been the state religion, and the church, France's dominant social institution. The separation of church and state in France is quite total. However, certain Catholic holy days, such as the Feast of the Assumption of Mary (August 15), are public holidays—a nod toward "cultural" tradition. Elected public officials do not take oaths of office with their hand on a Christian Bible or any other sacred book, sessions of parliament do not open with ecumenical prayers, and French presidents usually take great pains to keep their religious life (if any) private and as a general rule do not refer to God in even the most vague and ecumenical manner. Furthermore, separational laicism extends to all institutional and civic spaces of the Republic and to both representatives of the state and citizens while acting in those spaces (e.g., neither civil servants at work nor pupils attending public schools may wear articles of clothing deemed "religious" in nature).

Republican laicism has three additional meanings. It is *a civic and moral imperative* entailing an individual citizen's obligation to keep separate the private and public spheres of their own life—a responsibility that offsets and complements their right to freedom of religion *and* conscience as recognized in the 1789 Declaration of the Rights of Man and the Citizen and reaffirmed in the French constitution. Just as no government entity, group, self-styled authority, or person may interfere with an individual's total freedom of belief and conscience, no individual may interfere with the freedom of others. The private sphere is understood as the proper domain of that which is particular to individuals and groups of individuals (e.g., religious faith), whereas the public sphere, which includes political life, is the domain of that which is common to all individuals. Hence, whatever beliefs may shape the private life and identity of an individual, that person has a higher civic duty to use only the general criteria of reason as the basis of their deliberations and actions as a citizen in the public sphere. This is an ambitious expectation. Republican laicism is also *the driving force behind a historical and political struggle* to rid the political life of the nation, the broader public sphere of social life, and individual efforts of self-determination of clerical influence. This is consistent with the *Merriam-Webster* definition of the term "laicism": "a political system characterized by the exclusion of ecclesiastical control and influence." (From an etymological and historical perspective, the term refers to ordinary people, or *laymen*, as distinct from the clergy.) It is common in France to consider that clerical authority (i.e., clericalism) is intrusive, pernicious, and antithetical to carefully reasoned freethinking—a "Voltairean" attitude toward organized religion that developed during the Enlightenment and became more widespread in the modern era. This wariness toward organized religion is understandable given the power once wielded by the Catholic Church in France (with the formal support of the monarchy) and the great difficulty the French Republic had in the late nineteenth and early twentieth centuries establishing a secular public sphere and its own legitimacy outside a religious frame of references. However, some advocates of a more pragmatic, pluralistic, civil society-focused, and trusting form of laicism, like the historian and sociologist of religion, Jean Baubérot, believe that such ideological laicism no longer makes sense in the more complex social and religious environment of present-day France, particularly as it relates to Islam as the religion of a large and often unfairly treated minority. Other public intellectuals, like the philosopher Régis Debray, point with great concern to the widening appeal of religious fundamentalism and communitarianism both in France and worldwide, and suggest that a stricter and even somewhat "combative" interpretation of laicism is as relevant and necessary today as ever. Recent French history has seen the second position gain the upper hand. Examples include the 2004 law banning religious clothing (incl. esp. Muslim headscarves) in schools, the 2010 law banning face-covering clothing in public spaces (incl. esp. burkas), the 2013 "Charter of Laicity in School," the post-*Charlie Hebdo* attack (2015) emphasis on the idea that laicism and freedom of speech necessarily extended to speech that religious communities might deem blasphemous, and a 2021 law "reinforcing the respect of the principles of the Republic" (commonly known as the anti-religious separatist law). Finally, and perhaps paradoxically to some extent, laicism is *a key fixture of French republican civil religion*—a secular, humanistic, and patriotic set of beliefs, symbols, and rites that partially filled the void left in the public arena by the evacuation of other forms of religion. As such, *Laïcité* is for many French people as venerable—indeed, as *sacred*—as "Liberty, Equality, Fraternity," the Tricolor flag, the Marseillaise, the Declaration of the Rights of Man and of the Citizen, Marianne, Jules Michelet's "People," the Poilus who fought in the trenches of World War I, and Charles de Gaulle.

See also: Chapter 2: Timeline; Ferry (Jules) and the Third Republic; Napoleon Bonaparte (Napoleon I) and the First Empire; Robespierre (Maximilien) and the

French Revolution. Chapter 3: Left; Republic. Chapter 4: Catholicism; Islam; Rationalism and Universalism. Chapter 8: Republicanism and Public Schools.

Further Reading

Barras (2017); Baubérot (2009); Baubérot (2010); Charb (2016); Debray (2008); Fernando (2014); Fourest (2015); Jansen (2013); Kelly (2017); Kiwan (2020); Nilsson (2018); *What Do We Do?* (2008); Winter (2008).

RELIGIOSITY IN DECLINE

According to a 2012 WIN/Gallup International Poll, 29% of French people surveyed described themselves as "atheist"—the highest percentage of atheists in Western Europe and the fourth highest in the world; another 34% described themselves as "not religious." More recent polls offer somewhat different results. For instance, the 2017 Pew Global Attitudes Survey reports that 25% of the French population identifies as atheist, 5% as agnostic, and 8% as unaffiliated with a religion. Among French people who do identify with a particular religion, actual religious practice is infrequent. According to various polls, only 25% of French Catholics consider themselves practicing (although less than 5% attend Sunday regularly), 33% of Muslims consider themselves practicing (out of which 23% attend Friday prayer services), 24% of Protestants describe themselves as regularly practicing, and 36% of Jews describe themselves as practicing (but only 10% say they practice very often). As marriage rates in France are falling, so too are the number of religious marriage ceremonies; one report from 2017 estimated that only 28% of civil marriages (a requirement and the only legally recognized type of marriage) are followed by optional religious ceremonies.

Philosophy (Contemporary)

Contemporary French philosophy is known for the provocative and imaginative ways in which it rethinks the relationship between the human subject and society, culture, power, identity, alterity, empirical experience, ideas, and language in the context of the contradictions of modernity (e.g., astounding revolutions in technology and communication coupled with unprecedented threats to life, meaning, and autonomy). In the first half of the twentieth century, there were two distinct strands of French philosophy. The first was the continuation of a venerable French tradition in epistemology and the philosophy of science that began with Descartes. Henri Poincaré, Léon Brunschvicg, Gaston Bachelard (1884–1962), Jean Cavaillès, Georges Canguilhem (1904–1995), Jules Vuillemin, François Dagognet (1924–2015), Michel Serres (1930–2019), Jacques Bouveresse (b. 1940), and Pierre Jacob were among the leading figures of this strand. Starting with Henri Bergson (1859–1954), the second strand was a philosophy centering on human experience, vital interiority, and phenomenology that sought to distance itself from the legacy of Cartesian rationalism. Bachelard was a link between the two. He theorized the "epistemological obstacle" and the "epistemological break" as key to both the psychology and the history of science, and also contributed works on poetics and developed an alternative model of psychoanalysis because the Freudian model, in his view, failed to adequately address reverie and the workings of the imagination.

Bergson, whose most famous works were *Time and Free Will* (1889) and *Creative Evolution* (1907), was well versed in biology but broke with the scientific positivism of his era. He made key distinctions between the experiential reality of lived time, which he called "duration," and the spatialized and quantified "time" of clocks, science, and social life; and between the "intellect" (abstract, rational, and instrumental forms of intelligence) and "intuition" (holistic, sympathetic, and analogical forms of imagination). Phenomenology—which owed much to German thinkers like Hegel, Husserl, and Heidegger—approached reality from the standpoint of perception and subjective consciousness. Its leading practitioners in France were Maurice Merleau-Ponty (1908–1961), who discussed the thinking self's (*ego cogito*) dependence on the perceiving self (*ego percipio*); and Emmanuel Levinas (1906–1995), who theorized the self's encounter of "the Other." Exemplified by Jean-Paul Sartre (1905–1980), Simone de Beauvoir (1908–1986), and Albert Camus (1913–1960), French existentialism was in part an application of phenomenology to problems like human freedom, purposeful action, and the foundations of morality. It was also a politically engaged philosophical response to the absurdity of a modern world that had seen two world wars, colonialism, the holocaust, and the atomic bomb—and pervasive alienation in everyday life. Sartre (e.g., *Nausea* and *No Exit*) and Camus (e.g., *The Stranger* and *The Plague*) used literature to explore existentialist themes. Proclaiming that "existence precedes essence," that adherence to moral absolutes was a manifestation of "bad faith," and that people were "condemned" to be free and therefore solely responsible for the direction of their lives, Sartre's *Being and Nothingness* (1943) was the magnum opus of the movement that had made the cafés of Saint-Germain-des-Prés its home base and living laboratory. Beauvoir's groundbreaking feminist work, *The Second Sex* (1949), used existentialist concepts to analyze how "women" were a subordinate creation of a male-dominated society, male perception, and male mythology.

Alain Badiou (b. 1937), himself one of the most prominent and prolific thinkers of his generation (works on esthetics, politics, mathematics, cinema, ontology, religion, and other subjects), has described the fifty years between the publication of Sartre's *Being and Nothingness* and the last published works of Gilles Deleuze as one of the pivotal eras of western philosophy—comparable to the golden age of Ancient Greek philosophy and the era of German Idealism in the nineteenth century. Encompassing such divergent movements as existentialism, structuralism, and post-structuralism (popularized in American universities as "French Theory") and individual thinkers with strikingly different interests and styles, the gist of the French postmodern philosophical moment, according to Badiou, is the enunciation of a "new subject" that is no longer the robust rational and reflexive subject of Descartes but is nonetheless still defined by conceptuality in the form of mutable constructs that are entangled in complex relationships with power structures and dynamics, changing historical and political contexts, existential facticity, the body and its desires, the psycho-cognitive processes of conscious and subconscious thought, and language. Badiou calls this a "philosophy without wisdom" because the subject that it posits is eternally problematized. According to Badiou, this French moment changes philosophy in two additional ways. First, it takes philosophy out of the academy and forces it to encounter the most disconcerting and vigorous forms of modern life and culture—marginalized and minority social groups and movements, sexuality, contemporary art, militant politics, new media, and so on. Second, it experiments with new styles of philosophical writing that borrow from other disciplines (history, sociology, etc.) and in some instances resemble a sort of conceptual prose poetry.

Taking cues from linguists like Ferdinand de Saussure (1857–1913) and Roman Jakobson (1896–1982), and from Russian formalism (e.g., Viktor Shklovsky and Vladimir Propp), structuralism posited that culture was "structured" by socially and historically determined codes and systems of signs and that the human subject's perception, thought, action, and identity are consequently also determined (and limited) by the logic of such systems and the ideologies inherent to them. Its leading practitioners in France were the anthropologist Claude Lévi-Strauss (1908–2009) and the literary critic and semiotician Roland Barthes (1915–1980), who wrote an influential collection of essays on mass culture, *Mythologies* (1957). Structuralism also influenced the reformulations of psychoanalytic and Marxist theory by Jacques Lacan (1901–1881) and Louis Althusser (1918–1990), respectively. Post-structuralism—a label used more internationally than in France—adopted a more complex and nuanced view of how people interacted with, were shaped by, and could resist normative cultural systems. The leading figures of this more critical stance were Michel Foucault (1926–1984), Jacques Derrida (1930–2004), and Gilles Deleuze (1925–1995). Foucault has had perhaps the greatest influence through a series of books on the relationship between knowledge and power that dealt with the human sciences, madness, medical science, correctional practices (prisons and surveillance), sexuality, and biopower. His culturalist approach to epistemology was summarized in *The Archaeology of Knowledge* (1969). Derrida is best known as the developer of the form of critical analysis known as deconstruction. Deleuze wrote a series of reinterpretations of the works of major historical philosophers (e.g., Hume, Spinoza, Leibniz, Kant, Marx, Nietzsche, Descartes, and Bergson), but he is best known for his collaboration with Félix Guattari (1930–1992)—the two volumes of *Capitalism and Schizophrenia: Anti-Oedipus* (1972) and *A Thousand Plateaus* (1980). Luce Irigaray (b. 1930), Monique Wittig (1935–2003), Hélène Cixous (b. 1937), and Julia Kristeva (b. 1941) are among the influential feminist thinkers associated with post-structuralism. Contemporary French thinkers have also been among the most insightful analysts of what Jean-François Lyotard (1924–1998) famously termed the "postmodern condition." This includes Lyotard's influential reflection on the crisis of the "great narratives of modernity," Jean Baudrillard's (1929–2007) work on the pervasiveness of "simulacra" in media and consumer culture, and Paul Virilio's (1932–2018) treatment of technoculture and the paradigm of speed.

Contemporary French thought has also focused extensively on politics and religion. Influential political thinkers include Raymond Aron (1905–1983), Cornélius

Castoriadis (1922–1997), Claude Lefort (1924–2010), André Glucksmann (1937–2015), Bernard-Henri Lévy (b. 1948), and Pierre Manent (b. 1949). Aron and Manent are defenders of liberalism. Castoriadis was the cofounder of the libertarian socialist group "Socialisme ou Barbarie" (1948–1967). Lefort was a leading theorist and critic of totalitarianism. Glucksmann and Lévy achieved early notoriety in the late 1970s as leading examples of the young group of "Nouveaux Philosophes," who broke with the Marxism of their student days. French thinkers who have offered original perspectives on religion include Michel Henry, René Girard (1923–2015), Michel de Certeau, Jean-Luc Nancy, Régis Debray, Jean-Luc Marion, Marcel Gauchet, and Frédéric Lenoir. The best known among them is Girard, who taught at Stanford University in the United States and developed a wide-ranging anthropological philosophy centering on mimetic desire, violence, and the mechanism of the sacrificial victim.

The most influential French philosophers today are arguably Jacques Rancière (b. 1940) and Bruno Latour (b. 1947), whose work on democracy and esthetics (Rancière) and science, technology, and the Anthropocene (Latour) have implications for public debates on key issues of the day—as does the diverse work (on cybernetics, cognitive science, catastrophe theory, liberalism, the sacred, and evil) of Jean-Pierre Dupuy (b. 1941). Eclecticism and intersectionality are hallmarks of the work of many of the leading younger philosophers on the French scene—such as Yves Citton, Corinne Pelluchon, Pierre Zaoui, Paul B. Preciado, Pierre Cassou-Noguès, Élie During, Mehdi Belhaj Kacem, Cynthia Fleury, Nadia Yala Kisukidi, and Tristan Garcia.

See also: Chapter 5: Philosophy (Tradition). Chapter 7: Feminism and Women's Rights. Chapter 11: Literary Avant-Garde, 1950–1980; Literary Criticism and French Theory; Twentieth-Century Literature through Mid-Century (Novel and Theatre).

Further Reading
Angermuller (2015); Badiou (2012); Blakewell (2016); Cohen-Solal (2005); Collins (2020); Glendinning (2011); Gutting (2001); Gutting (2005); Gutting (2011); Jonkers and Welten (2005); Kritzman and Reilly (2006); Wicks (2003).

Philosophy (Traditional)

Philosophical thought is highly developed and valued in France. There is no better proof of this than the legendary philosophy section of the *baccalauréat* exam. The subject has been a key feature of the rigorous national high school diploma exam since its inception in 1809. Originally, it was covered in an oral exam *in Latin*; today, it takes the form of a single essay question that students have four hours to answer—a rite of passage for several hundred thousand young people each year. The questions treat big issues of life, knowledge, and society and form the capstone experience of a student's intellectual training to be a freethinking and thoughtful citizen of the Republic. "Does power exist without violence?" "Is a person's conscience only the reflection of the society they live in?" "Is desire a sign of our imperfection?" "Does culture make us more human?" "Is all truth final?" While sweeping changings have come to *baccalau-réat* via reforms implemented by the Macron administration, philosophy remains among subjects treated in the final written exams—not surprising given that Macron, a philosophy major at Nanterre University (Paris), once worked as an assistant to the eminent philosopher Paul Ricoeur (1913–2005), who was known for applying phenomenology (the study of human awareness) to hermeneutics (methodologies of interpretation). While it is a stretch to say that major French philosophers are household names (it depends on the household), many of the most prominent ones are indeed well known to the educated general public. Some may give their opinions on major political and social issues of the day or be the subject of profiles and interviews in *L'Obs* (the weekly news magazine formerly known as *Le Nouvel Observateur*). For readers looking for in-depth but accessible presentations of the latest developments in the field, there is *Philosophie Magazine*.

Paris was already a center of philosophical thought in the High Middle Ages. Better known for his love affair with Héloïse d'Argenteuil, Peter Abelard (1079–1142) was a Parisian logician and proponent of nominalism. He was also one of the founders of Scholasticism, which applied Aristotelian logic to Christian dogma. Other famous

A postage stamp honoring the French rationalist philosopher and mathematician René Descartes (1596–1650)—issued in 1937 to commemorate the 300th anniversary of the publication of his magnum opus, *Discourse on the Method of Rightly Conducting One's Reason and of Seeking Truth in the Sciences*. Certain features of his thought are thought to be so synonymous with the French mindset—critical thinking based on methodical doubt, faith in reason, and a penchant for clear and distinct ideas expressed in elegant French—that the French people are often described as "Cartesian." Descartes is also famous for his Cogito affirmation: "I think, therefore I am." (Fotomy/Dreamstime.com)

French and foreign Scholastic philosophers who either studied or taught in Paris were Peter Lombard, Albertus Magnus, Bonaventure, Thomas Aquinas, and Dun Scotus. As secular forms of thought developed during the French Renaissance, Michel de Montaigne (1533–1592) practiced an introspective and skeptical form of humanism in his *Essays*, which treated a wide range of subjects, including friendship, sorrow, passion, the sense of smell, conscience, human will, truth and uncertainty, solitude, aging, and cannibalism among the Indigenous people of Brazil. Other French thinkers of the sixteenth century, like Étienne de la Boétie and Jean Bodin, focused on questions of government. As important as these precursors may be, French philosophy truly begins with René Descartes (1596–1650) in the seventeenth century. In seminal works like the *Discourse on the Method* (1637), written in pristine French, Descartes, who was both a brilliant mathematician and a dualist (someone who believes that the immaterial mind and material body are fundamentally different states of being), broke with the Scholastic tradition to lay the foundations of an epistemological ontology that defined the self as the rational thinking subject ("I think, therefore I am") and outlined a method of deductive reasoning based on "clear and distinct ideas." French philosophers and their international counterparts still grapple with the legacy of Descartes' rationalist views of the human subject and cognition. In his own age, Descartes had both followers, like Nicolas Malebranche, and critics. The most prominent of the latter was the mathematician, physicist, moralist, and Catholic theologian Blaise Pascal (1623–1692). A follower of the morally rigorous form of Catholicism known as Jansenism, Pascal is most famous for his pragmatic "wager" about the existence of God—namely, that a rational person was better off living as if God existed because they would have much to gain by behaving thus, and comparatively little to lose. At the end of the seventeenth century and beginning of the eighteenth, Pierre Bayle pushed Cartesian methodological doubt in the direction of radical skepticism. A freethinker and rumored atheist, Bayle suggested that much of what was generally considered truth was just engrained opinion.

During the eighteenth and nineteenth centuries, the focus of French philosophy turned ostensibly to political and social issues. In the Age of Enlightenment (eighteenth century), during which polymath *philosophes* debated new ideas and the pressing issues of the day in urbane social gatherings known as salons, there was a widely shared optimistic belief that reason, education, informed public opinion, science, and technical advances could lead to political reforms consonant with respect for civil liberties and the common good and to human progress in general. Baron Montesquieu (Charles-Louis de Secondat, 1689–1755), author of *The Spirit of the Laws* (1738), argued that the separation of executive, legislative, and judicial power in government was a safeguard against tyranny and thought that governments needed to fit the societies over which they ruled. Jean-Jacques Rousseau (1712–1778) posited that humans were good in the state of nature but corrupted by society, developed the notion of government based on the consent of the governed (*The Social Contract*, 1762), was a precursor of modern notions of education emphasizing a balance of reason and sentiment and autonomous discovery of the world, and posited the salutary effects of "natural" religion. Voltaire (François-Marie Arouet, 1694–1778), was an ardent proponent of tolerance and justice and an ironic and acerbic social critic who was particularly harsh in his assessment of the arbitrary tyranny of the absolute monarchy and the clericalist obscurantism of the Catholic Church. Denis Diderot (1713–1784), like Voltaire, was a gifted author of literary works—an example of the French tradition of the use of literature to bring philosophical reflections to a wider audience—but is best known as the coeditor (with Jean-Baptiste le Rond d'Alembert) of the *Encyclopédie* (1751–1772), a progressive compendium of the arts, sciences, and industry that also advocated for freedom of thought and government in service of the common good. Other eighteenth-century French thinkers include Étienne Bonnot de Condillac (among the founders of the science of psychology), Nicolas de Condorcet (a proponent of a liberal economy, equal rights for women and other races, and public education), and Claude Adrien Helvétius (a censored author who denied the religious foundations of moral behavior and placed hedonistic emphasis on the senses).

The two major preoccupations of nineteenth-century French philosophical thought were the lessons to be learned from the French Revolution (1789–1799) about the limits of democracy and freedom and the social ramifications of industrialization and progress. France was home to a lively school of moderate liberal thought exemplified by Germaine de Staël (1766–1817), Benjamin Constant (1767–1830), and Alexis de Tocqueville (1805–1859). De Staël was a critic of Napoleon and champion of romanticism in France. Constant famously distinguished between the "liberty of the Ancients" and the "liberty of the Moderns." The former, lauded zealously by the dominant figures of the Revolution, was based on the Greco-Roman notion of the citizen's political rights and duty of active participation in public affairs—a paradigm that was ill-suited for large, modern nation-states in Constant's view. He believed that government intervention in the economy and civil society ought to be limited and respectful of the latter type of liberty, which includes civil liberties, the rule of law, and the private pursuit of happiness. Tocqueville was a comparative political philosopher best known for *Democracy in America* (1835–1840) and *The Old Regime and the Revolution* (1856). Another major school of thought in the first half of the nineteenth century was utopian socialism, which sought to imagine the ideal form of social organization. For Henri de Saint-Simon (1760–1825), who influenced both Emperor Napoleon III and Karl Marx, this was a society that was organized around the needs of the industrial class, which included business people, managers, financiers, scientists, and manual workers. For Charles Fourier (1772–1837), the ideal society was divided into cooperative and egalitarian communes called phalanxes, where labor would be just one means by which libidinal forces would be liberated. Experimental communities were set up following the principles of Fourier, as well as those of his contemporaries, Étienne Cabet (the Icarian movement) and Pierre-Joseph Proudhon (mutualist anarchism). The greatest nineteenth-century French social philosopher was Auguste Comte (1798–1857), a proponent of positivism (social evolution and progress based on the development of the sciences) and one of the founders of the discipline of sociology. Comte taught that human history was defined by a progression of three phases—the theological (defined by religion), the metaphysical (defined by abstract philosophical thought), and the positive (defined by the sciences)—and proposed a religion of humanity. Prominent French thinkers from the latter part of the century include Félix

Ravaisson (1813–1900), the author of the influential work *Of Habit* (1838) and proponent of spiritualist realism; Alfred Fouillée (1838–1912), an interpreter of the moral philosophy of Immanuel Kant who conceived of society as a complex organism; and Léon Bourgeois (1851–1925), who developed the doctrine of Solidarism as a middle ground alternative to capitalism and socialism, served as prime minister of France (1895–1896), and was awarded the Nobel Peace Prize in 1920 for his support for the League of Nations. Both Fouillée and Bourgeois had a significant influence over French republicanism.

See also: Chapter 5: Catholicism; Philosophy (Contemporary); Rationalism and Universalism. Chapter 11: Eighteenth-Century Literature.

Further Reading

Gaukroger and Peden (2020); Geenens and Rosenblatt (2012); Goodman (1994); Israel (2001); Moriarty (2003); Roche (1998); Shorto (2008); Taylor (1982); Wernick (2001).

PUBLIC INTELLECTUALS

The public intellectual—a respected writer who speaks out on social, political, and cultural questions of conscience—is a venerable French tradition. Historians Pascal Ory and Jean-François Sirinelli stress that the public intellectual is a French invention of the modern media era (e.g., novelist Émile Zola's scathing 1898 open letter to the president of the French Republic during the height of the Dreyfus Affair, "J'accuse!..."). Perhaps the most famous modern public intellectual was the philosopher and leftist political activist Jean-Paul Sartre (1905–1980), who spoke out on numerous issues throughout the 1950s, 1960s, and 1970s. His reputation was such that when he was arrested during the May 1968 student protests, President Charles de Gaulle ordered his release, quipping, "You don't arrest Voltaire." Leading examples from the 1980s and 90s include the philosophers Michel Foucault (1926–1984) and Régis Debray (b. 1940); and sociologists Pierre Bourdieu (1930–2002), Jean Baudrillard (1929–2007), Edgar Morin (b. 1921), and Alain Touraine (b. 1925). Public intellectuals have been criticized for ideological myopia (e.g., infatuation with Marxism and a rigid view of *Laïcité*), faulty analyses of complex issues they do not adequately master, and image-conscious publicity-seeking. They are still a vocal fixture of French culture. Prominent current examples include the philosophers Élisabeth Badinter (b. 1944), Bernard-Henri Lévy (b. 1948, known in France simply as BHL), Alain Finkielkraut (b. 1949), Michel Onfray (b. 1959), and Abdennour Bidar (b. 1971); the historians Gérard Noiriel (1950), Benjamin Stora (1950), Pascal Blanchard (1964), and Pap Ndiaye (b. 1965); the sociologists Luc Boltanski (b. 1940), Laurent Thévenot (b. 1949), Emmanuel Todd (b. 1951), Éric Fassin (b. 1959), and Karine Espineira (b. 1967); the political scientist Pierre Corcuff (b. 1960); the economist Thomas Piketty (b. 1971); and the journalists and essayists Éric Zemmour (b. 1958, a candidate for the French presidency in 2022), Caroline Fourest (b. 1975), Rokhaya Diallo (b. 1978), and Zineb El Rhazoui (b. 1982).

Protestantism

France was important for the development of the Protestant Reformation in the sixteenth century. Among the precursors of Protestant ideas in France include the humanist and translator of the Bible into French, Jacques Lefèvre d'Étaples (1455–1536) and the reform-minded bishop of Meaux, Guillaume Briçonnet (1470–1534). While Martin Luther's ideas were influential in France, Calvinism—the doctrine of the French theologian Jean Calvin (1509–1564), who broke with Roman Catholicism in 1530 and fled persecution to Switzerland in 1534—had even greater appeal in France, including among a large share of the nobility. However, neither the French monarchy nor the hardcore Catholic faction (led by Henry of Guise) was prepared to allow the spread of Protestantism. This led to eight bloody civil conflicts between 1562 and 1598, collectively known as the Wars of Religion, which included horrific massacres (e.g., the Saint Bartholomew's Day Massacre of 1572) and the assassinations of two French kings. The conflict ostensibly ended when Henry of Navarre, the leader of the Protestant faction, ascended to the French throne as Henry IV—a position secured by military force and a strategic abjuration of his Protestant faith—and issued the Edict of Nantes (1598) guaranteeing limited freedom and protections for Protestants. However, persecutions and royal belligerence toward Protestants (Huguenots) continued under Louis XIII (led by the king's prime minister, Cardinal Richelieu) and Louis XIV. The latter ended official tolerance of Protestantism by revoking the Edict of Nantes via Edict of Fontainebleau in 1685. As many as 200,000 Protestants went into exile during his reign. Twice as many converted to Catholicism under pressure. Some went underground during a period known as the "Desert" (1685–1787), a reference to the Jewish people's years of wandering in the Sinai Desert following their escape from captivity in Egypt. Others joined in a guerilla warfare campaign against the French crown in the rugged Cévennes region of southern France—War of the Camisards (1702–1710). This history of struggle and persecution is very important to the collective identity of the Protestant community of France. Freedom of religion for Protestants was reinstated during the Revolution and reaffirmed under Napoleon I, who officially recognized (and reorganized) France's Lutheran and Calvinist denominations. Under its new legitimized status, Protestantism thrived, attracting many new followers during the nineteenth century in what is called the "Awakening." In the nineteenth and twentieth centuries, Protestants rose to prominence in politics, government service, the military, business, academia, science, and letters—success that prompted jealousy, prejudice, and conspiracy theories about the influence of an allegedly powerful minority. French Protestants were among the firmest allies of the French Republic and its emphasis on *Laïcité*. In the twentieth century, many French Protestants evolved toward greater secularism. After a slow decline, the number of practicing Protestants has begun to grow again in recent decades due to the appeal of "evangelical" forms of Christianity, among other factors. Historically, Protestantism was more prevalent in the cities and larger towns, the Alsace region, and the South of France. However, this geography has been modified by the spread of Evangelical Christianity.

A wide array of Protestant denominations is present in France today, including Lutheranism, Calvinism, Evangelical Christianity, Pentecostalism, and an array of smaller denominations and independent forms of Christianity. The largest institutional church is the United Protestant Church of France, which was formed in 2013 through the merger of the Reformed Church of France (Calvinist) and the Evangelical Lutheran Church of France and claims 400,000 members. The Protestant Federation of France (FPF), founded in 1905, is an umbrella organization that represents nearly all French Protestants (each church and denomination maintains its own theological doctrine, liturgical practices, and structures of governance). Every four years, the Federation organizes *Les Protestants en Fête*, a festive multidenominational gathering of Protestants that attracts over ten thousand attendees. Jean-Paul Willaime, a sociologist and leading scholar of French Protestantism, estimates there are 2 million Protestants in mainland France—equal to 3% of the population. According to a major survey conducted in 2017 by IPSOS for the publication *La Réforme*, 26% of French Protestants identify as Evangelical Christians. According to the same poll, 50% of all French Protestants are nonpracticing (Willaime calls this segment "cultural Protestants"), 26% practice occasionally, and 24% practice regularly. The results for those who identified as Evangelical Christians were 30% nonpracticing, 17% occasionally practicing, and 53% regularly practicing. Protestants under the age of thirty-five were found to practice more regularly than their older counterparts. This represents a reversal of the dominant trend in the 1970s and 1980s and suggests a rekindling of religiosity among young Protestants in general and young Evangelicals in particular. Among Protestants in general, 75% were born into Protestant families, whereas 25% converted; among Evangelicals Christians, the results were 62% by birth and 38% by conversion. French Protestants tend to be slightly more conservative on issues of personal morality (e.g., making medically assisted procreation available to same-sex couples) than French people in general, but are more liberal politically than Catholics. However, French Evangelicals are not markedly more conservative politically, as their American counterparts tend to be. In the same IPSOS poll, 23% of Evangelicals expressed an affinity for centrist parties—a percentage several points higher than for both Protestants and French people in general.

See also: Chapter 1: North and South. Chapter 2: Francis I and the Renaissance. Chapter 5: Catholicism; Laïcité.

Further Reading
Fath (2005); Ruane (2010); Treasure (2013); Willaime (2010).

Rationalism and Universalism

The founding father and greatest embodiment of French rationalism was the seventeenth-century philosopher, mathematician, and scientist René Descartes (1596–1650), most famous for his metaphysical affirmation of the conscious self, "I think, therefore I am" (known as the "Cogito" because of its Latin version). The French penchant for rationalism is rooted in three further characteristics of Cartesian thought: unsparing methodological doubt (one begins by doubting, i.e., rationally critiquing everything commonly assumed to be true); a meticulous quest to isolate, articulate, and further refine clear and distinct ideas (there is a popular belief that the French language is uniquely suited to this task and a tendency to mistake the elegance of a formulation for the veracity of an assertion); and rigorous deductive reasoning from general truths to specific corollaries. Cartesian rationalism is reflected in the way French students are trained to write essays and in French politicians' limpid and confident justifications of their policies.

Cartesian rationalism is also a basis for the French penchant for universalism insofar as rational criteria of judgment are assumed to be common to all civilized minds. French universalism involves three additional assumptions:

1. That the achievements of French literature, art, thought, and politics are valid not just for France but for humankind;
2. That the universal validity of French culture is reflected in its actual *rayonnement* (influence compared to the outwardly radiating light and warmth of the sun) beyond France's borders; and
3. That a principled distinction is to be made between patriotism (which is inclusive, liberal-minded, and focused on the defense of national sovereignty and civil liberties) and nationalism (which is exclusive and chauvinistic, focused on the nation's alleged superiority and quest for wealth and power at the expense of other nations, and prone to militarism).

While French universalism did not begin with the Enlightenment and French Revolution, there is perhaps no better expression of French universalism than the 1789 Declaration of the Rights of Man and the Citizen—a foundational text of the French Revolution, which boldly asserted certain inalienable rights for all of humankind. The ironic and idiosyncratic musical celebration of the "world's tribes" (officially called "La Marseillaise") created by advertising filmmaker and former Grace Jones impresario Jean-Paul Goude in 1989 for the bicentennial of the French Revolution testified to the fact that such universalism was still alive and well in the minds of the French 200 years later. While the parade featured lots of questionable exoticism and neocolonial overtones, it also opened with a somber homage to the Chinese students of the Tiananmen Square pro-democracy protests of June 1989; culminated in a stirring rendition of the French revolutionary hymn and national anthem, the Marseillaise, by the African American soprano Jessye Norman (wearing an Azzedine Alaïa-designed gown in the colors of the French flag and thereby assuming the unofficial role of the Republic's first black "Marianne"); and included conspicuous nods to France's racial and ethnic minorities and their African countries of origin. Nearly thirty years after the Goude parade, French universalism was on display once again in 2018, in the speech given by President Emmanuel Macron in the presence of world leaders assembled to commemorate the centennial of the end of World War I. Macron reiterated the distinction between patriotism and nationalism by calling the latter a dangerous form of "selfishness" and a "betrayal of patriotism." The patriotism of the French and colonial soldiers who fought and died in the horrible conflict, Macron said, involved a vision of France as a "generous nation" and the defense of its "universal values." Still, universalism has both positive and negative ramifications. The former include a natural cosmopolitanism (esp. in Paris) and a bona fide humanitarian concern for the world's downtrodden and unfortunate; the latter include the disreputable invocation of universalism as an alibi for French colonialism in the nineteenth and twentieth centuries and the universalists' not infrequent insensitivity to the multicultural diversity of French society today.

See also: Chapter 2: Robespierre (Maximilien) and the French Revolution. Chapter 3: Republic. Chapter 5: Laïcité; Philosophy (Tradition). Chapter 9: Francophonie. Chapter 11: Eighteenth-Century Literature.

Further Reading

Hazareesingh (2015); Leruth (1998); Schor (2001); Scott (2004); Sepinwall (2005); Taithe (2004).

SELECTED BIBLIOGRAPHY

Ahearne, Jeremy. *Intellectuals, Culture, and Public Policy in France: Approaches from the Left*. Liverpool UP, 2010.

Angermuller, Johannes. *Why There Is No Poststructuralism in France: The Making of an Intellectual Generation*. Trans. Walter Allmand. Bloomsbury, 2015.

Arkin, Kimberly A. *Rhinestones, Religion, and the Republic: Fashioning Jewishness in France*. Stanford UP, 2013.

Badiou, Alain. *The Adventure of French Philosophy*. Trans. Bruno Bosteels. Verso, 2012.

Barras, Amélie. "Secularism in France." *The Oxford Handbook of Secularism*, eds. Phil Zuckerman and John R. Shook. Oxford UP, 2017, pp. 141–154.

Baubérot, Jean. "The Evolution of Secularism in France: Between Two Civil Religions." *Comparative Secularisms in a Global Age*, eds. Linell E. Cady and Elizabeth Shakman Hurd. Palgrave Macmillan, 2010, pp. 57–68.

Baubérot, Jean. "Laïcité and the Challenge of 'Republicanism.'" Modern & Contemporary France, vol. 17, no. 2, 2009, pp. 189–198.

Benbassa, Esther. *The Jews of France: A History from Antiquity to the Present*. Trans. M. B. DeBevoise. Princeton UP, 2001.

Bergeaud-Becker, Florence. "Social Definitions of *Halal* Quality: The Case of Maghrebi Muslims in France." *Qualities of Food*, eds. Mark Harvey, et al. Manchester UP, 2013.

Berkovitz, Jay R. *Rites and Passages: The Beginnings of Modern Jewish Culture in France, 1650–1860*. U Pennsylvania P, 2004.

Blakewell, Sarah. *At the Existentialist Café: Freedom, Being, and Apricot Cocktails*. Other P, 2016.

Bourg, Julian, ed. *After the Deluge: New Perspectives on the Intellectual and Cultural History of Postwar France*. Lexington, 2004.

Bowen, John R. *Can Islam Be French?: Pluralism and Pragmatism in a Secularist State*. Princeton UP, 2010.

Bowen, John R. *Why the French Don't Like Headscarves: Islam, the State, and Public Space*. Princeton UP, 2006.

Bréchon, Pierre, and Anne-Sophie Boutaud. "France in 2019: More Critical, More Altruistic." *CNRS News*, 6 Dec. 2019, https://news.cnrs.fr/articles/france-in-2019-more -critical-more-altruistic.

Byrnes, Joseph F. *Catholic and French Forever: Religious and National Identity in Modern France*. Penn State UP, 2005.

Césari, Jocelyne. "France." *The Oxford Handbook of European Islam*, ed. Jocelyne Césari. Oxford UP, 2014, pp. 23–63.

Chadwick, Kay, ed. *Catholicism, Politics and Society in Twentieth-century France*. Liverpool UP, 2000.

Chaplin, Tamara. *Turning on the Mind: French Philosophers on Television*. U Chicago P, 2007.

Charb [Stéphane Charbonnier]. *Open Letter: On Blasphemy, Islamophobia, and the True Enemies of Free Expression*. Engl. Trans. Little, Brown, 2016.

Cloots, André. "Christianity, Incarnation and Disenchantment: Marcel Gauchet on the 'Departurre' from Religion." *Radical Secularization?: An Inquiry into the Religious Roots of Secular Culture*, eds. Stijn Latré, et al. Bloomsbury, 2015, pp. 47–66.

Cohen, Erik. *The Jews of France Today: Identity and Values*. Brill, 2011.

Cohen-Solal, Annie. *Jean-Paul Sartre: A Life*. Trans. Anna Cancogni, new ed. New Press, 2005.

Collins, Jacob. *The Anthropological Turn: French Political Thought after 1968*. U Pennsylvania P, 2020.

Dargent, Claude. "Religious Practice versus Subjective Religiosity: Catholics and Those with 'No Religion' in the French 2017 Presidential Election." *Social Compass*, vol. 66, no. 2, 2019, pp. 164–181.

Davie, Grace. "Religion and Modernity: The Work of Danièle Hervieu-Léger." *Postmodernity, Sociology, and Religion*, eds. Kieran Flanagan and Peter C. Jupp. Palgrave Macmillan, 1999, pp. 101–117.

Debray, Régis. "God and the Political Planet." *New Perspectives Quarterly*, vol. 25, no. 4, 2008, pp. 33–35.

de Vries, Gerard. *Bruno Latour*. Polity, 2016.

Downing, Joseph. *French Muslims in Perspective: Nationalism, Post-Colonialism and Marginalisation under the Republic*. Palgrave Macmillan, 2019.

Drake, David. *French Intellectuals and Politics from the Dreyfus Affair to the Occupation*. Palgrave Macmillan, 2005.

Drake, David. *Intellectuals and Politics in Post-War France*. Palgrave Macmillan, 2002.

Fath, Sébastien. "Evangelical Protestantism in France: An Example of Denominational Recomposition?" *Sociology of Religion*, vol. 66, no. 4, 2005, pp. 399–418.

Fernando, Mayanthi L. *The Republic Unsettled: Muslim French and the Contradictions of Secularism.* Duke UP, 2014.

Fourest, Caroline. *In Praise of Blasphemy: Why Charlie Hebdo is not "Islamophobic."* Engl. Trans. Grasset, 2015.

Gadille, Jacques. "On French Anticlericalism: Some Reflections." *European Studies Review*, vol. 13, no. 2, 1983, pp. 127–144.

Garay, Alain. "New Religious Movements in France: The Legal Situation." *Minority Religions in Europe and the Middle East: Mapping and Monitoring*, ed. George D. Chryssides. Routledge, 2018, pp. 100–113.

Gaukroger, Stephen, and Knox Peden. *French Philosophy: A Very Short Introduction.* Oxford UP, 2020.

Geenens, Raf, and Helena Rosenblatt, eds. *French Liberalism from Montesquieu to the Present Day.* Cambridge UP, 2012.

Gemie, Sharif. *French Muslims: New Voices in Contemporary France.* U Wales P, 2010.

Geroulanos, Stefanos. *An Atheism that Is Not Humanist Emerges in French Thought.* Stanford UP, 2010.

Glendinning, Simon. *Derrida: A Very Short Introduction.* Oxford UP, 2011.

Goodman, Dena. *The Republic of Letters: A Cultural History of the French Enlightenment.* Cornell UP, 1994.

Gutting, Gary. *French Philosophy in the Twentieth Century.* Cambridge UP, 2001.

Gutting, Gary. *Michel Foucault: A Very Short Introduction.* Oxford UP, 2005.

Gutting, Gary. *Thinking the Impossible: French Philosophy Since 1960.* Oxford UP, 2011.

Harrison, Carol E. *Romantic Catholics: France's Postrevolutionary Generation in Search of a Modern Faith.* Cornell UP, 2014.

Hazareesingh, Sudhir. "The Dimming of the Light." *Aeon*, 22 Sep. 2015, https://aeon.co/essays/french-thought-once-dazzled-the-world-what-went-wrong.

Hazareesingh, Sudhir. *How the French Think: An Affectionate Portrait of an Intellectual People.* Basic, 2015.

Hecht, Jennifer. *The End of the Soul: Scientific Modernity, Atheism, and Anthropology in France.* Columbia UP, 2005.

Hervieu-Leger, Danièle. *Religion as a Chain of Memory.* Trans. Simon Lee. Rutlgers UP, 2000.

Horn, Gerd-Rainer, and Emmanuel Gerard, eds. *Left Catholicism, 1943–1955: Catholics and Society in Western Europe at the Point of Liberation.* Leuven UP, 2001.

Houtman, Dick, and Stef Aupers. "The Spiritual Turn and the Decline of Tradition: The Spread of Post-Christian Spirituality in 14 Western Countries, 1981–2000." *Journal for the Scientific Study of Religion*, vol. 46, no. 3, 2007, pp. 305–320.

Hyman, Paula. *The Jews of Modern France.* U California P, 1998.

Israel, Jonathan I. *Radical Enlightenment: Philosophy and the Making of Modernity, 1650–1750.* Oxford UP, 2001.

Jansen, Yolande. *Secularism, Assimilation and the Crisis of Multiculturalism: French Modernist Legacies.* Amsterdam UP, 2013.

Jonkers, Peter, and Ruud Welten. *God in France: Eight Contemporary French Thinkers on God*. Peeters, 2005.

Katz, Ethan B. *The Burdens of Brotherhood: Jews and Muslims from North Africa to France*. Harvard UP, 2015.

Kaufman, Suzanne K. *Consuming Visions: Mass Culture and the Lourdes Shrine*. Cornell UP, 2005.

Keaton, Tricia Danielle. *Muslim Girls and the Other France: Race, Identity Politics, & Social Exclusion*. Indiana UP, 2006.

Kelly, Michael. "Laïcité and Atheism in France." *French Cultural Studies*, vol. 28, no. 1, 2017, pp. 111–122.

Khosrokhavar, Farhad. "Islamic Radicalization in France." *Muslims in the West after 9/11: Religion, Politics, and Law*, ed. Jocelyne Cesari. Routledge, 2009, pp. 229–244.

Kiwan, Nadia. *Secularism, Islam and Public Intellectuals in Contemporary France*. Manchester UP, 2020.

Kors, Alan Charles. *Atheism in France, 1650–1729: The Orthodox Sources of Disbelief*. Princeton UP, 1990.

Kritzman, Lawrence D., and Brian J. Reilly, eds. *The Columbia History of Twentieth-Century French Thought*. Trans. M. B. DeBevoise. Columbia UP, 2006.

Laurence, Jonathan, and Justin Vaisse. *Integrating Islam: Political and Religious Challenges in Contemporary France*. Brookings Institution, 2006.

Leruth, Michael F. "François Mitterrand's 'Festival of the World's Tribes': The Logic of Exoticism in the French Revolution Bicentennial Parade." *French Cultural Studies*, vol. 9, no. 25, 1998, pp. 51–80.

Long, Imogen. *Women Intellectuals in Post-68 France: Petitions and Polemics*. Palgrave Macmillan, 2013.

Long, Kathleen Perry, ed. *Religious Differences in France: Past and Present*. Truman State UP, 2006.

Malinovich, Nadia. *French and Jewish: Culture and the Politics of Identity in Early Twentieth-Century France*. Littman Library of Jewish Civilization, 2008.

Mandel, Maud S. *Muslims and Jews in France: History of a Conflict*. Princeton UP, 2014.

Mathy, Jean-Philippe. *Extreme-Occident: French Intellectuals and America*. U Chicago P, 1993.

May, Todd. *Deleuze: An Introduction*. Cambridge UP, 2005.

McCaffrey, Enda. *The Return of Religion in France: From Democratisation to Postmetaphysics*. Palgrave Macmillan, 2009.

McMillan, James. "'Priest Hits Girl': On the Front Line of the 'War of the Two Frances.'" *Culture Wars: Secular-Catholic Conflict in Nineteenth-Century Europe*, eds. Christopher Clark and Wolfram Kaiser. Cambridge UP, 2003, pp. 77–101.

Meunier, Sophie. "The Distinctiveness of French Anti-Americanism." *Anti-Americanisms in World Politics*, eds. Peter J. Katzenstein and Robert O. Keohane. Cornell UP, 2006, pp. 129–156.

Moriarty, Michael. *Early Modern French Thought: The Age of Suspicion*. Oxford UP, 2003.

Moriarty, Michael, and Jeremy Jennings, eds. *The Cambridge History of French Thought.* Cambridge UP, 2019.

Nilsson, Per-Erik. *French Populism and Discourses on Secularism.* Bloomsbury, 2018.

Obadia, Lionel. "'Your Own Personal Buddha'? Contesting Individualism as the Main Feature of Modern Religious Experience: The Case of Buddhism in France." *Experiencing Religion: New Approaches to Personal Religiosity,* eds. Clara Saraiva, et al. LIT, 2016, pp. 105–117.

Palmer, Susan. *The New Heretics of France: Minority Religions, la République, and the Government-Sponsored "War on Sects."* Oxford UP, 2011.

Plenel, Edwy. *For the Muslims: Islamophobia in France.* Trans. David Fernbach. Verso, 2016.

Price, Roger. *The Church and the State in France, 1789–1870: 'Fear of God is the Basis of Social Order'.* Palgrave Macmillan, 2017.

Price, Roger. *Religious Renewal in France, 1789–1870: The Roman Catholic Church between Catastrophe and Triumph.* Palgrave Macmillan, 2017.

Roche, Daniel. *France in the Enlightenment.* Trans. Arthur Goldhammer. Harvard UP, 1998.

Roger, Philippe. *The American Enemy: The History of French Anti-Americanism.* Trans. Sharon Bowman. U Chicago P, 2005.

Roy, Olivier. *Secularism Confronts Islam.* Trans. George Holoch. Columbia UP, 2007.

Ruane, Joseph. "Ethnicity, Religion and Peoplehood: Protestants in France and in Ireland." *Ethnopolitics,* vol. 9, no. 1, 2010, pp. 121–135.

Samuels, Maurice. *The Right to Difference: French Universalism and the Jews.* U California P, 2016.

Sand, Shlomo. *The End of the French Intellectual: From Zola to Houellebecq.* Trans. David Fernbach. Verso, 2018.

Schnapper, Dominique, et al. *Jewish Citizenship in France: The Temptation of Being Among One's Own.* Routledge, 2010.

Schor, Naomi. "The Crisis of French Universalism." *Yale French Studies,* no. 100, 2001, pp. 43–64.

Scott, Joan Wallach. "French Universalism in the Nineties." *Differences: A Journal of Feminist Cultural Studies,* vol. 15, no. 2, 2004, pp. 32–53.

Scott, Joan Wallach. *The Politics of the Veil.* Princeton UP, 2007.

Sémelin, Jacques. *The Survival of the Jews in France, 1940–44.* Trans. Cynthia Schooch and Natasha Lehrer. Oxford UP, 2017.

Sepinwall, Alyssa Goldstein. *The Abbé Gregoire and the French Revolution: The Making of Modern Universalism.* U California P, 2005.

Shorto, Russell. *Descartes' Bones: A Skeletal History of the Conflict Between Faith and Reason.* Doubleday, 2008.

Taithe, Bertrand. "Reinventing (French) Universalism: Religion, Humanitarianism and the 'French Doctors.'" *Modern & Contemporary France,* vol. 12, no. 2, 2004, pp. 147–158.

Tallett, Frank, and Nicholas Atkin, eds. *Catholicism in Britain & France since 1789.* Hambledon, 1996.

Tallett, Frank, and Nicholas Atkin, eds. *Religion, Society and Politics in France since 1789.* Bloomsbury, 2003.

Tanke, Joseph J. *Jacques Rancière: An Introduction.* Continuum, 2011.

Taylor, Keith. *Political Ideas of the Utopian Socialists.* Routledge, 1982.

Tippett-Spirtou, Sandy. *French Catholicism: Church, State and Society in a Changing Era.* Palgrave Macmillan, 2000.

Treasure, Geoffrey. *The Huguenots.* Yale University Press, 2013.

Weitzmann, Marc. *Hate: The Rising Tide of Anti-Semitism in France (and What It Means for Us).* Houghton Mifflin, 2019.

Wernick, Andrew. *Auguste Comte and the Religion of Humanity: The Post-theistic Program of French Social Theory.* Cambridge UP, 2001.

What Do We Do with a Difference?: France and the Debate over Headscarves in Schools. Facing History and Ourselves Foundation, 2008.

Wicks, Robert. *Modern French Philosophy: From Existentialism to Postmodernism.* One World, 2003.

Wieviorka, Michel. *The Lure of Anti-Semitism: Hatred of Jews in Present-Day France.* Trans. Kristen Couper Lobel and Anna Declerck. Brill, 2007.

Willaime, Jean-Paul. "Protestantism in France: A Minority Defining Its Place in Catholic Culture." *Religious Newcomers and the Nation State: Political Culture and Organized Religion in France and the Netherlands*, eds. Erik Sengers and Thijl Sunier. Eburon, 2010, pp. 99–114.

Winter, Bronwyn. *Hijab & The Republic: Uncovering the French Headscarf Debate.* Syracuse UP, 2008.

Wolf, Joan B. *Harnessing the Holocaust: The Politics of Memory in France.* Stanford UP, 2003.

Wolfreys, James. *Republic of Islamophobia: The Rise of Respectable Racism in France.* Oxford UP, 2017.

Wolin, Richard. *The Wind from the East: French Intellectuals, the Cultural Revolution, and the Legacy of the 1960s.* Princeton UP, 2010.

Wright, Wynne, and Alexis Annes. "Halal on the Menu?: Contested Food Politics and French Identity in Fast-Food." *Journal of Rural Studies*, vol. 32, 2013, pp. 388–399.

Zuccotti, Susan. *The Holocaust, the French, and the Jews.* Basic Books, 1993.

CHAPTER 6

SOCIAL CLASS AND ETHNICITY

OVERVIEW

French society today is characterized by several paradoxes. It is the most racially and ethnically diverse society of continental Western Europe but does not openly celebrate its immigrant heritage and is generally suspicious of multiculturalism, which some believe may undermine the indivisibility and secularism of the Republic. It has a strong and widely shared egalitarian ethos, but this ethos does not replace deep-seated social hierarchy, classism, elitism, and status consciousness. The state and politicians across the spectrum are committed to social cohesion, accessible public services, and the country's social security system, which provides a safety net for all citizens—a culture of solidarity that helps make socioeconomic disparities less severe than in comparable wealthy countries; yet precariousness, poverty, and homelessness still exist. Finally, French society is generally liberal and individualistic but at the same time conspicuously resistant to change and organically grouped at the level of everyday life into protective social circles, from old-boy networks and political *groupuscules* to village café regulars and intimate friend groups—each with different traditions and value sets that individuals must learn how to navigate.

Profound social change has occurred in France over the course of the past several decades. Indeed, according to the sociologist Henri Mendras, a "Second French Revolution" occurred between 1965 and 1984, overlapping the final phase of the period of unprecedented economic development and modernization known as the "Glorious Thirty" (1945–1975). The overall thrust of this mostly nonviolent, but no less profound, sociopolitical transformation was France's abrupt and deep entry into what Mendras terms "late modernism." According to him, late modern French society is characterized by ten traits.

1. The underlying economic (greater wealth *and* inequality), political (assertion of the basic equality of all citizens), and cultural logic (encouragement of individual self-expression) of modern society (as defined by Daniel Bell) have become "disconnected" and no longer exert a moderating influence on one another.
2. Individualism has progressed to the point where a compensatory emphasis on intense forms of community and connection to others has developed.

3. Transversal and decentralized network-type structures (incl. modern communications networks and platforms) cut across traditional geographic and social boundaries.
4. Power is no longer wielded primarily from the top of the social hierarchy but is more diffused and omnipresent in daily life.
5. The general level of education and cultural capital has risen and given each individual both a better sense of their social worth and a better understanding of the workings of society.
6. Obedience to authority and its corollary, resentment of authority, have given way to negotiation as the default mode of social relations.
7. Society presents itself to the individual as a free marketplace of choices, such that each person now bears responsibility for the construction of his or her personality, identity, and lifestyle—a degree of apparent freedom that can be both exhilarating and exhausting.
8. Innovation in all forms—economic, political, social, technological, and cultural—has gained the upper hand over conformism and now emerges more readily from grassroots disruptors than from enlightened elites.
9. The influence of France's once symbolically potent "great institutions" and "ideological conflicts" has lessened considerably—a change that is both positive, because it leads to greater pragmatism, and negative, because it tends to make social reality less legible.
10. Collective identity—continental, national, regional, local, and communitarian—is now perceived as far more tentative and multifaceted, but national identity is far from obsolete despite being harder to define.

Furthermore, Mendras argues that traditional representations of society as driven by class conflict or hierarchically structured like a pyramid are inadequate to describe late modern French society, which he describes in terms of four overlapping and interacting constellations: a small "regulatory elite," a rather nebulous social mainstream that can be considered middle class despite differing degrees of financial comfort and cultural capital (Pierre Bourdieu) within it, an expanding *constellation populaire* comprised of working people of more modest means, and a fringe of the poor that is slowly drifting away from the other constellations. He also stresses that the major social transformations of the "Second French Revolution" were both felt most acutely and hastened most forcefully by students (e.g., those who took part in "May 68"), farmers, women, and senior citizens.

During the Middle Ages and up to the French Revolution, French society was divided into three caste-like orders: the clergy and nobility, who dominated society and enjoyed special privileges; and the commoners who "worked" for a living (including prosperous bourgeois merchants, office holders, modest tradesmen, laborers, and the mass of peasants)—lumped together in what was later called the "third estate." The Revolution upended this inegalitarian social structure but did not do away with its traces in French culture. Many of the values of the nobility, like elitism centering on family reputation, cultural refinement, and respect for tradition and good manners, were adopted by the upper echelons of the bourgeoisie, and some aspects of the aristo-cratic mindset, like an acute sense of one's implicit place in the social hierarchy and a "logic of honor" translating into resentment of the indignity of being placed in a pos-ition of subservience in one's work or in public, were (and still are) shared by people in the lower rungs of society. Moreover, other types of noble titles replaced those for-merly based on possession of a seigneurial estate or service to the monarch, such as the nominally meritocratic but no less elitist "nobility of diplomas." The descendants of the historical nobility are still around, although they represent less than 0.2% of the population of France (i.e., around 100,000 people). They are still allowed to use their titles publicly and in official documents, but noble status or lineage itself is no longer recognized by the French state and conveys no statutory special rights or privileges. Those members of the French nobility who are wealthy (not all of them are) form part of the social elite along with members of the *haute* (upper) and *grande* bourgeoisie, titans of industry, the political leadership, and people elevated by exceptional accom-plishments in prestigious fields (e.g., the arts). It is now less common to speak of the French bourgeoisie as a distinct social class than was the case in the nineteenth and most of the twentieth centuries (all but the top tier has been absorbed by the middle class, which has its own tiers determined by wealth, profession, and cultural capital). However, the cultural stereotype of the bourgeois—someone who is obsessed with material gain and comfort, generally conservative politically and conspicuously mor-ally upright (except for the "bourgeois bohemian" subtype), highly protective of pri-vate life, focused on the domestic sphere of the nuclear family, and prone to rational calculation of self-interest—still resonates (indeed, these are the mores of much of the middle class).

Similarly, it is now less common to speak of the "proletariat" as the social class adversaries of the bourgeoisie. The reasons for this trend include the diminished cur-rency of Marxist terminology and ideology; the wide dissemination of so-called middle-class attitudes, cultural tastes, and patterns of consumption; and the declin-ing share of industrial manufacturing in France's economic profile. The actual French working class has also changed. It now involves far more people in service industries and low-level "white-collar" jobs. As is the case elsewhere, the French working class—often called *la classe populaire*, which includes the lower rungs of the middle class and rural residents of modest means—is facing considerable internal and external pres-sures: competition from low-wage countries for jobs, chronic high unemployment and precariousness related to rampant restructuring, greater emphasis on highly skilled occupations that require more education at the tertiary level, declining pur-chasing power, and austerity-minded cuts to social programs and benefits. France's National Institute of Economic Statistics and Studies (INSEE) uses a more precise system of socio-professional nomenclature that divides the population into six main occupational groups and two groups of nonworking people: (1) farmers; (2) artisans/craftsmen, shopkeepers, and small business owners; (3) upper-level managers (*cadres supérieurs*) and intellectual professions; (4) intermediate professions (a range of occu-pations, including mid-level managers, supervisory personnel, and skilled self-employed service providers); (5) employees (office workers); (6) manual workers (*ouvriers*); (7) retirees; and (8) people without a defined occupation. While the nomenclature is used primarily by specialists and government officials, some of the terminology has become commonplace.

As recently as the early twentieth century, mainland France was a mosaic of culturally and linguistically distinct regions and local terroirs. The inhabitants of these different geographic areas today do not quite meet the common definition of ethnic or regional minorities, and French regional identities today coexist more or less peacefully with French national identity (regionalist sentiment tends to be stronger in more "peripheral" regions like Brittany, Alsace, the Basque Country, and Corsica). By comparison, immigration has dramatically increased the racial and ethnic diversity of French society—a fact that has still not been adequately recognized, let alone embraced. While France currently ranks seventh among the nations of the world (behind the United States, Russia, Saudi Arabia, Germany, the United Kingdom, and the United Arab Emirates) in terms of its current total immigrant population, it ranks alongside the United States, Canada, and Australia among the overall immigration leaders of the twentieth century. Belgians, Poles, and Eastern European Jews were among the major immigrant groups in the late nineteenth and early twentieth centuries. Large numbers of Spanish and Italians arrived from the 1920s through the 1960s. A particularly intense wave of immigration occurred between 1945 and 1975, chiefly from France's former colonies. In the 1960s and 1970s, Algerian and Portuguese immigrants arrived in roughly equal numbers. Moroccans and Tunisians came in large numbers in the 1980s. So, too, did many Turks and sub-Saharan Africans (from countries like Senegal, Ivory Coast, Cameroon, Mali, Mauritania, and the French Congo). The latter represent the most important regional cohort of immigrants in the 1990s and 2000s. Chinese, Vietnamese, and other Asians became a significant component of immigration to France beginning in the late 1970s and early 1980s. Finally, there has been much immigration from Central and Eastern Europe since the implementation of the Schengen Agreement in 1995. There are between 5.7 and 6 million immigrants residing in France today (including naturalized citizens)—close to 9% of the population. If one considers the first, second, and third generations (i.e., immigrants, children of at least one immigrant parent, and grandchildren of at least one immigrant), 40% of the population of France can be considered a product of immigration. While questions about a person's race and ethnicity are prohibited under French law and therefore not part of census data, it is estimated that there are between 5.5 and 6 million French citizens and residents of Arab origin in France (Maghrebi for the most part)—9% of the national population. Blacks make up the second largest minority group: between 3.0 and 5.5 million French citizens and residents (including people of color from the French Caribbean), which represents between 4.5% and 8% of the population.

French attitudes toward racial and ethnic diversity are complex. French society is generally liberal, tolerant, and supportive of an individual's "right to be different," regardless of how that difference is defined. It also has a strong republican tradition of anti-racism and support for civil rights for minorities. However, the same republican tradition purports to see all people as equal individuals who ought to be free of social and cultural determinism and not as members of particular racial, ethnic, or cultural communities, and it requires that all forms of "particularism" remain confined to the private sphere and out of politics. French liberal tolerance and republican universalism notwithstanding, racism, xenophobia, Islamophobia, and anti-Semitism exist in France and have become somewhat more widespread in recent years as anxieties about French national identity have been felt by ordinary people and exploited by political opportunists. Nonprofit organizations like the French Human Rights League, the International League against Racism and Anti-Semitism (LICRA), and SOS Racisme publicize and combat the most egregious and insidious forms of racism and discrimination. France also has laws that sanction hate speech. However, France generally does not favor the use of affirmative action (called *la discrimination positive* in French) as a remedy for systemic forms of discrimination based on race or ethnicity.

An extensive and generous social safety net is one reason why poverty and income inequality are less pronounced in France than in many comparable countries—France's 2019 poverty rate was 8.4%, compared to 18.0% for the United States (OECD), and its 2019 Gini coefficient, an indicator of income inequality based on five different variables, was 0.29, compared to 0.40 for the United States (OECD). However, poverty and homelessness still exist in France. According to the French government, 3.4% of the population live in acute poverty. Approximately 140,000 meet the official criterion for being considered "homeless" (*sans domicile fixe* [SDF]) and the number who have inadequate housing approaches 4 million according to some estimates. The French government takes these social problems seriously even though the concrete steps it has taken to alleviate them have been criticized by some as insufficient. Social inequality in France also has a geographical component: the major cities are generally vibrant and prosperous, but a number of rural areas are economically disadvantaged and depopulated, suburban zones with large public housing projects and minority populations have in some cases become "ghettoized" pockets of socioeconomic exclusion, and the standard of living and level of economic opportunity in France's overseas departments and territories are markedly lower than in the mainland.

Further Reading

Amselle (2003); Beaman (2019); Begag (2007); Chapman and Frader (2004); Dobbernack (2014); Forsé et al. (1993); Mendras and Cole (1991); Onishi (2021); Peabody and Stovall (2003); Schwartz (2014); Silverstein (2018); Weil (2008).

Arabs

Arabs represent the largest ethnic minority in France. The vast majority of French Arabs come from three countries in the Maghreb region of North Africa that were formerly French territories in the colonial era: Morocco (independence 1956), Algeria (independence 1962), and Tunisia (independence 1956). Algeria was an integral part of France until 1962 and is the source of the largest number of Maghrebi immigrants to France. A smaller number of French Arabs come from Syria and Lebanon, both of which were formerly (1923–1946) part of a French Mandate (the French presence in Lebanon was quite strong). Since the French state does not allow the official collection of data on race and ethnicity, estimating the size of this (or any other) ethnic minority remains imprecise. Some credible estimates report that there are between 5.5 and 6 million French citizens and residents of Arab origin in France—a figure equal to 9% of the national population. Many French people with North African/Maghrebi roots are not ethnic Arabs, but of Berber descent. This includes many people of Algerian origin whose ancestry is from the Kabyle subgroup of Berbers, from the Atlas Mountains region of northern Algeria. However, most French people of North African descent are commonly identified as "Arabs" or "Maghrebi," though they may self-identify by their familial country of origin (the Algerian, Moroccan, and Tunisian communities of France are distinct and, in some cases, rivalrous). While there has been a not insignificant number of Arabs living in France since the nineteenth century—the importance of Paris's Arab community was underscored in 1926 with the opening of the Grand Mosque of Paris, built as a tribute to the colonial Muslim infantrymen who had fought valiantly for France during World War I—most Arab immigrants came during the large wave of immigration that coincided with the period of sustained economic development known as the "Glorious Thirty" (1945–1975). They settled mainly in and around France's largest cities (e.g., Paris, Marseille, and Lyon) and in its industrial areas. There are also larger concentrations of people of Arab/North African descent in the south, especially along the Mediterranean coast. France's Arab minority has faced considerable racism and discrimination. For a long time, lingering bitterness over the bloody Algerian War for Independence (1954–1962) was a major contributing factor. To that were added negative stereotypes about immigrant manual laborers with large families who were allegedly not "well integrated" into French society and about rebellious Arab youths from the suburbs. More recently, however, Islamophobia—discrimination and negative perceptions motivated by Islam, often stereotyped as incompatible with French culture and tradition (e.g., secularism) and prone to extremism (incl. terrorism)—has been the leading source of animus, even though not all French Muslims are Arabs and not all French Arabs are practicing Muslims (indeed, their levels of belief in God and religious practice are close to those of compatriots nominally associated with other religions).

French Arabs stand up for their rights and identity and are involved in their local communities and in national politics. One watershed moment was the 1983 March for Equality and Against Racism, more commonly known as "La Marche des Beurs" due to the fact that most participants were second-generation North African immigrants, called "Beurs" (a slang term derived from the French word *Arabe* said backward). While the Beur movement's concrete impact on politics was slight, many children and grandchildren of North African immigrants have become successful professionally, leading some to speak of a "Beurgeoisie." Indeed, there have been many highly successful, famous, and esteemed French people of Arab descent in a wide range of fields—business, media, cinema (e.g., Isabelle Adjani, Jamel Debouuze, Rachid Bouchareb, Roschdy Zem, Kad Merad, Leïla Bekhti, Rachid Bouchareb, Abdellatif

Kechiche), music (e.g., Rachid Taha, Khaled, Magyd Cherfi, Juliette Noureddine, La Fouine), sports (e.g., Zinedine Zidane, Karim Benzema, Samir Nasri, Nordine Oubaali, Evan Fournier), fashion (e.g., Azzedine Alaïa, Hedi Slimane), literature (e.g., Amin Maalouf, Tahar Ben Jelloun, Abdellah Taïa, Leila Slimani, Faïza Guène, Riad Satttouf), art (e.g., Saâdane Afif, Kader Attia, Latifa Echakhch), academia, science, and politics. Several people of Arab descent have become cabinet ministers—Azouz Begag, Rachida Dati, Fadela Amara, Kader Arif, Najat Vallaud-Belkacem, Myriam El Khomri, Mounir Mahjoubi, Rima Abdul-Malak. Numerous elements of North African culture—including food (e.g., couscous and merguez sausages), music (e.g., raï), and linguistic expressions—have been incorporated into broader French culture.

See also: Chapter 2: Timeline; de Gaulle (Charles), World War II, and the Fifth Republic. Chapter 5: Islam. Chapter 6: Immigration; Suburbs. Chapter 9: Francophonie. Chapter 13: Rock, Pop, and Rap.

Further Reading

Beaman (2017); Ben Jelloun (1999); Blanchard (2016); Derderian (2004); Hussey (2014); Killian (2006); MacMaster (1997); Silverstein (2004).

Blacks

Exact figures concerning the size of the Black population in France do not exist because the official collection of data regarding a person's race or ethnicity is forbidden by law in France. General estimates vary from 3 to 5.5 million people, which would represent between 4.5% and 8% of the population (including overseas departments and territories with higher percentages of Black people). Further estimates suggest that approximately 80% of the Black population in France is of African origin with ties to countries that were formerly French colonies: Mauritania, Mali, Burkina Faso, Niger, Chad, Guinea (Conakry), Senegal, Ivory Coast, Togo, Benin, Cameroon, Central African Republic, Gabon, Congo (Brazzaville), Comoros Islands, and Madagascar. A smaller percentage are of Afro-Caribbean origin with ties to the islands of the French West Indies—Guadeloupe, Martinique, Saint Martin, and Saint Barthélemy—or from French Guiana. They are the descendants of African slaves brought to the Americas as part of the triangular Atlantic system of trade from the sixteenth through the early nineteenth century. Many present-day French Afro-Caribbeans (*Antillais*) are Creoles of mixed racial ancestry. French Blacks are sometimes also construed as including South Pacific island Melanesians, principally from New Caledonia, which is a semiautonomous French territory. Black people in metropolitan France arrived at different points in time, but many African immigrants came to France after 1980s. Africa continues to be a leading source of new immigrants to France. Migration is also a factor in the presence of many Afro-Caribbeans in metropolitan France even though they arrive in the French mainland as French citizens. For instance, many left their islands to live and work in the mainland as part of the BUMIDOM (Bureau for the Development of Migration in the Overseas Departments) program between 1963 and 1981. This program, which focused on Guadeloupe, Martinique, and Réunion (an island in the Indian Ocean), sought to alleviate overpopulation in the French overseas departments by bringing both unskilled and skilled French-speaking workers from the islands to the mainland. It included educated people for white-collar and civil service positions. In all, the program brought 70,000 islanders to the mainland, close to 45% of the total number of island migrants for the same period.

The idea that the Black population of France constitutes the Black "community" of France is not self-evident. Not only is identification with a racial or ethnic community not firmly anchored in the French social experience but there are also a lot of differences among French Blacks—region and country of origin, native language and citizenship status, religion, level of education, and so on. However, such community formation and identification is beginning to take place based on the common awareness of great historical traumas (slavery, colonialism, diaspora); the historical example of Black social, political, artistic, cultural, and literary movements in the United States, Africa, and broader Francophone world (e.g., Négritude, which began in the 1930s and was championed by Léopold Sédar Senghor of Senegal, Aimé Césaire of Martinique, and Léon Damas of Guiana); shared experiences of French racism and solidarity in resistance to it; social and cultural *métissage* in French cities and *banlieues* among people of color of diverse origins; and the creation of organizations that defend and represent the community like the Representative Council of France's Black Associations (CRAN, founded in 2005). Regardless of their degree of unity as a community, France's Black population has contributed a lot to French culture and diversity; and has produced highly successful individuals in a wide range of fields—tennis stars Yannick Noah and Gaël Monfils; figure skaters Surya Bonaly and Maé-Bérénice Méité; soccer stars Thierry Henry, Lillian Thuram, N'Golo Kanté, Paul Pogba, and Kylian Mbappé; basketball players Tony Parker, Rudy Gobert, and Nicolas Batum; authors Maryse Condé, Patrick Chamoiseau, Alain Mabanckou, Marie Ndiaye, and Fatou Diome; journalists Harry Roselmack, Rokhaya Diallo, and Audrey Pulvar; artists Barthélémy Togouo and Lask TWE; fashion designer Olivier Rousteing; actors Pascal Legitimus, Omar Sy, Fabrice Eboué, Firmine Richard, Aïssa Maïga, and Karidja Touré; film directors Ladj Ly and Pascal Zadi; rappers Abd al Malik, Kery James, Casey, and Sianna; activists Priscillia Ludosky and Assa Traoré; and politicians/government officials Christiane Taubira, Rama Yade, Danièle Obono, Sibeth Ndiaye, and Pap Ndiaye.

See also: Chapter 1: Overseas France. Chapter 5: Islam. Chapter 6: Immigration; Suburbs. Chapter 9: Francophonie. Chapter 11: Literary Avant-Garde, 1950–1980; Poetry (Modern and Contemporary). Chapter 13: Rock, Pop, and Rap.

Further Reading

Bass (2014); Beriss (2019); Collins (2020); Germain and Larcher (2018); Keaton et al. (2012); Thomas (2007); Thomas (2013); Tshimanga et al. (2009).

Bourgeoisie and Middle Class

The terms "bourgeois" and "bourgeoisie," which originated in France in medieval times, have several different connotations depending on their use in different contexts—historical, political, economic, sociological, cultural, and so on. Originally, a bourgeois, or burger, was a free inhabitant of a medieval town that had been granted a charter by the local feudal lord, who, in some cases, may have been the king. Between the eleventh and the thirteenth centuries, the towns grew rapidly, with the expansion of commerce and trade. Hence the broader economic meaning of the term as referring to merchants, craftsmen, guild members, financiers, office holders, and practitioners of other non-menial and nonagricultural occupations in the cities and towns. The bourgeois were members of the "third order" of feudal society (later called the "third estate")—the *laboratores*, or those who labor—along with the mass of peasants living in the countryside. However, over time, a bourgeois was understood to be an affluent member of the elite of that order, as socially distant from the urban working class as from the rural peasantry. Many members of the upper bourgeoisie aspired to join the nobility and did so by serving the king, acquiring a seigneurial estate, or marriage. Other bourgeois resented the power, prestige, and privilege of the ancien régime aristocracy and advocated political and social reforms, including civil and political rights and basic social equality—rights and equality they were not necessarily willing to share with women and non-property owners. During meetings of the Estates General in the early days (1789) of what was to become the French Revolution, bourgeois representatives of the third estate, joined by some progressive representatives of the clergy and the nobility, declared their order's deliberative body the National Assembly and set to work on a constitution that King Louis XVI would be forced to accept. Nonetheless, many historians today are more cautious about interpreting the French Revolution as a product of bourgeois class consciousness than their Marxist predecessors. Moreover, on the eve of the Revolution, perhaps no more than 8% of the population of France could be considered bourgeois (out of which just 2% were part of the upper bourgeoisie). Greater class consciousness would develop in the nineteenth century, when the upper bourgeoisie became the new dominant class.

Traditionally, there are four tiers of French bourgeoisie. The *petite bourgeoisie*, or petty bourgeoisie (i.e., lower middle class), is situated above the "lower" classes—the working class and peasants—and below the upper middle class, and is comprised of less affluent people who may have joined the middle class only recently, including shopkeepers, office workers, and lower-level civil servants. The *moyenne bourgeoisie*, or middle bourgeoisie, which corresponds approximately to the upper middle class, encompasses more affluent individuals—including members of the "intellectual" professions (e.g., professors, doctors, lawyers, and architects), mid-level managers and business executives, owners of small to midsized business, and upper-level civil servants—whose families have typically been bourgeois for three or more generations, but who have not yet attained the accumulated wealth and social prestige of the members of the upper tier of their class. The latter make up the *grande bourgeoisie*, whose families have been bourgeois for several generations (i.e., a century or more), have amassed considerable wealth, and who are members of the economic, social, political, and cultural elite of the nation. They tend to seek friends and marriage partners among other members of the elite and have a strong attachment to fine living and cultural distinction (according to sociologist Pierre Bourdieu). Finally, there is the quasi-noble *haute bourgeoisie*, the high or upper bourgeoisie, who are the members of "old" and very wealthy families and whose place at the pinnacle of French society dates back to the early nineteenth century (if not earlier). These families have a great degree of social prestige and cultural refinement, and are sometimes closely connected to the aristocracy, whose values and luxurious lifestyle they may share.

Identifying a common set of values shared by the French bourgeoisie involves more of a cultural stereotype than a sociological reality. Nonetheless, French bourgeois are often identified with their supposed obsession with social status, religious traditionalism, a sense of entitlement and moral superiority (compared to the "idle" and "obsolete" aristocracy and the "undisciplined" working class "rabble"), a strong work ethic, materialism and emphasis on material comfort, calculating rationality, political and cultural conservatism, and a protective view of private life. Elements of this cultural stereotype have been the fodder for social criticism and ridicule since the seventeenth century—like, for example, Molière's *The Bourgeois Gentleman* (1670), the novels of the nineteenth-century realists and naturalists (e.g., Stendhal, Balzac, Flaubert, and Zola), and surrealist filmmaker Luis Buñuel's late masterpiece, *The Discreet Charm of the Bourgeoisie* (1972). However, from the Revolution of 1789 to the present, there has been a progressive-minded faction of the French bourgeoisie that has played an important role in the development of French republicanism, scientific and technological progress, social democracy, modernism, liberalism, individualism, and European unity. These progressives, too, have been the objects of criticism and ridicule—from postmodern critics of the bourgeois "myth" of progress to unflattering caricatures of so-called "Bobos," or "Bourgeois Bohemians" (*les bourgeois bohèmes*)—relatively affluent young urban professionals who adopt some of the ideals, tastes, and lifestyle traits of countercultural hipsters without a radical or activist questioning of the current socioeconomic order.

Since the 1950s, it is more common to use the term "middle class" rather than "bourgeoisie." Like its counterparts in other countries, the economically diverse French middle class places a premium on education—beyond the indispensable baccalaureate (advanced high school diploma), earning at least one postsecondary diploma, if not several, is the most reliable means of cementing one's position in the middle class—and private property (the home ownership rate reached an all-time high of 65% of the French population in 2016). Its members are keen to follow the latest trends in consumer technology and communication. They vote across the political spectrum but tend to favor mainstream parties (e.g., Socialist Party, The Republic on the Move, The Republicans) and moderate candidates. They tend to be somewhat more socially liberal, secular, and concerned with ecology than their counterparts in the United States. They generally favor the consumer-oriented capitalist economy. However, they are increasingly anxious about the prospect of losing ground in terms of purchasing power and economic security and about France's ability to preserve its unique "social model" in the context of economic globalization.

See also: Chapter 2: de Gaulle (Charles), World War II, and the Fifth Republic; Louis XVI and the End of the Ancien Régime; Napoleon III and the Second Empire. Chapter 6: Income Distribution and Inequality; Nobility; Working Class. Chapter 10: Social Hierarchies.

Further Reading
Bidou-Zachariasen (2011); Boltanski (1987); Bourdieu (1984); Lamont (1992); Le Wita (1994); Maza (2003); Pech (2011); Pinçon-Charlot and Pinçon (2018); Seigel (2012).

Immigration

While the fact is not always acknowledged, let alone proudly incorporated into the national narrative and collective memory as it is in the United States, France is an immigrant melting pot and has been a magnet for foreign migrants since the nineteenth century. In fact, among major industrial countries, it ranks just behind the United States and Canada as a destination for immigrants in the modern period. At one point, in the 1920s and 1930s, it outpaced the United States in the number of immigrants it took in as share of the population. Belgians, Poles, and Eastern European Jews were among the major immigrant groups in the late nineteenth and early twentieth centuries. Large numbers of Spanish and Italians arrived from the 1920s through the 1960s. A particularly intense wave of immigration occurred between 1945 and 1975, during the period of extensive economic development known as the "Glorious Thirty." The leading sources of immigrants during this period were France's colonies and former colonies and overseas territories, beginning with the countries of the Maghreb region of North Africa, just across the Mediterranean Sea from France. During this period, male workers often arrived first and were later joined by their wives and families—a practice known as *le regroupement familial*, or family reunification, which continued after restrictions were placed on foreign worker immigration in the mid-1970s. These immigrants gradually became members of local French communities. In spite of prejudice and the illusory "myth of return" (i.e., the notion that their presence in France was temporary and that they would eventually return to their home countries after they had made enough money), their children became French through public school matriculation, native fluency in French, and exposure to French popular culture. In the 1960s and 1970s, Portuguese and Algerian immigrants settled in France in roughly equal numbers. Other Maghrebi—Moroccans and lesser numbers of Tunisians—came in the 1980s. So, too, did many Turks and sub-Saharan Africans (from countries like Mauritania, Mali, Niger, Chad, Senegal, Ivory Coast, Cameroon, and the French Congo). The latter represent the most important cohort of immigrants in the 1990s and 2000s. Chinese, Vietnamese, and other Asians became a significant component of immigration to France beginning in the late 1970s and early 1980s (Vietnam was also a former French colony and the fall of Saigon in 1975 triggered a large-scale exodus of migrants, whom the media sometimes characterized as "boat people"). Finally, one must not overlook significant immigration from countries in the EU other than Spain, Italy, and Portugal—especially from former Communist bloc countries in Central and Eastern Europe (e.g., Poland, Romania, ex-Yugoslavia, and Bulgaria). Immigration from within the EU was made considerably easier by the free circulation of people in the Schengen Area, instituted in 1995. There are between 5.7 and 6 million immigrants residing in France today (the term used most by the French is *immigrés*, which includes both foreign-born naturalized citizens and noncitizen foreign-born residents), close to 9% of the population. By country of origin, the eight largest immigrant groups in France today are Algerians, Moroccans, Portuguese, Italians, Turks, Tunisians, Spanish, and British. If one considers the first (immigrants themselves), second (people with at least one immigrant parent), and third generations (people with at least one immigrant grandparent), then approximately 40% of the population of France can be considered a product of immigration (*issu de l'immigration*).

Today, France places stringent limitations on legal immigration and makes the interdiction of illegal, or undocumented, immigration a major enforcement priority. Nonetheless, in 2017, France issued residency cards to over 260,000 foreigners and processed 100,000 asylum applications. In France, the right to French nationality and birthright citizenship is traditionally based on the principle of *jus soli*, or by virtue of having been born on French soil; however, there are additional qualifications, requirements, and restrictions. A child automatically acquires French citizenship if born in France (incl. overseas territories) to at least one parent who was also born in France or who is a naturalized French citizen (children born abroad to French citizens may also claim French citizenship). Children born in France to foreign parents do not automatically acquire French citizenship but may claim it if certain conditions are met—if stateless at birth; upon parental request in the case of a minor between the age of thirteen and sixteen if the beneficiary has been a resident of France continuously since the age of eight; and upon request of the beneficiary (minors between the age sixteen and eighteen or upon turning eighteen) themselves if they are residents of France at the time of the demand with at least five years residence since age eleven. Special rules apply to people whose parents came from France's former colonies and territories. For instance, a child born in France in 1963 or later to a parent born in Algeria—formerly an integral part of France—before independence is automatically a French citizen, as is a child born in France before 1994 to a parent born in a former French overseas colonial territory prior to its independence. If born in 1994 or later, children of such parents may request French citizenship at age eighteen. A foreign-born adult may seek French citizenship through naturalization after five years of continuous legal residence in France (the residency requirement is shortened to two years for members of highly skilled professions and other people with exceptional talents, and may be waived for refugees and people who have served in the French military). During the prerequisite residency period, one's primary source of income must be from France.

A man demonstrating for immigrant rights on May Day (French Labor Day). He is holding a T-shirt referring to the historical legacy of French colonialism in Africa and the daunting challenges faced by undocumented migrants in France today—with a slogan that reads "Yesterday colonized, today exploited, tomorrow legalized." Immigrants, including large numbers from France's former colonies, have contributed greatly to the French economy since the 1950s and 60s and have changed the face of French society and culture; however, they have also faced discrimination, social stigmatization, political scapegoating, economic precarity, police harassment, and outright racism. (Tom Craig/Dreamstime.com)

Additionally, one must demonstrate one's proficiency in the French language, understanding of the rights and responsibilities of a French citizen, and respect for French values (including secularism).

French attitudes toward immigration vary. Each wave and group of immigrants since the Belgians and Poles in the late nineteenth century has stirred some measure of xenophobic reaction. There is also a certain tendency to refer to people of certain races, religions, and ethnic groups as "foreigners" and/or *immigrés* after the first generation and regardless of citizenship status and degree of acculturation. However, France is an open-minded country with a proud tradition as a country of asylum, a strong attachment to "universalist" republican values like equality and fraternity, a tendency to view people as individuals and not members of particular ethnic communities, and a capital that is one of the most cosmopolitan cities in the world (Marseille and Lyon are also very diverse in terms of race and ethnicity). Still, immigration has been a contentious political and social issue since the 1980s. Several factors have made it so. One is the protracted sluggishness of the French economy and persistent high unemployment since the end of the "Glorious Thirty" period, which has led to racist and xenophobic accusations that "foreigners" are taking jobs from "native Frenchmen" (*Français de souche*) and straining the welfare system. Another is the coming-of-age of the second generation (e.g., the second-generation Maghrebi *Beurs* in the 1980s) and third generation of "immigrant" offspring and, with it, the undeniable reality that France has become a multicultural society—one in which younger members of the so-called *minorités visibles*, the children and grandchildren of immigrants, are as French as anyone else their age but no longer willing to relegate their roots, religious and cultural heritage, and hyphenated identities to the discrete precincts of private life. Another factor is the rise and influence of National Front party (now called the National Rally, or RN), which also dates from the 1980s. While the right-wing nationalist party has never had significant electoral success, its hard line on immigration and xenophobic rhetoric about a loss of French national identity due to unassimilated foreigners have found an echo, albeit in a somewhat more muted form, in French political discourse beyond the party. For example, the 2022 presidential campaign platform of the RN's Marine Le Pen included proposals to hold a national referendum on immigration and to restrict foreigners' access to welfare and other government subsidies and services. Finally, there has been considerable unease, much of it unfounded, about the extent to which Islam—the religion of many recent immigrants from the Maghreb and the rest of Africa—is compatible with the secular tradition of French Republic.

The Republic is thought to integrate individuals, not communities. It does not require total cultural assimilation (i.e., there is more than one way to be French), but civic integration. Hence, from a republican perspective, the individual right to be different (*le droit à la différence*), which may include racial identity and religious or ethnic heritage, is respected (esp. as an essentially private matter); however, the concept of multiculturalism (i.e., public recognition of society's cultural pluralism in general and of the cultural specificity and rights of minority groups in particular), tends to be considered an Anglo-American import and associated with fractious "communitarianism" (*le communautarisme*), and is therefore viewed with suspicion. On the other hand, the story of the nation's diversity (incl. that diversity's more problematic and traumatic historical antecedents, like slavery and colonialism) is now being more thoughtfully incorporated into the discourses of collective memory—as can be seen in a number of high-profile newer cultural institutions, like the Arab World Institute (Paris); the National Museum of the History of Immigration (Paris); Mucem, the Museum of Civilizations of Europe and the Mediterranean (Marseille), Memorial ACTe (Pointe-à-Pitre, Guadeloupe, focusing on slavery); and artist Kader Attia's café and postcolonial cultural venue, ~~La Colonie~~ (Paris, 2016–2020).

See also: Chapter 1: Overseas France; Population. Chapter 3: Far Right; Republic. Chapter 5: Overview; Islam; Judaism. Chapter 6: Arabs; Blacks; Refugee Crisis; Suburbs. Chapter 9: Regional and Minority Languages, Dialects, and Varieties of French.

Further Reading

Benson (2013); Freedman (2004); Hargreaves (2007); Noiriel (1996); Sayad (2004); Shain (2008); Ticktin (2011).

HATE SPEECH LAWS

Notwithstanding its strong traditions of freedom of expression and of the press, France has restrictions on hate speech unlike anything in the United States. There are four principal legal restrictions of this nature that are punishable by law, including when the speech occurs on the internet:

1. Public provocation of hatred, violence or racial discrimination (the original statute dates from 1972 but has been revised to include hate speech based on gender, sexual orientation, and disability);
2. Public defamation on the grounds of an actual or assumed membership or nonmembership in a specific ethnic group, nation, race, or religion;
3. Public slander on the grounds of an actual or assumed affiliation (or nonaffiliation) with a specific ethnic group, nation, race, or religion; and
4. Disputing the veracity of recognized crimes against humanity as defined by the Nuremburg Charter (incl. the Holocaust).

Additionally, one may be prosecuted for incitement to terrorism or public justification of terrorism (including praising specific acts of terrorism or idealizing their goals or their methods). National Front founder Jean-Marie Le Pen, controversial standup comic Dieudonné M'balla M'balla, and cultural commentator and 2022 presidential candidate Éric Zemmour are among the prominent public figures convicted of offenses under these statutes. Novelist Michel Houellebecq was acquitted on charges stemming from derogatory remarks about Islam.

Income Distribution and Inequality

Like other wealthy developed countries, France has its share of both very affluent individuals and families and people struggling to make ends meet or living precariously—including the working poor, the long-term and chronically unemployed, people without marketable skills or diplomas who are more susceptible to layoffs and economic downturns, individuals whose economic disadvantages are compounded by substance abuse and poor health, vulnerable migrants and undocumented immigrants, and homeless people. There is considerable anxiety in France about rising levels of inequality and precariousness. However, France does better than many peer nations in the developed world in terms of both poverty rates and income inequality. According to OECD statistics (2017), its overall poverty rate—the percentage of people whose income falls below the poverty line (half the national median household income)—of 8.1% is lower than that of the United States (17.8%), the United Kingdom (11.1%), and Germany (10.1%). Its poverty rate (OECD) for 2019 was slightly higher, 8.4%. In 2016, its Gini coefficient—an indicator expressed by a numerical value between 0 and 1 that factors in five different variables measuring income inequality—was 0.29, the same as Germany, but better than both the United States (0.39) and the United Kingdom (0.35). Its Gini coefficient in 2019 was the same. It fares better than the other three countries in terms of the ratio of the average income of the 20% richest to the 20% poorest (S80/S20): 4.4, compared to 8.5 for the United States, 6.0 for the United Kingdom, and 4.5 for Germany. According to the World Inequality Report (World Inequality Lab, 2018), the top 10% of French owned 55% of the nation's wealth; the top 1% owned 23%; and the top 0.01% owned 3%—the comparable statistics for the United States were 77%, 42%, and 11%, respectively. The average household net adjusted disposable income in France (OECD 2017) is $31,304 (slightly below the OECD average of $33,604); and the average household wealth is $280,604 (considerably lower than the OECD average of $409,880).

The reasons for France's comparatively lower rates of poverty and income inequality in spite of its lower average levels of household income and wealth include its high level of investment in public goods and services and high rate of social spending (31.5% of the GDP in 2016, compared to 19.3% for the United States, 21.5% for the United Kingdom, and 25.3% for Germany), including spending on family benefits. Indeed, the French are proud of and favor preserving the Republic's distinct social model, which also includes quality universal healthcare, accessible public transportation, and public universities that practice open admissions and charge only nominal tuition fees. Another example of the French republican emphasis on solidarity is the Revenu de Solidarité Active (RSA), or Active Solidarity Income, a benefit that is designed to help both the unemployed (e.g., those who have used up their unemployment benefits) and the underemployed (people in very low-wage jobs). The monthly RSA benefit decreases as the income from work increases. Single individuals lose RSA eligibility once they make the annual minimum wage. The benefit is higher for single parents and couples with children and varies according to the number of dependents in the household. At the other end of the spectrum, France has close to 2.2 million millionaires ($ USD) according to Crédit Suisse (2019)—ranking sixth among the nations of the world; and 38 billionaires according to Forbes (2019)—tied for eleventh in the world. According to OECD economists Laurence Boone and Antoine Goujard (2019) the real French inequality problem does not reside in income inequality per se. It resides in the fact that there has been virtually no increase in the average income of the bottom 20% of the population between 2008 and 2016. An even bigger problem for France, they say, is a very high level of intergenerational inequality of opportunity, which is exacerbated by the inherent weaknesses and biases of its educational system. They estimate that it takes six generations for a person at the bottom end of the income distribution to reach the mean—the second highest rate in the OECD (trailing only Hungary; the U.S. rate was five generations).

See also: Chapter 3: Protests. Chapter 4: Social Security and Healthcare; Unemployment. Chapter 6: Immigration; Poverty and Homelessness; Suburbs; Working Class. Chapter 10: Social Hierarchies.

Further Reading

Bozio et al. (2018); Frémeaux and Piketty (2014); Guilluy (2019); Jetten et al. (2020); Piketty (2018); Pinçon and Pinçon-Charlot (1996); Smith (2004).

Nobility

The French nobility, or aristocracy, is comprised of the descendants of the privileged classes of feudal and prerevolutionary (ancien régime) society and of people subsequently elevated to the nobility by any of the non-republican regimes of the nineteenth century (i.e., Bourbon Restoration, First Empire, July Monarchy, and Second Empire). The nobility has no legal status in France today. The titles and privileges of the old feudal and courtly aristocracy were first abolished in the early days of the French Revolution, on August 4, 1789—a decisive act that entailed the end of a centuries-old social hierarchy. Subsequently, many aristocrats were killed during the revolutionary period, including by guillotine during the Reign of Terror (1793–1794). However, Napoleon I established an imperial nobility in 1805 to honor those who had served the empire, and the old aristocracy was subsequently reestablished (without lands confiscated during the Revolution) by the restored monarchy. The privileges of all types of nobility were once again abolished in 1848, but hereditary titles were maintained and are still recognized today by the French government as honorary accessories to one's legal name (i.e., such titles no longer carry any special rights or privileges but are recorded in the civil registry, may be used publicly, and are listed on passports, etc.). A common misconception is that having the so-called nobiliary particle "de" in one's surname is a sign of noble ancestry. This is true only in 10% of the cases. On the other hand, there are people of verified noble descent without the particle in their names. Although estimates vary widely, there were perhaps 17,000 noble families before the French Revolution, but only 2,800 survived. Today, there are a little over 3,000 noble families in France representing perhaps 100,000 people (less than 0.2% of the population of France). The Association of Mutual Aid of the French Nobility (ANF, 1932) conducts genealogical research to verify the noble origins of people who apply for certification.

There were two main types of ancien régime nobility. The *noblesse d'épée*, or nobility of the sword, was the most ancient—in some cases tracing noble ancestry back to the time of the Frankish kings. These nobles were once an integral part of the feudal sociopolitical system. They swore fealty to the king and were required to serve him militarily (the so-called tax of blood). The most powerful had vassals of their own, owned vast seigneurial estates with imposing fortified châteaux, and had hereditary authority over the peasants of the surrounding area. They were exempt from paying most taxes to the king (e.g., the *taille*, a tax on property) but collected dues from their dependent peasants and made money off their land, on which others worked (they were forbidden to have a profession and engage in commerce). Members of the warrior caste (*bellatores* in Latin, or those who "fight"), they became more civilized over the centuries (e.g., the evolving concept of chivalry). The other main group, beginning in the fifteenth century, was the *noblesse de robe*, or nobility of the robe—people elevated to hereditary nobility by the king in compensation for civilian service to the crown or royal institutions such as the parlement courts. The sale of offices that carried with them hereditary nobility was a major (but unsustainable) source revenue for the monarchy. Other commoners (*roturiers*) bought their way into the aristocracy by acquiring seigneurial estates to which certain hereditary feudal rights and privileges were attached.

Today, some French nobles are members of the nation's political, economic, and social elite—including Parisian high society (*la société mondaine*). However, others quietly carry on family traditions in old country estates that are costly to maintain and are sometimes open to tourists; or they have simply blended into the mainstream of French society. Irrespective of the small size and current social position of the French aristocracy, aristocratic values have had a lasting impact on French civilization and still shape what it means to be a member of polite society today. These values include a strong sense of personal honor and family reputation, a corresponding sense of duty ("la noblesse oblige") to serve the greater good of society (e.g., in the military, diplomacy, other branches of government, the church, charitable and artistic organizations, etc.), the pursuit of prestige and grandeur, respect for social hierarchies and knowing one's place in them, impeccable manners and courteous behavior, cultural refinement, good taste and elegance in one's personal appearance and lifestyle, and excellence in the art of conversation. In early modern France, many members of the upper bourgeoisie aspired to join the aristocracy—Molière's famous play *The Bourgeois Gentleman* (1670) ridicules one pompous commoner's foolish attempt to do so. The highest military and civilian distinction in French society today is being made a member of the National Order of the Legion of Honor, which was founded in 1802 by Napoleon, who patterned it after a chivalrous order. Indeed, the first level of membership is that of "knight" (*chevalier*); the others are "officer," "commander," "grand officer," and bearer of the "grand cross." The president of the French Republic is the honorary grand master of the Legion of Honor.

See also: Chapter 2: Francis I and the Renaissance; Louis XIV and the Absolute Monarchy; Louis XVI and the End of the Ancien Régime; Napoleon Bonaparte (Napoleon I) and the First Empire. Chapter 6: Bourgeoisie and Middle Class. Chapter 10: Social Hierarchies; Social Importance of Good Manners. Chapter 12: Versailles.

Further Reading

Chaussinand-Nogaret (1985); Colchester (2011); Higgs (1987); Kuiper et al. (2015); MacKnight (2017); MacKnight (2018); Schalk (1986); Smith (2005).

Poverty and Homelessness

France is a wealthy country, but income inequality is less pronounced there than in many comparable countries. France spends a lot on social programs in the name of "solidarity" and has a comprehensive social safety net, universal healthcare, and a well-developed array of accessible public services. For these reasons, many people are surprised to learn that France also has a problem with poverty. According to recent statistics (2015) published by the National Institute of Statistics and Economic Studies (INSEE), there are 8.9 million poor people in France—defined in France as people living in households where the income is below 60% of the nation's median household income (the more common international metric is below 50% of median income). This number represents 14.2% of the population and an increase of 600,000 poor people compared to ten years before (12.6% of French people lived below the poverty line in 2004; 17.9% in 1970). In 2015, 3.4% of the population lived in severe poverty (below 40% of median household income).

Several factors are involved in these sobering statistics, including the lingering effects of the economic crisis of 2008, chronic high unemployment, and the severe social and economic handicap of leaving secondary school without a diploma (Bac, CAP, Brevet, etc.). Of the unemployed, 37.6% fall below the poverty line as opposed to 6.5% of the gainfully employed (France has an estimated 2 million working poor). Using the criterion of income less than 50% of median income, 33.2% of French adults without a secondary school diploma may be considered poor. INSEE also reports that there are higher rates of poverty among certain other demographic groups: 38.6% of members of immigrant households (44% of African immigrant households); 33% of people living in single-parent households; 25% of farmers and their dependents; 21% of artisans, shopkeepers, small business owners, and independent workers; and 20% of minors. By contrast, only 8% of retirees live below the poverty line—a figure considerably better than the over 30% of retirees in the 1970s. Another factor to be considered is that while the French government has multiple welfare and assistance programs, many of the poor do not utilize available forms of assistance. The aid organization Secours Catholique reports that 40% of people eligible to receive the RSA basic income supplement (a minimum revenue) do not collect it due to a failure to apply. Non-beneficiary rates are 31% among those who are eligible for family allocations and 23% among those eligible for housing allocations.

Homelessness is one of the most troublesome manifestations of poverty in France. The most recent comprehensive statistics, published by INSEE and the National Institute of Demographic Studies (INED), date from 2012. According to this report, there were 141,500 people without a permanent residence (*sans domicile fixe*, or SDF) in France that year, including 30,000 children. Of these, 50% were people of foreign origin; 40% were women; 25% were employed. The SDF category is rather broad insofar as it includes people who live transiently in hotels or with family members, people who rely on emergency housing provided by social services and charitable organizations, and people who spend the night in locations not meant for habitation (e.g., tents, subway stations, and the streets). This last category (*les sans-abri*, or those "without shelter") is considerably smaller: only about 13,000 according to the same report. On the other hand, the Fondation Abbé Pierre, a respected NGO named after a Catholic priest who was a lifelong advocate for the poor and homeless (Henri Grouès, 1912–2007), has reported (2017) that the total number of people in France who are either homeless or poorly/precariously housed is close to 4 million.

See also: Chapter 1: Overseas France. Chapter 4: Unemployment. Chapter 6: Income Distribution and Inequality; Suburbs; Working Class.

Further Reading
Allègre (2011); Gilbert and Parent (2017); Marpsat and Firdion (2004); Martin (2010).

Refugee Crisis

Beginning in 2014, spiking spectacularly in 2015, and continuing at a somewhat diminished pace in subsequent years, the EU faced an unprecedented crisis of migrants and asylum seekers attempting to enter the Schengen Area of free circulation by irregular means, many crossing stretches of the Mediterranean Sea in rickety craft. The migrant influx included large numbers of people fleeing civil war and violent persecution in Syria, Iraq, and Afghanistan, as well as political and economic refugees from sub-Saharan Africa, and an increase in the number of migrants from the Balkan region of southeastern Europe (e.g., Serbia, Kosovo, and Albania). Authorities characterized the crisis as part of the largest wave of refugees and displaced persons since the end of World War II. According to the office of the United Nations High Commissioner for Refugees (UNHCR), over 1,000,000 crossings were made in 2015, 362,000 in 2016, and 171,000 in 2017.

France did not have to deal with the influx of asylum seekers that Germany did—there were 110,000 asylum seekers in France in 2015, 86,000 in 2016, and 100,000 in 2017 (by contrast, Germany had 890,000 in 2015 alone). France was nonetheless one of the leading EU destinations for asylum seekers and was active both domestically and in EU diplomatic efforts to develop responses to the crisis. However, as is the case elsewhere in Europe, there was an anti-migrant sentiment in France, which conflicted with the country's reputation as a land of asylum and human rights. The French domestic approach was to improve conditions in which migrants were "welcomed" and to expedite the review of asylum applications while also taking a much tougher approach to the review process and to human trafficking of migrants to root out economic migrants without a legitimate claim to asylum. One of the most highly publicized aspects of the migrant crisis in France was the harsh living conditions and overcrowding in an illegal migrant camp near the city of Calais in northwest France known as the "Jungle"—a way station for migrants hoping to cross over into England. Dismantled in 2016, the camp had an estimated maximum population at one time ranging between 8,000 and 10,000. French NGOs like Doctors Without Borders were at the forefront of the humanitarian response to the international refugee crisis.

See also: Chapter 3: European Union. Chapter 6: Arabs; Blacks; Immigration.

Further Reading
Burgess (2019); Gattinara and Zamponi (2020); Ibrahim and Howarth (2016); McGee and Pelham (2018).

Senior Citizens and Elderly

The population of France is aging. There are now as many people over sixty as there are under twenty—24% of the total population. Of the total population, 9.2% is seventy-five or over. The mean age in France now stands at 41.4 and the median age at 40.5. By comparison, the median age was 34.9 in 1995. The average life expectancy in France is presently 79.5 for men, 85.3 for women (the gap between the two sexes is slowly closing), and 82.7 overall. In 1995, it was 77.8; and in 1970, 71.7. These trends are projected to continue becoming even more pronounced. According to a report by the French government's main statistics-gathering agency, INSEE, by the year 2050, 26.2% of the population will be sixty-five or over, compared to 18.4% in 2015. The aging of the French population presents a serious challenge for French social entitlement programs and raises questions about healthcare. It will also have a major impact on French society and culture in general. The sociologist Henri Mendras identified seniors—formerly called "third agers" (*le troisième âge*)—as one of the social groups (the others were farmers, women, and students) who were among the leaders and greatest beneficiaries of the period of profound sociocultural mutation that he called the "Second French Revolution" (1965–1984).

Being sixty years old in France today is not the same as it was a generation or two ago. If one has avoided serious illness in middle age and has had a relatively stable and decently paid working life, it often means that one is about to retire and embark on a period of twenty or more years of relative good health, leisure, and financial comfort before reaching a period of true old age, declining health, and dependency. Advertisers may still be obsessed with the youth market but cannot afford to ignore the fact that seniors now account for 50% of all consumer spending: they travel, take up hobbies, dine out, are big consumers of culture, and continue to spend money on stylish clothing and personal appearance. At sixty, one is likely to be surrounded by three other generations of one's family. Sunday dinners, holiday gatherings, and extended visits from grandchildren during the summer months are still culturally very important. One is usually not a financial burden on one's children. In fact, the opposite may be true, as many mature adults and younger seniors are called upon to provide financial assistance (if not a home) for a generation of younger adults (millennials and sometimes even middle-aged Gen Xers) who have found it harder to achieve financial, professional, and conjugal stability. On the other hand, some part of one's twenty years as a vigorous senior are more likely to be marked by care and concern for one's own aged parents. Today's French seniors are also more active in civic and cultural organizations and have greater political influence. For instance, close to one-third of all French mayors are seniors.

However, not all French seniors enjoy a life of relative comfort and freedom. Retired manual laborers tend to live almost ten years less on average than retired executives. Women who may have worked in less well-paid jobs are more likely to experience financial hardship after retirement due to insufficient pensions. There are also disparities across regions and between urban and rural seniors. In 2017, 436,000 people collected special welfare allocations for seniors—the "old age minimum income" or "supplemental invalidity allocations." Alzheimer's disease and dementia are serious healthcare issues among the elderly. Finally, experts predict that there will be 1.5 million dependent old people in France in ten to twenty years, compared to 1.1 million today—people who might not necessarily be able to count on family members for financial or emotional support.

See also: Chapter 1: Population. Chapter 4: Social Security and Healthcare. Chapter 7: Kinship and Family Structures.

Further Reading
Béland et al. (2013); Comité Consultatif National d'Ethique (2018); Desplanques (2005); Keller (2015).

Suburbs

"La banlieue" signifies the suburbs around French cities. It comprises both densely populated and highly urbanized areas closer to the outskirts of the city and peri-urban and quasi-rural areas farther away. The suburban landscape includes the remnants of older villages and towns with august nineteenth-century town halls and quaint cafés, massive concrete housing complexes built in the 1960s and 1970s (*les cités*), industrial parks, shopping zones with big-box chain retailers, transportation infrastructures (e.g., airports, highways, and commuter rail stations) that serve the central city, and bedroom community-type residential areas of single-family cottages (*zones pavillonnaires*). Essentially, these suburbs contain all the features of modern urban life that could not be squeezed into France's already densely built up and still mostly attractive cities. While some of the suburbs began to develop in the late nineteenth and early twentieth centuries (e.g., in the *petite couronne*, or first ring around Paris, including the Communist-voting working-class "red suburbs"), they grew spectacularly throughout the period known as the "Glorious Thirty" (1945–1975), during which rapid economic expansion fueled an influx of workers from rural areas and immigrants from other European countries (e.g., Italy, Spain, and Portugal) and overseas (e.g., former French territories in North and sub-Saharan Africa). The most immediate result of this growth was an acute housing crisis. In the 1950s and early 1960s, there were shantytowns in forlorn pockets near cities like Paris, home to some of the neediest of the working poor. The response was a massive housing building boom that included drab modern "rabbit-cage" apartment buildings in tower blocks on large, planned housing estates. These enclaves had basic amenities (e.g., schools, community centers, supermarkets, and green spaces) but were built on the cheap, surrounded by parking lots, poorly served by public transportation, and not well integrated into the surrounding metropolitan area. Many of the apartment buildings were subsidized, rent-controlled *habitations à loyer modéré*, or HLM. Famous examples in the Greater Paris region include Les Lochères in Sarcelles (Val-d'Oise department), La Cité des 4000 in La Courneuve (Seine-Saint-Denis department), and La Grande Borne in Grigny (Essonne department). These areas were originally working class and lower middle class but gradually became grittier and had higher concentrations of poor immigrant minorities, as those who could leave, left.

Not all French suburbs, nor HLMs, are problematic. However, the negative perception became a topic of discussion almost immediately. Concern about ghettoization of the *cités* intensified in the 1980s—a period of economic downturn and high unemployment that coincided with the coming-of-age of the immigrant second generation, an uptick in crime and juvenile delinquency (e.g., impromptu "rodeos" with stolen cars that were sometimes later burned), racial stereotyping of minorities, and the physical dilapidation of many HLMs. Relations between minority youths and the police in the suburban *cités* deteriorated and civil unrest there became more common, often prompted by police encounters marked by excessive use of force. This unrest and anger was the subject of director Matthieu Kassovitz's now-classic 1995 *banlieue* film, *La Haine* ("Hate"), and of the similarly themed and critically acclaimed 2019 film, *Les Misérables*, directed by Ladj Ly. In 2005, a police incident that led to the accidental deaths of two minority teenagers, Zyed Benna and Bouna Traoré, in the Paris suburb of Clichy-sous-Bois led to a nationwide wave of rioting (or "uprising") that lasted three weeks and resulted in the declaration of a state of emergency. The government response to the unrest, which included both reinforced policing and spending for social programs, has produced mixed results. Conditions are still challenging, and tensions high in many pockets of the French suburbs, including the 1,500 designated socioeconomically deprived and high-crime areas known as Urban Policy Priority Districts. It is important to stress that these areas are not "no-go zones," as some have suggested. Furthermore, many parts of France's multicultural suburbs are both calm and vibrant and have produced a highly influential and ingenious *banlieue* culture that ranges from hip-hop and fashion to film and literature.

See also: Chapter 1: Cities; Paris. Chapter 2: Sarkozy (Nicolas) and the Hyper Presidency. Chapter 3: Protests. Chapter 4: Unemployment. Chapter 5: Islam. Chapter 6: Arabs; Blacks; Immigration; Income Distribution and Inequality; Working Class. Chapter 12: Modern Architecture. Chapter 13: Rock, Pop, and Rap.

Further Reading
Carpenter (2018); Cartier et al. (2016); Cupers (2014); Dikec (2007); Fassin (2013); Moran (2012); Slooter (2019); Tetreault (2015); Wacquant and Howe (2008).

Working Class

The third order of medieval feudal society, or third estate, always contained a share of manual laborers working in cities, towns, and villages in nonagricultural occupations. By the time of the French Revolution, thanks to the growth of large workshops, a proto-working class already existed in France. This segment of society grew considerably in both numbers and class consciousness with the acceleration of the pace of industrialization and the advent of the factory system in France during the nineteenth century. During this time, many peasants left their homes in the country to take jobs in factories near French cities and in the industrial areas of north, northeast, and Rhône Valley. With industrialization came a heightened awareness on the part of workers of their exploitation at the hands of their bosses and growing frustration with the questions of social justice left unresolved by the French Revolution. Subsequent revolutions (the July Revolution of 1830, the Revolution of 1848, and the Paris Commune of 1871) were just as disappointing for French workers. Deservedly or not, workers had a reputation of being prone to insurrection and animosity toward the bourgeoisie and the state, which they did not trust to protect their rights and interests. In return, the bourgeoisie feared the so-called dangerous classes. There was nonetheless more room for compromise in the latter part of the nineteenth century and first half of the twentieth century as workers were given the right to vote (1848, universal suffrage for men), strike (1864), and form labor unions (1884)—although strikes could still turn into violent encounters. In response to the electoral victory of the leftist Popular Front coalition in 1936, striking workers pressed their advantage and obtained other concessions and rights, including the forty-hour workweek, collective bargaining, and two weeks' paid vacation. A decade later, the Provisional Government of the French Republic under Charles de Gaulle (with support and pressure from the French Communist Party) laid the foundation for France's current system of social security at the close of World War II. However, the French working class benefited perhaps most of all from the sustained economic expansion and rising standard of living that occurred during the thirty-year period (1945–1975) of the Glorious Thirty.

By comparison, the past thirty years have not been as kind to the French working class. Changes to the global (competition from low-wage countries) and French economies have meant the closure of numerous factories and a drastic decline in the share of industrial manufacturing and related activities in the French employment market and GDP—11% of the workforce and 10% of the GDP—half the levels in 1970. Unemployment increased dramatically and has been chronically high. The national unemployment rate was below 4% in 1975; whereas it has been mostly above 8% since the mid-1980s, was at or above 10% in 2015–2016, and was still above 9% in early 2018 before dipping markedly to 7.4% in the final quarter of 2021. In response to economic uncertainty and strict labor laws long perceived as a deterrent to private sector job creation, employers have tended to offer jobseekers precarious short-duration, fixed-term contracts instead of open-ended contracts with more job security. Meanwhile, politicians have, under pressure from financial markets and the EU to limit government expenditure and public debt, reformed the welfare state and social entitlements and adopted more pro-business policies—measures that might prove beneficial in the long run but have not yet provided a boost to the unemployed, underemployed, or unskilled workers most adversely affected by economic change. This has resulted in mistrust toward the political and economic elite and, increasingly, the EU and "foreigners." One concrete result has been a political shift among working-class voters from the left to the far right (e.g., the national-populist National Rally).

The French working class has a rich cultural heritage. Its values include solidarity and mutual aid; the strategic and tactical value of strikes, protest, and organized movements (incl. labor unions like the CGT and the CFDT); and enduring enmity for "big money" and politicians who spout shallow promises in intelligent-sounding double-talk (known as *la langue de bois*, or wooden language). While the lifestyle, consumption habits, and pop culture tastes of the working class are now quite similar to those of the lower and central tiers of the middle class, there is still a nostalgic attachment to humble pastimes (*loisirs populaires*) like *boules* (a bocce-like game also called *pétanque*) and a glass of anise-flavored pastis after work, at the "zinc" counter of a neighborhood café or bistro. Certain places, people, and things have enduring symbolic value for French workers—heroes like the early twentieth-century Socialist leader Jean Jaurès and the *métallos* (metal and steel workers) and *cheminots* (rail workers) whose labor movement exploits serve as a source of inspiration even for today's office workers; places like the Communards' Wall (Mur des Fédérés) in Père Lachaise Cemetery (the site of a massacre of insurgents during the Paris Commune) and the former "red suburbs" (working-class PCF-voting bastions) that once formed a sort of ring around Paris; and the symbolism of the Socialist hymn, "The Internationale," and of the iconic bright blue overalls and smocks worn by workers known as *bleus de travail*.

See also: Chapter 2: Timeline; Napoleon III and the Second Empire. Chapter 3: Far Right; Left; Protests. Chapter 4: Labor Relations; Social Security and Healthcare; Unemployment. Chapter 6: Immigration; Income Distribution and Inequality; Suburbs. Chapter 10: Social Hierarchies; Workplace Etiquette and Customer Relations.

Further Reading

Gadrey et al. (2006); Gilbert (2017); Kaplan and Koepp (1986); Lamont (2000); Lash (1984); McGraw (1992); Perrot (1986); Ray and Rojot (2015); Steinhouse (2001).

SELECTED BIBLIOGRAPHY

Allègre, Guillaume. "France: In-Work Poor or Poor Due to Lack of Work?" *Working Poverty in Europe. Work and Welfare in Europe*, eds. Neil Fraser, et al. Palgrave Macmillan, 2011, pp. 93–111.

Amselle, Jean-Loup. *Affirmative Exclusion: Cultural Pluralism and the Rule of Custom in France*. Trans. Jane Marie Todd. Cornell UP, 2003.

Bass, Loretta. *African Immigrant Families in Another France*. Palgrave Macmillan, 2014.

Beaman, Jean. "Are French People White?: Towards an Understanding of Whiteness in Republican France." *Identities*, vol. 26, no. 5, 2019, pp. 546–562.

Beaman, Jean. *Citizen Outsider: Children of North African Immigrants in France*. U California P, 2017.

Begag, Azouz. *Ethnicity and Equality: France in the Balance*. Trans. Alec G. Hargreaves. U Nebraska P, 2007.

Béland, Daniel, et al. "Aging in France: Population Trends, Policy Issues, and Research Institutions." *The Gerontologist*, vol. 53, no. 2, 2013, pp. 191–197.

Ben Jelloun, Tahar. *French Hospitality: Racism and North African Immigrants*. Trans. Barbara Bray. Columbia UP, 1999.

Benson, Rodney. *Shaping Immigration News: A French-American Comparison*. Cambridge UP, 2013.

Beriss, David. *Black Skins, French Voices: Caribbean Ethnicity and Activism in Urban France*. Routledge, 2019.

Bidou-Zachariasen, Catherine. "The Rise of the 'Middle Classes' or the Moyennisation of Society in Contemporary France: A Difficult Debate." *European and Chinese Sociologies: A New Dialogue*, eds. Laurence Roulleau-Berger and Peilin Li. Brill, 2011, pp. 127–136.

Blanchard, Pascal. "The Paradox of Arab France." *The Cairo Review of Global Affairs*, no. 21, 2016, pp. 62–71.

Boltanski, Luc. *The Making of a Class: Cadres in French Society*. Trans. Arthur Goldhammer. Cambridge UP, 1987.

Bourdieu, Pierre. *Distinction: A Social Critique of the Judgement of Taste*. Trans. Richard Nice. Harvard UP, 1984.

Bourdieu, Pierre. *The State Nobility: Elite Schools in the Field of Power*. Trans. Lauretta C. Clough. Stanford UP, 1996.

Bozio, Antoine, et al. "Inequality and Redistribution in France, 1990–2018: Evidence from Post-Tax Distributional National Accounts (DINA)." World Inequality Database Working Paper Series, no. 2018/10, 2018, https://wid.world/document/inequality-and-redistribution-in-france-1990-2018-evidence-from-post-tax-distributional-national-accounts-dina-wid-world-working-paper-2018-10/.

Burgess, Greg. *Refugees and the Promise of Asylum in Postwar France, 1945–1995*. Palgrave Macmillan, 2019.

Carpenter, Juliet. "The French Banlieue: Renovating the Suburbs." *The Routledge Companion to the Suburbs*, eds. Bernadette Hanlon and Thomas J. Vicino. Routledge, 2018, pp. 254–265.

Cartier, Marie, et al. *The France of the Little-Middles: A Suburban Housing Development in Greater Paris*. Trans. Juliette Radcliffe Rogers. Berghahn, 2016.

Chapman, Herrick, and Laura L. Frader, eds. *Race in France: Interdisciplinary Perspectives on the Politics of Difference*. Berghahn, 2004.

Chaussinand-Nogaret, Guy. *The French Nobility in the Eighteenth Century: From Feudalism to Enlightenment*. Trans. Willam Doyle. Cambridge UP, 1985.

Colchester, Max. "What's a Poor French Noble to Do without a King to Call His Own?" *The Wall Street Journal*, 5 Oct. 2011, https://www.wsj.com/articles/SB100014240531119 037036045765886715052108.

Collins, Lauren. "Assa Traoré and the Fight for Black Lives in France." *The New Yorker*, 18 Jun. 2020, https://www.newyorker.com/news/letter-from-europe/assa-traore-and-the-fight-for-black-lives-in-france.

Comité Consultatif National d'Ethique. "The Ethical Issues of Aging." Opinion no. 128, 15 Feb. 2018, https://www.ccne-ethique.fr/sites/default/files/publications/ccne_avis_12 8eng.pdf.

Cupers, Kenny. *The Social Project: Housing Postwar France*. U Minnesota P, 2014.

Derderian, Richard. *North Africans in Contemporary France: Becoming Visible*. Palgrave Macmillan, 2004.

Desplanques, Guy. "The Elderly Population in France." *Retraite et société*, vol. 45, no. 2, 2005, pp. 9–21.

Dikeç, Mustafa. *Badlands of the Republic: Space, Politics and Urban Policy.* Wiley-Blackwell, 2007.

Dobbernack, Jan. *The Politics of Social Cohesion in Germany, France and the United Kingdom.* Palgrave Macmillan, 2014.

Fassin, Didier. *Enforcing Order: An Ethnography of Urban Policing.* Trans. Rachel Gomme. Wiley, 2013.

Forsé, Michel, et al. *Recent Social Trends in France, 1960–1990.* Trans. Liam Gavin. Campus Verlag & McGill-Queen's UP, 1993.

Freedman, Jane. *Immigration and Insecurity in France.* Routledge, 2004.

Frémeaux, Nicolas, and Thomas Piketty. "France: How Taxation Can Increase Inequality." *Changing Inequalities and Societal Impacts in Rich Countries: Thirty Countries' Experiences,* eds. Brian Nolan, et al. Oxford UP, 2014, pp. 248–270.

Gadrey, Nicole, et al. "The Working Conditions of Blue-Collar and White-Collar Workers in France Compared: A Question of Time." *Decent Working Time: New Trends, New Issues,* eds. Jean-Yves Boulin, et al. International Labour Office, 2006, pp. 265–287.

Gattinara, Pietro Castelli, and Lorenzo Zamponi. "Politicizing Support and Opposition to Migration in France: the EU Asylum Policy Crisis and Direct Social Activism." *Journal of European Integration,* vol. 42, no. 5, 2020, pp. 625–641.

Germain, Félix, and Silyane Larcher, eds. *Black French Women and the Struggle for Equality, 1848–2016.* U Nebraska P, 2018.

Gilbert, Neil, and Antoine Parent, eds. *Welfare Reform: A Comparative Assessment of the French and U. S. Experiences.* New ed. Routledge, 2017; esp. ch. 10 ("Growth and Poverty in France").

Gilbert, Pierre. "The Working Classes in Contemporary France." *Books & Ideas,* Collège de France, 19 Oct. 2017, https://booksandideas.net/The-Working-Classes-in-Contemporary-France.html.

Guilluy, Christophe. *Twilight of the Elites: Prosperity, the Periphery, and the Future of France.* Trans. M. B. DeBevoise. Yale UP, 2019.

Hargreaves, Alec G. *Multi-Ethnic France: Immigration, Politics, Culture and Society.* 2nd ed. Routledge, 2007.

Higgs, David. *Nobles in Nineteenth-century France: The Practice of Inegalitarianism.* Johns Hopkins UP, 1987.

Hussey, Andrew. *The French Intifada: The Long War between France and Its Arabs.* Granta, 2014.

Ibrahim, Yasmin, and Anita Howarth. "Imaging the Jungles of Calais: Media Visuality and the Refugee Camp." *Networking Knowledge,* vol. 9, no. 4, 2016, https://doi.org/10.31165/nk.2016.94.446.

Jetten, Jolanda, et al. "How Economic Inequality Fuels the Rise and Persistence of the Yellow Vest Movement." *International Review of Social Psychology,* vol. 33, no. 1, art. 2, 2020, http://doi.org/10.5334/irsp.356.

Kaplan, Steven L., and Cynthia J. Koepp, eds. *Work in France: Representations, Meaning, Organization, and Practice.* Cornell UP, 1986.

Keaton, et al., eds. *Black France / France Noire: The History and Politics of Blackness*. Duke UP, 2012.

Keller, Richard C. *Fatal Isolation: The Devastating Paris Heat Wave of 2003*. U Chicago P, 2015.

Killian, Caitlin. *North African Women in France: Gender, Culture, and Identity*. Stanford UP, 2006.

Kleppinger, Kathryn, and Laura Reeck, eds. *Post-Migratory Cultures in Postcolonial France*. Liverpool UP, 2018

Kuiper, Yme, et al., eds. *Nobilities in Europe in the Twentieth Century: Reconversion Strategies, Memory, Culture, and Elite Formation*. Peeters, 2015.

Lash, Scott. *The Militant Worker: Class and Radicalism in France and America*. Fairleigh Dickinson UP, 1984.

Lamont, Michèle. *The Dignity of Working Men: Morality and the Boundaries of Race, Class, and Immigration*. Rev. ed. Harvard UP, 2000.

Lamont, Michèle. *Money, Morals, and Manners: The Culture of the French and the American Upper-Middle Class*. U Chicago P, 1992.

Le Wita, Béatrix. *French Bourgeois Culture*. Trans. J.A. Underwood. Cambridge UP, 1994.

MacKnight, Elizabeth C. *Aristocratic Families in Republican France, 1870–1940*. Manchester UP, 2017.

MacKnight, Elizabeth C. *Nobility and Patrimony in Modern France*. Manchester UP, 2018.

MacMaster, Neil. *Colonial Migrants and Racism: Algerians in France, 1900–62*. Macmillan, 1997.

Marpsat, Maryse, and Jean-Marie Firdion. "France" and "Paris." *Encyclopedia of Homelessness*, ed. David Levinson. Sage, 2004, 2 vols. pp. 171–175, 441–445.

Martin, Claude. "Feminization of Poverty in France: A Latent Issue." *Poor Women in Rich Countries: The Feminization of Poverty over the Life Course*, ed. Gertrude Schaffner Goldberg. Oxford UP, 2010, pp. 61–93.

Maza, Sarah. *The Myth of the French Bourgeoisie: An Essay on the Social Imaginary, 1750–1850*. Harvard UP, 2003.

McGee, Darragh, and Juliette Pelham. "Politics at Play: Locating Human Rights, Refugees and Grassroots Humanitarianism in the Calais Jungle." *Leisure Studies*, vol. 37, no. 1, 2018, pp. 22–35.

McGonagle, Joseph. *Representing Ethnicity in Contemporary French Visual Culture*. Manchester UP, 2017.

McGraw, Roger. *A History of the French Working Class*. Blackwell, 1992, 2 vols.

Mendras, Henri, and Alistair Cole. *Social Change in Modern France: Towards a Cultural Anthropology of the Fifth Republic*. Cambridge UP, 1991.

Mercat-Bruns, Marie. *Discrimination at Work Comparing European, French, and American Law*. Trans. Elaine Hultz. U California P, 2016.

Moran, Matthew. *The Republic and the Riots: Exploring Urban Violence in French Suburbs. 2005–2007*. Lang, 2012.

Noiriel, Gérard. *The French Melting Pot: Immigration, Citizenship, and National Identity*. Trans. Geoffroy de Laforcade. U Minnesota P, 1996.

Onishi, Norimitsu. "Will American Ideas Tear France Apart? Some of Its Leaders Think So." *New York Times*, 9 Feb. 2021, https://www.nytimes.com/2021/02/09/world/europe/france-threat-american-universities.html.

Peabody, Sue, and Tyler Stovall, eds. *The Color of Liberty: Histories of Race in France*. Duke UP, 2003.

Pech, Thierry. "Two Hundred Years of the Middle Class in France (1789–2010)." *L'Économie politique*, vol. 49, no. 1, 2011, pp. 69–97.

Perrot, Michelle. "On the Formation of the French Working Class." *Working-Class Formation: Nineteenth-Century Patterns in Western Europe and the United States*, eds. Ira Katznelson and Aristide R. Zolberg. Princeton UP, 1986, pp. 71–110.

Piketty, Thomas. *Top Incomes in France in the Twentieth Century: Inequality and Redistribution, 1901–1998*. Trans. Seth Ackerman. Belknap, 2018.

Pinçon, Michel, and Monique Pinçon-Charlot. *Grand Fortunes: Dynasties and Forms of Wealth in France*. Trans. Andrea Sengstacken. Algora, 1996.

Pinçon-Charlot, Monique, and Michel Pinçon. "Social Power and Power over Space: How the Bourgeoisie Reproduces Itself in the City." *International Journal of Urban and Regional Research*, vol. 42, no. 1, 2018, pp. 115–125.

Ray, Jean-Emmanuel, and Rojot, Jacques. "The Fissured Workplace in France." *Comparative Labor Law & Policy Journal*, vol. 37, no. 1, 2015, pp. 163–180.

Sayad, Abdelmalek. *The Suffering of the Immigrant*. Trans. David Macey. Polity, 2004.

Schalk, Ellery. *From Valor to Pedigree: Ideas of Nobility in France in the Sixteenth and Seventeenth Centuries*. Princeton UP, 1986.

Schwartz, Olivier. "Does France Still Have a Class Society?: Three Observations about Contemporary French Society." *Books & Ideas*, Collège de France, 3 Mar. 2014, https://booksandideas.net/Does-France-Still-Have-a-Class.html.

Seigel, Jerrold. *Modernity and Bourgeois Life: Society, Politics, and Culture in England, France and Germany since 1750*. Cambridge UP, 2012.

Shain, Martin. *The Politics of Immigration in France, Britain, and the United States: A Comparative Study*. Palgrave Macmillan, 2008.

Silverstein, Paul A. *Algeria in France: Transpolitics, Race, and Nation*. Indiana UP, 2004.

Silverstein, Paul A. *Postcolonial France: The Question of Race and the Future of the Republic*. Pluto, 2018.

Slooter, Luuk. *The Making of the Banlieue: An Ethnography of Space, Identity and Violence*. Palgrave Macmillan, 2019.

Smith, Jay M. *Nobility Reimagined: The Patriotic Nation in Eighteenth-Century France*. Cornell UP, 2005.

Smith, Timothy B. *France in Crisis: Welfare, Inequality, and Globalization since 1980*. Cambridge UP, 2004.

Steinhouse, Adam. *Workers' Participation in Post-liberation France*. Lexington, 2001.

Suleiman, Ezra N. *Elites in French Society: The Politics of Survival*. Princeton UP, 1978.

Tetreault, Chantal. *Transcultural Teens: Performing Youth Identities in French Cités*. Wiley, 2015.

Thomas, Dominic. *Africa and France: Postcolonial Cultures, Migration, and Racism*. Indiana UP, 2013.

Thomas, Dominic. *Black France: Colonialism, Immigration, and Transnationalism*. Indiana UP, 2007.

Ticktin, Miriam I. *Casualties of Care: Immigration and the Politics of Humanitarianism in France*. U California P, 2011.

Tshimanga, Charles, et al., eds. *Frenchness and the African Diaspora: Identity and Uprising in Contemporary France*. Indiana UP, 2009.

Wacquant, Loïc, and John Howe. *Urban Outcasts: A Comparative Sociology of Advanced Marginality*. Polity, 2008.

Weil, Patrick. *How to Be French: Nationality in the Making since 1789*. Trans. Catherine Porter. Duke UP, 2008.

CHAPTER 7

GENDER, SEXUALITY, MARRIAGE, AND FAMILY

OVERVIEW

Family is an extremely important concept in France. Well into the twentieth century, it was the overarching structure of one's life and value system and its interests far outweighed those of the individual. Moreover, despite regional variations—especially between the north and the south—in customs regarding marriage, kinship, inheritance, and household living arrangements, French families were patterned after the French royal house. They were multigenerational lines ruled by the male head of the household—or family patriarch—like an absolute monarch. Indeed, the father's authority and predominance in the family were written into the Napoleonic Civil Code of 1804 and were only diminished—that is, shared more equally with the mother—beginning in the late 1930s. A French family was also traditionally part of an extended network of grandparents, uncles, cousins, other relatives, and in-laws usually living in close proximity. Family gatherings, dinners, and paying one's respect to relatives were strict rituals. A number of societal trends dating back to the eighteenth century and intensified over the past sixty years have altered traditional family and kinship structures, like the modern notion of marriage for love instead of material advantage and family alliances, middle-class emphasis on the nuclear family, urbanization and greater mobility, greater equality for women and their joining the workforce in large numbers, declining marriage rates and rising divorce rates, declining birth rates (esp. with birth control) and smaller family sizes, longer life expectancy (making grandparents and even great-grandparents a regular part of one's life), declining religious practice and the sexual revolution of the 1960s and 1970s, individualism, consumerism, and advances in communication. Some 44% of all marriages now end in divorce. Single-parent families make up close to 25% of all family households, and blended families close to 10%. As many as 60% of children in France are currently born out of wedlock. Nonetheless, the family has retained its importance in French society. Evening dinners shared by the nuclear family unit and gatherings of the extended family on weekends and special occasions are still highly valued. The family has been recast as a nurturing and egalitarian framework that is essential to individual development and fulfillment. Furthermore, it remains a crucial safety net for its members in times of need—including, increasingly, for younger adults who take longer and have more difficulty "establishing" themselves "on their own" in an age of economic precariousness.

There is an overall trend toward fewer marriages in France; both the total number of marriages per year and the marriage rate have been steadily declining since 1970 (e.g., there were 3.6 new marriages per 1,000 inhabitants in 2016, compared to 7.8 in 1970), and people are getting married at a later age (the average age for a first marriage for men in 2017 was thirty-eight, compared to twenty-six in 1975; for women it was thirty-six, compared to twenty-four earlier). Marriage is no longer seen as the necessary final status of a couple. Since 2000, both different and same-sex couples have been able to contract a civil union. In 2016, there were 190,000 new civil unions formed, compared to 220,000 marriages. Most couples begin their lives together in cohabitation. More and more choose to stay this way. The French call this *l'union libre*, a freer form of union that is now widely accepted by society. Overall, 45% of all French committed couples forming households are married, 30% are in civil unions, and 25% are in state of *union libre*. Same-sex marriage was legalized in France in 2013. In the first five years since the law was passed, 30,000 same-sex marriages were celebrated in France.

French parents tend to be stern disciplinarians, especially with younger children (spanking and other forms of physical punishment used to be common) because they expect them to know how to behave in the adult world (e.g., know the rules of polite behavior) and are flattered when their children are complimented as *bien élévés*— literally, "well raised." Supporting families, in particular those in need, is a policy priority of the French government. This public commitment is demonstrated in the wide array of family benefits (*allocations familiales*) that constitute one of the main components of France's Social Security system, its generous paid parental leave policies, its strong support for early childhood education (nearly 100% of three-year-olds are in school), and the fact that there is regularly a cabinet-level position dedicated to families and children. Oral contraceptives have been legal in France since 1967, and abortion since 1975 (on demand up to fourteen weeks following conception and, with medical justification, in later stages in cases where pregnancy represents a serious health risk to the mother or the fetus has a grave and incurable condition). Both are covered by national health insurance. Previously, medically assisted procreation treatments were available only to different-sex couples. However, the law was changed in 2021 to make such treatments available to all women, including single women and women in same-sex unions. Surrogacy is against the law for in France.

France's reputation as a nation of lovers may be a somewhat hackneyed stereotype, but there is a highly developed notion of gallantry dating back to the medieval courtly love tradition and a generally liberal attitude toward sex dating back to the eighteenth-century libertines (e.g., amorous scenes depicted by Fragonard and the erotic literature of the Marquis de Sade). Today, France's liberal attitudes toward sexuality, which became even stronger in the decades after May 1968, can be seen in its widespread public acceptance of cohabitation, homosexuality, same-sex marriage (three-fourths of the public expressed acceptance of the second and two-thirds acceptance of the third when the 2013 "marriage for all" law was passed), public displays of affection, birth control counseling and availability of contraceptives in school clinics, the sexual indiscretions of public figures, casual nudity in advertising and on television, topless sunbathing by women at public beaches, and graphic sexual content in books and films that may be considered art. The French also tend to idealize the notion of seduction as something that involves more than sexual conquest and the open expression of one's desire (and desirability). It is seen as part of the inherent pleasure of interpersonal interactions. To be "seductive" also entails charisma, charm, bearing, articulate use of the French language, civilized manners, cultural capital, good taste, and stylishness; commanding attention in areas other than love and sex; and creating an aura of persuasiveness around one's person. Compelling ideas and successful politicians may also be qualified as *séduisants*. The negative implications of this French idealization of seduction include tacit justification of male privilege when it is exercised with the veneer of gallantry and a tendency to not take sexual harassment seriously as the rampant problem that it is in France. Finally, the reality of the love lives of the French is a bit more mundane. Surveys suggest that both men and women in France today have sexual relations for the first time on average around age seventeen—compared to age nineteen for men and twenty-one for women in the 1950s. Men report having had on average eleven to twelve sexual partners in their lives, compared to four to five for women. One-third of married people admit to having been unfaithful to their spouses.

The historical struggles for the rights of women and LGBTQ+ people in France are significant. Women involved in the Women's March on Versailles in October 1789 and in the Society of Revolutionary Republican Women were at the forefront of the French Revolution. Nonetheless, in spite of vigorous calls for equality for women on the part of people like the Marquis de Condorcet and Olympe de Gouges (author of the Declaration of the Rights of Women, 1791), equal rights for women were not recognized in the constitution, and their political involvement was curtailed by the Jacobins under the Reign of Terror. In fact, the Napoleonic Civil Code made the second-class status of French women the law of the land for well over a century. A wide range of groups and individuals (e.g., Flora Tristan, Clémence Royer, Maria Deraismes, Hubertine Auclert, Marguerite Durand, Cécile Brunschvicg, and Suzanne Lacore) fought for women's rights throughout the nineteenth and early twentieth centuries. However, women's suffrage was not obtained until 1944. In the 1960s, women joined the workforce, the sexual revolution gained momentum, and militant feminism started to flourish in France—exemplified by organizations like the Women's Liberation Movement and thinkers like Simone de Beauvoir, Antoinette Fouque, Monique Wittig, Hélène Cixous, and Luce Irigaray. Activists fought for bodily autonomy and equal pay and opportunity in the workplace and critiqued patriarchal power throughout society and culture. From the 1960s through the 1990s, numerous laws were passed that sought to give women greater equality and protection against discrimination, including a 2000 law that made gender parity a goal and legal norm in political life. Notwithstanding these gains, full equality between men and women has not yet been achieved in France and many still point to rampant sexism. One important focus of recent efforts and debates is the issue of sexual harassment. France's first law against sexual harassment in the workplace dates from 2002. In 2018, a new law was passed that sanctions sexual harassment of women in public.

Homosexuality was decriminalized in France—the first nation to do so—in 1791. However, a variety of laws (e.g., a 1960 law on public decency that singled out homosexuals for harsher punishments) were used to publicly persecute gays and lesbians, and homophobia has persisted to the present in spite of surveys suggesting generally tolerant public opinion. A militant gay rights movement emerged in France in the 1970s with groups like FHAR (Homosexual Front for Revolutionary Action). These groups and their successors have campaigned against homophobia and in favor of LGBTQ+ rights, for vigorous action to fight the HIV-AIDS epidemic, and in favor of marriage equality and reproductive rights. Paris has had a dynamic gay and lesbian culture since the nineteenth century and is today host to one of the largest pride parades in Europe. Other major French cities like Montpellier, Lyon, Toulouse, and Nice have important gay and lesbian communities and a reputation of LGBTQ+ tolerance. Laws protect French people against discrimination based on sexual orientation and gender identity. However, the trans and gender-nonconforming community in France still faces numerous challenges ranging from transphobic violence to the binary gendered conventions of the French language. Nonetheless, gains have been made recently in terms of acceptance and rights. For instance, since 2017, French people have had the right to change their legal gender without medical justification or without undergoing gender reassignment surgery.

Further Reading

Copley (1989); Desan (2004); Fishman (2017); Giroud and Lévy (1995); Hunt (1992); Nye (1998); Offen (2017).

Attitudes toward Sex

The stereotype of the "French lover" is an exaggeration. France is not a nation of suave lotharios and chic femmes fatales who enjoy the sport of seduction. However, there is a grain of truth beneath the layers of myth insofar as France is a nation with deeply rooted traditions of male gallantry (and privilege) and female coquettishness and generally liberal attitudes toward sex. The former originated in the Middle Ages with the notion of courtly love (i.e., ennobling passion that required devotion to the idealized object of one's affections), which was exemplified by the poems and love songs of the troubadours and critically reassessed by the poet and moral philosopher Christine de Pizan (1364–1430). The latter was given daring expression by the eighteenth-century libertines, who rejected conventional morality in the hedonistic pursuit of sexual pleasure. Historical examples of libertinage in art and literature include the amorous scenes (*scènes galantes*) painted by Antoine Watteau and Jean-Honoré Fragonard and erotic novels like *Dangerous Liaisons* (1782) by Pierre Choderlos de Laclos and *Justine* (1797) by the Marquis de Sade (1740–1814). Following the lead of precursors like the *poètes maudits* Charles Baudelaire (1821–1867) and Paul Verlaine, who wrote unabashedly of vices and sensual fixations, the "decadent" authors of the last decades of the nineteenth century, like Jules Barbey d'Aurevilly, Karl-Joris Huysmans, Léon Bloy, Auguste Villiers de l'Isle d'Adam, Pierre Louÿs, and Octave Mirabeau—reveled in moral decay, sexual perversion, and self-disgust. Sexual emancipation was a major undercurrent of the wave of social and cultural upheaval that swept through France in the late 1950s, 1960s and 1970s. Examples include Brigitte Bardot's character in Roger Vadim's 1956 film *And God Created Woman*; the slogans of the student protesters of May 68 (e.g., "It is forbidden to forbid"); influential work on gender, sexuality, and desire by philosophers like Simone de Beauvoir, Jacques Lacan, Gilles Deleuze, Félix Guattari, Monique Wittig, and Michel Foucault; and the political struggle for the reproductive rights culminating in the Veil Law that legalized abortion in France in 1975. Throughout the twentieth century, a celebration of passionate love persisted in French culture—as exemplified variously by the work of poets like Guillaume Apollinaire, Robert Desnos, Paul Eluard, Louis Aragon, and Jacques Prévert, and in the chanson tradition of popular song (e.g., Édith Piaf, Yves Montand, Jacques Brel, Barbara, Dalida, Charles Aznavour, and their heirs today). As discussed in a book by the American journalist Elaine Sciolino, the French concept of "seduction" goes beyond using physical attractiveness, sex appeal, and romantic prowess to one's advantage, with a sexual tryst as its final objective. To be "seductive" (*séduisant*) also entails charisma, charm, wit, confidence, bearing, good manners, articulate use of language, intellectual brilliance, cultural good taste, and stylishness, and its broader aims include commanding attention, creating an aura of overall attractiveness around one's person, and grounding persuasion in esthetics as much as logic.

France's liberal attitudes toward sexual behavior today are demonstrated in widespread public acceptance of cohabitation (*l'union libre*) as a normal life experience and permanent relationship structure for couples, of homosexuality and same-sex marriage, of public displays of affection, of birth control counseling and contraceptives in school clinics, of topless sunbathing at public beaches, and of nudity and sexual content in the media. Sexual themes are treated in frank and often graphic detail by authors like Michel Houellebecq (b. 1956) and Virginie Despentes (b. 1969); and in films like *Belle de Jour* (dir. Louis Buñuel, 1967), *Going Places* (dir. Bertrand Blier, 1974), *Betty Blue* (dir. Jean-Jacques Beineix, 1986), *Savage Nights* (dir. Cyrille Collard, 1992), *The Lover* (dir. Jean-Jacques Annaud, 1992), *Romance* (dir. Catherine Breillat, 1999), *Swimming Pool* (dir. François Ozon, 2003), *Blue Is the Warmest Color* (dir. Abdelattif Kechiche, 2013), *Stranger by the Lake* (dir. Alain Guiraudie), and *Elle* (dir. Paul Verhoeven, 2016), although these authors and films are by no means free of controversy. French notions of privacy favor discretion with respect to the sexual behavior of individuals and this extends to public figures. French public opinion does not expect the nation's political leaders to be paragons of monogamy and virtue. The French were not particularly upset by their belated discovery of President François Mitterrand's lifelong mistress and "second" family, who attended his 1996 funeral alongside his "legitimate" wife and family. However, they have been critical of some of their more recent leaders for not being more discreet about their relationships (e.g.,

Nicolas Sarkozy and François Hollande). In 2019, after the publication of a novel by one of his alleged victims (Vanessa Springora, *Consent*), there was a public outcry (and the opening of a criminal investigation) against the author Gabriel Matzneff, whose past literary awards and connections among the intelligentsia and cultural elite had served as cover in spite of the fact that his autobiographical works contained graphic accounts of sex with underage girls and boys (preadolescent in some cases). The legal status of prostitution in France is complicated. It is not illegal among consenting adults for a person to offer or provide sexual services in exchange for money, but it is illegal for a third party to profit from such a transaction. The operation of bordellos has been illegal in France since 1946 and procuring (proxenetism) is severely penalized under the law. Furthermore, the government is committed to aggressively fighting sex trafficking. The latter objective was part of the rationale for a new law in 2016 that includes fines and other penalties for the clients of prostitutes. The legal age of consent in France is fifteen. Recent surveys suggest that men in France today have sexual relations for the first time on average at age 17.2, and women at age 17.6—compared to age 18.8 for men and 20.6 for women in the 1950s (i.e., people are having sexual relations for the first time at a younger age and the age gap between the sexes is closing). Men report having had on average 11.6 sexual partners in their lives, compared to 4.4 for women.

See also: Chapter 5: Overview. Chapter 7: Feminism and Women's Rights; Gender Equality and Sexual Harassment; LGBTQ+ Community; Marriage, Divorce, Civil Unions, and Cohabitation Today. Chapter 10: Privacy and Personal Space. Chapter 11: Eighteenth-Century Literature; Houellebecq (Michel) and the Recent French Novel. Chapter 12: French Cinema II (since the Nouvelle Vague).

Further Reading
Bajos and Bozon (2012); Harp (2014); Iacub (2016); Mack (2017); Ollivier (2009); Saguy (1999); Sciolino (2011); Steintrager (2016); Yalom (2012).

Child Raising Practices

The French traditionally maintain a strict attitude with respect to child raising and discipline. There is no better compliment that one can make to a parent than to say that their child is *bien élévé* ("well raised"). The main emphasis is not on producing a child with healthy self-esteem, but on raising one who is disciplined and well mannered—especially in public. Such a child is polite, articulate, and deferential to adults, knows the rules of appropriate social behavior, has good table manners, and is well prepared for life in the adult world. Spanking and other forms of corporal punishment were still widely practiced as a form of parental discipline in France until recently; however, a new law in 2019 made France the fifty-sixth country to ban such practices. Polling data published at the time of parliamentary debate suggested that many as 70% of French people did not want the ban to include spankings; and only 7% were in favor of a ban of all forms of corporal punishment. France has had divergent views on raising and disciplining children since the Enlightenment. In his philosophical novel *Émile* (1762), Jean-Jacques Rousseau argued in favor of practices that would preserve the natural goodness and curiosity in children rather than reinforce the corrupting and stultifying influences of society. The theories of the pediatric psychoanalyst Françoise Dolto (1908–1988), who advocated a more permissive and child-centric approach to parenting (sometimes referred to derisively as the so-called *enfant-roi*, or child-as-king approach), have been particularly influential from the 1970s to the present.

French families attach great importance to their children's schooling. Virtually all French three-year-olds are in preschool—the great majority in the nation's excellent public *écoles maternelles*. The years spanning middle school, high school, and the national high school diploma exam (*le baccalauréat*) are particularly important, and intense, because the student's academic success at this level determines their postsecondary education options and ultimate social standing as much as anything else they may do later in life. The French school day is long and particularly grueling for adolescents and does not leave much room for extracurricular activities such as sports, music, theater, clubs, and community service. Since French children are raised to know how to act like adults and are expected to do so by their teen years, they are often trusted with greater autonomy in adolescence. This has included generally more liberal attitudes toward the sexual activity of teens. However, French young people may not obtain a full driver's license before the age of eighteen (though one may obtain a learner's permit at fifteen) and teenagers having their own car is not part of French culture. On the other hand, young people's use of computers and smartphones is as prevalent in France as in other wealthy countries, which raises questions of time spent online, appropriate use of social media, and cyberbullying. For example, according to a poll conducted in 2017 by Harris Interactive for the French Telecom Federation, the use of internet-connected devices by children between the ages of eight and fifteen was four hours or more per week in two-thirds of the households surveyed; and a 2015 poll conducted by IPSOS found that average internet (incl. social media) usage by French teenagers (age thirteen to nineteen) was 13.5 hours per week. Furthermore, in 2017, Association E-Enfance, which promotes safe internet use and operates a hotline for the victims of cyberbullying, reported that 40% of French young people between the ages of thirteen and seventeen had experienced some form of harassment online.

"Going away" for college is not the cultural phenomenon that it is in countries like the United States. Many French students live at home while completing their studies and those who live in student dormitories or apartments remain in close contact with their families. In either case, the general tendency is to attend university or a specialized institution of higher education close to home. Whether or not they continue their studies beyond the secondary level, young people today tend to remain in their parents' home until they are "well established" from a socio-professional standpoint. In fact, it is not uncommon to see employed adults in their thirties still living in their family homes—in some instances, with an intimate partner.

See also: Chapter 4: Social Security and Healthcare. Chapter 7: Kinship and Family Structures; Marriage, Divorce, Civil Unions, and Cohabitation Today. Chapter 8: Early Childhood Education and Elementary Schools; Secondary Schools. Chapter 10: Social Importance of Good Manners; Chapter 16: Internet, Social Media, and Video Games.

Further Reading

Claes et al. (2011); Druckerman (2012); Faircloth (2013); Gregory and Milner (2008); Gregory and Milner (2011); Heywood (2007); Jobs (2007); Martin (2017); Martin (2018a); Martin (2018b); Saint-Onge (2019); Suzzo (2004); Voléry (2016).

Feminism and Women's Rights

The history of feminism—a term first used in France in 1892—and of the struggle for equal rights for women in France is very rich. France was one of the centers of a long-running debate about the nature and societal role of women from the fifteenth through the eighteenth centuries that was called *la querelle des femmes*, or the "woman question." While many of the participants in this literary and intellectual debate were men, the Italo-French woman of letters Christine de Pizan (1364–1430) eloquently refuted notions of the intellectual and moral inferiority of women in influential works like *The Book of the City of Ladies* (1405). From the end of the eighteenth century through the middle of the twentieth century, the emphasis was on obtaining civic and political equality for women. Women were key participants in the early phases of the French Revolution. The market women of Paris, upset about the price of bread and other issues, led the Women's March on Versailles in October 1789 (also called the October March), forcing the king and the National Assembly to return to Paris for their deliberations on a new constitution. However, that constitution did not give women the rights of active citizens. Moreover, in 1793, the ruling Jacobin faction banned women's political clubs like the radical Society of Revolutionary Republican Women. Leading women revolutionaries included Pauline Léon, Madame (Marie-Jeanne) Roland, Anne-Josèphe Théroigne de Méricourt, and Olympe de Gouges. Gouges (1748–1793) was the author Declaration of the Rights of Woman and the Female Citizen (1791), a response to the Declaration of the Rights of Man and the Citizen (1789) that challenged male power and asserted equal rights for women. Both Roland and Gouges were sent to the guillotine during the Reign of Terror. In 1804, the Napoleonic Civil Code wrote the subservient position of women in marriage and society—they were required to obey their husbands and had fewer rights than minors—into law. In reaction to the contradictions of the French Revolution and the conservatism of both the Napoleonic Empire and the Restoration monarchy with respect to women's rights, the feminist cause gained momentum in the nineteenth and early twentieth centuries. Gender equality was defended by some of the utopian socialists (e.g., Saint-Simon and Fourier) and by feminist thinkers like Flora Tristan (1803–1844), Maria Deraismes (1826–1894), Clémence Royer (1839–1902), Hubertine Avalert (1848–1914), Marguerite Durand (1864–1936), Suzanne Lacore (1875–1975), and Cécile Brunschvicg (1877–1946). During the same period, a range of women's rights organizations were created—the Women's Union for the Defense of Paris and Care for the Wounded (1871), the French League for the Rights of Women (1882), the National Council of French Women (1901), and the French Union for Women's Suffrage (1909). These organizations fought for a range of goals, including political rights for women (esp. suffrage), equal pay, divorce, access to education, and the abolition of prostitution. Some tangible gains were made during this period. In 1880, the Sée Law opened access to secondary education to girls; and in 1884, the Naquet Law made divorce legal again (first legalized under the Revolution, it had been abolished in 1816). The National Assembly approved women's suffrage half a dozen times beginning in 1919 but the Senate blocked the legislation each time. Even some progressives were hesitant to support women's suffrage because they saw women as more susceptible to clerical influence. Part of the political program of the French Resistance, women finally gained the right to vote in 1944 under the Provisional Government of the French Republic. Wives' subservience to their husbands was removed from the Civil Code in 1938. However, women had to wait until 1965 to gain the right to take up a job or open a bank account without the approval of their husbands.

With these essential civil and political rights attained, attention in the 1960s, 1970s, 1980s, and 1990s turned to women's broader social empowerment and identity in a male-dominated society. It is in response to these issues that French feminism—more theoretical and radical than its pragmatic Anglo-American counterpart—emerged. Its foundational text was Simone de Beauvoir's (1908–1986) landmark philosophical essay, *The Second Sex* (1949), which argued that one was not born a woman but became one within the purview of male perception and power, which were to be combated. Radical French feminism developed largely in the wake of the wave of social and political agitation that spread beyond the protests of May 1968. Feminist philosophers, researchers, writers, and critics like Luce Irigaray (b. 1930), Monique Wittig (1935–2003), Anne Zelensky (b. 1935), Hélène Cixous (b. 1937), Christine Delphy (b. 1941), and Julia Kristeva (b. 1944) analyzed and critiqued the omnipresence of patriarchy in the structures of modern society and culture, deconstructed the phallocratic nature of language and literature, and grounded their theories in the experience of women's bodies. Their theoretical writing found a counterpart in the visual arts in the work of Louise Bourgeois (1911–2010), Nikki de Saint Phalle (1930–2002), Gina Pane (1939–1990), Annette Messager (b. 1943), and ORLAN (b. 1947), and in the militant actions of the MLF (Women's Liberation Movement)—founded in 1970 by a group of women that included Antoinette Fouque (1936–2014), Josiane Chanel, and Wittig. Reproductive rights and women's bodily autonomy were among the main objectives of feminist groups like the MLF and Choisir (Choose). Oral contraceptives were legalized in France through the Neuwirth Law of 1967, and abortion (usually called "IVG," which is the French acronym for "Voluntary Interruption of Pregnancy") through the Veil Law of 1975 (in reference to the minster of health, Simone Veil, 1927–2017). The latter law was enacted in the wake of memorable events like the 1971 "Manifesto of the 343" (signed by prominent French women who publicly admitted to having had abortions) and the highly publicized 1972 Bobigny Trial, which resulted in the acquittal of a young girl (defended by Gisèle Halimi) charged with having had an illegal abortion.

Beginning in the mid-1970s, the French government began to make women's rights a policy priority. Starting with Françoise Giroud, secretary of state for the condition of women from 1974 to 1976, most French governments have included a cabinet-level or sub-cabinet-level position focusing on women's issues. One of the most effective government advocates for women was Yvette Roudy, minister of women's rights from 1981 to 1986. Under Roudy, a landmark law against gender-based discrimination in the workplace was passed in 1983. It consolidated the gains made toward equal pay and against sexist biases in employment in earlier laws (1972, 1975) and also included broad provisions against sexual harassment and hostile workplace environments that were not retained in the final version of the bill that passed. The current ministerial position (since June 2022) is that of a junior minister for gender equality, diversity, and equal opportunity working directly under the prime minister.

French feminism has evolved further with the development of third wave feminism beginning in the mid-1990s, followed by a fourth wave in the 2010s. Diversity and intersectionality are common threads that run through these newer orientations of feminism—greater openness to both different understandings of what it means to be woman and women of diverse social, economic, cultural, religious, and national backgrounds; and awareness that the marginalization and subjugation of women involve interlocking systems of power and oppression that include historical and cultural constructions of race, class, sexual orientation, family, age, religion, esthetics, disability, political agency, and gender. One feminist organization that emerged in this context is Ni Putes, Ni Soumises (Neither Whores, Nor Submissive, founded in 2002), which advocates on behalf of immigrant women, particularly those who also come from religious, ethnic, and racial minorities and who live in the underprivileged suburbs. Another is Femen, an organization that started in Ukraine in 2008 and has been based in France, the home of its most active chapter, since 2013, and is known for its attention-getting and controversial protests involving topless militants.

See also: Chapter 2: Timeline. Chapter 5: Philosophy (Contemporary). Chapter 7: Gender Equality and Sexual Harassment; Marriage, Divorce, Civil Unions, and Cohabitation Today; LGBTQ+ Community. Chapter 9: Sexism and Gender Bias in French. Chapter 11: Literary Avant-Garde, 1950–1980. Chapter 12: Contemporary Art.

Further Reading
Cavallaro (2003); Duchen (1994); Duchen (2012); Fell (2019); Foley (2004); Greenwald (2018); McMillan (2000); Moses (1984); Scott (1996); Scott (2007); Smith (1996).

Gender Equality and Sexual Harassment

The strides toward gender equality made in France and elsewhere since the end of World War II (e.g., women were given the right to vote in France in 1944) is one of the great achievements of the modern era. Still, gender equality is far from complete in France. French girls excel in school—more so than their male counterparts—and are encouraged to do so by their families (esp. in the middle class and among the more affluent and educated). However, boys remain more prevalent in the more prestigious tracks in secondary and higher education—the STEM tracks of the high school baccalaureate curriculum and the prestigious *grandes écoles*, especially engineering schools. Women work in large numbers—67.6% of all women between the ages of fifteen and sixty-four in 2017 (83.3% of those between twenty-five and forty-nine), compared to 75.5% of all men of working age (and 93.3% of men aged between twenty-five and forty-nine). In 1985, the share of women aged between fifteen and sixty-four who worked was around 50% (compared to 72% for men), and in 1960—when married women still required the permission of their husbands to work or open a bank account (a law that was changed in 1965)—it was just 40% (compared to 90% of men). However, women today still lag behind men in terms of full-time employment, pay, and advancement. Currently, over 30% of all working women work part-time (the percentage is higher for women with children) compared to 7% of men. Men in France are still paid on average 9% more than women in the same types of positions and with the same educational credentials and experience. In 2016, women's overall gross hourly earnings were on average 15.2 % below those of men in France—only slightly better than the average EU unadjusted pay gap of 16% (although significantly better than both Germany and the United Kingdom, both of which have pay gaps of around 21%). In 2018, there was just one female chief executive of a CAC 40 company (the French equivalent of the Dow Jones companies). By contrast, thanks to a landmark 2000 law prescribing parity between men and women in electoral politics, women have made gains in terms of representation in the French parliament—they formed 38.7% of National Assembly delegates and 31.6% of senators in 2017, compared to 26.9% of National Assembly delegates in 2012 and 25% of senators in 2014 and 10.8% of delegates in 1997 and 5.6% of senators in 1995. Women have been finalists for the French presidency three times—Ségolène Royal (Socialist) in 2007 and Marine Le Pen (National Rally) in 2017 and 2022. There have been two female prime ministers—Édith Cresson (1991–1992) and Élisabeth Borne (since May 2022).

The roles of men and women in marriages and families have become progressively more equal since the 1970s. However, their roles are not entirely equal, as women still bear more of the burden for domestic tasks such as housekeeping, meal preparation, and the care of young children. Regrettably, there remains a considerable degree of everyday sexism against French women. They still face great pressure to conform to male notions of alluringness as a key component of their public perception and self-worth and are subjected to relatively frequent sexist treatment in public and the workplace. France's first sexual harassment legislation dates from 2002. It originally concerned overt abuse of power by superiors and quid pro quo forms of harassment (i.e., professional advancement in exchange for romantic and sexual favors). However, the laws have been strengthened several times since then and now include provisions for hostile environments of a sexist nature. In 2017, France saw the development of its equivalent of the #MeToo movement denouncing sexual harassment—#BalanceTonPorc (i.e., "expose your pig"). Revealingly, there was some pushback *by women* in France against these movements—for example, 100 French women, including film star Catherine Deneuve, signed an open letter in *Le Monde* that asserted, "Rape is a crime, but insistent or clumsy flirting is not an offense, nor is gallantry macho aggression," that "the right to bother" (*importuner*) was indispensable to sexual freedom," and that "seduction, based on respect and pleasure" was not to be confused with violence. It furthermore accused the movements of casting women as eternal helpless victims in their interactions with men. There was, however, also pushback against the pushback and Deneuve later apologized to women who felt aggrieved by the open letter and referred to sexual misconduct as "odious." Still, both the climate and law regarding sexual harassment in France is changing. In 2018, in response to an incident captured on video that quickly went viral around the world, the French parliament passed a law penalizing sexual harassment in public places, including aggressive "catcalling" of women in the street and other forms of verbal harassment.

See also: Chapter 3: Republic. Chapter 7: Attitudes toward Sex; Feminism and Women's Rights; Marriage, Divorce, Civil Unions, and Cohabitation Today. Chapter 9: Language Laws and Policies; Sexism and Gender Bias in French.

Further Reading
Allwood and Wadia (2009); Berrebi-Hoffmann et al. (2019); Colvin (2017); Donadio (2017); Donadio (2019); Faure (2020); Lehrer (2020); Onishi (2020); Saguy (2003); Saguy (2018); Weiner (2001).

Kinship and Family Structures

The French sociologist Henri Mendras quotes a knowledgeable observer of European societies and traditions who once asserted that the three greatest institutions created by Western European civilization were the Prussian army general staff, the Catholic Church, and the French family. This remark may be contrasted with the popular French saying, "One suffers one's family, but one chooses one's friends" ("On subit sa famille, on choisit ses amis"), to get a balanced sense of both the great importance that has been attached to the family in French culture through the ages and the sometimes oppressive nature of the French family structure as an inescapable reality and force of destiny—a complex subject that has provided the fodder for many of the great French writers (from Stendhal, Balzac, Flaubert, Zola, and Proust to Annie Ernaux and Édouard Louis). For many centuries, the French family was a strong institution because it was also an authoritarian one. There were different variations in the north and the south. In the south, where the *famille-souche* (i.e., "stem family," a close-knit and cohabitating multigenerational unit under the authority of a patriarch) prevailed, it was common for several generations to live together under one roof. In the past, the eldest son traditionally inherited both the ancestral homestead and other family property (esp. land)—so as not to fragment the patrimonial wealth of the family line in the passage from one generation to the next—and the position and authority as the head of the family line (the *oustal* was a house in the sense of both a "home" and a "dynasty"). Younger siblings could remain in the ancestral home under his authority or strike out on their own, or, in the case of girls, be married off. In the north, a more egalitarian model of inheritance was practiced (among males in particular) and each sibling lived in a separate conjugal household. Beyond these different practices, however, three things were both constant and certain—the individual and their freedom and desires mattered little when weighed against the material interests and reputation of the family; the family was thought of in broad terms that went far beyond the modern nuclear family to include the intergenerational line and the extended family (uncles, second cousins, etc.), and the father (or patriarchal grandfather) was the undisputed ruler of the family unit. The Napoleonic Civil Code of 1804 adopted the northern model of "egalitarian" treatment of heirs but unequivocally inscribed the supremacy of fathers over wives and children into the law of the land. Women had fewer rights than male minors. A married woman's "civil incapacity" and duty to obey her husband were not stricken from the French Civil Code until 1938 and her right to work without her husband's approval was only granted in 1965!

The French family has undergone sweeping changes in the twentieth century, especially in the wake of the wave of liberalism and generational conflict manifested in the student protests of May 1968. These changes are of a demographic, legal, political, social, economic, material, cultural, psychological, and attitudinal nature. Women are no longer constrained by reproductive biology; they have joined the workforce in large numbers and have an equal voice in family matters. There is considerable sharing of responsibilities between men and women in terms of decision-making, daily household tasks, and the care and education of children. However, the tendency to consider certain tasks as belonging to a distinctly gendered women's sphere (e.g., housekeeping, interior decoration, and meal preparation) or men's sphere (e.g., household repairs, automobile maintenance, and yard work) has not yet disappeared in French society. Sociologists describe the French family as having become more democratic and child-centered. It has been reconfigured as a close-knit and nurturing environment in which the individuality and autonomy of each member is respected. The education, material comfort, psychological development, empowerment, and pleasure of the family's children are now of paramount importance. French people are starting families and marrying at a later age than in the past and family size is getting smaller. People have become more mobile for reasons of economic opportunity and this has placed greater emphasis on the nuclear family unit, as contacts with the extended family have become more occasional. Generational differences between parents and children—and grandparents (now living much longer) and grandchildren—in matters of culture, mentalities, and consumption have not disappeared but are not as gaping as in the past. Grandparents are no longer the austere and distant patriarchal and matriarchal figures they once were. Especially when still in good health and financially secure, they have taken on new importance in their grandchildren's lives as a regular presence (both in person and digital) and as sources of affection and fun. For all of these changes, the family has remained a central focus of French life—family dinners (daily for the nuclear family, periodic for the extended family) are still very important, as are larger family gatherings on holidays, special occasions, and during the summer months. Living in relative proximity to members of one's extended family—with the maternal side of the family having grown in importance—is still relatively common and very desirable. Family solidarity has become increasingly important as a crucial support system for both older and younger members of a family. While France is no stranger to the (Western) trend of greater isolation of the elderly, many have come to rely on the care and support of their children and grandchildren. Younger adults today have become especially reliant on the continued support of their families (financial, emotional, and for a place to live) as the time spent as a student has gotten longer, finding good jobs and financial independence and stability harder, and "settling down" in a stable relationship and founding a family of one's own more complicated and precarious. This is a generational difference between young people today and those who came of age in the 1960s and early 1970s (sometimes called the "May 68 Generation"), who couldn't wait to distance themselves from their families and live by their own rules. The French family has also changed due to divorce and the greater instability of parental couples. Single-parent families now make up 22.5 % of all French families. Blended families—households formed by a couple and children from past unions in addition to their own, if any—represent 9.3% of all families (1.5 million, or 11% of minor children live in blended families).

See also: Chapter 4: Social Security and Healthcare. Chapter 6: Senior Citizens and Elderly. Chapter 7: Child Raising Practices; LGBTQ+ Community; Marriage, Divorce, Civil Unions, and Cohabitation Today.

Further Reading

Attias-Donfut (2003); Attias-Donfut and Segalen (2002); Boling (2015); Bonvalet and Lelièvre (2016); Burguière et al. (1996); Fuchs (2009); Köppen et al. (2017); Lefeuvre and Lemarchant (2007); Merchant (2019); Régnier-Loilier (2014); Robcis (2013); Thibeaud (2020).

FAMILY POLICY

The French government has an extensive array of policies that support families, children, and working mothers. Family benefits include the child benefit paid to all families beginning with the second child regardless of income, the family income supplement for qualified families with three or more children, and the back-to-school allowance to help qualified families with the purchase of school supplies and other school-related expenses. Social spending on family benefits (incl. housing subsidies) in 2015 represented nearly a 3% share of the GDP. A key component of the social security system is its generous paid maternity, paternity, and adoptive parental leave programs. An expecting mother is entitled to six weeks' prenatal leave and ten weeks' postnatal leave. Publicly funded daycare centers exist for younger children in most localities. Family policy is a major ministerial or sub-ministerial portfolio in French administrations. For instance, Prime Minister Édouard Philippe's cabinet (under President Emmanuel Macron) included a Ministry of Families, Children, and Women's Rights until May 2017, when responsibility for family policy was assigned to the Ministry of Solidarity and Health.

LGBTQ+ Community

France is a relatively tolerant country for lesbian, gay, bisexual, trans, and queer people, but this was not always the case in the past and instances of discrimination and anti-LGBTQ+ attitudes still present a problem. From the Middle Ages through the end of the eighteenth century, homosexuals could be put to death. A monument to the last two victims of such persecution, Bruno Lenoir and Jean Diot, who were burned at the stake in 1750, was dedicated near the location where the two were apprehended—Rue Montorgueil in the Les Halles district of Paris. In 1791, under the French Revolution, France became the first nation in the world to decriminalize homosexuality with the repeal of sodomy statutes. Homosexual acts between consenting adults in private were tolerated. However, other restrictions remained. Between 1942 and 1982, there were different ages of consent for sexual activity between heterosexuals (fifteen) and homosexuals (twenty-one until 1974, then eighteen). A public decency law enacted in 1960—repealed in 1980—included provisions for much harsher penalties for homosexuals and served as a legal pretext for their continued persecution, including police raids in bars, bath houses, and other gathering places. Discrimination on the grounds of sexual orientation was outlawed in 1985 and sexual orientation was included in anti-hate crimes legislation enacted in 2004. "Transsexualism" was delisted as a pathological condition in 2009 and "sexual identity" was included as grounds for protection in antidiscrimination laws in 2012 (subsequent revisions changed the language of the law to refer to "gender identity"). Same-sex couples in France have had the right to form civil unions since 1999 and to marry (and adopt children) since 2013. At the time of the discussion and passage of the marriage equality law, polls indicated that close to two-thirds of French people supported marriage rights for same-sex couples and over three-fourths of them expressed acceptance of homosexuality in general. Since 2017, French people have had the right to choose their legal gender without medical justification. Hormone replacement therapy and gender confirmation surgery is covered by national health insurance. LGBTQ+ people may serve openly in the French armed forces. Beginning with the Socialist mayor of Paris, Bertrand Delanoë (in office 2001–2014), France's first openly gay major political office holder, sexual orientation has generally not been a significant discriminatory factor in French electoral politics.

Paris has been a center of gay and lesbian life and culture since at least the seventeenth century (since the High Middle Ages, according to some historians). After the decriminalization of homosexuality in 1791, it became a place of even greater tolerance and attracted gay and lesbian expatriates from around the world. Between the Belle Époque (1871–1914) and the 1960s, gay, lesbian, and bisexual French and expatriate literary and cultural figures were at the forefront of the avant-garde in France. Among the most well known are the writers Paul Verlaine, Arthur Rimbaud, Oscar Wilde, Marcel Proust, André Gide, Colette, Gertrude Stein, Natalie Barney, Djuna Barnes, Janet Flanner, Jean Cocteau, Henry de Montherlant, Julien Green, James Baldwin, Simone de Beauvoir, Jean Genet, Michel Foucault, and Monique Wittig. The surrealist-affiliated photographer, sculptor, and writer Claude Cahun (Lucy Schwob,

1894–1954), known for gender nonconforming and transgressive self-portraits, is an important figure in both lesbian and transgender culture. Today, Paris (esp. the Marais district) is still considered one of the great LBTQ+ cities of Europe (along with Berlin, London, and Barcelona). Other LGBTQ+–friendly cities according to various polls include Montpellier, Lyon, Toulouse, Nice, and Lille. Paris is the site of France's largest Gay Pride parade, now officially known as "La Marche des Fiertés." With precursors back to 1981 (the first march was organized by CUARH, the Emergency Committee Against the Oppression of Homosexuals), it has been held annually since 2001—on the last Saturday in June, in commemoration of the Stonewall riots in New York on June 28, 1969—and regularly attracts over half a million participants and spectators. Numerous organizations have shaped the history of the LGBTQ+ rights movement in France. Through its influential journal of the same name and related endeavors, Arcadie (1954–1982) sought to present homosexuals as "respectable, cultured, and dignified individuals deserving of greater social tolerance." In the wake of the May 1968 protests, more radical groups took the lead in the 1970s—Front Homosexuel d'Action Révolutionnaire (FHAR, 1971–1976), Les Gazolines (1972–1974; incl. trans activist-performers Maud Molyneux, Hélène Hazera, and Jenny Bel'Air), Gouines

Young people at the 2021 Pride March (Marche des Fiertés LGBT) in Paris, formerly known as Paris Gay Pride—one of the largest Pride marches in Europe. While lesbian, gay, bisexual, trans, nonbinary, queer, and intersex people still face numerous forms of prejudice and discrimination (such as official hostility to gender-neutral language), France is nonetheless a relatively tolerant country for the LGBTQ community. Same-sex marriage was legalized there in 2013; the right to medically assisted procreation procedures was extended to all women, included married and single lesbians, in 2021. (Kovalenkov Petr/Dreamstime.com)

Rouges (Red Dykes), and Groupe de Libération Homosexuelle–Politique et Quotidien (GLH–Politics and Everyday Life). Founded by the queer theorist Guy Hocquenghem and the ecofeminist writer Françoise d'Eaubonne, the far-left FHAR was known for its radical public interventions, such as its disruption of a March 1971 live broadcast of an episode of a radio talk show on relationships and sex hosted by Ménie Grégoire, whom the FHAR militants denounced for her treatment of homosexuality as a "painful affliction." Some historians and activists consider this incident a "Stonewall moment" for the French LGBTQ+ movement. Beginning in the 1980s, considerable focus was placed on the HIV-AIDS epidemic, including via the militancy of groups like Act Up-Paris (founded 1989). Prominent groups today also include Association des Parents Gays et Lesbiens (APGL), SOS Homophobie, the LGBTQ+ and feminist-friendly mosque established by Imam Ludovic-Mohamed Zayed, and Bi'cause.

The trans community in France has long faced marginalization, discrimination, and violence. However, it has become increasingly vocal and militant in its campaign for acceptance and rights since the 1990s—a movement that has broadened its scope from people who formerly identified as "transsexuals" to a more diverse range of gender nonconforming individuals. The cabaret performers Coccinelle (Jacqueline Charlotte Dufresnoy, 1931–2006) and Bambi (Marie-Pierre Pruvot, b. 1935, later a high school literature teacher honored by the French government for her contributions to education) are pioneers who brought visibility to the transgender people in France in the late 1950s and early 1960s. The first fully accredited French medical team to offer gender confirmation surgery was formed in Paris in 1979 (Drs. Breton, Luton, and Banzet). However, candidates were subjected to rigid protocols established without input from the trans community and to often humiliating and dehumanizing treatment by officials both inside and outside of the medical establishment (e.g., until 2016, sterilization was a prerequisite for a legal change of gender). In 2010, transgenderism was officially declassified as a psychiatric illness in France—the first country to do so—although many militants argued that the change was more symbolic than real. Acceptess-T, Association Trans Aide, Observatoire des Transidentités, Ouest Trans, OUTrans, SoFECT, and the French chapter of Organisation Intersex International are among the organizations that offer support to gender nonconforming people in France. ExisTransInter is an annual Pride march held in October for people who identify as transgender, gender fluid/nonbinary, or intersex, and their allies. Slow progress is being made in France in terms of the acceptance and rights of trans and other gender nonconforming people, but daunting challenges remain in many areas—from transphobic violence, discrimination in employment, and very high rates of HIV infection and AIDS among trans people, to the rights of trans parents, the difficulties faced by gender nonconforming children and adolescents, and everyday problems posed by the deeply engrained binary gender conventions of the French language itself (and official resistance to the use of gender-neutral forms).

See also: Chapter 7: Attitudes toward Sex; Feminism and Women's Rights; Marriage, Divorce, Civil Unions, and Cohabitation Today. Chapter 9: Sexism and Gender Bias in French.

Further Reading

Broqua (2020); Espineira (2016); Espineira (2021); Foerster (2014); Gunther (2008); Jackson (2009); Mackenzie (2019); Martel (1999); Merrick and Ragan (1996); Merrick and Sibalis (2002); Perreau (2016a); Perreau (2016b); Provencher (2019); Puvot (2013); Reeser (2013).

MARRIAGE EQUALITY

Gay and lesbian rights advocates and their allies never accepted civil unions (PACS, legal since 1999) as a substitute for marriage equality. Legislation authorizing same-sex marriage passed—on a left-right vote—and took effect in 2013 under Socialist president François Hollande. At the time of its discussion in parliament, polls showed strong support for its main provision—60%–65% in favor of the right of same-sex couples to marry—and somewhat weaker support for extending adoption rights to same-sex married couples (45%–50% in favor). The law (commonly called the Taubira Law or "Marriage for All" Law) was still controversial and stirred massive protests. Many of the law's opponents were religious conservavtives, but they mainly avoided religious and moral arguments and focused instead on the law's redefinition of what a parent is and on a child's right to both a mother and a father. In the first five years since its passage, over 40,000 same-sex marriages were performed in France. The law did not give same-sex married couples legal access to "medically assisted procreation." Legislation extending access to such treatments to all women (incl. single women and lesbian women in same-sex couples) passed in 2021. Surrogacy, considered a form of human trafficking in France, remains illegal for all individuals and couples.

Marriage, Divorce, Civil Unions, and Cohabitation Today

Following a period of modest increase in the second half of the 1990s, and except for a very slight increase in the past few years that sociologists attribute to a "catching-up" effect in same-sex marriages since their legalization in 2013, marriage rates have been on a steady decline in France since 2000 and in a broader historical timeframe. The overall nuptiality rate—the number of new marriages per 1,000 inhabitants in a year—was 3.6 in 2016, 3.9 in 2010, 5.0 in 2000, 6.2 in 1980, and 7.8 in 1970. While demographic trends such as declining birth rates and an aging population have a part in this decline, its main cause is a social trend away from the institution of marriage itself. In 2017, there were 228,000 marriages in France, 7,000 of which were among same-sex partners. The number of marriages in 2000 was 298,000; in 1970, it was 394,000. Same-sex marriages in France are presently divided evenly among men and women. Another important marriage trend in France is that people are getting married at a later age. In 2017, the average age of first marriage for men was 38.1 years, compared to 32.9 in 1997 and 26.3 in 1975. For women the average age of first marriage in 2017 was 35.6, compared to 30.3 in 1997 and 23.9 in 1975.

More couples are living together without being joined by marriage or a civil union: *l'union libre*, formerly known somewhat pejoratively as *le concubinage*. In 1975, there were fewer than 450,000 couples living together; by 2012, the total was 8.5 million. Attitudes toward *l'union libre* in France are now very tolerant. Aside from being the preferred long-term arrangement for a growing number of couples, *l'union libre* is considered a normal early stage in the life of a couple. Close to 85% of French adults under the age of twenty-five who form a household as a couple in a committed relationship do so in *union libre*. And 90% of those who eventually marry have lived together prior to marriage; even among Catholics the rate is 75%. Presently, there are an estimated 500,000 *union libre* couples formed annually in France—significantly more than marriages and civil unions combined. Nonetheless, 45% of all French couples forming households (new + existing) are married, 30% are in civil unions, and 25% are in a state of *union libre*. Many young couples who are living together either marry or form a civil union approaching or after the birth of a child. Approximately one-third of marriages in France are between people who already have at least one child together. In 2016, 59.9% of all children in France were born out of wedlock. This figure compares to 54.9% in 2010, 48.4 in 2005, and 38.6 in 1995. There is no longer a significant social stigma in France concerning out-of-wedlock births and French law no longer makes distinction between "legitimate" and "illegitimate" or "natural" children. The number of civil unions (Pacte Civil de Solidarité, or PACS) has been in decline since 2010, following a period of rapid increase since their legalization in France in 1999 and changes in the legal status of civil unions in 2006 that gave them more of same rights as marriage. There were 192,000 new civil unions contracted in 2016, compared to 207,000 in 2010, 61,000 in 2005, and 22,000 in 2000. While one of the reasons for the creation of the PACS was to provide a legal status for same-sex couples at a time when their marriage was still not authorized, over 95% of the civil unions contracted in 2016 were for opposite-sex couples (compared to already over 90% in 2005). The option of civil unions is not thought to have had a major negative effect on the number of marriages—for the most part, couples not likely to marry choose the PACS, which is less costly and procedurally simpler in case of a breakup.

Except for a brief spike around 2005 due to a simplification of procedures, the number of divorces has been modestly but steadily declining in France since the mid-2000s—in direct correlation to the decline in marriages. However, the long-term trend is that of a significant increase in divorces. There were just 34,663 divorces in France in 1950, 55,612 in 1975, 100,505 in 1985, 133,909 in 2010, and 128,000 in 2016. Presently, 44% of all marriages end in divorce. Divorce laws were simplified significantly under President Giscard in 1975, including—for the first time since the Revolution—provisions for uncontested divorce by mutual consent. The number of single-person households and single-parent families is growing steadily. The former presently make up 30.8% of all French households (overall one out of seven French adults lives alone) and the latter make up 22.5% of all families (compared to 17.5% in 1999 and 10.2% in 1981).

See also: Chapter 2: Timeline; Napoleon Bonaparte (Napoleon I) and the First Empire. Chapter 6: Bourgeoisie and Middle Class. Chapter 7: Attitudes toward Sex; Feminism and Women's Rights; Gender Equality and Sexual Harassment; Kinship and Family Structures; LGBTQ+ Community; Marriage Traditions.

Further Reading

Béraud and Portier (2015); de Singly (1996); Fassin (2014); Gunther (2019); Maillochon (2019); Martin (2001); Martin and Théry (2001); Piazza (2017); Rault and Régnier-Loilier (2015); Régnier-Loilier (2016).

Marriage Traditions

For centuries, marriage was among the important social and religious institutions in France. Marriage was long considered primarily as a mutually beneficial alliance of families. What mattered most until the modern era was the preservation of social standing and enhancement of material wealth of the intergenerational family line, especially the patrilineal heritage estate. Marriage partners were often chosen by the parents or family elders. Brides—and their dowries—were part of a property transaction between families. Marriage was sanctioned as a sacrament by the Catholic Church, and there was no marriage outside of the church, which was the official keeper of family records. Specific marriage customs varied appreciably from one French region to the other. Since the eighteenth century, a number of factors have profoundly changed the way French people approach marriage—the advent of civil marriage (a key result of the Revolution, later juridically standardized in the Napoleonic Civil Code of 1804), declining religious practice, the spread of romantic notions of love, urbanization and a leveling of regional cultural traditions, the rise of individualism, greater legal and social equality of women, the sexual revolution of the 1960s, birth control (the "pill" was legalized in France in 1967), the legalization of abortion (1975), the legalization (1792, 1884) and simplification of divorce (1975, 2005), and contemporary consumer trends. Sexuality is no longer associated primarily with procreation, and life together as a couple is no longer associated primarily with marriage. Fewer French couples get married and, when they do, do so at a later age. Civil unions (PACS) are a popular alternative and living together—*l'union libre*—is now considered normal and acceptable. An individual may have several experiences of romantic couple cohabitation in his or her life and does not necessarily expect marriage to be for life. However, marriage and marital fidelity now take on added meaning as matters of individual lifestyle choice and strong personal commitment.

In France, civil marriages are the only legally recognized form of marriage. The various steps, including the civil marriage ceremony itself, take place at the local town hall—usually in the locality where one or both future spouses reside. Same-sex marriage in France is legal since 2013. One must first apply for marriage at the bureau of records (État Civil) of the town hall where the marriage is to take place at least ten days prior to ceremony, during which time the "marriage banns" (declaration of intent to marry) are published and publicly displayed at the town hall. The officiant at the civil ceremony is the mayor or a vice mayor, who wears the blue-white-and-red tricolor sash that is the symbol of their office. Each of the future spouses must have one witness but may have two. Serving as a marriage witness, *or témoin de mariage*, is a great honor that often goes to people who are important to the couple, such as siblings or close friends. Apart from the spouses' "I do's," the culmination of the civil ceremony is the speech given by the mayor or their delegate. The officiant reads the relevant section of the Civil Code that explains what marriage entails and what the obligations of the spouses are and then offers more personal reflections. At the conclusion of the ceremony, the married couple is given a government-issued *livret de famille*, or family booklet, in which their marriage is officially recorded and in which other important family events—births or adoption of children, the death of a spouse, and so on—are also officially recorded. Couples usually dress up for their civil ceremony (appropriate attire is required)—often in formal attire that includes a traditional white wedding dress for the bride. The couple is sometimes accompanied by a child dressed as a chimney sweep, who is thought to bring them good luck. A religious ceremony (or other type of personal ceremony or blessing) is optional and may only take place after the civil ceremony upon presentation of proof of marriage to the officiating member of the clergy. This practice is becoming less common, however. In 2017, only 28% of French people from Catholic backgrounds had church weddings after the required civil ceremony—compared to 56% in 1986 and 78% in 1965. France's ethnic and religious diversity, which includes the largest Muslim and Jewish communities in Europe, is a source of variety in both the nature of the religious marriage ceremony that may be held and the cultural traditions that characterize the subsequent wedding celebration. Almost 60% of French weddings take place during the summer months (June–September); 80% are held on a Saturday.

Weddings are the occasion for a celebration among the family, neighbors, and friends of the newlyweds. Following a period during which simpler celebrations were favored, "big" celebrations are now back in fashion. Such celebrations are now also a personal expression of the married couple and may reflect a specific theme. Acquaintances may receive an invitation for just the cocktail portion (*l'apéritif*) of the celebration, whereas as many as a hundred or so of the newlyweds' family members and close friends may be invited to the wedding dinner, which may be held in a restaurant or banquet hall—often followed by music and dancing late into the night. Since couples tend to get married at a later age, it is now more common for the newlyweds to pay for their own wedding celebration, or at least make a major contribution to it, although their families may still pay for all or part of the celebration (indeed, the wealth displayed in such celebrations is still socially important to some families). The average cost of a wedding in France is about €12,000. Other important wedding traditions in France are the bachelor or bachelorette parties—known as an *enterrement de vie de garçon* or *fille* (a "burial" of one's life as a single man or woman), which may include a festive or rowdy parade through town. Some young women still put together a collection (*un trousseau*) of personal and household items for their future new home as a married woman. The honeymoon (*voyage de noces*) is still a major part of a newlywed couple's new life together. The destinations vary according to the taste of the couple, but close to two-thirds opt for a seaside or tropical island destination. According to one 2018 poll, the three most cited dream destinations for honeymoons among French people were French Polynesia, Venice, and Bali.

See also: Chapter 7: LGBTQ+ Community; Marriage, Divorce, Civil Unions, and Cohabitation Today.

Further Reading

Chevalier-Karfis (2020); Monger (2004); Petyt (2013).

SELECTED BIBLIOGRAPHY

Allwood, Gill, and Kuesheed Wadia. *Gender and Policy in France*. Palgrave Macmillan, 2009.

Attias-Donfut, Claudine. "Family Transfers and Cultural Transmissions between Three Generations in France." *Global Aging and Its Challenge to Families*, eds. Vern L. Bengston and Ariela Lowenstein. New ed. Routledge, 2003, ch. 11.

Attias-Donfut, Claudine, and Martine Segalen. "The Construction of Grandparenthood." *Current Sociology*, vol. 50, no. 2, 2002, pp. 281–294.

Bajos, Nathalie, and Michel Bozon, eds. *Sexuality in France: Practices, Gender & Health*. Bardwell, 2012.

Béraud, Céline, and Philippe Portier. "Marriage pour tous : The Same-Sex Marriage Controversy in France." *The Intimate: Polity and the Catholic Church: Laws about Life, Death and the Family in So-called Catholic Countries*, eds. Karel Dobbelaere and Alfonso Pérez-Agote. Leuven UP, 2015, pp. 55–91.

Berrebi-Hoffmann, et al., eds. *Categories in Context: Gender and Work in France and Germany, 1900–Present*. Berghahn, 2019.

Boling, Patricia. *The Politics of Work–Family Policies: Comparing Japan, France, Germany and the United States*. Cambridge UP, 2015.

Bonvalet, Catherine, and Eva Lelièvre, eds. *Family beyond Household and Kin: Life Event Histories and Entourage, A French Survey*. INED-Springer, 2016.

Broqua, Christophe. *Action=Vie: A History of AIDS Activism and Gay Politics in France*. Trans. Jean-Yves Bart and Kel Pero. Temple UP, 2020.

Burguière, André, et al., eds. *A History of the Family: The Impact of Modernity*. Trans. Sarah Hanbury-Tenison. Belknap-Harvard UP, 1996.

Cavallaro, Dani. *French Feminist Theory: An Introduction*. Continuum, 2003.

Chevalier-Karfis, Camille. "What to Expect at a Typical French Wedding?" *FrenchToday*, 17 Jun. 2020, https://www.frenchtoday.com/blog/french-culture/expect-typical-french-wedding.

Claes, Michel, et al. "Adolescents' Perceptions of Parental Practices: A Cross-National Comparison of Canada, France, and Italy." *Journal of Adolescence*, vol. 34, no. 2, 2011, pp. 225–238.

Colvin, Kelly Ricciardi. *Gender and French Identity after the Second World War, 1944–1954: Engendering Frenchness.* Bloomsbury, 2017.

Copley, A. R. H. *Sexual Moralities in France, 1780–1980: New Ideas on the Family, Divorce, and Homosexuality: An Essay on Moral Change.* Routledge, 1989.

Desan, Suzanne. *The Family on Trial in the French Revolution.* U California P, 2004.

de Singly, François. *Modern Marriage and Its Cost to Women: A Sociological Look at Marriage in France.* Trans. Malcolm Bailey. U Delaware P, 1996.

Donadio, Rachel. "#BalanceTonPorc Is France's #MeToo." *The Atlantic*, 18 Oct. 2017, https://www.theatlantic.com/international/archive/2017/10/the-weinstein-scandal -seen-from-france/543315/.

Donadio, Rachel. "France's Fight over Sexual Freedom." *The Atlantic*, 11 Jan. 2019, https://www.theatlantic.com/international/archive/2018/01/me-too-france-le-monde-letter -backlash/550361/.

Druckerman, Pamela. *Bringing Up Bébé: One American Mother Discovers the Wisdom of French Parenting.* Penguin, 2012.

Duchen, Claire. *Feminism in France: From May '68 to Mitterrand.* Routledge, 2012.

Duchen, Claire. *Women's Rights and Women's Lives in France 1944–68.* Routledge, 1994.

Espineira, Karine. "Trans* Characters in French Series—An Obsolete yet Hegemonic Representation?" *Trans* Time: Projecting Transness in European (TV) Series*, ed. Danae Gallo Gonzalez. Campus, 2021, pp. 33–54.

Espineira, Karine. "Transgender and Transsexual People's Sexuality in the Media." *Parallax*, vol. 22, no. 3, 2016, pp. 323–329.

Espineira, Karine, and Marie-Hélène/Sam Bourcier. "Transfeminism: Something Else, Somewhere Else." *TSQ*, vol. 3, no. 1–2, pp. 84–94.

Faircloth, Charlotte. *Militant Lactivism?: Attachment Parenting and Intensive Motherhood in the UK and France.* Berghahn, 2013.

Fassin, Éric. "Same-Sex Marriage, Nation, and Race: French Political Logics and Rhetorics." *Contemporary French Civilization*, vol. 39, no. 3, 2014, pp. 281–301.

Faure, Valentine. "France Gets its Weinstein Moment." *The New York Times*, 20 Feb. 2020, https://nyti.ms/2HIYxdy.

Fell, Alison, F., eds. *Making Waves: French Feminisms and their Legacies 1975–2015.* Liverpool UP, 2019.

Fishman, Sarah. *From Vichy to the Sexual Revolution: Gender and Family Life in Postwar France.* Oxford UP, 2017.

Foerster, Maxime. "On the History of Transsexuals in France." *Transgender Experience: Place, Ethnicity, and Visibility*, eds. Chantal Zabus and David Coad. Routledge, 2014, pp. 19–30.

Foley, Susan. *Women in France since 1789: The Meanings of Difference.* Red Globe P, 2004.

Fuchs, Rachel G. *Contested Paternity: Constructing Families in Modern France.* Johns Hopkins UP, 2009.

Giroud, Francoise, and Bernard-Henri Lévy. *Women and Men: A Philosophical Conversation.* Trans. Richard Miller. Little Brown, 1995.

Greenwald, Lisa. *Daughters of 1968: Redefining French Feminism and the Women's Liberation Movement.* U Nebraska P, 2018.

Gregory, Abigail, and Susan Milner, "Fatherhood Regimes and Father Involvement in France and the UK." *Community, Work & Family*, vol. 11, no. 1, 2008, pp. 61–84.

Gregory, Abigail, and Susan Milner. "What Is 'New' about Fatherhood?: The Social Construction of Fatherhood in France and the UK." *Men and Masculinities*, vol. 14, no. 5, 2011, pp. 588–606.

Gunther, Scott. *The Elastic Closet: A History of Homosexuality in France, 1942-present.* Palgrave Macmillan, 2008.

Gunther, Scott. "Making Sense of the Anti-Same-Sex-Marriage Movement in France." *French Politics, Culture & Society*, vol. 37, no. 2, 2019, pp. 131–158.

Harp, Stephen L. *Au Naturel: Naturism, Nudism, and Tourism in Twentieth-century France.* LSU P, 2014.

Heywood, Colin. *Growing Up in France, from the Ancien Régime to the Third Republic.* Cambridge UP, 2007.

Hunt, Lynn. *Family Romance of the French Revolution.* Routledge, 1992.

Iacub, Marcela. *Through the Keyhole: A History of Sex, Space and Public Modesty in Modern France.* Trans. Vinay Swamy. Manchester UP, 2016.

Jackson, Julian. *Living in Arcadia: Homosexuality, Politics, and Morality in France from the Liberation to AIDS.* U Chicago P, 2009.

Jobs, Richard Ivan. *Riding the New Wave: Youth and the Rejuvenation of France after the Second World War.* Stanford UP, 2007.

Köppen, Katja, et al. "Childlessness in France." *Childlessness in Europe: Contexts, Causes, and Consequences*, eds. Michaela Kreyenfeld and Dirk Konietzka. Springer, 2017, pp. 77–96.

Lefeuvre, Nicky, and Chlotilde Lemarchant. "Employment, the Family, and 'Work-Life Balance' in France." *Women, Men, Work and Family in Europe*, eds. Rosemary Crompton, et al. Palgrave Macmillan, 2007, pp. 210–229.

Lehrer, Natasha. "*Ne me touche pas…* The Shift in Sex and Power Sweeping France." *The Guardian*, 23 Feb. 2020, https://www.theguardian.com/global/2020/feb/23/ne-me-touche-pas-the-shift-in-sex-and-power-sweeping-france.

Leturcq, Marion. "Competing Marital Contracts?: The Marriage after Civil Union in France." HAL Working Papers, 2001, halshs-00655585.

Mack, Mehammed Amadeus. *Sexagon: Muslims, France, and the Sexualization of National Culture.* Fordham UP, 2017.

Mackenzie, Louisa. "Beyond 'French-American' Binary Thinking on Non-Binary Gender." *H-France Salon*, vol. 11, no. 4, art. 7, 2019, https://h-france.net/Salon/SalonVol11no14.7.Mackenzie.pdf.

Maillochon, Florence. "From Tradition to Personalization: Changing Marriage Norms in France since the 1960s." *Population*, vol. 74, no. 1–2, 2019, pp. 41–70.

Martel, Frédéric. *The Pink and the Black: Homosexuals in France since 1968.* Trans. Jane Marie Todd. Stanford UP, 1999.

Martin, Claude. "Parenting as a Public Problem in a Neoliberal Era: A Changing Regime in France?" *Journal of Comparative Family Studies*, vol. 48, no. 3, 2018, pp. 303–314.

Martin, Claude. "Parenting Support in France: Policy in an Ideological Battlefield." *Social Policy and Society*, vol. 14, no. 4, 2018, pp. 609–620.

Martin, Claude. "(Re)-Discovering Parents and Parenting in France: What Really Is New?" *Journal of Family Research*, special issue 11 (*Parents in the Spotlight: Parenting Practices and Support from a Comparative Perspective*), 2017, pp. 273–292.

Martin, Claude, and Irène Théry. "The Pacs and Marriage and Cohabitation in France." *International Journal of Law, Policy and the Family*, vol. 15, no. 1, 2001, pp. 135–158.

McMillan, James. *France and Women, 1789-1914: Gender, Society and Politics*. Routledge, 2000.

Merchant, Jennifer. *Access to Assisted Reproductive Technologies: The Case of France and Belgium*. Berghahn, 2019.

Merrick, Jeffrey, and Bryant T. Ragan, eds. *Homosexuality in Modern France*. Oxford UP, 1996.

Merrick, Jeffrey, and Michael Sibalis, eds. *Homosexuality in French History and Culture*. Routledge, 2002.

Monger, George. *Marriage Customs of the World: From Henna to Honeymoons*. ABC-CLIO, 2004, esp. 131–132 ("France").

Moses, Claire Goldberg. *French Feminism in the 19th Century*. SUNY P, 1984.

Nye, Robert A. *Masculinity and Male Codes of Honor in Modern France*. U California P, 1998.

Offen, Karen. *The Woman Question in France, 1400-1870*. Stanford UP, 2017.

Ollivier, Debra. *What French Women Know: About Love, Sex, and Other Matters of the Heart and Mind*. Putnam, 2009.

Onishi, Norimitsu. "How Should Feminism Target Sexual Abuse?: A Battle in Patriarchal France." *The New York Times*, 10 Sept. 2020, https://nyti.ms/2FeAgi4.

Perreau, Bruno. "The Power of Theory: Same-Sex Marriage, Education, and Gender Panic in France." *After Marriage Equality: The Future of LGBT Rights*, ed. Carlos A. Ball. Oxford UP, 2016a, pp. 306–340.

Perreau, Bruno. *Queer Theory: The French Response*. Stanford UP, 2016b.

Petyt, Kimberly. *The Paris Wedding*. Gibbs Smith, 2013.

Piazza, Jo. *How to Be Married: What I Learned from Real Women on Five Continents about Surviving My First (Really Hard) Year of Marriage*. Harmony, 2017.

Provencher, Denis M. *Queer French: Globalization, Language, and Sexual Citizenship in France*. Routledge, 2007.

Provencher, Denis M. *Queer Maghrebi French: Language, Temporalities, Transfiliations*. Liverpool UP, 2019.

Puvot, Marie-Pierre. "Marie, Because It Is Beautiful." *Transgender Experience: Place, Ethnicity, and Visibility*, eds. Chantal Zabus and David Coad. Routledge, 2013, pp. 31–41.

Rault, Wilfried, et Arnaud Régnier-Loilier. "First Cohabiting Relationships: Recent Trends in France." *Population & Societies*, vol. no 521, no. 4, 2015, pp. 1–4.

Reeser, Todd W., ed. *Transgender France*. Special issue of *L'Esprit Créateur*, vol. 53, no. 1, 2013.

Régnier-Loilier, Arnaud, ed. *The Contemporary Family in France: Partnership Trajectories and Domestic Organization*. INED-Springer, 2014.

Régnier-Loilier, Arnaud. "Partnership Trajectories of People in Stable Non-Cohabiting Relationships in France." *Demographic Research*, vol. 35, 2016, pp. 1169–1212.

Robcis, Camille. *The Law of Kinship: Anthropology, Psychoanalysis, and the Family in France*. Cornell UP, 2013.

Saguy, Abigail. "Denouncing Denigration: #metoo and #balancetonporc." *Books & Ideas*, Collège de France, 27 Feb. 2018, https://booksandideas.net/Denouncing-Denigration .html.

Saguy, Abigail. "Puritanism and Promiscuity?: Sexual Attitudes in France and the United States." *Comparative Social Research*, vol. 18, 1999, pp. 227–247.

Saguy, Abigail. *What Is Sexual Harassment?: From Capitol Hill to the Sorbonne*. U California P, 2003.

Saint-Onge, Kathleen. *Discovering Françoise Dolto: Psychoanalysis, Identity and Child Development*. Routledge, 2019.

Sciolino, Elaine. *La Séduction: How the French Play the Game of Life*. Holt, 2011.

Scott, Joan Wallach. *Only Paradoxes to Offer: French Feminists and the Rights of Man*. Harvard UP, 1996.

Scott, Joan Wallach. *Parité!: Sexual Equality and the Crisis of French Universalism*. U Chicago P, 2007.

Smith, Paul. *Feminism and the Third Republic: Women's Political and Civil Rights in France, 1918–1945*. Clarendon P, 1996.

Steintrager, James A. *The Autonomy of Pleasure: Libertines, License, and Sexual Revolution*. Columbia UP, 2016.

Stokoe, Kayte. "A Transfeminist Critique of Drag Discourses and Performance Styles in Three National Contexts (US, France, UK): From *RuPaul's Drag Race* to Bar Wotever." *Contemporary Drag Practices & Performers: Drag in a Changing Scene, Volume 1*, eds. Mark Edward and Stephen Farrier. Methuen Drama, 2020, pp. 87–102.

Suzzo, Marie-Anne. "Mother–Child Relationships in France: Balancing Autonomy and Affiliation in Everyday Interactions." *Ethos*, vol. 32, no. 3, 2004, pp. 293–323.

Thibeaud, Matthias. "Same-Sex Families Challenging Norms and the Law in France." *Same-Sex Families and Legal Recognition in Europe*, ed. Marie Diogix. Springer, 2020, pp. 95–115.

Voléry, Ingrid. "Sexualisation and the Transition from Childhood to Adulthood in France: From Age-Related Child Development Control to the Construction of Civilisational Divides." *Childhood*, vol. 23, no. 1, 2016, pp. 140–153.

Weiner, Susan. *Enfants Terribles: Youth and Femininity in the Mass Media in France, 1945–1968*. Johns Hopkins UP, 2001.

Yalom, Marilyn. *How the French Invented Love: Nine Hundred Years of Passion and Romance*. Harper, 2012.

CHAPTER 8

EDUCATION

OVERVIEW

Education is extremely important in France. It is often at the center of public debates and is regularly the subject of major government reform initiatives, some of which lead to massive demonstrations on the part of students and teachers worried about the ramifications of the proposed changes. Education's importance in France is due, as it is elsewhere, to the need for an educated workforce in the context of a highly competitive global economy. However, in France, education is also important for more deep-seated reasons that have to do with national identity. France has been a great center of learning and intellect in the Western world through the Middle Ages, Renaissance, Enlightenment, and modern times. It respects public intellectuals, philosophers, writers, mathematicians, engineers, scientists, and teachers (from the revered *maîtres d'école* of yesteryear to the embattled *profs* of today). And it is rightfully proud of the prestige associated with such illustrious institutions of higher learning as the Sorbonne, the Collège de France, the École Normale Supérieure ("Normale Sup"), the École Polytechnique ("X"), and the École des Hautes Études en Sciences Sociales (EHESS). Moreover, public school is seen by many as the quintessential institution of the Republic—more so than the constitution, the legislature, or the armed forces. Public school—it is significant that the French commonly refer to it as "the *republican* school"—is credited with having turned millions of peasants into Frenchmen and made the Republic acceptable to the more conservative-minded inhabitants of France's rural areas and small towns. Even today, many insist that its primary *raison d'être* is not train young people for the labor market or help them develop a healthy and well-rounded sense of self, but to make them into citizens who are able to think—rationally and critically—for themselves, and who are imbued with the values of the Republic: liberty, equality, fraternity, and secularism (*Laïcité*). The recent emphasis on the latter is in a context of tensions related to French society's increasing racial, ethnic, and religious diversity, such that this principle of neutrality, tolerance, and civil peace preserved against the dangers of sectarianism has led some to treat the school as a temple of sacred secularism or the front line of an insidious culture war crystallized around headscarves worn by Muslim schoolgirls (banned in 2004). Finally, public schools are seen as exemplars of "republican elitism"—a particular ideal of meritocracy that attempts to reconcile unwavering commitments to equal opportunity within the institutional framework of a national public service and high standards of intellectual rigor that stubbornly ignore the varied social backgrounds and learning styles of the students. Republican elitism has led to the paradox of a society that views "selection" as a dirty word when used in reference to limited access to specific tracks and programs, university admissions in general, and the right to continue one's studies as long as possible, but has allowed a new "aristocracy of diplomas" to replace the old one based on lineage. Hence, many of the education reforms considered by the government deal with the challenge of reconciling excellence and equality, diversity and universality, pedagogical innovation and republican tradition.

Educational establishments at every level have a modicum of administrative autonomy, and decentralization has handed over responsibility for some aspects of running them—namely, operational budgets and physical plant—to authorities below the national level. Regions share responsibility for high schools, departments for middle schools, communes for elementary schools and preschools (public universities are now largely autonomous). Nevertheless, France's system of public education remains relatively centralized and uniform across the country. The national government establishes the curriculum at the primary and secondary levels, regulates national diplomas and university degrees, accredits universities, and plays a preponderant role in funding (especially in the payment of faculty and staff salaries). Unlike the United States, there are no local boards of education. The national government's authority over education at the local and regional levels is represented via thirty subregional academies grouped into seventeen academic regions, each run by a rector nominated by the council of ministers (i.e., at the highest level of the national executive branch of government). All French laws and regulatory decrees that apply to education are compiled in a nine-volume Code of Education, which is comparable to the Civil Code. Presently, there are two national government ministries with jurisdiction over education—the Ministry of National Education (for the primary and secondary levels) and the Ministry of Higher Education, Research, and Innovation. The education minister is traditionally one of the most prominent and difficult posts in the government. The Ministry of National Education has the largest share of the national budget of any ministry (€71.6 billion in 2018, compared to €42.6 for defense). With 1.5 million total employees (including 860,000 teachers), it is also the largest civilian employer in France and the sixth largest in the world! The Ministry of Higher Education, Research, and Innovation has the third largest budget of any government ministry (€27.7 billion in 2018). Overall, France spends around €148 billion on education annually (including money spent by families and the private sector), which represents 6.8% of its GDP. A 29% share of this money goes to the primary level (incl. preschools, €6,200 per child), 39% to the secondary level (middle schools and high schools, €8,500 per middle school student, €11,700 per high school student), 20% to higher education, 10% to adult and continuing education, and 2% to extracurricular expenses. The degree of centralization and uniformity has created a massive system that is quite slow and, in many instances, overtly resistant to change. However, the national government's strong financial commitment to education, tradition of oversight, abiding interest in the ideals of public service and equality in education, and willingness to implement bold reforms have combined to maintain high levels of quality and cohesion in public education. The National Center for Distance Learning (CNED), founded in 1939 as an institution offering correspondence courses, is the public provider of online education programs—the largest online education provider in Europe and in the Francophone world.

Instruction is compulsory in France for children from age three to sixteen. Additional training or education of some form (on-the-job training, civic/community service program, apprenticeship, special occupational transition and placement programs, or further schooling) is required for young people between the ages of sixteen and eighteen. Over 95% of three-year-olds attend public or private preschools/kindergarten and 92% of young people between sixteen and eighteen are still in school. France has an excellent system of public preschools serving children from age three to six (two-year-olds may be enrolled under certain conditions). Elementary schools in France serve children normally between the ages of six and eleven and are comprised of five grades divided into two cycles. French elementary schools are generally considered to be good. As is the case at the other levels of primary and secondary education, teachers at this level, called *professeurs des écoles*, are now required to have a postgraduate degree from a school of education (ESPE) and to pass a national recruiting and accreditation exam before they can teach. Middle schools in France are called *collèges*. They serve students who are typically between the ages of eleven and fifteen and are comprised of four grades. Middle school is the last stage at which all French students follow essentially the same curriculum. French officials have invested a lot of time and money into reforms designed to strengthen middle schools and to ease away from a one-size-fits-all approach without restoring separate tracks. At the end of middle school, all French students take their first national diploma exams, through which they may obtain either the brevet or the certificate. Based on their overall scholastic records and taking into consideration their personal preferences and educational goals, they are then placed in either a generalist *lycée* (LEGT) or a vocational *lycée* (LEP). Students who have struggled academically and do not wish to continue their formal education beyond age sixteen are channeled into apprenticeships, on-the-job training, and transitional programs. French high schools (*lycées*) serve students typically between the ages of fifteen and eighteen and are comprised of three grades (although LEP students interested in a quicker transition to the working world may earn a vocational certificate called the CAP after just two years)—*Seconde*, *Première*, and *Terminale*. In the LEGT, all students follow a common first-year (Seconde) curriculum, but they begin to specialize after that. LEGTs offer a traditional generalist track (i.e., liberal arts, social sciences, math, and science) and a technical track. Both the technical track in the LEGTs and the vocational track in the LEPs are further divided into several different concentrations. Up until 2021, the generalist track in the LEGT offered three main concentrations—STEM (S), economics and social sciences (ES), and humanities and languages (L). The separate tracks and concentrations led to different versions of the *Baccalauréat* exam at the end of high school. The new "bac" does away with the old concentrations and is organized around a common core curriculum for the final two years at the lycée coupled with specialty subjects chosen by the students according to their aptitudes and interests (three subjects in the second year, reduced to two in the third and final year). The rigorous bac is still a grueling ordeal and major milestone in a young person's life; however, the most recent reform of the bac includes 40% in-school testing and 60% national exams (in French, the student's final two specialty subjects, philosophy, and major oral exam) for the determination of the final result. Those who pass receive a national diploma that is considered university-grade and is the passport to higher education. In past generations, when fewer students went to university, getting one's bac was a prestigious crowning achievement of one's education. Presently, close to 80% of an age cohort obtain the bac—compared to 60% in 1994, 20% in 1970, and 3% in 1936. The success rate of students who actually sit for the bac is also climbing: 94% in 2021, compared to 86% in 2009, 76% in 1995, and 64% in 1980. The most recent reform aims to help students discover and develop their interests in a more flexible and practical framework, and also seeks to make sure that all students—and not just the academic overachievers of the former bac S (STEM concentration)—are prepared to succeed in higher education. Its critics—including many teachers, students, parents, defenders of the French republican tradition—counter that it will devalue the bac, lead to more surreptitious forms of elite clustering, strengthen the influence of marketplace paradigms over education, and result in cuts in course offerings.

The landscape of higher education has changed dramatically over the past decade and a half. Students counting on continuing their studies for a university degree or specialized diploma still face an almost bewildering array of choices. Most end up in a traditional degree program in one of France's public universities, where there are relatively open admissions among applicants at the undergraduate level (i.e., the *licence*, or bachelor's degree). Others enroll in the common first-year university program in health sciences (PACES) before taking the rigorous, competitive entrance exams that will allow them to enroll in a medical, dental, or pharmacy program. Many of the "best and brightest" are drawn to the CPGE/*grandes écoles* track, that is, two years of intensive study in the selective *classes préparatoires*, followed—if they score well in the competitive entrance exams—by three years in an elite specialized university-level school in a coveted field like engineering, business, and political science. For students interested in sciences and technical fields, there are three-year programs at the well-regarded University Institutes of Technology (IUT) and *lycée*-based Sections for Advanced Technical Studies (STS). Both types of tracks practice selective admissions. There are 112 IUTs nationwide offering degrees in over twenty different majors. BTS programs (in the STS) number around 2,400 nationwide. The two tracks attract 4.7% and 10% of all postsecondary students, respectively. Tuition in France's public universities and many elite *grandes écoles* (esp. the public ones) is close to nonexistent, which has made a good education affordable for those who know how to navigate the system. A lot has been done to strengthen *Licence* (B.A./B.S.) programs in the open admissions tracks of the public universities. However, the biggest changes have come as a result of structural changes built into sweeping reform legislation like the 2007 LRU Law, which gave universities real autonomy and room to innovate and the 2013 ESR Law, which made it possible for universities, *grandes écoles*, and research units to pool their resources, consolidate their governance and administration, and collaborate within integrated clusters called COMUE (university communities). As a result, there have been a series of mergers, consortium arrangements, and creation of new institutions that has led to a new nomenclature of big names in French higher education, for example, Sorbonne University, PSL University (Paris), University of Paris-Saclay, Polytechnic Institute of Paris, University of Strasbourg, Federal University of Toulouse Midi-Pyrénées, Grenoble-Alpes University, Aix-Marseille University, and so on.

While public establishments dominate education at all levels in France, French law guarantees freedom in education and the country has a vibrant private education sector as well. At the primary and secondary levels, 20% of French children attend private schools—17% go to private schools that have signed contracts with the state (including most run by the Catholic Church), whereby the schools receive significant government funding (including coverage of teacher salaries) in exchange for following the national curricula and opening their doors to students of all origins and religious backgrounds. Relations between church-run schools and state-run schools used to be very contentious and the full secularization of public schools under Jules Ferry in 1882 was hailed by Republicans as a victory of reason over obscurantism, but perceived by many Catholics as an act of anticlerical cultural warfare. Today, however, relations between church and state in matters of education are mostly placid and the two systems complement each other. Many French young people have had some experience in both systems and the reason for changing from one to the other often has little to do with religion. There are quite a few private establishments in higher education—most of them secular—including many top schools of business. French law does not allow private institutions take the name of university, but there are seven Catholic institutes—including the renowned Institut Catholique de Paris—that operate as universities. These private university-level institutes, like the private *grandes écoles* and specialized schools, also receive limited public subsidies.

Further Reading
Cornu (2015); d'Iribarne and Jolivet (2016); Dreux (2019); Duru-Bellat (2013); European Commission (2017); Hörner (2007); Lewis (1985); Ministère de l'Éducation Nationale (2012); Schreiber-Barsch (2015).

Early Childhood Education and Elementary Schools

Since 2019, compulsory schooling in France starts at age three. Parents may meet the requirement by enrolling their child in a public or private *école maternelle* (preschool/kindergarten), an accredited *jardin d'enfants* (nursery school), or homeschool program (under certain conditions). Even before the new rule took effect, over 95% of French children between the ages of three and six were enrolled in school—the majority at one of France's 14,000+ public *maternelles*. Two-year olds who meet certain criteria are accepted at public preschools if space is available and over 12% of two-year-olds are so enrolled. France's public preschools/kindergartens are among the most highly rated components of the French education system. Average class size is twenty-five. The teachers are highly trained, and the classroom assistants are fully licenced. French *maternelles* have three levels—*la petite section* typically for three-year-old children; *la moyenne section* for four-year-old children; and *la grande section* for five-year-old children. The curriculum varies from one level to the next but there is a general focus on oral language skills, introduction to written language, creative self-expression, discovery of the world, socialization, and physical activity.

French children typically attend elementary for five years, from age six to age eleven. The elementary school curriculum is organized into two different cycles. The lower cycle grades are known as "CP" (*le cours préparatoire*, equivalent to U.S. first grade, for children aged six/seven years), "CE1" (*le cours élémentaire 1*, age seven/eight), and CE2 (age eight/nine). The upper cycle is comprised of two grades: "CM1" (*le cours moyen 1*, age nine/ten) and "CM2" (the equivalent of U.S. fifth grade, age ten/eleven). The average class size in French elementary schools is twenty-three. Average spending at the primary level (*maternelles* and elementary schools) is approximately €6,200/pupil, which is 15% below the OECD average. A 2013 school reform law contained several

Young children in the playroom of a French school in Angers (Maine-et-Loire department, western France). Children start attending school at the age of three—the majority in public preschools (*écoles maternelles*) that are one of the strongest components of the national education system and consist of a three-year program. The first three grades of elementary school, beginning around age six, are called CP (Preparatory Class), CE1 (Elementary Class 1), and CE2 (Elementary Class 2). (Elena Abrosimova/Dreamstime.com)

important curricular and structural changes for elementary schools that took effect during the 2016–2017 school year. The most significant was the adoption of a common core curriculum focusing on seven areas: (1) Proficiency in French; (2) Acquisition of a first modern foreign language (now starting at age six in CP); (3) Math, natural science, and technology; (4) Communication and information gathering; (5) Humanistic culture (including art and music); (6) Social studies and civics (including basic notions of history and geography, etiquette, and the values of the French Republic); and (7) Individual autonomy and initiative. One in five French children repeats a year of school at the primary level. Grades and teacher comments are recorded in a booklet called le *livret scolaire*. The school week at the elementary level normally consists of four full school days during the week (no school on Wednesday) and an extra half-day on Saturday morning, but regulations now allow localities to opt for a four-day school week. According to the OECD, France has the lowest number of required school days per year among OECD member countries—162. However, its total number of school hours per year is higher than the OECD average—884 hours (France) compared to 800 (OECD). This means that French school days are long, which is a source of complaint among families and policy makers alike. The French school year is thirty-six weeks long, begins in early September, ends in early July, and is divided into five roughly equal periods separated by four two weeklong vacations: All Saints Break in late October, Christmas Break in late December, Winter Break in the middle of February, and Spring Break in the middle of April.

See also: Chapter 2: Ferry (Jules) and the Third Republic. Chapter 5: Laïcité. Chapter 7: Child Raising Practices. Chapter 8: Private Schools; Republicanism and Public Schools; Secondary Schools.

Further Reading
Brougère et al. (2008); Garnier (2011); Gumbel (2011); Melander (2018).

Erasmus and International Educational Exchange in France

France is one of the charter members of the Erasmus program (now called Erasmus+), the European structure for educational exchange and international mobility founded in 1987 that now includes all twenty-seven member countries of the EU as well as Iceland, Norway, Lichtenstein, the Republic of Macedonia, and Turkey (a consequence of Brexit, the United Kingdom has withdrawn from Erasmus+). Named for the Dutch Renaissance humanist Erasmus of Rotterdam (1466–1536), the program provides a European framework and funding for international travel, educational and cultural exchange programs, and collaboration among institutions for students (secondary through university), educators, scholars, young graduates, volunteers, professionals working with associations, and members of sports clubs and teams. At the higher education level, Erasmus-sponsored student exchanges range from two months to one year in length. It also aims to foster transparency and recognition of educational credentials within the EU and foster European unity and common identity (83% of participants report feeling "more European" because of their Erasmus program). Since its inception, it has benefited over 9 million people, including close to 4.5 million students. Nearly 300,000 people benefit from Erasmus exchanges annually. In 2016, over 71,000 people participated in Erasmus international mobility exchanges involving France (going to and coming from). France is currently the number one source of students participating in Erasmus exchanges and the number four destination for students from other Erasmus countries. As important as it is, Erasmus is just one institutional framework for international student exchanges in France. Others include direct exchange agreements between French institutions and counterparts abroad and government-sponsored foreign language teaching assistantships. Overall, about 4% of French students in higher education study abroad (78,000 in 2014–2015, 58% of whom stayed in Europe), which is a little below the OECD average (6%) and only half the EU average (8%)—a statistic that educational authorities are working to improve.

By contrast, 10% of the students enrolled in French universities and other institutions of higher education are foreigners—appreciably higher than the OECD average of 6%. In the 2015–2016 academic year, this represented 310,000 foreign students in France, a number that French education officials are hoping to double by 2025. France is the leading non-Anglophone country in terms of welcoming foreign students—fourth in the world overall after the United States, the United Kingdom, and Australia. The leading source of foreign students in France in 2015–2016 was the Maghreb region of North Africa (Morocco, Algeria, and Tunisia), accounting for 72,000 foreign students in France—nearly 25% of the total. Sub-Saharan Africa (esp. the former French colonies of Senegal, Cameroon, and Ivory Coast) accounted for 62,000 foreign students. A total of 59,000 foreign students came from Europe (Italy, Germany, and Spain leading the way). Asian countries (led by China, Vietnam, and India) contributed 50,000. The United States sent France close to 6,000 students. Paris and its surrounding region attract the most foreign students, followed by Lyon, Lille (close to the Belgian border), and Toulouse. Foreign students from the EU and students with French or European baccalaureate diplomas use the Parcourssup online platform to apply to study in France. Students from forty-one other countries use the "Études en France" platform, which they can access through their country-specific Campus France website (e.g., www.usa.campusfrance.org).

See also: Chapter 3: European Union. Chapter 8: Secondary Schools; Universities and Higher Education. Chapter 9: Francophonie.

Further Reading
Cairns (2017); Feyen and Krzaklewska (2013).

Grandes Écoles

France's *Grandes Écoles* are highly selective university-level schools in specialized fields that are historically and structurally not part of the French public university system. The oldest ones date back to the eighteenth century and the early 1800s. They were founded to teach modern subjects not offered in the universities, which remained bastions of traditionalism well into the nineteenth century, and thus to train a new national elite with practical expertise in science and technology and devotion to rational inquiry. Examples include some of France's leading engineering schools like École Nationale des Ponts et Chaussées (1747), École Nationale Supérieure d'Arts et Métiers (1780), École Nationale Supérieure des Mines de Paris (1787), École Polytechnique (1794, known familiarly as "X"), and École Centrale de Paris (1829, known as "CentraleSupélec" following its merger with another top school). The École Normale Supérieure de Paris was founded in 1794 as a school for training professors and has produced some of greatest French minds of the twentieth century and today in the humanities, social sciences, natural sciences, and mathematics. Many of France's winners of the Nobel Prize and the Fields Medal were students at "La Rue d'Ulm" (as ENS Paris is often called in reference to its historic location in the Latin Quarter of Paris). Another historic *grande école* is the École Nationale Supérieure des Beaux-Arts de Paris, France's leading school of art, which was reestablished in 1817 but traces its roots back to the Royal Academy of Painting and Sculpture (1648). New *grandes écoles* were founded to educate in fields like political science, public administration, and business, which were not yet taught in the universities though they were deemed important to the public life and industrial development of the nation. France's preeminent school of political science, the Insitut d'Études Politiques de Paris ("Sciences Po") was founded in 1872 and served as the model for the nine other IEP that were founded after World War II and in subsequent years. Created in 1945 and relocated to Strasbourg in 1991, the École Nationale d'Administration (ENA) produced many illustrious alumni (known as *énarques*), including four presidents of the Fifth Republic (Valéry Giscard d'Estaing, Jacques Chirac, François Hollande, and Emmanuel Macron), seven French prime ministers, numerous cabinet ministers, and quite a few titans of industry. It was permanently closed by Macron in 2021, in part in response to allegations (by the Yellow Vests protesters and other critics) that it produced an insulated ruling elite that was out of touch with the lives and needs of ordinary French people. France's three leading business schools, École Supérieure de Commerce de Paris (ESCP, 1819), École des Hautes Études Commerciales de Paris (HEC, 1881), and École Supérieure des Sciences Economiques et Commerciales (ESSEC, 1907)—collectively known as "the three Parisians"—also fall into this elite category. The graduate-only Institut Européen d'Administration des Affaires (INSEAD, 1957), with its main campus in Fontainebleau (near Paris), is a renowned business school with an international mission.

French universities operate as low-cost, open-admissions public institutions. Except in a small (but slowly growing) number of special programs, they are in principle open to all holders of the high school baccalaureate diploma (*bacheliers*). Space may be limited and priority for enrollment may be given to students residing in the same regional academic jurisdiction where a given university is located. However, *la sélection* (selective admissions) is a dirty word among university students, who see access to higher education as a right. In contrast, the *grandes écoles*, which may be private or public, are highly selective. Admissions for a very limited number of spots is normally based a competitive entrance exam (*un concours d'entrée*). Many *grandes écoles* (including the most prestigious) also require completion of affiliated preparatory classes, *or prépas*—rigorous two-year *post-bac* programs known officially as *Classes Prépartoires aux Grandes Écoles* (CPGE) that are offered in certain top *lycées*. Admission to the relevant CPGE is based on the strength of an applicant's file. While the CPGE curriculum is equivalent to the first two years at a university, the workload is famously heavy and the emphasis is on preparation for the *grande école* entrance exams. There are over 450 CPGE in France offering preparatory programs that fall into three broad disciplinary areas—science and math, literary studies and humanities (known as *khâgne*), and economics and business. The CPGE-*grande école* track pulls in 7–8% of all students newly entering the higher education system. Those who successfully complete this demanding "bac+5" program—two years of CPGE followed (normally) by three years in a *grande école*—receive a diploma that is highly valued in the job market and equivalent to a master's degree in the European "Bologna Process" framework. In certain fields, they may start a doctoral program in either a university or a *grande école* that offers one. There is a sense of group identity and solidarity among the alumni of specific *grandes écoles* that is absent among French university graduates. In addition to the *grandes écoles* in engineering (207 nationally accredited schools in 2017), business (230+ schools), politics, and fine arts (230+ schools)—and the four ultra-elite *écoles normales supérieures* (ENS Paris-Ulm, ENS Paris-Saclay, ENS Lyon, and ENS Rennes)—there are selective specialized schools in an array of other fields, including architecture, decorative arts, fashion, design, culinary arts, film, archaeology and art history (e.g., L'École du Louvre, founded 1882), civil aviation, applied science, computer science, telecommunications, agronomy, veterinary medicine, public health, social work, tourism, hospitality management, journalism, media and communication, and statistics and econometrics. The military service academies are also considered *grandes écoles*. The most famous is École Spéciale Militaire de Saint-Cyr (the French army academy, founded by Napoleon in 1802), known simply as "Saint-Cyr" in reference to its original location (it is now located in Coëtquidan, Brittany). France's other service academies include the École Navale (the naval academy, founded in 1827) and the École de l'Air (the Air Force Academy, founded in 1933).

The *grandes écoles* have a well-deserved reputation for excellence in France and several have appeared in the top tier of world university rankings—for example, ENS Paris-Ulm, Polytechnique, CentraleSupélec, ENS Lyon, and Ponts ParisTech. However, they are not generally well known abroad—a competitive disadvantage in the age of globalization. Various approaches have been taken to address the issue of global stature and visibility. One such effort (1991) involved institutional cooperation and rebranding in the form of a consortium of ten top Paris-based engineering schools collectively known as ParisTech. A 2006 law provided for more integrated forms of institutional cooperation and synergy among universities, *grandes écoles*, and research labs as Pôles de Recherche et d'Enseignement Supérieur (PRES). These arrangements, which also brought public and private institutions together under the same umbrella, were strengthened appreciably by the 2013 Law on Higher Education and Research (Loi ESR), which transformed the PRES into COMUE—Communautés d'Universités et d'Établissements. The university communities have the same legal status as individual universities, may pool their resources, develop coordinated hiring strategies, consolidate budgetary authority, grant degrees under one name, and merge institutionally to form single comprehensive universities.

ParisTech member schools have joined different COMUE without severing existing ties among them. For instance, Mines ParisTech and Chimie ParisTech are part of PSL University (Paris), as is ENS Paris-Ulm. In 2019, the illustrious École Polytechnique joined forces with four other top engineering to form the Polytechnic Institute of Paris (an independent part of the Saclay research campus project). While admissions to COMUE-member *grandes écoles* are still separate and selective, CPGE students must also maintain registration at an affiliated local university and there exist alternative means of *grande école* admission for qualified university students who have not first studied at a CPGE.

See also: Chapter 8: Private Schools; Republicanism and Public Schools; Secondary Schools; Universities and Higher Education. Chapter 10: Social Hierarchies.

Further Reading

Calmand et al. (2009); Deer (2009); Schippling (2018); van Zanten (2016); van Zanten and Maxwell (2015).

Private Schools

Although public institutions dominate education in France, the freedom to operate and attend a private school is a recognized right. However, the national government regulates all educational establishments and retains a monopoly in the granting of nationally recognized diplomas and degrees. About 20% of French students attend private schools at the primary and secondary levels. Most of them attend private schools that have signed agreements with the national government that allows them to receive public funding in exchange for agreeing to follow the national curriculum, employ qualified and certified teachers, and open their doors to all children regardless of race or religion. The government pays the salaries of the teachers in affiliated private schools, but the teachers do not have civil servant status. Almost all (95%) of state-affiliated and subsidized private schools are Catholic. The current affiliation framework dates to the Debré Law of 1959, which laid to rest (mostly) over a century of acrimonious competition between secular public schools and Catholic ones. The conflict flared up briefly in 1984 when the socialist Mitterrand administration proposed a merger of public and private schools. However, the plan was withdrawn after over one million people descended into the streets of Paris to defend *l'école libre*. Today, the French private sector of primary and secondary education involves approximately 5,300 primary schools, 1,800 middle schools, 1,600 high schools, 110,000 teachers, 800,000 families, and 2 million children. Private schools do not necessarily have the reputation of being academically superior to public ones. Religious faith plays an important role in the choice of private school over public school for some families, but others practice a sort of consumer-minded school zapping, switching back and forth between private and public schools when they think that one or the other gives their child a better environment at any particular stage. This zapping is particularly prevalent at the secondary level as the baccalaureate exam looms.

Private institutions play an important role in higher education, especially among *grandes écoles* and other specialized schools that are separate from universities. Most French business schools and many of its engineering schools are nonsectarian private institutions. Private institutions may receive government funds under certain conditions and new regulations allow some of them (e.g., the business schools) to join public institutions in "Communities of Universities and Establishments" (COMUE). Technically, there are no private universities in France. Although France's historic universities were originally institutions of the church (the University of Paris, founded in 1150, received a papal charter in 1215 and was home to the most illustrious faculty of theology in the Middle Ages), they were abolished during the French Revolution and later reestablished as public and secular institutions in the nineteenth century. The Walloon Law of 1875 authorized the establishment of private institutions of higher education, but such institutions are prohibited by law (1880) from calling themselves "universities" and cannot issue "national" diplomas like the *licence* (bachelor's degree). There are presently seven Catholic "institutes" in France—five that date from 1875 (Angers, Lille, Lyon, Paris, and Toulouse) and two newer ones founded in 1989 (Rennes and La Roche-sur-Yon). Relations between these institutions and the state are good. All are recognized as "Private Institutions of Higher Education that Serve the Common Good" (EESPIG) and receive limited government subsidies. They are home to over 40,000 French and foreign students. Unlike public universities, they practice selective admissions and charge tuition fees (although their tuition fee does not compare with that of private universities in the United States). Their academic programs are strong and attract students whose choice is not always motivated by religious identity. Some publicize themselves as universities (e.g., the Catholic University of Lyon) without interference from the state. The Catholic Institute of Paris, which has a fine international reputation, uses the term only in English. These institutes still do not issue national university degrees on their own authority, but their students may nonetheless earn them through cooperative agreements with local public universities or regional rectorates. France also has a small number of other private university-level institutions like the Pôle Universitaire Leonard de Vinci, which has a campus outside Paris and serves over 4,600 students.

See also: Chapter 2: Mitterrand (François) and France in the 1980s and 1990s. Chapter 5: Catholicism; Laïcité. Chapter 8: Early Childhood Education and Elementary Schools; Grandes Écoles; Republicanism and Public Schools; Universities and Higher Education.

Further Reading

Bertola (2017); Bourget (2019); Deer (2003); Moog (2016).

Republicanism and Public Schools

Public schools are the quintessential institutions of the French Republic. The "republican" values of the school include the fundamental equality of all students, the critical role that public services play in maintaining the said equality across the national territory, the combination of meritocracy and intellectual rigor known as "republican elitism," emphasis on individual autonomy as inseparable from critical thinking and rational judgment, secularism defined not just as the confessional neutrality of public institutions but as an individual civic duty and collective sacred trust, and an ideal of progress defined in terms of individual upward mobility and gradual social improvement through education and the advancement of knowledge. Furthermore, public education is often credited with giving the Republic widespread legitimacy during the Belle Époque (1871–1914) after over a hundred years of political turmoil, regime change, and ideologically polarized "culture wars" dating back to the French Revolution. The historical figure most closely associated with the republicanizing of public schools is Jules Ferry (1832–1893, three-time minister of public instruction (1879–1883), president of the council of ministers 1880–1881), who laid a new foundation for public education by making public primary schools *free*, instruction *compulsory* between the ages of six and thirteen (choice of the means of instruction was still left to parents), and public schools *secular* in nature—the main provisions of the "Ferry Laws" of 1881–1882. According to historian Pierre Chevallier, implementation of the secular mandate (*Laïcité*) entailed nothing less than a "Separation of Church and School" that served as a precursor of the more comprehensive separation of church and state instituted by the law of 1905. Crucifixes were removed from classrooms, religious content was taken out of the curriculum, and priests and members of religious orders were not allowed to teach in public primary schools without proper certification (and were later barred from teaching altogether). Compulsory secular instruction in "morals and civics" replaced religious instruction in the curriculum. Secularization proved controversial at first—in many small towns, the local schoolmaster and the parish priest vied for the hearts and minds of young people via competing public and parochial schools—however, in time, the "republican school" became one of the most respected public institutions in France.

Laïcité (secularism) in the schools is still a flashpoint today. Some, like the philosophers Régis Debray and Élisabeth Badinter, argue that strict adherence to the norm is as fundamental to France's republican identity as ever, while others, like the sociologists Jean Baubérot and Michel Wieviorka, warn that "absolutist" interpretations of the concept are actually a hindrance to civil peace and the integration of religious minorities. Tensions over *Laïcité* have been at the forefront of public debates over school and society since the first incidents associated with the Headscarf Affair in 1989—so named because female Muslim middle and high school students were suspended for refusing to take off the hijabs they wore to school—although they have subsided somewhat since the passage of a 2004 law banning in schools all articles of clothing that can be considered ostensible displays of religious identity. Public support for *Laïcité* and "republican values" as explicit components of the public school environment is on the rise and is often a subtext of discussions of other school-related issues such as curricular reforms, academic and career guidance, and student success rates. This is evident in both the name and some of the specific provisions of the 2013 school reform known as *La Refondation de l'École de la République*, which reestablished "moral and civic instruction" as part of the core curriculum of French schools and was followed up by the adoption of an official Secularism Charter (*Charte de la Laïcité à l'École*) designed as both a pedagogical tool and a set of ground rules for reinforced application of the norm. It features declarations such as: "Secularism safeguards freedom of conscience. Everyone has the freedom to believe or not to believe" (Art. 3); "Secularism in schools provides the conditions for pupils to shape their personality, exercise their free will and learn about citizenship. It protects them against any proselytism or pressures which could prevent them from making their own choices" (Art. 6); "Secularism gives pupils access to a common and shared culture" (Art. 7); "Secularism rejects all violence and discrimination. It safeguards gender equality and is based on a culture of respect for others and mutual understanding" (Art. 9); and "In their thought processes and activities, pupils help breathe life into secularism within their schools" (Art. 15).

See also: Chapter 2: Ferry (Jules) and the Third Republic. Chapter 3: Republic. Chapter 5: Catholicism; Islam; Laïcité. Chapter 8: Private Schools.

Further Reading

Chadwick 1997); Lizotte (2020); Mattei (2012); Mattei and Aguilar (2016); Roebroeck and Guimonda (2015); Soysal and Szakács (2010).

EDUCATION REFORMS

The size and degree of centralization of the French National Education system, the importance France attaches to excellence in education (e.g., the phenomenon known as "republican elitism") and the need to reconcile the egalitarian ethos of a public service to the changing demands of the modern economy and the increasing diversity of the French student population have made major nationwide education reforms and raucous protests against them recurring events in France since the 1950s. The names of French education ministers who have attempted such reforms and dealt with other contentious issues—sometimes successfully, other times not— are well known and seared into the collective memory of the generations of students, teachers, and families who grappled with them—for example, Edgar Faure, René Haby, Alain Savary, Jean-Pierre Chevènement, Alain Devaquet (higher education and research), Lionel Jospin, Jack Lang, François Bayrou, Claude Allègre, Luc Ferry, Luc Chatel, Valérie Pécresse (higher education and research), Vincent Peillon, and Jean-Michel Blanquer. Major initiatives in recent years have included the LRU reform (2007) giving more autonomy to universities, broad changes to primary and secondary education billed as the "Reorganization of the Schools of the Republic" (2013), and the Baccalaureate 2021 plan (2018) for reshaping the high school curriculum and diploma exam.

Secondary Schools

Secondary education in France is comprised of two cycles: lower secondary education involving four years (typically ages eleven to fifteen) at a *collège*, or middle school; and upper secondary education involving three years (typically ages fifteen to eighteen) at a *lycée*, or high school. All French young people follow the same core curriculum through middle school. From that point on, students begin to specialize and paths diverge. In principle, every French young person is required to stay in school (or enroll in an apprenticeship program) through age sixteen. While most French young people stay in school for two to three years (92% of young people aged sixteen to eighteen are still in school) and earn a diploma, and many continue their studies at the tertiary level (73% of all nineteen-year-olds in France are students, 44% of young people aged twenty-five to thirty-four have earned a postsecondary degree or professional qualification), there were still around 100,000 young people in 2017 who left school without any kind of diploma (the number was over twice that in the 1980s). In response to the problems this posed, since 2020, all French young people between the ages of sixteen and eighteen must continue their education or vocational training in some way— through on-the-job training, an apprenticeship, enrollment in a community service program, participation in an occupational counseling and placement program, or continuation of their schooling.

There is a major national examination at the end of both middle school and high school. At the conclusion of the lower secondary cycle, all middle school students take either the brevet exam for the Diplôme National du Brevet (DNB) or the Certificat de Formation Générale (CFP) exam, which is designed for students on a vocational track. Most, but not all, high school students take the baccalaureate exam at the end of their high school (*lycée*) years—a legendary rite of passage that looms large over the lives of French teenagers. The *baccalauréat*, or *bac*, is more than a high school diploma, it is the capstone experience of a rigorous curriculum (like the British A Level exams or a slate of Advanced Placement exams in the United States), a requirement for the continuation of one's studies at university level, and is a university-level credential in its own right. The type of *lycée* that one attends, the academic track one follows there, one's success or failure at the bac exam, and one's prospects for qualification for an elite track in higher education are all important considerations in a young person's life. Despite the existence of numerous viable vocational and postsecondary options, the entire French system is traditionally geared toward funneling students into higher education and the terminal diploma one eventually receives plays a decisive role in one's ultimate place in the social hierarchy. Consequently, a French student's years in secondary education tend to be highly competitive and stressful. Not surprisingly, the French spend a lot on secondary education—€8,500/student at the middle school level, €11,000/student in generalist *lycées*, and €12,400/student in vocational *lycées*. Overall, 39% of all money spent on education in France goes toward secondary education (compared to a 29% share for primary education and 20% for higher education). French per student spending on upper secondary education (i.e., the *lycée*/high school level) is 37% above the OECD average.

In secondary schools, levels are counted down to the final year of high school. Hence the four years of middle school are known as *Sixième* (sixth, which also happens to be the equivalent of sixth grade in the United States, typically age eleven/twelve), *Cinquième* (fifth, age twelve/thirteen), *Quatrième* (fourth, age thirteen/fourteen), and *Troisième* (third, age fourteen/fifteen). Following a curricular reform in 2015, middle school is presently divided into two cycles. The first year, *Sixième*, is part of the "Consolidation Cycle" along with the final year of elementary school, CM2. Here, the emphasis is on pedagogical continuity, the mastery of basic skills and proficiencies, and a gradual transition to the rigors of secondary school academics. *Cinquième*, *Quatrième*, and *Troisième* (the equivalent of ninth grade in the United States, which is typically part of high school) form the "Enhancement Cycle," where emphasis is on higher-level proficiencies, in-depth discipline-specific knowledge, preparation for high school, and early academic and career guidance. Middle schools follow a common core curriculum that includes French, continued study of the modern foreign language started in elementary school, math, artistic expression, art history, music, history-geography (taught together), and moral and civic education. In the Enhancement Cycle, students begin work on a second modern foreign language (or regional language) in *Cinquième*, science classes become more discipline-distinct, and students may take electives like theatre and dance. Students also have the option of joining special sections with a focus on European studies, bilingual studies, and classical languages and civilization. Another result of the middle school curricular reform of 2015 is that students work on one or more practical interdisciplinary projects (*Enseignements Pratiques Interdisciplinaires*). A new program rolled out in 2017–2018 was "Devoirs Faits," the reintroduction of daily homework assignments beginning in the final year of elementary school (CM2).

Middle School academics have proven to be one of the most problematic parts of the French education system. This is due to expected issues like the challenges of early adolescence, the growing diversity of the student population, budgetary constraints, ill-adapted curricula, and issues of teacher training. However, history must also be taken into consideration. Lower secondary education in France was not unified until 1975, when the Haby Law created *le collège unique*, or consolidated middle school. This reform involved the merger of two separate and different types of institutions—the *collèges d'enseignement général* (CEG), created in 1959 and known to be less rigorous (and to cater to a less affluent clientele), and the more highly regarded *collèges d'enseignement secondaire* (CES) created in 1963. A further peculiarity of the history of education in France is that throughout the nineteenth century and well into the twentieth, primary schools and secondary schools did not constitute different levels in a student's progression but different, implicitly class-based systems that each served students from age six through their teens—the elite and tuition-charging secondary schools for the bourgeoisie and the primary schools for everybody else. The former offered preparatory classes for younger students (antecedents of the CES), whereas the latter offered additional programs for older students (the basis for the CEG). Even after the different types of colleges merged and a common curriculum developed, student segregation persisted into the 1980s in the form of groupings by level of ability and achievement, which closely aligned with social class and income-level distinctions. Nowadays, a decisive moment comes at the end of the *Troisième* (final) year of middle school, when rising high school students are assigned to a traditional generalist high school, (*lycée d'enseignement général et technologique*, or LEGT) or a vocational high school (*lycée professionnel*, or LEP). The former places them on track for university-level work whereas the latter involves training in a skilled trade or practical field and implies a quicker transition to the working world. Another option available is placement in a nonacademic apprenticeship program, which consists of both on-the-job training and classes at a *centre de formation d'apprentis*, or CFA.

The standard French *lycée* program is for three years—*Seconde* (age fifteen/sixteen), *Première* (age sixteen/seventeen), and *Terminale* (age seventeen/eighteen). All students enrolled in LEGT-type *lycées* take essentially the same courses in the first year (*Seconde*) with the possibility of some exploratory electives. They then begin to personalize their studies and focus on certain subject areas. The first major decision is whether to pursue a course of studies that leads to a general or technical baccalaureate. Within each track, there is further specialization. Candidates for the *bac général* formerly enrolled in one of three disciplinary series, or concentrations—"S" (*Scientifique*, or STEM), "ES" (*Économique et Sociale*, or economics and social sciences), and "L" (*Littéraire*, or humanities and arts). The *bac S* was the most sought after and highly regarded. The Baccalauréat 2021 reform eliminated the series to make specialization less narrow and more gradual, to allow for a wider array of cross-disciplinary combinations based on student interest, and to better prepare all students for postsecondary academics.

All LEGT students still follow essentially the same curriculum during the first year (*Seconde*) as well as a common core curriculum in the second and third years comprised of French (second year), philosophy (third year), history-geography, moral and civic education, first and second modern foreign languages, physical education and sports, and interdisciplinary applied science and digital technology ("scientific and digital humanities"). Generalist track students then begin to personalize their studies through the choice of three specialty subjects in the second year (*Première*), two of which are continued in the third and final year (*Terminale*). Their options include fine arts; ecology, agronomy, and development; history-geography, geopolitics, and political science; humanities, literature, and philosophy; world/regional languages and literatures; mathematics; digital and information sciences; earth and life sciences; engineering; economics and social sciences; and physics and chemistry (however, not all schools offer all options). Additionally, they have academic and career advising and may take an optional elective in each of the final two years (fine arts, classical languages and civilizations, physical education and sports, third modern foreign language, "expert" math, supplementary math, and law/major contemporary issues). Technical track students focus on their concentration-specific curriculum during their second and third years in an LEGT—management (STMG); design and applied arts (STD2A); industry and sustainable development (STI2D); laboratory sciences (STL); public health and social work (ST2S); theatre, music and dance (TMD); hospitality (STHR); and agronomy and animal husbandry (STAV). Students at France's vocational high schools, or *lycées professionnels*, have a choice between a shorter, practical two-year program leading to a Certificate of Professional Aptitude (CAP), or a more traditional three-year program leading to the Professional Baccalaureate (*bac pro*). Created in 1911, the CAP track is focused on learning a trade (200 specialties are offered), but still includes a core of general education courses. Candidates for the *bac pro* (created in 1985) have a choice among seventy specialty fields (e.g., aeronautics, artistic trades, master butcher, sales, secretarial services).

All holders of the baccalaureate diploma are entitled to continue their studies at the university level. However, *bac pro* holders tend to do less well there than their peers with a *bac général* or *technologique*. According to the Ministry of Education, less than one-third (29%) of French high school students enroll in a vocational *lycée* (LEP) after middle school. Among those who do, 82% pursue the *bac pro* track and 18%, the CAP track. By contrast, over two-thirds of all high school students (71%) enroll in a generalist *lycée* (LEGT), where 72% choose the *bac général* track, compared to 28% for the *bac technologique* track. The Baccalauréat 2021 reform also modifies the examination process itself by incorporating a large component of regular in-school testing throughout high school. Critics of the reform fear that the changes will diminish the rigor and value of the bac, give a decisive upper hand to the short-sighted dictates of market-driven pragmatism at the expense of intellectual discovery and passion, lead inevitably to cuts in staff and course offerings, and do little to diminish socioeconomic inequality and privilege in school (e.g., because affluent families with more cultural capital will always be better equipped to navigate the system and seek out and benefit from its more elite and prestigious options).

The legendary "bac" exam is a big deal in the lives of French high school students and is likely to remain so for the foreseeable future. Clubs, sports, theater, and other extracurricular activities are not a major part of high schools in France, although they do exist. French students are quite politically active, however, and often take part in public protests of social and economic injustice, racism, and unpopular government policies.

See also: Chapter 3: Protests. Chapter 5: Laïcité. Chapter 8: Early Childhood Education and Elementary Schools; Grandes Écoles; Private Schools; Universities and Higher Education.

Further Reading

"Back to Bac" (2018); Dobbins and Martens (2012); El Atia (2004); El Atia (2008); Martin-van der Hagen and Deane (2003).

THE "BAC"

The high school diploma exam—the "bac"—is a big deal in the lives of French students. It is the passport to higher education, a mark of social distinction, and a rite of passage. The Baccalauréat 2021 reform made major changes to the exam process. Now, 40% of the overall exam grade comes from in-school testing, a combination of anonymous common final exams (30%) and course grade averages (10%). This *contrôle continu* component pertains to the common core subjects, the specialty subject not continued during the final year, and optional electives. The remaining 60% of the overall exam grade is determined by the results of traditional end-of-year national exams (*épreuves terminales*) in June. The subjects covered by these exams are French (taken at the end of the second year), philosophy, and two major specialty subject areas—all taken at the end of the third year. The terminal exams also include an oral exam on topics related to the student's areas of specialization. Students with a borderline non-passing overall exam grade (a passing grade is 10/20, borderline grades begin at 08/10) may take an additional compensatory oral later in the summer. Waiting for the results to be posted is a big (and nerve racking) moment in a young person's life. The rigorous nature of high school academics and focus on preparation for the "bac" leave little time for extracurricular activities. Presently, close to 80% of an age cohort obtain their bac—a long-standing government goal. However, the bac used to be more exclusive—in 1994, only 60% of an age cohort obtained the bac, compared to 20% in 1970 and 3% in 1936. Among actual bac candidates, the success rate is currently 94%, compared to 76% in 1995 and 64% in 1980.

Universities and Higher Education

French young people contemplating higher education face a wide array of choices. For the highest achievers, there are the small but highly selective quasi-graduate school-level *grandes écoles* in sought-after fields like engineering, business, and politics, as well as elite programs in the humanities, social sciences, math, and natural sciences at the prestigious *écoles normales supérieures*. Admittance to the *grandes écoles* is obtained via competitive entrance exams taken after two years of intensive preparatory studies at the undergraduate level in special *classes préparatoires* (CPEG) that are offered in a number of top high schools. For students interested in fields like journalism, communication, social work, public health, public works, architecture, art, performing arts, music, film, design, tourism, hospitality management, and agriculture, there are specialized schools that recruit holders of the baccalaureate diploma (*bacheliers*) directly out of high school based on an entrance exam, an application dossier, or both. For students interested in applied technology and a quicker transition to the workforce, there are two-year programs offered in the Sections for Advanced Technical Studies (STS) that lead to the Brevet de Technicien Supérieur (BTS) diploma. France's University Institutes of Technology (IUT) offer rigorous university-level three-year programs in technical fields that lead to a marketable professional bachelor's degree (*licence professionnelle*). However, for the majority of students—62% (over 1.5 million)—higher education is synonymous with studying at a public university, of which there are currently (Nov. 2021) 68 in France. French education officials have sought to make the varied institutional landscape of higher education more cohesive. One way has been to facilitate transfers from one type of institution to another. For example, students enrolled in a CPGE must maintain concurrent registration at a local university or some other accredited higher education establishment and there now exists an alternative path for admission to a *grande école* for qualified university students who have not studied in a CPGE. Recent landmark legislation allows different types of public institutions of higher education (as well as some private ones) and research centers, to become affiliated, pool their resources and fundraising efforts, consolidate their administrative structures, coordinate their academic and research programs, and offer degrees (e.g., through their joint doctoral schools) by forming consolidated "Communities of Universities and Institutions" (COMUE). In many cases, the affiliations have led to full mergers and the creation of new comprehensive research universities comprised of different colleges and schools along the lines of the American model. The COMUE structure replaced the looser form of university grouping known as the PRES (2006) in 2013. France presently counts twenty-five such "university communities." Since French higher education can seem like a confusing hodge-podge even to natives, the Repertoire National de Certification Professionnelle (RNCP) has created four levels of general qualification that correspond to the number of years of higher education one has successfully completed after having received a high school baccalaureate diploma: Level IV = bac; Level III = B + 2 (years of higher education); Level II = bac + 3 or 4; and Level I = bac + 5 (or more).

Unlike the other options in higher education, all of which practice a form of selective admissions, the undergraduate programs at French public universities are essentially open to all holders of the baccalaureate and are also very inexpensive—average annual tuition and fees for a bachelor's degree program is less than €200—thanks to public funding from the state, which considers them a public service. There may be limits on spots in an entering class and priority may be given to students who reside in the academic region in which a given university is located, but all *bacheliers* are still considered equal. Proposed reforms that include a degree of selectivity in admissions or higher tuition fees are usually met with fierce resistance on the part of students and the organizations—like UNEF, the largest student union in France, founded in 1907—that represent them. A certain (and growing) number of exceptions to the open admissions policy at the undergraduate level in public universities have been granted for innovative and high-demand programs. For instance, incoming students may freely enroll in the new common first-year university program in health sciences (PACES) before a highly competitive entrance exam that will allow only the best of them to enroll in a medical, dental, or pharmacy degree program. Recent high school graduates now "apply" for admission online via the "Parcourssup" platform by listing ten postsecondary institutions and programs of their choice. The site is a true application platform only for selective admissions options like the CPGE. Overall, it functions as a placement tool that uses an algorithm to assign the user to an institution in a way that takes into consideration a student's preference, interests, and qualifications, as well as general issues of supply and demand. Special consideration is given to the top 10% of students in each *lycée*. Given their mass audience, their open admissions policy, and their tradition of egalitarian uniformity, French universities have been unfairly portrayed as bureaucratic and impersonal, rather mediocre in terms of academic excellence, and ill-adapted to the needs of the job market. If there is a grain of truth in this uninspiring portrayal, it is perhaps only in the first cycle of university studies—the undergraduate programs leading to the *licence* (bachelor's) degree—where there have been high rates of failure and high concentrations of academically average and below-average students enrolled in *sciences humaines* (i.e., humanities and softer social sciences) majors that offer neither the intellectually versatile background of a true liberal arts degree nor marketable professional qualifications beyond generic "bac + 3" status. Still, even this narrow application of the stereotype is both inaccurate and misleading. There have always been areas of excellence in France's public service universities, in certain universities with excellent reputations, in specific disciplinary programs that attract top students, and at the master's and doctoral levels—where French universities are as strong as their international counterparts. Moreover, much has been done in recent years in the universities to develop new majors that both relate more directly to the job market and compare favorably to the offerings of the *grandes écoles*. The first semester of the first year of the *licence* track is now more general in nature and designed to allow students to explore different options and discover their interests. Student advising has also been made a priority. French higher education is now fully integrated into the European Credit Transfer System (ECTS) and has streamlined its offerings of diplomas and degrees to correspond to the common Bachelor-Master-Doctor framework developed under the Bologna Process: bachelor's degree (*Licence*) = first cycle = bac + 3 = 180 ECTS credits; master's degree = second cycle = bac + 5 = 120 additional ECTS credits; doctorate = third cycle = bac + 8 = 120 additional ECTS credits (with a successfully defended thesis).

The history of France's universities is complex and reflects that of the nation. The Middle Ages were a golden age of France's historic universities. The university structure itself emerged from the great cathedral schools as independent corporations of scholars divided into four faculties—an undergraduate faculty of liberal arts and

The courtyard of the Sorbonne in Paris. The Sorbonne was chartered in 1257 as a residential college for theology students attending the University of Paris (founded in 1150, chartered in 1200), with which it is still synonymous. Several institutions of higher education use buildings that are part of the historic Sorbonne campus. Following major restructuring of French universities in the 2000s and 2010s, present-day Sorbonne University regularly ranks in the top fifty universities worldwide and top three nationally. The chapel at the rear of the courtyard (arch. Jacques Lemercier, 1642) is a fine example of French Baroque-Classical architecture. (Rakonjac Srdjan/Dreamstime.com)

graduate faculties of law, medicine, and theology. The University of Paris, the second oldest in Europe, was founded in 1150, and given a royal charter in 1200 (and papal recognition in 1215). While often confused with the University of Paris as a whole, the Sorbonne (founded in 1257) was an endowed residential college for scholarship students at the university's faculty of theology—arguably the most prestigious in all of western Christendom. The University of Montpellier's Faculty of Medicine, chartered in 1220 but with roots dating back to 1137, is the oldest school of medicine in the western world still in operation. By the time of the French Renaissance (sixteenth century), the medieval universities of France had become bogged down in traditionalism and clericalism. In response, Guillaume Budé founded the Collège Royal (now called the Collège de France) in 1530 under the royal patronage of King Francis I in order to teach subjects ignored by the University of Paris (e.g., Greek, Hebrew, and natural sciences). The Collège de France still operates today as a special *grand établissment* of higher education that grants no degrees and has no registered students (lectures are free and open to the public) and currently has fifty-one tenured faculty chairs awarded to the most illustrious French thinkers, scholars, and scientists. Universities were abolished during the French Revolution in 1793, but Napoleon bought them back to life in 1806 in the form of the centralized Imperial University of France, which was divided into local teaching faculties. This structure was impractical and out of sync with modern developments (e.g., the rise of German universities), so it eventually gave way to a system of semiautonomous modern universities, which opened in 1896. In the aftermath of the student revolt of May 1968, these large entities were broken up and new universities were formed to meet the rising demand for higher education—usually along disciplinary lines. These universities were more democratic in their local governance but quite uniform in terms of their curricular offerings as parts of a massive national public service system.

Recent reforms (e.g., the LRU law of 2007 and the ESR law of 2013) have led to a new wave of consolidations and mergers in French higher education, which has increased institutional autonomy, fostered curricular innovation, and enhanced the international standing of French universities. In some cases, institutions resembling the pre-1968 universities reemerged through mergers. The University of Strasbourg and Aix-Marseille University (the largest university in the French-speaking world) are good examples of this type of structure. In other cases, consortium-like affiliations have federated most of the universities and institutions of higher education in an urban area. One successful example of this type is the Federal University of Toulouse Midi-Pyrénées, which affiliates three universities (Capitole, Jean Jaurès, and Paul Sabatier), twenty *grandes écoles* and specialized schools, seven research institutes, and a teaching hospital. The University of Lyon is another example of this type of collaborative structure without merger. The impact of the restructuring on the landscape of higher education has been the most spectacular in the Paris region, where the gigantic faculties of the University of Paris had been broken up into thirteen universities after May 1968 and there had been little interaction between them and the many prestigious Paris-based *grandes écoles*. The new names of Paris area universities include PSL University (collegiate university created by the merger of Paris-Dauphine, ENS Paris-Ulm, Mines ParisTech, and Collège de France), Sorbonne University (merger of Paris-Sorbonne and Pierre and Marie Curie + affiliates INSEAD and Panthéon-Assas), Paris Cité University (merger of Paris-Descartes and Paris-Diderot), Sorbonne Paris North University, Paris-Saclay University (merger of Paris-Sud, Versailles-Saint-Quentin-en-Yvelines, Agro ParisTech, CentraleSupélec, and ENS Paris-Saclay), and Polytechnic Institute of Paris (a collegiate university created by the merger of École Polytechnique and four other engineering schools + affiliate HEC). As university restructuring continues, the names and affiliations are changing. For instance, New Sorbonne University (formerly affiliated with Paris Cité), Panthéon-Sorbonne University, and ESCP business school are forming a new alliance without merging.

One of the motivations for all the changes has been to enhance the prestige and visibility of French institutions on the global stage, including in ranking systems like *U.S. News & World Report*, CUWR (Shanghai), *Times Higher Education* (*THE*), and *QS World University Rankings*. Although such rankings are notoriously subjective, the French strategy appears to be paying off. In the recent editions (2021–2022) of the four ranking systems, French institutions in the overall top 50 of at least one of the rankings were Paris-Saclay University, Sorbonne University, PSL University, and Polytechnic Institute of Paris. Other French universities and institutions of higher education landing in the overall top 200 of one of the four rankings were Paris Cité University, Aix-Marseille University, Grenoble Alpes University, University of Strasbourg, ENS Lyon, and University of Montpellier. Claude Bernard University (Lyon) and University of Bordeaux made the top 200 in natural sciences (QS 2022); Paul Sabatier University (Toulouse) made the top 200 in math; and Sciences Po-Paris was ranked third in the world for political science (QS 2022).

See also: Chapter 2: Timeline; de Gaulle (Charles), World War II, and the Fifth Republic; Sarkozy (Nicolas) and the Hyper Presidency. Chapter 3: Protests. Chapter 8: Erasmus and International Educational Exchange in France; Grandes Écoles; Private Schools; Secondary Schools.

Further Reading
Brinbaum et al. (2018); Chatelain-Ponroy (2014); Derouet and Normand (2008); Givord and Goux (2007); Musselin (2004); Musselin (2009); Pickard (2016); Pilkington (2012); Reisz (2017); Shavit and Smith (2020); Upton (2022); Weisz (1983); Zaretsky (2018).

NATIONAL CENTER FOR SCIENTIFIC RESEARCH

Founded in 1939, the National Center for Scientific Research, commonly known by its acronym, CNRS, is the largest research organization in Europe with 32,000 researchers, 950 laboratories and research units, and a budget of €3.2 billion. It is divided into ten disciplinary institutes—Biology, Chemistry, Earth Sciences and Astronomy, Ecology and Environmental Science, Engineering and Systems, Humanities and Social Sciences, Computational Science, Mathematics, Physics, and Nuclear and Particle Physics. Almost 97% of its units are partnered with universities, institutions of higher education, and other research organizations. University professors often hold joint appointments at CNRS labs and their teaching institutions. CNRS-sponsored research leads to the publication of over 40,000 scientific papers annually. CNRS-affiliated researchers have won twenty-one Nobel Prizes, twelve Fields Medals (Mathematics), and numerous other prizes and awards (Turing, Abel, Crafoord, Japan Prize, etc.). In recent years, it has fostered partnerships with industry, spawned innovative startups, and produced cutting-edge research on range of subjects—including life and its social implications; information, communication, and knowledge; the environment, energy, and sustainable development; nanotechnologies; and astroparticle physics. In the fields of public health and medical science, the National Institute of Health and Medical Research (INSERM), founded in 1964, is France's leading research body, and the number two ranking such institution in the world after the U.S. National Institutes of Health. It sponsors 339 research labs and produces 12,000 scientific papers per year; and has an annual budget of over €900 million.

SELECTED BIBLIOGRAPHY

"Back to Bac: Reforms to the Beloved Baccalauréat." *The Economist*, 10 Feb. 2018, p. 33.

Bertola, Giuseppe. "France's Almost Public Private Schools." *Labour*, vol. 31, no. 3, 2017, pp. 225–244.

Bourget, Carine. *Islamic Schools in France: Minority Integration and Separatism in Western Society*. Palgrave Macmillan, 2019.

Brinbaum, Yaël, et al. "50% to the Bachelor's Degree... But How?: Young People from Working Class Families at University in France." *Economie & Statistique*, no. 499, 2018, pp. 79–105.

Brougère, Gilles, et al. "*École maternelle* (Preschool) in France: A Cross-Cultural Perspective." *European Early Childhood Education Research Journal*, vol. 16, no. 3, 2008, pp. 371–384.

Cairns, David. "The Erasmus Undergraduate Exchange Programme: A Highly Qualified Success Story?" *Children's Geographies*, vol. 15, no. 6, 2017, pp. 728–740.

Calmand, Julien, et al. "Why Grandes Écoles Are So Valued? Youth Transitions at Risk?" Insecurity, Precarity and Educational Mismatch in the Youth Labour Market (conference), IREDU, Burgundy University, Dijon, France, Sep. 2009, halshs-00419388.

Chadwick, Kay. "Education in Secular France: (Re)defining *Laïcité*." *Modern & Contemporary France*, vol. 5, no. 1, 1997, pp. 47–59.

Chatelain-Ponroy, Stéphanie. "The Impact of Recent Reforms on the Institutional Governance of French Universities." *International Trends in University Governance: Autonomy, Self-government and the Distribution of Authority*, ed. Michael Shattock. Routledge, 2014, pp. 67–88.

Cornu, Bernard. "Teacher Education in France: Universitisation and Professionalisation—From IUFMs to ESPEs." *Education Inquiry*, vol. 6, no. 3, 2015, pp. 289–307.

Deer, Cécile. "Elite Higher Education in France: Tradition and Transition." *Structuring Mass Higher Education: The Role of Elite Institutions*, eds. David Palfreyman and Ted Tapper. Routledge, 2009, pp. 219–236.

Deer, Cécile. "Faith Schools in France: From Conflict to Consensus?" *Faith Schools: Consensus or Conflict?*, ed. Roy Gardner, et al. RoutledgeFalmer, 2003, pp. 181–190.

Derouet, Jean-Louis, and Romuald Normand. "French Universities at a Crossroads between Crisis and Radical Reform: Toward a New Academic Regime?" *European Education*, vol. 40, no. 1, 2008, pp. 20–34.

d'Iribarne, Alain, and Eric Jolivet. "Vocational Training in France: From the Margin of the French Education System to a Laboratory for Its Renewal." *Revista Española de Sociología*, vol. 25, no. 3, 2016, pp. 409–420.

Dobbins, Michael, and Kerstin Martens. "Towards an Education Approach *à la finlandaise*? French Education Policy after PISA." *Journal of Education Policy*, vol. 27, no. 1, 2012, pp. 23–43.

Dreux, Guy. "Great and Small Expectations: The French Education System." *Austerity and the Remaking of European Education*, eds. Anna Traianou and Ken Jones. Bloomsbury, 2019, pp. 73–92.

Duru-Bellat, Marie. "France: Permanence and Change." *Education Policy Reform Trends in G20 Members*, ed. Yan Wang. Springer, 2013, pp. 19–32.

El Atia, Samira. "The Baccalauréat Exam in France: History, Merit, and Passing." *Contemporary French Civilization*, vol. 28, no. 1, 2004, pp. 111–120.

El Atia, Samira. "From Napoleon to Sarkozy: Two Hundred Years of the Baccalauréat Exam." *Language Assessment Quarterly*, vol. 5, no. 2, 2008, pp. 142–153.

European Commission. "France Overview." EACA National Policy Platform, *Eurydice*, accessed Apr. 30, 2022, https://eacea.ec.europa.eu/national-policies/eurydice/content/france_en.

Feyen, Benjamin, and Ewa Krzaklewska, eds. *The ERASMUS Phenomenon: Symbol of a New European Generation?* Lang, 2013.

Garnier, Pascale. "The Scholarisation of the French *école maternelle*: Institutional Transformations since the 1970s." *European Early Childhood Education Research Journal*, vol. 19, no. 4, 2011, pp. 553–563.

Givord, Pauline, and Dominique Goux. "France: Mass and Class: Persisting Inequalities in Post-Secondary Education in France." *Higher Education: A Comparative Study*, eds. Yossi Shavit, et al. Stanford UP, 2007, pp. 220–239.

Gumbel, Peter. *They Shoot Kids, Don't They?* Grasset, 2011.

Hörner, Wolfgang. "France." *The Education Systems of Europe*, ed. Wolfgang Hörner. Springer, 2007, pp. 262–283.

Lewis, H. D. *The French Education System*. Routledge, 1985.

Lizotte, Christopher. "*Laïcité* as Assimilation, *Laïcité* as Negotiation: Political Geographies of Secularism in the French Public School." *Political Geography*, vol. 77, art. 102121, 2020.

Martin-van der Hagen, Françoise, and Michèle Deane. "The French Baccalaureates." *The Baccalaureate: A Model for Curriculum Reform*, eds. Graham Philips and Tim Pound. Kogan Page, 2003, pp. 73–88.

Mattei, Paola. "The French Republican School under Pressure: Falling Basic Standards and Rising Social Inequalities." *French Politics*, vol. 10, 2012, pp. 84–95.

Mattei, Paola, and Andrew S. Aguilar. *Secular Institutions, Islam and Education Policy: France and the U.S. in Comparative Perspective*. Palgrave Macmillan, 2016; esp. "The French Republican School: *l'École Laïque* and Its Historical Origins." pp. 60–79.

Melander, Ingrid. "'No Kid Left Behind': Macron Tries to Fix France's Education System." *Reuters*, 5 Jul. 2018, https://www.reuters.com/article/us-france-reforms-education/no-kid-left-behind-macron-tries-to-fix-frances-education-system-idUSKBN1JV0MM.

Ministère de l'Éducation Nationale. "School Education in France." *Eduscol*, 2012, https://cache.media.eduscol.education.fr/file/dossiers/07/3/2013_School_Education_in_France_244073.pdf.

Moog, François. "The Challenges Facing Catholic Education in France Today." *International Studies in Catholic Education*, vol. 8, no. 2, 2016, pp. 155–167.

Musselin, Christine. *The Long March of French Universities*. RoutledgeFalmer, 2004.

Musselin, Christine. "The Side Effects of the Bologna Process on National Institutional Settings: The Case of France." *European Integration and the Governance of Higher Education and Research*, eds. Alberto Amaral, et al. Springer, 2009, pp. 181–205.

Pickard, Sarah. "Higher Education in France: Social Stratification and Social Reproduction." *Routledge Handbook of the Sociology of Higher Education*, eds. James E. Cote and Andy Furlong. Routledge, 2016, pp. 223–233.

Pilkington, Marc. "The French Evolution: France and the Europeanisation of Higher Education." *Journal of Higher Education Policy and Management*, vol. 34, no. 1, 2012, pp. 39–50.

Reisz, Matthew. "France's Academy: Liberty, Autonomy or Permanent Bureaucracy?" *Times Higher Education*, 20 Apr. 2017, https://www.timeshighereducation.com/features /frances-academy-liberty-autonomy-or-permanent-bureaucracy.

Roebroeck, Elodie, and Serge Guimonda. "Schooling, Citizen-Making, and Anti-Immigrant Prejudice in France." *Journal of Social and Political Psychology*, vol. 3, no. 2, 2015, pp. 20–42.

Schippling, Anne. "Institutional Habitus of French Elite Colleges in the Context of Internationalisation: An In-Depth Look at the Écoles Normales Supérieures." *Elite Education and Internationalisation: From the Early Years to Higher Education*, eds. Claire Maxwell, et al. Palgrave Macmillan, 2018, pp. 279–296.

Schreiber-Barsch, Silke. *Adult and Continuing Education in France*. Bertelsmann, 2015.

Shavit, Helen, and Jude Smith. *Beyond the Bac: Higher Education in France and Abroad*. 2nd ed. Association of American Wives of Europeans, 2020.

Soysal, Yasemin Nuhoğlu, and Simona Szakács. "Reconceptualizing the Republic: Diversity and Education in France, 1945–2008." *The Journal of Interdisciplinary History*, vol. 41, no. 1, 2010, pp. 97–115.

Upton, Ben. "Liberté, Égalité, Autonomie: Do French Universities Want More Freedom?" *Times Higher Education*, 31 Mar. 2022, https://www.timeshighereducation.com/depth /liberte-egalite-autonomie-do-french-universities-want-more-freedom.

van Zanten, Agnès. "Promoting Equality and Reproducing Privilege in Elite Educational Tracks in France." *Education: International Perspectives*, eds. Claire Maxwell and Peter Aggleton. Routledge, 2016, pp. 114–125.

van Zanten, Agnès, and Claire Maxwell. "Elite Education and the State in France: Durable Ties and New Challenges." *British Journal of Sociology of Education*, vol. 36, no. 1, 2015, pp. 71–94.

Weisz, George. *The Emergence of Modern Universities in France, 1863–1914*. Princeton UP, 1983.

Zaretsky, Robert. "Liberté! Égalité! Overcrowded, Underfunded Universities!?" *Foreign Policy*, 18 Jul. 2018, https://foreignpolicy.com/2018/07/18/liberte-egalite-overcrowded -underfunded-universities/.

CHAPTER 9

LANGUAGE

OVERVIEW

French is the national language of France and a cornerstone of French identity. Few other nations have as strong a bond to a particular language as does France, where French has been treated as a high priority by the nation's leaders since the Middle Ages. French became the de jure official language of the French kingdom in 1539 via the edict of Villers-Cotterêts, which mandated its use by the royal administration and judiciary throughout the realm. One of the legacies of the French Revolution was the adoption of an ambitious language policy designed to generalize the use of French nationwide at the expense of regional languages and dialects, which the 1794 Grégoire Report treated condescendingly—and belligerently—as "patois" to be "annihilated." Grégoire's dream started to become a reality thanks in large part to the exclusive use of French in the public schools of the Third Republic. A century later, in 1992, in order to protect the status of French as the national language, a clause was added to Article 2 of the French constitution that proclaimed: "French is the language of Republic." In the modern era, French has served as a preeminent international language of culture and diplomacy and its literature and song traditions have been among the most admired and influential in the world. The global preeminence of French was particularly strong in the eighteenth, nineteenth, and early twentieth centuries—a period that overlaps France's two historical colonial empires. French remains a major world language today. It is the native language of over 87% of the population of France and of 77 million people worldwide. There is a combined total of 255 million L1 (native/first language) and fluent/daily L2 (second language) speakers of French—many of the latter in countries where French is an official national language (e.g., countries in Africa that were French colonies). It is the fifth most spoken language in the world (321 million speakers), the second most learned language by nonnative speakers, the second most used working language of many major international organizations, the third language of international business, and the fourth language for internet content worldwide. Since the 1970s, the concept of Francophonie, the global community of French-speaking nations and peoples has grown in importance. France treats the development of linguistic and political solidarity, economic and scientific cooperation, and cultural exchange among Francophone nations as a major foreign policy priority. Such cooperation and exchange takes place through a variety of means and structures, the most important of which is the Organisation Internationale de la

Francophonie (OIF), an international NGO with eighty-eight member states and governments, which holds a biannual Francophone Summit.

French is a romance language, that is, one of the modern languages (along with Italian, Occitan, Spanish, Catalan, Portuguese, and Romanian) primarily evolved from the Latin vernacular spoken in the areas of Europe colonized by Rome. More specifically, it is part of the Oïl (northern) regional subgroup of the Gallo-Romance branch of Western Romance languages. Modern French dates from the early to mid-seventeenth century. It was preceded by Middle French (fourteenth to seventeenth centuries) and Old French (eighth to fourteenth centuries). Portions of the Oaths of Strasbourg, recorded in 842 as part of a military alliance between two of the grandsons of Charlamagne against a third, are considered the first surviving text written in Old French. France is divided into two historical linguistic (and cultural) regions: the north, where varieties of Gallo-Romance dialects classified as *langues d'oïl* emerged; and the south, where *langues d'oc* dialects emerged (the oïl/oc distinction is based on the word used for "yes"). French descends from the langue d'oïl dialect spoken in the Paris region, the original stronghold of the Frankish monarchy, and it spread as the monarchy asserted its control over most of the territory of what used to be Roman Gaul, which subsequently became the Kingdom of France. Occitan, which is still spoken in parts of southern France, descends from langue d'oc dialects. Even today, there are noticeable differences in accent, cadence, and vocabulary in the French spoken in the north and the south, but these differences generally do not impede understanding. In fact, compared to many other countries (e.g., Belgium, Spain, Canada, China), mainland France does not have major linguistic divisions or minorities. However, it is more linguistically diverse than the dominance of French may lead one to believe. France was a patchwork of dialects through the middle of the twentieth century even though most people also spoke French. In 1999, the linguist Bernard Cerquiglini identified seventy-five regional and minority languages spoken throughout France, twenty-four of which are native to present-day mainland France (continental Europe and Corsica). The remaining such languages are spoken in France's overseas departments and territories. Updated figures reported by the Ministry of Culture now count a total of eighty-two "languages of France" (incl. overseas departments and territories). In mainland France, the surviving native regional and minority languages reflect both the historical north/oïl–south/oc divide and the specificity of "peripheral" regions that were integrated into France later. These prominent regional and minority languages and dialects are Corsican (Corsica), Breton (Brittany), Gallo (an Oïl language of western France), Basque (French Basque Country in the southwest), Franco-Provençal (an "Oc" language spoken in east-central France), Occitan (Occitania), Catalan (northern/French Catalonia), the Flemish dialect of Dutch spoken in northern France (near the border with Belgium), the Moselle and Alsatian dialects of German spoken in the Grand Est region, and the Ligurian spoken in a small area near Monaco on the Mediterranean coast. The French government has for long expressed animosity toward France's internal linguistic diversity, which has sparked political tensions at times—and still does to some degree in Brittany, French Basque Country, Corsica, and France's overseas departments and territories (e.g., Creole in the French

Caribbean and the Southern oceanic languages spoken by the Kanak population of New Caledonia). When the EU adopted the European Charter for Regional or Minority Languages in 1992, France resisted—it did not sign the charter until 1999 and still has not formally ratified it. However, the French government's attitude toward its regional and minority languages has evolved. Since 2008, they are recognized (in the French constitution) as part of the nation's heritage and are offered protection. However, they are endangered and now depend on people who learn them in school (e.g., Breton and Occitan).

Aside from regional differences (accents, etc.), the French language exhibits a large degree of sociolinguistic variety across the four main registers recognized by linguists— le français populaire ("working-class" French, i.e., nonstandard French spoken by lower socioeconomic groups and adolescents that contains a high percentage of slang), le français familier (a relaxed, colloquial form of French used by people belonging to the same social group or similar social standing), le français courant (everyday colloquial French generally perceived as acceptable usage in most contexts), and le français soutenu (highly formal French with strict adherence to grammatical rules and a more sophisticated vocabulary). Verlan is a widely known form of French slang that inverts the syllables of certain words.

Defending and promoting "good" French has been a preoccupation of the French literary intelligentsia and government authorities since the sixteenth century. In 1549, Joachim du Bellay wrote his Defense and Illustration of the French Language, which argued that French was as worthy a language for poetry and letters as Latin. In 1635, Cardinal Richelieu founded the Académie Française for the purpose of standardizing the lexicon, orthography, and grammar of French and promoting a "pure" and "eloquent" literary form of the language. Even today, its chief mission is the publication of the official dictionary of the French language—since 1992, the venerable institution, which also awards prestigious literary prizes and advises the government on language policy, has been working on the ninth edition of the dictionary, now two-thirds complete. In recent years, there has been great concern about protecting the integrity and global role of French, particularly against the encroachment and hegemony of English. Thus, in 1966, the French government created the High Commission for the Defense and Expansion of the French Language (replaced by the General Delegation for the French Language and the Languages of France in 2001). It has also enacted numerous laws to defend French against internal and external threats such as the insipid use of English in advertising, business, media, and popular culture. The most famous of these laws is the Toubon Law of 1994, which required the use of French in business, consumer information, advertising, and non-foreign language education (where English is used, a French translation must be provided), and set quotas for French songs in broadcast media. Authorities have also shown an interest in the modernization of the French language. In 1990, a reform of French orthography proposed by government experts received the endorsement of the Académie Française but its full implementation was delayed until 2016. Even then, it generated controversy, for example, among people reluctant to see the use of French's characteristic accent circonflexe (ˆ) diacritcal mark, severely curtailed. While the Académie and government have welcomed the feminization of the names of professions for which there were no feminine forms already in wide and/or accepted use, both have been reluctant to accept gender-neutral and inclusive forms, which have started to become more common in many spaces of civil society.

Further Reading

Adamson (2007); Ager (1999); Ayres-Bennett and Jones (2007); Barlow and Nadeau (2006); Harris and Vincent (1988); Henry (2008); Lodge (1993); Oakes (2001); Posner (1997); Walter (1994); Wise (1997); Wise et al. (1997).

Académie Française

The Académie Française was founded in 1635 by Cardinal Richelieu (Armand Jean du Plessis, 1585–1642), the prime minster of King Louis XIII (1601–1643). It was the first of several royal academies founded in the seventeenth century as a means by which the absolute monarchy could influence the development of the arts and sciences in France. It is the most authoritative national institution with respect to the French language and letters but is not an arm of the French government. French had become the official judicial and administrative language of the Kingdom of France via the edict of Villers-Cotterêts (1539). However, there was still very little standardization in spelling, lexicon, and grammatical usage even in the seventeenth century. Hence, the academy's mission, according to its official statues, was to give the French language well-defined rules to make it "pure, eloquent, and capable of serving the arts and sciences." Since its inception, the primary means by which the academy has carried out this mission has been to oversee the publication of the official dictionary of the French language, of which there have been eight editions to date—1694, 1718, 1740, 1762, 1798, 1835, 1878, and 1932–1935. The publication of the ninth edition, still under way, began in 1992. Portions of volume four (words beginning with the letter "r") were published in booklet format between 2012 and 2017. By the time of its completion, it is estimated that the ninth edition of the *Dictionnaire de l'Académie française* will contain definitions for over 60,000 words—almost double the number in the preceding edition (but far less than the 100,000 words in the most recent editions of *Le Grand Robert*, another highly respected unabridged dictionary). In addition to the official dictionary, the academy sponsors yearly literary prizes and language contests, is consulted on official reforms of the French language, and is tasked with coming up with viable French alternatives for widely used Anglicisms in lexically productive expanding fields like science and technology, business, and consumer goods (e.g., *logiciel* instead of "software," *courriel* instead of "email," *jeune pousse* instead of "start-up")—a task it has carried out with mixed results in terms of actual influence over the French vernacular. It has a reputation of being a bastion of linguistic and grammatical conservatism and exclusivity. For example, in 2008 it voiced opposition to the enactment of constitutional protections for French regional languages like Alsatian, Basque, Breton, Corsican, and Occitan because it feared that such protections might pose a threat to the preeminence of French as the national language. More recently, it has vigorously opposed efforts to adopt gender-neutral and inclusive constructions referring to persons.

The forty members of the academy, elected for life, are known as the "Immortals." They come from a wide range of fields but are always accomplished writers and exemplars of the French language. Upon election, they are outfitted with a ceremonial uniform consisting of a black coat embroidered with a green and gold leafy motif (for this reason, it is called the "green suit") and a personalized sword. Upon induction, they deliver a major speech to their fellow members. New members are elected to fill a specific numbered seat previously occupied by a recently deceased member and sometimes come from the same field or have another point in common with their predecessor. For instance, in 2013, the Haitian-born French Canadian author Dany Laferrière (b. 1953) was elected to fill the seat previously held by the Senegalese statesman, poet, and cofounder of the Négritude movement, Léoplold Sédar Senghor (1906–2001), the academy's first Black African member. The first woman elected to the academy, in 1980, was the Belgian-born French author (and U.S. citizen), Marguerite Yourcenar (1903–1987). The Algerian feminist author Assia Djebar (Fatima-Zohra Imalayen, 1936–2015) was the first Maghrebi and Muslim woman academician (elected in 2005). Along with the other existing royal academies, the Académie Française was abolished under the French Revolution, but was reestablished by Napoleon Bonaparte in 1803 as part of the Institut de France. The institute's other constituent academies are the Academies of Humanities (Inscriptions et Belles Letttres), Sciences, Fine Arts (incl. the fields of music and architecture), and Moral and Political Sciences. The French Academy is an honorary, advisory, literary, and intellectual body. The application of linguistic laws and policies in France is the prerogative of the General Delegation for the French Language and the Languages of France (DGLFLF), an interministerial agency created in 2001 (as the successor to a line of agencies dating back to 1966) and attached to the Ministry of Culture.

See also: Chapter 2: Louis XIV and the Absolute Monarchy. Chapter 9: Francophonie; Language Laws and Policies. Chapter 12: Ministry of Culture.

Further Reading
Amit (2016); De Witt (1983); Estival and Pennycook (2011); Fitzsimmons (2017); Traoré (2010).

Francophonie

The term "Francophonie" has several associated meanings. In its broadest understanding, it refers to French's status as a world language and to all those who speak it as a native or regular second language, or foreign language of particular historical or cultural significance. In spite of concerns about the importance of French in the modern world relative to English, French is still a widely spoken language of global significance. It has 77 million native speakers and a worldwide total of 321 million (L1 + L2) speakers—many of the latter regular users of the language in countries where French is one of the official national languages (e.g., numerous countries in Africa). It ranks as the third most prevalent "world language" (i.e., one widely used around the world as a means of international communication)—behind English and Spanish—and as the fifth most widely spoken language overall—behind English, Mandarin Chinese, Hindi, and Spanish. Depending on the criteria used, it also ranks as the second most learned language by foreigners (incl. 51 million current student learners), the second most commonly used official/working language of many international organizations (incl. the UN, EU, NATO, WTO, and OECD) after English, the third language of international business, and the fourth language for internet content. The French Ministry of Foreign Affairs projects that there will be 770 million Francophones in the world by the year 2050.

La Francophonie is also an international geopolitical and cultural space made up of the countries in which French is an official language, a widely used one, or where there are strong historical and cultural ties to the French language. Since the 1970s, a concerted effort has been made to increase trade, economic and technological cooperation, educational and cultural exchange, and geopolitical solidarity among these countries. Along with Canada, Belgium, and Switzerland, France has played a leading role in this effort, which it still considers a high priority in foreign policy. The Francophone community of nations and peoples is sometimes seen as a counterweight to Anglo-American dominance as well as a framework for north-south cooperation and the dissemination of democratic values. Many organizations are part of the structure of this international community. However, the most important is the Organisation Internationale de la Francophonie (OIF), an international NGO headquartered in Paris that was founded in 1970 as the Agence de Coopération Culturelle et Technique (ACCT). It adopted its present name with the ratification of the Charte (Charter) de la Francophonie in 1997 and now counts eighty-eight member and affiliated states and governments, which together represent more than one-third of UN member states and total a population of over 900 million people. In addition to the countries in which French is an official language (including most of the former African colonies of France and Belgium), full members include Romania, Bulgaria, Greece, Egypt, Lebanon, Armenia, Vietnam, Cambodia, and Laos. The U.S. state of Louisiana has observer status in the organization. The OIF's diverse activities go beyond language-specific endeavors. It hosts a biannual Francophone Summit of the leaders of member nations and governments—the first, in 1986, was held in Versailles; the 2018 edition was held in Yerevan, Armenia; and the 2020 one was to be held in Tunis but was postponed due to the worldwide COVID-19 pandemic. The OIF has also concluded over thirty cooperation agreements with international and regional organizations and sponsors the global French language television station TV5 Monde.

Finally, within the academic field of French studies, the concept signals greater emphasis on the literatures, cultures, and diverse societies of the broader Francophone world—a nonexclusively "hexagonal" (mainland/continental French) focus that factors in complex historical, political, economic, and cultural issues that underly and complicate French's global presence. The issues include slavery, colonialism and postcolonial realities, the wealth and development gap between the northern and southern hemispheres, immigration/migration, linguistic divisions and diversity in predominantly or partially Francophone countries, and the increasingly multicultural character of the northern Francophone countries and regions (i.e., France, Belgium, Switzerland, and Canada/Quebec). It is worth noting that the term "Francophonie" was first used in 1880 by the French geographer Onésime Reclus, who was also an ardent apologist of French colonialism.

See also: Chapter 1: Overseas France. Chapter 2: Timeline. Chapter 6: Arabs; Blacks. Chapter 9: Language Laws and Policies; Regional and Minority Languages, Dialects, and Varieties of French. Chapter 11: Overview; Houellebecq (Michel) and the Recent French Novel; Literary Avant-Garde, 1950–1980; Poetry (Modern and Contemporary). Chapter 13: Rock, Pop, and Rap.

Further Reading

Ager (1996); Alalou (2006); Apter (2005); Auplat (2003); Brown (2011); Dutton (2011); Forsdick and Murphy (2003); Little (2001); Marcoux and Konaté (2011); Moudileno (2010); Murdoch and Fagyal (2014); Neathery-Castro and Rousseau (2001); Neathery-Castro and Rousseau (2005); Rocheron and Rolfe (2004); Salhi (2002); Vigoureux (2013).

Language Laws and Policies

France has a long history of legislation and government policy pertaining to the French language. For the monarchy, such laws and policies, which generally promoted the official use of the French of the Paris region (the original stronghold of the Frankish monarchy) as opposed to both Latin and other vernacular languages spoken in the kingdom, were a means of consolidating power and augmenting French prestige in Europe. After the French Revolution (1789–1799), ensuring that French was the unrivaled national language spoken adequately by all citizens was key to the development and preservation of national unity and to social progress and equality. Today, defending the integrity and global reach of French is seen as integral to French identity and the *rayonnement* of French culture. However, there has also been a push to carefully adapt French to modern realities so as to ensure its viability and consistency.

King Philippe VI made French (as opposed to Latin) the primary language of the royal chancellery in 1330. Two centuries later, French was made the exclusive official language of all royal edicts and judicial rulings by Francis I through the Edict of Villers-Cotterêts (1539), essentially making it the official language of the kingdom. In 1635, the Académie Française was founded by Cardinal Richelieu under Louis XIII for the purposes of regulating the French language (spelling, lexicon, and grammar) and promoting it as a language of literature and high culture. The French Revolution initially showed democratic openness to France's regional languages and dialects, but this changed during the period of Jacobin rule. The Grégoire Report (1794), which proposed the "annihilation" of local "patois" and the vigorous promotion of French as the national language, was adopted by the National Convention. In the same year, it was made a punishable offense for any public official to create an official document in a language other than French and the Lakanal Decree affirmed that French was the obligatory language of instruction in French schools (but still allowed auxiliary use of regional languages for limited pedagogical purposes). Following the Ferry Laws (1880–1882) on public primary education during the second decade of the Third Republic, the exclusive use of French in schools was systematically enforced—including via humiliating punishments for students caught speaking other languages and dialects, even outside of class. In 1902, the Combes Circular forbade priests in Brittany to preach in Breton, having concluded that such use had become "excessive." This measure met with fierce opposition.

A more tolerant attitude toward France's regional languages was adopted in the post–World War II era. In 1951, the Deixonne Law authorized the teaching of four regional/minority languages in French secondary schools—Breton, Occitan, Catalan, and Basque. In the 1970s, private bilingual academies sprang up—called Diwan schools in Brittany and *calendratas* in the Occitan-speaking parts of the south. In 1976, the Haby Law allowed (in theory) regional languages to be taught at all levels of education. Around the same time, there was considerable concern about protecting the integrity of the French language, especially against the encroachment and hegemony of English. In 1966, the High Commission for the Defense and Expansion of the French Language was created as an agency of the French government—the first of several agencies with a similar purpose (e.g., the Superior Council of the French Language in 1989 and the General Delegation for the French Language and the Languages of France in 2001). In 1970, France joined Canada and other nations in setting up the Agency of Cultural and Technical Cooperation, which was designed to foster cooperation, cultural exchange, and solidarity among the French-speaking countries of the world—an organization that was later to become the OIF. In 1992, the European Charter for Regional or Minority Languages was adopted by the European Community, but over French opposition. It was finally signed by French representatives in 1999—in recognition of its general principles—but has never been formally ratified by the French. Significantly, also in 1992, when France made changes to the French constitution necessitated by its ratification of the Maastricht Treaty creating the EU, it also amended Article 2 of the constitution by inserting a phrase asserting that "French is the language of the Republic." However, in 2008, French regional languages were offered limited constitutional protections via the addition of new text (Art. 75-1) declaring that "Regional languages are part of the [cultural] heritage of France." The most ambitious law designed to protect the French language was the Toubon Law of 1994, which replaced the 1975 Bas-Lauriol Law. The new law required the use of

French in public postings and advertising (other languages may be used but a French translation must be provided), mandated the use of French in official written business communication (e.g., employment contracts, workplace rules, and product information addressed to consumers), and established broadcast quotas for French films and songs.

New policies have also been adopted to modernize French. In 1990, the Académie Française endorsed a government recommended reform of French orthography. Most of the changes are of a relatively minor nature—for example, simplified spellings of words like *oignon* (now *ognion*) and curtailed use of certain diacritical marks like the circumflex (e.g., the verb *disparaître* becomes *disparaitre*). However, implementation of the recommendations has been slow and the recent decision (2016) to mandate their application in school textbooks generated controversy, including a movement on Twitter around the hashtag "#JeSuisAccentCirconflexe." Gender has been a sensitive issue in French language policy. In 2019, the Académie Française—after years of hesitation and debate, long after other Francophone countries like Canada and Switzerland had already accepted the practice, and thirty years after the French government had started moving in this direction—finally approved the systematic feminization of the names of occupations and professions, many of which (esp. male-dominated ones) did not have standard feminine forms in wide use in France. For example, a woman author would be called *une auteure* and a woman boss, *une cheffe*. However, French officials have been less progressive when it comes to the use of gender-neutral or inclusive forms, such as nonbinary pronouns (e.g., *iel* in place of the third person singular masculine and feminine forms *il* and *elle*) and median-periods or standard periods to display the full range of endings for nouns and adjectives (e.g., *un.e étudiant.e*). The conservative official position is that French is inherently gendered, that the masculine form traditionally takes precedence as the de facto non-gender-specific form, and that such uses are cumbersome and undermine the clarity of French. For instance, in 2017, the Académie Française issued an official statement that declared gender-inclusive writing "an aberration that poses a mortal threat to the French language and for which the nation will have to account for to future generations." In 2021, MPs tabled a bill that would have banned the use of gender-neutral language among government officials and civil servants, while the education ministry formally forbid its use in the nation's schools. Government opposition notwithstanding, the practice is gaining ground in civil society.

See also: Chapter 2: Francis I and the Renaissance. Chapter 7: Gender Equality and Sexual Harassment; LGBTQ+ Community. Chapter 9: Académie Française; Regional and Minority Languages, Dialects, and Varieties of French; Sexism and Gender Bias in French.

Further Reading

Drackley (2019); Harrison and Joubert (2019); Judge (2007); Martin (2005); Oakes (2017); Schiffman (2002); Thody (2000).

FRANGLAIS

With a number of speakers that dwarf those of French and with the status of reigning global lingua franca, English is often seen as a threat to French. Its rise coincides with American hegemony as a superpower and the intensification of globalization via technology and economic interdependence. For example, 53% of the world's internet content is in English, compared to 4% in French. There has been longstanding concern about the encroachment of English in certain areas of life and culture in France—for example, business, tourism, science and technology, movies, advertising, mass media, and popular culture—and the corruption of French with anglicisms. This is the phenomenon known as "franglais." In 1964, René Étiemble published an essay that railed against the trend, *Parlez-vous franglais?* (fifteen years after a French Communist Party official first denounced "coca-colonization"). A more lighthearted take on the phenomenon can be found in singer Renaud's charming 1980 franglais love song, "It Is Not Because You Are." French alternatives to trendy anglicisms exist but the French often prefer to use Anglo-American terms like "DJ," "sitcom," "start-up," "downsizing," "think-tank," "webmaster," "software," and "mail" (i.e., "email"). The attitude in France has evolved on the issue of English in recent years; there is now greater acceptance of multilingualism and the mastery and use of English are seen as necessary for the global relevance of French diplomacy, business, scientific research, and culture. However, even when successful, France's cautious embrace of English is not without problems. President Emmanuel Macron uses the language regularly and conspicuously on the international stage—something that has irritated public opinion and political commentators, who have portrayed it as a sign of snobbery, if not an abdication of French linguistic sovereignty.

Regional and Minority Languages, Dialects, and Varieties of French

The status of French as the official national language of France is unassailable. It was legally made the official language of the royal administration in the sixteenth century and is recognized in Article 2 of the French constitution (1958) as the exclusive official language of the French Republic. It is the first language of over 87% of the population and is spoken fluently by well over 90% of the population. Arabic (esp. Maghrebi dialects), the native language of 3% of the population, is a very distant second. Unlike some of its neighbors (e.g., Belgium, Switzerland, and Spain), mainland France does not have major linguistic/regional divisions or numerically significant native linguistic minorities. However, there are political tensions over language in Corsica, the French Caribbean (i.e., the status of Creole in Martinique and Guadeloupe), New Caledonia, and other overseas departments and territories; and such tensions were felt periodically in the mainland itself throughout the twentieth century, particularly with respect to speakers of Occitan in the south, Alsatian in Alsace, Breton in Brittany, and

Basque in French Basque Country. The government's attitude toward regional languages and dialects has evolved. During the French Revolution, they were deemed relics of a primitive past and as unpatriotic obstacles to national unity. There is no more striking example of this attitude than the Grégoire Report (named for its author, the progressive French priest, Abbé Henri Grégoire), a linguistic survey and language policy proposal that was adopted by the National Convention in 1794—considered by some as the linguistic component of the Reign of Terror (its official title was *Report on the Necessity and Means to Annihilate Patois and Universalize the Use of the French Language*). Somewhat subdued echoes of this attitude are to be found in the tales of children from the countryside and provincial small towns who were punished for speaking their local dialects at school in the late nineteenth and early twentieth centuries; and in the French parliament's failure to ratify the 1992 European Charter for Regional or Minority Languages (which representatives of the French government nonetheless signed). Without challenging the status of French as the national language or recognizing speakers of regional languages as members of linguistic "minorities," the French government now sees these languages as a valued but threatened part of France's linguistic and cultural heritage and regional diversity, and offers some support—including limited protections written into the French constitution in 2008, authorization of bilingual schools, elective classes in the most important regional languages offered in high schools, and some programming in the languages on regional public television stations.

France exhibits a relatively high degree of linguistic diversity notwithstanding the current dominance of standard French. This diversity is to a considerable extent the result of the way the Latin vernacular spoken in Roman Gaul (i.e., most of present-day France) evolved in different parts of the country—interacting (first) with different Indigenous linguistic substrata and (later) regional Germanic influences—during and after Roman rule (first century BCE through fifth century CE), giving rise to two distinct regions of Gallo-Romance dialects on either side of a linguistic frontier—"oïl" dialects in the north (a designation that refers to the vernacular word for "yes"), including the dialect spoken in the Île-de-France (Paris) region that evolved into standard French, and "oc" dialects in the south. Remnants of this division are found today in different regional accents—especially in southern accents (often described as "singing" or "colorful") that contrast with the northern diction that has become standard. That standard is based largely on the speech of the Parisian bourgeoisie, whereas what is commonly thought of as the Parisian accent is based on working-class speech—in part a linguistic and cultural stereotype based on the bygone accents and speech of districts like Belleville and Ménilmontant and the style of mocking banter known as *la gouaille parisienne*. Other factors include subsequent geopolitical history (e.g., regions brought under French rule later such as Brittany, Alsace, and Corsica) and immigration. Building on the work of the linguist Bernard Cerquiglini, who studied the issue relative to the criteria of the abovementioned European charter, the French government (Ministry of Culture) presently recognizes a total of eighty-two "languages of France," fifty of which are native to France's overseas departments and territories. This leaves a legacy of thirty-two regional and minority languages native to

A bilingual road sign in French and Breton near the city of Vannes (Morbihan department, Brittany). While French is the official and undisputed national language of France, not to mention the subject of protectionist laws and considerable passion, the French government currently recognizes 82 "languages of France" (50 in the overseas departments and territories, 32 in the mainland), including Breton, a Celtic language that counts 250,000 fluent speakers. Signs like this one are also widespread in the South (dialects of Occitan, Catalan, and Basque), Alsace (Alsatian), and Corsica (Corsican). (Richard Villalon/Dreamstime.com)

and spoken in mainland (continental European) France. The most prominent are Corsican (Corsica), Breton (Brittany), Gallo (an oïl language of western France), Basque (French Basque Country in the southwest), Franco-Provençal (an "oc" language spoken in east-central France), Occitan (Occitania), and Catalan (northern/French Catalonia), and they have an official protected status in the regions where they are spoken. The other major regional languages and dialects spoken in mainland France include the Flemish dialect of Dutch spoken in northern France (near the border with Belgium), Moselle Franconian and the Alsatian dialect of German spoken in the Grand Est region, and the Ligurian spoken in a small area near Monaco on the Mediterranean coast. There are numerous smaller regional variants, or dialects, of Occitan (e.g., Gascon, Languedocien, Provençal, Auvergnat-Limousin, and Alpin-Dauphinois) and in the oïl language group (e.g., Walloon, Picard, Champenois, Norman, Angevin, Berrichon, Poitevin-Saintongeais, Franc-Comtois, Bourguignon-Morvandiau, and Lorrain). These languages were so prevalent at the beginning of the twentieth century that the courts in Paris employed an army of interpreters for defendants who could not speak or understand standard French. However, they are all seriously endangered today. Even the largest regional languages have relatively small numbers of native speakers in France—around 650,000 speakers of Alsatian, 600,000 speakers of Occitan (as well another 1,000,000 with some degree of proficiency in the language), 250,000 speakers of Breton (with another 400,00 with some degree of proficiency), and 125,000 speakers of Corsican. Native speakers of all oïl languages and dialects combined (excluding French) number fewer than 600,000. Overall, 400 languages are spoken in France, most of them the languages of France's immigrant groups—including Arabic (esp. North African dialects), Portuguese, Spanish, Italian, Turkish, Armenian, Yiddish, Romani, Chinese, and Vietnamese—and of its overseas departments and territories.

In addition to regional differences in accents and lexicon among speakers in French, there have been historically important class distinctions in the way French is spoken. While education and the media have worn away or softened these differences to a large extent, traces of them are still to be found in differences in phonetics, enunciation, grammatical usage, and vocabulary (esp. slang). *Verlan* is a well-known, inventive, and widely used (e.g., in the slang of young people) originally "lower-class" argot that relies on inverting the syllables of individual words to create slang terms (the term is itself based on a syllabic inversion of the French expression *à l'envers*, which means "backward"). For example, in Verlan, *femme* ("woman") becomes *meuf*, *Français* becomes *Çéfran*, and Arabe becomes *Beur*—a term that entered wide usage in the 1980s as means of self-designation among the then coming-of-age second generation of Maghrebi immigrants in France (often re-verlanized as *rebeu*). Verlan is a key part of the French used by multicultural youths from French suburbs and is prominent in French rap music. It has been widely popularized by the French media— so much so that some Verlan terms are now included in dictionaries and find their way into the everyday speech of users of standard French.

It is common among French linguists to distinguish among four main registers of French. The registers are a combination of levels of formality, degrees of conformity to the grammatical conventions of standard French, class identity, and sociolinguistic contextuality—*le registre populaire* (nonstandard French spoken by lower socioeconomic groups that contains a high percentage of group-specific slang and is perceived as transgressive), *le registre familier* (informal colloquial French used by people belonging to the same social group or between whom there is no hierarchical difference), *le registre courant* (simple but standard everyday French perceived as acceptable usage in most contexts), and *le registre soutenu* (formal French with strict adherence to rules of grammar, clear enunciation, and sophisticated vocabulary and structures).

See also: Chapter 1: North and South; Overseas France; Regional Identities. Chapter 6: Immigration. Chapter 9: Francophonie; Language Laws and Policies.

Further Reading
Blackwood (2008); Blackwood (2011); Costa (2016); Doran (2007); Harrison and Joubert (2019); Hornsby (2015); Jones and Hornsby (2013); Kluter (1989); Lefkowitz (1991); Lodge (2004); Lüdi (2013); Mooney (2018); Planchenault (2015); Pooley (1996); Sanders (1993); Vassberg (1993).

Sexism and Gender Bias in French

The putative inherent sexism and gender bias of the French language have become contentious issues in France and other Francophone countries. The debate is rooted in the fact that French has two grammatical genders—masculine and feminine (there is no "neuter" as in German). As a rule, nouns are therefore either masculine or feminine and other structures—including adjectives, personal pronouns, and articles—must "agree" with the gender of the nouns with which they are used and the persons to whom they refer. Exceptions are nouns, pronouns, and adjectives that are classified as "epicene" because they do not vary in form when referring to males or females (e.g., *enfant* = "child," regardless of gender). In most cases, however, epicene nouns are still used with gendered articles (e.g., *un enfant* = a male child, *une enfant* = a female child). By contrast, the epicene word *personne*, which is always used with a feminine article and variable adjectives in their feminine form (e.g., *une personne intéressante* = "an interesting person"), may refer to a male, a female, or a person of unspecified gender. Gender agreement affects both the orthography and pronunciation of words. Hence, binary gender is omnipresent in French and has many potentially problematic social repercussions. For instance, while common nouns that refer to people tend to have both a masculine and a feminine form (e.g., *un étudiant/une étudiante* = male/female "student"), nouns designating numerous traditionally male-dominated professions formerly did not. The French government has supported feminization of such nouns since the mid-1980s and issued a set of formal guidelines on nonsexist nomenclature in 2015. Feminized forms of the names of many such occupations and titles (e.g., *une professeure*) are now used more widely in France (other Francophone countries adopted them sooner). However, the masculine forms of the names of some occupations and titles (esp. very prestigious and/or ancient ones—e.g., *un/une médecin* = medical doctor) are still preferred even when referring to women despite the fact that feminine forms are grammatically possible (the masculine forms are thus de facto epicene terms). Feminists are divided over the issue. Some support feminization as an expression of gender equality, whereas others do not because they believe that gender should be deemphasized in French. Another manifestation of efforts to make French more gender neutral/inclusive is that it has become more common to see punctuation marks, such as median-periods or simple periods, used to display a neutral array of gendered declensions of a noun (e.g., *un.e citoyen.ne* for "citizen"). While authorities generally support feminization because it is in keeping with the conventional gender binary of French, the official response to efforts to make French more gender neutral/inclusive has been negative. The Académie Française has warned that conspicuous gender neutrality, including the use of median-periods is not only cumbersome but puts the French language in "mortal danger," and Édouard Philippe (French PM, 2017–2020) banned the use of gender-neutral French in official government documents and reaffirmed the traditional precedence of masculine forms, which make them the "default" neutral choice when gender is not specified.

The issue of gender bias in French is of particular importance to people who identify as trans, nonbinary, genderqueer, genderfluid, or *agenre*, who must contend with the problematic binary gendered conventions of the French language on an intimate and daily basis. An array of gender-neutral/nonbinary alternatives in French are currently in use among and with gender nonconforming people and depend to a large extent on individual preference. The most widespread gender-neutral third-person singular subject pronoun is *iel* (*al*, *ille*, *ol*, *ul*, *yel*, and *yul* are alternatives), which has been added to the online version of the authoritative French dictionary, *Le Robert*. *Iel* is also used as an indirect object pronoun (*ellui* is another option). In the case of singular definite articles and direct object pronouns, *lae* and *lea* are both used commonly (*lo* and *li* are alternatives). The gender-neutral ending *–xe* is sometimes used in the place of conventional masculine/feminine adjective agreement, where possible. A preference for the use of epicene terminology is another means of promoting gender neutrality and inclusiveness in spoken and written French.

Gendered titles of civility (i.e., *monsieur*/*madame*) are another sensitive issue. Some people refrain from using them, while others use gender-neutral alternatives like the anglicism *mix*. In 2012, the use of *mademoiselle* to refer to unmarried women was eliminated in official documents (there is no equivalent term used for unmarried men—as a sign of respect, all adult males are called *monsieur*). Now, all women are referred to as *madame* regardless of marital status. *Mademoiselle* is still used in everyday spoken French, especially to address young girls, just as the more informal *jeune homme* ("young man") is sometimes used to address young boys.

See also: Chapter 7: Feminism and Women's Rights; Gender Equality and Sexual Harassment; LGBTQ+ Community. Chapter 9: Language Laws and Policies.

Further Reading

Akhvlediani et al. (2021); Burr (2003); Fassin (2016); Fleischman (1997); Kosnick (2019); Piser (2020); Sarrasin (2012); Swamy (2019); Timsit (2017); Zaretsky (2017).

SELECTED BIBLIOGRAPHY

Adamson, Robin. *The Defense of French: A Language in Crisis?* Multilingual Matters, 2007.

Ager, Dennis E. *"Francophonie" in the 1990's: Problems and Opportunities.* Multilingual Matters, 1996.

Ager, Dennis E. *Identity, Insecurity and Image: France and Language.* Multilingual Matters, 1999.

Akhvlediani, Tsiuri, Giorgi Kuparadze, and Ketevan Gabunia. "Gender-Neutral Language in English and French Linguo-Cultures." *Language and Culture*, no. 26, 2021, pp. 18–22.

Alalou, Ali. "Language and Ideology in the Maghreb: Francophonie and Other Languages." *The French Review*, vol. 80, no. 2, 2006, pp. 408–421.

Amit, Aviv. "The Académie Française and Monocentricity in a Multicultural World." *Language Problems and Language Planning*, vol. 40, no. 3, 2016, pp. 235–249.

Apter, Emily. "Theorizing Francophonie." *Comparative Literature Studies*, vol. 42, no. 4, 2005, pp. 297–311.

Auplat, Claire. "The Commonwealth, the Francophonie and NGOs." *The Round Table*, vol. 92, 2003, pp. 368, 53–66.

Ayres-Bennett, Wendy, and Mari C. Jones. *The French Language and Questions of Identity.* Legenda, 2007.

Barlow, Julie, and Jean-Benoit Nadeau. *Plus Ça Change: The Story of French from Charlemagne to the Cirque Du Soleil.* Robson, 2006.

Blackwood, Robert J. "The Linguistic Landscape of Brittany and Corsica: A Comparative Study of the Presence of France's Regional Languages in the Public Space." *Journal of French Language Studies*, vol. 21, no. 2, 2011, pp. 111–130.

Blackwood, Robert J. *The State, the Activists, and the Islanders: Language Policy on Corsica.* Springer, 2008.

Brown, Peter. "La Francophonie: From the Postcolonial to the Post-Cold War Eras." *Australian Journal of French Studies*, vol. 48, no. 1, 2011, pp. 19–33.

Burr, Elisabeth. "Gender and Language Politics in France." *Gender Across Languages: The Linguistic Representation of Women and Men*, vol. 2, eds. Marlis Hellinger and Hadumod Bußman. Benjamins, 2003, pp. 19–140.

Costa, James. "Revitalising Language in Provence: A Critical Approach." *Proceedings of the Philological Society*, vol. 114, no. S1, 2016, pp. 1–184.

De Witt, Jean Zaun. "The Rhetoric of Induction at the French Academy." *Quarterly Journal of Speech*, vol. 69, no. 4, 1983, pp. 413–422.

Doran, Meredith. "Alternative French, Alternative Identities: Situating Language in *la Banlieue*." *Contemporary French and Francophone Studies*, vol. 11, no. 4, 2007, pp. 497–508.

Drackley, Patrick. "'*Je suis circonflexe*': Grassroots Prescriptivism and Orthographic Reform." *Language Policy*, vol. 18, 2019, pp. 295–313.

Dutton, Jacqueline. "Francophonie and Its Futures: Utopian, Digital, Plurivocal." *Australian Journal of French Studies*, vol. 48, no. 1, 2011, p. 3.

Estival, Dominique, and Alastair Pennycook. "L'Académie française and Anglophone Language Ideologies." *Language Policy*, vol. 10, 2011, pp. 325–341.

Fassin, Éric. "Gender is/in French." *Differences*, vol. 27, no. 2, 2016, pp. 178–197.

Fitzsimmons, Michael P. *The Place of Words: The Académie Française and Its Dictionary during an Age of Revolution.* Oxford UP, 2017.

Fleischman, Suzanne. "The Battle of Feminism and Bon Usage: Instituting Nonsexist Language in French." *The French Review*, vol. 70, no. 6, 1997, pp. 834–844.

Forsdick, Charles, and David Murphy, eds. *Francophone Postcolonial Studies: A Critical Introduction.* Routledge, 2003.

Harris, Martin, and Nigel Vincent, eds. *The Romance Languages. Routledge*, 1988; esp. "French" (Martin Harris, pp. 209–245), "Occitan" (Max W. Wheeler, pp. 246–278), and "The Romance Creoles" (John N. Green, pp. 420–474).

Harrison, Michelle, and Aurélie Joubert, eds. *French Language Policies and the Revitalisation of Regional Languages in the 21st Century.* Palgrave Macmillan, 2019.

Henry, Freeman G. *Language, Culture, and Hegemony in Modern France: 1539 to the Millennium.* Summa, 2008.

Hornsby, Michael. *Revitalizing Minority Languages: New Speakers of Breton, Yiddish, and Lemko.* Palgrave Macmillan, 2015.

Jones, Mari C., and David Hornsby, eds. *Language and Social Structure in Urban France.* Routledge, 2013.

Judge, Anne. *Linguistic Policies and the Survival of Regional Languages in France and Britain.* Palgrave Macmillan, 2007.

Kluter, Lois. "Breton vs. French: Language and the Opposition of Political, Economic, Social, and Cultural Values." *Investigating Obsolescence: Studies in Language Contraction and Death*, ed. Nancy C. Dorian. Cambridge UP, 1989, pp. 75–90.

Kosnick, Kiki. "The Everyday Poetics of Gender-inclusive French: Strategies for Navigating the Linguistic Landscape." *Modern & Contemporary France*, vol. 27, no. 2, 2019, pp. 147–161.

Lefkowitz, Natalie. *Talking Backwards, Looking Forwards: The French Language Game Verlan.* Narr, 1991.

Little, Roger. "World Literature in French; or Is Francophonie Frankly Phony?" *European Review*, vol. 9, no. 4, 2001, pp. 421–436.

Lodge, R. Anthony. *French: From Dialect to Standard.* Routledge, 1993.

Lodge, R. Anthony. *A Sociolinguistic History of Parisian French.* Cambridge, UK: Cambridge University Press, 2004.

Lüdi, Georges. "Communicative and Cognitive Dimensions of Pluricentric Practices in French." *Pluricentricity: Language Variation and Sociocognitive Dimensions*, ed. Augusto Soares da Silva. de Guyter-Mouton, 2013, pp. 49–82.

Marcoux, Robert, and Mamadou Kani Konaté. "Africa and the *francophonie* of Tomorrow: An Attempt to Measure the Population of the Francophonie from Now to 2060." *African Population Studies*, vol. 25, no. 2, 2011, pp. 215–225.

Martin, Elizabeth. *Marketing Identities through Language: English and Global Imagery in French Advertising.* Palgrave Macmillan, 2005.

Mooney, Damien. *Southern Regional French: A Linguistic Analysis of Language and Dialect Contact.* Legenda, 2018.

Moudileno, Lydie. "*Francophonie*: Trash or Recycle?" *Transnational French Studies: Postcolonialism and Littérature-monde*, eds. Alec G. Hargreaves, et al. Liverpool UP, 2010, pp. 109–124.

Murdoch, H. Adlai, and Zsuzsanna Fagyal. *Francophone Cultures and Geographies of Identity.* Cambridge Scholars, 2014.

Neathery-Castro, Jody, and Mark O. Rousseau. "Does French Matter?: France and Francophononie in the Age of Globalization." *The French Review*, vol. 78, no. 4, 2005, pp. 678–693.

Neathery-Castro, Jody, and Mark O. Rousseau. "Quebec, Francophonie, and Globalization." *Québec Studies*, vol. 32, 2001, pp. 15–35.

Oakes, Leigh. *Language and National Identity: Comparing France and Sweden.* Benjamins, 2001.

Oakes, Leigh. "Normative Language Policy and Minority Language Rights: Rethinking the Case of Regional Languages in France." *Language Policy*, vol. 16, no. 4, 2017, pp. 365–384.

Piser, Karina. "Aux Armes, Citoyen.nes! " *Foreign Policy*, 4 Jul. 2021, https://foreignpolicy.com/2021/07/04/france-gender-language-ecriture-inclusive-aux-armes-citoyennes/.

Planchenault, Gaëlle. *Voices in the Media: Performing French Linguistic Otherness.* Bloomsbury, 2015.

Pooley, Timothy. *Chtimi: The Urban Vernaculars of Northern France.* Multilingual Matters, 1996.

Posner, Rebecca. *Linguistic Change in French.* Clarendon, 1997.

Rocheron, Yvette, and Christopher Rolfe, eds. *Shifting Frontiers of France and Francophonie.* Lang, 2004.

Salhi, Kamal, ed. *French in and out of France: Language Policies, Intercultural Antagonisms, and Dialogue.* Lang, 2002.

Sanders, Carol, ed. *French Today: Language in Its Social Context.* Cambridge UP, 1993, esp. pp. 27–54 (Carol Sanders, "Socio-situational Variation") and pp. 55–85 (Roger Hawkins, "Regional Variation in French").

Sarrasin, Oriane, et al. "Sexism and Attitudes Toward Gender-Neutral Language: The Case of English, French, German." *Swiss Journal of Psychology*, vol. 71, no. 3, 2012, pp. 113–124.

Schiffman, Harold F. "French Language Policy: Centrism, Orwellian *dirigisme*, or Economic Determinism?" *Opportunities and Challenges of Bilingualism*, ed. Li Wei. Mouton de Gruyter, 2002, pp. 89–104.

Swamy, Vinay. "*Assignée garçon,* or Grappling with the Trans Question in the French Language." *H-France Salon*, vol. 11, no. 14, 2019, art. 8.

Thody, Philip. *Le Franglais: Forbidden English, Forbidden American: Law, Politics and Language in Contemporary France: A Study in Loan Words and National Identity.* Bloomsbury, 2000.

Timsit, Annabelle. "The Push to Make French More Gender-Neutral." *The Atltantic*, 24 Nov. 2017, https://www.theatlantic.com/international/archive/2017/11/inclusive-writing-france-feminism/545.

Traoré, Moussa. *One Story of Academia: Race Lines and the Rhetoric of Distinction through the Académie Française.* Lang, 2010.

Vassberg, Liliane Mangold. *Alsatian Acts of Identity: Language Use and Language Attitudes in Alsace.* Multilingual Matters, 1993.

Vigoureux, Cécile B. "Francophonie." *Annual Review of Anthropology*, no. 42, 2013, pp. 379–397.

Walter, Henriette. *French Inside Out: The Worldwide Development of the French Language in the Past, the Present, and the Future.* Trans. Peter Fawcett. Routledge, 1994.

Wise, Hilary. *The Vocabulary of Modern French: Origins, Structure, and Function.* Routledge, 1997.

Wise, R. Anthony, et al. *Exploring the French Language.* Arnold, 1997.

Zaretsky, Robert. "France Is Debating Whether French Is Sexist." *Foreign Policy*, 20 Nov. 2017, https://foreignpolicy.com/2017/11/20/france-is-debating-whether-french-is-sexist/.

CHAPTER 10

ETIQUETTE

OVERVIEW

Mastery of the rules of etiquette has been very important in France since the Renaissance—when self-control, correct understanding of social hierarchies and the dynamics and exigencies of specific situations, and polite and dignified behavior were the hallmark of an *honnête homme* and key to a nobleman's survival in the complex and high-pressure social arena of the court. Today, French parents invest significant time and effort in teaching their children the rules of etiquette and proper behavior in the adult world and it is a mark of distinction for them when their children are complimented as being *bien élévés* (well raised). While French social interactions have gradually become more informal and egalitarian, French etiquette is still more formal than in many other countries and the complexity and importance of getting things just right makes ownership of a *guide de savoir-vivre*, or etiquette primer, common in many French households.

Three important matters of etiquette among the French are greetings, the formal (*vous*) versus the informal (*tu*) form of address, and table manners. When being introduced to or interacting with strangers (and interacting with people with whom one's relationships are devoid of camaraderie or closeness), handshakes and profuse use of "monsieur" and "madame" are *de rigueur*. In many impersonal everyday interactions, handshakes are unnecessary but it is still important to greet, thank, and bid farewell to people respectfully (e.g., when entering or leaving a shop). When making a request to a stranger, the French will often begin by using a polite formula such as "Excusez-moi de vous déranger. . ." ("Forgive me for disturbing you…"). Shaking hands upon greeting or taking leave of others is also customary among colleagues, neighbors, and casual acquaintances, men and women alike. People who are close—such as friends, relatives, classmates (and young people in general), longtime coworkers of similar level—will greet one another with kisses on the cheek (*les bises*)—actually, near-kisses, during which one leans in close, brushing the other's cheek with one's own while making a faint kissing sound without touching the other person with one's lips. The number of kisses given varies across France but the most common practice is to kiss each cheek once. The formal *vous* (second personal singular pronoun) is the default form of address used to show respect for others and is always used for strangers and people one does not know very well (except for young children) and for people of a higher social status; it is also used generally for older people who are not family members or friends. Inappropriate use of the informal *tu* can be awkward or perceived as insulting. *Tu* is used widely with children, among the young, and with close friends, family members, regular coworkers of similar rank, and other people with whom one is chummy. Among people who are becoming friends (or whose relationship is becoming more casual or intimate in some other way), switching from *vous* to *tu* is something that must be agreed to—often quite simply but usually always explicitly. *Tu* may also be used in a more calculated fashion beyond its most typical justifications to create an atmosphere of informality or as a deliberate and unmistakable sign of disrespect.

Meals are very important to the French and so, too, are table manners. There are important rules to be observed when invited for dinner by a French person—bringing flowers or another appropriate gift for the host or hostess, contributing to the conversation, using cutlery (fork in the left hand and knife in the right, hands kept above the table when not holding cutlery) and eating bread correctly. There are similar rules of etiquette to be observed when dining in a restaurant, where servers are treated more formally and the service, or gratuity, is included in the price of the meal. Hosting people in one's home, especially for a dinner party, is both an art and a ritual that reflects significantly on one's social reputation and *savoir vivre* (according to *Merriam-Webster*, the "ability to live elegantly").

Beyond etiquette in the strict sense, one of the defining characteristics of the French in their social interactions is their protectiveness of privacy. This guardedness can be seen in the walls and privet hedges that surround their homes; extreme sensitivity to others prying into the details of their private lives (incl. matters of family, money, health, religion, and romantic relationships); strict privacy laws; less blurring of the public and private lives of politicians; and rising concerns about the threat posed to privacy, public reputation, and personal data by the internet and social media. Other traits of French behavior can give rise to misunderstandings with foreigners. One is the tendency to be frank, which is sometimes interpreted as rudeness, as can a greater tolerance of closer physical proximity in public places—although it is customary to utter a perfunctory *pardon* when accidently brushing against someone or needing to get around them quickly in a tight space—and their undisciplined and opportunistic (from an Anglo-American perspective) observance of lines. For the French, these behaviors are justifiable (or at least excusable) given the more crowded nature of many smaller public places and the need to be quick, resourceful (*débrouillard*), and assertive when competing for limited space and resources. Another behavior that sometimes strikes foreigners is the higher level of flirtatiousness between men and women in everyday life. It is often just an innocent effort to be charming that is thought of as part of the joy of life. Nonetheless, interactions between men and women in France are mostly courteous, cordial, neutral, and reflective of gender equality—particularly in professional contexts. Caddish treatment of women (once widely downplayed) is subject to increasing opprobrium. Sexual harassment is sanctioned by law—including a 2018 law that covers physical and verbal harassment in the street. The French workplace tends to be more formal and hierarchical; however, it is evolving in response to new theories of management and exposure to more casual styles through globalization and international commerce. Overall, the French are keenly aware of omnipresent social hierarchies and new forms of aristocracy (based on wealth, education, and socio-professional status) and seek both symbolic status and concrete personal advantage within this hierarchical system, but they also have a vigorous egalitarian ethos and a democratic sense of personal dignity as a fundamental attribute of citizenship. One French author explained this apparent contradiction—a legacy of the historical duality of ancien régime aristocracy and revolutionary republicanism—by quipping that what the French really believe in is "privileges for all."

Further Reading

Carroll (1992); Davetian (2009); de Rothschild (2015); Hacker (2016); Kerbat-Orecchioni (2012); Storti (2001).

Formal vs. Informal Forms of Address

An important question in interpersonal communication in French is the use of the informal (*tu*) vs. the formal (*vous*) form of the second person singular pronoun, for which there is only one equivalent in English—"you." The importance of the matter is reflected in the fact that the French even have nouns (and verbs) that signify using of one or the other—*tutoiement* (*tutoyer*) and *vouvoiement* (*vouvoyer*). As a general rule, *vous* is used whenever one wants or needs to show respect for the person one is addressing, which is very often—including strangers, people with whom one's relationship is of a more formal nature and devoid of connotations of friendship or camaraderie (incl. certain professional colleagues, casual acquaintances, and neighbors), people who are appreciably older than oneself, or people of a higher status in a particular context (e.g., a teacher, supervisor, or person of social prominence). Among strangers, *tu* is reliably used only when addressing children (stopping at older adolescents, who are treated as adults). It is used systematically among family members (one's immediate and extended family, but not necessarily one's in-laws) and friends; and widely among young people, coworkers of a similar hierarchical level with whom one works daily/frequently in a spirit of camaraderie and familiarity, and among members of the working class and people of lower status as a gesture of egalitarian fraternity (by contrast, the bourgeoisie uses *vous* more frequently).

Although there is a trend toward greater informality in interpersonal relations since the 1960s, and therefore toward broader and easier use of *tu, vous* remains the default form of address for adult individuals with whom there is no established or natural camaraderie or intimacy. Correct use of *tu* and *vous* is a sign of a good upbringing and mastery of the rules of etiquette. Inappropriate use of *tu* can cause awkwardness between two people or give offense. In fact, it is often used as a deliberate insult or provocation—for instance, when the police stop minority youths, or in verbal or physical confrontations. It is common for a person to ask another person if they may use *tu* with one another—or simply suggest that they do so—when such usage is natural or likely; and a person of higher status who would normally be addressed more politely as *vous* may tell another person that it is okay for them to use *tu*. Still, there are nuances that make the *tu/vous* distinction tricky. In some situations, a person of higher status will grant permission to another person to address them as *tu* but the other will nonetheless continue to use *vous* out of caution and deference (e.g., a pupil or student with their teacher). *Vous* is not necessarily a sign of a lack of closeness. Former French president Jacques Chirac addressed his wife, Bernadette, as *vous*—an upper-class convention of showing courtly respect for one's spouse.

In France, the use of another's first name is not practiced as widely as a sign of informality as in English-speaking countries. In general, the French call one another by their surnames, usually preceded by "Monsieur" or "Madame." In the workplace and in other formal situations, people occupying high-level positions are often addressed by their title, again preceded by "Monsieur" or "Madame." For instance, a managing director would be addressed as *Monsieur le Directeur*, and a CEO as *Madame la Présidente*. In public, one shows respect to strangers (and anyone with whom one would normally use *vous*) by the regular use of "Monsieur" and "Madame" throughout a conversation. "Mademoiselle" is still used for greeting girls and young women (i.e., through adolescence and presumably unmarried) in everyday situations but is no longer used on official forms for unmarried women because it is considered sexist (there is no equivalent for unmarried men, although *jeune homme*, or "young man," is used for boys and very young men in casual conversations). For anyone in their twenties, Monsieur or Madame is used as the default title.

Use of "Monsieur" or "Madame" is particularly important when first addressing someone, when greeting or bidding farewell to someone (including merchants and other businesspeople when entering or leaving their establishment), when making a request, and when thanking someone. When addressing a group of mixed gender, it is more formal to use the gendered singular or plural forms separately for the women and men (i.e., *Mesdames et Messieurs*) one is addressing. *Messieurs-dames* is a colloquial hybrid plural.

See also: Chapter 9: Sexism and Gender Bias in French. Chapter 10: Greeting Strangers, Acquaintances, Friends, and Family Members; Social Hierarchies; Social Importance of Good Manners; Workplace Etiquette and Customer Relations.

Further Reading
Beeching (2006); Coveney (2003); Dewaele (2005); Douglass (2009); Morford (2008); Warren (2006).

Greeting Strangers, Acquaintances, Friends, and Family Members

The French are known to maintain somber miens in public and in professional contexts; and there is nothing more "American" than flashing a big smile to everyone one meets. The somber mien connotes dignity, a guardedness with respect to one's

Two men shake hands by the Eiffel Tower in Paris. Shaking hands is customary when being introduced to people as well as when one greets business associates and colleagues, neighbors, and acquaintances who are not considered friends. (Nullplus/Dreamstime.com)

privacy, and the sober resolve needed to confront the challenges of daily life. On the other hand, the French are inveterate hand shakers. They shake hands when greeting strangers, work colleagues (especially at the start and close of a day), professional contacts, casual acquaintances, and neighbors. The handshake is especially important when greeting someone of higher social status or otherwise due one's respect. When greeting anyone with whom they are not on a first-name basis, they always use "Monsieur" or "Madame" with the word of greeting. In most instances, the handshake involves one quick, moderately firm grasp and shake. When greeting a group, each person in the group is normally greeted individually, with a handshake, unless the group is large and to do so would be cumbersome. Handshakes are not necessary when greeting someone with whom there is no expectation of a prolonged interaction (e.g., people in many simple public situations, such as shop clerks); however, one is expected to verbally greet, thank, and bid farewell to people in business establishments. The international business consultant Polly Platt recommends using what she calls the "magic words," when asking strangers for any kind of assistance: *Excusez-moi de vous déranger, monsieur (or madame)…*" ("Excuse me for disturbing you, Sir/ Madam. . ."). "Bonjour" is the default greeting before 6:00 p.m., and "Bonsoir" after 6:00 (or at dusk). When being introduced to someone for the first time, the most commonly used expression is *"Enchanté,"* which is a less formal, abbreviated form of *"Enchanté de faire votre connaissance"* ("Charmed to make your acquaintance"). After a greeting, it is traditional to inquire about the other person's health and well-being.

Among young people, more familiar acquaintances, colleagues, and friends, this can take the form of the very short and colloquial greeting, "*Salut, ça va?*" ("Hi, how's it going?"). An important cultural tradition is offering kisses on the cheek (*faire les bises*) when greeting one's friends and family members—a sign of closeness extended to casual acquaintances among the young and sometimes to coworkers to whom one is close. The *bises* greeting ritual is somewhat more common among women than men, particularly beyond the circle of people with whom one is truly close. Because it is a sign of intimacy and true feeling, it is less optional than the handshake, which can be dispensed with when greeting a large group or in situations where it is difficult to reach one's hand out to another. It is important to greet every person in a group of friends or family with the *bises*. One usually does not actually kiss the other person's cheek with one's lips; one leans in close, grazing the other's cheek while making a short, soft kissing sound with one's lips; then repeating the gesture on the opposite cheek. There are regional variations regarding the number of kisses one gives—one (traditional in Brittany), two (i.e., one on each cheek—the most common practice throughout France), three (more common in parts of the south), and sometimes even four (in parts of northern France except for the Paris region, where just two kisses are given). Close family members get one kiss on the cheek, whereas more distant members of one's extended family get the same number as friends. Hugging other people is considered a much more intimate form of embrace and is not a common form of greeting among friends, let alone mere acquaintances.

See also: Chapter 10: Formal vs. Informal Forms of Address; Privacy and Personal Space; Social Hierarchies; Social Importance of Good Manners; Workplace Etiquette and Customer Relations.

Further Reading
Lundmark (2009); Tessonneau (2005); Villeminot (2019).

Hosting and Gift Giving

Playing host to family, friends, neighbors, colleagues, and other guests is an important social act in France. Its most important manifestation is holding a dinner party in one's home, which may take on varying degrees of informality or formality depending on the occasion's significance and the importance of the guests. Entertaining people in one's home is an art, a ritual, and a form of social theater that significantly reflects both the regard one has for the guests and the host or hosts' *savoir vivre*, social standing, good taste, and capacity for friendship. The multicourse meals must be artfully prepared and pleasing to the guests; the wine must be good; the guests should be made to feel welcome; and both compatibility of the guests and overall atmosphere must be conducive to good conversation—it is the hosts' duty to keep the party running smoothly. French dinner parties typically start (8:00 p.m.) and run late due to the multiple courses and conversations to be savored. In other circumstances, people may be invited to one's home less formally for just *l'apéritif* (i.e., before-dinner drinks and refreshments c. 6:00 p.m.), which sometimes takes the form of a casual meal known as an *apéritif dinatoire*. Other informal occasions for entertaining include morning or afternoon coffee or tea, after-dinner desserts or drinks, backyard barbecues, and afternoon snacks (*un goûter*) for groups of children. It is also common for French people to get together with friends for drinks and/or dinner in a café, bistro, brasserie, or restaurant. French people signal their intention to host people outside of the home, that is, to treat people by paying for a café, restaurant, or cultural activity—by using the verb *inviter* ("to invite") when setting up the occasion (or spontaneously on the spot). The French are masters of protocol appropriate for large and formal banquets, social functions, and chic soirées, and excel in the art of hosting them. One historically and culturally important type of civilized social function for which France is well known is the salon—a gathering of intellectuals, literary and artistic figures, polymaths, and opinion makers for the sake of stimulating discussion of new ideas and lively debates on major issues of the day. Such salons have been held in France in various forms since the seventeenth century. Hosted by socially prominent women (and men) of great erudition and cultural refinement, they were an important cultural institution in the eighteenth and nineteenth centuries, when they played a crucial role in the emergence of the public sphere of opinion and social dialogue and the elaboration and dissemination of the ideas of both the Enlightenment and modernism. Great French salon hostesses (*salonnières*) include Madame (Marie Thérèse Rodet) Geoffrin, Madame (Françoise) de Graffigny, and Madame Necker (Suzanne Curchod) in the eighteenth century; Madame (Juliette) Récamier and Madame (Germaine) de Staël in the early nineteenth century; Nina de Villard and Countess Greffulhe (Élisabeth de Riquet de Caraman-Chimay) in the latter part of the century and Belle Epoque; and Vicomtesse (Marie-Laure) de Noailles in the twentieth century.

Gift giving in France is much like it is in other Western countries, in terms of both the type of gifts given and the occasions on which they are given, such as birthdays, weddings, wedding anniversaries, births of babies, religious holidays like Christmas, Saint Valentine's Day (but only among people who are romantically involved and certainly not more broadly among children), and special occasions. The French are prone to give small gifts of quality, esthetically elegant in their wrapping and general presentation, rather than large, very expensive gifts. This is because it is the thoughtful gesture that counts and because ostentatious gifts that are more expensive than either the occasion or the nature of the relationship between the giver and receiver calls for can be interpreted as showing off on the part of the giver and puts a burden on the receiver to reciprocate in kind. When given a gift, it is considered good form to call to offer thanks or, better still, to send a handwritten note of thanks. It is important to thank someone for any gesture of affection, appreciation, or esteem—including a birthday card or vacation postcard. Nonetheless, the French are not overly frequent card senders outside of major occasions. Flowers and food items, such as gift-wrapped chocolates and something from an artisanal pastry shop, are favorite gifts, for example, to bring to the home of someone who has invited you to dinner. Special occasions are often celebrated by inviting the honoree to a restaurant for lunch or dinner, a smaller one by inviting them to have a drink (*prendre un pot, boire un verre*) at a local café.

See also: Chapter 10: Greeting Strangers, Acquaintances, Friends, and Family Members; Privacy and Personal Space; Social Importance of Good Manners; Table Etiquette and Dinner Parties. Chapter 14: Overview.

Further Reading
Béal and Traverso (2010); Chevalier-Karfis (2020).

Privacy and Personal Space

The French do not have as expansive a notion of individual personal space (sometimes referred to as "body bubbles") as Americans, Britons, and northern Europeans. They have a more Latin sense of interpersonal proxemics and lifetimes of experience in crowded and bustling public spaces (where one often needs to jockey for position to gain access to limited space and resources). They press together and sometimes jostle one another in the street (and in public transportation and crowded shops), and are not very disciplined (from an American perspective) about waiting in lines—they are more prone to cut a line opportunistically if not ignore a line altogether (e.g., coming in at an angle to crowd around a service counter, ready to press their advantage over those farther back or allowing any gap to open up). It is nonetheless customary in France to say *pardon* when brushing up against someone inadvertently (and noticeably) or needing to get around someone in a tight space. While the French may have a higher degree of tolerance for physical promiscuity in public, they are much less understanding when people disturb the peace by talking loudly in public, and therefore generally speak in tones not likely to be overheard by others.

French personal spaces tend to be quite closed off. Open-space work areas have now become more common in French offices, but in traditional workspaces, office doors are not left open—though a closed door does not necessarily indicate that the person inside does not wish to be disturbed. In many instances, it simply takes a perfunctory knock before a coworker may open the door and enter, often without waiting for verbal permission to do so (especially when the hierarchical difference between the two is not too great). In crowded cafés and similar public spaces where people sit in close proximity (e.g., subway cars and buses), French people do not make small talk with people who are not part of their party and expect to be left alone as if in a world of their own, even when they are mere inches from strangers. One's home is considered a very private space and is protected as such. Individual residences are surrounded by walls of varying heights and tall privet hedges. Older apartment buildings often have an external *porte cochère*—an entrance with large, heavy doors, where passengers (formerly in carriages) were dropped off and picked up by drivers—and an outer courtyard or vestibule before one gains access to the residential part of the building. While the cultural institution of the concierge watching over an apartment building (and its residents) is waning, nearly all apartment buildings (and many individual homes) are equipped with intercom buzzer systems. The French do not easily open their homes to nonfamily members and people who are not close friends ("Make yourself at home" is a phrase that is used neither frequently or lightly). Guests are expected to stay in spaces reserved for guests and the rest of the residence is off-limits.

The French are very guarded about their privacy and private lives, especially concerning outsiders' intrusions into family affairs and private matters (and many public ones, too) that could cause scandals or loss of esteem. In premodern times (esp. among aristocrats at court), when the public and private spheres of life were more blended, people were protective of their public reputations, individual honor and dignity, and family reputations. Among aristocrats and other members of the social elite, a compromised reputation often led to a duel as an extreme means of defending one's honor, even as late as in the early twentieth century. In 1897, the author Marcel Proust, who was privately gay, fought an uneventful duel with pistols against a prominent literary critic, also gay, who had accused him of having a homosexual affair with the son of another well-known literary figure. The protective bubble of privacy expanded and grew stronger with the rise of bourgeois attitudes (e.g., outward moral austerity and the sanctity of the domestic sphere) in the nineteenth century. Examples range from a strong French aversion to the "indiscreet" discussion of matters considered private (e.g., religion, money, health, personal identity, romantic life, etc.) to extreme wariness about the exposure of private lives, and threats to personal information, which have increased with the proliferation of the internet and social media. France has strict laws concerning the invasion of privacy and the protection of personal data online. Created in 1978, the French data protection authority, officially known as the National Commission for Information Technology and Civil Liberties (CNIL), is a government agency tasked with the three-fold mission of protecting personal data, supporting innovation, and preserving individual liberties in the computer age. With recent advances in data collection technologies and the popularity of social media, France has been at the forefront of EU efforts to pressurize global internet giants like Google and Facebook to protect individuals and their personal data, including the delisting of defamatory and unwelcome private information about them in web searches. Provisions for a digital "right to be forgotten" were also included in a landmark 2016 "Digital Republic Law."

The protection of the private lives of celebrities and public figures is a trickier matter. Paparazzi stalk celebrities in France as they do elsewhere and the photos they take of them are published in gossip magazines and online, where they are followed by a curious and avid public. However, even people who lead ostensibly public lives are thought to deserve protection of their private lives. For example, the private lives of politicians—including their love lives and private transgressions—do not face the level of public scrutiny (and opprobrium) that they do elsewhere, except when they violate the law or represent a conflict of interest with their official duties. The French were mostly nonplussed by the revelations (1994) that President François Mitterrand had an illegitimate daughter with his longtime mistress and quite astonished that U.S.

president Bill Clinton faced removal from office (1999) over a consensual extramarital sexual relationship. While the role of presidential spouse has gradually become more public since the Pompidou administration (1969–1974), French presidents and presidential candidates generally do not put their families (esp. their minor children) in the spotlight. When François Hollande was inaugurated as president of the Republic in 2012, his children were not even present at the official ceremony at the Élysée Palace. While considerable attention has been paid to the fact that President Emmanuel Macron's wife, Brigitte, is 24½ years older than her husband and was his former high school teacher, the public has mostly respected the presidential couple's insistence that the details of their relationship history remain private. On the other hand, President Nicolas Sarkozy (2007–2012) was criticized by many for his calculated overexposure of his private life, including his courtship of and eventual marriage to the singer-songwriter and former high fashion model, Carla Bruni. French guardedness about the details of private life (esp. intimate life) extends to colleagues at work, except for coworkers who may also be friends.

See also: Chapter 6: Bourgeoisie and Middle Class. Chapter 7: Attitudes toward Sex. Chapter 10: Hosting and Gift Giving; Social Importance of Good Manners; Workplace Etiquette and Customer Relations. Chapter 16: Internet, Social Media, and Video Games.

Further Reading

De Gournay (2004); Krotoszynski (2016); Kuhn (2004); Prost (1991); Sarmiento-Mirwaldt et al. (2014); Trouille (2000); Wacks (2015); Whitman (2004).

MALE GALLANTRY AND FEMALE COQUETTISHNESS

Interactions between men and women have changed a great deal in France since the 1960s as a result of the sexual revolution, the weakening of the institution of marriage, the influx of women in the workplace, the achievements of feminism in all of its different forms, new laws, and changing attitudes as reflected in the media and popular culture. However, old notions of gallantry and coquettishness persist. Gallantry involves an obsequious respect and idealized affection for the supposed "fairer sex"—often mixed with more than a touch of supposedly harmless flirtation—and is seen as the mark of a true gentleman. It is a chivalrous and courtly variation of Latin/Gallic machismo, of which there is also a strong remnant in French culture. For their part, a large percentage of French women do not consider that equality and empowerment necessarily require abandoning the traditional attributes of femininity—including coquettishness, which entails dressing, acting, and conforming to norms of physical beauty in alluring ways that are designed to get the attention of and please men. Gallantry and coquettishness are often justified as complementary parts of the small pleasures of life. However, the pushback against this attitude has become increasingly fierce in the context of the #MeToo movement and its French equivalent, #BalanceTonPorc.

Social Hierarchies

Political historians and journalists are fond of describing France's democratic political institutions as constituting a "republican monarchy" because the office of the president has so much power and quasi-regal trappings. Similarly, one might characterize French society as an *egalitarian aristocracy*. The feudal privileges of the aristocracy were abolished in the first year of the French Revolution (1789) and despite attempts by subsequent monarchies and empires to revive an aristocratic order in the nineteenth century, no iteration of an actual nobility ever regained statutory privileges or the old aristocracy's place at the pinnacle of French society. However, neither the legacy nor the concept of aristocracy has completely died out in France. French people tend to be keenly aware of their place in the multitiered social hierarchy and the nation has a clearly identifiable social elite. Furthermore, the members of this elite—who benefit from accumulated wealth, prestige, a solicitous attitude on the part of politicians (many of whom are themselves part of the social elite), and numerous other social advantages, may be plausibly described as an aristocracy or cluster of overlapping aristocracies. Today's new "aristocratic" elite in France includes old families (of noble origin or part of the *haute* and *grande* bourgeoisie) with large inherited fortunes, individuals and households in the highest income and net worth brackets, top-level corporate executives and the top tier of people working in finance, owners of prospering larger businesses, highly educated people with the most valued degrees and diplomas (esp. the graduates of the ultra-selective *grandes écoles*), practitioners of highly skilled intellectual professions (e.g., doctors, engineers, lawyers, architects, accountants, etc.), high-level civil servants, politicians, members of the cultural elite (artists, writers, academics, Parisian intelligentsia, etc.), and the shapers of opinions and taste in the media and show business. The new "aristocracy" has its exclusive precincts and haunts (e.g., tony neighborhoods, exclusive clubs, high-priced restaurants and boutiques, and elite institutions) and is looked at with a mix of fascination and resentment by the rest of the population. Other broad-based hierarchical distinctions in French society may be expressed in a series of binaries—urban/rural, city/suburbs (i.e., *la banlieue*), Paris/provinces, men/women, people with French ancestry going back several generations (*Français de souche*)/people from immigrant backgrounds (*Français issus de l'immigration*), white people/racial minorities, mainlanders (*Français métropolitains*)/people residing in or recently arrived from the overseas departments and territories, and the Catholic majority/religious minorities (esp. Jews and Muslims). People who belong to the group identified by the first term in each binary have certain social advantages over those belonging to the group or category identified by the second term. Finally, from the top of the social hierarchy to the bottom, the French are prone to distinguish between those who are *pistonnés* in some way—people whose advantageous "place" in society was obtained with the help of connections (i.e., the extra thrust of a piston)—and those who are not. Traces of these hierarchical social distinctions are often subtle, if not masked, in everyday life notwithstanding a constant but latent tension between the privileged and the non-privileged. Nonetheless, the general ethos of French public space is democratic and inclusive, and it requires that all people treat one another in a civil manner in accordance with the rules of French etiquette. Moreover, a powerful counterweight to the persistent hierarchical and pseudo-aristocratic nature of French society is found in France's exceptionally strong egalitarian tradition. This tradition manifests itself in the fundamental tenet of the French Revolution's Declaration of the Rights of Man and the Citizen ("Men are born and remain free and equal in rights. Social distinctions may be founded only upon the general good."); in the French republican understanding of meritocracy as based on academic achievement in public schools and institutions of higher education (many of the *grandes écoles* are public and even those that are not base admissions largely on the results in competitive exams); in the equally republican stubborn refusal to make public distinctions among citizens based on what might characterize them in the private sphere (e.g., race, ethnicity, religion, gender, sexual orientation, or affiliation with a particular cultural community); in a comprehensive social safety net and extensive redistributive social spending on the part of the government in the name of solidarity; and in the propensity of *le Peuple* (sometimes also called *la France d'en bas*, or "France from down below") to rise up in revolt when it feels that inequality (or iniquity) has gotten out of hand—from the 1358 peasant uprising known as the Jacquerie to the unruly *Gilets Jaunes* (Yellow Vests) protests of 2018–2020. Put simply, France is a fundamentally democratic and civil society in which myriad subtle and conspicuous hierarchical distinctions, marked elitism with a lingering whiff of aristocracy, and passionate egalitarianism coexist.

See also: Chapter 2: Louis XIV and the Absolute Monarchy; Louis XVI and the End of the Ancien Régime. Chapter 3: Republic. Chapter 4: Labor Relations. Chapter 6: Overview; Bourgeoisie and Middle Class; Income Distribution and Inequality; Nobility; Working Class. Chapter 8: Grandes Écoles. Chapter 10: Formal vs. Informal Forms of Address; Workplace Etiquette and Customer Relations.

Further Reading
Birkelund and Lemel (2012); France (1992).

Social Importance of Good Manners

Knowing the social codes of etiquette and being perceived as well mannered is extremely important in France. A major historical source of this cultural fixation was the courtly behavior of the nobility, which followed strict rules of proper behavior seen as key to the preservation of the social hierarchy and to giving each person due respect. Mastery of the rules of polite behavior and the flawless demonstration of social graces in public was a large part of the seventeenth-century aristocratic ideal of the *honnête homme*—a courteous, civilized, earnest, honorable, decent, poised, disciplined, and self-possessed gentleman who easily adapts to a variety of social situations. Traces of the aristocratic origins of French etiquette are found everywhere—for example, in the use of "monsieur," which derives from *mon seigneur*, or "my lord." French parents (and schools) spend a considerable amount of time and effort teaching children the rules of etiquette from an early age. Children are expected to know how to follow the rules of the adult world and to interact politely with adults. They are permitted to "just be kids" (within reason, i.e., without disturbing adults) only when they are among themselves. A child lacking a minimum of requisite social graces and good behavior from an adult standpoint is sometimes described as *sauvage*, which means "wild" (i.e., not yet well trained). On the other hand, it is considered a great compliment when one's child is described as *bien élévé* (literally, well raised, or well trained).

Displaying good manners is demonstrated in a wide range of situations—by generally behaving in a way that is seen as unselfish and that does not attract undue attention to oneself (*se donner en spectacle*), discretion, knowing how to properly greet and thank people, knowing when and how one should excuse oneself, being able to make polite conversation that is context-appropriate and includes the right amount of flattery, appropriate usage of polite formulas in written correspondence (salutations like *Je vous prie d'agréer, Monsieur, l'expression de mes sentiments distingués*), impeccable table manners, appropriate use of the informal and formal forms of address in the second person (*tu* vs. *vous*), courteous behavior toward older people and individuals of the opposite sex, knowledge of gift-giving protocols, and proper understanding and observance of social hierarchies—including due deference to authorities and individuals occupying positions of social prominence—and expected use of honorary and professional titles. Mastery of etiquette is complicated; for this reason, a *guide de savoir vivre*, or etiquette and correspondence primer, is a fixture in many French homes and offices. The French are known to openly (and publicly) point out breaches of etiquette, often in a preachy way that people not used to such correction find unpleasant. However, such corrections are often preceded by a perfunctory and self-effacing apology on the part of the person making the observation. It is quite a misconception that the French are rude. Parisians are no ruder than New Yorkers or Londoners; and most French people are reasonably helpful to and tolerant of foreigners (those who are well behaved, at least) because hospitality is a part of *le savoir vivre*. However, the French also have a tradition of being frank and direct (incl. among close friends), which is sometimes misconstrued as harshness or rudeness. Democracy has not necessarily diminished the importance of politeness and good etiquette because it is part of the French democratic and egalitarian ethos that every individual, regardless of their social station, has a right to be treated with respect that reflects their inherent dignity. Nonetheless, there has been a trend toward greater informality in social interactions in France since the 1960s—a trend that has gained strength through foreign influences (including American casualness and informality) and the proliferation of rapid forms of electronic communication.

See also: Chapter 6: Bourgeoisie and Middle Class; Nobility. Chapter 7: Child Raising Practices. Chapter 10: Formal vs. Informal Forms of Address; Greeting Strangers, Acquaintances, Friends, and Family Members; Hosting and Gift Giving; Social

Hierarchies; Table Etiquette and Dinner Parties; Workplace Etiquette and Customer Relations.

Further Reading
Barlow and Nadeau (2016); Platt (2003).

Table Etiquette and Dinner Parties

Meals are very important in French culture and so, too, is displaying good table manners. If invited for a dinner in a French home, one should always bring a gift for the hosts, especially one that will please the hostess (if invited for an *apéritif*, cocktails with appetizers, a gift is still appreciated but not strictly necessary). Flowers are always a good gift, as are a bottle of wine, a cheese, or a dessert item (e.g., fine chocolates or something from an artisanal pastry shop). Upon arrival, one should sit where invited to do so by the host and stay there, moving around the home only when invited to do so by the host. One should use the bathroom before arriving; it is considered especially bad manners to leave the table to use the bathroom during a meal. One should take one's place at table where invited to do so by the host (there may be place markers). The guest of honor will be seated at the head of the table, usually to the immediate right of the primary host or hostess. If the hosts are a couple, the other host or hostess will usually sit at the other end of the table. Unless strict protocol is being observed, the other guests will be seated in a manner that is conducive to good conversation, which is an important part of a French meal. A guest should be prepared to be a good listener and to contribute to the conversation, which may include current events, cultural topics, and the personal experiences of the guests (indiscreet subjects excluded). Polite displays of wit are appreciated. One does not start eating until the hostess or host wishes the other diners "bon appétit."

A meal may be preceded by a toast, led by the host or hostess. A common toast involves drinking to the health of those at table (to which one can reply *à votre santé*, or simply *santé*). A more informal toast is *tchin tchin*. One should always make eye contact with the person one is toasting while gently clinking glasses and saying the phrase of the toast. It is considered polite for guests to make a toast later in the meal, especially to thank the hosts for their hospitality. One should always compliment the food. The hostess usually starts serving the guest of honor. Dishes are passed around the table in counterclockwise fashion. One is always served on one's left and passes serving dishes to one's right. A man should not serve himself before offering to serve a woman seated next to him first. In some cases, the men wait until all the women have been served, including the hostess (the last of the women), before serving themselves. In informal meals, the hostess may ask the guests to pass her their plates for her to serve them. Cutlery is arrayed around one's plate(s): forks to the left and knives and spoons to the right (dessert cutlery and/or a small knife for the bread and butter are placed in front of one's plate). For this reason, one always holds the fork in one's left hand and the knife in one's right hand (even if one is left-handed). One should set one's fork down when joining in the conversation and never speak with one's mouth full. There will be different glasses for water and wine (and separate glasses for different types of wine). If a separate plate is not used for bread, a piece of bread is placed on the tablecloth close to one's plate (never on the plate). One's piece of bread should be broken into bite-sized morsels (one never takes a bite from a larger piece of bread). One is expected to eat everything on one's plate and does not ask for seconds; however, one may be invited by the hostess or host to have seconds (one is not obliged to eat more, but refusal should always be polite). Except for bread, one normally never eats with one's fingers (including typical finger foods in other cultures, such as french fries and pizza). One uses cutlery to move food around one's plate. However, bread may be used to help scoop food onto one's fork, especially when cleaning one's plate before the next course. However, one generally does not use bread to soak up the remaining sauce, except during informal meals among family members and close friends (in which case, it is more polite to spear the bread with one's fork first). After finishing a course, one should place the fork and knife parallel next to one another diagonally on the plate. When not using cutlery, one should keep one hands in view above or resting on the table (never below the table); and one does not put one's elbows on the table. One should take one's time while eating, savoring each course. One should always think of other diners first (for example, offering to re-serve wine or water when a nearby dinner companion's glass is less than half full) and say *merci* ("thank you") when offered something and respond to being thanked with *je vous en prie* ("you are welcome"). After-dinner cheese(s) (usually a variety) is served only once. Round cheeses should be cut in wedges from the center. Among family members and close friends, it is polite to offer to help clear the table.

Restaurant etiquette is similar to that used for meals in French homes. However, it varies depending on the formality and elegance of the establishment. In a restaurant, one should never place a mobile phone or handbag on the table. Servers should be treated with respect, as they are professionals and practitioners of an art, and should never be called *garçon* (literally, "boy") but Monsieur (or Madame). Requests to servers—including for the check (*l'addition*)—should be made with the polite expression *s'il vous plaît* (literally, "if it pleases you"). In France, the service, or gratuity, is included in the price of the meal, so there is no need to leave a tip amounting to 15%–20% of the cost of the meal. However, one may leave some leftover change or a small bill as a gesture, particularly when one is pleased with the service. One should always thank and bid farewell to the restaurant proprietor or host (e.g., the *maître d'hôtel*) when leaving.

See also: Chapter 7: Child Raising Practices. Chapter 10: Hosting and Gift Giving; Privacy and Personal Space; Social Importance of Good Manners. Chapter 14: Gastronomy.

Further Reading
Sjögren-de Beauchaine (1988); Visser (1991); von Drachenfels (2000).

Workplace Etiquette and Customer Relations

French workplaces come in all shapes and sizes, ranging from very small businesses (incl. "mom-and-pop" shops) to state-of-the-art manufacturing facilities and the offices of large multinational corporations, both French and foreign. Not surprisingly, the workplace etiquette observed also varies considerably. Moreover, with the EU market and broader economic globalization, many French businesses have adapted to new modes of collaboration and management styles, some of which emphasize more casual types of interaction as well as increased pressures on individuals at all levels to be more productive, efficient, and self-motivated. Nevertheless, French workplaces tend be both more formal and more rigidly hierarchical than in other countries (e.g., the United States, the United Kingdom, Scandinavia, and Germany). It is helpful to keep in mind the lingering influence of France's aristocracy and absolute monarchy. A boss is a boss (the worst kind is the self-important and autocratic *petit chef*, who lords over underlings); everyone is keenly aware of their place in the company/workplace hierarchy (and of the rights, responsibilities, and limitations that come with that place); people of different hierarchical levels are generally not on first-name basis; and the titles of high-level managers and corporate executives are used in everyday interactions as a sign of respect (e.g., a company president is addressed as *monsieur le président*). In a major corporation, like at the royal court, there is marked distinction between the "commoners" and "nobility" (and among the different ranks of the latter), the CEO is the "monarch" at the center of all things, and one needs to know who is part of the inner circle, who is on the rise, and who has fallen out of favor. On the other hand, relations between labor and management are traditionally contentious, especially in the industrial sector—often with an unmistakable whiff of unresolved class conflict. The historical response to this tension has involved the development of an astoundingly complex corpus of labor laws that attempt to diffuse conflict by codifying in minute detail what is acceptable in employee-employer relations. This elaborate Labor Code—now undergoing changes as a result of government reforms and the pressure of global marketplace forces—also imposes a modicum of workplace democracy, including mandatory collective bargaining agreements that apply to all workers regardless of their union membership status and employee representation on enterprise councils.

France also has a distinct culture of customer service, which some have characterized as a national reluctance to be of service to customers. This negative assessment is based in part on exaggeration and misperception. However, it is true that the sayings "the customer is always right" and "the customer is king" do not reflect attitudes that come readily to the French. Customers and the representatives of businesses and public services interact more as equals, which means that the normal rules of etiquette and mutual respect are to be observed. Customers normally do not talk down to their business interlocutors or make capricious demands just because they are the ones who are paying. If anything, the onus is on them to be on their best (i.e., most courteous) behavior and to show due deference to professionals, especially when they are not on their home turf and/or the business person has the upper hand insofar as they have goods or services that the customer wants or needs. There has been a concerted effort made to change this culture given the increasing preponderance of services (incl. tourism) in the French economy, which makes the quality of customer service a key component of a company's business model, competitive advantage, and profitability. France has always had a strong culture of dignified and professional service in traditional hospitality industries like restaurants and hotels and among purveyors of high-end goods and services who cater to an elite clientele.

See also: Chapter 4: Labor Relations. Chapter 7: Gender Equality and Sexual Harassment. Chapter 10: Greeting Strangers, Acquaintances, Friends, and Family Members; Privacy and Personal Space; Social Hierarchies; Social Importance of Good Manners.

Further Reading

Alston et al. (2003); d'Iribarne (2003); Kerbat-Orecchioni (2005); Kerbat-Orecchioni (2006); Martin and Chaney (2008).

SELECTED BIBLIOGRAPHY

Alston, Jon P., et al. *A Practical Guide to French Business.* Writers Club, 2003; esp. pp. 114–132 ("Business Etiquette").

Barlow, Julie, and Jean-Benoit Nadeau. *The Bonjour Effect: The Secret Codes of French Conversation.* St. Martin's, 2016.

Béal, Christine, and Véronique Traverso. "'Hello, We're Outrageously Punctual': Front Door Rituals between Friends in Australia and France." *Journal of French Language Studies,* vol. 20, no. 1, 2010, pp. 17–29.

Beeching, Kate. "Politeness Markers in French: Post-posed *quoi* in the Tourist Office." *Journal of Politeness Research,* vol. 2, no. 1, 2006, pp. 143–167.

Birkelund, Gunn Elisabeth, and Yannick Lemel. "Lifestyles and Social Stratification: An Explorative Study of France and Norway." *GeWoP GEMASS* [Working Papers], no. 48, 2012, halshs-00870457.

Carroll, Raymonde. *Cultural Misunderstandings: The French-American Experience.* Trans. Carol Volk. U Chicago P, 1992.

Chevalier-Karfis, Camille. "14 Tips on How to Be a Polite Guest in a French Home." *French Today,* 4 Sep. 2020, https://www.frenchtoday.com/blog/french-culture/polite -guest-french-home.

Coveney, Aidan. "'Anything *You* Can Do, *Tu* Can Do Better': *Tu* and *Vous* as Substitutes for the Indefinite *On* in French." *Journal of Sociolinguistics,* vol. 7, no. 2, 2003, pp. 164–191.

Davetian, Benet. *Civility: A Cultural History.* U Toronto P, 2009.

de Gournay, Chantal. "The Pretense of Intimacy in France." *Perpetual Contact: Mobile Communication, Private Talk, Public Performance,* eds. James A. Katz and Mark Aakus. Cambridge UP, 2004, pp. 193–205.

de Rothschild, Nadine. *Savoir-Vivre in the 21st Century: A Guide to the Art of Living in France, for the French and Like the French.* Trans. Christine Mathieu. Littlefox, 2015.

Dewaele, Jean-Marc. "*Vous* or *Tu*?: Native and Non-Native Speakers of French on a Socio-linguistic Tightrope." *International Review of Applied Linguistics in Language Teaching*, vol. 42, no. 4, 2005, pp. 383–402.

d'Iribarne, Philippe. *The Logic of Honor: National Traditions and Corporate Management.* English trans. Welcome Rain, 2003.

Douglass, Kate. "Second-person Pronoun Use in French-language Blogs: Developing L2 Sociopragmatic Competence." *Electronic Discourse in Language Learning and Language Teaching*, eds. Lee B. Abraham and Lawrence Williams. Benjamins, 2009, pp. 213–240.

France, Peter. *Politeness and Its Discontents: Problems in French Classical Culture.* Cambridge UP, 1992.

Hacker, Maud. *Savoir Vivre: The Art of Fine Living by Ladurée.* Vendome Scriptum, 2016.

Kerbat-Orecchioni, Catherine. "From Good Manners to Facework: Politeness Variations in France, from the Classic Age to Today." *Understanding Historical (Im)Politeness: Relational Linguistic Practice Over Time and Across Cultures*, eds. Marcel Bax and Dániel Z. Kádár. Benjamins, 2012, pp. 131–152.

Kerbat-Orecchioni, Catherine. "Politeness in France: How to Buy Bread Politely." *Politeness in Europe*, eds. Leo Hickey and Miranda Stewart. Multilingual Matters, 2005, pp. 29–44.

Kerbat-Orecchioni, Catherine. "Politeness in Small Shops in France." *Journal of Politeness Research*, vol. 2, no. 1, 2006, pp. 79–103.

Krotoszynski, Ronald J. *Privacy Revisited: A Global Perspective on the Right to Be Left Alone.* Oxford UP, 2016.

Kuhn, Raymond. "'Vive La Différence'?: The Mediation of Politicians' Public Images and Private Lives in France." *Parliamentary Affairs*, vol. 57, no. 1, 2004, pp. 24–40.

Lundmark, Torbjörn. *Tales of Hi and Bye: Greeting and Parting Rituals around the World.* Cambridge UP, 2009.

Martin, Jeanette S., and Lillian H. Chaney. *Passport to Success: The Essential Guide to Business Culture and Customs in America's Largest Trading Partners.* Praeger, 2008, pp. 83–94.

Morford, Janet. "Social Indexicality in French Pronominal Address." *Journal of Linguistic Anthropology*, vol. 7, no. 1, 2008, pp. 3–37.

Platt, Polly. *French or Foe?: Getting the Most Out of Visiting, Living and Working in France.* 3rd ed. Culture Crossings, 2003.

Prost, Antoine, and Gérard Vincent. *A History of Private Life: Riddles of Identity in Modern Times.* Trans. Arthur Goldhammer. Belknap-Harvard UP, 1991.

Sarmiento-Mirwaldt, Katja, et al. "No Sex Scandals Please, We're French: French Attitudes towards Politicians' Public and Private Conduct." *West European Politics*, vol. 37, no. 5, 2014, pp. 867–885.

Sjögren-de Beauchaine, Annick. *The Bourgeoisie in the Dining-Room: Meal Ritual and Cultural Process in Parisian Families of Today.* Institutet för Folklivsforskning vid Nordiska Museet och Stockholms Universitet, 1988.

Storti, Craig. *Old World, New World: Bridging Cultural Differences: Britain, France, Germany, and the U.S.* Intercultural P, 2001.

Tessonneau, Alex Louise. "Learning Respect in Guadeloupe: Greetings and Politeness Rituals." *Politeness and Face in Caribbean Creoles*, eds. Susanne Mühleisen and Bettina Migge. Benjamins, 2005, pp. 255–282.

Trouille, Helen. "Private Life and Public Image: Privacy Legislation in France." *International & Comparative Law Quarterly*, vol. 49, no. 1, 2000, pp. 199–208.

Villeminot, Florence. "French Kissing Culture: The Ins and Outs of '*la bise*.'" Video, *French Connections*, France 24 English, 10 Oct. 2019, https://youtu.be/qm1SfpsItwQ.

Visser, Margaret. *Rituals of Dinner: The Origins, Evolution, Eccentricities, and Meaning of Table Manners.* Grove, 1991.

von Drachenfels, Suzanne. *The Art of the Table: A Complete Guide to Table Setting, Table Manners, and Tableware.* Simon & Schuster, 2000.

Wacks, Raymond. *Privacy: A Very Short Introduction.* 2nd ed. Oxford UP, 2015.

Warren, Jane. "Address Pronouns in French: Variation within and Outside the Workplace." *Australian Review of Applied Linguistics*, vol. 29, no. 2, 2006, pp. 16.1–16.17.

Whitman, James Q. "The Two Western Cultures of Privacy: Dignity Versus Liberty." *Yale Law Journal*, vol. 113, no. 6, 2004, pp. 1151–1221.

Williams, Lawrence, and Rémi A. van Compernolle. "*On* versus *Tu* and *Vous*: Pronouns with Indefinite Reference in Synchronous Electronic French Discourse." *Language Sciences*, vol. 31, no. 4, 2009, pp. 409–427.

CHAPTER 11

LITERATURE AND DRAMA

OVERVIEW

French literature is widely considered one of the greatest and most influential literary traditions of the world. It is particularly rich in classical theater, realist novels, romantic and modern poetry, avant-garde theatre, literary theory, and the literature of ideas. France claims more Nobel Prize laureates in literature than any other country, its two most recent being the novelists J. M. G. Le Clézio (2008) and Patrick Modiano (2014). Literature occupies an important place in the spiritual relationship between language and national identity in France. However, French literature is also synonymous with cosmopolitan diversity. France has attracted numerous foreign authors who have chosen to write much of their work in French (e.g., Tristan Tzara, Julien Green, Samuel Beckett, Eugène Ionesco, Edmond Jabès, Jorge Semprun, Milan Kundera, Amin Maalouf, Nancy Huston, and Andrei Makine). Furthermore, French literature is now viewed in the broader context of Francophone literature, or world literature in French, which encompasses not only Europe (incl. Belgium and Switzerland) and North America (incl. Québec and Louisiana), but also France's (and Belgium's) former colonies in the Caribbean, Africa, the Indian Ocean, and Southeast Asia. Of particular note is the pan-African and trans-Atlantic Négritude movement from the 1930s through the 1950s (e.g., Léopold Senghor, Aimé Césaire) and Maghrebi Francophone authors spanning several generations, like Mohammed Dib, Kateb Yacine, Assia Djebar, Leïla Sebbar, Rachid Boudjedra, Tahar ben Jelloun, Boualem Sansal, Yasmina Khadra, Kamel Daoud, Abdellah Taïa, and Leïla Slimani.

Literature is taken seriously in France. Some of France's greatest literary figures have become national heroes and cultural icons, like Molière, Voltaire, Victor Hugo, Charles Baudelaire, Arthur Rimbaud, Émile Zola, Marcel Proust, Antoine de Saint-Exupéry, Jean-Paul Sartre, Albert Camus, and Jacques Prévert. Prominent authors have taken part in the exchange of ideas and broader public discourse since the Renaissance. The eighteenth-century salons represent a high point in this ongoing dialogue, but modern equivalents can be found in the Parisian cafés of the twentieth century and influential book talk shows on television—like *Apostrophes* (1975–1990) and *La Grande Librairie* (2008–present). Fall is the apex of the literary year in France. The season begins with *la rentrée littéraire*—so named because it coincides with the weeks following the return from summer holidays—when many of the year's important new books are released, and concludes with the announcement of the winners of

France's most prestigious literary prizes (e.g., Prix Goncourt, Renaudot, and Femina) in November.

The first major works of literature written in French (dialects of Old French) date from the Middle Ages. They include *The Song of Roland* (c. 1098, France's national epic), the *Lais* (c. 1170) of Marie de France, the Arthurian romances of Chrétien de Troyes (twelfth century), the *Romance of the Rose* by Guillaume de Lorris and Jean de Meun (c. 1230/1275), and Christine de Pizan's *Book of the City of Ladies* (c. 1405). The notion of French national literature, however, started to take shape during the sixteenth and the seventeenth centuries. During the former (the French Renaissance period), Joachim du Bellay, one of the Pléiade group of poets argued (in his *Defense and Illustration of the French Language*, 1549) that French is as capable of literary greatness as Latin and Greek; and Michel de Montaigne's *Essays* (1580) offered an early example of characteristically French introspection and skepticism. During the latter, the monarchy used the power of the state to promote and regulate the French language and literature (e.g., the founding of the Académie Française by Cardinal Richelieu in 1635) for the greater glory of the crown and the nation. The result was some of the enduring masterpieces of French literature and an intense Quarrel of the Ancients and the Moderns (1687–1694) about whether newer works of literature and art could surpass those of classical antiquity.

There is perhaps no better way to get a sense of the evolution of French society—and of the mindset, desires, and sources of identity of the French people in different epochs—than the French novel. Great examples include *Gargantua and Pantagruel* (1532–1534) by François Rabelais, *The Princess de Clèves* (1678) by Madame de Lafayette, *Candide* (1759) by Voltaire, *Dangerous Liaisons* (1782) by Pierre Choderlos de Laclos, *The Human Comedy* (1829–1847) by Honoré de Balzac, *The Red and the Black* (1830) by Stendhal, *Madame Bovary* (1856) by Gustave Flaubert, *Les Misérables* (1862) by Victor Hugo, *The Rougon-Macquart* (1871–1893) by Émile Zola, *Claudine* (1900–1903) by Colette, *In Search of Lost Time* (1913–1927) by Marcel Proust, *Nadja* (1928) by André Breton, *Journey to the End of the Night* (1932) by Louis-Ferdinand Céline, *The Stranger* (1942) by Albert Camus, *The Voyeur* (1955) by Alain Robbe-Grillet, *La Place de l'Étoile* (1968) by Patrick Modiano, *Life: A User's Manual* (1978) by Georges Perec, *Shantytown Kid* (1986) by Azouz Begag, *The Elementary Particles* (1998) by Michel Houellebecq, *Black Bazaar* (2009) by Alain Mabanckou, and *Vernon Subutex* (2015–2017) by Virginie Despentes.

France's theatre scene is centered in Paris (e.g., the venerable Comédie-Française, founded in 1680), but there are high-quality companies in many other cities too. One of the most famous summer theatre festivals in the world takes place in Avignon. French theatres perform works by the country's celebrated classical (e.g., Racine, Molière, Beaumarchais, Marivaux), modern (e.g., Cocteau, Giraudoux, Ionesco, Sartre), and contemporary (Koltès, Reza, Zeller) playwrights.

Further Reading
Burgwinkle et al. (2011); Hollier (1989); Lyons (2010); McDonald and Suleiman (2010); Migraine-George (2013); Prendergast (2017).

Eighteenth-Century Literature

While the French eighteenth century is rightfully associated most closely with the intellectual legacy of the Enlightenment and the literature of ideas, it also gave rise to a rich and varied literary output marked by the development of modern genres like the novel and the affirmation of certain national traits in French letters—such as a free attitude toward sexuality and sensual pleasure and emphasis on the nimble and elegant use of the French language. The great French philosophers themselves were not just prolific literary writers but also very good ones. Montesquieu (1689–1755) deftly analyzed and critiqued French society from the perspective of two traveling Persian noblemen in his *Persian Letters* (1721). Voltaire (1694–1778), an author known for his incisive wit, wrote plays (e.g., *Zaire*, 1732; a reflection on religious bigotry) and philosophical tales, of which the most famous, *Candide* (1759), parodied the philosophical optimism of the German philosopher Leibniz. Denis Diderot (1713–1784) made a significant contribution to the development of the novel through such works as *Indiscreet Jewels* (1748), *The Nun* (1780), and *Jacques the Fatalist and His Master* (1788), and is best known for his philosophical dialogue *Rameau's Nephew* (1774). Genevan Jean-Jacques Rousseau (1712–1778) wrote novelistic philosophical narratives—*Émile* (1762), a detailed treatise on education packaged as a coming-of-age story; and *Julie, or The New Heloise* (1761), a precursor of romanticism's emphasis on feeling and authenticity.

The epistolary novel—where the narrative moves forward via the correspondence exchanged between characters—was arguably the period's most popular genre. Examples include Françoise de Graffigny's (1695–1758) *Letters from a Peruvian Woman* (1747) and Pierre Choderlos de Laclos's (1747–1803) *Dangerous Liaisons* (1787), the infamous tale of seduction, intrigue, and scandal among French aristocrats that has been made into several well-known films (including *Cruel Intentions*, 1999, set in modern-day New York). Numerous eighteenth-century novels employed exotic foreign settings as a foil for France, including *Manon Lescaut* (1731), a tale of socially unacceptable love partially set in New Orleans, by Antoine-François Prévost (1697–1763); and *Paul and Virginia* (1788), a love story set in Mauritius that charts the fate of two "children of nature," by Jacques-Henri Bernardin de Saint-Pierre (1737–1814).

Eighteenth-century French theatre may not have been as illustrious as that of the seventeenth century but included two prominent playwrights. One was Pierre de Marivaux (1688–1763), whose plays included *The Game of Love and Chance* (1730). Marivaux has been criticized by some for excessive flowery language and witty word play. However, his comedies are not devoid of psychological insight and social commentary, including the juxtaposition of the noble and the poor. Social commentary is at the forefront of the Figaro trilogy (1773–1791) by Pierre-Augustin Caron de Beaumarchais (1732–1799). The insubordinate barber turned valet, Figaro, became an international symbol of the spirit of freedom—and the subject of famous operatic adaptations by Rossini (*The Barber of Seville*) and Mozart (*The Marriage of Figaro*). The leading eighteenth-century French poet was André Chénier (1762–1794).

Libertine literature—in which libidinous characters disregard social and moral norms to freely engage in promiscuous sexual activity—had roots in the seventeenth century but developed as a genre in the more liberal context of the eighteenth century. The most infamous example was the work of Donatien Alphonse François de Sade (1740–1814), better known simply as the Marquis de Sade, whose works include *The 120 Days of Sodom* (1785), *Justine, or The Misfortunes of Virtue* (1791), *Philosophy in the Boudoir* (1795), and *Juliette* (1797–1801). Other notable authors of libertine literature include Claude Prosper Jolyot de Crébillon (1707–1777), and Nicolas-Edme Restif de La Bretonne (1734–1806).

See also: Chapter 2: Louis XVI and the End of the Ancien Régime. Chapter 5: Philosophy (Traditional); Rationalism and Universalism.

Further Reading

Darnton (1995); Davidson (2010); Delers (2015); Kjærgård (2018); Leigh (1999); Schaeffer (1999).

Houellebecq (Michel) and the Recent French Novel

Michel Houellebecq (Michel Thomas, b. 1956) is France's most famous and widely translated contemporary writer—and one of its most controversial. While primarily a novelist, he has also published poetry, essays, criticism, and correspondence. The crux of Houellebecq's work is his pessimistic and misanthropic analysis of French society in inexorable decline, mired in nihilistic and listless individualism since the hedonistic and countercultural 1960s and 1970s. In addition to this cynical view of contemporary society, Houellebecq's novels are criticized for their crass depictions of sex, misogyny, and negative portrayal of Islam. However, Houellebecq wins praise from other critics for his acute observation and uncompromising critique of a society that has been ravaged by free market fundamentalism, and for a subtle undercurrent of compassion and yearning for love overlooked by inattentive readers.

Houellebecq's debut novel was *Whatever* (*Extension du domaine de la lutte*, 1994), about the lives of two computer programmers. He first achieved notoriety for *The Elementary Particles* (1998, published in Great Britain as *Atomised*), a novel that tells the story of the bleak and lonely lives of two half-brothers and sons of an ex-hippie mother, Michel and Bruno, who share a dysfunctional view of love and sex. Michel is a molecular biologist who develops a method of cloning that promises to remove both sexual intercourse and romantic coupling from reproduction; Bruno finds no satisfaction in a life of promiscuous sex and ends up in a mental hospital. Sexual promiscuity and cloning were themes in Houellebecq's next two novels, too—*Platform* (2001), about sexual tourism in Thailand; and *The Possibility of an Island* (2005), a work of science fiction about a religious cult. Houellebecq won France's most prestigious literary award (Prix Goncourt) for *The Map and the Territory* (2010), a novel about an artist who finds unexpected fame and fortune in painting scenes of both traditional and modern professional activities (after an earlier series of photographs of hardware and iconic Michelin maps), and becomes embroiled in the police investigation of the brutal murder of a "Michel Houllebecq" character. Houellebecq's 2015 novel *Submission* imagines life in France following the election of a Muslim president from the perspective of an apathetic university professor specialized in the work of the decadent author Joris-Karl Huysmans. The protagonist converts to Islam after his lover, a former student, emigrates to Israel. Houellebecq's latest novel to date, *Serotonin* (2019), tells the story of a disenchanted agronomical engineer's struggle with chronic depression and withdrawal from social life—a personification of wounded white masculinity as unsuccessful in love as he is in defending French agriculture in the age of global free trade.

Michel Houellebecq (b. 1956) is one of France's most famous and controversial contemporary authors. His novels feature alienated and self-indulgent male characters and the theme of European decadence and decline. He won the coveted Prix Goncourt in 2010 for *The Map and the Territory*. (Kojoku/Dreamstime.com)

French contemporary literature has produced numerous noteworthy novelists and fiction writers besides Houellebecq and France's two most recent Nobel Prize winners, J. M. G. Le Clézio and Patrick Modiano. The most significant figures include Annie Ernaux (b. 1940—e.g., *A Woman's Story*, 1989); Jean Echenoz (b. 1940—e.g., *I'm Gone*, 1999); Leïla Sebbar (b. 1941—e.g., *Sherazade*, 1980); Daniel Pennac (b. 1944—e.g., *The Scapegoat*, 1985); Pierre Michon (b. 1945—e.g., *Small Lives*, 1984); Pascal Quignard (b. 1948—*The Roving Shadows*, 2002); Christian Oster (b. 1949—e.g., *My Big Apartment*, 1999); Philippe Delerm (b. 1950—e.g., *The Small Pleasures of Life*, 1997); Antoine Volodine (b. 1950—e.g., *Radiant Terminus*, 2014); Jean-Christophe Rufin (b. 1952—e.g., *Red Brazil*, 2001); Patrick Chamoiseau (b. 1953—e.g. *Texaco*, 1992); François Bon (b. 1953—e.g., *Daewoo*, 2004); Régis Jauffret (b. 1955—e.g., *Microfictions*, 2007); Azouz Begag (b. 1957—e.g., *Shantytown Kid*, 1986); Emmanuel Carrère (b. 1957—e.g., *Limonov*, 2011); Hervé Le Tellier (b. 1957—e.g., *The Anomaly*, 2020); Christine Angot (b. 1959—e.g., *Incest*, 1999); Delphine de Vigan (b. 1960—e.g., *Underground Time*,

2009); Linda Lê (b. 1963—e.g., *The Three Fates*, 1997); Frédéric Beigbeder (b. 1965—e.g., *99 Francs*, 2000); Alain Mabanckou (b. 1966—e.g., *Broken Glass*, 2005); Marie NDiaye (b. 1967—e.g., *Three Strong Women*, 2009); Virginie Despentes (b. 1969—e.g., *Vernon Subutex* trilogy, 2015–2017); Marie Darrieussecq (b. 1969—e.g., *Pig Tales*, 1996); and Muriel Barbery (b. 1969—e.g., *The Elegance of the Hedgehog*, 2006).

Much of French fiction of the last twenty years reflects both a refusal to choose between stylistic experimentation and a return to traditional narration and emphasis on fragile characters facing extreme disruptive situations. A promising younger generation of novelists includes Matthias Énard (b. 1972—e.g., *Zone*, 2008); Abdellah Taïa (b. 1973—e.g., *A Country for Dying*, 2015); Chloé Delaume (b. 1973—e.g., *Not a Clue*, 2004); David Foenkinos (b. 1974—e.g., *Delicacy*, 2009); Lola Lafon (b. 1974—e.g., *The Little Communist Gymnast Who Never Smiled*, 2014); Nicolas Mathieu (b. 1978—e.g., *And Their Children after Them*, 2018); Leïla Slimani (b. 1981—e.g., *The Perfect Nanny*, 2016); Faïza Guène (b. 1985—e.g., *Kiffe Kiffe Tomorrow*, 2004); Alice Zeniter (b. 1986—e.g., *The Art of Losing*, 2017); Édouard Louis (b. 1992—e.g., *The End of Eddy*, 2014); and Fatima Daas (b. 1995—e.g., *The Last One*, 2020). Éric-Emmanuel Schmitt (b. 1960), Marc Lévy (b. 1961), and Guillaume Musso (b. 1974) write works of fiction that regularly top French bestseller lists.

See also: Chapter 7: Attitudes toward Sex. Chapter 11: Literary Avant-Garde, 1950–1980; Nobel Prize Laureates in Literature: J. M. G. Le Clézio and Patrick Modiano; Novel in the Nineteenth Century; Poetry (Modern and Contemporary); Reza (Yasmina) and Recent French Theatre; Twentieth-Century Literature through Mid-Century (Novel and Theatre). Chapter 12: French Cinema II (since the Nouvelle Vague).

Further Reading
Best (2007); Betty (2016); Damlé and Rye (2013); Knepper (2012); Swamy (2012); Sweeney (2013); Ungureanu (2017); Wampole (2020).

CRIME FICTION

There is an avid audience in France for crime fiction (called *polars* in French) and several French authors have achieved classic status in the genre, like Georges Simenon (1903–1989), Léo Mallet (1909–1996), San Antonio (Frédéric Dard, 1921–2000), Sébastien Japrisot (1931–2003), Jean-Patrick Manchette (1942–1995), Jean-Claude Izzo (1945–2000), and Thierry Jonquet (1945–2009). Acclaimed crime fiction writers of today include Didier Daeninckx, Pierre Lemaître, Fred Vargas (Frédérique Audoin-Rouzeau), Bernard Minier, Franck Bouysse, Michel Bussi, Franck Thilliez, and Tanguy Viel. Five French works made the list of the 100 greatest crime novels and thrillers published since 1945 compiled by the *Sunday Times* (London) in 2019: *Maigret and the Headless Corpse* (Simenon, 1955), *The Lady in the Car with the Glasses and a Gun* (Japrisot, 1966), *Ghost Riders of Ordebec* (Vargas, 2011), *Alex* (Lemaître, 2011), and *The Frozen Dead* (Minier, 2011).

Literary Avant-Garde, 1950–1980

In the 1950s, 60s, and 70s, French literature became a showcase for avant-garde experimentation and radical critiques of modern life. In the Theatre of the Absurd, plot is secondary if not absent, language takes on a life of its own (often without clearly signifying anything), and the overall effect is one of existential anxiety and metaphysical uncertainty. Leading proponents of this style include Jean Genet (1910–1986—e.g., *The Maids*); Samuel Beckett (1906–1989—e.g., *Waiting for Godot*, 1952), and Eugène Ionesco (1909–1964—e.g., *The Bald Soprano*, 1950).

Authors associated with *Le Nouveau Roman*, or New Novel, also rejected traditional narrative in favor of disjunctive depictions of intricate states of mind. The leading exemplars of this current were Alain Robbe-Grillet (1922–2008—e.g., *Jealousy*, 1957), Claude Simon (1913–2005—e.g., *The Flanders Road*, 1967), Nathalie Sarraute (1900–1999—e.g., *The Planetarium*, 1959), Michel Butor (1926–2016—e.g., *Passing Time*, 1956), Robert Pinget (1919–1997—e.g., *The Inquisitory*, 1962), and Marguerite Duras (1914–1996—e.g., *Moderato Cantabile*, 1958). By comparison, writers affiliated with Oulipo (Workshop of Potential Literature, founded 1960) used arbitrary constraints, games, mathematical calculations, and other contrivances to stimulate their creativity by limiting their ability to write conventionally. For instance, Georges Perec's (1936–1982) mystery novel *A Void* (1969) was written without the letter "e." Perec was also a keen observer of everyday life, for example, *Things: A Story of the Sixties* (1965), and *Life, A User's Manual* (1978)—a 600-page novel about the lives and reminiscences of the residents of the same Paris apartment building, grasped in a single instant of time. Oulipo cofounder Raymond Queneau (1903–1976) produced the cult classic *Zazie in the Metro* (1959), a linguistically inventive, slang-filled account of an impudent preteen's escapades in Paris.

A significant development in the 1950s, 60s, and 70s was the opening of French literature to the voices of authors who were not native French, white, male, or straight. Of special importance were the authors from France's former colonies in the Maghreb (i.e., Morocco, Algeria, and Tunisia) and sub-Saharan Africa, many of whom lived in France or had their works published there. Présence Africaine (founded in Paris in 1947 by Alioune Diop) was among the first houses to publish the works of important African Francophone writers like Birago Diop (Senegal, 1909–1986), Jacques Rabemananjara (Madagascar, 1913–2005), Cheikh Anta Diop (Senegal, 1923–1986), Ousmane Sembène (Senegal, 1923–2016), Mongo Beti (Cameroon, 1932–2001), and Ken Bugul (Senegal, b. 1947). It also published Martinican writer Aimé Césaire's (1913–2008) blistering *Discourse on Colonialism* (1950). A culmination of this postcolonial awakening came in 1983, when Léopold Senghor (Sénégal, 1906–2001)—like Césaire, one of the pillars of the Négritude movement in the 1930s—became the first African elected to the Académie Française. In the 1980s, France would also see the first noteworthy literary works by the children of North African immigrants, young "Beur" authors who grew up in the suburbs, like Mehdi Charef (b. 1952—e.g., *Tea in the Harem*, 1983) and Farida Belghoul (b. 1958—e.g., *Georgette!*, 1986).

Écriture féminine, or women's writing, was pioneered by radical feminists in the 1960s and 1970s, who explored the relationship between women's bodies, gender, sexuality, power, language, and textuality. Leading examples include Monique Wittig (1935–2003—e.g., *Les Guerillères*, 1971), Hélène Cixous (b. 1937—e.g., *The Laugh of the Medusa*, 1975), and Chantal Chawaf (b. 1943—e.g., *Redemption*, 1988). Since then, the category has broadened to include the voices of women of color like Maryse Condé (b. 1937—e.g., *Crossing the Mangrove*, 1985) and Assia Djebar (1936–2015—e.g., *Women of Algiers in Their Apartment*, 1980). One of the most radical voices from the period was the bisexual writer Pierre Guyotat (1940–2020), known for provocative and transgressive novels characterized by linguistic inventiveness, dehumanizing brutality, and quasi-pornographic depictions of sex, like *Tomb for 500,000 Soldiers* (1967), *Eden Eden Eden* (1970), and *Prostitution* (1975). Hervé Guibert (1955–1991) was a major gay male writer of the period. His works include *Arthur's Whims* (1983) and *To the Friend Who Did Not Save My Life* (1990), one of the most significant works dealing with the HIV/AIDS epidemic.

Not all of the literature of the 1950s, 1960s, and 1970s was experimental or radical. Many fine writers in a more conventional vein published significant works during the period. One was Julien Gracq (1910–2002), whose notable works include the novels *A Dark Stranger* (1945) and *The Opposing Shore* (1951), and the collection of literary essays *The Dark Waters* (1976). Another is Marguerite Yourcenar (1903–1987), the first woman elected to the Académie Française (1980), best known for historical novels like *Memoirs of Hadrian* (1951) and *The Abyss* (1968). A third is Michel Tournier (1924–2016), the author of *Friday* (1967), *The Erl-King* (1970), and *The Four Wise Men*, 1980. Tournier's work—often cited as an example of postmodernism—used mythology and traditional Western stories and characters to challenge the cultural and moral status quo of contemporary society.

See also: Chapter 7: Feminism and Women's Rights. Chapter 9: Francophonie. Chapter 11: Houellebecq (Michel) and the Recent French Novel; Literary Criticism and French Theory; Poetry (Modern and Contemporary); Reza (Yasmina) and Recent French Theatre; Twentieth-Century Literature through Mid-Century (Novel and Theatre).

Further Reading

Babcock (1997); Becker (2012); Bredeson (2018); Cazenave (2005); Conley (1991); Essif (2013); Esslin (2001); Kleppinger (2019); Norrish (1988); Smith (2000); Taylor (2003–2011); Willging (2019).

Literary Criticism and French Theory

France has an influential tradition of literary criticism that is particularly noteworthy for its theoretical reflections on the formal properties, underlying semiotic processes, and sociocultural determinants of literature. Following precursors like Nicolas Boileau-Despréaux (1636–1711—e.g., *The Art of Poetry*, 1674), literary criticism truly emerges as a distinct field of intellectual inquiry in France in the nineteenth century, encompassing three strands. First, literary authors themselves wrote a lot about literature and other writers, like François-René de Chateaubriand (1768–1848), Théophile Gautier (1811–1872), Charles Baudelaire (1821–1867), Edmond (1822–1896) and Jules (1830–1870) de Goncourt, Paul Bourget (1852–1935), and Remy de Gourmont (1858–1915). Next, there were theorists Like Charles-Augustin de Saint-Beuve (1804–1869), a proponent of biography as the key to understanding an author's work and the most influential critic of his era. Others include Ferdinand Brunetière (1849–1906) and Jules Lemaître (1853–1914). Finally, there were the academic historians of literature like Hyppolite Taine (1828–1893) and Gustave Lanson (1857–1954).

An array of writers, scholars, intellectuals, journalists, and philosophers made significant contributions to French literary criticism and theory in the twentieth century, including Paul Valéry, Paul Léautaud, Gaston Bachelard, Jean Paulhan, Jean Guéhenno, Georges Bataille, Lucien Goldmann, Maurice Blanchot, Roger Caillois, Jean-Pierre Richard, Édouard Glissant, Serge Doubrovsky, and Jean Ricardou. Jean-Paul Sartre (1905–1980) applied an existentialist type of psychoanalysis to modern authors like Charles Baudelaire (*Baudelaire*, 1947), Jean Genet (*Saint Genet: Actor and Martyr*, 1952), and Gustave Flaubert (*The Family Idiot*, 1971). From the 1960s through the 1990s, two intellectual trends that originated largely in France—structuralism and post-structuralism—have exerted enormous influence around the world on literary theory and criticism and adjacent fields like linguistics, anthropology, psychoanalysis, semiotics, philosophy, sociology, and cultural studies. The (chic) French provenance, broad interdisciplinary scope, and predilection for conceptual abstraction and arcane jargon of the two trends led to the coinage of umbrella term "French Theory."

Building on the theories of Ferdinand de Saussure (1857–1913), Roman Jakobson (1896–1982), and Claude Lévi-Strauss (1908–2009), structuralism posits that thought, perception, and cultural production—including literature—are sociocultural constructs involving complex systems of codes in which any component derives meaning from its relationship to the system and its various components. The leading proponent of a structuralist approach to literature was Roland Barthes (1915–1980), whose most famous works include *The Death of the Author* (1967) and *S/Z* (1970). In the former, he argues against the idea that the meaning of a work is to be deciphered primarily in terms of the intentions and experiences of its "author," because any text is in reality a multilayered nexus of language that derives relational meaning from other systems, including other literary texts (intertextuality), language, social structures, and ideologies. The text is "made" as much by these different systems as by its titular author. More importantly, it is *remade* each time it is read, decoded, and interpreted by a reader. Other prominent French structuralist literary critics include A. J. Greimas (1917–1992), Gérard Genette (1930–2018), Tzvetan Todorov (1939–2017), and Julia Kristeva (b. 1941).

Unlike structuralism, post-structuralism is more of a label than a movement or school of thought. It refers to the work of iconoclastic thinkers like the psychoanalyst Jacques Lacan (1901–1981); the philosophers Michel Foucault (1926–1984), Jacques

Derrida (1930–2004), and Gilles Deleuze (1925–1995); and the sociologist Jean Baudrillard (1929–2007)—and to academics who use their theories to interpret literary texts and other forms of cultural production, like the "mirror stage" in the development of the self (Lacan), "archaeology of knowledge" and "biopolitics" (Foucault), "deconstruction" (Derrida), "schizoanalysis" (Deleuze and Félix Guattari), and "simulacra" and "hyperreality" (Baudrillard). Radical feminist philosophers and literary theorists such as Kristeva, Luce Irigaray (b. 1930), and Hélène Cixous (b. 1937) are also associated with the concept. Post-structuralism is a critique of structuralism insofar as it acknowledges that the culturally conditioned underlying structures of any text are more knotty and unstable than the structuralists thought; indeed, they are rife with unresolved contradictions, latent power dynamics (e.g., those related to class, race, gender, and colonialism), and libidinal impulses.

Cofounded by Guy Debord (1931–1994) and Asger Jorn (1914–1973), situationism (i.e., the Situationist International [SI], 1957–1972) is sometimes placed under the umbrella of French Theory. Combining Marxism, anarchism, Dada, surrealism, and media theory, its central insight was that control in postindustrial societies comes via pervasive "spectacle" in everyday life (e.g., media, advertising, the superficial trappings of democracy, mass culture, consumerism, and contemporary urbanism), which keeps people from meaningful political and cultural agency (c.f. Debord, *The Society of the Spectacle*, 1967). The SI was in the vanguard of the French student uprising of May 1968 and several of its practices—e.g., *le détournement* (the hijacking of mainstream culture)—have had significant influence over activists, artists, writers, and critics.

See also: Chapter 5: Philosophy (Contemporary). Chapter 11: Literary Avant-Garde, 1950–1980; Poetry (Modern and Contemporary).

Further Reading
Bertens (2014); Compagnon (2004); Culler (2001); Cusset (2008); Jefferson (2007); Nesbitt (2013); Sokal and Bricmont (1998).

Nobel Prize Laureates in Literature: J. M. G. Le Clézio and Patrick Modiano

France counts more winners of the Nobel Prize for Literature than any other country— Sully Prudhomme (1901), Frédéric Mistral (1904), Romain Rolland (1915), Anatole France (1921), Henri Bergson (1927), Roger Martin du Gard (1937), André Gide (1937), François Mauriac (1952), Albert Camus (1957), Saint-John Perse (1960), Jean-Paul Sartre (1964), Claude Simon (1985), Gao Xingjian (2000), J. M. G. Le Clézio (2008), and Patrick Modiano (2014). Le Clézio and Modiano may be seen as part of a shift in the 1970s and 1980s away from the nontraditional narrative structure and willfully incoherent characterization of the *Nouveau Roman* (New Novel), which was highly influential in the 1950s and 1960s.

Jean-Marie Gustave Le Clézio (b. 1940) has been profoundly shaped by his own multicultural background and world travels. The descendant, on his father's side, of a Breton family that left France at the start of the French Revolution and settled in the Indian Ocean island of Mauritius, Le Clézio spent part of his childhood in Nigeria, studied in England, conducted research in Mexico, is married to a Moroccan woman, has held professorships in South Korea and China, and has been a regular resident of Albuquerque, New Mexico since the 1990s. The Swedish Academy, which awards the Nobel Prize, cited his work for its expression of "poetic adventure and sensual ecstasy." Le Clézio is also interested in the lives of displaced and marginalized people who live in the shadow of dominant cultures, and in the complex relationship between the past and the present. His most famous works include the novels *The Interrogation* (1963), *Terra Amata* (1967), *Desert* (1980), *The Prospector* (1985), *Onitsha* (1991), *Ourania* (2006), and *Alma* (2017). He has also written the short story collections *Mondo and Other Stories* (1978) and *The Round and Other Cold Hard Facts* (1982).

The parents of Jean Patrick Modiano (b. 1945)—a Jewish Italian businessman (with Sephardic Greek roots) and a Flemish Belgian actress—met in Occupied Paris during World War II. The wartime experiences of his parents remained shrouded in mystery—a fact that was to exert a strong influence over Modiano's work as a novelist. That work has sometimes been compared to Marcel Proust's and was specifically praised by the Swedish Academy for "the art of memory" with which Modiano "has evoked the most ungraspable human destinies and uncovered the life-world of the Occupation." Modiano's major works include *La Place de l'Étoile* (1968), *The Night Watch* (1969), *Ring Roads* (1972), *Villa Triste* (1975), *Missing Person* (1978), *Suspended Sentences* (1988), *Dora Bruder* (1997), *Paris Nocturne* (2003), *In the Café of Lost Youth* (2007), and *So You Don't Get Lost in the Neighborhood* (2014).

Two French writers regularly mentioned in recent years as among the leading contenders for the Nobel Prize in literature are Annie Ernaux (Annie Duchesne, b. 1940) and Maryse Condé (b. 1937). Ernaux is known for her sociologically astute and emotionally complex autobiographical fiction and memoirs like *Cleaned Out* (1974), *A Man's Place* (1983), *A Woman's Story* (1987), *Simple Passion* (1991), *Shame* (1997), *Happening* (2000), *The Years* (2008), and *A Girl's Story* (2016). Condé, from Guadeloupe, writes compellingly about race and gender in colonial and postcolonial contexts in acclaimed fictional works like *Heremakhonon* (1976), *Tituba: Black Witch of Salem* (1986), *Tree of Life* (1987), *Crossing the Mangrove* (1989), *Windward Heights* (1995), *Victoire* (2006), and *The Wondrous and Tragic Life of Ivan and Ivana* (2017).

See also: Chapter 11: Houellebecq (Michel) and the Recent French Novel; Literary Avant-Garde, 1950–1980; Poetry (Modern and Contemporary); Twentieth-Century Literature through Mid-Century (Novel and Theatre).

Further Reading
Cooke (2005); Day (2007); Duncan (2003); Fulton (2008); Kawakami (2015); Kemp (2010); Martin (2012); Moser (2012).

Novel in the Nineteenth Century

There are great French novels associated with each of the four major literary trends of the century—romanticism, realism, naturalism, and symbolism. Early romantic novels include *Atala* (1801) and *René* (1802) by François-René de Chateaubriand (1768–1848); *Corinne, or Italy* (1807) by Germaine de Staël (1766–1817); and *Adolphe* (1816) by Benjamin Constant (1767–1830). Chateaubriand's protagonist René is the prototype of the romantic hero—a sensitive, conflicted, and melancholy young man who is desperately disillusioned with the cold and prosaic era in which he was born—an affliction called *le mal du siècle*—and has sought adventure in the exotic setting of America among the Natchez people of Louisiana. French romantic writers were particularly skilled in writing grand historical novels. Famous examples include *The Three Musketeers* (1844) and *The Count of Monte Christo* (serialized, 1844–1856) by Alexandre Dumas (1802–1870); and *The Hunchback of Notre-Dame* (1831) and *Les Misérables* (1862) by Victor Hugo (1802–1885), featuring the immortal characters of Jean Valjean, Cosette, Inspector Javert, and Gavroche and considered by many to be the greatest novel in French literature. Another prominent French romantic novelist is George Sand (Amantine Dupin, 1804–1876), the author of *Indiana* (1832) and *Little Fadette* (1851)—works that take a sympathetic view of common people.

Realism took on the task of closely observing people and society during an age of tumultuous change in politics, the economy, social hierarchies, values, material culture, and everyday life. Its leading proponents in France were Stendhal (Marie-Henri Beyle, 1783–1842), Honoré de Balzac (1799–1850), and Gustave Flaubert (1821–1880). The author of *The Red and the Black* (1830) and *The Charterhouse of Parma* (1838), Stendhal created characters (e.g., Julien Sorel, the ambitious protagonist of *The Red and the Black*) and intrigues that were consistent with romanticism. However, he subjected his characters to a proto-modern, probing psychological analysis. Balzac was not only the quintessential realist, he also undertook one of the most ambitious projects in all of modern literature—*La Comedie humaine*—a sprawling series of novels, stories, and essays (over ninety works in all) divided into several thematic cycles, offering an exhaustive literary study of post-Napoleonic society. Among the most famous novels in the series are *The Skin of Sorrow* (1831), *The Unknown Masterpiece* (1831), *Eugénie Grandet* (1833), *Old Goriot* (1835), and *Lost Illusions* (serialized, 1837–1843). Balzac's novels deal extensively with money, power, marital life, family relations, country vs. city life, love, sex, and class. Flaubert's two greatest novels are *Madame Bovary* (1857) and *The Sentimental Education* (1869). Emma Bovary, the romantically deluded, profligate, and tragically disaffected wife of a mediocre country doctor is one of the greatest characters in all western literature. Another noteworthy French realist novelist was Eugène Sue (1804–1857), best known for *The Mysteries of Paris* (serialized, 1842–1843), a sensational exploration of the lower depths of Parisian society.

Naturalism developed in the latter part of the century as a more "scientifically" rigorous extension of realism that placed greater emphasis on the role that environmental factors played in determining individual and social behavior, and displayed a particular interest in exposing the living conditions and suffering of the working classes. The greatest French naturalist was Émile Zola (1840–1902), author of the "Rougon-Macquart" series of twenty interlinked novels described as "The Natural and Social History of a Family under the Second Empire." The most famous novels in the series include *The Belly of Paris* (1873—set in the markets in Paris), *The Drinking Den* (i.e., *L'Assomoir*, 1877—about the debilitating effects of alcoholism and poverty), *Nana* (1880—about a prostitute), *Ladies' Delight* (1883—set in a Parisian department store), *Germinal* (1885—about a miners' strike), and *The Beast Within* (i.e., *La Bête humaine*, 1890—about the murderous impulses of a disturbed train engineer). Other authors associated with naturalism include Alphonse Daudet (1840–1897) and Guy de Maupassant (1850–1897), both of whom are better known for their short stories: for example, Maupassant's "Ball of Lard" (1880) and "The Necklace" (1884).

Emile Zola (1840–1902) was one of the greatest French writers of the nineteenth century. His novels about French society in his era were examples of literary naturalism (e.g., the "Rougon-Macquart" series). As a courageous and controversial public intellectual, he championed social reform and intervened in the Dreyfus Affair in defense of French army captain Alfred Dreyfus (1859–1945), wrongfully accused of espionage and a victim of vicious anti-Semitism. (Library of Congress)

Symbolism, which focused on individual emotional experience and "truer" realities accessed through art, was a reaction against naturalism's obsession with mundane social reality. The most famous symbolist novel is *Against the Grain* (i.e., *A rebours*, 1884) by Joris-Karl Huysmans (1848–1907), who is also associated with decadentism. It is the story of Des Esseintes, a neurasthenic esthete who retreats from society into a private haven of sensual pleasure. Maurice Barrès (1862–1923) had ties to both symbolism and decadentism in his younger years but is best known for his promotion of nationalism. He was the author of two novel trilogies—*The Cult of the Self* (1888–1891) and *The Novel of National Energy* (1897–1902).

Nineteenth-century French literature also gave rise several major works of what was later to be called science fiction, the most famous being the novels of Jules Verne (1828–1905), *Journey to the Center of the Earth* (1864) and *Twenty Thousand Leagues under the Sea* (1870). Another noteworthy example is *The Future Eve* (1886) by the symbolist author Auguste Villiers de l'Isle-Adam (1838–1889).

See also: Chapter 6: Bourgeoisie and Middle Class. Chapter 11: Eighteenth-Century Literature; Houellebecq (Michel) and the Recent French Novel; Literary Avant-Garde, 1950–1980; Nobel Prize Laureates in Literature: J. M. G. Le Clézio and Patrick Modiano.

Further Reading
Farrant (2007); Lehan (2005); Levin (1963); Robb (1997); Unwin (1997).

Poetry (Modern and Contemporary)

France has produced some of the most highly acclaimed and influential poets of the modern era. One of the greatest of all was Charles Baudelaire (1821–1867), whose masterpiece, *Les Fleurs du mal* (1857, *The Flowers of Evil*), offered evocative tableaux of the seedier side of Parisian street life; probed the highs (e.g., the freedom of movement, contemplation, and reverie of the "flaneur") and lows (e.g., the idle melancholy and lonely dejection of "spleen") that characterized the life of a socially isolated city dweller; and chronicled the poet's efforts to escape mundane (bourgeois) reality through various decadent and transcendent means—art, alcohol, drugs, sensuality, and exoticism. Baudelaire's work is to be placed in the broader context that encompasses the French romantic poets (e.g., Alphonse de Lamartine, Alfred de Vigny, Victor Hugo, Gérard de Nerval, Alfred de Musset, and Théophile Gautier); the Parnassians (e.g., Charles-Marie Leconte de Lisle, Théodore de Banville); and the later symbolists (e.g., Auguste Villiers de l'Isle-Adam, Stéphane Mallarmé, Charles Cros, Paul Verlaine, Arthur Rimbaud, and Pierre Louÿs), many of whom are also identified as *poètes maudits* ("accursed poets") or decadents. While the styles of these poets varied, many shared a common sensibility that included the poet's responsibility to reflect on the essential realities of human existence (helping to fill a void left by the waning influence of religion), devotion to the autonomy of art ("art for art's sake"), commitment to exploring new forms of beauty (modern as opposed to classical, Dionysian as well as Apollonian), and rebellion against bourgeois norms. Among the symbolists, the works of Rimbaud (1854–1891), author of the prose poems *Illuminations* (1886), and Mallarmé (1842–1898), author of the free-verse poem "A Throw of the Dice Will Never Abolish Chance" (1897/1914), have been particularly influential in terms of subsequent modern poetry. The same can be said of the poetry of a young visionary who had lived earlier in the century, Comte de Lautréamont (Isidore Lucien Ducasse, 1846–1870), whose long prose poem *The Songs of Maldoror* (1868) was a delirious and transgressive work that inspired the surrealists.

In the early decades of twentieth century, the works of the so-called cubist poets (e.g., Guillaume Apollinaire [1880–1913], Max Jacob, Blaise Cendrars, and Pierre Reverdy) and later surrealist ones (André Breton, Paul Éluard, Tristan Tzara, Philippe

Soupault, Louis Aragon, Benjamin Péret, Robert Desnos, and René Char) are particularly noteworthy. The former, like their famous namesakes in painting, experimented with form (e.g., Apollinaire's free-verse image-poems, *Calligrammes*, 1918) in order to capture some of the most novel and most unsettling aspects of modern life—industry, technology, speed, trains, automobiles, airplanes, war, social upheaval, popular culture, advertising, and mass media (e.g., "Zone" by Apolllinaire, 1913). Led by Breton (1896–1966), the surrealist movement (esp. in the 1920s and 1930s) was dedicated to the liberation of the subconscious and the revelation of a more oneiric and libidinal super-reality hidden below the surface of mundane reality via openness to chance (e.g., experiments in automatic writing and the parlor game known as "the exquisite corpse"). Some of the poetry of Éluard (1895–1952) and Aragon (1897–1992) could be surprisingly idealistic and quasi-romantic, whereas Char (1907–1988) was aphoristic and existential. Poets Léopold Sédar Senghor (1906–2001, from Senegal), Aimé Césaire (1913–2008, from Martinique), and Léon Damas (1912–1978, from French Guiana) were at the forefront of Négritude, a movement that began among Black students in Paris influenced by surrealism. It sought to give voice to a pan-African and trans-Atlantic Black consciousness and culture of resistance in the decades before, during, and after decolonization (e.g., Césaire's powerful and visionary *Notebook of a Return*

A bust of the Martinican poet, playwright, and politician Aimé Césaire (1913–2008) in Le Diament, Martinique. Césaire was one of the founders of the pan-Africanist Négritude movement, a militant critic of French colonialism (e.g., *Discourse on Colonialism*, 1950), and a member of the French National Assembly. His best-known literary work is his long poem, *Notebook of a Return to the Native Land* (1939). The bust is the work of Thybel. (Philippehalle/Dreamstime.com)

to the Native Land, 1939). Other noteworthy French poets of the first half of the twentieth century include Paul Valéry, Charles Péguy, Léon-Paul Fargue, Victor Segalen, Valéry Larbaud, Jules Supervielle, Saint-John Perse, and Pierre-Jean Jouve.

Prominent contemporary poets (i.e., active from 1945 to the present) include Francis Ponge, Jacques Prévert, Raymond Quéneau, Jean Follain, Eugène Guillevic, Edmond Jabès, Jean-Paul de Dadelsen, Claude Vigée, Yves Bonnefoy, André du Bouchet, Jacques Dupin, Roger Giroux, Jacques Réda, Michel Deguy, Jacques Roubaud, Henri Meschonnic, Annie Salager, Franck Venaille, Anne-Marie Albiach, Emmanuel Hocquard, Alain Veinstein, and Philippe Denis. Prévert (1900–1977) is the most popular poet of his generation—due in large part to the fact that his work has been set to music and sung by performers like Yves Montand. Bonnefoy (1923–2016), whose work combined misleadingly simple language with a philosophical interest in the tension between presence and absence, the revealed and the concealed, is the most critically acclaimed of his generation. The interplay of language and the body is a preoccupation of Albiach's (1937–2012) visually and verbally spare work.

Leading poets who came of age in the 1970s and 1980s include Serge Pey, Christian Bobin, Yvon Le Men, Antoine Émaz, Béatrice Bonhomme, Olivier Barbarant, Valérie Rouzeau, and Frédérick Houdaer. Among younger poets, standouts include Thomas Vinau, Laura Vazquez, Rim Battal, and Cécile Coulon. Rapper and spoken word artist Abd al Malik (b. 1975) and slam poets Marc-Alexandre Oho Bambe (b. 1976) and Grand Corps Malade (Fabien Marsaud, b. 1977) have reached a broader audience with their work. Le Printemps des Poètes ("The Spring of Poets") is an annual celebration of poetry writing and reading organized around a specific theme, like Courage (2020), Ardor (2018), Africa (2017), Poetic Insurrection (2015), Infinite Landscapes (2011), A Woman's Perspective (2010), Laughter (2009), and Songs of Cities (2006).

See also: Chapter 9: Francophonie. Chapter 11: Houellebecq (Michel) and the Recent French Novel; Literary Avant-Garde, 1950–1980 (Novel and Theatre); Novel in the Nineteenth Century; Reza (Yasmina) and Recent French Theatre; Twentieth-Century Literature through Mid-Century (Novel and Theatre). Chapter 13: Chanson.

Further Reading

Azérad and Collier (2010); Balakian (1986); Barda (2019); Bishop (1993); Dickow (2015); Little (1996); Lloyd (2002); Porter (1990); Rabaka (2015); Thomas and Winspur (1999); Wilder (2005); Wilder (2015).

Reza (Yasmina) and Recent French Theatre

Yasmina Reza (b. 1959) is France's most celebrated living playwright. Her most successful plays—Conversations after a Burial (1986), Winter Crossing (1989), "Art" (1994), The Unexpected Man (1995), Life × 3 (2000), God of Carnage (2006), and How You Talk the Game (2011)—have been performed around the world. Most of them fall in the "comedy of manners" (*comédie de mœurs*) genre since they expose and ridicule the anxieties and hang-ups of the bourgeoisie. *Conversations after a Burial* makes a spectacle of the range of emotions—not only mourning and regret but also petty bickering and uncontrollable lust—that rise to the surface when people gather for a loved one's funeral. *"Art"* centers on the bitter argument that takes place among three friends—a cynical and domineering philistine, an ostensibly phony arriviste esthete, and a wishy-washy sad sack—when the second, Serge, purchases a virtually monochromatic (and manifestly insipid) abstract painting. It is as much a reflection on the fragility and complex power dynamics of friendship as it is a questioning of esthetic judgment and the inflated value of contemporary art. *Gods of Carnage* focuses on the descent into chaos that occurs when two civilized but tense middle-class couples meet for what is supposed to be a polite discussion of a fight that has taken place between their two young sons. Reza has also written critically acclaimed fiction—*Hammerklavier* (1997), *Desolation* (1999), *Adam Haberberg* (2003), *Happy Are the Happy* (2013), and *Babylon* (2016), and a probing portrait of the notoriously ambitious and psychologically complex Nicolas Sarkozy—*Dawn, Evening, or Night* (2007)—during his successful first campaign for the French presidency.

France has produced several other critically acclaimed playwrights since the 1970s. Michel Vinaver (b. 1927) has had an illustrious career that began in the 1950s. His best works deal with latent social and socioeconomic tensions, like *Situation Vacant* (1971, about the tortured psyche of an unemployed man), *The Neighbors* (1984), and *The Television Program* (1988). Vinaver also wrote a bilingual oratorio comprising newspaper and documentary accounts of the 9/11 terrorist attacks in the United States, *11 septembre 2001* (2002)—one of several French noteworthy French works that deal with this tragedy (cf. Frédéric Beigbeder's searing and controversial novel *Windows on the World* [2003]). The plays of Bernard-Marie Koltès (1948–1989) focus on the struggles of alienated individuals crushed by society—*Black Battles with Dogs* (1979, about racial tension in West Africa), *The Night Just before the Forests* (1979), *West Pier* (1985), *In the Solitude of the Cotton Fields* (1986, a one-act play about the encounter between nameless characters known simply as the "Dealer" and the "Client"), and *Roberto Zucco* (1988, based on the story of a notorious serial killer). Jean-Luc Lagarce (1957–1995) is best known for *It's Only the End of the World* (1990), a play about a gay playwright who returns home to visit to his family after a long absence to announce that he is dying. Noteworthy French playwrights of today include Éric-Emmanuel Schmitt (e.g., *The Visitor*, 1993), Joël Pommerat, Xavier Durringer, Marion Aubert, Florian Zeller (e.g., *The Father*, 2012), Mariette Navarro, and Magali Mougel (e.g., *Suzy Storck*, 2014).

See also: Chapter 11: Houellebecq (Michel) and the Recent French Novel; Literary Avant-Garde, 1950–1980; Seventeenth-Century Theatre; Twentieth-Century Literature through Mid-Century (Novel and Theatre).

Further Reading
Bradby and Chéreau (1997); Carroll (2002); Finburgh and Lavery (2011); Giguere (2014); Glynn (2020); Tilger (2016); Turk (2011).

THEATRE IN FRANCE

The French Ministry of Culture supports live theatre through ARTCENA (National Center for Circus, Street Performance, and Theatre), a branch of the Ministry of Culture. France has hundreds of theatres—large, small, traditional, experimental, and popular. The most prestigious are its five national theatres—the Comédie-Française (founded in 1680 on the basis of Molière's royal troupe), the Théâtre National de l'Odéon-Théâtre de l'Europe, the Théâtre National de la Colline, and Théâtre National de Chaillot—all in Paris; and the Théâtre National de Strasbourg. The ministry also funds thirty-eight "national centres for the dramatic arts" (CDN) throughout the country. Paris also has a lively Broadway/West End-type scene, known as "boulevard theatre." France's second capital of theatre is Avignon, the site of the world-famous Festival d'Avignon, an annual festival of theatre and the performing arts held in July, which was founded in 1947 by Jean Vilar. Renowned directors of the contemporary era include Peter Brook, Robert Hossein, Antoine Vitez, Roger Planchon, Jacques Lassalle, Ariane Mnouchkine, Patrice Chéreau, Alain Fançon, Gérard Désarthe, Georges Lavaudant, and Olivier Py. Outstanding achievements in theatre are honored by the annual Molière Awards, France's equivalent of the Tony Awards (United States) and the Laurence Olivier Awards (United Kingdom). Leading theatre arts schools include CNSAD (National Conservatory of the Dramatic Arts) and the Cours Florent, both in Paris.

Seventeenth-Century Theatre

Seventeenth-century French theatre—classical theatre—is one of the pillars of French literary greatness. Three things define it as "classical." First, like most elite literature and art of the period, a large share of its subject matter, esthetic models, and cultural ideals were drawn from classical antiquity (i.e., Greece and Rome). Second, it endeavored to illustrate a set of noble values by which every respectable gentleman should strive to live—orderliness, good measure, devotion to honor and duty, self-control, social refinement, ideal believability (*vraisemblance*), respect for decorum (*les bienséances*), and practical knowledge of the general traits of human character and behavior (both vices and virtues). Additionally, theatre in the "grand century" served the greater glory of king and nation.

Seventeenth-century French theatre has a "big three" made up of Pierre Corneille (1606–1684) and Jean Racine (1639–1699)—both tragedians; and Jean-Baptiste Poquelin (1622–1673), known universally by his stage name, Molière—a comedic playwright. Corneille's early work, *Le Cid*, a tragicomedy about a legendary medieval Spanish military commander, created a controversy in French literary circles because it violated a number of rules of classical theatre. However, it is still a staple of the French canon and contains perhaps the most famous line in all of French theatre: "O rage! O despair! O age my enemy! Have I lived simply to know this infamy?" Corneille went on to write three great classical tragedies—*Horace* (1640), *Cinna* (1643), and *Polyeucte* (1643). Racine is considered one of the greatest French literary writers of all time. His tragedies—*Andromaque* (1667), *Bérénice* (1670), *Phèdre* (1677), and *Athalie* (1691)—demonstrate a masterful use of dodecasyllabic alexandrine verse. The most famous is *Phèdre*, which tells the story of the mythical Queen of Athens, who falls in love with her stepson Hippolytus during the absence of her husband, King Theseus. After many twists and turns, Hippolytus drowns at sea and Phaedra confesses to Theseus, ultimately committing suicide by poison. Molière's comedies—many of which were created as *comédies-ballets* for the court—often satirize the phony and exaggerated affectations of characters who strive to be something they were never meant to be (as such, they are known as "comedies of manners"). Still widely performed today, his best known works include *The Affected Young Ladies* (1659), *Tartuffe, or The Imposter* (1664—the name of the title character is still synonymous in French with a religious hypocrite), *Don Juan* (1665), *The Misanthrope* (1666), *The Miser* (1668), *The Bourgeois Gentleman* (1670—Molière's most famous play, about the universal figure of the obtuse commoner who foolishly attempts to pass himself off as an aristocrat), *The Learned Ladies* (1672), and *The Imaginary Invalid* (1673).

Other major seventeenth-century French authors include the poets François de Malherbes and Nicolas Boileau-Despréaux; the playwright Jean Rotrou; the moralist Jean de La Rochefoucaud; the novelists Honoré d'Urffé, Madeleine de Scudéry, and Madame de Lafayette (e.g., *The Princesse de Clèves*, 1678); the fabulist Jean de La Fontaine and the author of fairy tales Charles Perrault; and the satirist Jean de la Bruyère. The collected sermons of Jacques-Bénigne de Bossuet and the collected correspondence of Madame de Sévigné are also considered among the literary masterpieces of the period.

See also: Chapter 2: Louis XIV and the Absolute Monarchy. Chapter 11: Literary Avant-Garde, 1950–1980; Reza (Yasmina) and Recent French Theatre; Twentieth-Century Literature through Mid-Century (Novel and Theatre). Chapter 12: Versailles. Chapter 13: Dance; Opera.

Further Reading
Brown (2005); Goldmann (1964); Howarth (1997); Scott (2000).

Twentieth-Century Literature through Mid-Century (Novel and Theatre)

The years just before the outbreak of World War I (1914) offered a varied assortment in terms of literary production. There were mature works by symbolist, naturalist, and decadent writers. There were the great innovations in form and subject matter of the "cubist" poets like Guillaume Apollinaire and Blaise Cendrars. In theatre, there were the popular farces of Georges Feydeau, Edmond de Rostand's *Cyrano de Bergerac*

(1897), the Catholic and patriotic writer Charles Péguy's *Joan of Arc* (1897), and the raucous absurdity and of radical puerility of *Ubu the King* (1896) by Alfred Jarry. In the novel, there was André Gide's *The Immoralist* (1902)—the controversial orientalist story of a young man's journey of self-discovery and awakening to sensualism and homosexual desire; and Alain-Fournier's wistful coming-of-age story, *Le Grand Meaulnes* (1913). In *The Banquet Years: The Origins of the Avant-Garde in France, 1885 to World War I*, Roger Shattuck summarized the avant-garde art and literature of the French Belle Époque as driven by four related strategies for achieving a sort of transcendence in a "godless universe" by "dredging up" new material from the subconscious—the cult of the primitive child-man; humor taken to the absurd; the eruption of dreams, magnified as hallucination, into waking experience; and the embrace of polysemic ambiguity. These traits lingered in the literary and cultural production of the rest of the century. However, they lost their epiphanous quality as they were forced to contend with a collapse of western humanism.

The ravages of World War I (1914–1918) caused an astounding shock to the system, which, in the arts and literature, produced Dada and surrealism. Headed by André Breton (1896–1966), who had also been a member of Dada, surrealism was conceived as a revolutionary movement complementary to communism insofar as it sought to liberate the subconscious from bourgeois oppression and soulless materialism just like the communism sought to liberate the proletariat. Its approach included "automatic writing" (e.g., *The Magnetic Fields*, 1920, by Breton and Philippe Soupault) and openness to dreams, desire, and the uncanny—all hidden just behind the façades of everyday reality. While both Dada and surrealism were focused more on the visual arts and poetry, they were not without an effect on theatre and the novel. Dada-affiliated artists staged performances (e.g., the Salle Gaveau Dada "festival" in 1920 and the "Bearded Heart" *soirée* in 1923) that were precursors of the performance art and experimental theatre of 1960s and 1970s. There were a number of surrealist "novels," the most famous of which were Louis Aragon's *Paris Peasant* (1926), Breton's *Nadja* (1928), Georges Bataille's *Story of the Eye* (1928), and René Daumal's *A Night of Serious Drinking* (1939).

Many great French novels were written in the 1920s, 1930s, and 1940s. Arguably the greatest of all was Marcel Proust's (1871–1922) seven-volume exploration of memory and subjectivity, *In Search of Lost Time* (1913–1927). It is also during this period that Gide (1869–1951) published his mature work, *The Pastoral Symphony* (1919) and *The Counterfeiters* (1925). Other important novelists of the period include Colette (Sidonie-Gabrielle Colette—e.g., *Chéri*, 1920); Roger Martin du Gard (e.g., *The Thibaults*, 1922–1940); François Mauriac (e.g., *Thérèse Desqueyroux*, 1927); Jules Romains (*Men of Good Will*, 1932–1946); Georges Bernanos (e.g., *Under the Sun of Satan*, 1926); Louis-Ferdinand Céline (e.g., *Journey to the End of the Night*, 1932); André Malraux (e.g., *Man's Fate*, 1933); and Vercors (Jean Bruller—e.g., *The Silence of the Sea*, 1941). Many of the novels dealt unsparingly with the extreme moral dilemmas of the era.

The leading dramatists were Paul Claudel (e.g., *The Satin Slipper*, 1931), Jean Giraudoux (*Electra*, 1937), and Jean Anouilh (e.g., *Antigone*, 1944). Claudel's works were inspired by his Catholic faith. Giraudoux (1882–1944) and Anouilh (1910–1987) reworked classical material to examine modern problems. Antonin Artaud (1898–1906) developed his concept of the "Theatre of Cruelty," which is intended to "shock the spectator into seeing the baseness of his world" (*The Theatre and Its Double*, 1938). One of the most talented literary figures of the twentieth century was Jean Cocteau (1889–1963). In addition to collaborating with the Ballets Russes, Cocteau wrote novels (e.g., *The Holy Terrors*, 1929), plays (e.g., *The Infernal Machine*, 1934), and poetry. He also directed several acclaimed films, like *The Blood of a Poet* (1930), *Beauty and the Beast* (1946), and *Orpheus* (1949).

Novels and plays were important means of expression for the writers associated with French existentialism (1930s–1960s). A reflection of the tumultuous times and a philosophical offshoot of phenomenology, existentialism rejected various forms of essentialism (e.g., religion) on the grounds that human existence was patently absurd. It viewed individuals as "condemned to be free" and tackled the problem of autonomous moral agency in opposition to conformist "bad faith." Jean-Paul Sartre (1905–1980) treated these issues in his novels *Nausea* (1938), *The Age of Reason* (1945), and *Troubled Sleep* (1949); in his collection of short stories *The Wall* (1939); and in his plays *The Flies* (1943), *No Exit* (1945), *Dirty Hands* (1948), and *The Condemned of Altona* (1959). Although better known for her essays (e.g., *The Second Sex*, 1949) and autobiography (*Memoirs of a Dutiful Daughter*, 1958), Simone de Beauvoir (1908–1986) also wrote several novels (e.g., *The Mandarins*, 1954). Perhaps the best writer among the existentialists was Albert Camus (1913–1960), author of *The Stranger* (1942) and *The Plague* (1947). The alienated and impassive Meursault, the protagonist of the former, ranks as one of the most famous characters in modern literature.

See also: Chapter 11: Literary Avant-Garde, 1950–1980; Novel in the Nineteenth Century; Poetry (Modern and Contemporary). Chapter 12: French Cinema I (through the Nouvelle Vague); Modern Art and the School of Paris.

Further Reading

Best (2002); Gransard (2020); Guicharnaud (1967); James (2020); Kaplan (2016); Shattuck (1968); Shattuck (2000).

SELECTED BIBLIOGRAPHY

Azérad, Hugues, and Peter Collier, eds. *Twentieth-Century French Poetry: A Critical Anthology*. Cambridge UP, 2010.

Babcock, Arthur E. *The New Novel in France: Theory and Practice of the Nouveau Roman*. Twayne, 1997.

Balakian, Anna. *Surrealism: The Road to the Absolute*. 3rd ed. U Chicago P, 1986.

Barda, Jeff. *Experimentation and the Lyric in Contemporary French Poetry*. Palgrave Macmillan, 2019.

Becker, Daniel Levin. *Many Subtle Channels: In Praise of Potential Literature*. Harvard UP, 2012.

Bertens, Hans. *Literary Theory: The Basics*. 3rd ed. Routledge, 2014; esp. 46–66 and 102–149.

Best, Victoria. *An Introduction to Twentieth-century French Literature*. Duckworth, 2002.

Best, Victoria, and Martin Crowley, eds. *The New Pornographies: Explicit Sex in Recent French Fiction and Film*. Manchester UP, 2007.

Betty, Louis. *Without God: Michel Houellebecq and Materialist Horror*. Penn State UP, 2016.

Bishop, Michael. *Nineteenth-century French Poetry*. Twayne, 1993.

Bradby, David, and Patrice Chéreau. "Bernard-Marie Koltès: Chronology, Contexts, Connections." *New Theatre Quarterly*, vol. 13, no. 49, 1997, pp. 69–90.

Bredeson, Kate. *Occupying the Stage: The Theater of May '68*. Northwestern UP, 2018.

Brown, Gregory S. *A Field of Honor: Writers, Court Culture, and Public Theater in French Literary Life from Racine to the Revolution*. Columbia UP, 2005.

Burgwinkle, William, et al., eds. *The Cambridge History of French Literature*. Cambridge UP, 2011.

Carroll, Noël. "Friendship and Yasmina Reza's *Art*." *Philosophy and Literature*, vol. 26, no. 1, 2002, pp. 199–206.

Cazenave, Odile M. *Afrique sur Seine: A New Generation of African Writers in Paris*. Lexington, 2005.

Compagnon, Antoine. *Literature, Theory, and Common Sense*. Trans. Carol Cosman. Princeton UP, 2004.

Conley, Verena Andermatt. *Hélène Cixous: Writing the Feminine*. Rev. ed. U Nebraska P, 1991.

Cooke, Dervila. *Present Pasts: Patrick Modiano's (Auto)biographical Fictions*. Rodopi, 2005.

Culler, Jonathan. *Barthes: A Very Short Introduction*. Oxford UP, 2001.

Cusset, François. *French Theory: How Foucault, Derrida, Deleuze, & Co. Transformed the Intellectual Life of the United States*. Trans. Jeff Fort. U Minnesota P, 2008.

Damlé, Amaleena, and Gill Rye, eds. *Women's Writing in Twenty-first-century France: Life as Literature*. U Wales P, 2013.

Darnton, Robert. *The Forbidden Best-Sellers of Pre-Revolutionary France*. Norton, 1995.

Davidson, Ian. *Voltaire*. Pegasus, 2010.

Day, Loraine. *Writing Shame and Desire: The Work of Annie Ernaux*. Lang, 2007.

Delers, Olivier. *The Other Rise of the Novel in Eighteenth-Century French Fiction*. U Delaware P, 2015.

Dickow, Alexander. "Yves Bonnefoy and the 'Genius' of Language." *SubStance*, vol. 44 no. 2, 2015, pp. 158-171.

Duncan, Alastair. *Claude Simon: Adventures in Words*. 2nd ed. Manchester UP, 2003.

Essif, Les. *American "Unculture" in French Drama: Homo Americanus and the Post-1960 French Resistance*. Palgrave Macmillan, 2013.

Esslin, Martin. *The Theatre of the Absurd*. 3rd ed. Vintage, 2001.

Farrant, Tim. *An Introduction to Nineteenth-Century French Literature*. Bloomsbury, 2007.

Finburgh, Clare, and Carl Lavery, eds. *Contemporary French Theatre and Performance*. Palgrave Macmillan, 2011.

Fulton, Dawn. *Signs of Dissent: Maryse Condé and Postcolonial Criticism*. U Virginia P, 2008.

Giguere, Amanda. *The Plays of Yasmina Reza on the English and American Stage*. McFarland, 2014.

Glynn, Dominic. "Yasmina Reza and Florian Zeller: The Art of Success." *Contemporary European Playwrights*, eds. Maria M. Delgado, et al. Routledge, 2020, pp. 261–276.

Goldmann, Lucien. *The Hidden God: A Study of Tragic Vision in the Pensées of Pascal and the Tragedies of Racine*. Trans. Philip Thody. Routledge, 1964; new ed. Verso, 2016.

Gransard, Marie-José. *Twentieth-Century Paris, 1900–1950: A Literary Guide for Travellers*. Bloomsbury, 2020.

Guicharnaud, Jacques. *Modern French Theatre from Giraudoux to Beckett*. Rev. ed. Yale UP, 1967.

Hollier, Denis, ed. *A New History of French Literature*. Harvard UP, 1989.

Howarth, William D. *French Theatre in the Neo-classical Era, 1550–1789*. Cambridge UP, 1997.

James, Alison. *The Documentary Imagination in Twentieth-Century French Literature: Writing with Facts*. Oxford UP, 2020.

Jefferson, Ann. *Biography and the Question of Literature in France*. Oxford UP, 2007.

Kaplan, Alice. *Looking for the Stranger: Albert Camus and the Life of a Literary Classic*. U Chicago P, 2016.

Kawakami, Akane. *Patrick Modiano*. 2nd ed. Liverpool UP, 2015.

Kemp, Simon. *French Fiction into the Twenty-First Century: The Return to the Story*. U Wales P, 2010.

Kjærgård, Ross. *Reimagining Society in 18th Century French Literature: Happiness and Human Rights*. Routledge, 2018.

Kleppinger, Kathryn A. *Branding the "Beur" Author: Minority Writing and the Media in France*. Liverpool UP, 2019.

Knepper, Wendy. *Patrick Chamoiseau: A Critical Introduction*. U Mississippi P, 2012.

Lehan, Richard Daniel. *Realism and Naturalism: The Novel in an Age of Transition*. U Wisconsin P, 2005.

Leigh, John. *The Search for Enlightenment: An Introduction to Eighteenth-Century French Writing*. Rowman & Littlefield, 1999.

Levin, Harry. *The Gates of Horn: A Study of Five French Realists*. Oxford UP, 1963.

Little, Roger. *Shaping of Modern French Poetry: Reflections on Unrhymed Poetic Form, 1840–1990*. Carcanet P, 1996.

Lloyd, Rosemary. *Baudelaire's World*. Cornell UP, 2002.

Lyons, John D. *French Literature: A Very Short Introduction*. Oxford UP, 2010.

Martin, Bronwen. *The Fiction of J. M. G. Le Clézio: A Postcolonial Reading*. Lang, 2012.

McDonald, Christie, and Susan Suleiman, eds. *French Global: A New Approach to Literary History*. Columbia UP, 2010.

Migraine-George, Thérèse. *From Francophonie to World Literature in French: Ethics, Poetics, and Politics*. U Nebraska P, 2013.

Moser, Keith. *J. M. G. Le Clézio: A Concerned Citizen of the Global Village*. Lexington, 2012.

Nesbitt, Nick. *Caribbean Critique: Antillean Critical Theory from Toussaint to Glissant*. Liverpool UP, 2013.

Norrish, Peter. *New Tragedy and Comedy in France, 1945–1970*. Barnes & Noble, 1988.

Platten, David. *The Pleasures of Crime: Reading Modern French Crime Fiction*. Rodopi, 2011.

Porter, Laurence. *The Crisis of French Symbolism*. Cornell UP, 1990.

Prendergast, Christopher, ed. *A History of Modern French Literature: From the Sixteenth Century to the Twentieth Century*. Princeton UP, 2017.

Rabaka, Reiland. *The Negritude Movement: W.E.B. DuBois, Léon Damas, Aimé Césaire, Léopold Senghor, Frantz Fanon, and the Evolution of an Insurgent Idea*. Lexington, 2015.

Robb, Graham. *Victor Hugo: A Biography*. Norton, 1997.

Schaeffer, Neil. *The Marquis de Sade: A Life*. Knopf, 1999.

Scott, Virginia. *Molière: A Theatrical Life*. Cambridge UP, 2000.

Shattuck, Roger. *The Banquet Years: The Origins of the Avant Garde in France, 1885 to World War I*. Rev. ed. Vintage, 1968.

Shattuck, Roger. *Proust's Way: A Field Guide to* In Search of Lost Time. Norton, 2000.

Smith, Roch C. *Understanding Alain Robbe-Grillet*. U South Carolina P, 2000.

Sokal, Alan, and Jean Bricmont. *Fashionable Nonsense: Postmodern Intellectuals' Abuse of Science*. Picador, 1998.

Swamy, Vinay. *Interpreting the Republic: Marginalization and Belonging in Contemporary French Novels and Films*. Lexington, 2012.

Sweeney, Carole. *Michel Houellebecq and the Literature of Despair*. Bloomsbury, 2013.

Taylor, John. *Paths to Contemporary French Literature*. Transaction, 2003–2011. 3 vols.

Thomas, Jean-Jacques, and Steven Winspur. *Poeticized Language: The Foundations of Contemporary French Poetry*. Penn State UP, 1999.

Tilger, Lauren. "Gender: The Hidden God in Yasmina Reza's *Le Dieu du Carnage*." *Studies in 20th & 21st Century Literature*, vol. 40, no. 1, 2016, art. 4.

Turk, Edward Baron. *French Theatre Today: The View from New York, Paris, and Avignon*. U Iowa P, 2011.

Ungureanu, Camil. "Michel Houellebecq's Shifting Representation of Islam: From the Death of God to Counter-Enlightenment." *Philosophy and Social Criticism*, vol. 43, no. 4–5, 2017, pp. 514–528.

Unwin, Timothy. *The Cambridge Companion to the French Novel: From 1800 to the Present*. Cambridge UP, 1997.

Wampole, Christy. *Degenerative Realism: Novel and Nation in Twenty-first-century France*. Columbia UP, 2020.

Wilder, Gary. *Freedom Time: Negritude, Decolonization, and the Future of the World*. Duke UP, 2015.

Wilder, Gary. *The French Imperial Nation-State: Negritude and Colonial Humanism between the Two World Wars*. U Chicago P, 2005.

Willging, Jennifer. *Telling Anxiety: Anxious Narration in the Work of Marguerite Duras, Annie Ernaux, Nathalie Sarraute, and Anne Hébert*. U Toronto P, 2019.

CHAPTER 12

ART AND ARCHITECTURE

OVERVIEW

The history of French art and architecture contains outstanding and trendsetting works in every period and style from the Middle Ages to the present. Throughout that history, Paris has stood out as an international hub in the arts and can rightly be considered the capital of the avant-garde from the mid-nineteenth century through World War II. France's sustained excellence in art and architecture owes a lot to the central role that the state has played in these areas dating back to the Carolingian Renaissance of the early 800s. Today, this role is played by the national Ministry of Culture, created in 1959. Appreciation of the arts—and the corollary notion that creative works must be treated as "exceptions" to the pure logic of the global marketplace—are widely thought of as components of French national character.

Identifying common denominators of the "French tradition" in art and architecture across the ages is a highly speculative undertaking, but art historian André Chastel proposed four prevalent traits. One is the persistence of the classical tradition. While the seventeenth century is rightfully seen as the golden age of French classicism (e.g., the paintings of Nicolas Poussin and the Palace of Versailles), the French passion for the classical is a much broader megatrend. It is the dominant artistic discourse from the sixteenth through the nineteenth centuries. In architecture, it reaches as far back as the Romanesque style. In painting, it lives on in the twentieth century in the work of the late Pierre-Auguste Renoir, Pablo Picasso, André Derain, Balthus, Martial Raysse, and Gérard Garouste. Indeed, French artists have positioned themselves as the most rigorous and inspired interpreters of the classical tradition. Another trait identified by Chastel is the paradox wherein French art is both quintessentially in the service of power (e.g., the painter David staging the Festival of the Supreme Being for Robespierre in 1794) and the source of emblematic social and political resistance and critique (e.g., Eugène Delacroix, *Liberty Leading the People*, 1830). Another French duality identified by Chastel is the coexistence of an artistic cult of happiness and pleasure verging on frivolity and decadence (e.g., Jean-Honoré Fragonard, *The Swing*, 1767) and a "Cartesian" rationalist obsession with straight lines, order, and symmetry on a monumental scale, like the placing of the Louvre Pyramid and Grande Arche de la Défense—both presidential building projects of the Mitterrand era (1980s) and grandiose geometrical hybrids of the modern and the classical—on the same Parisian *Axe historique* that also contains the Tuileries Gardens, the classical Place de la

Concorde, the Champs-Élysées, and the neoclassical Arc de Triomphe. Finally, Chastel stressed that France has long been a cosmopolitan artistic melting pot, where foreign artists have played a pivotal role in the development of "French" art. Italians helped launch the School of Fontainebleau (c. 1530–1610). Four centuries later, artists of many different nationalities formed the core of the School of Paris (prolonged by the "New School of Paris" in the years following World War II)—the Spaniards Pablo Picasso, Juan Gris, Joan Miró, and Salvador Dalí; the Russian Empire Jews Marc Chagall, Ossip Zadkine, Chaïm Soutine, and Jacques Lipchitz; the Germans Max Ernst and Hans Hartung; the Swiss Alberto Giacometti; the Italian Amedeo Modigliani; the Dutchman Piet Mondrian; the Romanian Constantin Brâncuşi; the Americans Man Ray and Kay Sage; the Chilean Roberto Matta; the Japanese Tsuguharu Foujita, the Chinese Zao Wou-Ki (… and the list goes on).

The artistic and architectural heritage of France includes many fine examples from the Gallo-Roman era (125 BCE–450 CE)—especially in southern cities like Arles, Orange, and Nîmes (e.g., the Roman temple known as the Maison Carrée and the nearby Pont du Gard aqueduct bridge). However, one can make the case that the story of *French* art and architecture per se begins during the High Middle Ages (1000–1250), when the Kingdom of France established itself as a distinct geopolitical entity. There were two prominent architectural (and artistic) styles in medieval France—Romanesque (950–1150) and Gothic (1150–1500). The former derives its name from its Roman-inspired rounded arches and was more prevalent in eastern, western, central, and southern France. The Gothic style—known for its pointed arches and other features that allowed for high vaults and capacious, light-filled interiors—originated in the Paris region and was first more prevalent in northern France before spreading to the rest of the country and throughout Western Europe. Religious edifices offer the best examples of both styles. The abbey churches of Aurillac, Caen, Conques, Cluny, Moissac, and Vézelay, the basilica of Saint-Sernin (Toulouse), and Notre-Dame la Grande (Poitiers) are among the best examples of Romanesque. Gothic is best exemplified by the stunning cathedrals of Amiens, Beauvais, Chartres, Laon, Paris, Reims, Rouen, and Strasbourg. Both styles are known for their statuary; Gothic also excelled in illuminated (illustrated) manuscripts, tapestry, and radiant stained-glass windows (e.g., the Rose Window of Chartres and the Sainte Chapelle in Paris).

Classicism dominated art and architecture in France from the sixteenth through the eighteenth centuries and was still both highly influential and officially supported in the nineteenth century. It was not just a style, but a set of cultural paradigms and a world view in which models for literature, art, architecture, philosophy, and behavior were found primarily in classical antiquity. It originally made its way to France in the early sixteenth century via the imitation of the art and architecture of the Italian Renaissance. While based on emulation and imitation, the classicism of the French Renaissance (sixteenth century) served as the foundation for the first conspicuously national styles in France, exemplified in the Cour Carrée of the Louvre in Paris, Fontainebleau Palace, and the Loire Valley châteaux (e.g., Blois, Chambord, Chenonceau, Azay-le-Rideau)—still considered among the greatest masterpieces of French architecture. The leading sculptors of the French Renaissance were Jean Goujon and Germain Pilon. Its leading painters include the members of the School of Fontainebleau, Jean Cousin the Elder, François Clouet, and Antoine Caron (Mannerism).

In the seventeenth century, classicism became a highly regulated, rational, orderly, and all-encompassing system. While French classicism sought to set itself apart from the more ornate baroque style prevalent in Italy and elsewhere, it shared the baroque's penchant for complexity, grand scale, and dynamic synthesis. For this reason, the greatest achievement of French classical architecture, the Palace of Versailles (expanded 1661–1715), may also be described as baroque. The seventeenth century was particularly rich in painting. The greatest master of the era was Nicolas Poussin (e.g., *The Arcadian Shepherds*, 1638). Other major painters of the era were Georges de la Tour, Claude Lorrain, and Philippe de Champaigne. Seventeenth-century French architecture is further exemplified by the Place des Vosges, Institut de France, and Hôtel des Invalides—all in Paris. Compared to the severity and spectacle of the seventeenth century, art in the eighteenth century was both lighter (rococo) and more restrained and civic-minded (neoclassicism). The greatest painters of the era were Jean-Antoine Watteau (e.g., *The Embarkation for Cythera*, 1717), François Boucher, Jean-Honoré Fragonard, Jean-Baptiste-Siméon Chardin, Jean-Baptiste Greuze, and Jacques-Louis David (e.g., *Oath of the Horatii*, 1784). Its leading sculptor was Jean-Antoine Houdon. Noteworthy examples of French architecture of the period include the Petit Trianon at Versailles, Place de la Bourse in Bordeaux, Place Stanislas in Nancy, Panthéon in Paris, and Royal Saltworks at Arc-et-Senans.

Following the French Revolution, which disrupted the system of royal patronage and ultimately led to a rethinking of the role of art and artists in society, French art in the nineteenth century pointed in several different directions. Neoclassicism was to remain an influential part of the esthetic and cultural code throughout the century (e.g., Jean-Auguste-Dominique Ingres and the less-inspired academic painters). Nevertheless, artistic revolution was underfoot. It was present in the disorderly passion and interest in current events of the great romantic painters like Eugène Delacroix and Théodore Géricault (e.g., *The Raft of the Medusa*, 1819) and in the more naturalistic landscapes and plein air painting of the Barbizon School (e.g., Jean-Baptiste-Camille Corot, Jean-François Millet). It expressed itself categorically in the documentary style and lower-class subject matter of the realists like Gustave Courbet (e.g., *A Burial at Ornans*, 1850) and Honoré Daumier; and in the daring works of the impressionists, who applied realism to the urban milieu to create evocative tableaux of modern life (Gustave Caillebotte, *Paris Street, Rainy Day*, 1877) and freed their brushwork to capture the nuances of perception on the fly (Claude Monet, *Impression, Sunrise*, 1874). Édouard Manet, Frédéric Bazille, Camille Pissarro, Pierre-Auguste Renoir, Edgar Degas, and Berthe Morisot were the other major impressionists. Later, both the oneiric fantasies and metaphysical yearnings of the symbolists (Paul Gauguin, *Where Do We Come From? What Are We? Where Are We Going?*, 1897) and the stylistic and expressionistic experiments of the postimpressionists (Georges Seurat, Paul Signac, Henri de Toulouse-Lautrec, Vincent Van Gogh, and Paul Cézanne) anticipated the avant-garde art of the twentieth century. Known for audacious works like *The Thinker* (1879–1889), Auguste Rodin was a disruptor who similarly paved the way for modern sculpture.

The dominant architectural style in France from the 1830s through the end of the century was the Beaux-Arts style, a pompous variation on neoclassicism taught in France's leading school of architecture, the École des Beaux-Arts. The century's most impressive building, the new Paris Opera (completed 1875) by Charles Garnier, was an eclectic blend of Beaux-Arts academicism and baroque revival. By contrast, the upscale apartment buildings built on the *grands boulevards* that constituted the crux of the sweeping rebuilding of Paris (1853–1870) overseen by Prefect Eugène Haussmann during the reign of Emperor Napoleon III were rather conservative in style. They reflected the bourgeois esthetic of the ambitious plan, which was undertaken to make Paris into a showcase of Bonapartist order and capitalist prosperity. Synonymous throughout the world with the elegant modern look and feel of Paris, its other features included a new sewer system and central market, posh sidewalk cafés, popular entertainment venues, public parks, strategically located army barracks, and glitzy department stores.

France was one of the incubators of modernist art and architecture in the twentieth century—a deep rethinking of the responsibilities and possibilities of art and architecture in an age of mechanical reproduction, technological progress, speed, democracy, individualism, mass culture and media, materialism, social upheaval, alienation, and global war that also gave the artist (and architect) the freedom to create works that express a unique personal vision in defiance of convention. In the visual arts through the 1950s, much of this ferment and innovation was the product of the School of Paris. The movements, styles, and groups associated with the French avant-garde scene during this period include cubism, fauvism, Orphism, Esprit Nouveau, Dada, surrealism, expressionism, tachisme, lyrical abstraction, and art brut. The most influential were cubism and fauvism before World War I and Dada and surrealism in the Interwar Period (1919–1939). As the prolific leaders of cubism and fauvism, respectively, Pablo Picasso (e.g., *Les Demoiselles d'Avignon*, 1907) and Henri Matisse (e.g., *The Red Studio*, 1911) are two of the towering figures of modern art. Led by André Breton, surrealism set about liberating the unconscious mind by turning art and poetry over to automatic processes, chance, dream life, irrational impulses, and sexual desire. In France, the movement's leading painters included Max Ernst, André Masson, Joan Miró, and Salvador Dalí (e.g., *The Persistence of Memory*, 1931). After World War II, the painters of the School of Paris and related groups (e.g., Georges Mathieu, Nicolas de Staël, Jean Dewasne, Hans Hartung, Simon Hantaï, and Pierre Soulages) embraced abstraction, whereas the earlier "ready-mades" (e.g., the ironic and provocative *Fountain*, 1917) of the independent-minded Marcel Duchamp, formerly affiliated with both cubism and Dada, proved influential in the subsequent conceptual turn of contemporary art after 1960.

Beginning in the 1960s, both in France and elsewhere (especially in the United States, which had supplanted France as the most influential artistic nation), contemporary art set itself apart from modern art in a number of ways—its embrace of unconventional media and forms of expression (e.g., installations, performance, happenings, public interventions, mail art, body art, land art, conceptual art, minimalism, optic and kinetic art, video art, telecommunications art, digital art, etc.); its critical engagement with the everyday, mass culture, and controversial issues (giving it a countercultural ethos at odds with its being accepted quickly by elite art institutions); and a high degree of individualism. A corollary of this last point is that while contemporary art in France has had no shortage of collectives, informal groups sharing certain ideological and/or esthetic principles, and media-fed trends, the modern era of major avant-garde movements like cubism and surrealism was over. Between 1960 and 1990, the French groups and trends had names like Lettrisme, Nouveau Réalisme, GRAV, Situationist International, Supports/Surfaces, Figuration Narrative, Sociological Art Collective, Figuration Libre, and Aesthetics of Communication.

After Duchamp, the most influential figure of emergent French contemporary art was Yves Klein, a founding member of the Nouveaux Réalistes with an interest in Zen Buddhism. Klein painted striking monochromatic works using his patented International Klein Blue (IKB) and was a pioneer of conceptual art and performance (e.g., *The Void*, 1958; *Zones of Immaterial Pictorial Sensibility*, 1959–1962). Other major French and France-based contemporary artists of the past sixty years include Arman, François Boisrond, Christian Boltanski, Daniel Buren, Sophie Calle, Christo, Robert Combas, Jean Dubuffet, Fred Forest, Gérard Garouste, Pierre Huyghe, Fabrice Hyber, Michel Journiac, Jacques Monory, François Morellet, Tania Mouraud, Gina Pane, Pierre & Gilles, Bernard Rancillac, Martial Raysse, Sarkis, Nicolas Schöffer, Franciso Sobrino, Jean Tinguely, Victor Vasarely, Claude Viallat, Ben Vautier, and Bernar Venet. While most of the above-mentioned artists are men, some of France's most innovative and audacious contemporary artists have been women who have incorporated feminist themes in their work. Examples include Niki de Saint Phalle (e.g., the "Nana" figures in *Tarot Garden*, 1978–1998), Louise Bourgeois (e.g., the *Cells* series in the 1980s and 1990s), Annette Messager (e.g., *My Vows*, 1988–1991), and ORLAN (e.g., *The Reincarnation of Saint Orlan*, 1990–1995). The best-known younger French artists of today include JR, famous for his participatory street photomural projects (e.g., *Inside Out*, 2011–present); Kader Attia, who explores the themes of injury and repair in connection to colonialism, postcolonialism, and migration, among other issues (e.g., *The Repair: From Occidental to Extra-Occidental Cultures*, 2012); and the New York-based sculptor and videographer Camille Henrot (*Grosse fatigue*, 2013).

The leading styles of French architecture in the first half of the twentieth century were Art Nouveau (e.g., Hector Guimard), art deco (e.g., Auguste Perret), and the international style as represented by the work of the Swiss architect Le Corbusier (e.g., Villa Savoye, 1931) and of his French contemporary, Robert Mallet-Stevens. Leading architects of the 1950s, 1960s, and 1970s include Jean Prouvé, Claude Parent (associated with brutalism), Jean Balladur, and Émille Aillaud. Contemporary architecture in France exhibits an eclectic array of styles while remaining for the most part boldly modern. It has been given impetus by major government-sponsored building projects in Paris and elsewhere. While some of the most emblematic of these *grands travaux* have been designed by renowned international architects, like the Centre Pompidou

(Richard Rogers and Renzo Piano, 1977), the Pyramide du Louvre (I. M. Pei, 1989), and the Centre Pompidou-Metz (Shigeru Ban, 2010), other major commissions have gone to French architects. Jean Nouvel designed the Institut du Monde Arabe (Paris, 1987) and Musée du Quai Branly-Jacques Chirac (Paris, 2006); Dominique Perrault, the Bibliothèque Nationale François Mitterrand (Paris, 1995); Christian de Portzamparc, the Cité de la Musique (Paris, 1984–1995); and Rudy Ricciotti, the Musée des Civilisations de l'Europe et de la Méditerranée (Marseille, 2013).

The French have a broad view of art that extends to cinema, fashion, industrial design, and comics. Cinema and fashion have a special place in France's artistic sense of self. The Lumière brothers invented motion pictures at the end of the nineteenth century. At the beginning of the twentieth, Georges Méliès was the first filmmaker to make artistic films using special effects (e.g., *A Trip to the Moon*, 1902). Through World War II, three movements dominated French cinema—impressionist cinema (e.g., Abel Gance), surrealism (e.g., René Clair and Jean Cocteau), and poetic realism (e.g., Jean Vigo, Julien Duvivier, Jean Renoir, and Marcel Carné). Taking inspiration from these movements as well as from the postwar minimalists (Robert Bresson, Henri-Georges Clouzot, and Jean-Pierre Melville), the directors of the French Nouvelle Vague created a revolution in film in the late 1950s and 60s with their concept of the *film d'auteur*, their innovative camera work and editing, their frank social critique, and their nontraditional approach to storytelling. The Nouvelle Vague's leading directors include François Truffaut (e.g., *The Four Hundred Blows*, 1959), Jean-Luc Godard (e.g., *Breathless*, 1960), Claude Chabrol, Alain Resnais, Chris Marker, Agnès Varda, Jacques Demy, Éric Rohmer, and Louis Malle. While current French cinema is eclectic and individualistic, there have been a few noteworthy trends since the Nouvelle Vague, such as the *Cinéma du Look* in the 1980s and early 1990s (e.g., Luc Besson) and the New French Extremity (also called the Cinema of the Body) of the 2000s and 2010s. Leading French filmmakers of the present include Olivier Assayas, Jacques Audiard, Claire Denis, Arnaud Desplechin, Julia Ducourneau, Mia Hansen-Løve, Michel Hazanavicius, François Ozon, and Céline Sciamma. From the great fashion houses of the late nineteenth and early twentieth centuries (Worth, Rouff, Lanvin, Paquin, Poiret, Vionnet, and Patou) to the golden age of the 1920s and 1930s (Coco Chanel, Elsa Schiaparelli, and Nina Ricci) and the innovators of the postwar years (Gaby Aghion, Hubert de Givenchy, and Christian Dior), and from Yves Saint Laurent and his 1960s–1990s contemporaries (André Courrèges, Pierre Cardin, Sonia Rykiel, Karl Lagerfeld, Azzedine Alaïa, Thierry Mugler, Jean-Paul Gaultier, and Christian Lacroix) to the leading younger designers of today (e.g., Nicolas Ghesquière, Alexis Mabille, Maxime Simoëns, Hedi Slimane, Anthony Vaccarello, and Virginie Viard), France, via Paris, has maintained its status as the epicenter of world fashion.

Further Reading

Chastel (1994–1996); Fournier-Lanzoni (2015); Golbin (2017); Hanser (2005); Hayward (2005); Hunt and Conan (2002); Kirkland (2013); Lemoine (1998); Martigny (2008); Morrison and Compagnon (2010); Sutcliffe (1993); Williams (1992).

Contemporary Architecture

A good place to start when discussing French architecture of the past forty years is the series of presidential building projects that the French call *les grands travaux présidentiels*—a modern version of a tradition that dates back centuries (e.g., Louis XIV's expansion of Versailles in the seventeenth century and Napoleon III's transformation of Paris in the nineteenth). The prototype for this type of undertaking is the Centre Georges Pompidou in Paris, the ultramodern home of France's National Museum of Modern Art, designed by Renzo Piano and Richard Rogers. Presidential building projects were taken to a new height under François Mitterrand (1981–1995). Although many of the architects for the new monuments and cultural institutions were selected via international competitions, Mitterrand's personal preference was for stately yet unequivocally modernist buildings that reflected his administration's democratic ideal of "transparent" public access to art and culture. The list of Mitterrandian *grands travaux* in Paris includes the Institut du Monde Arabe (Jean Nouvel), Louvre Pyramid (I. M. Pei), Opéra Bastille (Carlos Ott), Grande Arche de La Défense (Johan Otto von Spreckelsen), the new Bibliothèque Nationale de France (Dominique Perrault), and Cité de la Musique (Christian de Portzamparc) located in La Villette park, also noteworthy for its deconstructed red "Follies" (Bernard Tschumi). The presidential building frenzy calmed somewhat after Mitterrand but did continue. The Musée du Quai Branly (Nouvel) was the pet project of Jacques Chirac. Nicolas Sarkozy spearheaded the Grand Paris initiative (announced 2007), an urban renewal and public transportation master plan designed to transform the Greater Paris area into a coherent, sustainable, and cutting-edge global metropolis by the year 2030. Sarkozy's successor, François Hollande, made a campaign promise to build Mémorial ACTe (Jean-Michel Mocka-Célestine, Pascal Berthelot, Mikaël Marton et Fabien Doré), a museum of the trans-Atlantic slave trade in Pointe-à-Pitre, Guadeloupe.

Portzamparc (b. 1944) and Nouvel (b. 1945) have both won the Pritzker Prize for architecture. The former designs buildings with an artistic flair (often white) and an integral sense of urban space and context and is considered the leading example of postmodernism among French architects. Noteworthy examples of his work include LVMH Tower in New York and *Le Monde* headquarters in Paris. The latter favors complex modern designs with unique atmospheric quality. Nouvel's other major projects include the Euralille center (Lille), Torre Glòries (Barcelona), Guthrie Theater (Minneapolis), Abu Dhabi Louvre, and Philharmonie de Paris concert hall. This prestigious prize was again awarded to French architects in 2021—partners Anne Lacaton (b. 1955) and Jean-Philippe Vassal (b. 1954), known for their stunning renovations, like the transformation of an industrial site into the FRAC Nord-Pas-de-Calais contemporary art center (Dunkirk), the renovation and expansion of the Art Deco Palais de Tokyo (Paris), and the modernist transformation of the Grand Parc social housing estate in Bordeaux. The prize citation lauded the duo for the "democratic spirit" of their work; their "commitment to a restorative architecture that is at once technological, innovative, and ecologically responsive" and "pursued without nostalgia"; and

The Institut du Monde Arabe (Arab World Institute, 1987) in Paris, designed by the Pritzker Prize-winning architect Jean Nouvel (b. 1945) in association with Architecture-Studio. It incorporates geometric patterns inspired by Islamic art with a sleek and high-tech modernist esthetic. The new building for the cultural institute was one of President François Mitterrand's "Grand Travaux" projects. The abstract sculpture in the foreground, *Geometry of the Spirit* (1987), is the work of the Jordanian artist Mona Saudi (1945–2022). (Jean Luc Azou/Dreamstime.com)

their renewal of the "legacy of modernism" and its "hopes and dreams to improve the lives of many."

Other renowned present-day French architects include Paul Andreu (CDG Airport Terminal 2E, Paris), Frédéric Borel (131 rue Pelleport, Paris); Patrick Bouchain (CCN dance center, Rieux-la-Pape [Lyon]); Anne Démians (Quai-Ouest, Nancy); Jean-Marie Duthilleul (train station addition, Strasbourg); FREAKS (MECA cultural center, Bordeaux); Jean de Gastines (Seine Musicale, Paris, with Shigeru Ban); Manuelle Gautrand (C42 Citroën showroom, Paris); Rudy Ricciotti (MuCEM, Marseille); Denis Valode and Jean Pistre (Tour Saint-Gobain, Paris), Jean-Paul Viguier (Tour Majunga, Paris), and Jean-Michel Wilmotte (Allianz Riviera Stadium, Nice). France is also known for its interior and industrial designers. The two most influential French designers of the past fifty years are Andrée Putman and Philippe Starck. The former was an avant-garde minimalist, whereas the latter is best known for his concept of "democratic design."

See also: Chapter 1: Cities; Paris. Chapter 2: Mitterrand (François) and France in the 1980s and 90s. Chapter 6: Suburbs. Chapter 12: Contemporary Art; Modern Architecture.

Further Reading
Fierro (2002); Jodido (2012); Jodido (2016); Jodido and de Portzamparc (2017); Yaari (2008).

Contemporary Art

Both in France and elsewhere, contemporary art emerged starting in the 1960s, when certain factors set it apart from the modern art that came before it. One was the proliferation of nontraditional media and practices, which supplanted painting and sculpture in critical significance. The inspiration for this revolution in media was a Frenchman, Marcel Duchamp (1887–1968), who pioneered the use of found objects (e.g., *Fountain*, 1913) and emphasized concept and context over the esthetics of the art object. In the 1960s and 1970s, this led to experiments with repurposed everyday materials (Arman, Jean Tinguely, Raymond Hains, Annette Messager); installations (Tania Mouraud, Christian Boltanski, Jean-Pierre Raynaud); happenings (Jean-Jacques Lebel, Robert Filliou); performances and body art (Gina Pane, Michel Journiac, ORLAN); public interventions (GRAV, Sociological Art Collective); video art (Jean-Luc Godard, Fred Forest, Carole Roussopoulos, Jean Dupuy, Thierry Kuntzel, Catherine Ikam); telecom, cybernetic, and interactive art (Aesthetics of Communication, Nicolas Schöffer, Jean-Louis Boissier, *Les Immatériaux* [exhibition] at the Centre Pompidou); land art (Christo and Jeanne Claude); opto-kinetic art (Victor Vasarely, Francisco Sobrino, Julio Le Parc, Jesús Rafael Soto, Yaacov Agam, Sarkis [Zabunyan]); conceptual art (Daniel Buren, Ben [Vautier], Bernar Venet, André Cadere, Philippe Thomas); and so on. These alternative forms of expression also pushed the traditional ones in the direction of less lyrical forms of abstraction and minimalism (Jean Dewasne, François Morellet, Simon Hantaï), deconstruction (Supports/Surfaces painters like Claude Viallat and Marc Devade), and conceptualism (Roman Opalka, Jean-Luc Vilmouth, Jean-Marc Bustamente, Bertrand Lavier). A second factor is the paradoxical status of much of this art with respect to the notion of the avant-garde. On the one hand, the driving force of much of contemporary art is systematic transgression that took aim at both art itself (e.g., the myths of modernist artistic freedom and individual genius) and prevailing social norms of good taste, morality, and even legality. A good example of the first type of transgression is Fred Forest's 1977 media operation, *The Artistic Square Meter* (based on advertisements that enticed people to buy tiny plots of rural land as dual investments in both real estate and art). Memorable examples of the second type include Michel Journiac's 1969 performance *Mass for a Body* (a parody of the Catholic mass in which the "eucharistic host" was a blood sausage made with the artist's own blood) and Sophie Calle's 1979 enigmatic photo-narrative *Suite Vénitienne* (for which the artist followed and photographed a stranger in the streets of Venice). On the other hand, countercultural transgression became no less a tradition than the history painting of old (Nathalie Heinich)—especially given the fact that while the general public and even some intellectuals remained dubious about the esthetic merits of contemporary art (e.g., the French contemporary art controversy, or *Querelle de l'art contemporain*, of the 1990s), art institutions were seemingly quick to accept anything and everything. In France, this paradox of esthetic doubt and institutional consecration is compounded by the degree to which the government is implicated in the art arena (e.g., the purchasing power of the FRACs, or Regional Funds for Contemporary Art, established in 1982). One reason for this public investment in contemporary art is to preserve the independence and uniqueness of the French art scene in the face of American hegemony and the globalization of taste and style (which does not mean that French artists do not closely follow and adopt international trends).

The emblematic figure of French contemporary art is Yves Klein (1928–1962). Klein made monochromatic paintings and mixed media works using his patented IKB (blue) paint, created conceptual artworks (e.g., sales of *Zones of Immaterial Pictorial Sensibility*, 1959–1962), experimented with performance (e.g., *Leap in the Void*, 1960), and staged public painting ceremonies involving nude models who became human brushes by smearing their bodies with IKB and leaving imprints on the canvas (*Anthropométries*) while musicians played a one-note score. Klein was a judo master and follower of Zen Buddhism for whom both the Void and IKB had spiritual connotations.

Following Klein's quasi-ascetic approach, one of the main preoccupations of French art in the 1960s and 1970s was the attempt to reconcile art with everyday life. One approach taken was that of Nouveau Réalisme (new realism), a group founded in 1960 by Pierre Restany and spearheaded by Klein. The Nouveaux Réalistes made art out of the commodities and detritus of mass culture—accumulations of discarded objects (Arman), junked cars (César), stripped away layers of street posters (Hains), objects or monuments wrapped in tarps (Christo), and paintings inspired by the old masters done in the kitsch style of advertising (Martial Raysse). Another approach was that of Narrative Figuration, a style of painting similar to American pop art, albeit more militant in its political and social critique. Representative works by members of this group include *Our Holy Mother the Cow* (1966) by Bernard Rancillac, *American Interior No. 1* (1968) by Erró, *Murder No. 10/2* (1968) by Jacques Monory, and *Boulevard des Italiens* (1971) by Gérard Fromanger.

The 1980s and 1990s were an eclectic period in French art. One important trend was multimedia fabrications of personal mythologies—idiosyncratic expressions of identity, enigmatic glimpses of the private lives and obsessions of artists, and ambiguous sites of memory. Examples include Boltanski's works dealing with the Holocaust (e.g., *Lycée Chases Altar*, 1986–1987), Anne and Patrick Poirier's sculptures and installations incorporating fragments of faux ancient ruins, the kitschy and erotic gay iconography of Pierre et Gilles, and much of the work of Calle (b. 1953), who explores issues related to intimacy, loss, and ephemeral connectedness. For *The Sleepers* (1979), she photographed strangers she had invited to sleep in her bed; for *The Hotel* (1981), she took a job as a housekeeper in a hotel and photographed the personal effects of the occupants of the rooms she cleaned; for *Take Care of Yourself* (2007), she solicited a series of videos in which over 100 different women interpreted a break-up email that she had received from her lover. A second major trend of the postmodern decades was Figuration Libre (launched in 1981), an individualistic approach figurative painting often in sync with both art history and the edgier side of popular culture (e.g., graffiti and comics). The movement's representative artists included Robert Combas (e.g., *Couple psychopatex*, 1995), Hervé Di Rosa, François Boisrond, Jean-Michel Alberola, and Jean-Charles Blais. Although not affiliated with Figuration Libre, Gérard Garouste (b. 1946) is often mentioned in the same context, although his inspirations include classicism, mythology, religion, and popular legends (e.g., *Chartres*, 2007). A third important trend of the period was the growing interest French artists took in digital media and the internet. Forest (b. 1933) was a pioneer in this respect. Following his involvement as a cofounder of the Sociological Art Collective (1970s) and the Aesthetics of Communication group (1980s), Forest was one of the first French artists to create participatory works/events on the internet that reflected on the medium's social and existential impact (e.g., *Time-Out*, 1998; *The Center of the World*, 1999). Other noteworthy French digital artists include Maurice Benayoun, Grégory Chatonsky, and Miguel Chevalier.

From the 1960s to the present, some of the most groundbreaking French artists have been women, including Louise Bourgeois (1911–2010), Niki de Saint Phalle (1930–2002), Annette Messager (b. 1943), ORLAN (Mireille Porte, b. 1947), and Calle. Known for the recurring motif of the spider (a maternal image) in her work, Bourgeois's later installations, like *The Destruction of the Father* (1974) and the *Cells* series of the 1980s and 1990s, offer compelling glimpses into the artist's inner world, memories, domestic life, and identity as a woman. Saint Phalle was affiliated with the Nouveaux Réalistes and collaborated with major American avant-garde figures like John Cage, Jasper Johns, and Robert Rauschenberg. Early in her career, she "painted" by using a shotgun to explode paint cans placed in front of assemblages (e.g., *Tirs*, 1961). She went on to create her "Nana" series featuring colorful sculptures of curvaceous goddess-like women (e.g., *Hon*, 1966; *Tarot Garden*, 1998). In the early phase of her career, Messager focused on cultural projections of women's social identity and body image in a series of scrapbook-like themed albums (1971–1974) with titles reminiscent of articles in women's magazines (e.g., *Handbook of Everyday Magic, My Guide for Knitting, Practical Life, Women I Admire, Before and After*) and in groups of small framed pictures of body parts, usually suspended from the ceiling (e.g., *My Vows*, 1988–1991). Later, she created installations in which deceptively childish, enigmatic, and disconcerting arrays of everyday objects (e.g., articles of clothing and stuffed animals) are suspended in a gallery or hung on the walls. ORLAN's early work consisted of striking feminist performances centered on her body (e.g., *MesuRAGEs*, c. 1968; *The Artist's Kiss*, 1977). She later took this focus on the body to an extreme with a series of plastic surgery performances called *The Reincarnation of Saint Orlan* (1990–1995), during which her body was reshaped according to stereotypes of feminine beauty from the history of art.

A visitor explores a photographic installation by the street artist and photo-muralist known simply as JR (b. 1983). Part of his ongoing community-based public participation project, *Inside Out* (2011–present), *To the Pantheon!* (2014) consisted of self-portraits and selfies of ordinary people uploaded to the project website or made in JR's travelling photo van at different national monuments. It derives special significance from the fact that the Pantheon in Paris, an eighteenth-century neoclassical former church (arch. Jacques-Germain Soufflot), is a secular shrine where many of France's great men and women are buried: e.g., Josephine Baker (1906–1975) was reinterred there in 2021. (Minacarson/Dreamstime.com)

Among the younger generation of French artists, those with the highest profile internationally include Pierre Huyghe (b. 1962), Kader Attia (b. 1970), Lili Reynaud-Dewar (b. 1975), Camille Henrot (b. 1978), and JR (b. 1983). Huyghe's early work included site-specific conceptual installations (e.g., *Billboards*, 1994–1995) and film "remakes" that revealed complex layers of narratives and temporalities (*The Third Memory*, 2000—based on *Dog Day Afternoon*). More recent work involves complex, open systems that take on a life of their own in space and time (*UUmwelt*, 2018–2019). Attia's acclaimed work explores the themes of injury and repair with a particular focus on colonialism, postcolonialism, and migration (e.g., *The Repair: From Occidental to Extra-Occidental Cultures*, 2012; *Reflecting Memory*, 2016). The winner of the 2021 Prix Marcel Duchamp, Reynaud-Dewar reflects on the vulnerability of the marginalized and combines choreographic performances, installations, and films (e.g., *Teeth, Gums, Machines, Future, Society*, 2018; *Beyond the Land of Minimal Possessions*, 2019). Henrot is a sculptor, videographer (e.g., *Grosse Fatigue*, 2013), and creator of immersive environments that deal with existential and anthropological questions like the origins of the universe and the nature of myth. JR is a world-famous street artist whose large-scale communal/public participation photomural projects include *Face2Face* (2007), *Women Are Heroes* (2010), and *Inside Out* (begun in 2011). Other critically acclaimed French (and France-based) artists of the past two decades include Saâdane Afif, Gilles Barbier, Claude Closky, Clément Cogitore, Dominique Gonzalez-Foerster, Laurent Grasso, Thomas Hirschhorn, Fabrice Hybert, Marion Laval-Jeantet, Philippe Parreno, Bruno Peinado, Abraham Poincheval, Pierrick Sorin, Agnès Thurnauer, Barthélémy Toguo, Tatiana Trouvé, Nicole Tran Va Bang, Sarah Trouche, and Xavier Veilhan.

See also: Chapter 11: Literary Avant-Garde, 1950–1980. Chapter 12: Contemporary Architecture; French Cinema I (through the Nouvelle Vague); French Cinema II (since the Nouvelle Vague); Modern Art and the School of Paris.

Further Reading
Banai (2014); Bishop (2008); Cabañas (2013); DeRoo (2006); Dossin (2018); Ford (2005); Gumpert (1997); Heinich (2000); Killiam (2011); Leruth (2017); Millet (2006); Nayeri (2019); Storr (2016); Thompson and Remnant (2019); Wilson (2010); Woodruff (2020).

Fashion

Fashion (incl. designer *haute couture*) has a rich history in France, where it is viewed as both art and a major industry. Paris is not the only French city with a fashion scene, but it is still considered the epicenter of international fashion even though it faces stiff competition from New York, Milan, London, and other cities. Paris Fashion Week is highly anticipated the world over. It is overseen by the Fédération de la Haute Couture et de la Mode, which includes the Chambre Syndicale de la Haute Couture and two other bodies for ready-to-wear fashion and menswear.

Distinctly French fashion dates to the fifteenth century. Its economic importance was recognized in France in the seventeenth century by the royal finance minister Jean-Baptiste Colbert (1619–1683). Famous eighteenth-century fashion trendsetters include Queen Marie-Antoinette (1755–1793) and the male Incroyables and female Merveilleuses ("Incredibles" and "Marvelous") of the 1790s, whose extravagant dress represented a rebuke to the egalitarian austerity of the French Revolution. Modern French haute couture begins with the first great Parisian fashion houses founded in the latter part of the nineteenth and early twentieth centuries—Worth, Doucet, Rouff, Lanvin, Paquin, Poiret, Cheruit, Vionnet, and Patou. Women—Jeanne-Marie Lanvin (1867–1946), the four Callot sisters, and Madeleine Vionnet (1876–1975)—were the driving forces behind several of these prestigious houses.

Another woman, Gabrielle Bonheur "Coco" Chanel (1883–1971), was France's first great national fashion icon—and is still considered relevant. Chanel founded her house in 1909 and rose to prominence in the Roaring Twenties for her boyish *garçonne* look. She went on to champion simple elegance and a confident modern look that fitted the new roles that women were beginning to play in society. Iconic Chanel creations include her striped "Breton" shirts, versatile little black dresses, and tweed skirt suits—still a favorite of upscale working women. Chanel's contemporaries (and rivals) include the Italian-born designers Elsa Schiaparelli (1890–1973, house founded in 1927) and Nina Ricci (1883–1970, house founded in 1932). The former was close to artists like Jean Cocteau and Salvador Dali and infused high fashion with an avant-garde esthetic. Leading houses of the 1940s and 1950s include Balmain, Dior, Céline, Chloé, and Givenchy. Gaby Aghion of Chloé and Hubert de Givenchy were both forward-looking designers, but it was Christian Dior (1905–1957) who had the biggest impact in the late 1940s with his "New Look" style featuring rounded shoulders, cinched waists, and full A-line skirts evoking a bolder notion of femininity.

The greatest French fashion designer from the 1960s, 1970s, and 1980s is undoubtedly Yves Saint Laurent (YSL—1936–2008), who got his start with Dior and founded his own house in 1961. Saint Laurent revolutionized fashion by creating visionary designs inspired by the hip youth culture, avant-garde artists ranging from Piet Mondrian to Andy Warhol, North Africa and other global cultural influences, and a more androgynous view of women's fashion. Working with Pierre Bergé, YSL also revolutionized the fashion business by making designer *prêt-à-porter* (ready-to-wear) more important and implementing a modern marketing strategy that centered on the personality of the designer. Other leading Paris designers of the 1960s and 70s include André Courrèges (known for his space-age designs and as one of the inventors of the miniskirt), Pierre Cardin, Sonia Rykiel (known for her knitwear and "poor boy sweater"), and "agnès b." (Agnès Troublé—also very successful in *prêt-à-porter*.) A new generation of talented designers rose to fame in the 1980s and 1990s, including Azzedine Alaïa (known for his body-hugging designs in black), Thierry Mugler (the proponent of a structured and sometimes hard-edged sexiness), Jean-Paul Gaultier (an *enfant terrible* of fashion who created androgynous designs and was inspired by street fashion and popular culture), and Christian Lacroix (an eclectic designer known for his elegant prints and use of vivid Mediterranean colors). The 1990s and 2000s are also known for consolidation in the fashion industry. As a result, most of the great French houses and other famous creators of fashion, luxury goods, perfumes, and cosmetics (e.g., Louis Vuitton, Hermès, Laboutin, Bulgari, Piaget, Guerlain, and L'Oréal) are now part of international conglomerates. Throughout the present era, numerous talented foreign designers have come to Paris to work and make their name—Karl Lagerfeld (Germany), Paco Rabanne (Spain), Kenzo Takada (Japan), John Galliano (Great Britain), Tom Ford (United States), Raf Simons (Belgium), Alexander McQueen (Great Britain), Zuhair Murad (Lebanon), and Tuomas Merikoski (Finland).

There is no shortage of talented younger French designers working today. Some of the most acclaimed are Virginie Viard, Isabel Marant, Hedi Slimane, Nicolas Ghesquière, Alexandre Vauthier, Julie Fournié, Alexis Mabille, Guillaume Henry, Christelle Kocher, Anthony Vaccarello, Maxime Simoëns, Olivier Rousteing, Sébastien Meyer, Simon Porte Jacquemus, Arnaud Vaillant, and Marine Serre.

See also: Chapter 1: Paris. Chapter 4: Luxury Goods.

Further Reading

Charles-Roux (2005); Dimant (2016); Drake (2006); English (2013); Gautier (2011); Loriot (2011); Müller (2016); Parkins (2012); Steele (2017); Steele (2019); Troy (2002).

French Cinema I (through the Nouvelle Vague)

French cinema has a rich history and is highly regarded internationally for its artistic quality. The Lumière brothers—Auguste and Louis—invented the cinematograph and first used it to project a motion picture in 1895. Georges Méliès (1861–1938) was the first great French filmmaker, best known for his early experiments with special effects (e.g., *A Trip to the Moon*, 1902). The three most important styles in French cinema from the 1920s to the 1940s were impressionism, surrealism, and poetic realism. French impressionism placed emphasis on visual beauty and on the use of the camera and editing to evoke psychological moods. The term was applied to the silent films of Louis Delluc, Abel Gance (e.g., *Napoleon*, 1927), Jacques Feyder, Jean Epstein, Germaine Dulac, and Jean Renoir. Surrealist filmmakers were interested in the cinema's capacity to evoke subconscious thought and dreamlike states and emphasized jarring juxtapositions of images over the development of plot and character psychology. Notable surrealist filmmakers include René Clair (e.g., *Entr'acte*, 1924), Fernand Léger (e.g., *Magnetic Ballet*, 1924), and Luis Buñuel (e.g., *An Andalusian Dog*, 1929). Surrealism also influenced the films of Jean Cocteau (e.g., *The Blood of a Poet*, 1930; *Beauty and the Beast*, 1946; *Orpheus*, 1949). Approaching their work as proto-*auteurs*, the poetic realists of the 1930s and 1940s cast a critical eye on society, featured marginalized and working-class characters, and dealt extensively with the themes of hardship, disillusionment, nostalgia, fate, and death—often in a lyrical fashion. The leading representatives of this style were the later Feyder and Renoir, Jean Vigo, Julien Duvivier, and Marcel Carné. The poetic realists are responsible for some of the greatest films in cinema history—Vigo's *Zero for Conduct* (1933) and *L'Atalante* (1934); Duvivier's *They Were Five* (1936) and *Pépé le Moko* (1937); Renoir's *The Grand Illusion* (1937), *The Human Beast* (1938), and *The Rules of the Game* (1939); and Carné's *Port of Shadows* (1938), *Daybreak* (1939), and *The Children of Paradise* (1945). One of the most popular filmmakers of the 1930s and 1940s is Marcel Pagnol, who is best known for his Marseille Triology—*Marius*, 1931; *Fanny*, 1932; and *César*, 1937. A plethora of French film stars emerged from this first era of French cinema and became national cultural icons—Max Linder, Raimu, Fernandel, Jean Gabin, Jean Marais, Gérard Philippe, Arletty, Danièle Darrieux, Michèle Morgan, and Simone Signoret.

The 1950s and 1960s were a period of great artistic innovation in French cinema. On the one hand, there were the minimalists, known for their gritty thrillers and *film noir* crime dramas. The most noteworthy examples were Robert Bresson (e.g., *Pickpocket*, 1959), Henri-Georges Clouzot (e.g., *The Wages of Fear*, 1953; *Diabolique*, 1955), and Jean-Pierre Melville (e.g., *Bob the Gambler*, 1956; *The Red Circle*, 1970). On the other hand, there were the great comic films of Jacques Tati (1907–1982), who was known for his virtually silent Monsieur Hulot character—a clumsy and good-natured man hilariously ill at ease with modern life (e.g., *Monsieur Hulot's Holiday*, 1953; *My Uncle*, 1958; *Playtime*, 1967; and *Traffic*, 1971). Finally, and most importantly, there was the Nouvelle Vague (New Wave) revolution. Leading directors associated with the Nouvelle Vague were Claude Chabrol (1930–2010), Jacques Demy, Jean-Luc Godard (b. 1930), Chris Marker, Louis Malle, Alain Resnais, Jacques Rivette, Éric Rohmer, François Truffaut (1932–1984), and Agnès Varda (1928–2019). Another important figure in the movement was the film critic André Bazin, one of the cofounders of the influential journal *Les Cahiers du cinéma*. The movement's signature début films were Chabrol's *Le Beau Serge* (1958); Truffaut's *The Four Hundred Blows* (1959)—a semi-autobiographical coming-of-age story that was the first installment in a series of films that captured different moments in the life of Truffaut's Antoine Doinel character (played by Jean-Pierre Léaud); Resnais's *Hiroshima, Mon Amour* (1959, screenplay cowritten by Marguerite Duras); and Godard's *Breathless* (1960)—the story of a petty criminal (played by Jean-Paul Belmondo) and his idealistic American girlfriend (played by Jean Seberg). One of the defining features of the Nouvelle Vague was its insistence on artistic independence. In practical terms, this involved independence from the major studios (and hence low budget productions). In esthetic terms, it involved the concept of the director as *auteur*, whereby the director is the primary source of the film's concept and story and their personal artistic vision is valued over commercial success. Another feature was the iconoclastic break with the filmic and storytelling conventions of the film industry. This entailed prevalent use of hand-held cameras (i.e., the camera was not inconspicuous and thus made the visual experience more self-conscious), shooting on location (greater immediacy and naturalness), the expression of complex ideas without sacrificing visual directness, and explicit (and sometimes radical) social and political critique. Finally, the Nouvelle Vague was known for its distinctive style of editing, which included abrupt and sometimes disorienting transitions from one scene to the next (jump cuts). The production of the Nouvelle Vague filmmakers was prolific, diverse, and extended well into the 1970s, 1980s, and 1990s—and, in some cases, right up to the present, for example, Godard's *Goodbye to Language* (2014). They made films in nearly every genre—surrealistic narratives (e.g., Resnais's *Last Year at Marienbad*, 1961), romantic dramas (e.g., Truffaut's *Jules and Jim*, 1962), crime stories (e.g., Chabrol's *The Butcher*, 1970), science fiction (e.g., Marker's *La Jetée*, 1962; Godard's *Alphaville*, 1965), social satire (e.g., Godard's *Weekend*, 1967), comedy of manners (e.g., Rohmer's series, *Six Moral Tales*, 1963–1972; and later, *Comedies and Proverbs*, 1981–1987), historical films (e.g., Malle's *Lacombe Lucien*, 1974), literary adaptations (e.g., Rivette's *The Nun*, 1963), feminist cinema (e.g., Varda's *One Sings, the Other Doesn't*, 1977), documentary (Marker's *The Lovely Month of May*, 1963), fantasy (e.g., Rivette's *Céline and Julie Go Boating*, 1974), and even musicals (Demy's *The Umbrellas of Cherbourg*, 1964). It is hard to underestimate the influence that the Nouvelle Vague has had on independent filmmaking around the world.

See also: Chapter 11: Literary Avant-Garde, 1950–1980. Chapter 12: French Cinema II (since the Nouvelle Vague); Modern Art and the School of Paris. Chapter 15: Movies. Chapter 16: Television.

Further Reading
Abel (1984); Abel (1994); Andrew (1995); Crisp (1993); Turk (1989).

French Cinema II (since the Nouvelle Vague)

There were many talented directors working in a more conventional narrative vein in the 1970s, such as Claude Sautet (e.g., *Vincent, François, Paul, and the Others*, 1974), Bertrand Blier (*Going Places*, 1974), and Diane Kurys (*Peppermint Soda*, 1978). Their work offered insightful depictions of contemporary life and challenged social conventions. The 1980s featured well-made period films and literary adaptations such as Bertrand Tavernier's *A Sunday in the Country* (1984), Claude Berri's *Jean de Florette* (1986), Louis Malle's *Au Revoir, les Enfants* (1987), and Maurice Pialat's *Under the Sun of Satan* (1987). The two decades also produced a string of now-classic, popular comedies such as *Delusions of Grandeur* (Gérard Oury, 1971); *The Tall Blond Man with One Black Shoe* (Yves Robert, 1972); *The Wing or the Thigh* (Claude Zidi, 1976); *La Cage aux Folles* (Édouard Moulinaro, 1978); *The ComDads* (Francis Veber, 1983); *Three Men and a Cradle* (Coline Serreau, 1985); and *Life Is a Long Quiet River* (Étienne Chatiliez, 1988). Several of these comedies were remade in English by Hollywood.

Recent French filmmaking has been stylistically eclectic and individualistic, often striking balance between artistic invention and coherent storytelling. However, two trends have attracted special attention in the decades after the New Wave. One is the *cinéma du look* of the 1980s and early 1990s, which featured stylish hyperreal visuals, attractive and alienated young characters, a characteristically postmodern blend of high and pop culture, and a punkish attitude. The three directors most closely associated with the trend are Jean-Jacques Beneix (e.g., *Diva*, 1981), Luc Besson (e.g., *Subway*, 1985), and Leos Carax (e.g., *Bad Blood*, 1986). Besson later directed several successful films in English (e.g., *The Fifth Element*, 1997). The other trend, prevalent in the 2000s and 2010s, is referred to as the "New French Extremity" (James Quandt) or "Cinema of the Body" (Tim Palmer). Its hallmarks include graphic/provocative emphasis on the body, visceral sensation, extreme/transgressive sexuality, horror, violence, the weird, and deviant behavior. Directors associated with the trend include Alexandre Aja, Catherine Breillat, Bertrand Bonello, Carax, Claire Denis, Virginie Despentes, Julia Ducournau, Bruno Dumont, Christophe Honoré, Xavier Gens, Pascal Laugier, Gaspard Noé, François Ozon, Quentin Dupieux, and Marina de Van.

There are many other talented French directors who have made remarkable films since 1990. Examples include Olivier Assayas, Jacques Audiard, Xavier Beauvois (e.g., *Of Gods and Men*, 2010), Rachid Bouchareb, Laurent Cantet (e.g., *The Class*, 2008), Arnaud Desplechin, Philippe Garrel (*Jealousy*, 2013), Alain Giraudie, Lucile

Hadžihalilović, Mia Hansen-Løve, Michel Hazanavicius (e.g., *The Artist*, 2011), Agnès Jaoui (e.g., *The Taste of Others*, 2000), Jean-Pierre Jeunet, Mathieu Kassovitz (e.g., *La Haine*, 1995), Abellatif Kechiche (e.g., *Blue Is the Warmest Color*, 2013), Cédric Klapsich (e.g., *When the Cat's Away*, 1996), Mélanie Laurent, Patrice Leconte (e.g., *Ridicule*, 1999), Ladj Ly (*Les Misérables*, 2019), Katell Quillévéré (e.g., *Love Like Poison*, 2010), Céline Sciamma (e.g., *Tomboy*, 2011; *Portrait of a Lady on Fire*, 2019), André Techiné (e.g., *Wild Reeds*, 1994), and Rebecca Zlotowski (e.g., *Grand Central*, 2013).

The strength of current French cinema is demonstrated by the twenty-seven films made since 2000 that appeared on the list of the 100 greatest French-language films of all time compiled by *Paste* magazine (2018). They are: *The Gleaners and I* (Agnès Varda, 2000), *Hidden* (Michael Haneke [Austria], 2005), *Evolution* (Hadžihalilović, 2016), *Trouble Every Day* (Denis, 2001), *Beau Travail* (Denis, 2000), *Holy Motors* (Carax, 2012), *Elle* (Paul Verhoeven [Netherlands], 2016), *The Kid with a Bike* (Jean-Pierre and Luc Dardenne [Belgium], 2011), *Flight of the Red Balloon* (Hou Hsiao-Hsien [Taiwan], 2007), *Raw* (Ducournau, 2017), *A Christmas Tale* (Desplechin, 2008), *Things to Come* (Hansen-Løve, 2016), *Amour* (Haneke, 2012), *Girlhood* (Sciamma, 2014), *Fat Girl* (Breillat, 2001), *A Prophet* (Audiard, 2010), *Faces Places* (Varda and JR, 2016), *Stranger by the Lake* (Guiraudie, 2014), *The Triplets of Belleville* (Sylvain Chomet, 2003 [animated]), *Summer Hours* (Assayas, 2008), *Persepolis* (Marjane Satrapi and Vincent Paronnaud, 2007 [animated]), *Amélie* (Jeunet, 2001), *Martyrs* (Laugier, 2008), *Nocturama* (Bonello, 2016), and *Breathe* (Laurent, 2014).

Maintaining an economically strong and artistically independent French cinema and pushing for recognition that films should be treated differently than other goods freely traded in the global marketplace according to the logic of supply and demand are national domestic and foreign policy priorities in France. Government assistance to French filmmakers is provided through the National Center for Cinema and Animation, or CNC, an agency of the Ministry of Culture. The results have been mixed— while the dominance of Hollywood is undeniable, the French film industry today nonetheless ranks among the top ten in the world in terms of both the number of films produced and box office revenue. France's most prestigious film school is La Fémis (École Nationale Supérieure des Métiers de l'Image et du Son, founded in 1943 as IDHEC), now part of PSL Research University in Paris. Another major film institution is the Cinémathèque Française in Paris, one of the largest film archives in the world—founded in 1936 by Georges Franju and Henri Langlois. Major French film stars of the past fifty years include Jean-Paul Belmondo, Vincent Cassel, Alain Delon, Gérard Depardieu, Louis de Funès, Jean-Pierre Léaud, Thierry Lhermitte, Jean Reno, Pierre Richard, Michel Serrault, Isabelle Adjani, Stéphane Audran, Juliette Binoche, Sandrine Bonnaire, Marion Cotillard, Catherine Deneuve, Isabelle Huppert, Anna Karina, Sophie Marceau, and Audrey Tautou.

See also: Chapter 11: Reza (Yasmina) and Contemporary French Theatre. Chapter 12: French Cinema I (through the Nouvelle Vague); Ministry of Culture. Chapter 15: Movies. Chapter 16: Pop Culture Icons; Television.

Further Reading

Austin (2003); Austin (2008); Bey-Rozet (2021); Chareyron and Viennot (2019); Fox et al. (2015); Higbee (2013); Horeck (2011); LaSalle (2012); Marie (2003); Met and Schilling (2018); Neupert (2007); Neupert (2011); Palmer (2006); Palmer (2011); Powrie (1997); Quandt (2004); Rees-Robert (2008); Sellier (2008); Smith (2005); Tarr and Rollet (2016); West (2016).

CANNES FILM FESTIVAL

Founded as an alternative to the Venice Film Festival and first held in 1946, the Cannes Film Festival is one of the world's premier international film festivals. It is known for championing the artistic quality of films and is held annually in the month of May. The festival's juries—including its main jury—vary from one edition to the next and are comprised of and presided by respected film professionals (directors, producers, actors, cinematographers, critics, etc.). It screens films in several different categories. The official selection includes films in competition for the Palme d'Or (Golden Palm)—the festival's top prize (awarded to the best film)—as well as "Un Certain Regard" (unique works that reflect an wide array of cultural perspectives) and Out of Competition films. Parallel selections include the films featured in the International Critics Week and Directors' Fortnight series. The festival's other prestigious awards include the Grand Prix (second place); Prix du Jury (third place); Caméra d'Or (best first film); and awards for best director, actor, actress, screenplay, and short film.

Gothic Cathedrals

Gothic architecture originated in the Île-de-France region in the twelfth century, flourished in the northern part of France—agriculturally rich, economically prosperous, full of growing towns, and firmly under the control of the assertive Capetian monarchy—throughout the thirteenth, gradually spread to the rest of France and Europe, and became more ornate in the fourteenth century, before losing momentum in the fifteenth. The style's main structural feature was a ribbed vault consisting of intersecting pointed/broken arches, which, along with exterior flying buttresses, directed the weight away from the vaults. This allowed the vaults to be built higher and with more and larger stained-glass windows (e.g., circular rose windows), thereby creating spiritually stirring interior spaces that were soaring, vast, largely open, and often dazzlingly luminous. Based on a theology that associated God with light, luminosity was a property that was highly stressed by the style's first theorist and promoter, the abbot of Saint-Denis and royal advisor Suger (1081–1151). The term "Gothic" originated in the sixteenth century (i.e., French Renaissance) and was pejorative

The soaring interior and famous stained-glass windows of the cathedral of Chartres (1194–1220, Eur-et-Loir department, Centre-Val de Loire region). Chartres displays the pointed (ogival) arches and high ribbed vaulting characteristic of the gothic style. Chartres (91 km/56 mi from Paris) is located in the agriculturally rich natural region of the Beauce (still known as France's breadbasket), which is in the northern part of France, where gothic architecture got its start and first thrived before spreading to the rest of the country and throughout western Europe. (Claudio Giovanni Colombo/Dreamstime.com)

(a reference to the primitive Germanic Goths). In its own age, however, it was called the "modern style" and was the reflection of a humanistic form of Christianity that emphasized the imitation of a just and compassionate Christ, a balance of reason and emotion, and the maternal qualities of the Virgin Mary (many cathedrals were named for "Notre Dame," or "Our Lady"). Stained-glass windows offered edifying portrayals of the life and teachings of Christ, the lives of the apostles and saints, stories of Old Testament figures, and images of Christian society that were accessible to the faithful. Sculptures offered lessons about man's ultimate fate (e.g., portrayals of the Last Judgment) as well as images of optimism (e.g., the "Smiling Angel" of Reims) and beauty (ubiquitous statues of the Virgin and Child, the former elegantly posed and often wearing a queen's crown). The Annunciation was a favorite theme of altarpiece paintings, which included several fifteenth-century masterpieces (e.g., Aix and Moulins).

Gothic architecture is commonly divided into three periods—early Gothic (sometimes called "classical" Gothic, c. 1120–1200), high Gothic (or "rayonnant" Gothic, c. 1200–1350), and late Gothic (often called "flamboyant" Gothic, c. 1280–1500). Cathedrals took decades to build and were often started in one style and finished, or updated, in another. Notable examples of early Gothic architecture include the basilica of Saint-Denis (begun c. 1135), and the cathedrals of Noyon, Laon, and Paris (1160–1260), the last one being nearly destroyed by a fire that started in the roof (while the building was undergoing renovation) on April 15, 2019. Examples of high Gothic include the cathedrals of Chartres (1194–1220), Bourges, Amiens, Reims (1211–1345), and Strasbourg; and the Sainte Chapelle (part of the medieval royal palace complex on the Île de la Cité) in Paris. Examples of flamboyant Gothic include the north spire of Chartres, the cathedral of Rouen (western façade and towers, 1234–1530), the basilica of Notre-Dame d'Épine (Châlons-sur-Marne), and the church of Saint-Maclou (Rouen). Rediscovered by the romantics, Gothic architecture was revived in the nineteenth century. Leading examples include the final phase of the reconstruction of the cathedral of Orléans and the restoration of Notre-Dame de Paris (1845–1864) by Eugène Viollet-le-Duc.

See also: Chapter 1: Historical Sites; Paris. Chapter 2: Louis IX and the Capetian Dynasty. Chapter 4: Tourism. Chapter 5: Catholicism. Chapter 12: Loire Valley Châteaux; Versailles.

Further Reading

Ball (2008); Duby (1981); Frankl (2001); Poirier (2020); Sandron and Tallon (2020); Scott (2003); Sekules (2001).

Impressionism

Throughout the nineteenth century, French art was still largely in thrall to classicism. Some of the neoclassical painters produced compelling work (e.g., Jean-Auguste-Dominique Ingres, Pierre Puvis de Chavannes, Thomas Couture). However, for the most part, this persistent neoclassicism took the form of polished but uninspired academicism, the kind of pompous art on conventional historical and mythological themes and trending orientalist ones that was championed by the Académie des Beaux-Arts, which controlled access to the annual Paris Salon. Examples include the work of Alexandre Cabanel, Jean-Léon Gérôme, and William-Adolphe Bouguereau. The forward momentum that leads (in hindsight) to modern art thus begins with a break with classicism. One part of this break was romanticism, offering emotionally charged depictions of current events and exotic far-away lands (through the lens of French colonialism) that shook up classicism's emphasis on timeless archetypes, decorum, orderly compositional structure, and the restrained use of color—for example, the work of Eugène Delacroix (1798–1863; e.g., *Liberty Leading the People*, 1830, Théodore Géricault, and Théodore Chassériau). An arguably bigger break was caused by the realists, who stressed contemporaneity—namely that an artist "should be of his times" (in the words of Édouard Manet, 1832–1883)—and put this principle into practice by attempting to offer non-idealized and quasi-documentary depictions of the surroundings and lives of rural people and the working classes, among other real-life subjects. The most radical French realist in terms of both esthetics and politics was Gustave Courbet (1819–1877; e.g., *A Burial at Ornans*, 1849–1850). Other leading French realists include Honoré Daumier, Jean-Baptiste-Camille Corot, Théodore Rousseau, Jean-François Millet, Rosa Bonheur, and Jules Breton.

French impressionism is to be understood in the context of this break with classicism and the academy. The impressionists admired the iconoclastic audacity of Delacroix, continued the experiments in plein air painting and the immediate capture of visual experience of Camille Corot and the Barbizon School (portable easels and tubes of premixed paint facilitated this endeavor), and were interested in the implications of photography (e.g., their friend and patron Nadar). Above all, they were realists who trained their gaze on modern urban life—a new and quintessentially modern subject for art—and painted with approximate brushstrokes that captured evanescent nuances of light and color in specific circumstances as well as the energy and constant motion of the big city. This was all quite revolutionary and not infrequently considered bad art by establishment critics and the public—hence the need for the 1863 Salon des Refusés, a conciliatory gesture after works by Manet (*The Luncheon on the Grass*) and other progressive artists had been rejected by the conservative selection committee of the official salon. Moreover, the term "impressionism" itself was originally a derogatory reference to *Impression, Sunrise* (1874) by Claude Monet (1840–1926). The most prominent impressionist painters were Manet, Monet, Camille Pissarro (1830–1903), Edgar Degas (1834–1917), Pierre-Auguste Renoir (1841–1919), and Gustave Caillebotte (1848–1894). Other notable painters affiliated with the movement include, Alfred Sisley, Frédéric Bazille, Bethe Morisot, and Mary Cassatt. Manet defied esthetic and moral convention with *Olympia* (1863) and excelled at revealing snapshots of the Parisian social life (e.g., *A Bar at the Folies-Bergère*, 1882). Monet was a sensitive painter of outdoor scenes of all types (landscapes, seascapes, cityscapes, gardens)—for example, *La Grenouillère* (1869) and *Gare Saint-Lazare* (1877). Later in his career, he systematically painted the cathedral of Rouen (1892–1894) and the water lilies in his Japanese garden pond at Giverny (1899–1919) in all sorts of light and weather—leading to works that verged on the abstract. Degas was famously fascinated by horse races, the ballet (e.g., *The Dance Class*, 1874), and music hall scenes. However, he also made compelling images of modern urban *ennui* (e.g., *The Absinthe Drinker*, 1875–1876) and of nude bathers in intimate everyday poses. Possessing a delicate touch, Renoir excelled at portraits, domestic scenes (e.g., *Madame Georges Charpentier and Her Children*, 1878), images of leisure (e.g., *Luncheon of the Boating Party*, 1881). Caillebotte was an engineer by training, which perhaps accounts for his unique geometrical and structural sense of urban spaces (e.g., *Paris Street; Rainy Day*, 1877). His *Floor Scrapers* (1875) is one of the most famous depictions of manual labor in the century.

While impressionism was focused on capturing the real, it also liberated painting in terms of composition, color, the painter's subjectivity, and the physicality of touch as part of the final product. The varied painters who are loosely grouped together under postimpressionism pushed these innovations further in the direction of modernism. Key figures include Georges Seurat (e.g., *A Sunday Afternoon on the Island of La Grande Jatte*, 1884–1886), Paul Signac (e.g., *Portrait of Félix Fénéon*, 1890), Henri de Toulouse-Lautrec (e.g., *At the Moulin Rouge*, 1892), Vincent van Gogh (1853–1890; e.g., *The Starry Night*, 1889), Paul Gauguin (1848–1903; e.g., *Where Do We Come From? What Are We? Where Are We Going?*, 1897), and the later Paul Cézanne (1839–1906; e.g., *Mont Sainte-Victoire and Château Noir*, 1904–1906).

See also: Chapter 1: Paris. Chapter 2: Napoleon III and the Second Empire. Chapter 11: Novel in the Nineteenth Century. Chapter 12: Modern Art and the School of Paris.

Further Reading
Clark (1984); King (2006); King (2016); Loyrette (2007); Roe (2006); Shiff (2014); Thomson (2000).

Loire Valley Châteaux

Elegant examples of classically inspired French Renaissance architecture, the châteaux of the Loire Valley region in north-central France, are among the architectural wonders of the world (42 of them are part of the Loire Valley UNESCO world heritage site, but there are close to 300 throughout the region). Built or renovated mostly in the sixteenth century, the châteaux reflect two major cultural shifts in French history—a broader shift in the political and cultural center of gravity from Paris and the church to the Loire Valley and the monarchy (i.e., secular art and culture centered around the royal court and driven by renewed interest in classical antiquity and the spread of humanism), as well as the transformation of the castle from a warlord's stronghold into a luxurious residence for civilized princes and aristocrats. The Loire Valley was the primary locus of these shifts because it was located close to Paris and was one of the first areas brought under royal control—much of it held directly by the French kings as part of the royal domain—outside the Paris region (Île-de-France). It was also prosperous due to its fertile land and renowned vineyards and was covered in lush forests that were rich in game and therefore prized as hunting grounds by the kings and their traveling entourage.

Numerous Loire Valley châteaux were royal residences. Amboise was the boyhood home of Francis I and is the place where Leonardo da Vinci, a royal artist-in-residence, is buried. Originally a medieval fortress, it was given a large addition under Charles VII in the Italianate style beginning in 1495—the first such construction project in France. Blois is known for the spiral staircase that was built as part of its Renaissance-era wing during the reign of Francis I. Chambord (1514–1545) is the largest of the Loire Valley châteaux and the epitome of French Renaissance architecture (e.g., pitched roof of black slate and decorative turrets). Chenonceau was presented as a gift from King Henry II to his mistress and favorite, Diane de Poitiers. It is known for its arched gallery over the Cher River—designed by Philibert de l'Orme. Other notable royal châteaux in the Loire Valley include Angers, Chinon, Langeais, Loches, Saumur, and Tours. Many more Loire Valley châteaux were built and owned by prominent members of the nobility. The most famous is Azay-le-Rideau (1518–1527), the embodiment of French Renaissance refinement. Other noteworthy nonroyal châteaux in the region include Chaumont-sur-Loire, Gien, Sully-sur-Loire, Ussé (a source of inspiration for Disney's *Sleeping Beauty*), and Vallandry (known for its French gardens).

Geographically not part of the Loire Valley region, Fontainebleau is undoubtedly the most important of all French Renaissance châteaux. Its main phase of construction and decoration took place between 1528 and 1547, under Francis I. Nearly three centuries later, it became the favorite residence of Emperor Napoleon I. Under Francis, a lover of art and supporter of the humanists, it was an epicenter of the French Renaissance. The main architect was a Frenchman, Gilles Le Breton, who adapted classical influences to the French context. Francis brought in Italians like Rosso Fiorentino and Francesco Primaticcio for the important interior work (e.g., the Francis Gallery, 1533–1539). This blend of French and Italian elements gave rise to the influential School of Fontainebleau, the harbinger of a distinctively French national style in art. Major artists associated it include Jean Cousin the Elder, François Clouet, Antoine Caron, Germain Pilon, Ambroise Dubois, and Toussaint Dubreuil. However, some of the school's most famous paintings are by artists who have remained anonymous— for example, *Diana the Huntress* (c. 1550) and *Gabrielle d'Estrées and One of Her Sisters* (c. 1594). The precursors of French Renaissance painting include Enguerrand Quarton and Jean Fouquet, and the manuscript illuminations of the *Très Riches Heures du Duc de Berry* (1412–1416, 1440–1489) by the Limbourg brothers.

See also: Chapter 1: Historical Sites; Regional Identities; Rivers. Chapter 2: Francis I and the Renaissance. Chapter 4: Tourism. Chapter 12: Gothic Cathedrals; Versailles.

Further Reading

Marsh (2018); Pérouse de Montclos and Polidori (1997); Usher (2013); Zerner (2003); Zorach (2005).

Ministry of Culture

France has had a Ministry of Culture since 1959 when President Charles de Gaulle created it and appointed the writer André Malraux (1901–1976) as minister. However, the importance accorded to art and culture at the highest level of the French state has a much longer history. For instance, Alcuin of York (735–804) advised Charlemagne, and Abbot Suger of Saint-Denis (1081–1151) Louis VI and VII, on matters ranging from education to architecture. The Bourbon kings of the seventeenth and eighteenth centuries relied on both the royal academies and specially designated officeholders at court to ensure that the best in art and literature also served the greater glory of the king and absolute monarchy (e.g., Charles Le Brun, 1619–1690, First Painter to the King under Louis XIV). Prior to the creation of the modern ministry, various high-level officials (usually attached to the Ministry of Public Instruction) served as de facto ministers of culture, like Jean Zay (1904–1944), who served as minister of national education and fine arts in the Popular Front government (1936–1939); and Jeanne Laurent (1902–1989), who was in charge of theatre and music (1946–1952) at the Secretariat of State for Fine Arts.

The two most influential ministers of culture were Malraux (1959–1969) and Jack Lang (b. 1939), under François Mitterrand (1981–1986, 1988–1993). Malraux had an elitist view of culture that stressed the universal canonical great works of human civilization and modernism, and also shared de Gaulle's belief in France's *grandeur*. However, he also asserted that ordinary people had a right to great art and culture, and created a network of local *maisons de culture*. The charismatic Lang defended a more pluralistic notion of cultural democracy—one that blurred the line between high culture and popular culture and emphasized the spectacular. He was also one of the framers of the "cultural exception"—that in a globalized economy based on profit and free trade, cultural works ought not to be treated just like other goods. Lang's other priorities included carrying out Mitterrand's monumental building projects (e.g., Louvre Pyramid and Bastille Opera), support for contemporary creators in all fields, the decentralization of cultural institutions and policy making, and framing culture as an integral part of economic policy. While the ministry's mission has been scaled back somewhat in recent years, its interventionist approach and assertion of culture's centrality to France's identity as a democratic nation that both Malraux and Lang championed are well woven into the fabric of French public life, including among regional and local public officials.

The Ministry of Culture and its affiliated agencies have jurisdiction over a range of matters, including the national archives, monuments, and museums; national cultural celebrations (e.g., Printemps des Poètes, Fête de la Musique, Journées Européennes du Patrimoine); grants and subsidies for artists; the performing arts (e.g., orchestras, opera, dance, theater, and circus); public broadcasting; support for critical cultural industries like film, publishing, and popular music; advanced research in cultural fields; promotion of French culture abroad (via the Institut Français, jointly operated with the Ministry of Foreign Affairs); and statistical studies of French cultural practices. In 2019, the ministry's total budget was €10 billion, of which €3.86 billion was earmarked for public broadcasting and €3.63 billion for the ministry's core missions (incl. related personnel and pension costs). Using the latter figure as the reference, 0.93% of the budget was to be spent on culture—very closed to the symbolic yet budgetarily significant 1% target first set by Mitterrand and Lang. The budget included €899 million for the preservation of France's national heritage (incl. €456 million for national monuments); €780 million for artistic creation; €695 million in support of film, audiovisual, and video/computer game production; and €541 million for spending on cultural education and the "democratization" of culture. Another large budget line entailed €1.482 in culture-related tax credits.

See also: Chapter 1: Historical Sites. Chapter 2: Mitterrand (François) and France in the 1980s and 90s. Chapter 4: Budget, Debt, and Taxes. Chapter 12: Contemporary Art. Chapter 13: Fête de la Musique. Chapter 15: Movies; Museums. Chapter 16: Radio; Television.

Further Reading

Ahearne (2002); Bickerton (2016); Eling (1999); Lebovics (1999); Looseley (1995); Martin (2014); Pfleiger (2013); Poirrier (2003); Thévenin and Moeschler (2018).

Modern Architecture

The story of French modern architecture can be told through a look at the work of nine leading figures. Hector Guimard (1867–1942) is the most prominent French exponent of the Art Nouveau style characterized by elegant plant-like lines and a rhythmic fusion of structure and ornament. Guimard is remembered especially for his iconic Paris Métro entrances (1899–1900). By contrast, Tony Garnier (1869–1948) is better known for his theoretical work (e.g., functional zoning and the utopian *Cité industrielle*, 1904/1917). Auguste Perret (1874–1954) was a pioneer of the use of reinforced concrete (with Garnier) and practiced a sober and classically inclined version of the art deco style (sleek, sharp angles, abstract geometrical forms, exquisite modern decorative details). His early works include the Théâtre des Champs-Élysées (Paris, 1913) and Notre-Dame du Raincy church (suburban Paris, 1923). After World War II, Perret oversaw the rebuilding (1945–1964) of the center of the port city of Le Havre, which had been devasted by bombing raids. The towering figure of twentieth-century French architecture is Swiss-born Charles-Édouard Jeanneret (1887–1965), better known as Le Corbusier. A proponent of L'Esprit Nouveau, or new spirit, Le Corbusier took cues from industrial design (he famously declared that a house was a "machine for living in"); eschewed ornamental clutter and traditionalism; implemented "five points" of modern architectural design (reinforced concrete columns to relieve the need for load-bearing walls, open floor plans, façade design freed from structural constraints, horizontal windows for even interior light, and roof gardens); and adopted an integral approach to design that included the décor, objects for daily use, and broader urban fabric. His Modular Man human figure embodied a universal system of ideal proportions and was a key component of his designs. Le Corbusier's most famous projects include the Pavilion of the Esprit Nouveau (Paris, 1925), Villa Savoye (Poissy, 1931), Unité d'Habitation apartment building (Marseille, 1952), and planned city of Chandigarh, India (1951–1961). Le Corbusier's designs are sometimes criticized for being too rational and acontextual (e.g., the unrealized Plan Voisin [1925] and Ville Radieuse [1930]). However, he was also capable of poetry (e.g., Notre-Dame-du-Haut chapel in Ronchamp, 1955). Le Corbusier's contemporary, Robert Mallet-Stevens (1886–1945), created a synthesis of cubist influences, art deco, and the international style. He is best known for his designs for private residences (e.g., Villa Noailles, Hyères, 1928).

In the postwar years, the self-taught architect and industrial designer Jean Prouvé (1901–1984) designed prefabricated modernist gas stations (1953) and an easy-to-assemble modular home (the so-called "Better Days" house, 1956) as a means to alleviate a housing and homelessness crisis. Claude Parent (1923–2016) was the most influential avant-garde French architect of the 1960s and 1970s. He was associated with oblique function (the evocative use of inclined walls), brutalism (geometrical buildings that make abundant use of exposed raw [brut] reinforced concrete), and deconstructivism (asymmetrical, fragmented, and free-form designs). His noteworthy projects include Sainte Bernadette du Banlay church (Nevers, 1966; with Paul Virilio, his partner in Architecture Principe) and GEM shopping center (Sens, 1970). Jean Balladur (b. 1924) is best known as the architect of La Grande Motte (1965–1973), a resort community on the Mediterranean coast near the city of Montpellier. Émile Aillaud (1902–1988) was a utopian architect who attempted to disrupt the monotony and isolation of suburban housing projects with innovative designs (e.g., La Grande Borne, Grigny, 1971; and the so-called Cloud Towers, Nanterre, 1976).

See also: Chapter 1: Cities; Paris. Chapter 6: Suburbs. Chapter 12: Contemporary Architecture; Modern Art and the School of Paris.

Further Reading
Britton (2001); Cohen (2015); Curtis (2015); Lemoine (2000); Parent (2018).

Modern Art and the School of Paris

The term "School of Paris" ("École de Paris") refers not to a particular style or movement in the fine arts, but rather to Paris's ongoing status as the capital of the international avant-garde in the first half of the twentieth century, and to the wide range of artists (esp. painters) both French and foreign who lived and worked in Paris in those decades (e.g., the Montmartre and Montparnasse districts)—exchanging ideas about art and its role in society, moving between styles and movements, and pushing modern artistic expression beyond the limits of esthetic convention and bourgeois taste. Before the outbreak of World War I in 1914, Paris was a laboratory of artistic experimentation that included representatives of postimpressionism (Paul Cézanne); members of the Nabis group (e.g., Paul Sérusier, Pierre Bonnard, Édouard Vuillard); protomodern sculpture (Antoine Bourdelle, Aristide Maillol); fauvism (Henri Matisse, André Derain, Maurice de Vlaminck, Raoul Dufy); and cubism (Pablo Picasso, Georges Braque, Marie Laurencin, Juan Gris, Jean Metzinger, Robert Delaunay). It also included artists with distinctive individual styles like Marc Chagall, Fernand Léger, Tamara de Lempicka, Amedeo Modigliani, Chaïm Soutine, and Maurice Utrillo. Arguably, the two most influential artists of the era were the friends and rivals, Picasso (1881–1973) and Matisse (1869–1954), who embodied different paths for modern art. In Picasso, we find clinical decomposition (analytical cubism) and subjective recomposition (synthetic cubism) of the real based on multiple and relative points of view, formal innovation verging on abstraction, and esthetic engagement with the material and popular culture of the modern age (e.g., *Les Demoiselles d'Avignon*, 1907; *Ma Jolie*, 1911–1912; *The Guitar*, 1913; *Three Musicians*, 1921). In Matisse, we find the liberation of color and line, "primitive" simplicity, sensualism, and a utopian yearning for something beyond the soulless materialism of modernity (e.g., *Luxe, calme et volupté*, 1904; *View of Collioure*, 1905; *Harmony in Red*, 1908; *Dance*, 1910). Throughout the 1910s, 1920s, and 1930s, a number of Paris-based artists also experimented with abstraction. Among them, one finds the painters Sonia Terk-Delaunay (e.g., *Electric Prisms*, 1914; an example of Orphism), Sophie Taeuber-Arp (e.g., *Composition with Diagonals and Cross*, 1916), Auguste Herbin (e.g., *Composition monumentale*, 1919), Piet Mondrian (e.g., *Tableau 1*, 1921), and Jean Hélion (*Equilibre*, 1933–1934), and; and the sculptors Constantin Brâncuşi (e.g., *Bird in Space*, 1928), Jean Arp (e.g., *Human Concretion*, 1935), and Alberto Giacometti (e.g., *Woman with Her Throat Slit*, 1932). Sculptors working in a cubist vein include Henri Laurens, Jacques Lipchitz, and Ossip Zadkine (e.g., *The Beautiful Servant Girl*, 1928).

The senseless carnage of World War I (1914–1918) profoundly shook the Parisian avant-garde. One result was the emergence of two artistic movements that represented radical critiques of society and the humanist tradition. In the case of Dada, this meant anti-art that sought to destroy the myths of art itself (i.e., beauty, vision, originality, craft, coherence, progress, etc.). Among French adherents to Dada, Francis Picabia was known for his quasi-sexual imagery of machine parts, provocative antics, and derisive mixed media works like *Portrait of Cézanne, Portrait of Renoir, Portrait of Rembrandt* (1920) featuring a monkey doll. Foreshadowing the conceptual turn, embrace of the mundane, and institutional critique in contemporary art, Marcel Duchamp (1887–1968) created tongue-in-cheek conversation pieces that made use of found objects (e.g., the upside-down urinal called *Fountain*, 1917). Led by the poet André Breton (1896–1966), surrealism made an emancipatory appeal to the subconscious, the irrational, psychic automatism, chance, dreams, desire, phantasm, and the non-Western through literature, periodicals (e.g., *La Révolution surréaliste*, 1924–1929), graphic arts, photography (e.g., the work of the iconoclastic nonbinary artist Claude Cahun [Lucy Schwob, 1894–1954]), film, parlor games (e.g., the *cadavre exquis*), and assemblages of objects (e.g., Meret Oppenheim, *Luncheon in Fur*, 1936). Surrealism proved to be an especially fruitful source of inspiration for painters of various nationalities. The Paris surrealist group's leading painters were Max Ernst (e.g., *The Elephant Celebes*, 1921; *Europe after the Rain II*, 1942), Joan Miró (e.g., *The Harlequin's Carnival*, 1924–1925), Salvador Dali (e.g., *The Persistence of Memory*, 1931), André Masson (e.g., *Gravida*, 1939), and Yves Tanguy (e.g., *Indefinite Indivisibility*, 1942). The great Belgian surrealist René Magritte (1898–1967) had a three-year stay in Paris before returning to Brussels, where he painted his most famous works (e.g., *The Key to Dreams*, 1930). There were remarkable women artists affiliated with the Paris surrealists such as Leonor Fini (e.g., *The End of the World*, 1949), Dora Maar, Remedios Varo, Dorthea Tanning, Leonora Carrington (e.g., *Self-Portrait*, 1938), and Kay Sage.

Remnants of the School of Paris regrouped or returned from exile after World War II (1939–1942). They had to contend not only with the barbarism and devastation of the war, but also with new challenges such as the Cold War, decolonization, and the first inklings of a mass consumer society. Furthermore, the center of gravity of the art world was shifting away from Paris—most notably to New York, where many of the luminaries of the school had spent part of the war years. However, a younger generation of artists picked up the mantle of modernism and the term "New School of Paris" was applied loosely to much of the art produced in France in the latter part of the 1940s and 1950s. Three new trends merit special attention. First, there were the styles of abstract painting—Art Informel, Tachisme, Abstraction Lyrique—seen as the French response to American abstract expressionism. Representatives of this trend include Jean Bazaine, Jean Fautrier, Hans Hartung, Jean Messagier, Georges Mathieu (e.g., *The Battle of Hastings*, 1956), Serge Poliakoff, Pierre Soulages (e.g., *Peinture, 195 x 130 cm, mai 1953*), Nicolas de Staël (e.g., *Le Lavendou*, 1952), and Maria Helena Vieira da Silva. Second, there was art brut, a subcurrent of outsider art. The leader of the movement was Jean Dubuffet (1901–1985), most famous for his *Hourloupe* cycle (1962–1974). For Dubuffet (other representatives include Gaston Chaissac, Roger Chomeaux, and Robert Tatin), art brut involved the kind of "raw" and untrained expression of emotion that one found in primitivism (e.g., works by prison inmates and the insane), graffiti, and the artwork of children. Third, there were artists creating novel sorts of figurative works, for instance, the "miserabilist" paintings of the neo-expressionist Bernard Buffet, the political works of the neo-realist André Fougeron (e.g., *Atlantic Civilization*, 1953), and the now controversial eroticized depictions of young girls spied in moments of reverie by Balthus (Balthasar Klossowski de Rola). It was also during the late 1940s, 1950s, and 1960s that France's two greatest humanist photographers and pioneers of photojournalism, Henri Cartier-Bresson (1908–2004) and Robert Doisneau (1912–1994), did their best work.

See also: Chapter 1: Paris. Chapter 11: Literary Avant-Garde, 1950–1980; Poetry (Modern and Contemporary); Twentieth-Century Literature through Mid-Century (Novel and Theatre). Chapter 12: Contemporary Art; French Cinema I (through the Nouvelle Vague). Chapter 13: Overview; Classical Music; Dance.

Further Reading

Antliff and Leighten (2001); Birnbaum (2011); Caws (2004); Green (2001); Hopkins (2016); Kuenzli (1990); Meisler (2015); Roe (2015); Roe (2019); Scott (2007); Seigel (1986); Wilson et al. (2002).

Versailles

Located approximately 19 km (12 mi) south of Paris, the Palace of Versailles was France's primary royal residence, center of court life, and seat of government from 1682 until 1789. Today, it is one of the most visited tourist sites in France. It began (1623–1624) as a hunting lodge under King Louis XIII, who later transformed it into a small chateau (1631–1634). Following the civil war and rebellion against the monarchy known as the Fronde (1648–1653), his son, Louis XIV, embarked on the first (1664–1668) of four massive expansion projects at the chateau and surrounding estate. It was in the third phase (1678–1684), that Louis made Versailles his primary residence and moved the royal court and government there. At its height, over 3,000 members of the royal family, courtiers, government officials, and servants lived in the 700-room palace. The total cost of the expansion and renovations was staggering and placed great strain on royal finances. For Louis XIV, Versailles was intended as an overwhelming illustration of royal absolutism and a testimony to his own personal glory and refinement—a microcosm of the sovereign imposing his will and sense of order on the kingdom that would awe visitors. It was also the backdrop for a never-ending series of carefully choreographed rituals and elaborate spectacles that revolved around the king's every move and were meant to occupy the prestige-hungry upper tier of the nobility (and thereby neutralize potential rivals to the king).

Versailles is an example of the French baroque style (from the 1610s to the 1770s). Compared to the variations of the style in Germany, Italy, and Spain, French baroque adhered more closely to the models provided by classical antiquity and placed greater emphasis on sober authority, harmony, symmetry, and uncompromising geometrical rigor (for these reasons, it is also called French classicism and classical baroque). What made it baroque was its ornate ornamentation and carefully constructed aura of dramatic tension—as well as its totalistic, theatrical, and ultimately plastic approach to space. As such, it is a prime example of Christian Norberg-Schulz's assertion that the *capital city* as a comprehensive whole is the highest expression of the baroque vision. The individuals most responsible for the look of Versailles were the architects Philibert Le Roy, Louis Le Vau, Jacques Hardouin-Mansart (1646–1708), and Ange-Jacques Gabriel; the painter and decorator Charles Le Brun (1619–1690); and the landscape architect André Le Nôtre (1613–1700). The major architectural features of Versailles include the immense royal courtyard and smaller marble courtyard, the sumptuous royal apartments, the hall of mirrors (with allegorical ceiling paintings by Le Brun celebrating the accomplishments of Louis XIV, presented in the guise of a Roman emperor), the royal opera, the floral *parterres* and fountains of its gardens (incl. the fountain of Apollo, featuring the Greek sun god rising from the sea in a four-horse chariot), grand canal (creating an illusion of infinite extension), and the more intimate Grand Trianon and Petit Trianon (best known as the private retreat of Queen Marie Antoinette, the wife of Louis XVI).

There are many other illustrious examples of seventeenth-century classical baroque architecture in France. In Paris, there is the Place des Vosges, Luxembourg Palace, Palais-Royal, Hôtel de Sully, Sorbonne chapel, Val-de-Grace church, Institut de France, Hôtel des Invalides, and Place Vendôme. Beyond Paris, major examples include Vaux-le-Vicomte château, Place de la Bourse (Bordeaux), and Place Stanislas (Nancy).

See also: Chapter 1: Historical Sites; Paris. Chapter 2: Louis XIV and the Absolute Monarchy. Chapter 6: Nobility. Chapter 11: Seventeenth-Century Theatre. Chapter 12: Loire Valley Châteaux. Chapter 13: Classical Music; Dance; Opera.

Further Reading

Goldstein (2008); Jones (2018); Mérot (1995); Norberg-Schulz (2003); Spawforth (2008); Tadgell (2020); Thompson (2006).

LOUVRE

France's longtime official royal palace, the Louvre (Paris) dates to a medieval fortress that Philip Augustus began building in the late twelfth century. It was expanded multiple times from the sixteenth through the nineteenth centuries. Its noteworthy features are its Renaissance Lescot wing (1546–1551), designed by Pierre Lescot; its baroque Pavillon de l'Horloge (1624–1645), designed by Jacques Lemercier; and the classical colonnaded east façade (1665–1668), designed by Claude Perrault. In the 1850s, Napoleon III built two new wings in the ornate Beaux-Arts style. They connected the Old Louvre to the sixteenth- and seventeenth-century Tuileries Palace (arch. Philibert de l'Orme et al.), the customary residence of French kings and emperors. The latter was burned to the ground during the Commune of 1871. The Louvre Museum, a creation of the French Revolution, grew out of the former royal art collection. The transformation of the entire Louvre into a museum (Grand Louvre) began in the 1980s with the evacuation of the Ministry of Finance and the construction of I. M. Pei's at first highly controversial glass pyramid.

SELECTED BIBLIOGRAPHY

Abel, Richard. *The Ciné Goes to Town: French Cinema, 1896–1914*. U California P, 1994.

Abel, Richard. *French Cinema: The First Wave, 1915–1929*. Princeton UP, 1984.

Ahearne, Jeremy, ed. *French Cultural Policy Debates: A Reader*. Routledge, 2002.

Andrew, Dudley. *Mists of Regret: Culture and Sensibility in Classic French Film*. Princeton UP, 1995.

Antliff, Mark, and Patricia Leighten. *Cubism and Culture*. Thames and Hudson, 2001.

Austin, Guy. *Contemporary French Cinema: An Introduction*. 2nd ed. Manchester UP, 2008.

Austin, Guy. *Stars in Modern French Film*. Bloomsbury, 2003.

Ball, Philip. *Universe of Stone: Chartres Cathedral and the Invention of the Gothic*. Harper Collins, 2008.

Banai, Nuit. *Yves Klein*. Reaktion, 2014.

Bey-Rozet, Maxime. "Cycles of Death and Rebirth in Twenty-first Century French Horror." *French Screen Studies*, vol. 21, no. 3, pp. 191-203.

Bickerton, Emilie. "Has the French Culture Ministry Lost Its Way?" *Apollo*, 27 Jun. 2016, https://www.apollo-magazine.com/has-the-french-culture-ministry-lost-its-way/.

Birnbaum, Paula J. *Women Artists in Interwar France: Framing Femininities*. Routledge, 2011.

Bishop, Michael. *Contemporary French Art 1: Eleven Studies*. Rodopi, 2008.

Britton, Karla. *Auguste Perret*. Phaidon, 2001.

Cabañas, Kaira M. *The Myth of Nouveau Réalisme: Art and the Performative in Postwar France*. Yale UP, 2013.

Caws, Mary Ann. *Surrealism*. Phaidon, 2004.

Chareyron, Romain, and Gilles Viennot, eds. *Screening Youth: Contemporary French and Francophone Cinema*. Edinburgh UP, 2019.

Charles-Roux, Edmonde. *Chanel and Her World*. Vendome, 2005.

Chastel, André. *French Art*. Trans. Deke Dusinberre. Flammarion, 1994–1996. 4 vols.

Clark, T. J. *The Painting of Modern Life: Paris in the Art of Manet and His Followers*. Knopf, 1984.

Cohen, Jean-Louis. *France: Modern Architectures in History*. Trans. Christian Hubert. Reaktion, 2015.

Crisp, Colin. *The Classic French Cinema, 1930–1960*. Indiana UP, 1993.

Curtis, William J. R. *Le Corbusier: Ideas & Forms*. 2nd rev. ed. Phaidon, 2015.

DeRoo, Rebecca. *The Museum Establishment and Contemporary Art: The Politics of Artistic Display in France after 1968*. Cambridge UP, 2006.

Dimant, Elyssa. *The New French Couture: Icons of Paris Fashion*. Harper, 2016.

Dossin, Catherine, ed. *France and the Visual Arts since 1945: Remapping European Postwar and Contemporary Art*. Bloomsbury, 2018.

Drake, Alicia. *The Beautiful Fall: Fashion, Genius, and Glorious Excess in 1970s Paris*. Little Brown, 2006.

Duby, Georges. *The Age of the Cathedrals: Art and Society, 980–1420*. Trans. Eleanor Levieux. U Chicago P, 1981.

Eling, Kim. *The Politics of Cultural Policy in France*. Palgrave Macmillan, 1999.

English, Bonnie. *A Cultural History of Fashion in the 20th and 21st Centuries: From Catwalk to Sidewalk*. 2nd ed. Bloomsbury, 2013.

Fierro, Annette. *The Glass State: The Technology of the Spectacle, Paris 1981–1998*. MIT P, 2002.

Ford, Simon. *The Situationist International: A User's Guide*. Black Dog, 2005.

Fournier-Lanzoni, Rémi. *French Cinema from Its Beginnings to the Present*. 2nd ed. Bloomsbury, 2015.

Fox, Alistair, et al., eds. *A Companion to Contemporary French Cinema*. Wiley-Blackwell, 2015.

Frankl, Paul. *Gothic Architecture*. 2nd rev. ed. Yale UP, 2001.

Gautier, Jérôme. *Chanel: The Vocabulary of Style*. Yale UP, 2011.

Golbin, Pamela, ed. *Fashion Forward: 300 Years of Fashion*. Rizzoli, 2017.

Goldstein, Claire. *Vaux and Versailles: The Appropriations, Erasures, and Accidents That Made Modern France*. U Pennsylvania P, 2008.

Green, Christopher. *Art in France, 1900–1940*. Yale UP, 2001.

Gumpert, Lynn, ed. *The Art of the Everyday: The Quotidian in Postwar French Culture*. New York UP, 1997.

Hanser, David A. *Architecture of France*. Greenwood, 2005.

Hayward, Susan. *French National Cinema*. 2nd ed. Routledge, 2005.

Heinich, Nathalie. "From Rejection of Contemporary Art to Culture War." *Rethinking Comparative Cultural Sociology: Repertoires of Evaluation in France and the United States*, eds. Michèle Lamont and Laurent Thévenot. Cambridge UP, 2000, pp. 170–210.

Higbee, Will. *Post-Beur Cinema: North African Emigré and Maghrebi-French Filmmaking in France since 2000*. Edinburgh UP, 2013.

Hopkins, David, ed. *A Companion to Dada and Surrealism*. Wiley, 2016.

Horeck, Tanya, ed. *The New Extremism in Cinema: From France to Europe*. Edinburgh UP, 2011.

Hunt, John Dixon, and Michel Conan. *Tradition and Innovation in French Garden Art: Chapters of a New History*. U Pennsylvania P, 2002.

Jodido, Philip. *Architecture in France*. Taschen, 2016.

Jodido, Philip. *Nouvel*. Tachen, 2012.

Jodido, Philip, and Christian de Portzamparc. *Portzamparc Buildings*. Rizzoli, 2017.

Jones, Colin. *Versailles: Landscape of Power and Pleasure*. Head of Zeus, 2018.

Kirkland, Stephane. *Paris Reborn: Napoléon III, Baron Haussmann, and the Quest to Build a Modern City*. St. Martin's, 2013.

Killiam, Marie-Therese. *The End of Art: A Comparative Analysis of French Postmodern Art Theorists*. Common Ground, 2011.

King, Ross. *The Judgment of Paris: The Revolutionary Decade That Gave the World Impressionism*. Walker, 2006.

King, Ross. *Mad Enchantment: Claude Monet and the Painting of the Water Lilies*. Bloomsbury, 2016.

Kuenzli, Rudolf E., and Francis M. Naumann. *Marcel Duchamp: Artist of the Century*. MIT P, 1990.

Lankarani, Nazanin. "French-Algerian Artist Explores Identity and Repair." *The New York Times*, 11 Jun. 2013, https://nyti.ms/19heyS1.

LaSalle, Mick. *The Beauty of the Real: What Hollywood Can Learn from Contemporary French Actresses*. Stanford UP, 2012.

Lebovics, Herman. *Mona Lisa's Escort: Andre Malraux and the Reinvention of French Culture*. Cornell UP, 1999.

Lemoine, Bertrand. *Architecture in France 1800–1900*. Trans. Alexandra Bonfante-Warren. Abrams, 1998.

Lemoine, Bertrand. *Birkhauser Architectural Guide: France 20th Century*. Trans. Sarah Parsons. Birkhauser, 2000.

Leruth, Michael F. *Fred Forest's Utopia: Media Art and Activism*. MIT P, 2017.

Looseley, David L. *The Politics of Fun: Cultural Policy and Debate in Contemporary France*. Bloomsbury, 1995.

Loriot, Thierry-Maxime, ed. *The Fashion World of Jean Paul Gaultier: From the Sidewalk to the Catwalk*. Abrams, 2011.

Loyrette, Henri, ed. *Nineteenth Century French Art: From Romanticism to Impressionism, Post-Impressionism and Art Nouveau*. Trans. David Radzinowicz. Random House, 2007.

Marie, Michel. *The French New Wave: An Artistic School*. Trans. Richard Neupert. Blackwell, 2003.

Marsh, Terry. *Châteaux of the Loire*. Michelin, 2018.

Martigny, Vincent. "The Importance of Culture in Civic Nations: Culture and the Republic in France." *Studies in Ethnicity and Nationalism*, vol. 8, no. 3, 2008, pp. 543–559.

Martin, Laurent. "The Democratisation of Culture in France in the Nineteenth & Twentieth Centuries: An Obsolete Ambition?" *International Journal of Cultural Policy*, vol. 20, no. 4, 2014, pp. 440–455.

Meisler, Stanley. *Shocking Paris: Soutine, Chagall and the Outsiders of Montparnasse*. St. Martin's, 2015.

Mérot, Alain. *French Painting in the Seventeenth Century*. Trans. Caroline Beamish. Yale UP, 1995.

Met, Philippe, and Derek Schilling, eds. *Screening the Paris Suburbs: From the Silent Era to the 1990s*. Manchester UP, 2018.

Millet, Catherine. *Contemporary Art in France*. Trans. Charles Penwarden. Flammarion, 2006.

Morrison, Donald, and Antoine Compagnon. *The Death of French Culture*. Trans. Andrew Brown. Polity, 2010.

Müller, Florence, ed. *Yves Saint Laurent: The Perfection of Style*. Skira Rizzoli, 2016.

Nayeri, Farah. "We Need to Talk about Colonialism, This Artist Says." *The New York Times*, 25 Feb. 2019, https://nyti.ms/2GKWY0C.

Neupert, Richard. *French Animation History*. Wiley, 2011.

Neupert, Richard. *A History of the French New Wave Cinema*. 2nd ed. U Wisconsin P, 2007.

Norberg-Schulz, Christian. *Baroque Architecture*. 3rd ed. Phaidon, 2003.

Palmer, Tim. *Brutal Intimacy: Analyzing Contemporary French Cinema*. Wesleyan UP, 2011.

Palmer, Tim. "Style and Sensation in the Contemporary French Cinema of the Body." *Journal of Film and Video*, vol. 58, no. 2, 2006, pp. 22–32.

Parent, Chloé, ed. *Claude Parent: Visionary Architect*. Rizzoli, 2018.

Parkins, Ilya. *Poiret, Dior and Schiaparelli: Fashion, Femininity and Modernity*. Bloomsbury, 2012.

Pérouse de Montclos, Jean-Marie, and Robert Polidori. *Chateaux of the Loire Valley*. Trans. Paul Aston. Könemann, 1997.

Pfleiger, Sylvie. "Financing the Arts in France." *ENCATC: Journal of Cultural Management and Policy*, vol. 3, no. 1, 2013, https://www.encatc.org/media/2692-encatc_journal_vol3_issue_1_2013415.pdf.

Poirier, Agnès. *Notre-Dame: The Soul of France*. One World, 2020.

Poirrier, Philippe. "Heritage and Cultural Policy in France under the Fifth Republic." *International Journal of Cultural Policy*, vol. 9, no. 2, 2003, pp. 215–225.

Powrie, Phil. *French Cinema in the 1980s: Nostalgia and the Crisis of Masculinity*. Clarendon P, 1997.

Quandt, James. "Flesh & Blood: Sex and Violence in Recent French Cinema." *Artforum International*, vol. 42, no. 6, 2004, pp. 126-132.

Rees-Roberts, Nick. *French Queer Cinema*. Edinburgh UP, 2008.

Roe, Sue. *In Montmartre: Picasso, Matisse and the Birth of Modernist Art.* Penguin, 2015.

Roe, Sue. *In Montparnasse: The Emergence of Surrealism in Paris, from Duchamp to Dalí.* Penguin, 2019.

Roe, Sue. *The Private Lives of the Impressionists.* Harper, 2006.

Sandron, Dany, and Andrew Tallon. *Notre Dame Cathedral: Nine Centuries of History.* Trans. Lindsay Cook. Penn State UP, 2020.

Scott, Clive. *Street Photography: From Atget to Cartier-Bresson.* Tauris, 2007.

Scott, Robert A. *The Gothic Enterprise: A Guide to Understanding the Medieval Cathedral.* U California P, 2003.

Seigel, Jerrold. *Bohemian Paris: Culture, Politics, and the Boundaries of Bourgeois Life, 1830–1930.* Viking, 1986.

Sekules, Veronica. *Medieval Art.* Oxford UP, 2001.

Sellier, Geneviève. *Masculine Singular: French New Wave Cinema.* Trans. Kristin Ross. Duke UP, 2008.

Shiff, Richard. *Cezanne and the End of Impressionism: A Study of the Theory, Technique, and Critical Evaluation of Modern Art.* U Chicago P, 2014.

Smith, Alison. *French Cinema in the 1970s: The Echoes of May.* Manchester UP, 2005.

Spawforth, Tony. *Versailles: A Biography of a Palace.* St. Martin's, 2008.

Steele, Valerie, ed. *Paris, Capital of Fashion.* Bloomsbury, 2019.

Steele, Valerie. *Paris Fashion: A Cultural History.* 3rd ed. Bloomsbury, 2017.

Storr, Robert. *Intimate Geometries: The Art and Life of Louise Bourgeois.* Monacelli, 2016.

Sutcliffe, Anthony. *Paris: An Architectural History.* Yale UP, 1993.

Tadgell, Christopher. *The Louvre and Versailles: The Evolution of the Proto-typical Palace in the Age of Absolutism.* Routledge, 2020.

Tarr, Carrie, and Brigitte Rollet. *Cinema and the Second Sex: Women's Filmmaking in France in the 1980s and 1990s.* Bloomsbury, 2016.

Thévenin, Olivier, and Olivier Moeschler. "The Changing Role of the Cultural State: Art Worlds and New Markets—A Comparison of France and Switzerland." *Art and the Challenge of Markets: National Cultural Politics and the Challenges of Marketization and Globalization*, eds. A. Alexander, et al. Palgrave Macmillan, 2018, pp. 125–153.

Thompson, Ian. *The Sun King's Garden: Louis XIV, Andre Le Nôtre and the Creation of the Gardens of Versailles.* Bloomsbury, 2006.

Thompson, Nato, and Joseph Remnant. *JR: Can Art Change the World?* Rev. ed. Phaidon, 2019.

Thomson, Belinda. *Impressionism: Origins, Practice, Reception.* Thames & Hudson, 2000.

Troy, Nancy J. *Couture Culture: A Study in Modern Art and Fashion.* MIT P, 2002.

Turk, Edward Baron. *Child of Paradise: Marcel Carné and the Golden Age of French Cinema.* Harvard UP, 1989.

Usher, Philip John. *Epic Arts in Renaissance France.* Oxford UP, 2013.

West, Alexandra. *Films of the New French Extremity: Visceral Horror and National Identity.* McFarland, 2016.

Williams, Alan. *Republic of Images: A History of French Filmmaking.* Harvard UP, 1992.

Wilson, Sarah. *The Visual World of French Theory: Figurations.* Yale UP, 2010.

Wilson, Sarah, et al., eds. *Paris: Capital of the Arts, 1900–1968.* Royal Academy of Art, 2002.

Woodruff, Lily. *Disordering the Establishment: Participatory Art and Institutional Critique in France, 1958–1981.* Duke UP, 2020.

Yaari, Monique. *Rethinking the French City: Architecture, Dwelling, and Display after 1968.* Rodopi, 2008.

Zerner, Henri. *Renaissance Art in France: The Invention of Classicism.* Trans. Deke Dusinberre, et al. Flammarion, 2003.

Zorach, Rebecca. *Blood, Milk, Ink, Gold: Abundance and Excess in the French Renaissance.* U Chicago P, 2005.

CHAPTER 13

MUSIC AND DANCE

OVERVIEW

The musical culture of France is rich and encompasses a wide variety of traditions, genres, and styles ranging from traditional folk music and dance and classical music and ballet to *chanson*, *bal-musette*, jazz, rock, pop, and hip-hop. Public support for music and dance is demonstrated by Ministry of Culture programs and subsidies for the arts, the construction of impressive new concert venues like the Philharmonie de Paris, the existence of hundreds of music and dance festivals throughout the country (including the annual nationwide celebration of the Fête de la Musique on June 21), and laws that are designed to protect the linguistic and musical heritage of France by ensuring that songs in French get a fair share of airtime. Music and dance have long been showcases of cultural diversity and *métissage* in France. This diversity encompasses the traditions of France's regions and far-flung overseas departments and territories as well as the contributions of expatriates, immigrants, and ethnically diverse artists through the centuries (e.g., Lully, Gluck, Offenbach, Diaghalev, Piaf, Rossi, Brel, Dalida, Moustaki, Khaled, Solaar, etc.). Artists from around the world come to Paris to perform, collaborate, and record. France's multicultural suburbs are incubators of talented artists and new styles in sync with global trends. Furthermore, France embraces the music of other French-speaking countries and regions of the world (e.g., Québec, Louisiana, Belgium, Switzerland, and the former French colonies of the Maghreb and sub-Saharan Africa). Music helps to forge a bond among French people that spans generations, ethnicity, and genres. This can be seen in the popular musical variety shows on French television, which are fond of staging reviews of the "classics" of French songs in which one is as likely to find Belgian pop sensation Stromae's global hit "Tous les mêmes" (2013), rapper MC Solaar's cheeky "Bouge de là" (1991), and Renaud's tongue-in-cheek ode to a housing project apartment building "Dans mon HLM" (1980) as Claude François's searing "Comme d'habitude" (1967), Johnny Hallyday's rock ballad "Que je t'aime" (1969), pop crooner Joe Dassin's charming "Le petit pain au chocolat" (1969), and Charles Trenet's ebullient "Y' a de la joie" (1938).

Although France's rich, varied, and centuries-old folk music heritage eroded considerably in the face of migration, urbanization, and the advent of national mass culture in the nineteenth and twentieth centuries, it experienced a resurgence in the 1950s, 1960s, and 1970s that included both "traditionalists" and "modernists." Certain French regions have maintained more vibrant traditional music scenes. These regions include Brittany, the mountainous central part of France (e.g., Auvergne and Limousin), French Basque Country, Gascony, Provence, and Corsica. The music of Brittany is Celtic and has points in common with the music of Ireland and Great Britain. The traditional music of Auvergne is one of the sources of the Parisian popular musical genre of bal-musette, known for its use of accordions (an Italian contribution to the genre). Corsican music is known for a style of polyphonic singing called *paghjella*.

With antecedents stretching back to the Middle Ages and Renaissance, French classical music took shape at the French court in the seventeenth century, where composers wrote music for *ballets de cour* (King Louis XIV was a skilled dancer who took part in many productions), operas, and royal ceremonies and celebrations. The leading French composers of the baroque and classical eras (1600–1750 and 1750–1820, respectively) were Jean-Baptiste Lully, Marc-Antoine Charpentier, Jean-Philippe Rameau, François Couperin, Jean-Marie Leclair, François-Joseph Gossec, and André Grétry. The later history of musical theater in France encompasses Italian-style *opera seria* (a French version of which was called *tragédie en musique*), French-style *opéra comique* (which used spoken dialogue rather than recitative), grand opera, and operetta (e.g., the work of Jacques Offenbach). The romantic era (1820–1900) was a period of greatness in French music. Leading French romantic composers include Hector Berlioz, Charles Gounod, César Franck, Camille Saint-Saëns, Georges Bizet, Jules Massenet, and Emmanuel Chabrier. The romantic era also saw a great resurgence of French ballet in which prima ballerinas emerged as the stars. French composers played an important part in the modernization of Western classical music from the 1880s through the 1930s. Examples include the work of Claude Debussy, Gabriel Fauré, Maurice Ravel (like Debussy, often identified as a musical impressionist), Erik Satie, and the composers known as Les Six (incl. Darius Milhaud and Francis Poulenc). During the same era, France (esp. Paris) was also a locus of innovation in choreography, for example, the innovative productions of Sergei Diaghalev's Paris-based Ballets Russes and later choreographers like Serge Lifar and Maurice Béjart. The most noteworthy French figures in music in the latter part of the twentieth century include the composer Olvier Messaien, the electronic music pioneer Pierre Schaeffer (one of the originators of *musique concrète*), and the composer and conductor Pierre Boulez. Jazz has found receptive audiences in France. With the help of American expatriates, France developed its own jazz scene in the 1920s and numerous major American jazz greats, from Sydney Bechet to Bud Powell and Miles Davis, have made France their home for a time. The most famous French style of jazz is the so-called gypsy jazz style (*jazz manouche* in French) made famous in the 1930s by the Belgian-born French Romani guitarist Django Reinhardt and his violinist, Stéphane Grappelli. The manouche style still has many talented French practitioners today.

A wide variety of genres and styles of popular music are prevalent in France today. The most French is chanson, a style of song that has its roots in the Parisian music halls and cabarets of the nineteenth century. Chanson places greater emphasis on the quality of the song lyrics—stories of passionate love, tales of the triumphs and travails of Bohemian artists and working-class people, odes to liberty and resistance, and poetic or humorous observations about everyday life—with music that essentially follows the rhythm of the French text. The 1950s and 1960s were a golden age of chanson. Leading artists of the era include Charles Aznavour, Barbara, Georges Brassens, Jacques Brel, Léo Ferré, Serge Gainsbourg, Yves Montand, and the legendary Édith Piaf. Following a period in the shadow of rock and pop, chanson experienced a resurgence beginning in the 1990s and is now attracting a new generation of talented young artists (e.g., Bénabar, Vincent Delerm, Renan Luce, Juliette Noureddine, Zaz, Pomme, Leïla Huissoud).

France's first native rock and roll-inspired style of pop music was *yé-yé* in the early 1960s—a cultural phenomenon that helped to launch the careers of Sheila, Sylvie Vartan, France Gall, Françoise Hardy, Johnny Hallyday (the "French Elvis"), Eddy Mitchell, and Claude François. From the 1970s to the present, France has seen a steady stream of talented performers who have achieved national—and, rarely, international—fame in various genres of rock and pop music, including singer-songwriters, pop-inflected *chanson de variété*, punk, disco, R&B, heavy metal, new wave, alternative rock, world music, and neo-musette. Contemporary French artists have shown particular strength in two areas—electronic/electro/techno/house/synth-pop music (e.g., Daft Punk, David Guetta, St. Germain, Air, Jacques, Sébastien Tellier) and hip-hop/rap (beginning with iconic 1990s acts like MC Solaar, Assassin, Suprême NTM, Ministère AMER, IAM, and Fonky Family and continuing through current artists like Keny Arkana, Bigflo & Oli, Booba, Casey, Chilla, La Fouine, Maître Gims, Kery James, Abd al Malik, Médine, MHD, Nekfeu, PNL, Sexion d'Assault, Sianna, and Soprano). A product *la banlieue*, the French rap scene is one of the most dynamic and creative in the world outside the United States.

Further Reading

Guibert and Rudent (2018); Jones (2022); Kelly (2008); Looseley (2003); Pasler (2009); Portis (2004); Trezise (2015); Watkins (1994).

Chanson

The French popular song tradition of chanson (*chanson* is the French word for "song")—featuring solo singers performing lyrical works that treat themes of love, social critique, and everyday life in a poetic, realistic, or satirical fashion—has roots that date back to the Middle Ages and the courtly love ballads of the *trouvères*, the twelfth- and thirteenth-century northern counterparts of the southern French troubadours (who sang in Occitan). Burgundian songs of the fourteenth and fifteenth centuries—typically in one of the three traditional medieval formats (*ballade, rondeau*, and *virelai*)—and Parisian songs of the sixteenth century, which were homophonic, are other important precursors to the chanson tradition. The genre developed considerably with urbanization in the nineteenth and twentieth centuries. The greatest *chansonnier* (songwriter) of the first half of the nineteenth century was Pierre-Jean de Béranger (1780–1857), whose works expressed a liberal and populist attitude and often criticized the government (esp. the monarchy), the clergy, and the bourgeoisie. The Parisian *cafés-concerts* (music halls) and cabarets (e.g., Le Moulin Rouge and Le Chat Noir, both in the Bohemian district of Montmartre) during the Belle Époque (1871–1914) were very important for the development of French chanson and also gave rise to the related genre of cabaret song. In this milieu, romantic ballads, humorous vaudeville-inspired musical numbers, social satires in the tradition of Béranger, and more radical protest songs coexisted alongside the emergent *chanson réaliste* genre. While the legendary cabaret performer Aristide Bruant (1851–1925) is often considered the genre's founder, its most famous practitioners were women like Thérésa, Mistinguett (Jeanne-Marie Bourgeois, 1875–1956), Fréhel, Yvonne George, and Édith Piaf (1915–1963). Realist songs dealt with the hardships of the inhabitants of the poorer Parisian faubourgs, the colorful life of the streets, prostitution, and the criminal underworld, as well as with stories of passionate love and the suffering endured in its loss. Piaf, the greatest French *chanteuse* of all time, touched on these themes in her iconic songs—"Les Mômes de la cloche," "L'Accordéoniste," "La Vie en rose," "Hymne à l'amour," "La Foule," "Milord," and "Non, je ne regrette rien." Charles Trenet (1913–2001), who was known for a light-hearted, whimsical, and sentimental style (e.g., "Boum!," "La Mer," "Y'a d'la joie," "Que reste-t-il de nos amours?," "Ménilmontant," and "Douce France"), was arguably the greatest male *chanteur* of the 1940s. Maurice Chevalier (1888–1972) was an international ambassador of French cabaret singing and had a prosperous career in Hollywood from the 1930s through the 1960s.

In the twentieth century, French chanson intersected with the musical style known as *musette* (also called *bal-musette*), which is known for its characteristic use of accordions and is widely identified as the sound of Paris. The genre's name derives from the colloquial name for a type of bellows-based bagpipe that was widely used in the folk music of the Auvergne region. Auvergnats migrated to Paris in large numbers during the industrial revolution. Many became proprietors of cafés, which often provided musical entertainment in the Auvergnat style. This music absorbed many influences in the course of its development into *musette*—including that of American jazz, gypsy music (especially in the *manouche* style of guitar playing), and Italian folk music (Italian immigrants were responsible for the introduction of the accordion, which later replaced the bagpipes). *Bal-musette* is closely associated with the java style of dancing popular from the 1910s through the 1950s—a fast-paced type of waltz that used small steps and was markedly sensual (e.g., the once scandalous placement of the male dancer's hands on the hips or buttocks of his female partner).

The golden age of French chanson spans the 1950s to the early 1970s, between the end of World War II and the emerging dominance of rock and roll and commercial pop music. In addition to established artists like Piaf and Trenet, the leading representatives of this golden age include Salvatore Adamo, Hugues Aufray, Charles Aznavour (1924–2018), Barbara (Monique Andrée Serf, 1930–1997), Guy Béart, Gilbert Bécaud, Georges Brassens (1921–1981), Jacques Brel (1929–1978), Jean Ferrat (1930–2010), Léo Ferré (1916–1993), Juliette Gréco, Mireille Mathieu, Yves Montand (1921–1991), Georges Moustaki (1934–2013), Serge Reggiani, Serge Rezvani, and Boris Vian (1920–1959). Many of these artists were known for the poetic quality of the lyrics they sang—in some instances, adapted from the works of well-known poets like Louis Aragon and Jacques Prévert. A writer, friend of Left Bank intellectuals like Jean-Paul Sartre and Simone de Beauvoir, and major figure of the French jazz scene, Vian is best known for his antiwar song "Le Déserteur." Brel (e.g., "Ne me quitte pas"—widely considered the greatest love song in the French language) was Belgian but did most of his recording in Paris, where he lived for many years. Brassens, a French southerner, was known for songs that exemplified an independent spirit and often included an element of tongue-in-cheek social satire (e.g., "La Mauvaise reputation"). Ferré (e.g., "Avec le temps"), was steeped in classical music and is considered a fine poet in his own right. Ferrat (e.g., "Nuit et brouillard") was a leftist and sang about political and social issues. Montand, best known for his rendition of "Les Feuilles mortes" ("Fallen Leaves"), also had an illustrious career as an actor. Aznavour (e.g., "La Bohème") had a career that spanned eight decades—he achieved international superstardom later in life and was given a state funeral in 2018. Barbara wrote and sang songs of great emotional depth and delicate melancholy (e.g., "L'Aigle noir," "La Solitude," "Ma plus belle histoire d'amour," and "Göttingen").

The chanson tradition opened itself to new influences and trends in the 1970s, 1980s, and early 1990s through the work of artists like Pierre Bachelet, Michel Berger, Francis Cabrel, Alain Chamfort, Dalida (Iolanda Gigliotti), Joe Dassin, Brigitte Fontaine, Serge Gainsbourg (1928–1991), Jacques Higelin, Maxime Le Forestier, Claude Nougaro, Renaud (Renaud Séchan), Véronique Sanson, Michel Sardou, and Alain Souchon. Gainsbourg's work incorporated the stylings of jazz, pop, rock, reggae, new wave, disco, and hip-hop, and challenged societal norms with eccentric and sexually explicit content (e.g., "Je t'aime ... moi non plus") in a series of critically acclaimed concept albums. Souchon produced a string of fine songs (e.g., "J'ai dix ans" and "Ultra moderne solitude") and albums, many in collaboration with fellow singer-songwriter Laurent Voulzy—a successful long-standing partnership for which they have been called "the French Lennon & McCartney" (Peter Hawkins). Dassin incorporated an easy listening pop musical esthetic ("L'Été indien"); Cabrel (e.g., "L'Encre de tes yeux" and "Je l'aime à mourir") and Renaud (e.g., "L'Hexagone," "Laisse béton," and "Mistral gagnant") were influenced by American popular music, including country and folk-rock; Nougaro ("Tu verras") was an accomplished jazz singer; Higelin recorded some fine rock-inspired music before returning to chanson ("Tombé du ciel"). By contrast, Pierre Perret's extensive body of work dating back to the 1950s represented continuity with tradition.

Since the late 1990s, the chanson genre has enjoyed a resurgence and has been embraced by a new generation of artists—hence the label *nouvelle chanson* is sometimes used—including Juliette Armanet, Bénabar (Bruno Nicolini), Benjamin Biolay, Mathieu Boogaerts, Françoiz Breut, Anne Cherhal, Coralie Clément, Pauline Croze, Camille (Dalmais), Daniel Darc, Vincent Delerm, Thomas Fersen, Christina Goh, Arthur H (Higelin), Hoshi (Mathilde Gerner), Leïla Huissoud, Indila (Adila Sedraïa), Keren Ann (Zeidel), Renan Luce, Maëlle (Pistoia), Ben Mazué, Christophe Miossec, J.P. Nataf, Juliette Noureddine, Pomme (Claire Pommet), Olivia Ruiz, Émilie Simon, Mano Solo (Emmanuel Cabut), and Zaz (Isabelle Geffroy). Compared to other

French singer-songwriter Zaz (Isabelle Geffroy, b. 1980) performing on stage in 2016 at the Francofolies music festival in Bulgaria (an associate member country of the Organisation Internationale de la Francophonie). One of the most popular French musical artists of today, Zaz's style ranges from jazzy pop to chanson. Her bestselling studio albums include her self-titled début, *Zaz* (2010), featuring the hit single "Je veux" ("I want"), and her Paris-themed album of covers of iconic French songs from 1930s to the 1960s, *Paris* (2014). (Sergey Kan/Dreamstime.com)

members of their generation who are immersed in the international pop-rock culture, these artists are drawn to chanson out of a commitment to the poetic quality of their lyrics and the unique rhythms of the French language. In addition to its importance to French linguistic heritage, chanson is culturally significant other ways. Beloved French songs from earlier decades, which are frequently featured on French musical variety shows on television and covered by younger artists, contribute to an intergenerational cultural bond. Furthermore, artists of various national and ethnic origins—Piaf had Italian and Moroccan Berber roots on her mother's side, Aznavour was Armenian, Montand was Italian, Dalida was born in Egypt to Italian parents, Dassin was a Brooklyn-born American with Ukrainian and Polish Jewish roots, Moustaki was Egyptian with Italo-Greek Jewish roots (origins he famously sang about in "La Métèque"), Indila's roots are very multicultural (Indian, Algerian, Egyptian, and Cambodian), and Karen Ann is Israeli—have found a musical home and an inclusive form of Frenchness in the genre.

See also: Chapter 1: Paris. Chapter 9: Francophonie; Language Laws and Policies. Chapter 13: Fête de la Musique; Folk Music; Jazz; Rock, Pop, and Rap. Chapter 15: Cafés. Chapter 16: Pop Culture Icons; Radio.

Further Reading

Bret (1999); Cordier (2013); Cordier (2014); Hawkins (2017); Haworth (2015); Haworth (2018); Lebrun (2014); Looseley (2015); Papanikolaou (2007); Salie (2022); Tinker (2006).

Classical Music

The French tradition of classical music—broadly understood as encompassing all conventional art music dating back to the Middle Ages—is rich and innovative. While many of the most famous household names among classical composers are Germanic (e.g., Bach, Handel, Mozart, Beethoven, Brahms, and Wagner), music critic Igor Toronyi-Lalic has written in *The Spectator* (2014) that French composers like Berlioz, Debussy, and Boulez actually did "most of the heavy lifting" to move classical music forward, and credits the under-recognized eighteenth-century French composer Jean-Philippe Rameau in particular for having "invented the French sound world" and initiated his compatriots' longstanding and fruitful "obsession with color, melodic heartache, and formal weirdness."

French contributions to the music of both the Middle Ages—*ars antiqua*, the Notre Dame School of polyphony, the development of the motet, the ballads of the troubadours and trouvères, *ars nova*, Guillaume de Machaut, *ars subtilor*, the Avignon School, and Baude Cordier—and the Renaissance—the Burgundian School, Josquin des Prez, Clément Janequin, Claudin de Sermisy, and Parisian chanson—are noteworthy. However, the French tradition in classical music truly began to take shape at the court of Louis XIV during the baroque era, when leading composers wrote music for *ballets de cour*, operas, and other musical genres that entertained the king and the rest of the aristocratic elite, but also glorified the former and celebrated absolute monarchy. Part of the monarchy's wide-ranging efforts to both exert control over and foster well-ordered excellence in the arts was the founding of the Académie d'Opéra in 1669, renamed the Académie Royale de la Musique in 1671. The leading French composers of the baroque era (i.e., the seventeenth and the first half of the eighteenth centuries) were Jean-Baptiste Lully (1632–1687), Marc-Antoine Charpentier, Marin Marais, Jean-Philippe Rameau (1683–1764), François Couperin, and Jean-Marie Leclair. Lully and Rameau were the dominant musical figures at the court. While music for ballet and opera were of paramount importance, major French schools of musical composition for the organ, harpsicord, violin, and lute also flourished during the same period.

France did not produce a noteworthy crop of composers in the properly classical vein, the dominant style from 1750 to 1820—attributable in part to the disruption caused by the French Revolution (1789–1799). However, its most prominent composers of the latter part of the eighteenth century and first two decades of the nineteenth wrote extensively for the opera. They include François-Joseph Gossec (1734–1829), André Grétry, Étienne-Nicolas Méhul, and Daniel Auber. By contrast, the romantic era (roughly 1830–1900) was a time of brilliance for French music. The four giants of French romantic music are Hector Berlioz (1803–1869), Georges Bizet (1838–1875), Camille Saint-Saëns (1835–1921), and Gabriel Fauré (1845–1924). Famous as the author of *La Symphonie fantastique* (1830), Berlioz was a radical in his time as well as a consummate romantic who believed that music should be driven by intense emotion and dramatic storytelling. Bizet is best known for his legendary Spanish-themed opera *Carmen* (1875). Saint-Saëns wrote a wide range of works, including the violin showpiece *Introduction and Rondo Capriccioso* (1863), the eerie tone poem *La Danse macabre* (1878), five symphonies (the most famous being No. 3, the "Organ Symphony" of 1886), and the whimsical *Carnival of the Animals* (1886). While Fauré wrote some major orchestral works (e.g., *Pavane*, 1887) too, he is best known for his songs (e.g., "Après un rêve," 1878) and chamber works (esp. for piano). Fauré's daring harmonic progressions helped pave the way for more modern musical experimentation but were always softened by an unostentatiousness and elegant touch. Other noteworthy French composers of the romantic era and style include Emmanuel Chabrier, Cécile Chaminade, Ernest Chausson, Vincent d'Indy, Paul Dukas, Charles Gounod, César Franck, Édouard Lalo, Jules Massenet, Jacques Offenbach, and Charles-Marie Widor.

Hector Berlioz (1803–1869) is the greatest French classical composer of the early Romantic era. His most famous works are his *Symphonie Fantastique* (1830) and *Requiem* (1837). France's other acclaimed composers include Lully, Charpentier, Rameau, and Couperin in the Baroque era; Grétry in the Classical era; Bizet, Massenet, Saint-Saëns in the later Romantic era; Fauré, Debussy, and Satie in the transition from romanticism and musical impressionism to modernism during the Belle Époque (late nineteenth and early twentieth century); Ravel and Poulenc in the early twentieth century, and Messiaen in the postwar era. (Musée Carnavalet)

During the Fin de Siècle and first decades of the twentieth century, Claude Debussy (1862–1918), Erik Satie (1866–1925), and Maurice Ravel (1875–1937) helped push classical music in the direction of modernism. The work of Debussy, arguably the most influential French composer of all time, is often characterized as "impressionist" (a term the composer loathed) and atmospheric (accurate, albeit simplistic). A better comparison would be to the symbolists and decadents—he was a friend of Stéphane Mallarmé, whose work (like Debussy's) was alternately spiritual, oneiric, sensual, synesthetic, iconoclastic, free-form, and abstract. Debussy may have had a painter's sensibility, but his evocative soundscapes ultimately exemplified music for music's sake and challenged audiences to listen closely. Debussy sought to break free of Western conventions of structure and tone (e.g., he was influenced by non-Western musical traditions like Javanese Gamelan and his works incorporate elements of dissonance) in order to express fine nuances of light, color, movement, and mood. His major compositions include *Prélude à "l'Après-midi d'un faune"* (*Prelude to "The Afternoon of a Faun,"* 1894), *Nocturnes* (1899), *Pelléas et Mélisandre* (1902), and *La Mer* (*The Sea*, 1905). Satie, who was expelled from the Paris Conservatory for a supposed lack of talent, is considered a precursor of surrealism and minimalism. His most famous works include his compositions for solo piano, *Les Gymnopédies* (1888) and *Les Gnossiennes* (1893), and his music for the ballet *Parade* (1917). A genius in orchestration, Ravel, like Debussy, is often considered a musical impressionist. His finely crafted and tonally inventive compositions display a wide range of outside influences, including American jazz. Ravel's best-known works include *String Quartet in F* (1903), *Rapsodie espagnole* (1907), *Gaspard de la nuit* (1908), *Valses nobles et sentimentales* (1911–1912), *Daphnis et Chloé* (1912), *Tzigane* (1924), *L'Enfant et les sortilèges* (1925), and *Boléro* (1928).

Inspired by Satie and critical of the lush and complex orchestrations of Debussy, a group of French composers known as "Les Six" advocated a more resolute form of musical modernism (minimalist, polytonal, jazzy, and attentive to the sounds of modern life) in the early twentieth century. The group's members were Arthur Honegger, Darius Milhaud (1892–1974), Germaine Tailleferre, Francis Poulenc (1899–1963), Georges Auric, and Louis Durey. An accomplished composer, Nadia Boulanger is better known as the teacher of many great twentieth-century composers and musicians (e.g., Milhaud, Aaron Copland, Virgil Thomson, Astor Piazzolla, Philip Glass, Daniel Barenboim, and Quincy Jones). Another influential twentieth-century French composer is Edgar Varèse (1883–1965), a precursor of contemporary music (e.g., soundmasses and experiments with electronic media) who spent most of his professional life in the United States. Albert Roussel (1869–1937) was a leading French composer of the 1920s and 1930s who wrote in a more traditional style. The most celebrated French composer of the second half of the twentieth century is Oliver Messaien (1908–1902). Massaien's style was complex, personal, and exhibited a wide range of influences (e.g., serialism, microtonality, Eastern music, and birdsong). He was also a devout Catholic whose music was often profoundly spiritual. His most famous works include *Quatuor pour la fin du temps* (*Quartet for the End of Time*, 1941; composed in a German POW camp); *Le Réveil des oiseaux* (*The Awakening of the Birds*, 1953), *Chronochromie* (1960), *La Transfiguration de Notre Seigneur Jésus-Christ* (1969), and *Des canyons aux étoiles. . .* (*From the canyons to the stars. . .*, 1974; inspired by Brice Canyon in Utah). Two noteworthy movements in French contemporary music (i.e., avant-garde music from 1950 to the present) are *musique concrète* and *musique spectrale*. The former, closely associated with the pioneering work of Pierre Schaeffer (1910–1995), who worked in the research department of French National Radio from the 1940s through the 1960s, involved the creation of electronic sound montages based on recorded material. The latter, which dates from the 1970s, involved computer analysis of the timbre of both acoustic and synthesized music. One of the staunchest advocates of contemporary music was the composer and conductor Pierre Boulez (1926–2016), a student under Messaien and former collaborator of Scheaffer. Boulez created influential institutions and ensembles—for example, L'Esemble Intercontemporain—and was the author of the nine-part song cycle *Le Marteau sans maître* (*The Hammer without a Master*, 1955). Other esteemed contemporary French composers include Henri Dutilleux, Iannis Xenakis, Betsy Jolas, Eliane Radige, Yves Prin, Ida Gotkovsky, Gérard Grisey, Tristan Murail, Edith Canat de Chizy, Jean-François Durand, Pascal Dusapin, Nicolas Bacri, and Eric Tanguy. France has also produced notable composers of music for films, including Joseph Kosma, Maurice Jarre, Michel Legrand, Philippe Sarde, Alexandre Desplat, Ludovic Bource, and Yann Tiersen.

France is well equipped in state-supported professional symphony orchestras. Aside from the Paris-based flagship Orchestre National de France and the Orchestre de Paris, twenty are located in other cities throughout France—including nine other "national orchestras" (Alfortville, Angers, Bordeaux, Lille, Lyon, Metz, Montpellier, Strasbourg, and Toulouse). The advanced study of music is offered in hundreds of institutions, including the country's two prestigious national conservatories of music and dance, located in Paris and Lyon. France has produced many outstanding conductors and instrumental soloists. Radio stations France Musique and Radio Classique and the television station Arte are the leading broadcasters of classical music.

See also: Chapter 2: Louis XIV and the Absolute Monarchy. Chapter 11: Seventeenth-Century Theatre. Chapter 12: Ministry of Culture. Chapter 13: Dance; Opera. Chapter 16: Radio.

Further Reading
Anthony (1997); Bloom (1998); Born (1995); Caballero (2001); Dingle (2007); Fulcher (2005); Isherwood (1973); Kelly (2013); Larner (1996); Mellers (1987); Nichols (2002); Potter (2016); Shapiro (2011); Smith and Potter (2006); Walsh (2018).

THE MARSEILLAISE

France's national anthem was written during the French Revolution by Claude Joseph Rouget de Lisle in 1792, right after France declared war on Austria. Its original title was "War Song for the Army of the Rhine," but it gained its more common name due to its popularity among volunteers from Marseille who marched to Paris to join the war effort. Its bellicose rhetoric and violent lyrics offer an urgent plea to French patriots to rise up to defend their nation's sovereignty and their newly won liberty. It has been featured in popular culture from the opening bars of the Beatles'

"All You Need Is Love" to Serge Gainsbourg's reggae-inspired "Aux armes, etc." ("To Arms, etc."). Along with the blue-white-red "Tricolor" flag, the motto of "Liberté, Égalité (Equality), Fraternité," and the allegorical figure of Marianne, it is one of the official symbols of the French Republic. Translated, its first stanza is—"Arise, children of the Fatherland / The day of glory has arrived! / Against us, tyranny's / Bloody flag is raised / The bloody flag is raised / Do you hear, in the countryside / Those ferocious soldiers roar? / They're coming right into your arms / To cut the throats of your sons, your women!" Its famous refrain is: "To arms, citizens / Form your battalions, / Let's march, let's march! / That an impure blood / Should soak our furrows!"

Dance

Dance was perhaps the most important of all art forms at the French royal court in the seventeenth century, where it served as a living embodiment of social grace and hierarchy among the aristocracy, an emphatic expression of political power for the absolute monarchy, and a chief means of transmission of the classical heritage that underpinned French civilization. Ballet traces its roots back to the Italian Renaissance, but it was at the French court in the baroque-classical era that it became a highly codified art form. *Ballets de cour*—a hybrid genre of performance that included dance, theatrical decor, lavish costumes, orchestral music, song, poetry, allegory, and pageantry—were a popular form of entertainment at the court. King Louis XIV (reign 1643–1715) was an accomplished dancer who owed his "Sun King" alias to having danced the role of Apollo (among other attributes, the god of the sun in Greek mythology) in a resplendent sun-emblazoned costume at age fourteen in the 1653 production of the *Ballet Royal de la Nuit* in Paris, an allegorical statement of his absolute power. One of the first official acts of his personal reign in 1661 was the founding of the Académie Royale de Danse, an example of the monarchy's desire to tighten state control over the arts. Three years later, in 1664, to mark the start of the massive building project that would transform Versailles into the most glorious royal palace in all of Europe, Louis held a five-day extravaganza of art and pageantry, *Les Plaisirs de l'Île Enchantée* (*The Pleasures of the Enchanted Island*), which included *comédie-ballets* by the comedic playwright Molière (Jean-Baptiste Poquelin, 1622–1673; dance was an integral part of his stage productions) and the court composer and dancer Jean-Baptiste Lully (1632–1687). The elite school of dance—affiliated with the Académie Royale de la Musique—that Lully directed is the precursor of the modern Paris Opera Ballet, which is thus considered the oldest ballet company in the world still in operation. It was also during this period that the characteristic French terminology of ballet and the Beauchamp-Feuillet system of choreographic notation were established. These developments helped to underpin enduring French dominance in dance. Ballet further developed as a high art form in eighteenth-century France as a result of the influence of people like Jean-Georges Noverre (1727–1810), who pioneered the *ballet d'action*, an ancestor of modern narrative ballet driven by plot and character development. In addition to the professional performances, dancing at formal balls and other social events was also very important in France during the ancien régime period. Guests performed refined versions of the Allemande, Bourrée, Chaconne, Courante, Gigue, Hornpipe, Loure, Menuet, Passepied, Rigaudon, Sarabande, and Tarantelle—dances popular throughout Europe.

Since it was so closely associated with the monarchy and the aristocracy, ballet suffered in the aftermath of the French Revolution. However, it rebounded in the first half of the nineteenth century as an expression of romanticism, which favored lush and passionate music, expressive and athletic choreography, and moving stories based on mythology and folklore. In the nineteenth century, ballet was marked by the rise of ballerinas, who replaced male dancers as the star performers; and by the generalization of pointe work. Great ballerinas who danced with the Paris Opera Ballet in the nineteenth century include Geneviève Gosselin, Marie Taglioni, Fanny Elssler, and Emma Livry. Famous ballets include *La Sylphide* (Paris premiere in 1832, music by Jean-Madeleine Schneitzhoeffer, choreography by Filippo Taglioni) and *Giselle* (Paris premiere in 1842, music by Adolphe Adam, choreography by Jean Coralli and Jules Perrot). Russia was the preeminent balletic nation in the latter half of the nineteenth century, and Russian expatriates helped to make Paris the ballet capital of the world once again in the early twentieth century through the bold and groundbreaking modernist productions of the Paris-based Ballets Russes (1909–1924)—founded by Sergei Diaghalev (1872–1929) and featuring the work of choreographers like Michel Fokine, Léonide Massine, and George Ballanchine, and of legendary dancers like Vaslav Nijinsky and Anna Pavlova. The next great force in French ballet was the Russian-born (Ukrainian) French dancer and choreographer Serge Lifar (1905–1986), who was a member of the Ballets Russes and later served as artistic director (ballet master) of the Paris Opera Ballet for nearly three decades (1929–1945, 1947–1958). Lifar restored the company's reputation for excellence while also championing modern ballets.

Beginning in the 1970s, the avant-garde contemporary dance movement sought to break free of the conventions of both the classical ballet tradition and modernism. Its leading proponents in France were associated with La Nouvelle Danse Française—a movement that gained influence in the Centres Chorégraphiques Nationaux (created in 1984). Key dancers and choreographers of French contemporary dance include Yvette Chauviré, Jean Babilée, Janine Charrat, Roland Petit, Maurice Béjart (1927–2007, the most acclaimed and influential French choreographer since Lifar), Odile Duboc, Jean-Claude Gallotta, Dominique Bagouet, Maguy Marin, Patrick Dupond, Alain Buffard, Philippe Decouflé, Sylvie Guillem, Agnès Letestu, Nicolas Le Riche, Laëtitia Pujol, Marie-Agnès Gillot, Benjamin Millepied, Alice Renavand, and Matthieu Ganio.

See also: Chapter 2: Louis XIV and the Absolute Monarchy. Chapter 11: Seventeenth-Century Theatre. Chapter 12: Ministry of Culture; Modern Art and the School of Paris. Chapter 13: Classical Music; Folk Music; Opera.

Further Reading
Garafola (1997); Garafola (1998); Harris-Warrick (2016); Homans (2010); Karthas (2015); Robinson (1997); Smith (2000).

Fête de la Musique

The Fête de la Musique, also known as Music Day and Make Music Day, is an annual public celebration of music in France that is held on the day of the summer solstice (June 21 in the northern hemisphere) in cities and towns throughout the country. Thousands of affiliated performances are free and open to the public. The event lasts all day but many performances take place outdoors in the evening in a festive atmosphere that attracts large crowds. The celebration historically embraces all musical genres and practices without hierarchical distinctions and includes both professional and amateur musicians—indeed, the event is construed as an invitation for ordinary people to make music (in French, *faites de la musique*—a homophonic play on words implicit in the event's title). Held for the first time in 1982, the event was largely the brainchild of three officials of the Mitterrand presidency—minister of culture Jack Lang (b. 1939); the ministry's director of music and dance, Maurice Fleuret; and Christian Dupavillon, Lang's advisor. The celebration reflected the administration's emphasis on cultural democratization and pluralism, its taste for the spectacular (also reflected in Mitterrand's Parisian building projects, such as the Louvre Pyramid), and adherence to a French republican tradition of civic festivity dating back to the French Revolution and seen as an effective means to fortify the civic bond among citizens. The model caught on and was imported to other countries (now over 120) beginning in 1985, which coincided with the European Year of Music. The 2018 edition of the Fête de la Musique featured 4,663 officially recognized free events throughout France (over 1,000 in Paris and the Île-de-France region alone). These events included *concerts de poche* (pop-up concerts) and workshops designed to bring classical music, jazz, and folk music to rural areas and isolated urban neighborhoods. Each year, the celebration attracts an estimated 10 million spectators in France. The celebration has served as a template for other national cultural celebrations in France devoted to everything from cinema to the internet, architectural heritage to bread, and science to secularism.

See also: Chapter 1: Cities. Chapter 2: Mitterrand (François) and France in the 1980s and 90s. Chapter 4: Tourism. Chapter 12: Ministry of Culture. Chapter 13: Chanson; Classical Music; Jazz; Rock, Pop, and Rap. Chapter 15: Holidays.

Further Reading
Bulger (2019); Looseley (1990); Williamson (2019).

Folk Music

The traditional (folk) musical heritage of France—which includes distinctive dances, songs, instruments, and musical styles—reflects the country's rich history and extraordinary regional diversity. In the nineteenth and early twentieth centuries, it was subjected to two contradictory trends. On the one hand, scholars and enlightened members of the cultural elite showed great interest in preserving France's musical heritage. For example, in 1839, the scholar Théodore Hersart de la Villemarqué published *Barzaz Breiz*, a compilation of the traditional popular songs of Brittany; and between 1923 and 1930, the composer-musicologist Joseph Canteloube (1879–1957) wrote a series of acclaimed and still widely performed classical arrangements of the folksongs of the Auvergne region, *Chants d'Auvergne*. On the other hand, in same era, powerful forces like industrialization, urbanization, migration, and republican nation building—which placed a premium on national unity and the French language in opposition linguistic and cultural "particularism"—seriously threatened the cultural survival and intergenerational transmission of this musical heritage among ordinary people. There was a strong revival of interest in France's folk music heritage in the 1950s, 1960s, and 1970s—a movement that included both rigorous traditionalists and innovators like the influential Breton musician and master of the Celtic harp, Alain Stivell (b. 1944), who explored intersections between folk and rock. French folk music today has the strongest presence in Brittany, western France (Vendée, Anjou, Maine, Poitou-Charentes), Auvergene, Limousin, Gascony, Basque Country, Languedoc-Roussillon, Provence, and Corsica—regions that are geographically isolated (e.g., mountainous Auvergne, the island of Corsica), have a history of strong regionalist and autonomist sentiment (e.g., Brittany, Basque Country), or a highly developed tourist industry that lends itself to demonstrations of local traditions and cultural flavor (e.g., Provence).

The music of Brittany, which has Celtic roots and displays similarities to the music of Ireland and Scotland, is justifiably famous. The traditional instruments of Brittany include the high-pitched type of bagpipe called the *biniou* and the double-reed alto-range shawm called the *bombard*. Played together, these instruments make up a *couple de sonneurs*. Along with drums, these instruments form the core of a *bagad* ensemble. Breton music is often played at a lively type of traditional festival of folk music and dance called a *festoù-noz*, or *fest noz*. In mountainous central France, which includes Auvergne and Limousin, the folk music prominently features a different type of bagpipe (*cornemuse* in French) called the *cabrette* and the hurdy-gurdy (*vielle à roue*, or wheel fiddle in French)—a round string instrument that is played by turning a hand crank that causes a rosined wheel to turn, producing sound as it rubs against the strings (a keyboard alters the pitch of the sound). This music lends itself to lively dances (e.g., bourrées, gavottes, etc.). It is also at the root of the traditional popular music of Paris, known as *musette* (a name derived from a colloquial term for the *cabrette*), or *bal-musette*. Many inhabitants of Auvergne relocated to Paris in the nineteenth century. By the end of the century, quite a few became proprietors of cafés, where Auvergnat-style music was played. This music evolved into Parisian *musette*, which came to use the accordion—introduced by Italian musicians—in the place of the hurdy-gurdy and lent itself to waltzes (including the fast-paced *java*). Along the way, musette absorbed other influences (e.g., from American jazz and gypsy music). Virtuoso accordionist Émile Vacher (1883–1963) is widely considered the father of the *bal-musette* genre. Other legendary musette-style accordionists include Gus Viseur, Jo Privat, Yvette Horner (1922–2018), and Marcel Azzola. Horner played at the Tour de France, with President Giscard and the British pop star Boy George, and was a

CHILDREN'S SONGS

One of the best-known parts of France's musical heritage are the folksongs that are part of the childhood of so many French people. The most famous songs include "Frère Jacques" ("Brother John"), "Au clair de la lune" ("In the Moonlight"), "Sur le pont d'Avignon" ("On Avignon Bridge"), "Le Roi Dagobert" ("Good King Dagobert"), "Cadet Rousselle" ("Young Rousselle"), "Gentil coquelicot" ("Pretty Poppy"), "Savez-vous planter les choux?" ("Do You Know How to Plant Cabbage?"), "J'ai du bon tabac" ("I've Good Tobacco"), "Meunier, tu dors" ("Miller, You're Sleeping"), and "Auprès de ma blonde" ("By My Fair One's Side"). Some of these traditional songs reference historical periods and events such as the waning of the Merovingian dynasty of kings ("Le Roi Dagobert"), the Franco-Dutch War ("Auprès de ma blonde"), and the French Revolution ("Cadet Rousselle").

muse to the brash 1980s and 90s fashion designer Jean-Paul Gauthier. She helped to make the accordion "cool" again. The musette style has been rediscovered by a new generation of musicians beginning in the 1980s and 1990s—like Yann Tiersen, François Hadji-Lazaro, Les VRP, Les Ogres de Barback, Les Têtes Raides, Les Hurlements d'Léo, La Tordue, La Rue Kétanou, Le Balluche de la Saugrenue, Le Petit Bal de Poche, Les Croquants, Les P'tits Yeux, Les Doigts Tordus, Acorps de Rue, Une Touche d'Optimisme, Picon Mon Amour, Les VRP, Délinquante, and Émeline Tout Court. One of the most distinctive features of Corsican music is a form of polyphonic singing in three voices known as *paghjella*, which has been recognized by UNESCO as part of the intangible heritage of humanity.

See also: Chapter 1: North and South; Overseas France; Regional Identities. Chapter 9: Regional and Minority Languages, Dialects, and Varieties of French. Chapter 13: Chanson; Dance.

Further Reading
Bithell (2007); Ling (1997); Revill (2004); Wilkinson (2016); Winick (1995); Wright (1983).

Jazz

France has an important jazz scene. Jazz was introduced in France by American soldiers during World War I (e.g., the concert tours of 369th Infantry "Harlem Hell Fighters" Band, led by Lt. James Reese Europe) and France's native jazz scene began to develop with the help of American expatriates (like the entertainer Josephine Baker, 1906–1975). Not only have touring American jazz performers found receptive audiences in France, but some have also made France (esp. Paris), their temporary or permanent home, including a number of African American jazz greats who sought greater racial tolerance and artistic recognition there. Among them are Sydney Bechet, Coleman Hawkins, Benny Carter, Don Byas, Kenny Clarke, Lester Young, Dexter Gordon, Bud Powell, Miles Davis, Eric Dolphy, and Dee Dee Bridgewater. The African American expatriate jazz scene in Paris is evoked in Bertrand Tavernier's acclaimed 1986 film *Round Midnight*, starring Gordon and based on the lives of Powell and Young (with an Oscar-winning original score by Herbie Hancock). The style of jazz for which France is best known is gypsy jazz, or *jazz manouche*, exemplified by the legendary Belgian-born Romani-French guitarist and composer Django Reinhardt (1910–1953). Along with violinist Stéphane Grappelli (1908–1997), Reinhardt founded the Quintette du Hot Club de France (1934–1948), arguably the greatest French ensemble of all time. The jazz clubs of Paris (e.g., Le Caveau de la Huchette, Le Duc des Lombards, La Cave du 38 Riv, and New Morning) and festivals throughout the country (e.g., Paris, Nice, Juan-les-Pins) are important parts of the French jazz scene.

There are noteworthy French contemporary and current jazz performers in every instrumental discipline. Guitarists include Christian Escoudé, cousins Tchavolo and Dorado Schmitt, Nguyên Lee, Angelo Debarre, Biréli Lagrène, and Thomas Dutronc. Violinists include Jean-Luc Ponty, Didier Lockwood, Régis Huby, Aurore Voilqué, and Scott Tixier. Accordionists include Marcel Azzola, Richard Galliano, Marc Berthoumieux, Vincent Peirani, and Laurent Derache. Pianists include Martial Solal, Claude Bolling, Jean-Michel Pilc, Michel Petrucciani, Jacky Terrasson, Benoît Delbecq, Baptiste Trotignon, Eve Risser, and Tony Tixier. Sofiane Pamart is a classically trained pianist who records and performs with leading rappers but whose solo work has elements in common with jazz. Drummers include Michel Denis, Manu Katché, Xavier Desandre Navarre, Christophe Marguet, Patrice Héral, and Vincent Tortiller. Saxophonists include Michel Portal, Pascal Parisot, David El Malek, Sophie Alour, Sylvain Rifflet, and Christophe Panzani. Trumpet players include Éric Le Lann, Jean-Sébastien Simonoviez, Stéphane Belmondo, Ibrahim Maalouf, and Antoine Berjeaut. Double bass players include François Rabbath, Henri Texier, Renaud Garcia-Fons, and Simon Tailleu.

See also: Chapter 1: Paris. Chapter 13: Chanson; Rock, Pop, and Rap.

Further Reading
Braggs (2016); Dregni (2008); Jackson (2003); Jordan (2010); Mawer (2014); McGregor (2016); Perchard (2015).

Opera

French opera is one of the great operatic traditions of the world alongside Italian and German opera. Opera in the traditional sense made its first appearance in France at the court of Louis XIV (seventeenth century) as an Italian import. However, there was already a precedent for opera-like singing as part of the spectacular *ballets de cour* (which later evolved into *opéras-ballets*) that were held at Versailles. The mixing of dance, singing, and pageantry is an integral part of the French tradition of high musical theater. The Italian-born composer Jean-Baptiste Lully (1632–1637) and the Frenchmen Jean-Philippe Rameau (1683–1764) developed a French genre of serious opera called *tragédie en musique* (lyric tragedy). Rameau's preeminence in French opera was followed by that of the German composer Christoph Willibald Gluck (1714–1787), who composed eight operas for the Paris stage, including a French version of *Orfeo ed Euridice*. Gluck fused elements of the French and Italian styles along with his own dramatic approach. During the second half of the eighteenth century, a new genre of musical theater, *opéra comique*, flourished. Its chief exemplar during the period was the composer André Grétry (1741–1813). While French comic opera traces its roots back to the vaudeville tradition and was generally lighter in tone, it could also treat serious subject matter, and its chief differences with Italian *opera seria* and French *tragédie en musique* was that its protagonists were not drawn from the heroes of classical antiquity and that it featured spoken dialogue rather than recitative.

The Revolution (1789–1799) disrupted French opera and its traditional sources of patronage. However, it also emphasized patriotic music and songs, like "La Marseillaise," composed by Claude Joseph Rouget de Lisle in 1792; and François-Joseph Gossec's propagandistic opera, *Le Triomphe de la République*. This patriotic use of opera was maintained throughout the nineteenth century as French music sought to assert the French national character. Indeed, even in 1989, "opera" was used to convey a patriotic and political message in the quirky multicultural parade that Jean-Paul Goude created as the climax of the celebration of the bicentennial of the French Revolution—a spectacle that its government promoters and the media commonly referred to as "L'Opéra Goude" and featured the soprano Jessye Norman singing the "Marseillaise" at the Place de la Concorde in an Azzedine Alaïa gown inspired by the French flag.

This is not to say that Italian opera was not popular in France in the nineteenth century. Indeed, following a reorganization of theaters by Napoleon Bonaparte, three Parisian theaters had a monopoly on opera productions in the French capital—the Paris Opéra (the main theater for serious operas in French with recitative dialogue and narrative), the Opéra Comique (for works in this French genre employing spoken dialogue), and the Théâtre Italien (for imported Italian works). Indeed, the leading composer of operas in the early part of the nineteenth century, Gioachino Rossini (1792–1868), served as the Théâtre Italien's director (1824–1829) and composed a number of French operas (e.g., *Guillaume Tell*). Rossini was influential in the development of the French style of grand opera, which is known for its grandiosity, heroic subject matter, and large orchestras and casts. The leading composer of grand operas for the French stage was a German, Giacomo Meyerbeer (1791–1864), whose best known works are *Robert le diable* and *Les Huguenots*. Meyerbeer's contemporary, the visionary romantic composer Hector Berlioz (1803–1869), composed the music for three operas. However, they were not well received at the time. Still, Berlioz influenced the operatic works of a later generation of French romantic composers like Georges Bizet (1838–1875), Charles Gounod, and Jules Massenet. Known for its unbridled romantic passion, earthy realism, and Spanish exoticism, Bizet's *Carmen*, which premiered in 1875, is the most famous and best loved French opera of all time. As the bourgeois demand for entertainment grew in the Haussmann-remade Paris of the second half of the nineteenth century, another new genre of light opera flourished—operetta. The best-known composer of operettas was Jacques Offenbach (1819–1880). The latter part of the nineteenth century was marked by the challenge posed by the towering influence of the German composer Richard Wagner. Wagner had French defenders (Charles Baudelaire) and imitators (Emmanuel Chabrier and Ernest Chausson), but his music also generated considerable controversy and hostility. Ultimately, the best French response to Wagner was the sole opera written by Claude Debussy (1862–1918)—*Pelléas et Mélisande* (1902)—which incorporated some Wagnerian elements but ultimately exemplified a symbolist style of its own. Other twentieth-century French opera composers include Maurice Ravel (1875–1937) (e.g., the childhood fantasy *L'Enfant et les sortilèges*), Darius Milhaud, Francis Poulenc (e.g., the surrealist comic opera *Les Mamelles de Tirésias*), and Olivier Messiaen.

Built between 1861 and 1875, the ornate Palais Garnier (now named for Charles Garnier, its architect) was the epicenter of the Paris opera scene for over a century, until the inauguration of the Opéra Bastille in 1989. The French government, via the Ministry of Culture, funds seventeen companies, including seven that are officially designated as "national operas"—Paris (Palais Garnier and Opéra Bastille), the Théâtre National de l'Opéra-Comique (Paris), Bordeaux, Lyon, Opéra de Lorraine (Nancy), Montpellier, and Opéra du Rhin (Strasbourg). France has produced many great opera singers. Leading artists of today include Gaëlle Arquez, Mireille Delunsch, Véronique Gens, Patricia Petibon, Sandrine Piau, Lea Desandre, Roberto Alagna, Christophe Dumiaux, and Philippe Jaroussky.

French musical theater has a rich tradition of "American-style" musical comedies. The best known internationally are Jacques Demy's (1931–1990) classic film musicals, *The Umbrellas of Cherbourg* (1964) and *The Young Girls of Rochefort* (1967). Beginning in the 1970s, there have been numerous of pop-accented stage productions. A leading early example was *Starmania*, a rock opera (music by Michel Berger, lyrics by Luc Plamondon) that premiered in Paris in 1979. More recently, *Notre-Dame de Paris* (music by Riccardo Cocciante, lyrics by Plamondon, 1998), *Le Roi-Soleil* (2005), *Les Chansons d'Amour* (2007), *Mozart, L'Opéra Rock* (2009), *1789: Les Amants de la Bastille* (2012), and *Demain Commence Ici* (2020) have been big successes.

See also: Chapter 2: Louis XIV and the Absolute Monarchy. Chapter 11: Seventeenth-Century Theatre. Chapter 13: Classical Music; Dance.

Further Reading

Bloechl (2017); Fulcher (1987); Giroud (2010); Huebner (1999); Thomas (2002); Verba (2013).

Rock, Pop, and Rap

The French pop music scene is both dynamic and diverse. In addition to traditional French genres of popular music—*chanson, chanson de variété* (a more commercial and musically hybrid subgenre of chanson), cabaret, musette, jazz manouche, and regional folk music-based styles—which have attracted a new generation of talented interpreters—virtually every genre and subgenre that has had an impact on the international scene has been adopted and reinterpreted by French musicians.

France's response to the irresistible rise of American rock and roll in the late 1950s and 1960s was the French style of pop known as *yé-yé*, which was popularized by the radio program *Salut, les copains* (first aired in 1959). The show made stars out of performers like Johnny Hallyday (Jean-Philippe Smet, 1943–2017), Christophe (Daniel Bevilacqua, 1945–2020), Eddy Mitchell (Claude Moine), Dick Rivers (Hervé Forneri), Claude François (1939–1978), France Gall, Sheila (Annie Chancel), Sylvie Vartan, and Françoise Hardy. Hallyday, known as the "French Elvis" and for a pastiche Americana persona consistent with his stage name, later adopted a more hard rock style (e.g., "Noir, c'est noir" and "Que je t'aime"), whereas Hardy ("Tous les garçons et les filles" and "Comment te dire adieu") moved in the direction of chanson ("Message personnel"), and François, affectionately known to his fans as Cloclo, in the direction of *chanson de variété* and disco (e.g., "Alexandrie Alexandra"). François also cowrote and performed "Comme d'habitude," one of the most famous heartache songs in the French pop repertoire—later made famous in its English version, "My Way" (lyrics by Paul Anka), as interpreted by Frank Sinatra. Critically acclaimed artists like Jacques Dutronc, Serge Gainsbourg, Jacques Higelin, Gérard Manset, and Michel Polnareff championed a nonderivative form of French rock in the 1960s and early 1970s. Important French rock groups of the 1970s, 1980s, 1990s, and early 2000s include Ange (progressive rock), Oberkampf (punk rock), Métal Urbain (punk rock), Trust (heavy metal), Téléphone (pop rock), Indochine (pop rock), Niagra (new wave), Taxi Girl (New Wave), Carte de Séjour (so-called Arab [Beur] rock from the suburbs), Les Rita Mitsouko (alternative rock), Magma (progressive rock), Mano Negra (alternative rock, fronted by Manu Chao), Zebda (multicultural alternative rock), Noir Désir (hard rock), Louise Attaque (folk-rock), and Micky3D (folk-rock). Leading pop-rock solo performers whose careers date back to the 1980s include Charlélie Couture, Bernard Lavilliers, Daniel Balavoine (1952–1986), Alain Bashung (1947–2009), Étienne Daho, Jean-Jacques Goldman, Patrick Bruel, Marc Lavoine, Jean-Louis Murat, Desireless (Claudie Fritsch-Mentrop), Jeanne Mas, Vanessa Paradis, Mylène Farmer, and Patricia Kaas. Solo performers and groups that have fused traditional French popular music genres like musette and manouche (gypsy) music with a rock and roll (and in certain cases punkish) attitude—a trend that gained momentum in the late 1980s and early 1990s—include Les VRP, Les Têtes Raides, Les Ogres de Barback, Pigalle, Les Négresses Vertes, Sanseverino, Les P'tits Garçons Laids, and Bob's Not Dead.

In 2010, the French edition of *Rolling Stone* published a list of the "100 Essential Albums of French Rock" featuring all music recorded before 2000. The top fifteen albums in the ranking were: (1) Alain Bashung, *Osez Joséphine* (1991); (2) Noir Désir, *Tostaky* (1992); (3) Téléphone, *Dure limite* (1982); (4) Serge Gainsbourg, *Histoire de Melody Nelson* (1971); (5) Jacques Higelin, *BBH 75* (1974); (6) Johnny Hallyday, *Rivière … ouvre ton lit* (1969); (7) Les Rita Mitsouko, *The No Comprendo* (1986); (8) Mano Negra, *Puta's Fever* (1989); (9) Bashung, *Fantaisie militaire* (1998); (10) Noir Désir, *Veuillez rendre l'âme (à qui elle appartient)* (1989); (11) Trust, *Répression* (1980); (12) Noir Désir, *666.667 Club* (1996); (13) Téléphone, *Au cœur de la nuit* (1980); (14) Gainsbourg, *Initials B.B.* (1968); and (15) Jacques Dutronc, *L'Intégrale des EP Vogue* (2009).

Popular solo performers and groups on the French pop and rock scene of the past two decades and today include Anggun, BB Brunes, Ben l'Oncle Soul, Amel Bent, Matthieu Chedid ("-M-"), Christine and the Queens, Corneille, Anaïs Croze, Lou Doillon, Julien Doré, La Femme, Feu! Chatterton, Fishbach, Grégoire (Boissenot), L'Impératrice, Izïa (Higelin), Jenifer (Bartoli), Joyce Jonathan, Juniore, (Philippe) Katerine, Nolwenn Leroy, Lorie, Clara Luciani, Christophe Maé, Nâdiya, Pascal Obispo, Eddy de Pretto, Sh'ym, La Grande Sophie, Thérapie TAXI, Cléa Vincent, Ophélie Winter, Yelle, and Zazie. Talent contests on French television, such as *Star Academy* and *The Voice: La plus belle voix*, have played an increasingly important part in launching the careers of young artists like Leroy. The French are also loyal viewers of the Eurovision Song Contest, which was first held in 1956.

Two genres in which French artists have excelled are hip-hop/rap and electronic/techno/house. France has had a thriving hip-hop scene—one of the most active and creative outside the United States—since the mid-1980s. French rap derives its energy and relevance as an expression of the nation's multiethnic suburbs (*la banlieue*). Seminal early groups include DJ Dee Nasty, Assassin, Suprême NTM (the group's 1995 album, *Paris sous les bombes*, was the highest rated French rap LP of all time in a ranking published by *Les Inrocks* magazine in 2017), Ministère AMER, Doc Gynéco, Mafia K-1 Fry, and Lunatic (from the Paris suburbs); and IAM, Fonky Family, PSY4 de la Rime, 113, and Bouga (from Marseille). The early years of French rap were characterized by a rivalry between the Paris and Marseille rap scenes that was similar to the East Coast/West Coast divide in the United States. Artists like MC Solaar (Claude M'Barali, b. 1969)—the proponent of a mellow style and whimsical word play who was France's first rap superstar—and Diam's (Mélanie Georgiades) had considerable crossover success in the pop mainstream. Major hip-hop/rap artists of today include Keny Arkana, Bigflo & Oli, Booba (formerly of Lunatic), Casey, Chilla, Gaël Faye, La Fouine, Maître Gims, Kery James, Jul, Lacrim, Lomepal, Abd al Malik, Médine, MHD, Nekfeu, Niska, OrelSan, Oxmo, PNL, Sexion d'Assault, Sianna, Sniper, Sofiane, and Soprano. In the field of electronic, electro, techno, house, and synth-pop, influential French artists of the past and present include Air, Daft Punk, Laurent Garnier, David Guetta, Bob Sinclair, Jean-Michel Jarre, M83, Phoenix, Danger (Franck Rivoire), St. Germain (Ludovic Navarre), Kavinsky (Vincent Belorgey), Télépopmusik, Justice, Busy P (Pedro Winter), Mr. Oizo (Quentin Dupieux), Yuksek (Pierre-Alexandre Busson), French 79, Sébastien Teller, Grand Blanc, Hyphen Hyphen, Salut C'est Cool, Polo & Pan, and Jacques. The global appeal of French house music was such that critics and fans coined the term "French Touch" to describe it. Guetta, a DJ, producer, and songwriter who is one of the style's leading exemplars, is one of the best-selling French artists outside of France and has collaborated with groups and solo artists like The Black Eyed Peas, Nicki Minaj, Rihanna, and Lady Gaga.

French pop music reflects the multicultural realties of French society today and its ties to other countries and cultures. French artists of many different origins have given new twists to French and international genres like chanson, rock, pop, hip-hop, and rhythm and blues. Leading artists from other Francophone countries and regions—such as Sénégal's Youssou N'Dour, Algeria's Khaled (a leading exemplar of

North African raï), Québec's Cœur de Pirate and Pierre Lapointe, Belgium's Stromae, and Angèle—tour extensively in France. Finally, there is the significant musical contribution of France's overseas departments and territories. The French Caribbean island departments of Guadeloupe and Martinique, for example, are the birthplace of the style of dance music known as Zouk. Legendary bands from the 1980s include Kassav' and Zouk Machine. Current practitioners of the style include Thierry Cham, Medhy Custos, Christiane Vallejo, Princess Lover (Nicole Nérêt), and Perle Lama.

See also: Chapter 6: Immigration. Chapter 9: Francophonie; Language Laws and Policies. Chapter 13: Chanson; Fête de la Musique; Folk Music; Jazz. Chapter 16: Pop Culture Icons; Radio.

Further Reading

Berrian (2000); Briggs (2015); Dauncey and Cannon (2003); Deluxe (2014); Durand (2002); Durand (2012); Gross et al. (2002); Huq (1999); Kangansky (2020); Lebrun (2014); Looseley (2003); Looseley (2005); Looseley (2018); Marc (2020); McCarren (2013); Swedenburg (2010); Tinker (2002); Tinker (2006); Verlant (2012).

SELECTED BIBLIOGRAPHY

Anthony, James R. *French Baroque Music: From Beaujoyeulx to Rameau.* Rev. ed. Amadeus, 1997.

Berrian, Brenda F. *Awakening Spaces: French Caribbean Popular Songs, Music, and Culture.* U Chicago P, 2000.

Bithell, Caroline. *Transported by Song: Corsican Voices from Oral Tradition to World Stage.* Scarecrow P, 2007.

Bloechl, Olivia. *Opera and the Political Imaginary in Old Regime France.* U Chicago P, 2017.

Bloom, Peter. *The Life of Berlioz.* Cambridge UP, 1998.

Born, Georgina. *Rationalizing Culture: IRCAM, Boulez, and the Institutionalization of the Musical Avant-Garde.* U California P, 1995.

Braggs, Rashida K. *Jazz Diasporas: Race, Music, and Migration in Post-World War II Paris.* Stanford UP, 2016.

Bret, David. *Piaf: A Passionate Life.* Robson, 1999.

Briggs, Jonathyne. *Sounds French: Globalization, Cultural Communities and Pop Music, 1958–1980.* Oxford UP, 2015.

Bulger, Anthony. "La Fête de la Musique: How France's Annual Musical Jamboree Enchanted the World." *France-Amérique*, 20 Jun. 2019, https://france-amerique.com/en/la-fete-de-la-musique-how-frances-annual-musical-jamboree-enchanted-the-world.

Caballero, Carlo. *Fauré and French Musical Aesthetics.* Cambridge UP, 2001.

Cordier, Adeline. "Chanson and Tacit Misogyny." *Journal of European Popular Culture*, vol. 4, no. 1, 2013, pp. 37–49.

Cordier, Adeline. *Post-War French Popular Music: Cultural Identity and the Brel-Brassens-Ferré Myth.* Ashgate, 2014.

Dauncey, Hugh, and Philippe Le Guern, eds. *Stereo: Comparative Perspectives on the Sociological Study of Popular Music in France and Britain.* Ashgate, 2011.

Dauncey, Hughes, and Steve Cannon, eds. *Popular Music in France from Chanson to Techno: Culture, Identity and Society.* Ashgate, 2003.

Deluxe, Jean-Emmanuel. *Yé-Yé Girls of '60s French Pop.* Feral House, 2014.

Dingle, Christopher. *The Life of Messiaen.* Cambridge UP, 2007.

Dregni, Michael. *Gypsy Jazz: In Search of Django Reinhardt and the Soul of Gypsy Swing.* Oxford UP, 2008.

Durand, Alain-Philippe, ed. *Black, Blanc, Beur: Rap Music and Hip-Hop Culture in the Francophone World.* Scarecrow, 2002.

Durand, Alain-Philippe, ed. *Hip-Hop en Français: An Exploration of Hip-Hop Culture in the Francophone World.* Rowman & Littlefield, 2012.

Fulcher, Jane F. *The Composer as Intellectual: Music and Ideology in France, 1914–1940.* Oxford UP, 2005.

Fulcher, Jane F. *The Nation's Image: French Grand Opera as Politics and Politicized Art.* Cambridge UP, 1987.

Garafola, Lynn. *Diaghilev's Ballets Russes.* Da Capo, 1998.

Garafola, Lynn, ed. *Rethinking the Sylph: New Perspectives on the Romantic Ballet.* UP New England, 1997.

Giroud, Vincent. *French Opera: A Short History.* Yale UP, 2010.

Gross, Joan, et al. "Arab Noise and Ramadan Nights: Rai, Rap, and Franco-Maghrebi Identities." *The Anthropology of Globalization: A Reader*, eds. Jonathan Xavier Inda and Renato. Wiley-Blackwell, 2002, pp. 198–230.

Guibert, Gérôme, and Catherine Rudent, eds. *Made in France: Studies in Popular Music.* Routledge, 2018.

Harris-Warrick, Rebecca. *Dance and Drama in French Baroque Opera: A History.* Cambridge UP, 2016.

Hawkins, Peter. *The French Singer-Songwriter from Aristide Bruant to the Present Day.* Routledge, 2017.

Haworth, Rachel. "French *chanson.*" *French Studies*, vol. 72, no. 1, 2018, pp. 87–96.

Haworth, Rachel. *From the* Chanson française *to the* Canzone d'autore *in the 1960s and 1970s Authenticity, Authority, Influence.* Routledge, 2015.

Homans, Jennifer. *Apollo's Angels: A History of Ballet.* Random House, 2010.

Huebner, Steven. *French Opera at the Fin de Siècle: Wagnerism, Nationalism, and Style.* Oxford UP, 1999.

Huq, Rupa. "Living in France: The Parallel Universe of Hexagonal Pop." *Living through Pop*, ed. Andrew Blake. Routldege, 1999, pp. 131–145.

Isherwood, Robert M. *Music in the Service of the King: France in the Seventeenth Century.* Cornell UP, 1973.

Jackson, Jeffrey H. *Making Jazz French: Music and Modern Life in Interwar Paris.* Duke UP, 2003.

Jones, Gareth. *French Pop: From Music Hall to Ye-Ye.* Music Mentor, 2022.

Jordan, Matthew F. C. *Le Jazz: Jazz and French Cultural Identity.* U Pennsylvania P, 2010.

Kagansky, Serge. "Oh les Filles: Meet the Badass Women of French Rock." *France-Amérique*, 21 May 2020, https://france-amerique.com/en/oh-les-filles-meet-the-badass -women-of-french-rock/.

Karthas, Ilyana. *When Ballet Became French: Modern Ballet and the Cultural Politics of France, 1909–1939*. McGill-Queen's UP, 2015.

Kelly, Barbara L., ed. *French Music, Culture, and National Identity, 1870–1939*. U Rochester P, 2008.

Kelly, Barbara L. *Music and Ultra-Modernism in France: A Fragile Consensus, 1913–1939*. Boydell, 2013.

Larner, Gerald. *Maurice Ravel*. Phaidon, 1996.

Lebrun, Barbara. "Beyond Brassens: Twenty-First Century *Chanson* and the New Generation of Singer-Songwriters." *Modern & Contemporary France*, vol. 22, no. 2, 2014, pp. 159–175.

Lebrun, Barbara. *Protest Music in France: Production, Identity and Audiences*. Routledge, 2009.

Ling, Jan. *A History of European Folk Music*. U Rochester P, 1997.

Looseley, David L. *Edith Piaf: A Cultural History*. Liverpool UP, 2015.

Looseley, David L. "Fabricating Johnny: French Popular Music and National Culture." *French Cultural Studies*, vol. 16, no. 2, 2005, pp. 191–203.

Looseley, David L. "Jack Lang and the Politics of Festival." *French Cultural Studies*, vol. 1, no. 1, 1990, pp. 5–19.

Looseley, David L. *Popular Music in Contemporary France: Authenticity, Politics, Debate*. Berg, 2003.

Looseley, David L. "'Une Passion Française': The Mourning of Johnny Hallyday." *French Cultural Studies*, vol. 29, no. 4, 2018, pp. 378–388.

Marc, Isabelle. "Around the World: France's New Popular Music Diplomacy." *Modern & Contemporary France*, vol. 28, no. 3, 2020, pp. 253–270.

Mawer, Deborah. *French Music and Jazz in Conversation: From Debussy to Brubeck*. Cambridge UP, 2014.

McCarren, Felicia. *French Moves: The Cultural Politics of Le Hip Hop*. Oxford UP, 2013.

McGregor, Elizabeth Vihlen. *Jazz and Postwar French Identity: Improvising the Nation*. Lexington, 2016.

Mellers, Wilfrid. *François Couperin and the French Classical Tradition*. 2nd ed. Faber and Faber, 1987.

Nichols, Roger. *The Harlequin Years: Music in Paris, 1917–1929*. U California P, 2002.

Papanikolaou, Dimitris. *Singing Poets: Literature and Popular Music in France and Greece*. Legenda, 2007; esp. pp. 11–60.

Pasler, Jann. *Composing the Citizen: Music as Public Utility in Third Republic France*. U California P, 2009.

Perchard, Tom. *After Django: Making Jazz in Postwar France*. U Michigan P, 2015.

Portis, Larry. *French Frenzies: A Social History of Popular Music in France*. Virtualbookworm, 2004.

Potter, Caroline. *Erik Satie: A Parisian Composer and His World*. Boydell, 2016.

Revill, George. "Cultural Geographies in Practice: Performing French Folk Music: Dance, Authenticity and Nonrepresentational Theory." *Cultural Geographies*, vol. 11, no. 2, 2004, pp. 199–209.

Robinson, Jacqueline. *Modern Dance in France, 1920–1970: An Adventure.* Harwood, 1997.

Salie, Olaf. *Chanson: A Tribute to France's Most Romantic and Poetic Musical Tradition.* Prestel, 2022.

Shapiro, Robert, ed. *Les Six: The French Composers and Their Mentors Jean Cocteau and Erik Satie.* Owen, 2011.

Smith, Marian Elizabeth. *Ballet and Opera in the Age of Giselle.* Princeton UP, 2000.

Smith, Richard Langham, and Caroline Potter, eds. *French Music since Berlioz.* Ashgate, 2006.

Swedenburg, Ted. "Khaled and the Myth of Rai." *Foreign Policy*, 10 Sep. 2010, https://foreignpolicy.com/2010/09/10/khaled-and-the-myth-of-rai/.

Thomas, Downing. *Aesthetics of Opera in the Ancien Régime, 1647–1785.* Cambridge UP, 2002.

Tinker, Chris. *Georges Brassens and Jacques Brel: Personal and Social Narratives in Post-War Chanson.* Liverpool UP, 2006.

Tinker, Chris. "Serge Gainsbourg and *Le défi américain*." *Modern & Contemporary France*, vol. 10, no. 2, 2002, pp. 187–196.

Tinker, Chris. "Shaping Youth in *Salut les copains*." *Modern & Contemporary France*, vol. 15, no. 3, 2007, pp. 293–308.

Trezise, Simon, ed. *The Cambridge Companion to French Music.* Cambridge UP, 2015.

Verba, Cynthia. *Dramatic Expression in Rameau's Tragédie en Musique: Between Tradition and Enlightenment.* Cambridge UP, 2013.

Verlant, Gilles. *Serge Gainsbourg: The Biography.* Trans. Paul Knobloch. Tamtam, 2012.

Walsh, Stephen. *Debussy: A Painter in Sound.* Knopf, 2018.

Watkins, Glenn. *Pyramids at the Louvre: Music, Culture, and Collage from Stravinsky to the Postmodernists.* Belknap-Harvard UP, 1994.

Wilkinson, Desi. *Call to the Dance: An Experience of the Socio-cultural World of Traditional Breton Music and Dance.* Pendragon, 2016.

Williamson, Alissa. "Fête de la Musique, the Worldwide Midsummer Musical Bash, Explained." *Vox*, 21 Jun. 2019, https://www.vox.com/culture/2019/6/21/15872430/fete-de-la-musique-festival-june-21.

Winick, Stephen D. "Breton Folk Music, Breton Identity, and Alan Stivell's *Again*." *The Journal of American Folklore*, vol. 108, no. 429, 1995, pp. 334–354.

Wright, John. "Traditional Dance in France." Smithsonian Folklife Festival, French/French-American Program, 1983, https://festival.si.edu/articles/1983/traditional-dance-in-france.

CHAPTER 14

FOOD

OVERVIEW

France has often been called a nation of gourmets. While a connoisseur's appreciation of haute cuisine may not be quite universal, there is no denying that the nation has incomparably rich culinary traditions, that it has been a world leader in gastronomical excellence for centuries, that food occupies a central place in its cultural identity, and that the average French person attaches a great deal of importance to good food and the pleasure of eating well. French gastronomy began to take shape during the Middle Ages and Renaissance, when Italian influences at court and local traditions were intertwined. However, a truly distinct French art of fine cooking first asserted itself in the seventeenth century via the contributions of the master chef François Pierre de la Varenne (1615–1687). It achieved its dominant international reputation for excellence and was codified in its modern traditional form between the early nineteenth and early twentieth centuries through the work of influential chefs like Marie-Antoine Carême (1784–1833) and Auguste Escoffier (1846–1935). National awareness of France's culinary excellence and traditions was advanced through the publication of cookbooks and the Michelin Red Guides, which date back to 1900 and took their current form in the 1920s and 1930s, and whose three-star rating system is still the gold standard in restaurant ratings. The most recent edition of the guide lists 27 three-star, 86 two-star, and 503 one-star restaurants in France—more than any other nation in each category. Gault-Millau, founded in 1965 and using a twenty-point scale and also awarding one to five chef's toques, is another authoritative French restaurant guide. The existence of a classic French tradition of gastronomy has not hindered innovation. From the 1960s through the 1990s, the proponents of nouvelle cuisine, led by the Lyon-based chef Paul Bocuse (1926–2018), challenged orthodoxy by offering lighter dishes with restrained herbal seasonings (in contrast to the traditional rich sauces championed by Escoffier), coupled with greater emphasis on fresh market ingredients, regional and local inspirations, inventive flavor combinations, and esthetic presentation.

Each part of France has its own rich culinary traditions and many of the great recipes from each region have become favorites nationally and the world over. Among them are the hearty dishes of northern, eastern, and central France—*blanquette de veau* (veal in creamy white sauce) from Nord-Pas-de-Calais; *choucroute garnie* (sauerkraut served with cured meats) from Alsace; beef bourguignon (beef stew marinated in red wine), *coq au vin* (chicken stew marinated in red wine), and *escargots à la bour-gignonne* (snails prepared with garlic and white wine) from Burgundy; and *andouil-lette* (pig intestine) sausage from Lyon, which is considered by many the true culinary capital of France. The cooking of southern France reflects a Mediterranean heritage and many iconic southern French dishes are equally beloved and famous—for exam-ple, ratatouille (spicy vegetable stew) from Provence, Niçoise salad (with anchovies) from Nice, *bouillabaisse* (spicy fish stew) from Marseille, or *cassoulet* (white bean cas-serole served with pork sausage) from Occitanie. Finally, what tourist has gone to France without hoping to savor authentic crêpes and apple cider (Brittany), onion soup (Paris), or goose liver *pâté de foie gras* (Gascony)? The culinary diversity of France is further enhanced by traditional recipes from its overseas departments and territories in the Caribbean, the Indian Ocean, and the Pacific; and of its immigrants and ethnic minority communities (e.g., North African dishes like couscous and slow-cooked tajine lamb stew).

The French strongly associate food quality and cultural authenticity with its regional and local place of origin. This concern manifests itself in the concept of terroir—the notion that the regional or local natural environment in which a particu-lar crop or other food or beverage is produced, including the soil, topography, climate, and surrounding plants, as well as the traditional savoir faire that is part of the cul-tural heritage of the same area—give quality foods and beverages a unique character and savor that ought to be protected. Geographical quality control and local culinary heritage protection come in the form of France's system of certified origin appella-tions, including the highest category—the *Appellation d'Origine Contrôlée*, or AOC (equivalent to the EU norm designation of *Appellation d'Origine Protegée*, or AOP). Certified origins, which include two lower-tier categories, were first used for French wines in the 1930s but now apply to other types of foods and beverages, including ciders, cheeses, and poultry. French excellence in wine and cheese production is unsurpassed. There are ten different grape-growing and wine-producing regions of France and the wines of each are distinct. The most famous regions are Bordeaux, Burgundy, the Loire Valley, and Rhône Valley–Provence. The best wines from these and other regions—including the sparkling wines of Champagne and Cognacs—are appreciated by wine connoisseurs the world over. The overall emphasis on quality in the French wine industry is reflected in the fact that over 50% of French production falls in the AOC category. France is the world's largest exporter of wine (nearly 30% of all global exports), the second largest producer of wines, the second largest producer of organic wines, and the second largest consumer of wine. France has an equally strong reputation for cheese production and its artisanal AOP cheeses are appreciated around the world. It ranks as the largest consumer and third largest producer of cheese in the world, and boasts a stunning 1,200 officially registered varieties of cheese of every type—from bloomy-rind soft cheese (like Camembert and Brie) to blue cheese (like Roquefort), cooked pressed cheese (like Emmental, Beaufort, and Comté), goat's milk (*chèvre*), and sheep's milk (*brebis*) cheese.

France's third food passion is good bread, ranging from the ubiquitous long and narrow sticks of crusty white bread known as baguettes (representing 70% of French bread production and over 10 billion loaves sold annually), to breads in different shapes and sizes (e.g., *flûtes*, *bâtards*, *ficelles*, *boules*, and *couronnes*), bread made from different sorts of grains and flours (whole wheat, sourdough, multigrain, and rye), and specialty breads like brioche (sweet bread) and southern-style fougasse (similar to focaccia). The search for good bread to be served at every meal is one reason why neighborhood artisanal bakeries (*boulangeries*) are still popular (albeit declining in number) even in an age of massive supermarkets (leading French chains include Carrefour, Auchun, Leclerc, Intermarché, and Casino/Géant). The same can be said of other types of boutique food stores specializing in red meat and poultry, sausages and charcuterie, fish, cheese, wine, and fresh produce; and for France's 10,000+ public markets, which have a reputation for offering high-quality products that are fresh, flavorful, locally sourced, and steeped in tradition.

The importance that the French attach to food comes through in recent polls (e.g., OpinionWay 2018 and BVA 2019) on the subject. It was found that 86% of French people report paying attention to the food they eat (21% close attention, 57% more attention than they used to). While 46% of French people think that diversity of food products has improved in recent years, 49% believe that food quality relative to price has declined, as has overall taste of food according to 46%. In terms of food quality and safety, the French have the most confidence (82%) in small producers (91% for taste). They have more confidence in the quality of the food found in public markets (74%) than in supermarket chains (51%). Some 67% consider official labels (Red Label, AOP/AOC, etc.) a sign of quality. And 86% report buying organic food products (34% weekly). Organic foods are growing in popularity as concerns about the safety and naturalness of food rise. Another sign of the same concern is France's strong resistance to genetically modified organisms (GMOs) in the food they eat. The French also place importance on eating a balanced and healthy diet. Around 45% say that fruits and vegetables are a part of their daily diet (92% of consumers pay attention to the seasonality of the produce they eat, 90% to its French origin). However, only 2% and 3% of people surveyed report adhering to vegetarian and vegan diets, respectively. While French traditionalists (and nutritionists) may decry the popularity of "American-style" fast food, it too is on the rise. Concerns about the role that junk food, processed foods, and foods high in fat, sugar, and salt play in rising obesity rates and other associated health risks (e.g., diabetes, heart disease, cancer) have led to conspicuous labeling of such foods and large-scale public service advertising campaigns promoting healthier eating habits.

Further Reading

Abramson (2007); Behr (2016); Flandrin (2007); Hénaut and Mitchell (2018); Mennell (1996); Pitte (2002); Root (1992); Scannavino (2011); Scher and Weiss (2001).

Bread

Bread is truly a French passion. In 1788–1789, a combination of factors, including bad weather, poor grain harvests, and rampant speculation led to severe bread shortages and skyrocketing prices. Only the rich could afford to eat white bread; people of modest means had to make do with substandard bread or go hungry. This in turn led to widespread bread riots that were a key contributor to the violent upheaval that was the French Revolution (1789–1799). No French food item is as iconic as the baguette, the long, thin loaf—the French word means "stick"—of white bread that is crusty and firm on the outside and soft (but not spongy) on the inside. Current regulations (dating from 1993) specify that a baguette must be 55–65 cm long (22–26 in), 5–6 cm (2–2.5 in) in diameter, and 250–300 g (9–11 oz) in weight. To qualify as "de tradition française" (a protected designation), a baguette must be made using only wheat flour, water, yeast, and common salt (only minute quantities of other ingredients may be used: e.g., 0.5% soy flour and 0.3% wheat malt flour). Baguettes account for 70% of all French bread production. Every year, over 10 billion baguettes are sold in France, including 6 billion from specialty bakeries, or *boulangeries*. They are commonly served with every meal (sometimes with breakfast but always with lunch and dinner), where a hand-sized slice is usually placed directly on the table next to one's plate and broken up into bite-sized morsels to be eaten throughout the meal. The average French person eats half a baguette per day (average consumption was one per day in 1970 and three around 1900). Long, thin loaves of bread were already popular in France in the eighteenth century, but the modern baguette came into existence in the nineteenth century as a result of standardization in the type of flour and fermentation (yeast) used and the method of baking the bread in brick "deck" ovens using steam. The baguette was first officially defined by regulatory law in 1920—around that time bakers were required to do their work between 4:00 and 10:00 a.m., which further contributed to the prevalence of the fast-baking stick-like loaves.

Other common French types of bread by shape are the *bâtard* (half the length of a baguette) and a bit thicker, the *ficelle* (the same length as a baguette but half the diameter and weight), the *flûte* (the same length as a baguette but twice the diameter), the *boule* (shaped like a flattened ball), and the *couronne* (ring-shaped). Whole wheat bread is called *pain complet*, rye is *pain de seigle*, and sourdough bread is *pain au levain*. A traditional kind of rustic bread that is regaining popularity is the *pain de campagne*, a roundish loaf often made using a mixture of refined white flour, whole wheat, and sourdough with higher bran and germ content and a somewhat chewier consistency. While France has numerous specialty pastry shops (*pâtisseries*), combined bread and pastry shops—*boulangeries-pâtisseries*—are the norm. Popular pastries include croissants, *pains au chocolat* (typically called chocolate croissants in English), and brioche (a moist sweet bread). All are examples of *viennoiseries* (i.e., Viennese pastries)—puff pastry with flaky crusts baked like bread but with added ingredients (eggs, butter, milk, cream, and sugar)—which are typically eaten at breakfast or during coffee breaks. *Fougasse*, from Provence, is a focaccia-type flat bread traditionally baked in the form of an ear of wheat that is seasoned with salt, garlic and herbs, and (sometimes) garnished with olives and anchovies.

Neighborhood bread bakeries are a fixture of French cities and towns. The Fédération Nationale de la Boulangerie-Pâtisserie estimates that there are currently 32,000 of them, many of which owned and operated by independent artisan bakers—equal to

A traditional artisanal *boulangerie-pâtisserie* (bakery-pastry shop) in the old quarter of Nice (Alpes-Maritimes department, Provence). Here, one can buy a variety of breads and pastries, including the ubiquitous baguette—a long and thin crusty bread that is made using a process that includes steam baking (national laws regulate both the ingredients and baking process of the traditional French baguette and French authorities applied for UNESCO world cultural heritage designation for the baguette in 2021). The number of traditional bakeries in France is in decline and bread vending machines have appeared in some underserved urban areas and small towns. (VVShots/Dreamstime.com)

one bakery for every 1,800 inhabitants. Their number has slowly decreased over the years—there were 36,500 neighborhood bakeries in 1990—largely the result of competition from supermarket chains that have their own in-store bakeries. However, specialized local bakeries still represent a 60% share of French bread production, register €11 billion in annual sales, are visited by 12 million customers daily, and employ 180,000 people (incl. 22,000 apprentices). Increasingly, neighborhood bakeries are seen as cultural institutions and bread bought there is viewed as a small luxury rather than just an everyday staple. French excellence in the art of baking bread is demonstrated in several annual competitions, such as the Concours des Meilleurs Jeunes Boulangers de France (best young bread baker) and the Concours National de la Meilleure Baguette de Tradition Française (best French traditional baguette). The nation's passion for bread is celebrated yearly during the weeklong Fête du Pain, or Bread Week, which takes place in mid-May to coincide with the Feast of Saint Honoré, the traditional patron saint of millers and bakers.

See also: Chapter 2: Louis XVI and the End of the Ancien Régime. Chapter 10: Table Etiquette and Dinner Parties. Chapter 14: Cheese; Shopping for Food; Wine.

Further Reading

Barboff (2018); Chevallier (2012); Chevallier (2019); Kaplan (2006); Nurra et al. (2017); Onishi (2019); Poilâne (2019); Rambali (1994).

Cheese

French President Charles de Gaulle once famously asked, "How can anyone be expected to govern a country where there exist 258 varieties of cheese?" De Gaulle may have been right about how hard it can be to govern France, but he was a little off on his number of cheeses. According to the French National Dairy Products Professional Federation, there are 1,200 different varieties of cheese made in France. The French are the world's leading consumers of cheese—26.2 kilograms (57.8 pounds) per person per year. France also ranks third in the world in both overall cheese production (close to 2 million metric tons annually)—behind the United States and Germany—and cheese exports ($3.5 billion in 2017)—behind Germany and the Netherlands. Cheese production is a major part of France's thriving dairy industry. Over two-thirds of all milk produced in France is used for cheese production. Dairy is France's second leading agricultural sector (tied with wine), behind meat production, accounting for €30 billion in annual sales (equal to 13% of the total for the agricultural sector), an annual trade surplus of €4.0 billion, and 300,000 jobs. France is home to five of the world's twenty-five largest dairy industry conglomerates, including world no. 1 Lactalis and no. 6 Danone.

France produces many different types of cheese that vary in terms of aging, texture, animal milk used, and methods of production—including unripened cheese (e.g., *fromage blanc* and *fromage frais*), bloomy-rind soft cheese, washed-rind soft cheese, blue cheese, cooked and uncooked pressed cheese, goat and sheep milk cheese, and processed cheese. Quality is as important as quantity and variety in French cheese production. Forty-five French cheeses have *Appellation d'Origine Protégée*, or AOP, designation (formerly, *Appellation d'Origine Contrôlée*, or AOC), which means that to use the name of a protected variety, the cheese must be produced according to strict standards in a specific local geographical area (*terroir*). The most well-known protected varieties of French cheese include Saint-Marcellin, Neufchâtel, Brie de Meaux, and Camembert de Normandie (bloomy rind soft); Sablé de Wissant, Vacherin, and Rollot (washed rind soft); Fourme de Montbrison, Bleu de Bonneval, and Roquefort (blue); Emmental, Beaufort, and Comté (cooked pressed); Saint-Nectaire, Echourgnac, and Tomme des Pyrénées (uncooked pressed); and Selles-sur-Cher and Bouton de Culotte (goat). Camembert and Brie, which are popular French exports, are similar cheeses but come from different regions: Camembert from Normandy and Brie from Seine-et-Marne. Gruyère (a name regulated since 1951), sometimes commonly called "Swiss cheese" in English, is a type of cooked pressed cheese that comes from a specific region of France and Switzerland. Since 2013, France has used the special, regulated designation *fermier* ("farmhouse") for artisanal cheeses made according to traditional methods by a farmer on site with milk produced solely on their farm. A course of cheeses is often served after the main course of a French meal, either before or after (and sometimes in place of) a dessert.

See also: Chapter 1: Mountains; Regional Identities. Chapter 4: Agriculture; Trade. Chapter 10: Table Etiquette and Dinner Parties. Chapter 14: Bread; Food Quality, Organic Products, and GMO Resistance; Shopping for Food; Wine.

Further Reading
Boisard (2003); Bouchait (2018); Lison (2013); Percival and Percival (2019).

Food Quality, Organic Products, and GMO Resistance

Food quality and wholesomeness are very important to the French. One indication of this is the growing emphasis placed on locally sourced food that reflects the environment, character, and traditions of a particular terroir. Via the Ministry of Agriculture-affiliated National Institute of Origins and Quality (INAO, founded in 1935), the French government certifies several levels and types of protected designations of origin that are coupled with standards of quality and other regulations. The two top categories, which correspond to EU norms adopted in 2009, are AOP (*Appellation d'Origine Protégée*) and IGP (*Indication Géographique Protégée*). AOP is the highest category and pertains to true terroir-sourced foods and beverages—for beverages, the older AOC (*Appellation d'Origine Contrôlée*) label is still in use—produced using traditional methods and exacting standards of quality. According to the INAO (2017), AOP/AOC designation is currently awarded to 363 wine appellations, 17 appellations for other types of alcoholic beverages, and 4 cider appellations. Beverages represent 78% of AOP production and a market worth €21.2 billion (2016). AOP designation is also awarded to 50 dairy product appellations and 100 appellations for other types of food products ranging from apples to chickens. IGP designation concerns products sourced from larger geographical areas that conform to high quality standards—currently, 110 beverage product appellations (incl. 74 wines) and 140 other agricultural food appellations. Additional superior quality assurance is provided through Label Rouge ("Red Label") designation for products that may not fit the emphasis on terroir or geographic origin. The largest Label Rouge category is comprised of poultry and eggs (the standard is pasture-based production that is respectful of animal welfare). Seafood, other meats, and charcuterie are also covered. Food quality is enforced by a host of other government regulations as well.

Another sign of the French interest in high-quality, natural food is the growing popularity of organic food (*biologique* in French, commonly shortened to *bio*). France presently has the third largest surface area devoted to organic food production in the EU and the EU's second largest market (behind Germany) for organic food—worth €8 billion in 2017 (3.5% of French food purchases). Organic food in France involves roughly 36,000 agricultural producers, 2 million hectares (5 million acres) of farmland, 12,000 processers, and 5,000 distributors. A major impetus for greater emphasis on natural agricultural production, including certified organic production, and on stricter food quality and safety standards in general, was the epidemic of so-called mad cow disease (Bovine spongiform encephalopathy) from the mid-1980s to the early 2000s, which is caused by infected proteins (prions) that some believe can be traced to animal feed containing infected animal by-products. Additionally, French opposition to GMOs, or genetically modified organisms, in food production is substantial. Activists and many consumers tend to view the use of GMOs—especially in plant crops (including grains like corn)—as a threat to both public health and biodiversity. Others—including scientists (there are divergent opinions on the issue within the scientific community), farmers, and industry representatives—claim that fear of GMOs has been greatly exaggerated. GMO use is limited and strictly regulated under EU directives, but French laws and regulations go further. Limited experiments with GMOs may be conducted (but not in an open field, to prevent contamination of neighboring fields) and certain kinds of GMO food may be imported provided they conform to EU regulations and are clearly labeled as such. However, commercial production of food using GMOs is banned by national law in France.

See also: Chapter 4: Agriculture; Trade. Chapter 10: Table Etiquette and Dinner Parties; Chapter 14: Bread; Cheese; Shopping for Food; Wine.

Further Reading

Ayres and Bosia (2014); Fantasia (2018); Hayes (2007); Heller (2007); Hoquette et al. (2013); Kuntz (2014); Stapleton (2011); Sukapdjo (2013); Trubek et al. (2010).

Gastronomy

French gastronomy is recognized (since 2010) by UNESCO as part of the world's "intangible cultural heritage" and is widely considered as the most influential and exemplary of culinary excellence in the world. Four moments stand out in the history of French gastronomy. The first, from the fourteenth through the sixteenth centuries, is when it begins to take shape at court. A popular myth suggests that fine cuisine in France dates back to 1533, when the young Catherine de Medici arrived at the French court to wed the future King Henry II and, finding French cooking lacking refinement, placed Italian chefs in charge of her kitchen. Although Italian cooking indeed exerted considerable influence on French cooking at the time, the story of Catherine's Italian chefs is an exaggeration since a French tradition of fine cooking was already well established by then. That tradition is represented by the first noteworthy compilations of recipes, or cookbooks, published in France, like *Le Viandier* (fourteenth century), attributed to Guillaume Tirel (known as "Taillevent"), one of the first true master chefs in modern history; and *On Cookery* (1420) by Master Cliquart. Still, the high art of French cooking truly distinguished itself in the second historical moment, from the mid-seventeenth through the early nineteenth century. Two figures stand out. The first is François Pierre de la Varenne (1615–1678), a master chef who decisively broke with Italian approaches and played a major role in codifying distinctively French cuisine in the golden age of Louis XIV, the chief result of which was his highly influential cookbook, *The French Cook* (1651). The other is Marie-Antoine Carême (1784–1833), known for his elaborate and highly artistic style and his legendary five-volume, mostly posthumous *The Art of French Cuisine in the Nineteenth Century* (1833–1847). Carême is also widely credited with having invented the modern chef's hat (*la toque* in French) and may be considered the world's first celebrity chef.

The third great moment in the history of French gastronomy took place in the early twentieth century. During this period, the great chef, restaurateur, and culinary writer Auguste Escoffier (1846–1935) shaped the modern orthodox view of French *haute cuisine*. Among other contributions, he simplified and updated the work of Carême, was a global ambassador of French cuisine (e.g., he operated renowned restaurants in two Ritz hotels in London), developed the "brigade" system of kitchen organization that is still in wide use today and promoted classic recipes for five major sauces that were long the hallmark of French cuisine. Around the same time, the Michelin guides promoted gastro-tourism and the best restaurants all over France. The first guide was published in 1900, when automobiles and tires—the main source of income for Michelin—were still quite new. The guide series began using its iconic red covers (for hotels and restaurants) in 1926 and finalized its famous and highly influential zero to three-star rating system in 1931. The final great historical moment began in the 1960s (and spanned four decades) with the emergence of "nouvelle cuisine." Led by the legendary Lyon-based chef Paul Bocuse (1926–2018) and by several others (e.g., Alain Chapel, Jean and Pierre Troisgros, Michel Guérard, Roger Vergé, and Raymond Oliver), and championed by the food critics Henri Gault and Christian Millau (the creators of an authoritative restaurant guide and rating system of their own), the movement rebelled against the Escoffier orthodoxy. Their new approach was summarized in a ten-part "formula" that included emphasis on lighter dishes, the freshest local market ingredients, local and regional dishes as inspiration, artistic presentation, use of modern equipment, inventive flavor pairings, and simple herbal seasonings (as opposed to heavy sauces that sometimes mask natural flavors). Some critics argue that nouvelle cuisine lost its edge by the late 1980s. However, somewhat younger chefs like Joël Robuchon (1945–2018) and Alain Ducasse (b. 1956) carried on the tradition of inventive French cooking beyond the height of the nouvelle cuisine craze. Noteworthy chefs of today include Yannick Alleno, Michel Bras, Hélène Darroze, Fabrice Desvignes, Philippe Labbé, Arnaud Lallement, Jean-Michel Lorain, Édouard Loubet, Thierry Marx (a leading practitioner of "molecular gastronomy" as theorized by Hervé This, a French research chemist at the Institut National de la Recherche Agronomique [INRA]), Jean-Christophe Novelli, Alain Passard, Anne-Sophie Pic,

Laurent and Jacques Pourcel, Thibaut Ruggeri, Jean Sulpice, and Jean-Georges Vongerichten.

Several influential French guides offer ratings of French restaurants, including Michelin Red Guide, Gault & Millau (held in high esteem by foodies), and Relais et Châteaux; however, Michelin remains the gold standard. Its coveted three-star (highest) rating was awarded to just twenty-seven French restaurants in its 2019 edition, nine of them in Paris. Even one or two Michelin stars is a great honor. Consider the example of two of the most legendary Parisian restaurants—La Tour d'Argent currently has one Michelin star and Le Grand Véfour has two. France's reputation as a center of the culinary world is also exemplified by the biennial Bocuse d'Or competition in Lyon. Winning the top prize is one of the highest honors in the culinary world. Scandinavian chefs have been quite dominant in recent editions of the competition, but its top prize was won by American chef Mathew Peters in 2017. Not surprisingly, France has some of the top culinary schools in the world. Those with the best reputations include Ferrandi Paris (considered "the Harvard of Gastronomy"), Le Cordon Bleu (established in 1895 and now encompassing thirty-five affiliated schools in twenty countries), Institut Paul Bocuse, École Ritz Escoffier, École Lenôtre, École Vatel, and Ducasse Éducation.

The art of French cooking is not the exclusive domain of experts; it is a cherished cultural tradition that is practiced daily and on special occasions at home by many enthusiastic and skilled amateurs equipped with cookbooks and recipes passed down through generations. Between 2011 and 2018, it was the subject of an annual nationwide celebration in September called La Fête de la Gastronomie, which merged with Goût de France (officially "Good France" in English but literally "Taste of France") in March 2019. Gastronomy and restaurants are a regular theme of French films like *My Wife's Husband* (1963); *The Wing or the Thigh* (1976); *A Chef in Love* (1996); *Haute Cuisine* (2012); *The Chef* (2012); and *Delicious* (2021). They also figure prominently in Marie Ndiaye's critically acclaimed 2016 novel, *The Cheffe*.

See also: Chapter 10: Table Etiquette and Dinner Parties. Chapter 14: Bread; Cheese; Food Quality, Organic Products, and GMO Resistance; Regional Culinary Traditions; Wine.

Further Reading
Booth (2008); Buford (2020); Davis (2013); Ferguson (2006); Gillespie (2016); James (2002); Macdonald (2012); Pinkard (2009); Pitte (2002); Rao et al. (2003); Spang (2001); Steinberger (2009); Trubek (2000).

Regional Culinary Traditions

Entire volumes are devoted to the unique culinary traditions and world-famous dishes of French regions. These extremely varied regional specialties bear the influence of local ingredients and traditional ways of making food, as well as the influence of neighboring countries. Many of France's best-known regional dishes have originated as the hearty fare of common country folk but have since been given upscale renditions and new twists by France's inventive chefs. This is true of what has been called France's national dish—the beef stew known as *pot-au-feu* (beef slowly cooked with carrots, turnips, leeks, onions, and [often] oxtail for flavor), which has several different regional variations. In the west, the region of Brittany is known for its crêpes (thin wheat flour pancakes)—known as *galettes* when prepared with buckwheat flour as a savory dish and filled with cheese, ham and eggs, mushrooms, artichokes, and/or other meats—and tart cider. Specialties in neighboring Normandy include mussels (*moules*) stewed in white wine and *blanquette de veau*, a veal and mirepoix vegetable-base ragout in white sauce made with butter and cream. In the Nord–Pas-de-Calais, as in nearby Belgium, creamy *waterzooï* stew, which can be made with either fish or chicken, is a traditional favorite. The cuisine of Alsace, in the northeastern part of the country, is Germanic in nature. Characteristic dishes include *choucroute garnie*, sauerkraut served with cured meats and potatoes (the taste of the cabbage is not as sweet as in the German variety); and *flammekueche* (*tarte flambée* in French)—the thin, pastry-like tart covered with *fromage blanc* or *crème fraîche*, thinly sliced caramelized onions, and lardons (smoked bacon) that is sometimes called "Alsatian pizza." Not surprisingly, wine figures prominently in the regional cuisine of Burgundy, including in beef bourguignon—a hearty beef and potato stew marinated in red wine. *Coq au vin*, a classic French chicken stew is another dish that is cooked with Burgundy red wine (and a bit of Cognac). The region is also home to one of France's most popular snail dishes—*escargots à la bourguignonne*—traditionally using wild local snails prepared with white wine, butter, garlic, and parsley. The city of Lyon is often considered the gastronomic capital of France but is also known for its variety of *andouillette*, a sausage made from pig intestine. In the French Alps of southeastern France, the predictably hearty fare includes *fondue savoyarde* (typically using melted Comté, Emmental, or Beaufort cheese) and gratin dauphinois—a casserole made with sliced potatoes baked in milk and heavy cream.

Seafood and regional herbs and spices are the main ingredients in the cuisine of the South of France. Examples include ratatouille, the spicy stewed vegetable dish (made with tomatoes, onions, zucchini, eggplant, and peppers) that is popular throughout Provence; and *bouillabaisse*, the traditional spicy fish stew of Marseille. Ingredients vary but traditionally include mussels, red scorpionfish, red mullet, sea robin, monkfish, skate, Conger eel, and/or John Dory fish, but may also include other types of fish and shellfish, sea urchin, and octopus. Other southern dishes include Niçoise salad (with olives and anchovies), tapenade (made with finely chopped olives, capers, and olive oil), and *pistou* soup (a minestrone-like soup made with an olive oil-based basil sauce similar to pesto). *Cassoulet*, a white bean casserole served with pork sausages is common fare that originated in the Occitanie region (e.g., the cities of Castlenaudary, Carcassonne, and Toulouse). *Foie gras*, duck or goose liver—prepared as is or in the form of pâté from fowl specially force-fed via tubes (a controversial process known as *le gavage*, which is prohibited by regulation or law in multiple countries

Ratatouille is a famous vegetable stew dish from Provence, a region in southern France known for its distinctive cuisine. Ratatouille's ingredients typically include tomato, bell pepper, garlic, onion, zucchini, eggplant, and regional spices. Bouillabaisse fish stew (from Marseille) is the region's other iconic dish. (Robinstewart/Dreamstime.com)

in the EU and beyond)—is one of the leading products of Gascony. In the central Auvergne region, *aligot* is Tomme cheese blended into mashed potatoes and served with a Toulouse sausage—comfort food formerly served to religious pilgrims on the road to Santiago de Compostela. Another hearty dish of the Auvergne-Rhône-Alpes region in central France is *soupe vichyssoise* (also called *potage parmentier*)—a creamy leek and potato soup served cold. Local freshwater fish and game—including *sandre* (pikeperch), *brème* (bream), *anguille* (eel), rabbit, venison, wild boar, deer, duck, quail, pheasant, and pigeon—figure quite prominently in the regional cuisine of the Loire Valley. All regional cuisines converge in Paris, which is also known for simple popular dishes like the toasted cheese and ham sandwich known as the *croque monsieur* and, perhaps most famously, rich onion soup made with beef or chicken stock. One common way of generalizing about regional culinary differences in France (first popularized by the American food writer Waverley Root in the 1950s) is according to the type cooking fat that is most commonly used. Using this criterion, France may be divided into three food regions—the domain of butter (Paris, Burgundy, the Alpine region in the southeast, the Bordeaux wine region, and the western coastal regions of Brittany and Normandy), the domain of lard (Alsace and Lorraine), and the domain of olive oil (virtually the entire south, including Provence in the southeast and Gascony in the southwest).

RATATOUILLE

Recipe for four servings by Dawn Perry (www.bonappetit.com). Ingredients: 1 large globe eggplant, peeled, coarsely chopped; 1 large zucchini, sliced into ¼-inch-thick rounds; 2 teaspoons kosher salt; ¾ cup olive oil, divided; 5 sprigs thyme; 1 large onion, halved, sliced ½ inch thick; 1 red bell pepper, ribs and seeds removed, coarsely chopped; 2 garlic cloves, thinly sliced; 2 pints cherry tomatoes, divided; freshly ground black pepper; 1 cup torn basil leaves. Preparation: (1) Preheat oven to 400°F. (2) Toss eggplant, zucchini, and 2 tsp. salt in a colander. Let sit 30 minutes, then pat dry with paper towels. (3) Heat ¼ cup oil in a large Dutch oven or other heavy oven-proof pot over medium-high heat. (4) Add half of eggplant and zucchini and cook, stirring constantly, until vegetables begin to take on color, about 5 minutes. Transfer to a medium bowl. (5) Repeat with ¼ cup oil and remaining eggplant and zucchini. (6) Tie thyme sprigs together with kitchen twine. (7) Heat remaining ¼ cup oil in same pot and cook onion, bell pepper, garlic, and thyme, stirring occasionally, until onion begins to brown and is softened, 8–10 minutes. (8) Add half of tomatoes and cook, stirring occasionally, until just beginning to soften, about 5 minutes. (9) Stir in zucchini and eggplant, then top with remaining 1 pint tomatoes (do not stir); season with salt and pepper. (10) Transfer pot to oven and roast until all vegetables are softened and tomatoes begin to burst, 15–20 minutes. (11) Remove thyme bundle. (12) Transfer to a serving platter and top with basil.

See also: Chapter 1: North and South; Regional Identities; Overseas France. Chapter 14: Cheese; Gastronomy; Wine.

Further Reading

Chevallier (2018); Downie (2017); Long and Long (1996); Pettinger et al. (2006); Robuchon and Bienassis (2014); Young (2001).

Shopping for Food

The French have an array of choices available to them when it comes to shopping for food. One popular option is public markets, which may take the form of either covered market halls or open-air markets. One recent estimate found that there were over 10,000 public markets in France. A sign of their growing popularity is that hundreds of new ones are opened each year. Almost every town of a certain size has its public market. Larger cities have several located in different neighborhoods. Well-known outdoor markets in Paris include Enfants Rouges (located in the Marais district and dating back to the seventeenth century), Mouffetard (located in the Latin Quarter and immortalized in the children's stories by Pierre Gripari), Aligre, Bastille, and Batignolles (specialized in organic products). Markets are appreciated for their farm-direct and local products, fresh fruits and vegetables, organic foods, and artisanal specialty items. They also offer small slices of country life in town and reflect the French emphasis on food as part of a larger and pleasurable cultural experience. Large supermarkets have registered a slight decline in relative share of per capita food shopping in recent years, while public markets have registered an increase. This is due to the fact that public markets have a positive reputation in terms of the food quality issues that matter most to French consumers—natural or organic produce, origin (French, local, or protected terroir appellation), and—above all—taste. A 2018 Opinion Way survey noted that 74% of French people trusted public markets for good tasting food products, compared to 51% for big supermarket chains. Market days for open-air markets vary from location to location, but Saturday is usually a market day. Small specialty food stores used to reign supreme in French commerce and their proprietors were familiar figures in small towns and big city neighborhoods. While their numbers have progressively declined in the face of changing lifestyles and competition from big supermarket chains, they are still holding their own—valued by consumers for their proximity, the artisanal savoir faire of their proprietors and employees, the tradition they embody, and their reputation for offering products that are high-quality, locally sourced, expertly made, and unique. While most French consumers do the bulk of their regular food shopping in big box-type supermarkets, which are frequently located in the suburbs, many do at least some of their shopping in specialty stores—for particular items (like fresh-baked bread) and when quality is more important than price. In cities and larger towns, these small businesses are sometimes grouped together in market streets. Among the most common French food specialty shops, an *épicerie* is a small neighborhood grocery and may be open till late; a *boucherie* (butcher shop) offers fresh meats; a *boulangerie* (bakery) offers fresh-baked bread; a *pâtisserie* sells pastry items, cakes, and other desserts (when combined with a bread bakery, it is called a *boulangerie-pâtisserie*); a *poissonnerie* sells fresh fish and other types of seafood; a *charcuterie* sells pork and delicatessen-type products, including sausages and cold cuts; a *traîteur* (equivalent to a caterer) offers a range of prepared dishes (the modern restaurant, an eighteenth-century invention, traces its roots back to this type of business); a *crémerie* (also called a *laiterie*) sells dairy products; a *fromagerie* specializes in cheeses; a *marchand de vins* offers a wide selection of wines; a *magasin de fruits et légumes* (greengrocer) sells fresh produce (a *marchand de primeurs* specializes in fruits and vegetables available early in the season); a *confiserie* (candy store) offers an array of sweets; and a *chocolatier* specializes in fine chocolates. In France, beer, wine, and spirits are available in supermarkets, grocery stores, and specialty shops.

When more supermarkets began to pop up in France in the 1950s, they were greeted with suspicion (e.g., as yet another American cultural import), the hostility of small shopkeepers (some of whom supported the right-wing populist and antiparliamentary movement known as Poujadism), and government regulations designed to protect smaller businesses (e.g., the 1973 Royer Law). However, the French soon embraced the supermarket concept with both passion and impressive expertise. The French were early proponents of big box everything-under-one-roof combined supermarket/discount department stores—stores so big that they had to be located on the outskirts of town and in the concrete-and-asphalt commercial zones of the suburbs, and were called "hypermarkets" (*hypermarchés* in French). Smaller versions of these types of stores are located in town. The largest French chains are Carrefour (the fifth largest food retailer in the world), E. Leclerc, Intermarché, Casino/Géant/Franprix, Système U (Hyper U/Super U), Leader Price, and Monoprix. France counts 2,000 hypermarkets—stores with a sales floor $\geq 2,500$ m² (8,200 ft²)—and 10,000 supermarkets, which together do €110 billion in business annually. Hypermarkets respond to consumer demand by offering a wide array of products at low prices. By law and longstanding tradition, these large stores were normally closed on Sundays, but this is slowly changing. For example, the 2015 Macron Law increased the number of "Mayor's Sundays" permitting Sunday store openings until 12:00 p.m. and revamped the system of special commercial and tourist zones in which Sunday store openings for large stores is generally permitted—albeit on a voluntary basis on the part of employees pursuant to collective bargaining agreements and compensated with significant overtime pay increases. In 2016, France also enacted a law—the first in the world—to prevent food waste by supermarkets in the form of throwing away food approaching its expiration date (and deliberately spoiling food to prevent foragers from salvaging it). The law requires that such unsold food must now be donated to charities such as food banks.

See also: Chapter 14: Bread; Food Quality, Organic Products, and GMO Resistance; Gastronomy.

Further Reading
de la Pradelle (2006); Jacques (2018); Lescent-Giles (2005); Pettinger et al. (2008); Picot-Coupey et al. (2009); Tchoukaleyska (2014); Téchoueyres (2007).

Wine

Wine and winemaking have been an integral part of Gallic culture since before the existence of France as a nation. Today, France is a leading wine producing and exporting country. Its winemaking regions are legendary; its expertise in the art, science, and business of making wine is recognized the world over; and its top wines are among the most highly coveted by connoisseurs. Wine is an important part of daily life for the French, for whom no proper meal is complete without the right wine. There is archaeological evidence that the ancient Gauls harvested grapes for winemaking 12,000 years ago and the Phocean Greek colony of Massilia (present-day Marseille) was well known as a wine producing and exporting center in the sixth century BCE. Winemaking spread throughout France during the period of Roman rule. In the Middle Ages, French wines already had an international reputation for quality and the wine trade was a lucrative business—for instance, exports to England from the Bordeaux region, then under English control. French winemaking reached another illustrious peak in the nineteenth century. Hence, it was in 1855 that the influential Bordeaux system of rating wines by quality, or *crus*—still in use—was adopted. However, French vineyards were devastated in the second half of the century by a series of plagues, including downy mildew, black rot, and phylloxera—an insect parasite from North America that attacks the rootstock of grapevines. The phylloxera problem was dealt with through hybrids and grafts with resistant plants (the preferred remedy). In the same era, famed microbiologist Louis Pasteur made major scientific contributions to wine quality through his research into fermentation and spoilage.

France's climate, soil, and topography all lend themselves to the production of a variety of fine wines. There are ten major wine-producing regions in France and the wines of each are distinct. The four largest in terms of volume of production are Languedoc-Roussillon (28% of all French wine), Charentes-Cognac (19%), Bordeaux-Bergerac-Aquitaine (14%), and Rhône Valley-Provence (11%). The other major regions are the Southwest, Loire Valley-Centre, Champagne, Burgundy-Beaujolais-Savoie-Jura, Alsace-East, and Corsica. Still wines account for 75% of French production, of which 48% is red, 20% white, and 32% rosé. Wine used in the making of Cognac accounts for 18% of production and sparkling wines the remaining 7%. Wines priced at €3 or less per bottle account for over 50% of production, but only 20% of sales, whereas wines priced at or above €17/bottle represent 10% of volume and 50% of sales. The finest Bordeaux (e.g., Haut Médoc, Margaux, Pauillac, Pessac-Léognan, Pomerol, Saint-Emilion, and Sauternes appellations) and Burgundy vintages, champagnes, and cognacs are world famous and belong to the category of luxury goods. The French wine industry is the source of 600,000 jobs, represents €11.5 billion of value added to the French economy, totals close to €12 billion in annual exports (attaining record levels in recent years), is the second largest positive contributor to France's balance of trade (behind aeronautics), and is its second largest sector of agricultural production (following livestock/meat). France is the world's second largest producer of wine (trailing only Italy and ahead of Spain, the United States, and Australia), but it is by far the world's largest exporter—it accounts for 29% of global sales (ahead of no. 2 Italy by €3 billion; Spain, Australia, Chile, and the United States round out the top six). About 54% of French wine exports stay within the EU, while 46% go to countries outside the EU. In 2016, the largest importers of French wine were the United States, the United Kingdom, Germany, China, and Belgium. French vineyards represent 10% of the global total. Independent grower producers—the majority of which are rather small in scale—account for 57% of French production, cooperatives 37%, and non-grower producers (including large corporate brands) only 6%. Wine tourism is a major industry, involving 10,000 tourist-oriented cellars throughout France and attracting 10 million visitors annually (40% of whom are foreigners). France is also the world's second largest producer of organic wine (behind Italy), accounting for 20% of global production.

The French government and wine industry have a longstanding commitment to promoting quality in winemaking. The first laws linking standards of quality and certified locality of origin date from the early twentieth century and the official AOC ("Appellation d'Origine Contrôlée") designation bestowed on high-quality wines produced using traditional methods (and conforming to additional regulations) in a particular geographical terroir—that is, wines whose character reflects local conditions and grape varieties—was first implemented in 1935. The AOC designation still exists as part of a three-tiered classification system that conforms to European norms adopted in 2009—the official EU equivalent designation is AOP, or "Appellation d'Origine Protégéé," although both designations are used on French wine. AOC/AOP wines number in the 400s and represent the majority of French production. The second level of quality is comprised of the "Indication Géographique Typique," or IGP designation, which certifies that the wine comes from a particular region and still meets high quality standards. The bottom category bears the "Vin de France" label and may be made from grapes from different regions of France. Under an earlier system of classification, which also included a now eliminated category (VDQS, or "Vin Délimité de Qualité Supérieure") situated between the current VOC/VOP and IGP categories. The current "Wine of France" category used to be known as "Table Wine"—a class of less expensive wines for everyday use that are often also quite good for the price. The continued emphasis on quality coincides with the fact that the French are themselves now drinking less wine. The French are now the world's second leading overall consumers of wine (3.5 billion bottles annually, behind the United States and ahead of Italy, Germany, and China) and were still the largest consumers per capita in 2016, but more recent statistics suggest that it has slipped to third place in per capita consumption. In 2016, the French consumed 42 liters of wine per person annually compared to 55 liters/person per year in 2000, 80 liters in 1980, and 100 liters in 1960—a significant downward trend that reflects changing lifestyles, awareness of the health risks of alcohol consumption, and competition from a wider variety of beverages.

See also: Chapter 1: Climate; Mountains; North and South; Regional Identities. Chapter 4: Agriculture; Tourism; Trade. Chapter 14: Bread; Cheese; Food Quality, Organic Products, and GMO Resistance; Gastronomy; Regional Culinary Traditions.

Further Reading
Bohling (2018); Coates (2000); Demossier (2010); Frankel (2014); Guy (2003); Harvey et al. (2014); Loubère (1990); Mazzeo (2008); Paul (1996); Phillips (2016); Smith (2016); Wilson (1999).

TERROIR

A *terroir* is a small rural region as defined by the set of ecological traits (topography, soil, terrain, geology, climate, indigenous plants and animals, etc.), agricultural practices and know-how, and local cultural heritage. The term is used most commonly in reference to wine and other products (e.g., cheese, butter, poultry, fruits, and spirits) that exhibit a distinct local character and savor (esp. those with the "Appellation d'Origine Contrôlé," or AOC, geographical designation). Public support for France's *terroirs*, their agricultural products, and their traditional cuisine is not just a question of business, but also a matter of preserving the nation's locally diverse cultural heritage. The precise number and boundaries of France's *terroirs*, also called *pays* (a word with different historical connotations dating back to the Roman Empire), are matters of discussion—experts identify between 400 and 550 specific local *pays* in France. However, local residents usually know which one they and/or their forebears belong to and refer proudly to *mon pays* ("my country") to signify both their "little homeland" (*terroir*) and "big homeland" (France).

SELECTED BIBLIOGRAPHY

Abramson, Julia. *Food Culture in France*. Greenwood, 2007.

Ayres, Jeffrey, and Michael J. Bosia. "Food Sovereignty as Localized Resistance to Globalization in France and the United States." *Globalization and Food Sovereignty: Global and Local Change in the New Politics of Food*, eds. Peter Andrée, et al. U Toronto P, 2014.

Barboff, Mouette. *French Regional Breads*. Gourcuff Gradenigo, 2018.

Behr, Edward. *The Food and Wine of France: Eating and Drinking from Champagne to Provence*. Penguin, 2016.

Bohling, Joseph. *The Sober Revolution: Appellation Wine and the Transformation of France*. Cornell UP, 2018.

Boisard, Pierre. *Camembert: A National Myth*. Trans. Richard Miller. U California P, 2003.

Booth, Michael. *Sacre Cordon Bleu: What the French Know about Cooking*. Cape, 2008.

Bouchait, Dominique. *Fromages: A French Master's Guide to the Cheeses of France*. Rizzoli, 2018.

Buford, Bill. *Dirt: Adventures in Lyon as a Chef in Training, Father, and Sleuth Looking for the Secret of French Cooking*. Knopf, 2020.

Chevallier, Jim. *About the Baguette: Exploring the Origin of a French National Icon*. Chez Jim, 2012.

Chevallier, Jim. *Before the Baguette: The History of French Bread*. Chez Jim, 2019.

Chevallier, Jim. *A History of the Food of Paris: From Roast Mammoth to Steak Frites*. Rowman & Littlefield, 2018.

Coates, Clive. *An Encyclopedia of the Wines and Domaines of France*. U California P, 2000.

Davis, Jennifer J. *Defining Culinary Authority: The Transformation of Cooking in France, 1650–1830*. LSU P, 2013.

de La Pradelle, Michèle. *Market Day in Provence*. Trans. Amy Jacobs. U Chicago P, 2006.

Demossier, Marion. *Wine Drinking Culture in France: A National Myth or a Modern Passion?* U Wales P, 2010.

Downie, David. *A Taste of Paris: A History of the Parisian Love Affair with Food*. St. Martin's, 2017.

Fantasia, Rick. *French Gastronomy and the Magic of Americanism*. Temple UP, 2018.

Ferguson, Priscilla Parkhurst. *Accounting for Taste: The Triumph of French Cuisine*. U Chicago P, 2006.

Flandrin, Jean-Louis. *Arranging the Meal: A History of Table Service in France*. Trans. Julie E. Johnson, et al. U California P, 2007.

Frankel, Charles. *Land and Wine: The French Terroir*. U Chicago P, 2014.

Gillespie, Cailein. *European Gastronomy into the 21st Century*. Routledge, 2016.

Guy, Kolleen M. *When Champagne Became French: Wine and the Making of a National Identity*. Johns Hopkins UP, 2003.

Harvey, Matt, et al., eds. *Wine and Identity: Branding, Heritage, Terroir*. Routledge, 2014.

Hayes, Graeme. "Collective Action and Civil Disobedience: The Anti-GMO Campaign of the *Faucheurs Volontaires*." *French Politics*, vol. 5, no. 4, 2007, pp. 293–314.

Heller, Chaia. "Post-Industrial 'Quality Agricultural Discourse': Techniques of Governance and Resistance in the French Debate over GM Crops." *Social Anthropology*, vol. 14, no. 3, 2007, pp. 319–334.

Hénaut, Stéphane, and Jeni Mitchell. *A Bite-Sized History of France: Gastronomic Tales of Revolution, War, and Enlightenment*. New P, 2018.

Hoquette, Jean-François, et al. "Quality of Food Products and Consumer Attitudes in France." *Consumer Attitudes to Food Quality Products*, eds. Marija Klopčič, et al. European Federation of Animal Science-Wageningen, 2013, pp. 67–82.

Jacques, Tristan. "The State, Small Shops and Hypermarkets: A Public Policy for Retail, France, 1945–1973." *Business History*, vol. 60, no. 7, 2018, pp. 1026–1048.

James, Kenneth. *Escoffier: The King of Chefs*. Hambledon Continuum, 2002.

Kaplan, Steven Laurence. *Good Bread Is Back: A Contemporary History of French Bread, the Way It Is Made, and the People Who Make It*. Duke UP, 2006.

Kuntz, Marcel. "The GMO Case in France: Politics, Lawlessness and Postmodernism." *GM Crops & Food*, vol. 5, no. 3, 2014, pp. 163–169.

Lescent-Giles, Isabelle. "The Rise of Supermarkets in Twentieth-Century Britain and France." *Land, Shops and Kitchens: Technology and the Food Chain in Twentieth-Century Europe*, eds. Peter Scholliers, et al. Brepols, 2005, pp. 188–211.

Lison, Kathe. *The Whole Fromage: Adventures in the Delectable World of French Cheese*. Broadway, 2013.

Long, Dixon, and Ruthanne Long. *Markets of Provence: A Culinary Tour of Southern France*. Collins, 1996.

Loubère, Leo A. *The Wine Revolution in France: The Twentieth Century*. Princeton UP, 1990.

Macdonald, Bob. *Knives on the Cutting Edge: The Great Chefs' Dining Revolution*. Red Portal-Scarlatta, 2012.

Mazzeo, Tilar J. *The Widow Clicquot: The Story of a Champagne Empire and the Woman Who Ruled It*. Harper, 2008.

Mennell, Stephen. *All Manners of Food: Eating and Taste in England and France from the Middle Ages to the Present*. U Illinois P, 1996.

Nurra, Rina, et al. *French Pâtisserie: Master Recipes and Techniques from the Ferrandi School of Culinary Arts*. Flammarion, 2017.

Onishi, Norimitsu. "French Baguettes from a Vending Machine? 'What a Tragedy.'" *The New York Times*, 10 Nov. 2019, https://nyti.ms/2NxG1Zt.

Paul, Harry H. *Science, Vine, and Wine in Modern France*. Cambridge UP, 1996.

Percival, Bronwen, and Francis Percival. *Reinventing the Wheel: Milk, Microbes, and the Fight for Real Cheese*. U California P, 2019.

Pettinger, Clare, et al. "'All under One Roof?': Differences in Food Availability and Shopping Patterns in Southern France and Central England." *European Journal of Public Health*, vol. 18, no. 2, 2008, pp. 109–114.

Pettinger, Clare, et al. "Meal Patterns and Cooking Practices in Southern France and Central England." *Public Health Nutrition*, vol. 9, no. 8, 2006, pp. 1020–1026.

Phillips, Rod. *French Wine: A History*. U California P, 2016.

Picot-Coupey, Karine, et al. "Grocery Shopping and the Internet: Exploring French Consumers' Perceptions of the 'Hypermarket' and 'Cybermarket' Formats." *The International Review of Retail, Distribution and Consumer Research*, vol. 19, no. 4, 2009, pp. 437–455.

Pinkard, Susan. *A Revolution in Taste: The Rise of French Cuisine, 1650–1800*. Cambridge UP, 2009.

Pitte, Jean-Robert. "French Gastronomy Faced with Globalization." *Phi Kappa Phi Forum*, vol. 82, no. 3, 2002, pp. 34–38.

Pitte, Jean-Robert. *French Gastronomy: The History and Geography of a Passion*. Trans. Jody Gladding. Columbia UP, 2002.

Poilâne, Apollonia. *Poilâne: The Secrets of the World-Famous Bread Bakery*. Houghton Mifflin, 2019.

Rambali, Paul. *Boulangerie: The Craft and Culture of Baking in France*. Macmillan, 1994.

Rao, Hayagreeva, et al. "Institutional Change in Toque Ville: Nouvelle Cuisine as an Identity Movement in French Gastronomy." *American Journal of Sociology*, vol. 108, no. 4, 2003, pp. 795–843.

Robuchon, Joël, and Loic Bienassis. *French Regional Food*. Frances Lincoln, 2014.

Root, Waverley. *The Food of France*. Knopf, 1958; Vintage, 1992.

Saporta, Isabelle. *Vino Business: The Cloudy World of French Wine*. Grove, 2015.

Scannavino, Martine I. "France." *Food, Cuisine, and Cultural Competency for Culinary, Hospitality, and Nutrition Professionals*, ed. Sari Edelstein. Jones & Bartlett, 2011, pp. 133–144.

Scher, Lawrence R., and Allen S. Weiss, eds. *French Food: On the Table, on the Page, and in French Culture*. Routledge, 2001.

Smith, Andrew W. M. *Terror and Terroir: The Winegrowers of the Languedoc and Modern France*. Manchester UP, 2016.

Spang, Rebecca L. *The Invention of the Restaurant: Paris and Modern Gastronomic Culture*. Harvard UP, 2001.

Stapleton, Patricia A. "Contested Technology, Contested Governance: The Fight Over GMO Regulation in France." *Social Science Research Council*, 21 Aug. 2011, https://ssrn.com/abstract=1913996.

Steinberger, Michael. *Au Revoir to All That: The Rise and Fall of French Cuisine*. Bloomsbury, 2009.

Sukapdjo, Amye. "*La Restauration Rapide*: An Affront to the Collective Cultural Memory of French Cuisine." *The Coastal Review*, vol. 4, 2013, no. 1, art. 10, https://doi.org/10.20429/cr.2013.040102.

Tchoukaleyska, Roza. "Outdoor Food Markets as Community Spaces in France." *Geography*, vol. 99, 2014, pp. 99–103.

Téchoueyres, Isabelle. "Food Markets in the City of Bordeaux—From the 1960s until Today: Historical Evolution and Anthropological Aspects." *Food and the City in Europe since 1800*, eds. Peter Lummel, et al. Routledge, 2007, pp. 239–250.

Trubek, Amy B. *Haute Cuisine: How the French Invented the Culinary Profession*. U Pennsylvania P, 2000.

Trubek, Amy B, et al. "Terroir: A French Conversation with a Transnational Future." *Contemporary French and Francophone Studies*, vol. 14, no. 2, 2010, pp. 139–148.

Wilson, James E. *Terroir: The Role of Geology, Climate, and Culture in the Making of French Wines*. U California P, 1999.

Young, Daniel. *Made in Marseille: Food and Flavors from France's Mediterranean Seaport*. Harper Collins, 2001.

CHAPTER 15

LEISURE AND SPORTS

OVERVIEW

The French are productive, value hard work, and are as subject to the hectic pace and stressful demands of modern life as any other people. On the other hand, they also have a long-standing attachment to *la joie de vivre* (joy of living). Leisure time therefore takes on added significance for them. Life cannot be reduced to the grinding routine of what the Parisians call *métro, boulot, dodo*—subway, working, and sleeping. This means that time must be set aside regularly for a slower pace, for family and friends, for good food and conversation, for culture, for fun, and for taking care of oneself—and such time is sacred. To begin with, most places of businesses (not just offices) are closed on Sundays and most people therefore do not work on that day. There have been limited measures loosening some restrictions on work and commerce associated with *le repos dominical* (i.e., Sunday as a day of rest) and polls show that French public opinion favors greater access to certain goods and services on Sunday (esp. in retail commerce). However, there is strong opposition to making major changes to the traditional prohibition of Sunday work.

The most important "time out" for the French is their annual vacation. The first guaranteed paid vacations for French workers date from the 1930s (two weeks), and five weeks have been the rule since the 1980s. While many French people may take a week off at different times of the year—for example, to coincide with their children's school breaks—most French people take a big chunk (if not the majority) of their paid vacation time as part of an extended summer holiday—a major French cultural phenomenon. During July and August, when there are two distinct waves of holiday departures, the pace and feel of life of the entire nation changes palpably—small businesses schedule annual closures and larger ones may scale back production and big projects; airports, train stations, and highways are jammed with vacationers; and people flock to the beaches, countryside, mountains, and cultural heritage sites.

Specific holidays also punctuate the year. The national holiday, July 14, which commemorates the storming of the Bastille in 1789 during the French Revolution, also marks the beginning of summer and is celebrated with parades, fireworks, picnics, and public dancing. Due to France's predominantly Catholic religious heritage, certain Christian/Catholic religious holidays, like Easter Monday, the Ascension, Pentecost Monday, the Assumption (August 15), and All Saint's Day (November 1) are also legal holidays. While these days remain meaningful for France's shrinking number of

413

practicing Catholics, for many other French people they simply represent a welcome day off. On the other hand, Christmas (December 25) is at the heart of a joyous end-of-the-year holiday season with special festive traditions—Christmas markets in public squares, lights in the streets, Provençal manger scenes with their traditional figurines, chocolate cake Yule logs (*bûches de Noël*) for desert on Christmas Eve, and the *galette des rois* pastry with its hidden trinket (whose lucky finder is crowned king) served on the Epiphany—and is celebrated by millions and not just observant Christians. France's major secular holidays are Labor Day (May 1, also called May Day), Victory Day (May 8, commemorating the end of World War II in Europe), and Armistice Day (November 11, commemorating the end of World War I). However, the French do not need holidays to take time to relax and enjoy life. This is also accomplished by dinners with family and friends (Sunday dinners remain a major social ritual but informal gatherings are also relished) and going out to restaurants and cafés. Cafés are an ubiquitous institution in big cities and small towns alike and serve multiple functions, for example, as urban refuges, convenient public meeting places, hubs of neighborhood social life, places of idle leisure, and forums for the exchange of ideas.

France is a land of great natural beauty and diverse landscape, which includes thousands of miles of coastline, numerous rivers and streams, extensive forests, and five major mountainous regions (the Vosges, the Jura, the Alps, the Pyrenees, and the Massif Central). Not surprisingly, the French love activities amid nature, including hiking, camping, hunting, fishing, gliding, sailing, rowing, wind surfing, and skiing and other winter sports. Hunting has declined but is still steeped in tradition. Gardening and leisurely walks in the country are outdoor pastimes appreciated by the less adventurous.

The French love competitive sports and excel in a wide range of them. The most important and iconic sporting event of the year is the Tour de France bicycle race—a twenty-one-stage road race held annually over a twenty-three-day period in July covering 3,500 km (2,200 mi). It is not only the world's most prestigious cycling event but also a sacred annual ritual that celebrates the French countryside and diversity of the national territory. The tour is known around the world for the yellow jersey worn by its leader and its grueling mountain stages. While the French passion for cycling goes well beyond the tour, soccer is the most popular sport in France—played by millions of men, women, and youngsters on every sort of pitch imaginable. France has produced a steady stream of soccer talent since the 1980s—Michel Platini, Jean-Pierre Papin, Éric Cantona, Zinedine Zidane, Fabien Barthez, Thierry Henry, Franck Ribéri, Antoine Griezmann, Paul Pogba, N'Golo Kante, and Kylian Mbappé. This has led to a rising level of play in the French top division professional league (Ligue 1), French stars on the rosters of leading club teams throughout Europe, and—most notably—to two men's FIFA World Cup championships—in 1998 and 2018. Other popular competitive sports in France include rugby (especially in the south), basketball (including a recent spike of French players with successful careers in the American NBA), team handball (France is a perennial world power), tennis (esp. with the French Open, a Grand Slam tournament also called "Roland-Garros"), skiing (with numerous world-class resorts in the Alps), figure skating, swimming, track and field, competitive sailing, judo, and Formula 1 (i.e., Grand Prix-style) automobile racing.

The French are also devoted to cultural pastimes. There is a strong interest in the performing arts, including theater, dance, orchestral and popular music, and circus. A particular French specialty in the performing arts is the cultural festival. There are hundreds of festivals focusing on virtually every field of culture and the performing arts held in cities and towns all over France throughout the year, with a swell of outdoor festivals in the summer. Some of the best known festivals are held outside Paris, for example, in Angoulême (comics), Avignon (theater), Beaune (opera), Bourges (rock), Cannes (cinema), Juan-les-Pins (jazz), La Rochelle (Francophone music), Lyon (contemporary art biennial), Nice (carnival), Nîmes (bullfighting), and Sète (Saint Louis festival). France has also given the world a new model of seasonal, nationwide celebrations of specific fields of culture and creativity starting with the Fête de la Musique (first held in 1982)—an eclectic evening of free open-air concerts held on the day of the summer solstice (June 21).

Museums, books, and movies also figure prominently among French cultural pastimes. There are over 10,000 museums in France, out of which 1,200 are officially designated "museums of France" by the Ministry of Culture. Of the latter, 34% are devoted to the arts, 32% to history, 22% to society and civilization, and 11% to science and technology. Art museums attract two-thirds of all museum visitors—60 million people in 2016, a number nearly equivalent to the national population. Like the peoples of other nations, the French do not read quite as much as in the past. However, they are still among the most avid readers in Europe, third in terms of the average number of hours spent reading for pleasure per person per week (and eighth in the world). Close to three-fourths of all French people age fifteen and above read at least one book for pleasure per year. The most popular categories among new books purchased in 2016 were literature (22% market share), scholastic books, humanities and social sciences, children's books, practical books, and comic book albums. By contrast, the French still go to the movies in near record numbers—in 2016, a total of 213 million people went to the movies in France, the second highest total ever. Over two-thirds of French people went to the movies at least once during the year in 2016. Such devotion to the movies (as well as some help from the French government) has helped the French film industry stay afloat—50% of the full-length commercially shown new releases in 2016 qualified as French. However, Hollywood films still dominate the box office—in the same year, eight out of the top ten films in terms of ticket sales, representing 20% of the total, were American—and just one was French. Art house films (*art et essai*) accounted for one-third of total audience share in 2016.

Further Reading
Christin and Donnat (2014); Haine (2006); Samuel (2005).

Books and Reading

The French have a reputation for taking books seriously, and reading is still an important leisure activity in France. In one recent survey (NOP World Culture Index Score,

2016), France ranked eighth in the world in hours spent reading (print and digital formats) per week per person at 06:54 hours. It was tied with Sweden for third place in Europe—behind the Czech Republic (07:24) and Russia (07:06). The most recent French Ministry of Culture statistics available for the number of books read annually for pleasure are older. The ministry reports that in 2012, 73% of French adults (age fifteen and up) read at least one book for pleasure annually. This was five points higher than the EU average for the same year (68%), three points higher than French average for 1973 (70%), but comparable to the French averages for 1981 and 1997 (74%). Other statistics suggest a gradual downward trend in reading for pleasure. The French read on average five fewer books in 2008 than in 1973. Comparing the same two years, the number of voracious readers is also in decline—16% of French people reported having read twenty or more books for pleasure in 2008, compared to 28% in 1973. Money spent on books and other print media (newspapers and periodicals) also represents a declining share of household cultural budgets, as spending on audiovisual and multi-media content, computers, and mobile telephony has risen—books represented 8% of money spent on culture content and accessories by French households in 2016; and other print media, 14%—compared to 8% (books) and 19% (print media) in 2000 and 13% and 29%, respectively, in 1980. Furthermore, paid readership of daily newspapers and other periodicals has dropped by 50% since the 1970s as more people get their information for free via broadcast media and online.

The French book publishing industry is still relatively healthy—€2.8 billion in sales in 2015 (representing a 7% decline over ten years); 78,000 new French titles legally deposited at the Bibliothèque Nationale de France; 103,000 total titles published (47,000 first editions, 56,000 reprints); translation rights sold for 12,300 titles (54% in Europe, 19% for Mandarin); 87% of sales attributed to the ten largest French publishers (38% to Hachette, the largest French publisher and sixth largest in the world). The most popular categories in 2016 in terms of market share were literature (22% of total sales); textbooks and scholastic titles (15%); humanities, social sciences, and law (14%); children's books (13%); books for practical uses, including leisure and tourism (13%); and comic book albums, graphic novels, and manga (9%). The Ministry of Culture counts over 3,600 bookstores in France (including 500 larger independent ones). Bookstores account for 22% of all new book sales; big box retailers specialized in media and culture (e.g., the Fnac and Cultura chains) account for 24%; generalist supermarket and department stores account for most of the rest. France is also well equipped with public libraries and other public points of access to books (reading rooms, cultural centers, etc.)—7,700 of the former and 8,800 of the latter, well distributed throughout the national territory. France's proactive public policy on everything pertaining to books, publishing, bookstores, authors, and reading is coordinated by the Centre National du Livre (CNL, founded in 1946), a branch of the Ministry of Culture.

See also: Chapter 9: Overview; Francophonie. Chapter 11: Overview. Chapter 15: Movies; Museums. Chapter 16: Internet, Social Media, and Video Games; Press.

Further Reading

Helling (2012); Jeantheau and Johnson (2016); Merfeld-Langston (2010); Ouvry-Vial (2003); Sciolino (2012); Smith (2004); Southerton et al. (2012); Tandé (2020); Villate (2020).

Cafés

The café is a definitive French cultural institution. French cafés come in all shapes and sizes—from the chic Parisian sidewalk cafés popular among tourists and Parisians, with their broad awning-covered outdoor terrasses buzzing with conversation and discreet people watchers; to simple neighborhood haunts with a working-class clientele and tiny family-run establishments with just a few tables and chairs outside on village squares in rural France. In its varied forms, the French café has been depicted

The outdoor terrace of Les Deux Magots, a famous Parisian sidewalk café in the Saint Germain des Près district of the Left Bank—frequented by many famous writers and intellectuals like Ernest Hemingway, James Baldwin, Bertolt Brecht, Jean-Paul Sartre, Simone de Beauvoir, and Albert Camus. French people love to meet in cafés for a leisurely coffee or glass of wine, good conversation, and discreet people-watching. A national institution, sidewalk cafés with awning-covered terraces grew in popularity in Paris in the latter half of the nineteenth century, during and after the transformation of the urban landscape (e.g., the elegant grand boulevards) overseen by Baron Eugène Haussmann. (Kovalenkov Petr/Dreamstime.com)

by poets and artists from Edgar Degas to Robert Doisneau. The modern café traces its roots back to the establishments that first started serving coffee—originally, an exotic drink looked upon as a powerful stimulant—in Paris in the latter part of the seventeenth century. However, the modern French café is unlike a "coffee house" in that it serves both alcoholic beverages (beer, wine by the glass, aperitif drinks like anise-based pastis, etc.) and light meals, as well as pastries and desserts. On the other hand, bistros and brasseries, many of which also feature café-like terrasses where a customer may sit for hours with just something to drink, are full-service informal restaurants.

French cafés serve many different social functions—they are urban refuges (public spaces where one may enjoy a modicum of privacy and calm); convenient meeting places; hubs of local and neighborhood social life; bricks-and-mortar precursors of today's social media that are used for making different types of connections (romantic, professional, political, etc.); places of leisure where one can read, play cards, or watch a sporting event on television in the company of other fans; and important loci for the discussion and dissemination of ideas on politics, society, philosophy, literature, and the arts. They have played an important role in the lives of intellectuals, students, and working people. Café Procope in Paris, which opened in 1686 and still operates today, was frequented by the likes of Voltaire, Rousseau, Diderot, and d'Alembert in the eighteenth century. The famous cafés of the Montparnasse district of Paris (La Rotonde, Le Dome, Le Select, La Coupole, and La Closerie des Lilas) and of the more intimate Saint-Germain-des-Prés neighborhood (Les Deux Magots and Café de Flore) were the meeting places of wide array of international avant-garde figures of the twentieth century. Cafés had a profound effect on the literary and philosophical writings of the existentialists, most notably Jean-Paul Sartre and Simone de Beauvoir. This intellectual heritage is carried on today in the meetings of "philosophical cafés" in many French cities where members of the general public and local intellectuals meet to discuss specially chosen themes. Cafés meant something else to members of the lower classes in the nineteenth century. They were homes away from home for people who lived in dank, dilapidated, and crowded flats and furnished rooms—they were places where people could socialize in the evening and get around restrictions on political meetings, voice their opinions and grievances, and even plot. This gave the cafés something of a bad reputation among conservative members of the bourgeoisie. However, this perception changed somewhat with the addition of many more respectable establishments along the new boulevards created by Baron Haussmann in Paris in the second half of the nineteenth century. Around the same time, the café-concert grew as a quintessentially Parisian cabaret-style entertainment establishment frequented by a broader social range of customers. While people of diverse origins, including many Algerians and Vietnamese, may run small cafés and bistros today, historically, Auvergnats were very prominent in this line of work, particularly in Paris. Many French cafés provide other services too—most notably through their on-site government-licensed tobacconist shop or counter, which typically sells cigarettes and other tobacco products as well as lottery tickets, prepaid phone refill coupons and cards, and postage stamps. A café that is so equipped is called a *café-tabac* and displays an iconic red lozenge-shaped sign. French cafés have adapted to changing times, including offering free Wi-Fi.

However, the traditional image of the café as a place for leisurely face-to-face socialization still resonates. One example is the fictitious Bar du Mistral, which is the center of communal life in the Marseille neighborhood that is the setting for the long-running French soap opera *Plus belle la vie* ("Life More Beautiful").

See also: Chapter 1: Cities; Paris. Chapter 2: Napoleon III and the Second Empire. Chapter 5: Philosophy (Traditional). Chapter 10: Privacy and Personal Space; Table Etiquette and Dinner Parties. Chapter 13: Chanson.

Further Reading
Bisserbie (2020); Boyer (1994); Fitch (2007); Haine (1998); Kleinman (2006); Rittner et al. (2016).

Holidays

There are eleven major legal public holidays in France. On these days, shops and schools are closed and people enjoy time off from work and celebrate with family and friends. Of these, six are related to the Christian (Catholic) faith, which is historically the majority religion of France—Easter Monday, the Feast of the Ascension, Pentecost Monday, the Feast of the Assumption (August 15), All Saint's Day (November 1), and Christmas (December 25). Three of the remaining public holidays are of a patriotic nature—Victory Day (May 8), the National Holiday (July 14), and Armistice Day (November 11). Labor Day (May 1) honors working people. New Year's Day (January 1) is a celebration of the Western new year and the culmination of "the end-of-the-year holidays." There has been some debate about continuing the holiday status of some of the Christian holidays in a country that is strictly secular in a legal sense, and where Christian religious practice is in decline and overall religious diversity is on the rise (incl. a substantial Muslim community). This is especially true of the Ascension (a celebration of Christ's ascent into Heaven on the fortieth day after the Resurrection on Easter Sunday) and the Assumption (a celebration of Mary's bodily assumption into Heaven following her death). These holidays are sacred to practicing Catholics but are just days off for most other French people. Still, these holidays are deeply engrained cultural fixtures in France. Easter is triply important for its religious signification for Christians, as a secular celebration of springtime, and as the basis of a relaxing three-day weekend. Easter is preceded by the forty days of prayer and reflection known as Lent, which begins on Ash Wednesday—the day after Mardi Gras or Fat Tuesday (so named because it is traditionally the last day to enjoy fatty foods before the austerity of Lent). Mardi Gras is the occasion of the joyous carnival celebration, when children dress up in costumes and fanciful, satirical parades are held throughout France (the most famous one is in Nice). All Saint's Day is also a primarily a Catholic holiday as well but has broader meaning as a commemoration of deceased loved ones.

A sacred celebration among Christians of the birth of Jesus Christ, Christmas is the high point of a more-than-a-month-long holiday season that also includes Advent (i.e., the period leading up to Christmas and encompassing the four preceding Sundays), Saint Nicolas Day (December 6, when children receive treats, including gingerbread figures of the saint, who was the inspiration for Santa Claus), New Year's Eve (known in France as Saint Sylvester's Day), New Year's Day, and the Feast of the Epiphany (January 6, a commemoration of the three kings' visit to the Infant Jesus). The entire atmosphere of French cities and towns changes during this period and even non-Christians (and nonpracticing ones) partake in the festive atmosphere, which includes bright lights on homes and in the streets (and on Christmas trees), decorated shops, the buying of presents for loved ones (esp. children who eagerly await the Christmas Eve arrival of Le Père Noël, or Father Christmas), the singing of hymns, and numerous parties and family gatherings.

Aside from the predictable reveling, a unique French New Year's tradition is a televised address to the nation given by the French president on New Year's Eve (*les vœux du président*). The ostensible purpose of the speech is to wish the French people the best in the upcoming year. However, it also offers a retrospective assessment of the action taken by the presidential administration and challenges faced by the nation during the previous year and outlines policy priorities for the upcoming year, rather like a U.S. president's January State of the Union address to Congress.

July 14 is France's national holiday and leading secular holiday. Referred to as Bastille Day in the English-speaking world and simply as *Le Quatorze-Juillet* in French, the date was chosen as France's national holiday in 1880 by the moderate leaders of the Third Republic—primarily in commemoration of the people's storming of the hated Bastille prison in the early days of the French Revolution (July 14, 1789). The violent nature of the original event is mitigated by the fact that the holiday also commemorates the Festival of the Federation, a grand celebration of national unity that took place on the Champs de Mars in Paris in the presence of King Louis XVI, members of the National Assembly, and national guard units from throughout France on the day of the first anniversary of the storming of the Bastille. The celebration of the holiday, which also coincides with the first weeks of summer vacation for school children and the first wave of summer holiday departures, is celebrated in typical fashion with parades, picnics, and fireworks displays. Two unique French July 14 traditions are the massive morning military parade on the Champs-Élysées in Paris and the *bals populaires*, or open-air dances (the most famous ones are hosted by firefighters). May 8 and November 11, which commemorate the Allied victory in Europe in World War II (1945) and the signing of the Armistice putting an end to World War I (1918), respectively, are more solemn events given the great loss of life and national trauma that these two conflicts brought about. May 8 also coincides with the liberation of Orléans by Joan of Arc in 1429 (Hundred Years' War). However, France's secular national holiday of Joan of Arc and Patriotism (an official holiday but not a legal public one with time off from work), which also commemorates this victory, always falls on the second Sunday in May (the Catholic feast day for Saint Joan, patron saint of France, is May 30). As in many other Western countries, Labor Day falls on May 1 and is important for the trade union movement, which holds large rallies on the day. The socialist hymn "The Internationale" is sung at many of these events. Another May Day tradition is to offer someone, even a stranger, a sprig of lilies of the valley (*muguets* in French) as a gesture of good luck and in celebration of the return of spring.

Other important secular holidays in France—without legal days off—include Mother's Day (traditionally, the final Sunday in May); Father's Day (the third Sunday in June); and the Fête de la Musique (Music Day, June 21), which is celebrated by an evening of free open-air concerts. The Fête de la Musique has served as the template for a series of annual nationwide cultural celebrations tied to specific dates, which can be treated a new type of quasi-holiday. The French Ministry of Culture website lists no fewer than twelve official "national events" of this type devoted to other subjects like poetry (March), the French language (March), artistic professions (April), gardens (June), books (July), and cultural/architectural heritage (September). Beyond this list of ministry-sponsored national events, similar cultural celebrations have been created for everything from cinema and contemporary art to the internet, and from gastronomy and bread to secularism. The major religious holidays of France's other prominent religious communities, most notably its large Jewish and Muslim communities, are also widely celebrated and socially significant. For French Jews, this includes Rosh Hashana (Jewish New Year), Yom Kippur (Day of Atonement), Chanukah, Purim, and Pesach (Passover). Chanukah is a more modest celebration for French Jews and does not reach American "Christmas-like" levels of festivity and rampant commercialization. Given that Islam is now the second largest religion in France, Muslim holidays are major events in France that have an impact beyond the community of believers. This is particularly true of the holy month of Ramadan, which is one of the Five Pillars of Islam. Observance of Ramadan—including fasting from dawn until sunset—is growing among formerly nonpracticing and especially younger French Muslims. The end of Ramadan is marked by the celebration of Eid al-Fitr, which is a now a major event throughout France. Two charming French holiday traditions are the April Fool's Day (April 1) practice of sticking a picture or cut-out shape of a fish (*un poisson d'avril*) on a friend's back as a practical joke and the observance of the Feast of Saint Catherine (November 25) by young, unmarried women. Formerly, such young women, known as "Catherinettes" (also a slang term for "spinster"), would honor Saint Catherine (their patroness) by placing a specially made hat, or headdress, on the head of a statue of the saint. However, this practice later waned and the holiday gave rise to more jocular rituals as French society became more secular and women more emancipated. Today, some unmarried French women under the age of twenty-five mark the day—and affirm their individuality and freedom—by wearing elegant, unusual, or comical hats.

See also: Chapter 2: Louis XVI and the End of the Ancien Régime. Chapter 4: Tourism. Chapter 5: Overview; Catholicism. Chapter 8: Early Childhood Education and Elementary Schools. Chapter 13: Fête de la Musique. Chapter 15: Vacations.

Further Reading
Aben (2017); "FrancoFiles #011" (2020); Lestz (2014); Liubchenkova (2020); Pendergast (2008); Salzberg (2020); Simon (2008).

CHRISTMAS TRADITIONS

The following French Christmas traditions are noteworthy. One is Christmas markets in city and town squares—especially prevalent in the north and northeast of France. The most famous one is in Strasbourg. Another is the somewhat sinister legend of "Le Père Fouettard," or "Old Man Whipper," an unkempt figure with a bearded, soot-covered face who accompanies Saint Nicholas on his rounds and distributes lumps of coal—and, according to legend, beatings—to the bad children. *Santons*, tiny figures representing various characters of traditional village life that fill manger scenes (*crèches*) in the Provence region of southern France are a third. Favorite Christmas carols include "Il est né, le divin enfant" (sacred) and "Petit Papa Noël" (secular). Midnight mass is a Christmas Eve tradition for many Catholics. No Christmas Eve celebration would be complete without a *bûche de Noël*, or Yule log, for dessert after an impressive meal—a chocolate sponge cake in the form of a log. The final treat of the season is the *galette des rois* eaten on the Feast of the Epiphany—a flat round pastry with a frangipani filling and a little trinket hidden inside called the *fève*. The person who finds the trinket in their piece is crowned king (or queen).

Movies

French cinema has a deep history—from the Lumière brothers (inventors of the *cinématographe*) in the 1890s to the groundbreaking *films d'auteur* of the Nouvelle Vague in the 1960s (e.g., Chabrol, Truffaut, Godard, Rohmer, and Varda)—and France's role as a center of the film-making industry is taken seriously. The latter point is demonstrated by the global importance of the Cannes Festival and the government's support for the French film industry (via subsidies and grants for young filmmakers) in the face of Hollywood dominance. While the French film industry is undergoing significant economic and technological changes (e.g., the impact of streaming), movies are still a popular form of entertainment in France. According to the French Ministry of Culture, 68% of French people went to the movies at least once in 2016 (the national average was five films per year)—88% of people of age fifteen to nineteen (an average of seven films) and 78% of people of age twenty to twenty-four. The same year, a total of 213 million people went to the movies in France—the second highest total ever. The ministry counted a total of 2,045 movie theaters and 5,843 screens in metropolitan France in 2016 (19% of screens are in the Île-de-France region that includes Paris). Not all cinemas are multiplexes and not all films are industrially made blockbusters. In fact, 60% of all cinemas, 40% of the total number of screens, and 32% of the audience share fall into the *art et essai* (art house) category. In 2016, 716 full-length new release films were shown commercially in France. Of these new releases, 50% qualify as French films (including 40% international coproductions in French and eighty directorial first films of French provenance); 20% were American and 30% were from other countries. American films still dominated in terms of ticket sales and box office—111 million tickets sold for American films compared to 75 million for French ones. Moreover, the top ten films in 2016—eight American and one French film—accounted for 20% of all ticket sales.

The French film industry and cinema arts are supported by the National Center for Cinema and the Moving Image (CNC, founded 1946). Cinema is promoted through hundreds of film festivals held throughout the year in Paris and every corner of France that cover every genre and type of film imaginable as well as the cinema of scores of countries and regions. Aside from the Cannes Festival, other major annual film festivals include Deauville (American), Alpe d'Huez (comedy), Annecy (animation), Bastia (Italian), Beaune (crime films), Clermont-Ferrand (short films), Créteil (women's), Dieppe (Canadian), Dinard (British), Gérardmer (fantasy), Lausanne (African), Montpellier (Mediterranean), Nantes (science fiction), Paris (Arab, Brazilian, documentary, gay and lesbian, German, human rights, Israeli, Iranian, new cinema and contemporary art, Quebecois, Russian, Turkish, etc.), Toulouse (Spanish), and Vesoul (Asian). Two other major yearly events that are important for French cinema and movie goers are the César Awards, France's version of the Oscars (U.S. Academy Awards), held in February; and the Fête du Cinéma, a yearly multiday celebration of movies featuring special reduced ticket prices.

See also: Chapter 12: French Cinema I (through the Nouvelle Vague); French Cinema II (since the Nouvelle Vague); Ministry of Culture. Chapter 16: Internet, Social Media, and Video Games; Pop Culture Icons; Television.

Further Reading
Buchsbaum (2017); Debenedetti and Larceneux (2011); Michael (2019); Roy (2014); Ulff-Møller (2001); Walkley (2018).

Museums

There are over 1,200 museums in France that are officially included in the category *musées de France* by the French Ministry of Culture and a grand total of 10,000 museums. Among the former, over 82% are run by agencies of regional and local government, 13% by private associations and foundations, and 5% by the national government. The number of titular "national" museums is forty. The largest museum umbrella organization in Europe is the Réunion des Musées Nationaux–Grand Palais, which runs thirty-four museums, most of which are in Greater Paris. The capital region has the largest concentration of museums overall and its museums attract close to 60% of all visitors. Of the 1,200 officially recognized museums, 34% are devoted to the arts, 32% to history, 22% to society and civilization, and 11% to science and technology. However, the French art museums attract a 68% share of total visitors. In 2016, France's museums were visited by close to 60 million visitors—34 million were paid entries and 26 million free.

France's ten most visited museums in 2018 were the Musée du Louvre (10.2 million visitors), the Centre Pompidou (3.5 million), the Musée d'Orsay (3.2 million), the City of Sciences and Industry (2.2 million), the Museum of European and Mediterranean Civilizations (MuCEM, 1.3 million), Musée du Quai Branly (1.26 million), the Petit Palais (1.21 million), the Musée de l'Armée (1.2 million), the Grand Palais (1.1 million), and the Orangerie (1 million). Located in Marseille, MuCEM is the only museum in this elite group outside Paris. Other major museums include the Musée Picasso, the Musée Rodin, Palais de Tokyo, Musée Marmotton Monet, Fondation Louis Vuitton, Museum of Decorative Arts, Palais Galliera (Paris Fashion Museum), Musée de Cluny (National Museum of the Middle Ages), Naional Air and Space Museum, National Museum of Natural History, Musée de l'Homme (Museum of Man), National Museum of the History of Immigration, and Museum of the History of France (located at the Palace of Versailles) in or near Paris; and Bayeux Tapestry Museum (Normandy), Charles de Gaulle Memorial (Colombey-les-Deux-Églises, Champagne), Carreau Wendel Mine Museum (Petite-Roselle, Lorraine, part of the European Route of Industrial Heritage), rail (Cité du Train) and automobile (Collection Schlumpf) museums of Mulhouse, Fondation Maeght (Saint-Paul-de-Vence, near Nice); and art museums of Lille, Colmar, Strasbourg, Lyon, Nice, Marseille, Nîmes, Montpellier, Toulouse, and Bordeaux. France has made a concerted effort to decentralize its major cultural institutions. This is the reason why there is a major branch of the Centre Pompidou in Metz (Lorraine, Grand Est region) and a branch of the Louvre in Lens (Pas-de-Calais, Hauts-de-France region). France has also excelled in the development of museums devoted to contemporary art, including fifty-one *centres d'art* and the collections of twenty-three Fonds Régionaux d'Art Contemporain (FRAC). In addition to museums, the French are ardent visitors of national monuments and historical and cultural heritage sites—from the megalithic stones of Carnac (Brittany) to the World War I battlefield and military cemetery of Verdun (Meuse, Grand Est region) and the D-Day beaches of Normandy, and from sites devoted to lace making to ones devoted to wine making. Its medieval cathedrals and Renaissance châteaux are the most treasured of its architectural monuments.

See also: Chapter 1: Historical Sites; Paris. Chapter 4: Tourism. Chapter 12: Overview; Contemporary Architecture; Ministry of Culture.

Further Reading

Benhamou and Moureau (2006); Bodenstein (2011); Eidelman (2018); Greffe et al. (2017); Oliver (2007); Pauget et al. (2021).

Outdoor Pastimes

France is a country of great natural beauty and topographical variety, with 3,400 km (2,100 mi) of coastline in the mainland, 150,000 hectares (380,000 acres) of inland waterways, 16 million hectares (40 million acres) of forests (covering 31% of the territory of the mainland and representing 13% of the European total), five mountain ranges (Vosges, Massif Central, Jura, Alps, Pyrenees), ten national parks (including two in overseas departments) covering a total area of 54,000 km² (34,000 mi²), fifty-one regional natural parks covering 15% of the total national land area, six maritime natural parks, 167 national nature reserves covering 68 million hectares (168 million acres), and 162 regional nature reserves (not counting an additional 7 Corsican nature reserves). With these resources, an ancient and deeply engrained cultural appreciation for the land and sea, and progressive ecological policies, it is not surprising that nature-focused outdoor sports and pastimes are very popular in France. They include hiking, rock climbing, mountain climbing, skiing, hunting, fishing, camping, bird watching, star gazing, biking, ATV (all-terrain vehicle) outings, boating, sailing, various types of surfing, diving, gliding, various types of gathering (wild berries, flowers, herbs, truffles, and mushrooms), and gardening.

Hiking (*la randonnée*) and nature walks are extremely popular pastimes that appeal to both occasional weekend practitioners equipped with picnic baskets or headed for a nearby charming country or mountain *auberge* (inn) and serious hikers (*randonneurs*). There are over 100,000 km (62,000 mi) of walking and hiking trails throughout the mainland, including a 35,000 km (22,000 mi) national network of long-distance trails known as *Sentiers de Grande Randonnée* (SGR) and many more modest and local *Chemins de Grande Randonnée* (CGR). The former are marked (e.g., on trees and stones) by a red band above a white band, whereas the latter are marked by a yellow band. High-quality trail maps are published by the Institut Géographique National (IGN). The Jura, Alps, and Pyrénées contain numerous famous peaks that are challenging even for highly trained and experienced climbers. The French Alps are home to some of the most famous ski resorts in the world. They include Alpe d'Huez, Avoriaz, Chamonix, Courcheval, La Clusaz, La Plagne, Les Deux Alpes, Méribel, Serre Chevalier, Val d'Isère, and Val Thorens. Hunting is deeply engrained in French history and culture. It was once largely limited to the aristocracy. Consequently, the right of ordinary people to hunt was a big political issue at the time of the French Revolution. France still has a political party devoted to defending the interests of hunters and rural traditionalists—the Rurality Movement (founded in 1989 as Hunting, Fishing, Nature and Traditions [CPNT]); current name adopted in 2019. France's National Federation of Hunters estimates that there are 1.1 million licensed hunters in France today. The sport is especially popular in the southwest and along the Mediterranean coast. However, the number of hunters has been in steady decline and the sport is the target of vocal opposition. A wide range of game is hunted in France, including foxes, deer (red, fallow, roe), wild boar, rabbits, Pyrenean and Alpine chamois (goat antelope), mouflon (wild sheep), and birds (pheasants, pigeons, partridge, ducks, and geese). Fishing has become more popular in recent years and ranges from tranquil fishing on the banks of local streams or in small watercraft to serious fly fishing and various types of big-game fishing (e.g., swordfish, bluefin tuna, and sharks) off France's mainland coasts and in the waters around its island departments and territories. Gardening takes many different forms in France, from

---

PÉTANQUE

Pétanque, also called *boules*, is a Provençal/French game that resembles both lawn bowling and horseshoes. It is typically played on hard dirt or gravel—but may also be played on grass or soft dirt at home—using a set of heavy, hand-sized metal balls (650–800 g, 70.5–80 mm diameter) with distinctive markings. Players score points in several rounds by throwing or rolling the balls closer to the small, round target *(cochonnet)* than their opponents. They may also use their turns to knock opponents' balls away from the target. Players must remain inside a circle with both feet planted on the ground while throwing. The games are a fixture of small-town squares and parks, as well as specialized venues called *boulodromes*. Official tournament games are played on lanes measuring 4 × 15 m. French national and world championship tournaments are held biannually. One of the greatest players of the current era is twelve-time world and national champion, Philippe Quintais (b. 1967).

---

backyard vegetable and flower gardens to esthetic landscaping that takes inspiration from the great French classical gardens of the seventeenth century (e.g., the work of André Le Nôtre, 1613–1700). France has a tradition of worker and family gardens—tiny parcels of land grouped together that localities set aside and allot to people who cannot have gardens at home and who tend to their plots (often equipped with individual sheds) on weekends and days off.

See also: Chapter 1: Mountains; Natural Resources and Environment; Overseas France; Rivers. Chapter 4: Tourism. Chapter 15: Sports; Vacations.

Further Reading

Bel et al. (2015); Ducros (2017); Gentin (2011); Lee (2010); Nilsen (2014); Perrin-Malterre et al. (2019); Rogers (2002); Torres et al. (2018).

Sports

Soccer is France's leading team sport. The French national federation (Fédération Française de Football, or FFF) reports close to 2.2 million registered members (including 160,000 women), 15,000 licensed clubs (including forty teams in the top two professional divisions), thirteen regional leagues in the mainland and nine in overseas departments and territories, and over 800,000 federation-sanctioned games played annually. Millions more play the game informally on public pitches and playgrounds, in the streets and vacant lots, and in backyards everywhere. Many more watch games in stadiums and on television. The French have always been competitive in international soccer but have been world powers since the mid-1980s. France's national teams are called Les Bleus. The men's national team won the FIFA World Cup for the first time in 1998, when a multicultural side—euphemistically described as "Black-Blanc-Beur"—led by the attacking midfielder, Zinedine Zidane (widely considered one of the all-time best players in the world), defeated Brazil 3-0 before a home crowd. It won the World Cup for the second time in 2018 behind the brilliant play of Kylian Mbappé (voted the tournament's best young player) and Antoine Griezmann (with strong performances turned in by N'Golo Kante, Paul Pogba, Hugo Lloris, Olivier Giroud, and others)—defeating Croatia 4-2 in the final in Moscow. France finished second in the World Cup in 2002 and third in 1986. Among other international successes, the men's national team won the European Cup in 1984 and 2002.

Individual great players include Ballon d'Or winners Raymond Kopa (1958), Michel Platini (1983–1985), Jean-Pierre Papin (1991), and Zidane (1998); and legends Larbi Benbarek, Just Fontaine, Marius Trésor, Alain Giresse, Jean Tigana, Éric Cantona, Laurent Blanc, Didier Deschamps, Fabien Barthez, Lilian Thuram, Thierry Henry, Marcel Desailly, Youri Djorkaeff, Patrick Vieira, Franck Ribéry, Claude Makelele, and Karim Benzema. France's recent excellence in soccer owes a lot to its strong youth academy and team system, which is especially adept at identifying and developing promising young players from France's suburbs. French-born players have been key to the national teams of Morocco, Algeria, Tunisia, Senegal, Ivory Coast, Cameroon, and Portugal—all significant sources of immigrants to France. At the 2018 FIFA men's World Cup, twenty-nine French players—including a large contingent from the Paris suburbs—competed for other countries' national teams. French professional players are stars in the English Premier League, Spain's La Liga, and for Italy's Serie A, and Germany's Bundesliga. The caliber of play in France's top-tier professional league, Ligue 1, is also high. Legendary French clubs include Paris Saint-Germain, Olympique de Marseille, Olympique Lyonnais, AS Monaco, FC Nantes, FC Girondins de Bordeaux, and AS Saint-Étienne. The French women's national team, which has finished fourth in both the FIFA women's World Cup (2012) and the Olympic Games (2012), has developed into a consistently strong team. France has also produced top-level women's professional club teams and individual stars like Amandine Henry and Wendie Renard, who were both nominees for the inaugural women's Ballon d'Or award (2018). France hosted the FIFA women's World Cup tournament in 2019, won by the United States.

Several other team sports are popular in France. With close to 450,000 registered players and 1,900 licensed clubs, rugby football—introduced in France by the British in the 1870s—is the second most popular team sport and is particularly popular in the south. The top French professional league, the Top 14, plays at a very high level. The second division league is called Rugby Pro D2. Legendary French club teams include Stade Toulousain (Toulouse), Stade Français (Paris), Racing 92 (Greater Paris), USA Perpignan, ASM Clermont Auvergne, Biarritz Olympique, and Béziers. France's men's national team has been competitive internationally. It participates in the annual Six Nations Tournament (along with teams representing England, Scotland, Wales, Ireland, and Italy), which it has won five times. It won the previous version of the tournament—the Five Nations Tournament (without Italy)—twelve times (including shared titles). It has appeared in eight rugby World Cup tournaments, finishing second three times. France is slated to host the tournament in 2023. Basketball has grown tremendously in popularity in France in the past thirty years. The men's national team has performed well in international tournaments like the Olympic Games (ten appearances, three silver medals), the FIBA World Cup (seven appearances, two bronze medals), and the EuroBasket championship (numerous appearances, gold medal in 2013). The team is regularly in the top five of the FIBA world rankings and lost a close game to the United States in final of the 2020 Summer Olympics in Tokyo (held in 2021 due to the COVID-19 pandemic), after having beaten the Americans in the preliminary round. France's top-tier professional league, LNB Pro A, was started in 1921 and features a high caliber of play. However, many of the best French players have had successful careers in the American NBA. Famous current and former French NBA players include Nicolas Batum, Boris Diaw, Evan Fournier, Rudy Gobert, Killian Hayes, Timothé Luwawu-Cabarrot, Théo Maledon, Frank Ntilikina, Joakim Noah, Tony Parker, and Kevin Séraphin. Volleyball and handball are also popular team sports in France. It has a high-level professional league and is an international power in the latter. France has won the biannual IHF World Men's Handball Championship six times—more than any other nation—including four of the last seven times (2009, 2011, 2015, and 2017).

France has a strong tradition in a range of individual sports. It has produced Olympic medalists and international champions in track and field, cycling, fencing, ice skating, skiing, swimming, judo, boxing, sailing, and tennis. France's strong interest in Olympic sports owes something to the fact that the modern Olympic Games (1896–present) were started by a Frenchmen, Pierre de Coubertin (1863–1937), the founder of the International Olympic Committee (IOC). Paris has hosted the Summer Olympic Games twice (1900 and 1924) and will do so again in 2024. Three French cities have hosted the Winter Olympic Games—Chamonix (1924), Grenoble (1968), and Albertville (1992). The French Open—also called Roland-Garros in reference to the stadium complex where its matches are played (late May–early June)—is one of the four Grand Slam events of men's and women's professional tennis. The last French players to win Grand Slam singles titles in tennis are Marion Bartoli (Wimbeldon, 2013—women) and Yannick Noah (Roland-Garros, 1983—men). Motor sports are also very popular in France. Leading races include the French Grand Prix (Formula 1 automobile racing), which was first held in 1906, ceased operations after 2008, and was revived in 2018 (at Circuit Paul Ricard in Le Castellet, near Marseille); and the 24 Hours of Le Mans automobile endurance race, which is held annually since 1923. The Monaco Grand Prix is one of the most prestigious F1 automobile races in the world. The greatest French F1 racer of all time is Alain Prost (b. 1955), a four-time Formula 1 World Drivers' Champion and winner of 51 Grand Prix races. The Dakar Rally (sponsored by a French promoter), formerly known as the Paris–Dakar Rally, was a legendary annual off-road race for cars, trucks, and motorbikes across the desert in Africa. Since the cancellation of the 2008 race due to security concerns, it has been held in South America.

See also: Chapter 1: Mountains; Rivers. Chapter 6: Immigration. Chapter 15: Outdoor Pastimes; Tour de France. Chapter 16: Pop Culture Icons; Television.

Further Reading

Beydoun (2018); Chavinier-Réla et al. (2015); Dauncey and Hare (1999); Didierjean (2008); Dine (2001); Dine (2012); Dubois (2010); Hare (2003); Kilcline (2019); Krasnoff (2012); MacAloon (2008); Matthew (2020); Scelles (2017); Violette and Attali (2018); von Tuyckom (2016).

Tour de France

Started in 1901, the Tour de France bicycle race—a twenty-one-stage road race held annually over a twenty-three-day period in July covering 3,500 km (2,200 mi)—is the world's most prestigious cycling race and the most important sporting event of the year in France. Nicknamed *La Grande Boucle* (the "Great Loop") in French, it has a strong resonance with French national identity as an annual rite of summer, an epic demonstration of individual endurance and team solidarity—qualities that are highly valued in France—before the eyes of thousands of fans who line its route without needing to pay for a ticket (which makes it democratic as well), and a celebration of communion with the French countryside and of the great diversity of the French landscape. The race's circuit varies from year to year and traverses many different parts of France; since 1954, it has regularly incorporated stages in neighboring

Riders pass through the streets of Larchamp (pop. 1,100, Mayenne department, northwest France) during the seventh stage of the 2018 Tour de France bicycle race, to the cheers of spectators. The Tour is not only the world's premier bicycle road race, but also a national cultural institution and sporting rite of summer (over the course of three weeks in July) that showcases the varied topography of France, its diverse regions, and small towns like Larchamp. The 2018 Tour was won by Egan Bernal (Colombia). (Zhbampton /Dreamstime.com)

countries. The race is most famous for its grueling mountain stages in the Pyrenees and Alps—where legends are born, and races won or lost—and for its final stage on the Champs-Élysées. It also includes several time trials.

For each edition of the race, approximately twenty teams of eight riders each compete. The most important objective of each team is to support its designated leader. In regular road stages, the stage and overall leaders ride ahead of the *peleton*, or pack. Winning any stage is a great individual accomplishment. The overall leader based on fastest cumulative time wears the coveted *maillot jaune*, or yellow jersey, and the rider who dons it at the conclusion of the final stage is the overall winner—one of the greatest feats in sports. However, the best overall individual time (general classification) is not the only aspect of the race for which a prize is given. There is also a points competition based on the order in which riders finish each stage. The current race leader and final winner on points don the green jersey. The red-and-white polka-dot jersey (*le maillot à pois*) is worn/won by the best mountain stage racer; and the white jersey is donned by the best young racer. The greatest heroes of the Tour are its four five-time winners—Jacques Anquetil (France), Eddy Merckx (Belgium), Bernard Hinault (France), and Miguel Indurain (Spain). Still active, Chris Froome (Great Britain) has won it four times. The first non-European winner was Greg LeMond (United States) in 1986. Raymond Poulidor (France) is a legendary and popular hero in France and arguably the most acclaimed cyclist never to have won the Tour—he finished second three times and third five times. The 2020 and 2021 editions of the Tour were both won by Tadej Pogačar of Slovenia. Questions of doping (e.g., blood transfusions and performance enhancing drugs) have plagued the race since its early days but were pervasive in the 1990s and 2000s, resulting in several high-profile disqualifications and suspensions. The most notorious example was the American racer Lance Armstrong, who was stripped of his seven consecutive Tour wins (1999–2005) in 2012. There has been no consistent women's equivalent of the Tour de France although several attempts have been made beginning in 1955. Since 2014, the organizers of the men's Tour have sponsored La Course, an elite race for women that is currently a one-day event held in conjunction with one of the stages of the men's Tour.

See also: Chapter 1: Overview; Mountains; North and South; Regional Identities. Chapter 4: Tourism. Chapter 15: Outdoor Pastimes; Sports.

Further Reading

Andreff (2016); Dauncey (2012); Dauncey and Hare (2003); Hamilton and Coyle (2012); Reed (2015); Schneider (2007); Sidwells (2010); Thompson (2008).

Vacations

Vacations are very important to the French people. The first legally mandated paid vacations in France date from 1936—originally, two weeks annually—during the

Socialist-led progressive coalition government known as the Popular Front. People who work full time in France are currently (since 1982) entitled to five weeks' paid vacation annually in addition to national public holidays. Some salaried employees accumulate additional paid time off to offset having worked more than the legal maximum thirty-five-hour workweek over given stretches (such extra days off are called "RTT" days in reference to the *Réduction du Temps de Travail*, or "work time reduction" arrangements under which they are taken).

French people take vacations at various times throughout the year. Families with children in school often plan their vacations to coincide with school-year breaks (*les vacances scolaires*), like the February winter break, which is a popular time for skiing and winter sports holidays. However, the main vacationing time of the year is during the summer months of July and August, when most French people who can afford to do so go somewhere for an extended summer holiday—often two or more weeks long. There is a palpable change in the rhythm of French life during the summer vacation season—so much so that September is considered the time of *La Rentrée* ("The Return") because it is a return to normal routines for more than just the children who must come to terms with going back to school. During July and August, cities are emptied of a good proportion of their residents, small businesses typically close completely for a few weeks annually, and large businesses either slow down production or carefully calibrate the departures of employees in order to keep functioning with minimal disruption. Airports, train stations, and highways are notoriously clogged—especially during the first weekend after the July 14 national holiday and in early August, when returning *Juilletistes* (people who take their summer holidays in July) and departing *Aoûtistes* (those who prefer August) cross paths, and seaside destinations are crowded. Summer destinations vary according to personal preference and household budget. France's Mediterranean and Atlantic beaches are among the most popular, as are similar locations elsewhere in the EU (esp. Spain, Italy, and Greece). Those with more money to spend seek out more distant and "exotic" locations like the Caribbean or Tahiti. The French are fond of so-called green tourism, which includes camping, hiking, other close-to-nature activities in the mountains, and peaceful stays at a *gîte rural* in the country. Other French people are drawn to cultural tourism (e.g., summer festivals, museums and historical sites, and the vibrant cities of France and the EU), theme parks (e.g., Disneyland Paris, Parc Astérix near Paris, Futuroscope near Poitiers, Puy du Fou in the Vendée region, and Space City in Toulouse), and foreign travel to visit relatives in the homeland for families with immigrant backgrounds.

The French passion for vacation (and France's status as the number one tourist destination in the world) has had a profound impact on the French economy and culture. French tourist and vacation infrastructures are highly developed, the French excel in the hospitality industry, and French people have created some of the most innovative and iconic businesses in the field (e.g., Club Med, cofounded in 1950 by the Belgian Gérard Blitz and the Frenchman Gilbert Trigano).

Summer holidays are a frequent subject of books, songs, television shows, and films—including the iconic *Monsieur Hulot's Holiday* (directed by and starring Jacques Tati, 1953); Roger Vadim's Brigitte Bardot bombshell classic *And God Created*

Woman (1956); Jean-Luc Godard's caustic *Weekend* (1967); Jacques Deray's sultry psychological thriller starring Alain Delon and Romy Schneider, *La Piscine* (1969); the three movies in the cult *Les Bronzés* series of comedies (*French Fried Vacation*, 1978, 1979, 2006); the Claude Zidi comedy (starring Coluche) about a travelers' aid service, *Banzaï* (1983); Eric Rohmer's moody *Pauline at the Beach* (1983), *The Green Ray* (1986), and *A Summer's Tale* (1996); François Ozon's disturbing thriller *See the Sea* (1997); the ensemble comedy *Hikers* (dir. Philippe Harel, 1997); the summer camp comedy (an entire subgenre) favorite *Those Happy Days* (2006); thoughtful portrayals of youthful summer love like *Goodbye First Love* (dir. Mia Hansen-Løve, 2011) and *Summer of 85* (dir. Ozon, 2020); Antonin Peretjatko's snarky satire *The Rendez-Vous of the Déja-Vu* (2013); the wholesome and nostalgic *Nicholas on Holiday* (dir. Laurent Tirard, 2014), an installment in a film franchise based on the *Petit Nicholas* children's book series by René Goscinny and Sempé); and stories of family/intergenerational conflict against the backdrop of summer holidays like *The Great Highway* (dir. Hubert, 1987), *My Summer in Provence* (dir. Rose Bosch, 2014—starring Jean Reno) and *The Summer of All My Parents* (dir. Diastème, 2016).

See also: Chapter 1: Overview; Climate; Historical Sites; Mountains; North and South; Overseas France; Paris; Regional Identities; Rivers; Transportation. Chapter 4: Tourism. Chapter 8: Early Childhood Education and Elementary Schools. Chapter 15: Holidays; Outdoor Pastimes.

Further Reading
Furlough (1993); Furlough (1998); Furlough (2001); Manera and Pohl (2009); Onishi (2019); Renaut (2011).

SELECTED BIBLIOGRAPHY

Aben, Jacques. "The 14 July Parade, or the Military Ceremonial as a Political Instrument." *Review of the Air Force Academy*, vol. 15, no. 3, 2017, pp. 15–26.

Andreff, Wladimir. "The Tour de France: A Success Story in Spite of Competitive Imbalance and Doping." *The Economics of Professional Road Cycling*, eds. Daam Van Reeth and Daniel Joseph Larson. Springer, 2016, pp. 233–255.

Bel, François, et al. "Domestic Demand for Tourism in Rural Areas: Insights from Summer Stays in Three French Regions." *Tourism Management*, vol. 46, 2015, pp. 562–570.

Benhamou, Françoise, and Nathalie Moureau. "From Ivory Towers to Museums Open to the Community: Changes and Developments in France's Cultural Policy." *Museum International*, vol. 58, no. 4, 2006, pp. 21–28.

Beydoun, Khaled, "Les Bleus and Black: A Football Elegy to French Colorblindness." *Minnesota Law Review*, vol. 103, 2018, pp. 20–27.

Bisserbie, Noemie. "France Says Au Revoir to the Cafe." *The Wall Street Journal*, 7 Feb. 2020, https://www.wsj.com/articles/france-says-au-revoir-to-the-cafe-11581091992.

Bodenstein, Felicity. "National Museums in France." *Building National Museums in Europe 1750–2010*, eds. Peter Aronsson and Gabriella Elgenius. Routledge, Conference proceedings from European National Museums: Identity Politics; the Uses of the Past, and the European Citizen, Bologna, Apr. 2011, EuNaMas Report no. 1, Linköping Electronic Conference Proceedings, No. 64, pp. 289–326.

Boyer, Marie-France. *The French Café*. Thames & Hudson, 1994.

Buchsbaum, Jonathan. *Exception Taken: How France Has Defied Hollywood's New World Order*. Columbia UP, 2017.

Chavinier-Réla, Sabine, et al. "Sport Clubs in France." *Sport Clubs in Europe. A Cross-National Comparative Perspective*, eds. Christoph Breuer, et al. Springer, 2015, pp. 161–185.

Christin, Angèle, and Olivier Donnat. "French and American Cultural Participation: Elements of Comparison, 1981–2008." *Culture études*, vol. 1, no. 1, 2014, pp. 1–16.

Dauncey, Hugh. *French Cycling: A Social and Cultural History*. Liverpool UP, 2012.

Dauncey, Hugh, and Geoff Hare, eds. *France and the 1998 World Cup: The National Impact of a World Sporting Event*. Cass, 1999.

Dauncey, Hugh, and Geoff Hare, eds. *The Tour de France, 1903–2003: A Century of Sporting Structures, Meanings and Values*. Cass, 2003.

Debenedetti Stéphane, and Fabrice Larceneux. "'The Taste of Others': Divergences in Tastes between Professional Experts and Ordinary Consumers of Movies in France." *Recherche et Applications en Marketing* (English Edition), vol. 26, no. 4, 2011, pp. 71–88.

Didierjean, Romaine. "Sport, Gender and Migration in France." *Sport, Integration, Europe: Widening Horizons in Intercultural Education*, eds. Petra Gieß-Stüber and Diethelm Blecking. Trans. Julia Thornton and Rachel Ives. Schneider, 2008, pp. 268–274.

Dine, Philip. *French Rugby Football: A Cultural History*. Berg, 2001.

Dine, Philip. *Sport and Identity in France: Practices, Locations, Representations*. Peter Lang, 2012.

Dubois, Laurent. *Soccer Empire: The World Cup and the Future of France*. U California P, 2010.

Ducros, Hélène. "Wayfinding Design for Rural Flânerie in France." *The Routledge International Handbook of Walking*, eds. C. Michael Hall, et al. Routledge, 2017, pp. 340–349.

Eidelman, Jacqueline. "What Museums Do We Want in France in the Future?" *Museum Management and Curatorship*, vol. 33, no. 6, 2018, pp. 585–593.

Fitch, Noel Riley, and Rick Tulka. *Paris Café: The Sélect Crowd*. Soft Skull, 2007.

"FrancoFiles #011: Bastille Day—Then & Now—The History & Present Culture of France's National Day." *France in the United States*, Embassy of France in Washington, D.C., 2 Jul. 2020, https://franceintheus.org/spip.php?article9803.

Furlough, Ellen. "Making Mass Vacations: Tourism and Consumer Culture in France, 1930s to 1970s." *Comparative Studies in Society and History*, vol. 40, no. 2, 1998, pp. 247–286.

Furlough, Ellen. "Packaging Pleasures: Club Méditerranée and French Consumer Culture, 1950–1968." *French Historical Studies*, vol. 18, no. 1, 1993, pp. 65–81.

Furlough, Ellen. "Vacations and Citizenship in Post-War France." *Sites*, vol. 5, no. 1, 2001, pp. 121–129.

Gentin, Sandra. "Outdoor Recreation and Ethnicity in Europe: A Review." *Urban Forestry & Urban Greening*, vol. 10, no. 3, 2011, pp. 153–161.

Greffe, Xavier, et al. "The Future of the Museum in the Twenty-first Century: Recent Clues from France." *Museum Management and Curatorship*, vol. 32, no. 4, 2017, pp. 319–334.

Haine, W. Scott. *Culture and Customs of France*. Greenwood, 2006; esp. pp. 87–106 ("Social Customs: Leisure, Holidays, Sports, and Festivals").

Haine, W. Scott. *The World of the Paris Café: Sociability among the French Working Class, 1789–1914*. Johns Hopkins UP, 1998.

Hamilton, Tyler, and Daniel Coyle. *The Secret Race: Inside the Hidden World of the Tour de France: Doping, Cover-ups, and Winning at All Costs*. Bantam, 2012.

Hare, Geoff. *Football in France: A Cultural History*. Berg, 2003.

Helling, John. *Public Libraries and Their National Policies: International Case Studies*. Chandos, 2012; esp. 101–116 ("France").

Jeantheau, Jean-Pierre, and Sandra Johnson. *Literacy in France: Country Report, Short Version*. European Literacy Project Network, 2016, https://orbi.uliege.be/bitstream/2268/203615/1/France_Short_Report1.pdf.

Kilcline, Cathal. *Sport and Society in Global France: Nations, Migrations, Corporations*. Liverpool UP, 2019.

Kleinman, Sharon S. "Cafe Culture in France and the United States: A Comparative Ethnographic Study of the Use of Mobile Information and Communication Technologies." *Atlantic Journal of Communication*, vol. 14, no. 4, 2006, pp. 191–210.

Krasnoff, Lindsay Sarah. *The Making of Les Bleus: Sport in France, 1958–2010*. Lexington, 2012.

Lee, Il-Yul. "Calmness and Recreation: The Role of Regional Nature Park in the Ile-de-France Region." *International Journal of Tourism Sciences*, vol. 10, no. 1, 2010, pp. 13–22.

Lestz, Margo. *French Holidays & Traditions*. Boo-Tickety, 2014.

Liubchenkova, Natalie. "Bastille Day in Pictures: 100 Years of France's National Celebration." *Euronews*, 23 Jul. 2020, https://www.euronews.com/2020/07/14/bastille-day-in-pictures-100-years-of-france-s-national-celebration.

MacAloon, John J. *This Great Symbol: Pierre de Coubertin and the Origins of the Modern Olympic Games*. Routledge, 2008.

Manera, Carles, and Manfred Pohl. *Europe at the Seaside: The Economic History of Mass Tourism in the Mediterranean*. Berghahn, 2009.

Matthew, Spiro. *Sacre Bleu: Zidane to Mbappé—A Football Journey*. Biteback, 2020.

Merfeld-Langston, Audra L. "Celebrating Literature to Shape Citizenship: France's 2007 'Lire en fête.'" *Modern & Contemporary France*, vol. 18, no. 3, 2010, pp. 343–356.

Michael, Charlie. *French Blockbusters: Cultural Politics of a Transnational Cinema*. Edinburgh UP, 2019.

Nilsen, Micheline. *The Working Man's Green Space: Allotment Gardens in England, France, and Germany, 1870–1919*. U Virginia P, 2014.

Oliver, Bette Wyn. *From Royal to National: The Louvre Museum and the Bibliothèque Nationale*. Lexington, 2007.

Onishi, Norimitsu. "Holidays Are a Way of Life in France in August: Yellow Vests Can't Afford Them." *The New York Times*, 29 Aug. 2019, https://nyti.ms/2ZHTjd3.

Ouvry-Vial, Brigitte. "Small and Big Publishers in France: Is Literature a Rare Species?" *Publishing Research Quarterly*, vol. 19, 2003, pp. 31–44.

Pauget, Bertrand, et al. "The Future of French Museums in 2030." *Technological Forecasting and Social Change*, vol. 162, 2021, https://doi.org/10.1016/j.techfore.2020.120384.

Pendergast, Chritopher. *The Fourteenth of July and the Taking of the Bastille*. Profile Books, 2008.

Perrin-Malterre, Clémence, et al. "Outdoor Recreation in a Regional Park: Types of Hikers, Ski Tourers and Snowshoers in the Hautes-Bauges (Savoie, France)." *Annals of Leisure Research*, Oct. 2019, https://doi.org/10.1080/11745398.2019.1682016.

Reed, Eric. *Selling the Yellow Jersey: The Tour de France in the Global Era*. U Chicago P, 2015.

Renaut, Christian. "Disneyland Paris: A Clash of Cultures." *Disneyland and Culture: Essays on the Parks and Their Influence*, eds. Kathy Merlock Jackson and Mark I. West. McFarland, 2011.

Rittner, Leona, et al., eds. *The Thinking Space: The Café as a Cultural Institution in Paris, Italy and Vienna*. Routledge, 2016.

Rogers, Susan Carol. "Which Heritage?: Nature, Culture, and Identity in French Rural Tourism." *French Historical Studies*, vol. 25, no. 3, 2002, pp. 475–503.

Roy, Pierre. "When Disruption Is Driven by Established Firms: The Case of French Multiplex Theatres." *International Perspectives on Business Innovation and Disruption in the Creative Industries: Film, Video, and Photography*, eds. Robert DeFellippi and Patrik Wikström. Edward Elgar, 2014, pp. 88–104.

Salzberg, Alysa. "These Are the Surprising Differences between Christmas in France and Abroad." *French Together*, 17 Jan. 2020, https://frenchtogether.com/christmas-france.

Samuel, Nicole. "France." *Free Time and Leisure Participation: International Perspectives*, eds. Grant Cushman, et al. CABI, 2005, pp. 75–100.

Scelles Nicolas. "France: Organisation of Sport and Policy Towards Sport Federations." *Sport Policy Systems and Sport Federations*, eds. Jeroen Scheerder, et al. Palgrave Macmillan, 2017, pp. 133–155.

Schneider, Angela J. "Cultural Nuances: Doping, Cycling and the Tour de France." *Doping in Sport: Global Ethical Issues*, eds. Angela J. Schneider and Fan Hong. Routledge, 2007, pp. 36–50.

Sciolino, Elaine. "The French Still Flock to Bookstores." *The New York Times*, 20 Jun. 2012, https://nyti.ms/MMb7m2.

Sidwells, Chris. *A Race for Madmen: The History of the Tour de France*. Collins, 2010.

Simon, Vera C. "Nations on Screen: Live Broadcasting of Bastille Day and Reunification Day." *European Review of History*, vol. 15, no. 6, 2008, pp. 615–628.

Smith, Kelvin. "Why French Publishing Is Different. Or Is It?" *Logos*, vol. 15, no. 4, 2004, pp. 203–208.

Southerton, Dale, et al. "Practices and Trajectories: A Comparative Analysis of Reading in France, Norway, the Netherlands, the UK and the USA." *Journal of Consumer Culture*, vol. 12, no. 3, 2012, pp. 237–262.

Tandé, Alexandre. "Cultural Policies Mixing Commonality and Difference?: The Case of Public Libraries in French Cities." *Ethnic and Racial Studies*, vol. 43, no. 11, 2020, pp. 2062–2079.

Thompson, Christopher S. *Tour de France: A Cultural History*. U California P, 2008.

Torres, Ana Cristina, et al. "Small but Powerful: The Importance of French Community Gardens for Residents." *Landscape and Urban Planning*, vol. 180, 2018, pp. 5–14.

Ulff-Møller, Jens. *Hollywood's Film Wars with France: Film-Trade Diplomacy and the Emergence of the French Film Quota Policy*. U Rochester P, 2001.

Urbain, Jean-Didier. *At the Beach*. Trans. Catherine Porter. U Minnesota P, 2003.

Villate, Pascale. "A Further Tale of Two Cities: Bookselling in London and Paris." *Publishing History*, vol. 82, 2020, pp. 49–75.

Violette, Louis, and Michaël Attali. "Sporting Memory and its Heritagisation: The Example of Roland-Garros." *French Cultural Studies*, vol. 29, no. 3, 2018, pp. 279–289.

von Tuyckom, Charlotte. "Youth Sport Participation: A Comparison between European Member States." *Routledge Handbook of Youth Sport*, eds. Ken Green and Andy Smith. Routledge, 2016, pp. 61–71.

Walkley, Sarah. *Cultural Diversity in the French Film Industry: Defending the Cultural Exception in a Digital Age*. Palgrave Macmillan, 2018.

CHAPTER 16

MEDIA AND POPULAR CULTURE

OVERVIEW

Freedom of speech and of the press are important to French democracy and republicanism. They are among the fundamental rights protected in the 1789 Declaration of the Rights of Man and the Citizen. The rights and responsibilities of a free press were further spelled out in the landmark 1881 French press freedom law and have been put to the test on numerous occasions. For instance, during the Dreyfus Affair, which was hotly debated in the French press, the novelist Émile Zola published "J'accuse...!," his famous open letter to the French president on the front page of *L'Aurore* (January 13, 1898). The letter accused the French government of anti-Semitism and willfully perpetrating a miscarriage of justice in the case of the Jewish army captain Alfred Dreyfus's dubious prosecution for espionage. Zola was tried and convicted for libel, but his letter helped turn the tide of the affair in favor of Dreyfus. The rights and responsibility of the free press were once again thrust into the forefront of public debate after two gunmen killed twelve people in a terrorist attack on the Paris headquarters of the satirical newspaper *Charlie Hebdo* on January 7, 2015 in retaliation for its publication of provocative cartoons ridiculing the Islamic prophet Muhammad. Rallying behind the "Je suis Charlie" slogan, there was a wave of public support for the slain cartoonists and journalists, and for freedom of the press, including of content critical of religion that might deemed blasphemous by believers. However, others critiqued the publication's crass and offensive portrayals of Islam, the religion of a large and mistreated minority in France.

As is the case in many other countries, paid subscriptions and readership of print copies of newspapers and magazines in France are in steep decline as readers and content have shifted to online platforms. This has led to major structural changes in journalism and the periodicals publishing industry in France. However, all of France's leading print publications also have extensive websites and offer electronic subscriptions. News coverage is dominated nationally by daily newspapers like *Le Monde*, *Le Figaro*, *Libération*, *La Croix*, and *L'Humanité*; and by weekly newsmagazines like *L'Obs*, *L'Express*, and *Le Point*. *Le Canard Enchaîné* is a national weekly newspaper known for its satirical commentary and investigative reporting. *Médiapart* and *Rue 89* are leading exclusively online sources of quality journalism. One of France's most iconic publications, the weekly magazine *Paris Match*, combines current events coverage with illustrated features about celebrities. France also has a highly developed regional press. Every major French city has a daily newspaper of its own. Leading examples include *Ouest-France* (western France), *Le Parisien* (Paris), *Le Progrès* (Lyon), and *La Provence* (Marseille). There are daily, weekly, and monthly publications in France that specialize in a wide range of subject matter and appeal to every type of reader. Examples include the dailies *L'Équipe* (sports) and *Les Échos* (business), the weeklies *Télé Loisirs* and *Télérama* (television listings and entertainment), and the monthlies *Le Monde Diplomatique* (commentary on politics, foreign affairs, society, and culture) and *Les Inrocks* (music and popular culture). Agence France-Presse, better known as AFP, is one of the world's leading news gathering organizations alongside the Associated Press and Reuters.

The landscape of French television and radio has changed considerably as result of government deregulation and privatization in the 1980s and the rise of the internet in the 2000s. France has hundreds of television channels that offer general and specialized content via free-to-air digital terrestrial televisions (twenty-six national channels and forty-one local ones), cable, satellite, and streaming. France has maintained a strong offering of public television via the France Télévisions group, which includes France 2 (primary flagship station), France 3 (secondary flagship station and regional programming), France 4 (young viewers and live performance), and France 5 (educational TV). France's leading TV broadcaster is the privately held national channel TF1 (20% audience share). Other major channels include Canal+, M6, and Arte (a Franco-German joint venture that offers high-quality arts and cultural programing). Leading twenty-four-hour all-news channels are BFM TV, Cnews, France 24, LCI, and France Info. TV5 is a global Francophone satellite TV channel.

The audience for French radio has shrunk over the past decades. However, the medium (including its satellite and internet streaming offshoots) remains important for news, information, entertainment, and popular music. Leading radio channels include RTL, France Inter, RMC, NRJ, France Bleu, Europe 1, Nostalgie, France Info, Skyrock, Fun Radio, Chérie, France Culture, Radio Classique, Rire et Chansons, and France Musique. The Conseil Supérieur de l'Audiovisuel is France's independent television and audiovisual media regulatory agency.

France was once known for a certain ambivalence with respect to the internet. In the 1990s, concerns focused on the existential threat it posed to France's videotext-based precursor online network, Minitel (1982–2012), American and Anglophone hegemony in cyberspace, and the protection of individual privacy online. The latter two topics are still of great concern because American companies like Google, Facebook, Twitter, and Amazon dominate the French market and threats to personal data privacy have grown with the proliferation of social media platforms. The National Commission on Information Technology and Civil Liberties (CNIL) is the independent French regulatory agency tasked with protecting personal data and civil liberties online and is a leader in the fight waged by the EU to hold global conglomerates like Google and Facebook responsible for the protection of the privacy and personal data of their users. France's landmark Digital Republic Law (2016) includes provisions that acknowledge an individual "right to be forgotten" online (e.g., delisting of compromising and false information about oneself in web searches) and equal access to online resources and communication. France is also a leading proponent of net neutrality. These concerns, however, have not prevented the internet and social networks from flourishing in France. It has the fourth highest number of internet users in Europe and French is the fourth most used language on the internet. Almost 86% of French households have access to the internet, 78% of French people (age twelve and up) have personal computers, 94% have a mobile phone, 75% have smartphones (98% of eighteen- to twenty-four-year-olds), 58% have access to 4G broadband network service. About 89% of French people are internet users (close to 100% for people under the age of sixty) and 80% of French people use it daily (close to 100% for people between the ages of eighteen and thirty-nine). On average, French people spend eighteen hours per week online—a national average now equal to the average amount of time spent watching television. The internet is a common means of shopping (59% of the general population make purchases online, totaling over €80 billion in sales in 2017), filling out official forms and completing other administrative tasks (65% of the population), and looking for a job (27% of the population). France has 38 million regular users of social networks—59% of the general population, 76% of twelve- to seventeen-year-olds, and 93% of eighteen- to twenty-four-year-olds. The fifteen leading social networks in France (by percentage of use among users, 2021) are Facebook, Facebook Messenger, WhatsApp, Instagram, Snapchat, TikTok, Twitter, Pinterest, LinkedIn, iMessage, Skype, Discord, Telegram, Reddit, and Signal. Young people are particularly avid users of social networks—a generational trend that has raised concerns in France about cyberbullying and other forms of online harassment, the protection of minors, identity theft, account hacking, and the effects on cognitive and psychological development.

The media and entertainment industries are the two pillars of France's vibrant popular culture. While the media, performing arts, and entertainment industries—including the French film and music industries—are still largely based in Paris, this does not mean that France's other regions and cities do not have their fair share of theater and performing arts, live music, museums, arts and cultural festivals, nightlife, and other types of popular entertainment. In fact, cultural decentralization has been a government policy priority since the 1980s. Another policy priority has been the French defense of the so-called cultural exception—that cultural products are not like other commercial goods and services and therefore merit certain protections in an age of global free trade and American cultural hegemony. The main French focus in this respect has been on movies and popular music, which have benefited from government subsidies and quotas. The underlying principle of the protections is that a nation has a right to moving images and songs that reflect the culture and language of its people. While such measures have not slowed the appeal of Hollywood movies and international pop music (much of it in English), it has helped the French national film and music industries remain relatively viable (e.g., half of the over 700 new full-length feature films commercially released in France in 2016 were French). Culture is an important component of the French economy. According to the Ministry of Culture, in 2016, it contributed €44.5 billion of value added to the French economy and represented a 2.2% share of France's GDP. As significant as this is, it represents a decline compared to 2003 (2.5% of GDP). Detailed statistics show that major structural changes in the press were responsible for a large part of the modest overall decline. However, growth in other fields is comparatively strong, like in audiovisual (including significant gains in video/computer games and television production), live spectacle, the visual arts, and design. The French reputation for artistic quality and avant-garde panache, which extends to popular culture, sometimes called the "French Touch," is viewed as a competitive advantage that can help the French arts and entertainment industry thrive in the context of globalization.

Icons of French popular culture come from many fields, including film, popular music, comic books, comedy, television, sports, humanitarian activism, politics, the arts, and fashion. The intergenerational cultural resonance of the most widely acclaimed figures in the performing arts and popular entertainment was confirmed in the massive public response that followed the recent deaths of two great stars of French popular music—Johnny Hallyday (d. 2017), the rocker known as the "French Elvis," and Charles Aznavour (d. 2018), one of the great practitioners of the French chanson tradition.

Further Reading

Badillo et al. (2016); Cicchelli and Octobre (2018); Coulangeon (2017); Dauncey (2003); DeJean (2005); Ervine (2019); Fortunati et al. (2014); Grove (2010); Holmes and Looseley (2012); Ibarra (2015); Kuhn (2011); Kuisel (1993); Kuisel (2011); Lamizet and Tétu (2007); Laurent (2014); Martin (2014); Screech (2004); Singer (2013); Vessels (2010).

Internet, Social Media, and Video Games

In the 1990s, there was great concern in France about the strategic, political, economic, social, cultural, and ethical implications of the internet. Part of the concern arose from the competition that the internet represented for France's internet precursor, videotext-based Minitel online network (nationwide availability 1982–2012), which offered services ranging from informational pages for specific businesses and organizations and telephone listings to e-commerce and erotic message services for adults. Indicative of the broader concerns, an opinion piece in *Le Monde* by the renowned public intellectual and former presidential advisor Jacques Attali likened the internet to a virtual seventh continent that had already been colonized by the Americans. In response, a thoughtful government-commissioned report by Patrick Bloche, *Le Désir de France*, made a case for a French and Francophone cultural exception in cyberspace that echoed then prime minister Lionel Jospin's concept of an "information society based on solidarity." Even the 1998 inaugural edition of France's national Internet Day Celebration (Fête de l'Internet), which was created to popularize the internet (still held annually on or around March 21), included a mock trial (in a real Paris courtroom) of the internet, which stood accused of various offenses ranging from spreading hate speech to invasion of privacy. France is still concerned about linguistic and cultural pluralism online, American corporate domination of web search engines and social media platforms, net neutrality, and threats to privacy and personal data in the era of "life on the screen" (Sherry Turkle). For instance, the landmark 2016 Digital Republic Law includes provisions that stress universal access, establish a "right to be forgotten" online, and strictly regulate how web and social media companies can utilize user information. Established in 1978, CNIL is an independent government agency tasked with protecting personal data and individual freedom in the computer age. France has been at the forefront of EU efforts to pressure global internet giants like Facebook and Google to protect individuals and their personal data. The inter-ministerial Digital Agency coordinates the government's internet and digital policy, which includes a comprehensive "Digital Society Initiative."

France has the fourth highest number of internet users in Europe (and the seventeenth highest number in the world), while French is the fourth most used language in the world for internet content (4% of internet content, compared to 53% for English, the undisputed top online language). French households are well equipped with computers, smartphones, tablets, and internet service. According to French government statistics for the years 2016–2018 (sources: INSEE, Ministry of Culture, 2018 "Digital Barometer" published by the Ministry of Economy and Finance), 86% of French households have access to the internet and 58% have access to 4G broadband cellular network service. Of the French people, 78% (age twelve and up) have personal computers; 94% have a mobile phone; 75% have smartphones (83% of twelve- to seventeen-year-olds and 98% of eighteen- to twenty-four-year-olds); and 30% have a personal computer, tablet, *and* smartphone. About 41% of French people send one or more text messages daily (79% of eighteen- to twenty-four-year-olds do so). And 89% of French people are internet users. The percentage is close to 100% for people under sixty, 82% for people in the sixty to sixty-nine age group, and 60% for seventy- to seventy-nine-year-olds. People without the high school baccalaureate diploma or college degrees (53%), who live alone (73%), and do not work outside the home (79%) have lower percentages of internet use. The device used most often to access the internet is now the smartphone (for 46% of French people), followed by the personal computer (35%), and the tablet (7%). Young people are the most likely to rely on smartphones for internet access (e.g., the preferred device for 83% of eighteen- to twenty-four-year-olds), whereas middle-aged French people (aged forty to fifty-nine) use smartphones and computers equally, and people in the sixty to sixty-nine age group tend to use computers more often (57%). Almost 80% of French people use the internet daily. The percentage is close to 100% for people between the ages of eighteen and thirty-nine and 91% for twelve- to seventeen-year-olds (perhaps reflecting some parental reticence about allowing young people constant internet access via smartphones). French people spend on average eighteen hours per week on the internet (twenty-one hours is the average among internet users). This weekly average is equal to that for television viewing. Not surprisingly, young people are the most voracious internet users in France. About 41% of twelve- to seventeen-year-olds, 62% of eighteen- to twenty-four-year-olds, and 36% of twenty-five- to thirty-nine-year-olds spend over twenty-one hours online per week. Children between the ages of seven and twelve spend on average six hours online per week, and younger children spend an average of close to 4.5 hours online per week. In each case, the latest statistics show significant increases in time spent online compared to just five years before—a trend that is likely to continue growing.

The streaming of video content online represents an increasing share of internet usage. The national average for video streaming (population as a whole, including nonusers of the internet) is five hours per week (the average is ten hours per week among internet users). One-third of French people stream videos for three hours or more per week (but 52% never stream video content). The development of e-commerce in France has been impressive. About 61% of French internet users (59% of the general population) now make at least one online purchase annually (2018), compared to just 30% in 2007—a trend that is projected to increase significantly in the future. The per person average among those who do shop online is thirty-three purchases per year. In 2017, French e-commerce (1.2 trillion purchases) amounted to €82 billion in sales (a 14% increase over the previous year). Almost 78% of French internet users consume cultural goods and services online (e.g., music, videos, films, TV series, games, books, and software)—much of it illicitly (reportedly 75% of music, films, and videos; and 68% of TV content). And 65% of the general population (compared to 36% in 2007) now use the internet for administrative procedures; 27% use it for job searches—with much higher percentages among the young and more highly educated. Google occupies a dominant position in France among search engines (92% market share in January 2018). Among web browsers (personal computers and smartphones combined), Google Chrome was in first position with a 50% share, followed by Safari (22%), Firefox (12%), and Internet Explorer + Edge (8%).

France has 38 million users of social networks—59% of the general population, 66% of internet users, 76% of twelve- to seventeen-year-olds, 93% of eighteen- to twenty-four-year-olds, and 82% of twenty-five- to twenty-nine-year-olds. The national average is one hour per week spent on social networks (however, regular users spend an average of 1.5 hours/day on social networks). In terms of market penetration (percentage of social media users who use a given platform), the leading social media platform in France is Facebook with 73.2% use reported (Kepios survey, Q3 2021), followed by Facebook Messenger (59.5%), WhatsApp (55.7%), Instagram (54%), Snapchat (41%), TikTok (29.9%), Twitter (28.6%), Pinterest (27.9%), LinkedIn (23.6%), iMessage (21.7%), and Skype (18.3%). According to a study commissioned by the nonprofit organization Génération Numérique (2021), the three most popular online platforms among young people age eleven to fourteen are currently YouTube (#1), Snapchat (#2), and Instagram (#3); and the three most popular among fifteen to eighteen year-olds are Instagram (#1), Snapchat (#2), and YouTube (#3). TikTok is gaining rapidly among French adolescents—from 31% reported usage among young people age eleven to eighteen in 2020 to 49% in 2021 (60% among girls compared to just 35% among boys). The most common reason for the use of social media platforms among French adolescents was for talking to friends and family (75%), followed by watching videos (54%) and exchanging information about school and homework (29%). Among eleven to fourteen-year-olds, 69% of boys and 75% of girls surveyed reported having at least one social media account; among fifteen- to eighteen-year-olds, the results are 95% and 96%, respectively. About 19% of French young people report having experienced problems on social media platforms (46% of the problems involved strangers)—including online disputes (58% of those reporting problems), insults (46%), ridicule (22%), cyberbullying, harassment by strangers, hacked accounts, theft of personal data, and unauthorized publication of personal photos. Among fifteen- to eighteen-year-olds, 75% report having communicated with or "friended" a stranger and 30% reported either staying awake or waking up at night to be on their screens.

According to the Ministry of Culture, 70% of French people between the ages of ten and sixty-five play video/computer games at least occasionally. The percentage is 90% for those under the age of twenty-four. And 52% of French people report being regular players (i.e., at least two times/week). Sales of physical copies of games for use on computers and other gaming devices are in decline (–56% between 2008 and 2016), whereas digital downloads, which are somewhat harder to track, are on the rise and now represent an estimated two-thirds of all game sales. Electronic game production is an important business in France. While the sector involved just 2,300 people and 225 companies in 2015, it registered €1.6 billion in sales in the same year. The French industry leader is Ubisoft (the maker of *Assassin's Creed*). The most popular games (in terms of sales) vary according to platform. According to French gaming industry statistics (Syndicat des Éditeurs de Logiciels de Loisirs, 2018 annual report), the top ten console games were: (1) *FIFA 19*, (2) *Red Dead Redemption 2*, (3) *Call of Duty: Black Ops 4*, (4) *Mario Kart 8 Deluxe*, (5) *Super Mario Party*, (6) *Spider-Man*, (7) *Super Smash Brothers Ultimate*, (8) *Super Mario Odyssey*, (9) *Assassin's Creed Odyssey*, and (10) *Gods of War*. On personal computers, the top five games were: (1) *The Sims 4*, (2) *Farming Simulator 19*, (3) *Overwatch 3*, (4) *World of Warcraft: Battle for Azeroth*, and (5) *Call of Duty: Black Ops 4*. The top ten mobile gaming applications for the same year were: (1) *Dragon Ball Z: Dokkan Battle*, (2) *Clash Royale*, (3) *Candy Crush Saga*, (4) *Clash of Clans*, (5) *Summoners War*, (6) *Lords Mobile*, (7) *Candy Crush Soda Saga*, (8) *Gardenscapes*, (9) *Pokemon Go*, and (10) *Homescapes*. These statistics predate *Fortnite*, which counted 250 million registered players worldwide in 2019 and is now the most downloaded game application in France. A French team led by "Kouto" (Issam Tanguine) took second place in the 2019 Fortnite World Cup (creative) in New York.

See also: Chapter 4: Innovation and Startups. Chapter 9: Overview. Chapter 10: Privacy and Personal Space. Chapter 15: Movies. Chapter 16: Press; Radio; Television.

Further Reading
Alderman (2019); Breton (2011); Brown and Michinov (2017); Cardon and Granjon (2005); Chrisafis (2020); Eko (2013); Flichy (2007); Jöuet (2009); Kharazian (2017); Koc-Michalska et al. (2013); Maarek (2015); Rubin (2017); Rufat et al. (2014); Satarino (2020); Schafer and Thierry (2017); Strode (1999); Warlaumont (2010).

Pop Culture Icons

Pop culture icon status is notoriously subjective and depends on a number of variables, including the media visibility of certain fields (film, television, music, and sports are among the most visible and therefore the source of the greatest number of icons), changing cultural norms and tastes, and demographics (different subsets of the population have different notions of who is an icon). Despite such obvious vagueness, a famous person's putative iconic status in a given society says something about that society's culture and values. Since 1998, a key indicator of cultural icon status in France has been the annual poll conducted by IFOP for the French national Sunday newspaper *Le Journal du Dimanche*, which results in the publication of a list of France's fifty favorite (living) personalities. The poll traditionally separates favorite men and women into two separate lists. The top twenty in the December 2020 edition of the IFOP-JDD poll were: (1) Jean-Jacques Goldman (singer-songwriter), Sophie Marceau (actress); (2) Thomas Pesquet (astronaut), Marion Cotillard (actress); (3) Omar Sy (actor and humorist), Florence Foresti (humorist and actress); (4) Soprano (rapper), Louane (singer-songwriter); (5) Francis Cabrel (singer-songwriter), Alexandra Lamy (actress); (6) Florent Pagny (singer-songwriter), Josiane Balasko (actress and filmmaker); (7) Dany Boon (humorist, actor, and filmmaker), Mimie Mathy (actress); (8) Teddy Riner (judo champion), Mylène Farmer (singer-songwriter); (9) Philippe Etchebest (celebrity chef and television personality), Valérie Lemercier (actress); (10) Jean-Pierre Pernault (television journalist and author), Karine Le Marchand (television personality); (11) Renaud (singer-songwriter), Anne Roumanoff (humorist and actress); (12) Cyril Lignac (celebrity chef and television personality), Françoise Hardy (singer-songwriter); (13) Vianney (singer-songwriter), Line Renaud (singer, actress, and activist); (14) Jean Reno (actor), Evelyne Dhéliat (television weather forecaster); (15) Jean-Luc Reichmann (radio and television personality), Vanessa Paradis (singer and actress); (16) Michel Sardou (singer-songwriter), Michèle Laroque (actress and humorist); (17) Zinedine Zidane (soccer star and coach), Muriel Robin (actress and humorist); (18) Jean Dujardin (actor), Nolwenn Leroy (singer-songwriter); (19) Kylian Mbappé (soccer star), Zazie (singer-songwriter); and (20) Kad Merad (actor and filmmaker), Ingrid Chauvin (actress). A few observations might be made about this list. One is that the French value those who make them laugh and who carry on the traditions of French song and cuisine. Another is that France's increasing racial and ethnic diversity is reflected in its cultural icons. A third is that while many of the names on the list have found fame relatively recently, quite a few have been French favorites dating back to the 1980s, 1970s, and even 1960s (e.g., Goldman, Cabrel, Renaud, Reno, and Sardou among the men; Marceau, Balasko, Farmer, Hardy, L. Renaud, and Paradis among the women). In 2017, the newspaper published an overall ranking of France's favorite personalities (men and women together) over the thirty-year period since the first IFOP-JDD poll was first published in 1988. The top ten personalities of the past three decades were: (1) Jacques Cousteau (oceanographer and explorer), (2) Abbé Pierre (Catholic priest and advocate for the homeless), (3) Sy, (4) Haroun Tazieff (geologist), (5) Boon, (6) Michel Cymes (physician and media personality), (7) Zidane, (8) Foresti, (9) Goldman, and (10) Sœur Emmanuelle (Catholic nun and humanitarian).

Assessing broader iconic status is more subjective. One noteworthy attempt is a 2010 book by Denis C. Mayeur, *Clés pour la France en 80 icônes culturelles*. Mayeur identifies eighty cultural icons that are emblematic of French culture from the standpoint of foreigners. While a survey of cultural icons from the French perspective might well differ, one suspects that many of the icons Mayeur lists would also be considered important by the French themselves. Most involve things, institutions, and symbols seen as characteristically French—the Académie Française, Astérix and Obélix, champagne, cheese, the Citroën 2 CV automobile, the Eiffel Tower, the Légion d'Honneur, *Le Monde* (daily newspaper), Marianne (personification of the French Republic), May 68 (student protests), Michelin, Perrier, *pétanque* (bowling game), snails (as a gastronomic delicacy), Social Security, the Sorbonne, summer vacations, *Tiercé* (a popular form of off-track betting) and *Loto* (the national lottery), the TGV (high-speed train), tobacconist shop signs, the Tour de France, village church bell towers, Vuitton (luxury goods), and wine. A number of prominent historical and cultural figures are also named, like Abbé Pierre, Brigitte Bardot (actress), Roland Barthes (literary critic), Jean-Paul Belmondo and Alain Delon (actors), Simone de Beauvoir (philosopher), Napoleon Bonaparte (emperor), Coco Chanel (fashion designer), Maurice Chevalier (singer and actor), Coluche (humorist and humanitarian), Catherine Deneuve (actress), Jacques Derrida (philosopher), Serge Gainsbourg (singer), Charles de Gaulle (statesman), Victor Hugo (writer), the impressionist painters (collectively), Joan of Arc (military hero and saint), Marcel Marceau (mime), Yannick Noah (tennis champion and singer), Edith Piaf (singer), and Yves Saint Laurent (fashion designer). Other French historical and cultural figures could be added to the list of icons—Louis XIV, Molière, Voltaire, Victor Hugo, Louis Pasteur, Jules Ferry, Claude Debussy, Marie Curie, Marcel Proust, Jean-Paul Sartre, Michel Foucault, and Bernard-Henry Lévy (there are wax figures of both Lévy and Sartre in the Musée Grévin wax museum in Paris). So, too, could a number of other famous actors and singers—Jean Gabin, Charles Trenet, Fernandel, Bourvil, Louis de Funès, Yves Montand, Jacques Tati, Georges Brassens, Charles Aznavour, Jeanne Moreau, Claude François, Johnny Hallyday, Gérard Depardieu, Isabelle Adjani, and Isabelle Huppert. The top ten French historical figures of all time according to the viewers of a 2005 France 2 television documentary series *Le plus grand Français* ("The Greatest Frenchman") were: (1) de Gaulle, (2) Pasteur, (3) Abbé Pierre, (4) M. Curie, (5) Coluche, (6) Hugo, (7) Bourvil, (8) Molière, (9) Cousteau, and (10) Piaf—a result that curiously underrated a number of major historical figures (e.g., Napoleon [#16], Joan of Arc [#31], and Louis XIV [#50]) while skewing in favor of more contemporary celebrities.

The deaths of national idols are major events in the eyes of the French government and people. Victor Hugo was given a grand national funeral in 1885. When the rock star Hallyday (b. Jean-Philippe Smet, 1943) died in 2017, an estimated 800,000 mourners lined the Champs-Élysées to watch his body be taken to the Madeleine Church for the funeral service, which was attended by the current and two former French presidents. Similarly, when Aznavour, the last of the great practitioners of the French chanson tradition from its golden age, died in 2018, he was given a state funeral at Les Invalides in Paris, where he was eulogized by President Macron.

See also: Chapter 12: French Cinema I (through the Nouvelle Vague); French Cinema II (since the Nouvelle Vague) Chapter 13: Chanson; Rock, Pop, and Rap. Chapter 15: Movies; Sports. Chapter 16: Internet, Social Media, and Video Games; Television.

Further Reading

Chrisafis (2018); Gaffney and Holmes (2007); Glaser (2009); Kovacs and Marshall (2015); Mutta (2016); Vincendeau (2000); Willsher (2017).

Press

The internet has revolutionized the world of the press in France. Sales of hard copies of newspapers and magazines have fallen, whereas readership of media content online has increased. Most major French publications that started in print now have online editions that complement their print editions and compete with electronic-only publications and social media for the attention of readers and advertising dollars. This shift to online platforms has changed both the business model and the journalistic practice of the French press. According to the French Ministry of Culture, the total number of journalists and editors in France declined by 24% between 2008 and 2015, whereas the number working in audiovisual media increased by 14%. Over the past twenty years, the GDP impact of newspaper and periodical publication has dropped by one-third. To promote an economically viable free press, the French government awarded €79.6 million in press subsidies in 2016. On the other hand, readership of the national press is actually rising if one factors in readership of online content. The ten most popular press websites in February 2018 were: LeFigaro.fr (world and national news, 50.0 million visits), L'Équipe.fr (sports, 44.9), LeMonde.fr (world and national news, 44.1), Tele-Loisirs.fr (TV listings and entertainment, 39.7), LeParisien.fr (national and Paris news, 29.0), Ouest-France.fr (national and regional news, 27.8), 20minutes.fr (world and national news, 25.9), Femmeactuelle.fr (women's content, 15.4), L'Obs.com (world and national news, 14.8), and Lexpress.fr (world and national news, 14.8). There is a slightly different top ten ranking for visits via mobile phone application.

Freedom of the press is deeply engrained in French values. Freedom of expression is protected under Article 11 of the Declaration of the Rights of Man and the Citizen (1789). However, even after the French Revolution, there was persistent censorship until the passage of the 1881 law on press freedom. The January 2015 terrorist attack that claimed the lives of cartoonists, journalists, and staff members at the Paris headquarters of the satirical weekly *Charlie Hebdo*—known for its self-declared "stupid and mean" style of humor and its defiant, irreverent, and highly controversial cartoon depictions of the Islamic prophet Muhammad—stirred both a renewed national commitment to the defense of freedom of the press and a passionate debate about the limits and responsibilities of a free press in a multicultural society.

Five influential national daily newspapers dominate coverage of world and national affairs, including French politics. *Le Monde* (founded by Hubert Beuve-Méry in 1944, 2.2 million readers) is France's most prestigious and authoritative national daily. Displaying a left-of-center editorial line, it is widely read among the French elites. Its rival is *Le Figaro*, France's oldest major newspaper (founded in 1826, 1.9 million readers), which stakes out a right-of-center line and is known for its coverage of business and economic news. The other three are *Libération* (founded in 1973 by a group that included Jean-Paul Sartre and Serge July, left-liberal line), *La Croix* (founded in 1880, Catholic perspective), and *L'Humanité* (founded in 1904 by Jean Jaurès, formerly an organ of the French Communist Party). The dailies *20 Minutes* and *CNEWS Matin* are free daily newspapers that are popular among commuters. *Le Journal du Dimanche* (founded in 1948), is a weekly national newspaper published on Sundays, when France's major national and regional dailies traditionally do not publish an edition. Specialized national dailies include *L'Équipe* (founded in 1946, 2.8 million readers, sports news) and *Les Échos* (founded in 1908, 1.1 million readers, business and financial news). Other leading business and financial publications in France include

A woman reading an issue of *Le Monde* newspaper (c. August 2021) at her kitchen table. The main headline refers to the health passes then required in France as proof of COVID-19 vaccination or negative status. Founded in 1944 by Hubert Beuve-Méry, the respected Paris-based national daily is one of France's newspapers of record. It generally takes a center-left editorial line and is particularly popular among intellectuals and members of the elite. (Ifeelstock/Dreamstime.com)

Le Nouvel Économiste, La Tribune, and *Challenges* (weekly); and *Alternatives éconon-omiques, Capital,* and *L'Usine nouvelle* (monthly). France's major generalist weekly newsmagazines are *L'Obs* (formerly *Le Nouvel Observateur,* founded in 1964), *L'Express* (founded in 1953), and *Le Point* (1973)—respectively liberal, centrist, and conservative in their editorial stances. Headquartered in Paris, Agence France-Presse (AFP) is the world's oldest news agency (founded in 1835) and currently the world's third largest (after the Associated Press and Reuters). It comprises 1,500 staff journalists and 2,200 affiliated reporters reporting from 200 bureaus worldwide. Leading French news web-sites include *Rue89, Mediapart,* and the French affiliates of *HuffPost* and *Slate.* The French press includes publications that cater to every interest and demographic group. *Têtu* and *Jeanne Magazine* are leading gay and lesbian periodicals. Founded in Tunis (1960) but now published in Paris, *Jeune Afrique* is a Francophone pan-African news weekly. France's most famous magazine is *Paris Match* (founded in 1949), which covers news and social issues but is best known for its glossy features on the lifestyles of celebrities. *Le Monde Diplomatique, Esprit, Études, Les Temps Modernes, Commentaire, Cités,* and *La Revue des Deux Mondes* are important opinion journals among intellectuals.

See also: Chapter 3: Overview; Republic. Chapter 15: Books and Reading. Chapter 16: Internet, Social Media, and Video Games; Radio; Television.

Further Reading

Benson (2004); Eko (2019); Le Vaillant (2015); Rouger (2013); Thogmartin (1998).

REGIONAL AND LOCAL PRESS

France has a strong tradition of regional daily newspapers—although these publications are facing some of the same challenges as the national press in print. Still, according to a 2018 study (ACPM One Global), 41 million French people consult a regional daily at least once per month (monthly readership is 51 million for all types of regional press). And 38% of readers still rely on print editions exclusively, whereas 77% of French people consult the regional press on varied digital platforms at least once per month. The four leading regional dailies are *Le Parisien/Aujourd'hui en France* (Paris, 20.7 million readers—all formats), *Ouest-France* (multiple editions incl. Rennes and Nantes, 16.3 million), *Sud-Ouest* (Bordeaux, 7.6 million), and *La Dépêche du Midi* (Toulouse, 6.9 million). Other leading regional daily newspapers are *La Voix du Nord* (Lille), *Les Dernières Nouvelles d'Alsace* (Strasbourg), *L'Alsace* (Mulhouse), *L'Est Républicain* (Nancy), *La République du Centre* (Orléans), *La Montagne* (Clermont-Ferrand), *Le Progrès* (Lyon), *Le Dauphiné Libéré* (Grenoble), *Le Midi Libre* (Montpellier), *La Provence* (Marseille), *Nice-Matin* (Nice), *Corse-Matin* (Ajaccio), *France-Antilles* (separate editions for Guadeloupe, Martinique, and French Guiana), and *Le Quotidien* (Réunion and Indian Ocean region).

Radio

Like television, radio broadcasting was for a long time a tightly controlled state monopoly in France. Historically, there were two main ways to get around the monopoly. One was "peripheral radio"—commercial radio stations that broadcasted primarily for French audiences from locations in neighboring countries (hence legally) near the French border. This was how the current major stations RTL (Radio Télévision Luxembourg), RMC (Radio Monte Carlo), and Europe 1 got their start. The other method was through unauthorized "pirate" or "free" FM radio stations (*radios libres*), which represented a countercultural movement in the 1960s and 1970s. Such renegade stations operated clandestinely, from broadcast studios set up in apartments and other locations. Their operators faced prosecution and broadcasts were regularly jammed by French authorities. Following the election of François Mitterrand, a Socialist, as president, *radios libres* were authorized to operate locally on a nonprofit basis in 1981. Broader freedom to operate, and privatization, came in the following years. Today, the radio landscape in France resembles that in other Western countries.

The leading French radio stations in terms of cumulative audience (third quarter 2018) are RTL, France Inter, RMC, NRJ, France Bleu, Europe 1, Nostalgie, France Info, Skyrock, RFM, Fun Radio, RTL2, Virgin Radio, Chérie, France Culture, Radio Classique, Rire et Chansons, and France Musique. According to the French Ministry of Culture, the average number of hours spent listening to the radio per person has remained relatively stable (02:50 hours per day during weekdays), but the overall number of radio listeners in France is in decline (77% of people age thirteen and above listened to the radio at least once during the first trimester of 2017 compared to 82% over a comparable period in 2007). Generalist (41%) and music (24%) format stations represent a combined three-fourths audience share. Radio stations continue to play an important role in the diffusion of recorded music—especially French songs, which are covered by quotas instituted by the 1994 Toubon Law. In terms of categories, international pop/rock leads the way (23% of all music broadcast time), followed by dance music (20%) and French songs (*variété française*, 18%). However, French radio broadcasts of music increasingly reflect corporate consolidation and homogenization of taste in the music business—the 2% most played titles took a 71% share of total music airtime. Major pop/rock format stations like NRJ, Fun Radio, and Skyrock have seen losses in total cumulative audience due to competition from music streaming applications and websites. French public radio, represented by the Radio France group of stations, is an important means to ensure a diversity of voices, sounds, and perspectives on the airwaves. Radio France encompasses seven national radio channels with different programming formats—France Inter (generalist with popular music, news, talk, and special programs), France Info (24-hour news), France Culture (culture, arts, history, ideas, and in-depth public affairs), France Musique (classical music and jazz), France Bleu (regional stations featuring popular music, news, and local programming), FIP (eclectic and alternative musical programming, including classical, jazz, blues, rock, French chanson, and world music), and Mouv' (cutting-edge pop music). Radio France International (RFI) is a global French language station operated by the French Ministry of Foreign Affairs that broadcasts in French and twelve other languages. It is one of the most listened to radio stations in the world.

See also: Chapter 2: Mitterrand (François) and France in the 1980s and 90s. Chapter 4: Public Sector and Privatization. Chapter 13: Chanson; Classical Music; Jazz; Rock, Pop, and Rap. Chapter 16: Internet, Social Media, and Video Games; Television.

Further Reading

Glevarec (2005); Glevarec and Pinet (2008); Miller (1992); Neulander (2009); Schmidt (2011).

Television

As in many other countries, broadcast television has changed significantly in France over the past three decades. Until 1975, all French television was a tightly controlled state monopoly under the authority of the ORTF (Office de Radiodiffusion Télévision Française). During the transitional period that followed, France's major television broadcasters remained state-owned but operated independently. However, in 1986–1987, a major shift in favor of privatization occurred—France's first privately owned channel, La Cinq, began broadcasting in 1986 (it ceased operation in 1992); and in 1987, France's first national channel was privatized as TF1, privately owned channel M6 started broadcasting (its original format focused on music videos); and France's first premium subscription-based encrypted channel, Canal+, was launched. Now, France counts hundreds of mostly privately owned channels that reach viewers via broadcast, satellite, cable, and streaming platforms. France's major broadcasters support the European Hybrid Broadcast Broadband TV (HbbTV) initiative in favor of an open standard for digital TV and broadband media delivered via a single user interface. While there is vigorous free competition in the French television market, the public interest is represented by the CSA (Conseil Supérieur de l'Audiovisuel), France's independent television and audiovisual media regulatory body.

Founded in 1992, public broadcaster France Télévisions (also called France.tv) consists of six main channels—France 2 (its primary flagship station), France 3 (its secondary flagship station, with an emphasis on regional programming, including broadcasts in regional languages), France 4 (programming for children during the day under the Okoo brand and cultural programing with an emphasis on live performance during the evening under the Culturebox brand), France 5 (educational TV, documentaries, and societal issues), La Première (programming for and from France's overseas departments and territories), France Info (24-hour news), and Slash (programing for adolescents and young adults, including popular series like *Skam France*—France's first fully digital channel [2018] available on various platforms, including Snapchat). France's other major all-news channels are BFM TV, CNews,

France 24, and LCI (La Chaîne Info). High-quality arts and cultural programming is offered by Arte, a Franco-German joint venture. LCP-Assemblée Nationale (La Chaîne Parlementaire) and its sister channel, Public Sénat, offer extensive live and recorded coverage of parliamentary debates and committee meetings as well as other public affairs programming. In terms of audience share (2017) among free-to-air television channels, France's leading channel is TF1 (20% audience share), followed by France 2 (13%), M6 (10%), France 3 (9%), France 5 (4%), Arte (2%), and unencrypted Canal+ (1%). The other free-to-air French channels (numbering over twenty) that are now digitally broadcast (digital terrestrial television)—including C8, W9, TMC, NRJ12, Gulli, L'Équipe, RMC Découverte, Chérie 25, and 6ter—have a combined 31% audience share.

French television viewing habits are evolving. In 2017 (according to the Ministry of Culture), the average French person watched 03:42 hours of television daily—about the same as in 2011. However, television viewing is declining somewhat among children between the ages of four and fourteen (01:46 hours in 2017, compared to 02:18 in 2011) and among younger and middle-aged adults age fifteen to forty-nine (02:54 in 2017, compared to 03:16 in 2011)—due mostly to the growing prevalence of other types of digital content (e.g., internet, social media, and gaming). It is only among older adults and seniors (age 50 and above) that a modest increase in television viewing has been registered (05:12 hours/day in 2017, compared to 04:59 in 2011). Two other viewing trends are noteworthy. First, an increasing share of "television" content is consumed on demand via online streaming—a four-fold increase in viewing in 2017 compared to 2011 (offerings doubled over the same period). Second, whereas home computers were the leading platform for streamed content in 2011, smartphones and tablets now lead the way (39% of all streamed content in 2017). Major sporting events and presidential election broadcasts (every five years) are among the most watched programming. Other popular types of programming include reality TV (including talent competitions), the annual Eurovision song contest, police/crime dramas, situation comedies (including American imports), soap operas, films, variety shows, talk shows, game shows, documentaries and special reports on societal issues, animation (esp. for children), cultural programming (e.g., performing arts), and "shortcoms" (i.e., concept comedies with three to seven minute episodes) that are used as fillers between other programs.

Shortcoms and crime/thriller shows are two French specialties. Successful past examples of the former include *Un gars, une fille* (trans. "A Guy and a Girl," 1999–2003), *Caméra café* (trans. "Coffee Break Camera," 2001–2003), *Samantha Oups!* (2004–2007), *Kamelott* (2004–2009), *Bref* (trans. "To Make a Long Story Short," 2011–2012), *Nos chers voisins* (trans. "Our Dear Neighbors," 2012–2017), *Parents mode d'emploi* (trans. "User's Manual for Parents," 2013–2018), *Bloqués* (trans. "Slackers," 2015–2016), *Serge le Mytho* (trans. "Serge the Fibber," 2016–2017), *Family Business* (2019–present), and *La Flamme* (2020–present). The French do crime TV as well as anyone. This excellence was revealed to the broader international public when *Lupin* (2021–present), a series starring Omar Sy loosely based on a classic series of early twentieth-century novels about a gentleman burglar, became one of the most watched shows on the Netflix platform when it premiered. Other noteworthy recent French crime/thriller series include *Maigret* (1991–2005), *Julie Lescaut* (1992–2014), *Spiral* (2005–2020), *Blood on the Vine* (2011–present), *Captain Sharif* (2013–2018), *Murder in . . .* (2013–present), *Candace Renoir* (2013–present), *Captain Marleau* (2014–present), *Witnesses* (2014–present), *The Art of Crime* (2014–present), *The Bureau* (2015–2020), *Black Spot* (2017–present), *War on Beasts* (2018), *Alexandra Ehle* (2018–present), and *Paris Police 1900* (2021–present).

See also: Chapter 3: Elections. Chapter 4: Public Sector and Privatization. Chapter 7: Child Raising Practices. Chapter 12: French Cinema I (through the Nouvelle Vague); French Cinema II (since the Nouvelle Vague). Chapter 15: Movies; Sports; Tour de France. Chapter 16: Internet, Social Media, and Video Games; Pop Culture Icons; Press; Radio.

Further Reading

Chaplin (2007); Dauncey (2020); Fache (2018); Ghosn (2014); Kuhn (2010); Kuhn (2013); Lafon (2010); Lévy (1998); Mazdon (2001); McCabe (2012); Palmeri and Rowland Jr. (2011); Scriven and Lecomte (1999); Scriven and Roberts (2003); Tinker (2008); Tinker (2012); Villez (2016).

SELECTED BIBLIOGRAPHY

Alderman, Liz. "France Moves to Tax Tech Giants, Stoking Fight with White House." *The New York Times*, 11 Jul. 2019, https://nyti.ms/2Lh1iXo.

Badillo, Patrick-Yves, et al. "Media Ownership and Concentration in France." *Who Owns the World's Media?: Media Concentration around the World*, ed. Eli M. Noam. Oxford UP, 2016, pp. 80–96.

Benson, Rodney. "La Fin du Monde?: Tradition and Change in the French Press." *French Politics, Culture & Society*, vol. 22, no. 1, 2004, pp. 108–126.

Breton, Philippe. *The Culture of the Internet and the Internet as Cult: Social Fears and Religious Fantasies*. Trans. Ronald E. Day. Litwin, 2011.

Brown, Genavee, and Nicolas Michinov. "Cultural Differences in Garnering Social Capital on Facebook: French People Prefer Close Ties and Americans Prefer Distant Ties." *Journal of Intercultural Communication Research*, vol. 46, no. 6, 2017, pp. 579–593.

Cardon, Dominique, and Fabien Granjon. "Social Networks and Cultural Practices: A Case Study of Young Avid Screen Users in France." *Social Networks*, vol. 27, no. 4, 2005, pp. 301–315.

Chaplin, Tamara. *Turning on the Mind: French Philosophers on Television*. U Chicago P, 2007.

Chrisafis, Angelique. "France's Digital Minister Says Tax on Big Tech Is Just the Start." *The Guardian*, 12 Jan. 2020, https://www.theguardian.com/world/2020/ jan/12/frances -digital-minister-tax-on-tech-giants-just-the-start-cedric-o-gafa.

Chrisafis, Angelique. "'In France, Poets Never Die': Macron Pays Tribute to Aznavour." *The Guardian*, 5 Oct. 2018, https://www.theguardian.com/world/2018/oct/05/in-france -poets-never-die-france-pays-homage-to-aznavour-funeral.

Cicchelli, Vincenzo, and Sylvie Octobre. *Aesthetico-Cultural Cosmopolitanism and French Youth: The Taste of the World*. Trans. Sarah-Louise Raillard. Palgrave Macmillan, 2018.

Coulangeon, Philippe. "Cultural Openness as an Emerging Form of Cultural Capital in Contemporary France." *Cultural Sociology*, vol. 11, no. 2, 2017, pp. 145–164.

Dakhlia, Jamil. "Humor as a Means of Popular Empowerment: The Discourse of French Gossip Magazines." *Language and Humour in the Media*, eds. Jan Chovanec and Isabel Ermida. Cambridge Scholars, pp. 231–248.

Dauncey, Hugh, ed. *French Popular Culture: An Introduction*. Arnold, 2003.

Dauncey, Hugh. "Regulation of Television in France: Reality Programming and the Defense of French Values." *Reel Politics: Reality Television as a Platform for Political Discourse*, eds. Lemi Baruh and Ji Hoon Park. Cambridge Scholars, 2020, pp. 302–320.

DeJean, Joan. *The Essence of Style: How the French Invented High Fashion, Fine Food, Chic Cafes, Style, Sophistication, and Glamour*. Free P, 2005.

Eko, Lyombe. *American Exceptionalism, the French Exception, and Digital Media Law*. Lexington, 2013.

Eko, Lyombe. *The Charlie Hebdo Affair and Comparative Journalistic Cultures: Human Rights Versus Religious Rites*. Palgrave Macmillan, 2019.

Ervine, Jonathan. *Humour in Contemporary France: Controversy, Consensus and Contradictions*. Liverpool UP, 2019.

Fache, Caroline. "Beur and Banlieue Television Comedies." *Reimagining North African Immigration: Identities in Flux in French Literature, Television, and Film*, eds. Véronique Machelidon and Patrick Saveau. Manchester UP, 2018, pp. 97-117.

Flichy, Patrice. *The Internet Imaginaire*. Trans. Liz Carey-Libbrecht. MIT P, 2007.

Fortunati, Leopoldina, et al. "The New About News: How Print, Online, Free, and Mobile Coconstruct New Audiences in Italy, France, Spain, the UK, and Germany." *Journal of Computer-Mediated Communication*, vol. 19, no. 2, 2014, pp. 121–140.

Gaffney, John, and Diana Holmes. *Stardom in Postwar France*. Berghahn, 2007.

Ghosn, Catherine. "Entertainment on French Television." *Handbook of Research on the Impact of Culture and Society on the Entertainment Industry*, ed. Gulay Ozturk. IGI Global, 2014, pp. 145–160.

Glaser, Stephanie A. "The Eiffel Tower: Cultural Icon, Cultural Interface." *Cultural Icons*, eds. Keyan G. Thomaselli and David Scott. Intervention, 2009, ch. 3.

Glevarec, Hervé. "Youth Radio as 'Social Object': The Social Meaning of 'Free Radio' Shows for Young People in France." *Media, Culture & Society*, vol. 27, no. 3, May 2005, pp. 333–351.

Glevarec, Hervé, and Michel Pinet. "From Liberalization to Fragmentation: A Sociology of French Radio Audiences since the 1990s and the Consequences for Cultural Industries Theory." *Media, Culture & Society*, vol. 30, no. 2, 2008, pp. 215–238.

Grove, Laurence. *Comics in French: The European Bande Dessinée in Context*. Berghan, 2010.

Holmes, Diana, and David Looseley, eds. *Imagining the Popular in Contemporary French Culture*. Manchester UP, 2012.

Ibarra, Karen Arriaza. *Public Service Media in Europe: A Comparative Approach*. Routledge, 2015.

Jöuet, Josiane. "The Internet as a New Civic Form: The Hybridisation of Popular and Civic Web Uses in France." *Javnost-The Public: Journal of the European Institute for Communication and Culture*, vol. 16, no. 1, 2009, pp. 59-72.

Kharazian, Zarine. "Yet Another French Exception: The Political Dimensions of France's Support for the Digital Right to Be Forgotten." *European Data Protection Law Review*, vol. 3, no. 4, 2017, pp. 452–462.

Koc-Michalska, Karolina, et al. *Mapping Digital Media: France*. Open Society Foundations, 2013.

Kovacs, George, and C. W. Marshall, eds. *Son of Classics and Comics*. Oxford UP, 2015; esp. ("All Gaul"), pp. 113–160.

Kuhn, Raymond. "France 24: Too Little, Too Late, Too French?" *The Rise of 24-hour News Television: Global Perspectives*, eds. Stephen Cushion and Justin Lewis. Lang, 2010, pp. 265–281.

Kuhn, Raymond. *The Media in Contemporary France*. Manchester UP, 2011.

Kuhn, Raymond. "Private Television in France: A Story of Political Intervention." *Private Television in Western Europe: Content, Markets, Policies*, eds. Karen Donders, et al. Palgrave Macmillan, 2013, pp. 56–69.

Kuisel, Richard F. *The French Way: How France Embraced and Rejected American Values and Power*. Princeton UP, 2011.

Kuisel, Richard F. *Seducing the French: The Dilemma of Americanization*. U California P, 1993.

Lafon, Benoît. "France 3, a State Institution: The French Model of Regional Television." *Media History*, vol. 16, no. 1, 2010, pp. 103–108.

Lamizet, Bernard, and Jean-François Tétu. "The French Media Landscape." *European Media Governance: National and Regional Dimensions*, ed. Georgios Terzis. Intellect, 2007, pp. 213–224.

Laurent, Roxane. "The Cultural Industries in France and Europe: Points of Reference and Comparison." *Culture chiffres*, vol. 7, no. 7, 2014, pp. 1–20.

Le Vaillant, Anne-Lise. "France." *The European Newspaper Market: Social Media Use and New Business Models*, eds. Bettina Schwarzer and Sarah Spitzer, Nomos, 2015, pp. 49–71.

Lévy, Marie-Françoise. "Television, Family, and Society in France, 1949–1968." *Historical Journal of Film, Radio, and Television*, vol. 18, no. 2, 1998, pp. 199–212.

Maarek, Philippe J. "Political Communication, Electronic Media, and Social Networks in France." *Political Parties in the Digital Age: The Impact of New Technologies in Politics*, eds. Guy Lachapelle and Philippe J. Maarek. de Gruyter, 2015, pp. 165–180.

Martin, Laurent. "The Democratisation of Culture in France in the Nineteenth & Twentieth Centuries: An Obsolete Ambition?" *International Journal of Cultural Policy*, vol. 20, no. 4, 2014, pp. 440–455.

Mazdon, Lucy. "Contemporary French Television, the Nation, and the Family: Continuity and Change." *Television & New Media*, vol. 2, no. 4, 2001, pp. 335–349.

McCabe, Janet. "Exporting French Crime: The *Engrenages/Spiral* Dossier." *Critical Studies in Television*, vol. 7, no. 2, 2012, pp. 101–118.

Miller, James. "From Radios Libres to Radios Privées: The Rapid Triumph of Commercial Networks in French Local Radio." *Media, Culture & Society*, vol. 14, no. 2, 1992, pp. 261–279.

Mutta, Maarit. "The Asterix Series: Gallic Identity in a Nutshell?" *Scandinavian Journal of Comic Art*, vol. 3, no. 1, 2016, pp. 64–75.

Neulander, Joelle. *Programming National Identity: The Culture of Radio in 1930s France*. LSU P, 2009.

Palmeri, Hélène, and Willard D. Rowland, Jr. "Public Television in a Time of Technological Change and Socioeconomic Turmoil: The Cases of France and the U.S." *International Journal of Communication*, vol. 5, 2011, pp. 1082–1137.

Rouger, Aude. "What Future for Local News?: The Crisis of the French Regional Daily Press." *The Future of Newspapers*, ed. Bob Franklin. Routledge, 2013, pp. 193–202.

Rubin, Alissa J. "France Lets Workers Turn Off, Tune Out and Live Life." *The New York Times*, 2 Jan. 2017, https://nyti.ms/2hM3kyZ.

Rufat, Samuel, et al. "Playing Videogames in France. Social Geography of a Cultural Practice." *L'Espace géographique*, vol. 43, no. 4, 2014, pp. 308–323; English trans.

Satarino, Adam. "'This Is a New Phase': Europe Shifts Tactics to Limit Tech's Power." *The New York Times*, 30 Jul. 2020, https://nyti.ms/2D1uiQy.

Schafer, Valérie, and Benjamin G. Thierry. "From the Minitel to the Internet: The Path to Digital Literacy and Network Culture in France (1980s–1990s)." *The Routledge Companion to Global Internet*, eds. Gerard Goggin and Mark McLelland. Routledge, 2017, pp. 77–89.

Schmidt, Blandine. "Interactivity on Radio in the Internet Age: A Case Study from France." *Radio Content in the Digital Age: The Evolution of a Sound Medium*, eds. Angeliki Gazi, et al. Intellect, 2011, pp. 25–36.

Screech, Matthew. *Masters of the Ninth Art: Bandes Dessinées and Franco-Belgian Identity*. Liverpool UP, 2004.

Scriven, Michael, and Monia Lecomte, eds. *Television Broadcasting in Contemporary France and Britain*. Berghahn, 1999.

Scriven, Michael, and Emily Roberts, eds. *Group Identities on French and British Television*. Berghahn, 2003.

Singer, Barnett. *The Americanization of France: Searching for Happiness after the Algerian War*. Rowman & Littlefield, 2013.

Strode, Louise. "French Identity in the Information Society: The Challenge of the Internet." *Modern & Contemporary France*, vol. 7, no. 3, 1999, pp. 319–328.

Thogmartin, Clyde. *The National Daily Press of France*. Summa, 1998.

Tinker, Chris. "Âge Tendre et Têtes de Bois: Nostalgia, Television and Popular Music in Contemporary France." *French Cultural Studies*, vol. 23, no. 3, 2012, pp. 239–255.

Tinker, Chris. "'One State, One Television, One Public': The Variety Show in 1960s France." *Media History*, vol. 14, no. 2, 2008, pp. 223–237.

Vessels, Joel E. *Drawing France: French Comics and the Republic*. U Mississippi P, 2010.

Vigoureux, Céclie B. "Genre, Heteroglossic Performances, and New Identity: Stand-up Comedy in Modern French Society." *Language and Society*, vol. 44, 2015, pp. 243–272.

Villez, Barbara. "French Television Crime Fictions: The Case of *Spiral* (*Engrenages*)—Coming Out of the Confusion." *Crime Fiction and the Law*, eds. Maria Aristodemou, et al. Birkbeck, 2018, pp. 43-54.

Vincendeau, Ginette. *Stars and Stardom in French Cinema*. Bloomsbury, 2000.

Warlaumont, Hazel G. "Social Networks and Globalization: Facebook, YouTube and the Impact of Online Communities on France's Protectionist Policies." *French Politics*, vol. 8, 2010, pp. 204–214.

Willsher, Kim. "A Million Take to Paris Streets for Johnny Hallyday's Funeral." *The Guardian*, 9 Dec. 2017, https://www.theguardian.com/music/2017/dec/09/johnny-hallyday-funeral-paris-tributes-emmanuel-macron.

APPENDIX A

A DAY IN THE LIFE

A DAY IN THE LIFE OF A CAFÉ OWNER

Arnaud owns and operates a café in the center of Nevers, a small city in central France (Nièvre Department, Bourgogne-Franche-Comté). It's hard work and long hours—the café is open from 6:00 a.m. to 9:00 p.m. and Arnaud often arrives early and stays late—but he loves his profession because of family tradition (his father owned and operated the café before him) and also because of what the café represents in French society ... and what his café represents to the city and its local clientele. It's a place to have one's morning coffee before the start of another work day or a drink (*un apéro*) after work before heading home for dinner; a place where strangers can feel at home, locals can take a break from a busy day, tourists can have a light lunch, teenagers can hang out after school, people can meet business associates and friends, retired people can play cards and talk about the old days, and sports fans can watch a big game on TV. Arnaud loves chatting with his clients—especially his regulars, who form a sort of extended family. He likes to think of his establishment as a place where people of different backgrounds and points of view can feel welcome—from the devout Catholic pilgrims who have come to visit the uncorrupted body of Saint Bernadette Soubirous in the chapel of the nearby convent of Saint Gildard to local members of the "Gilets Jaunes" protest movement—with whom Arnaud sympathizes—before or after a rally. A day in Arnaud's life intersects with different moments in the daily lives of his customers centered on his three rush hours—early morning (7:00–9:00 a.m.), noontime (12:00–1:30 p.m.), and late afternoon/early evening (4:30–7:00 p.m.). Noontime is especially busy since he and his wife Isabelle prepare and serve light lunches—soups, salads, sandwiches, steak and fries platters, omelets, and so on. Throughout the day, Arnaud orders stocks of supplies, supervises his small staff of servers, mans the cash register, and does the books. When his kids were small, they did their homework after school on one of the back tables. When they were older, they helped behind the counter. They are now grown and live out of town. Arnaud and Isabelle still live in the small apartment above the café. Like many others of its kind, the café is a multiservice establishment—it holds a government-issued concession as a *bureau de tabac*, or tobacconist shop—where people can buy cigarettes and other regulated products—as well as other items like candy, newspapers and magazines

(Presse), stamps, and phone cards. It is also an official outlet for lottery ticket and game card sales (Loto) and limited off-track betting on horse races (PMU). Normally, Isabelle runs the Tabac and Arnaud, the café. Although Arnaud's life is centered around the café, he is an outspoken member of the local small business association, which supports businesses like his own and is concerned about closings in their ranks as more commerce is based on the big-box retail zones on the outskirts of the town. He also volunteers at a local "Resto du Cœur," a national charity founded in 1985 by the comedian Coluche (1944–1986)—one of Arnaud's heroes, alongside Michel Platini, the greatest French soccer player of the 1980s. It serves as a food bank and provides hot meals for the needy. After the café closes, Arnaud has quite a late dinner at home with Isabelle and watches a little television or does a crossword puzzle before going to bed.

A DAY IN THE LIFE OF A HIGH SCHOOL STUDENT

Khadijah is in her final year of high school, *Terminale*, in Strasbourg. She attends the Lycée Kléber (one of the city's best generalist high schools, or *lycées d'enseignement general et technologique*) and is part of the first graduating class under the recently restructured *Baccalauréat* curriculum and diploma exams. Under the new format, students like Khadijah no longer specialize quite so early by choosing a track, or major, leading to a different battery of terminal exams—L (Literary Studies/Humanities), S (STEM), and ES (Economics and Social Sciences). Instead, all students who are candidates for the traditional generalist "bac" follow a common core curriculum throughout their three years of high school but they also select three areas of concentration for the second year and continue coursework in two of these areas during the final year. Khadija's two final areas of concentration are "physics-chemistry" and "earth and life science." She is also taking an additional math course as an elective. Khadija's first two years of lycée were challenging not only because of the transition to the new bac, but also due to the COVID-19 pandemic, which necessitated online classes. She is happy that her final year has been mostly normal, with in-person classes. Khadijah has her sights set on medical school, which in France begins in the second year of university studies following a common first-year program for prospective health sciences students and a competitive entrance exam. This means that Khadijah works very hard both during and after school and, like many fellow French *lycée* students, does not have much time for extracurricular activities. Khadijah gets up at 6:00 a.m. and leaves the house at 7:15 a.m. to take public transportation—a bus and a tram—to get to school. On certain days, she arrives early to meet up with friends at a neighborhood café near her school. Classes begin at 8:15 a.m. and end at 5:50 p.m.—a typically long (nearly nine hours) French school day! Thankfully, there are breaks during the day—fifteen-minute breaks at 10:00 a.m. and 3:00 p.m. and one-and-a-half hours for lunch—and no school on Wednesday (on Saturday, she goes to school for half a day in the morning). Khadijah has over thirty hours of classes weekly (in addition to an hour and half of academic and career counseling), although twenty-seven hours is a more typical high school load. Her courses throughout the school year include four hours (weekly) of philosophy, two hours of history/geography, four hours of two foreign languages (English and Arabic), two hours of physical education, two hours of interdisciplinary applied science and digital technologies (with a focus on contemporary issues), half an hour of ethics and civics, six hours of physics and chemistry, six hours of life/earth sciences, and three hours of advanced math. She misses the concentration courses in fine arts that she had to give up after her second year. On most days, she eats lunch at the cafeteria, which serves mostly organic, locally sourced food. Once a week, Khadijah has lunch in the center of Strasbourg with her friends—a great chance to get away from the stress of school, look at the shop windows, or sit and talk with her friends in a park. Occasionally, she spends her lunch break at the home of a friend who lives closer to school. Khadijah has been elected a class delegate—an important position in which she represents the student perspective in discussions with the faculty and administration. It is also part of her responsibilities to attend meetings of the school's Class Council and Disciplinary Council. Her other school-related extracurricular activity is her membership in the school's film club, for which she helped to organize a series of films from Algeria, where her grandparents were born. Khadijah leaves school around 6:00 p.m. and gets home around 7:00 p.m. Before dinner at 8:00, she helps her younger siblings with their homework and catches up with friends on social media. She watches the lead stories on the evening news while eating dinner with her family and helps clear the table and do the dishes. After dinner, she studies and does her homework. The multipart bac exam in June looms large. She did well in the French exam, which is given after the second year of high school (*Première*), but this year's terminal exams will be more extensive even though the restructured bac includes more in-school testing as part of the final result (it also includes a terminal oral exam on topics related to her two concentrations). Khadijah does a lot of practice for the exam in philosophy, her weakest subject. Her usual bedtime on school nights is midnight. On Wednesdays, she attends a judo class. Khadijah's favorite things to do on weekends are sleeping late on Sunday morning and streaming her favorite French and American TV series during the day. Many of Khadijah's classmates are politically active and participate in protest marches but Khadijah prefers to stay focused on her academics. Like many of her peers, Khadijah will attend university in her hometown and live at home (at least during her first year).

A DAY IN THE LIFE OF A WINEGROWER

Julien is a *viticulteur*, or *vigneron*—a winegrower who runs a medium-sized, family-owned vineyard in Aude Department, which is part of the historic Languedoc winegrowing region in the South of France. He does not make wine himself (except for small batches for family use)—his profession involves the growing of grapes that others use to make wine. There are two principal clients for the grapes he produces. The first is a local *cave cooperative vinicole*, or winemaking cooperative, which produces mostly Corbières AOC wines—medium-high-quality wines bearing the *Appellation d'Origine Contrôlée* that certifies their source and production in the Corbières local terroir. The second is a regional wine merchant, or *négociant*, who uses the grapes harvested by Julien to make a wide range of wines and sells some of the grapes it buys to larger commercial producers. Julien's vineyard produces several of the grape varieties for which the Languedoc region is best known (esp. in full-bodied and fruit-forward blends)—Syrah, Grenache, Carignan, and Mourvèdre. Like other farmers, Julien gets up early so that he can be out in the field at sunrise during growing season. He supervises the work of his employees and addresses problems that arise. At 10:30 a.m., he has an appointment with an oenologist, an agronomical engineer specialized in the cultivation of grapes and winemaking. The oenologist helps Julien to address technical issues and to apply the latest scientific research to care of his vineyard. Before lunch, Julien spends between an hour and an hour and a half attending to some of the most urgent aspects of the business side of his vineyard, such as sending emails, returning phone calls, and making plans for the grape harvest (*vendange*) in September. He usually eats a hearty lunch between 1:00 and 2:00 p.m. After lunch, he heads into town for a round of business meetings, the most important of which are a meeting with his banker about a loan for the purchase of some new equipment and a meeting of the board of directors of the cooperative, on which he sits. The board discusses a wide range of issues, including sales, marketing campaigns, new export markets, foreign competition, EU directives, and efforts to improve environmental sustainability. Julien is back home by 5:00 p.m. and checks in on both work at the vineyard and his four children, who have returned from school. Then, from 6:00 p.m. to dinner at 8:00 p.m., he attends to the more mundane aspects of running the vineyard, such as bills, contracts, and bookkeeping. After dinner, he relaxes by reading before going to bed at 10:30. Literature has remained a passion since his lycée days and he tries to keep up with the latest from France's leading novelists. Julien is thankful that on this particular day, there was no weekly meeting of the local town council (*conseil municipal*), of which he is a member—elected on the slate of Emmanuel Macron's centrist party, Renaissance (formerly known as La République en Marche). Even though the commune is small and the issues that it deals with are rather straightforward, Julien takes his duties on the council seriously. This means that part of every day is for talking to constituents—online, on the phone, and in person—about their concerns. Some friends and community members think that Julien should run for mayor. Julien likes the idea of being able to marry people in civil ceremonies at the town hall but doubts that he would have time for the added responsibilities given how labor-intensive running a vineyard is on a daily basis.

A DAY IN THE LIFE OF A WORKING MOTHER

Coralie is a young working mother who lives with her husband Thierry in Massy, a suburb south of Paris. She works in the human resources department of a large corporation at its headquarters in one of the glass towers in La Défense, the business district just west of the city. Her life is not the perfect embodiment of the popular French expression of "Métro, Boulot, Dodo" ("Subway, Work, Sleep")—but it does seem to her that it comes close at times. This is because her day begins with a substantial commute to work—either sixty minutes by the RER commuter-rail system (usually quicker but also more crowded) or ninety minutes via train and tram (a longer trip but also less crowded). She therefore gets up at 5:45 a.m. in order to get to work by 8:30. If the commute goes well, she has thirty minutes before work starts to gather her thoughts, check her schedule, and answer a few emails. The thirty-nine-year-old mother of a four-year-old and a nine-year-old, Coralie is lucky in two respects. In the first place, public policy in France is helpful to working parents—especially in terms of parental leave after the birth or adoption of a child, the availability of convenient and affordable childcare at municipal care centers (*crèches*), and high-quality public preschools (*écoles maternelles*), which children begin attending full time at age three. In the second place, her husband works as a civil servant for the local government and has a more flexible schedule that allows him to drop off and pick up the children before and after school. On days that Thierry is too busy, a sitter picks the children up and stays with them until Thierry gets home. Coralie usually gets home between 6:30 and 7:00 p.m. At work, her day is filled with the usual sorts of activities for a person in her position—emails and phone calls, paperwork, individual interviews, team meetings, training sessions, projects, and reports. Since Coralie's company is multinational in scope, it helps that she also speaks English proficiently, as well as some Spanish and German. Her favorite time of the day is her ninety-minute-long lunch, which she usually takes in the company cafeteria. At least once or twice a week, however, she uses the last half of her lunch break to go out for a coffee with her best friend from work, Florence. During the day, Coralie always makes two FaceTime video calls—a lunchtime chat with Thierry and a quick afternoon call to her children while they are having their after-school snack, or *goûter*. Since she gets home from work late, Coralie's priority is to spend quality time with her children—giving them their baths is so soothing—while Thierry gets dinner ready. Thierry and Coralie are traditional when it comes to dinner—everybody sits down for a well-balanced home-cooked meal and conversation. It is also very important to them that their children learn proper table etiquette and join in the conversation. After dinner and putting the children to bed, Coralie does thirty minutes of yoga before relaxing with Thierry, sometimes with an after-dinner drink and some music on in the background. There's little time for TV unless one of their favorite films or a major soccer game is on. Coralie goes to bed around 11:30 p.m. Saturdays are hectic days, filled with shopping (at the open-air market in Massy for fresh produce and a big-box supermarket for everything else) and other errands. Every now and then, however, the couple gets a babysitter and goes to Paris for a museum visit, a play, or a concert. Sunday is for rest and relaxation—perhaps a nature outing with the children. The family has Sunday dinner once a month with both Thierry's parents in the 20th Arrondissement of Paris and Coralie's, in a small town near Amiens, about 150 km north of Paris. These larger family gatherings, which sometimes involve siblings and cousins, are very important.

APPENDIX B

GLOSSARY OF KEY TERMS

#BalanceTonPorc: Translated "#ReportYourPig," a public and social media campaign against the sexual harassment of women similar to #MeToo.

Ancien régime: The political and social system of France from the 1500s to the Revolution of 1789, characterized by the remnants of feudalism, aristocratic and ecclesiastical dominance, hereditary (absolute) monarchy, and court society.

Anticlericalism: Animosity toward the Catholic Church and clergy and their alleged influence over French society—particularly strong in France from the Age of Enlightenment (eighteenth century) through the passage of the Law of Separation of Churches and State in 1905.

Antilles: The Antilles archipelago (island group) and surrounding Caribbean region, especially the French overseas departments in the region: Martinique and Guadeloupe, sometimes also used to refer to the Atlantic coastal French department of Guiana in South America.

Apéritif: An alcoholic drink consumed before dinnertime thought to stimulate the appetite, often with light snacks; also a time to relax in the presence of family and friends, at home or in a café or similar establishment, at the end of the day (equiv. to cocktail hour).

Appellation: A registered and legally protected designation of local origin for a specific variety of wine, cheese, or other food products.

Arrondissement: An administrative subdivision of a French department, used especially to refer to the twenty districts of the city of Paris and to similar subdivisions of Marseille and Lyon.

Art Deco: A modern style of art, architecture, and design prominent in France from the 1910s through the 1930s—characterized by sleek and streamlined forms, bold geometric shapes, luxurious decoration that took inspiration from industrial design, and (in the case of French Art Deco architecture) a synthesis with neoclassical elements (e.g., Auguste Perret).

Art Nouveau: An international style in art, architecture, and design prominent in France from the 1880s through World War I (i.e., the Belle Époque). Its rich and fanciful decorative elements and emphasis on elegant and flowing forms inspired by nature (e.g., curving plant stems), geometry, and Japanese motifs represented a modernistic break with classicism and other Western historical styles. Major representatives of the style in France include Émile Gallé, Hector Guimard, René Lalique, Jules Lavirotte, Louis Majorelle, Alphonse Mucha, and Henri de Toulouse-Lautrec.

Ashkenazi: Eastern European Jews (incl. Jews originally settled in the Rhineland and northern France who fled eastward to escape persecution there). Until the 1950s and 1960s, the majority of French Jews were of Ashkenazi origin.

Bac: A colloquial abbreviation of *Baccalauréat* (Baccalaureate), the French advanced high school diploma earned after passing a battery of rigorous exams and constituting a passport to university-level higher education.

Baguette: Iconic French bread characterized by its long and thin shape, crispy and relatively hard crust that seals in flavor and aroma, and baking process incorporating basic lean wheat flour dough and steam.

Banlieue: Suburban areas outside French cities; used especially to refer to communities just outside the city limits that are characterized by large and sometimes blighted social housing projects, racially and ethnically diverse populations that are the product of immigration, and social tension due to economic marginalization and discrimination.

Bastille: A medieval fortress and prison in the eastern part of Paris that was a symbol of royal despotism and was stormed by a mob in search of gunpowder on July 14, 1789—an event traditionally considered the beginning of the French Revolution.

Belle Époque: The period of peace, prosperity, elegant living, and avant-garde experimentation in literature and the arts (the "Beautiful Era") from 1871 to 1914 (i.e., the outbreak of World War I); overlaps with the latter Victorian Era in Great Britain and the Gilded Age in the United States.

Beur: A verlan slang term in French for "Arab," used (sometimes pejoratively) since the 1980s to designate the children—and, later, the grandchildren (esp. in the derivative double verlan form *rebeu*)—of Maghrebi (Muslim North African, e.g., Algerian) immigrants to France.

Bises: A series of platonic pecks on the cheek (and, more likely, air kisses in the vicinity of the cheeks) given as a gesture of greeting among family members, close friends, people on a very familiar basis, and young people.

Bleus, Les: In English, "the Blues"—the nickname given to France's national sports teams, especially its national soccer teams.

Bobo: An abbreviated form of *bourgeois bohème* (bourgeois bohemian) in colloquial French, used to refer to educated, liberal city dwellers whose lifestyle combines middle-class comfort and privilege and countercultural eclecticism (a cross between a "yuppie" and a "hipster").

Boulangerie-Pâtisserie: A combined bread bakery and pastry shop, especially of the traditional artisan variety.

Boulevard theatre: Popular theatrical productions, including dramas and comedies, as opposed to the literary theatre of the elites. At its most sophisticated, it is similar to Broadway theatre in the United States and West End theatre in Great Britain.

Bourbons: The royal dynasty (and former cadet branch of the Capetian dynasty) that ruled France from 1589 to 1792 and again from 1815 to 1830. It included Louis XIV, the ultimate practitioner of royal absolutism; and Louis XVI, deposed and guillotined during the French Revolution.

CAC 40: The leading stock index on the Euronext Paris Stock Exchange, comprised of the stocks of forty large companies and seen as a major economic indicator in France.

Camembert: A soft, moist, and creamy surface-ripened cheese from the Normandy region of northwest France characterized by a white bloomy rind, a pungent aroma, and a sweet and milky taste. Traditional camembert is made from raw cow's milk, but pasteurized varieties are now more widespread.

Capetians: The ruling royal dynasty of France during the Middle Ages from 987 to 1328. The Capetian kings (incl. Hugues Capet, Philip Augustus, Saint Louis, and Philip the Fair) consolidated the power of the French monarchy at the expense of their regional feudal rivals.

Carte Vitale: The national health insurance card linked to the healthcare branch of the French social security system. Now computer chip equipped, it can be used at a healthcare provider's for invoicing and reimbursement and for accessing a patient's records.

Cartesian: Adjective derived from the name of the seventeenth-century French philosopher and mathematician René Descartes—used to describe his style of thought, his followers and their work, and (more widely) the rigorous rationalist mindset of the people, institutions, and culture of France.

Césars: Annual awards (incl. for Best Picture, Best Original Screenplay, Best Actor in a Leading Role, etc.) given in the French motion picture industry. Similarly to the

Oscars in the United States, the common name for the award is based on the trophies handed out to winners (designed by the sculptor César).

Chanson: A French tradition of popular song that emphasizes poetic lyrics over rhythm; realistic depictions of life, love, heartache, loss, simple pleasures, everyday travails of working-class people, and bohemian/liberal ideals; and artful singing in clear, standard French. It traces its roots back to the Middle Ages and experienced Golden Ages in the 1880s, 1930s, 1960s, and present (e.g., Fréhel, Mistinguett, Édith Piaf, Charles Trenet, Georges Brassens, Charles Aznavour, Yves Montand, Léo Ferré, Barbara, Georges Moustaki, Bénabar, Vincent Delerm, Juliette Noureddine, Ben Mazué, and Pomme).

Chanson de geste: Traditional epic poetry that celebrates the exploits (esp. military) of French heroes from the latter part of the Early Middle Ages. The most prominent French example is the *Chanson de Roland* (*Song of Roland*), composed between 1040 and 1115.

Charlie Hebdo: Weekly satirical newspaper known for its "stupid and mean" style of humor, crude satirical attacks on politicians and religion, and publication of controversial cartoons featuring the prophet Muhammad. The latter were the motivation for a murderous retaliatory attack on the publication's Paris headquarters by Islamist terrorists on January 7, 2015.

Ch'ti: Shortened form of *Ch'timi*, a colloquial name for speakers of the Picard dialect—and, by extension, native inhabitants of the Hauts-de-France region of northern France; portrayed in popular culture as a rural working-class stereotype.

Classe préparatoire aux grandes écoles: A rigorous program of postsecondary studies offered in certain lycées that is designed to prepare students for the competitive exams for admission to France's elite university-level *grandes écoles*; also referred to as CPGE and *prépa*.

Classicism: An esthetic culture that found inspiration in Greco-Roman antiquity, prevalent in France from the sixteenth through the nineteenth centuries. In various iterations (incl. the Baroque Classicism exemplified by Versailles), classicism sought order, propriety, and sober illustrations of heroic virtues and the mastery of individual passions.

CNRS: Acronym for Centre National de la Recherche Scientifique, France's largest and most prestigious publicly funded institute of scientific research.

Cohabitation: Term used in French politics to designate a situation of divided government, wherein a new majority in the National Assembly opposed to the president (head of state) obliges the latter to share executive power with a prime minister (head of government) and cabinet supported by and beholden to that majority.

Collège: French middle school (three grades comprising the first level of secondary education), typically serving students ages twelve to fifteen.

Comédie de mœurs: A genre of witty comedy popular in France since the sixteenth century that satirizes and criticizes the society of the present era via characters that serve as stereotypes displaying the characteristic vices and failings of the era and its dominant classes.

Communautarisme: French term equivalent to "communitarianism," often used pejoratively in reference to allegedly fractious racial, ethnic, religious, and cultural communities, and social minorities, thought to give precedence to group interests and grievances over the national interest and "universal" principles.

Commune: An administrative subdivision of the territory of the French Republic that represents local government and public administration in cities, towns, and rural townships.

COMUE: Acronym for *Communauté d'universités et établissements,* or "community of universities and institutions"—a grouping of local universities, research institutes, and other types of higher education establishments under the provisions of a 2013 law with the authority to grant degrees and manage budgets as a collective entity. Formulas range from consortium-like arrangements to fuller integration (often a prelude to formal merger).

Conseil Français de Culte Musulman: CFCM—French Council of the Muslim Faith, a national elected body of Islamic religious leaders founded in 2003 as the official interlocutor with the French government on matters pertaining to Islamic religious affairs in France.

Cordon Bleu, Le: An international network of prestigious gourmet culinary, restaurant management, and hospitality schools (currently thirty-five institutes in twenty countries)—founded in Paris in 1895; the name means "the Blue Cord."

Côte d'Azur: French name for the French Riviera, the Mediterranean coastal region of southeastern France (mostly in the historic region of Provence), known for its sunny beaches, luxurious resorts, vibrant port cities (Toulon, Cannes, Antibes, Nice, and Monte-Carlo [Monaco]), and beautiful landscapes.

CRS: Acronym for *compagnies républicaines de sécurité,* elite reserve units of the French national police specialized in crowd control, security at large public demonstrations, quelling social unrest, highway patrol in urban areas, and the protection of national monuments and other high-profile sites.

Department: Historically, the most important administrative subdivision of the territory of the French Republic, created during the Revolution to replace the provinces of the monarchy. At a level between the larger regions (13 in metropolitan France) and the much smaller local communes (34,836 in metropolitan France), there are 96 departments in metropolitan France, as well as 5 combined overseas department-regions. Most are named for rivers and other local geographical features.

Dirigisme: A French tradition of activist government intervention in an otherwise capitalist economy that goes beyond regulation to include planning, the strategic role of state-held companies and state-directed investments in key sectors, and significant incentives for research and development. It dates to the rebuilding and modernization of the French economy after World War II and is the opposite of a laissez-faire approach.

Dreyfus Affair: A protracted public controversy (1894–1906) in France involving the trial and wrongful conviction of French Jewish captain Alfred Dreyfus for espionage. The trial brought into the open undercurrents of vicious anti-Semitism and reactionary nationalism and sharply divided the defenders and opponents of French republican values (equality, justice, secularism).

DROM-COM: French acronym for "Overseas Departments and Regions—Overseas Collectivities." It encompasses the range of political and administrative statuses that apply to parts of France that are distant from the European mainland ("metropolitan" France)—the vestiges (mostly islands) of French colonialism. The most fully integrated have dual status as departments and regions of the French Republic.

École maternelle: School for young children between the ages three and six. Since 2019, instruction is compulsory for children beginning at age three. The three grades of the *maternelle*, span nursery school and kindergarten and together make up the first cycle of the French common core education system.

Élysée (Palace): The official Paris residence of the president of the French Republic. The name is used metonymically to refer to the presidential administration.

Eurovision: A popular music song contest, held annually since 1956, in which representatives from different European countries (and several non-European ones) compete on live television. The contest is very popular in France (which has won it five times) and is the world's most watched nonsporting televised event.

Existentialism: A philosophical school of thought that emphasizes the radical freedom of the individual outside a priori moral frameworks and humanist idealism in a world that may seem absurd. With ties to nineteenth-century precursors and early twentieth-century phenomenology, it was particularly prevalent in France during the late 1930s, 1940s, and 1950s due to the writings of Jean-Paul Sartre, Simone de Beauvoir, and Albert Camus.

Family Reunification (Immigration): In French, *le regroupement familial*—beginning in the mid-1970s, after large-scale economic immigration of foreign workers had been stopped, a main source of legal immigration to France, whereby family members could rejoin a foreigner already in France and holding a residency permit, with certain conditions (e.g., time living in France, housing, financial resources, etc.).

Ferry Laws: A set of laws passed in 1881–1882 at the instigation of Jules Ferry (minister of public instruction) that made primary instruction compulsory and established public schools as free (publicly funded) and secular (with civic and moral instruction as part of the curriculum). The laws were contested by the Catholic Church but seen by republicans (and later by a majority of the population) both as a foundation of modern public education in France and as key to broader support for the institutions and values of the Republic itself.

Fête de la Musique: Called World Music Day internationally, an annual celebration of music of all types with numerous free concerts on the day of the summer solstice, June 21—created by the French Ministry of Culture in 1982.

Fifth Republic: The current constitutional regime of France—a parliamentary democracy with a strong president at the top of the executive. The new constitution took effect in 1958 after the Fourth Republic (1946–1958) had proved itself unable to deal with the Algerian War and its domestic repercussions.

Fonctionnaires: Civil service (*fonction publique*) employees of the national government, regional and local administrations (territorial collectivities), and the public hospital system. The *fonction publique* sector encompasses 5.6 million salaried employees—20% of the total number in the French economy.

FRAC: Acronym for Fonds Régional d'Art Contemporain (founded in 1982)—one of the current twenty-three regional public collections of contemporary art across France. The collections reflect a policy of decentralization in cultural affairs, make contemporary art part of the national heritage, and have a major impact on the French art market.

Françafrique: Term that refers to France's special (neocolonial) ties to and cultivated sphere of influence among many of its former colonies in sub-Saharan Africa (independence gained in the 1960s). Its tools have included currencies pegged to the former French franc and euro, development aid, special relations among heads of state, educational and cultural exchange, close economic ties, French military intervention, and immigration.

France Télévisions: France's national public television broadcaster (founded in 1992), including its flagship channel, France 2, and six other channels with a focus on regional programming, children's programming and live performance, educational documentaries and societal issues, overseas markets, news, and programming for adolescents and young adults.

France Unbowed: Translation of La France Insoumise (LFI), a populist, progressive, and anti-capitalist party of the hard left, currently led by Jean-Luc Mélenchon.

Francophonie: The global community of nations, regions, and people who speak French as a native, official, or culturally important language. The shared linguistic, literary, and cultural heritages of the community form a basis for exchange and cooperation among its members and solidarity in the defense of those heritages on the international stage (e.g., via the Organisiation Internationale de la Francophonie).

French Exception/Cultural Exception: The former is used to refer to French exceptionalism and France's propensity to stake out independent/outlier positions (esp. among Atlantic allies) in world affairs. The latter is used (by France in particular) primarily in the context of trade policy to assert that cultural products (esp. in the field of arts and entertainment) should not be treated like other goods that are subjected to deregulated trade and the free play of the forces of the global marketplace but deserve reasonable protections due to their importance to collective identity and heritage and to global cultural diversity.

French Touch: Term used broadly to signify a characteristic national esthetic flair in music, arts, fashion, and other creative fields on the part of contemporary French creators. Qualities include chic elegance, sensual pleasure of experience, technological modernity, sophisticated sense of humor and irony, the blending of pop and avant-gardism, and cosmopolitan mixing of borrowed elements. It is used primarily to refer to the distinctive sound of French electronic music (esp. house) of the 1990s and 2000s (e.g., Daft Punk, David Guetta).

Gallantry: Behavior of a man who pays special attention to women, chivalrous and/or flirtatious in nature—thought to be a characteristic of French male behavior. Seen by some as part of the pleasure of everyday interactions between the sexes and by others as a sign of male privilege that regularly gives rise to harassment.

Gaul: Ancient homeland of the Gauls (a Celtic people) before and during the period of Roman conquest, colonization, and rule (50 BCE–486 CE). It encompassed much of the territory of present-day metropolitan France. Gaul and its inhabitants are traditionally considered the ancestral precursors of the modern-day French nation and people. By extension, "Gaul" is a popular substitution to refer to France itself; similarly, things quintessentially French are often referred to as "Gallic."

Gaullism: Political philosophy associated with General Charles de Gaulle, leader of Free France during World War II and first president of the Fifth Republic (1958–1969). Gaullism prioritizes French independence and grandeur on the international stage, advocates vigorous action on the part of state to modernize French society and maintain order, stresses national unity, and combines conservatism (traditional values) and republicanism (incl. a social welfare).

Gendarme: A law enforcement agent who is a member of the Gendarmerie Nationale, which is a branch of the French armed forces although partially under the jurisdiction of Ministry of the Interior. Compared to the National Police, which focuses on urban areas, gendarmes patrol the countryside, small towns, and highways. The Gendarmerie also has special forces (GIGN), counterterrorism, crowd control, ceremonial (Republican Guard), and cybercrime units.

Grandes écoles: Elite establishments of higher education that are distinct from the public university system. Admission is typically based on highly competitive national exams taken after two to three years of postsecondary preparatory classes. This category includes France's prestigious *écoles normales supérieures* (e.g., Paris "Ulm," Lyon) and many top schools in STEM (esp. engineering), business, and political science (e.g., École Polytechnique, Mines Paris Tech, HEC, "Sciences Po" Paris).

Grands travaux: Large and prestigious public building projects, especially facilities for cultural institutions characterized by bold modern designs, such as the presidential *grands travaux* in Paris (e.g., Centre Pompidou, Louvre Pyramid, Quai Branly Museum).

Halal: An Arabic word designating that which is lawful or permitted, used especially for food that is allowed under Islamic religious dietary laws, such as meat from animals slaughtered using methods in accordance with those laws. The availability of halal foods is an important issue for France's Muslim community.

Haussmannization: The transformation of Paris (incl. gentrification of many older, socially mixed neighborhoods) undertaken during the years of the Second Empire (1852–1870) and Napoleon III, overseen by Paris Prefect Eugène Haussmann—characterized by broad boulevards lined with stylistically uniform upscale apartment buildings and fashionable sidewalk cafés.

Haute couture: High fashion, of which Paris is a global center—especially exquisite custom-made garments created by top designers that reflect an esthetic vision that evolves from season to season.

Hexagon: Nickname for France based on the geometric shape outlined by the borders of continental France.

Hijab: Headscarf worn by Muslim women and girls—prohibited in French primary and secondary schools under a 2004 law as contrary to the French legal and civic norm of secularism. A provision of a proposed "anti-separatism" law (2021) would extend the prohibition to minors in all public spaces.

HLM: Acronym for *habitation à loyer modéré* (lit. moderate-rent housing)—publicly subsidized housing for people in lower income brackets, including large housing estates in the suburbs outside French cities, some of which are comprised of drab tower blocks constructed in the 1960s, 1970s, and 1980s.

Huguenots: The French Protestant (esp. Calvinist) community that faced religious persecution in the sixteenth and seventeenth centuries, including the diaspora that fled the country after King Louis XIV rescinded the 1598 Edict of Nantes (limited tolerance and protections) in 1685.

Hypermarket: Translation of *hypermarché*, a French term for a big-box retail outlet that combines a full-service supermarket with a low-cost department store—typically located on the outskirts of French cities and towns.

Iel: Most widely used gender-neutral third-person singular personal pronoun (a combination of the masculine "Il" and the feminine "Elle").

INSEE: Acronym for Institut National de la Statistique et des Études Économiques, or National Institute of Statistics and Economic Studies (founded in 1946)—France's leading source of official statistics alongside the Institut National d'Études Démographiques (INED).

Institut Universitaire de Technologie: IUT; translation of University Institute of Technology. A school offering three-year bachelor's degree programs (formerly two-year diplomas) in a broad range of technical fields—a branch of the French public university system.

Jacobin: Originally refers to the member of a radical left-wing political party during the French Revolution (in power during the Reign of Terror [1793–1794]). Because of that party's support for a centralized, unitary republic and extensive use of state power, the term is now used more generally to refer to a French tradition of bureaucratic centralization and top-down "big government" at the national level that dates back to the absolute monarchy.

La Défense: A business district of gleaming skyscrapers just outside the western city limits of Paris that includes the monumental Grande Arche de la Défense (1989).

Laïcité: In English, "laicity" or "laicism." The French republican legal and cultural norm that encompasses the Separation of Churches and State (Law of 1905), the strict neutrality of the public sphere with respect to private matters of religion and conscience, religious liberty and tolerance as guaranteed by the 1789 Declaration of the Rights of Man, and a historical aversion to clerical influence over French politics, society, and free thought. The concept implies an individual obligation as well as an institutional mandate.

Langue d'oïl–Langue d'oc: Distinction between the romance languages and dialects that evolved from Latin in the north of France (*oïl*—e.g., French, Picard, Gallo) and in the south (*oc*—e.g., Occitan, Provençal, Auvergnat) during the Early Middle Ages. The terms are based on the different words used for "yes" in the two linguistic regions.

Left Bank–Right Bank: The two sections of Paris as determined by their situation north (Right Bank) or south (Left Bank) of the Seine River. The centers of political and economic power as well as major monuments and museums are mostly found in Right Bank districts, while the Left Bank is known for its concentration of universities and schools and as the location of the Eiffel Tower.

Legitimist: Refers to a faction of the reactionary right after the French Revolution that maintained that the divine-right monarchy and the Bourbon dynastic line were the sole rightful basis of national sovereignty and government. Legitimists were also closely tied to the Catholic Church and espoused very conservative moral values and social views.

Liberal: In the context of French politics and economic life, someone who espouses a laissez-faire philosophy with respect to free enterprise, deregulated marketplaces, and unfettered capitalism—usually alongside support for representative democracy, civil liberties, individual autonomy, an open society, cultural pluralism, the rule of law, fiscal conservatism, and moderate forms of social welfare.

Liberation: France's emancipation from German military occupation in concert with the soon victorious Allied powers and return to national independence and republican self-government at the end of World War II (June 1944–May 1945)—a major turning point in French history and the beginning of a period of postwar reconstruction, economic development, political renewal, social reforms, modernization, and decolonization.

Libertine: Someone whose ideas and lifestyle with respect to sex and emphasis on personal pleasure are very liberal—sometimes to the point of recklessness—and who exhibits "enlightened" and open disregard for societal moral conventions. Libertine culture was particularly strong in France during the eighteenth century, the early twentieth century, and the 1960s and 1970s.

Licence: A three-year bachelor's degree from a French university or other accredited institution of higher education.

Ligue 1: The league at the highest level of professional soccer/football in France—including legendary teams like Paris Saint-Germain, Olympique de Marseille, Olympique Lyonnais, and FC Girondins de Bordeaux.

Lycée: French high school (upper-level secondary school): consisting of three grades, serving students ages fifteen to eighteen, and typically leading to a *baccalauréat* diploma after passage of a battery of exams. There are two types of *lycées* in France: ones that offer a traditional liberal arts and STEM curriculum (LEGT) and ones that offer specialized vocational and professional programs (LEP).

Maghrebi: A person from, or who ethnically and culturally identifies with, the countries of Northwest Africa, or the Arab and Berber peoples who inhabit them. In France, the term is used to refer to immigrants and the descendants of immigrants from the former French colonies of Morocco, Algeria, and Tunisia.

Manouche: A French term for Gypsy (Romani/Roma) people and culture. The term is also widely used for a French style of jazz exemplified by Django Reinhardt in the 1930s and 1940s.

Marianne: The name traditionally given to the female personification of the French Republic, which derives from eighteenth-century (esp. French Revolution) allegorical personifications of Liberty. Marianne is typically depicted wearing the red Phrygian cap of liberty and is widely represented in public statues, town hall busts, postage stamps, and official logos of the French government.

Matignon (Hôtel de): The official residence of the Prime Minister of France, used metonymically to refer to the prime minister's office and administration.

May 68: The massive wave of radical student protests and worker strikes that took place in France in May and June of 1968. The "events" of May 68 profoundly marked a generation and have a quasi-mythical status in France. They were a failure as a political revolution but crystallized a groundswell of social and cultural change. May 68 ideals include individualism, leftism, sexual freedom, women's liberation, LGBT rights, anti-Establishment thinking, anti-racism, the rejection of organized religion, critiques of capitalism and consumerist materialism, opposition to government paternalism, identification with the struggles of the peoples of the developing world and postcolonial nations, and the exaltation of self-expression.

Métropole: A term that has two distinctive meanings in the French context: (1) mainland France in continental Europe as opposed to the nation's far-flung overseas departments and territorial collectivities (the vestiges of French colonialism); (2) a special category within French territorial administration that applies to a certain number of cities and surrounding urban areas and facilitates a high level of intercommunal consolidation of local government and public administration.

Midi: French name for the South of France. It is sometimes used broadly to refer to the parts of the country that lie south of the Loire River. More specifically, it pertains to a distinct cultural space comprised of the historic regions of Aquitaine (Guyenne and Gascony), Languedoc, Rousillon, and Provence.

Musette: A traditional genre of popular Parisian dance music with Auvergnat roots that prominently features accordions (also called *bal-musette*).

Napoleonic Code: Name given to France's extensive and frequently updated written civil code, which was first compiled and implemented by Napoleon Bonaparte in 1804.

National Rally: Rassemblement National (RN), formerly Front National—a nationalist and populist party of the far right founded by Jean-Marie Le Pen in 1972. Focus on immigration, French identity, crime, economic protectionism, and denunciations of the political establishment. Marine Le Pen took over as party leader in 2011. Current acting president is Jordan Bardella (b. 1995).

Naturalism: An offshoot of Realism in French literature in the latter part of the nineteenth century that strives for quasi-scientific observation and detailed, critical, and progressive-minded depictions of the society of its era—especially the lives of the working class, the poor, rural people, and the marginalized. The novelist Zola was a key theorist and the leading practitioner of the style.

Négritude: A literary and intellectual concept and movement that first developed among Black Francophone students, writers, intellectuals, and political activists based in Paris in the 1930s. Key concepts include Black consciousness, esthetics, shared cultural heritage across Africa and throughout the diaspora, and resistance to European colonialism. Leading figures include Paulette and Jane Nardal, Aimé Césaire, Léopold Sédar Senghor, Léon Damas, and Cheikh Anta Diop. Frantz Fanon was influenced by Négritude but also critiqued its essentialism.

New French Extremity: Term coined by critic James Quandt to describe French independent films from the 2000s to 2010s that were graphic in nature and nonhumanist in spirit, many of which dealt with themes of horror, violence, sexual exploitation and promiscuity, the abject, and the distasteful. Representative directors include Catherine Breillat, Léos Carax, Claire Denis, Virginie Despentes, Julia Ducournau, Bruno Dumont, Xavier Gens, Gaspar Noé, François Ozon, and Marina de Van.

Nouveau Roman: Translated "New Novel." A French school of avant-garde experimental novelists in the 1950s and 1960s who rejected the traditional modes of narration and characterization generally associated with the realist novel. Leading representatives include Michel Butor, Marguerite Duras, Alain Robbe-Grillet, Robert Pinget, Nathalie Sarraute, and Claude Simon.

Nouvelle Cuisine: Trend in French gastronomy that began in the 1960s and emphasized lighter fare (as opposed to traditional rich sauces), fresh local market ingredients, innovative flavor combinations, and esthetic presentation. Leading examples among chefs include Paul Bocuse, Alain Chapel, Michel Guérard, Jean and Pierre Troisgros, and Roger Vergé.

Nouvelle Vague: Translated "New Wave." French school of avant-garde independent filmmaking in the late 1950s, 1960s, and early 1970s that rejected the filmic and dramatic conventions of traditional quality cinema. Nouvelle Vague innovations included positioning the filmmaker as an *auteur* (author), location filming, use of handheld cameras, jump cuts and other creative editing techniques, unconventional narrative structure, and critical (and sometimes politicized) commentary on contemporary French society and bourgeois values. Leading directors include Claude Chabrol, Jean-Luc Godard, Alain Resnais, Eric Rohmer, François Truffaut, and Agnès Varda.

NUPES: Acronym for Nouvelle Union Populaire Écologique et Sociale, or New Ecologic and Social People's Union—a coalition of left-wing parties formed in May 2022 to compete in the June 2022 French legislative (National Assembly) elections under the leadership of Jean-Luc Mélenchon. The dominant party in the coalition at its founding was Mélenchon's La France Insoumise (France Unbowed). Other members of the original alliance included the Socialist Party, EELV (Ecologists/Green Party), and French Communist Party. Leading opposition bloc in the NA after the 2022 elections.

Occitan: Langue d'oc–evolved romance language spoken in the South of France and some areas of Italy and Spain. It has multiple dialects and regional variants such as Auvergnat, Gascon, Languedocien, Limousin, Provençal, Vivaro-Alpine, and Niçard.

Outre-mer: French for "Overseas," formerly used to refer to France's far-flung colonial empire; now used to refer to the overseas departments and territorial collectivities that are the remnants of that empire.

PACS: French acronym for *pacte civil de solidarité*, a contractual civil union available since 1999 to adults who elect to organize their domestic life as partners. The rights and responsibilities associated with the PACS are not quite the same as those of marriage. The PACS was originally created for same-sex couples who later obtained the right to marry (2013). It is still a popular alternative to marriage for both opposite and same-sex couples.

Paysan: French for "peasant," still used for small-scale farmers and rural people who do manual work in agriculture or identify with a traditional rural way of life.

Petite bourgeoisie: A historical term for members of the lower rungs of the bourgeoisie, such as self-employed artisans, small shopkeepers, office clerks, and autonomous peasants who may own some land. One step removed from the working class and the peasantry, the members of this subgroup tend to be politically conservative and emulate (unevenly) the values and behaviors of the upper middle bourgeoisie.

Pieds-Noirs: European settlers in France's colonial territories of North Africa, especially Algeria, where they had French citizenship long before Indigenous majority. The term is also used for Algerian Jews who were considered French citizens since 1871. There was a massive exodus of *Pieds-Noirs* following Algerian independence in 1962.

Poète maudit: French term for an "accursed poet"—a poet who lives on the margins of mainstream (bourgeois) society, feels rejected or unrecognized by it (alienation), and is opposed to its stifling norms and moral hypocrisy; such a poet lives a Bohemian lifestyle that may include alcohol and drug abuse, other illicit activities, and promiscuous sexual liaisons and makes these experiences a theme of their poetry. The term is used specifically to refer to the French nineteenth-century poets Charles Baudelaire, Paul Verlaine, Arthur Rimbaud, and Comte de Lautréamont. François Villon was a late medieval precursor. Provocative singer-songwriter Serge Gainsbourg was a contemporary example.

Post-Structuralism: A trend in philosophical thought and critical theory in the 1960s, 1970s, and 1980s in which French thinkers played a prominent role. Similarly to earlier structuralism, it pays special attention to language, discourse, and the codified systems that underpin culture and knowledge; however, it differs from its predecessor insofar as it does not see those systems as self-sufficient and open to universal interpretation but as unstable reflections of conflicting forces, mutable power dynamics, cultural hegemony and resistance, and socially determined interpretative practices that can only be partially uncovered or deconstructed. Leading post-structuralist thinkers include Roland Barthes, Jean Baudrillard, Hélène Cixous, Michel de Certeau, Gilles Deleuze, Jacques Derrida, Michel Foucault, and Julia Kristeva.

Prêt-à-porter: Ready-to-wear clothing, especially that designed by leading fashion houses.

Prix Goncourt: The most prestigious French literary prize awarded annually to the most outstanding work of imaginative prose in French, almost always a novel. Spinoff Goncourt prizes are awarded for first novels, short stories, poetry, and biography.

Quai d'Orsay: The headquarters of the French Ministry of Foreign Affairs is located on the Quai d'Orsay, customarily used to refer to the ministry itself, the French foreign service, and the shapers of French foreign policy.

Quatorze-Juillet: The Fourteenth of July, France's national holiday, the anniversary of the storming of the Bastille in Paris in 1789—the reason for its being called "Bastille Day" outside of France—and the beginning of popular involvement in the French Revolution.

Renaissance: The centrist liberal political party founded by Emmanuel Macron in 2016, formerly known as La République en Marche! (LREM), or The Republic on the Move! The new name dates from May 2022.

Rentrée: A return from a vacation or holiday period—used especially for the period in September when people have returned from their long summer holidays, children are heading back to school, and a range of other activities that have slowed down during the summer months—from industry to politics to publishing—return to their normal rhythm of operation.

Republic: The French democratic system of government without a monarch or other hereditary ruler; since 1789, an aspirational identity for the French nation that has its roots in the Enlightenment and is based on the principles of liberty, equality, fraternity, indivisibility, secularism, social solidarity, justice, the rule of law, individual autonomy, civil rights, civic virtues, reason, and progress. The French Republic faced opposition from both the far right and elements of the far left during the nineteenth and early twentieth centuries; however, it came to be broadly accepted and revered in the latter half of the twentieth century (esp. during the period of the Fifth Republic, founded in 1958).

Republicans, The: Translation of Les Républicains (LR)—France's main center-right political party, renamed as such in 2015 (previously Union pour un Mouvement Populaire). It has moderate, conservative, and nationalist wings and traces its roots back to the neo-Gaullist Rassemblement pour la République, founded by Jacques Chirac in 1976.

Roland-Garros: French name for the French Open tennis tournament (one of the four Grand Slam tournaments), based on the name of the Paris stadium in which its main matches are played (on clay courts)—itself named after a pioneer aviator and French World War I fighter pilot, shot down and killed in combat in 1918.

Roquefort: A pungent, tangy, crumbly, and semimoist sheep's milk blue cheese from the South of France (EU and French regulations stipulate that cheese bearing this protected name must be naturally aged in the caves of Roquefort-sur-Soulzon).

Sans-culottes: Radical republican militants from the lower rungs of Parisian society that played an active role in the French Revolution. The name refers to the fact that they did not wear the silk knee britches of the aristocratic and bourgeois elites, but the long trousers of working men.

Savoir-vivre: French term for "knowledge of living"—basic knowledge of the rules of etiquette and how to comport oneself in polite society.

School of Paris: The avant-garde modern artists—French as well as numerous foreign émigrés—who worked in Paris in the first half of the twentieth century, forming a loose cosmopolitan community whose members frequented one another, followed each other's work, sometimes collaborated, and discussed and debated art and esthetics. Numerous schools and trends were represented (Cubism, Fauvism, Expressionism, Surrealism, etc.) and the artists often shifted between them. The most famous figures of the School of Paris include Pablo Picasso, Henri Matisse, Marc Chagall, Amadeo Modigliani, and Fernand Léger. The School's work was twice disrupted by world war. It was revived as the New School of Paris from the late 1940s through the 1970s by the practitioners of abstraction, by which time Paris's status as the capital of the art world was in dispute.

SDF: Acronym for *sans domicile fixe* (without a fixed place of residence)—that is, a homeless person.

Sécu: Abbreviation of Sécurite Sociale—France's comprehensive social safety net, which was set up as a mostly unified system in 1945 and has been both expanded and reformed several times since then. French Social Security has six branches: Family (incl. support for children, welfare for the poor and vulnerable, and housing subsidies), Illness (incl. health insurance and maternity), Workplace Accidents and Occupational Health, Retirement (and old age), Personal Autonomy (for the elderly and the disabled), and Collections. Unemployment benefits in France are handled by a separate independent agency, Pôle Emploi (Employment Hub), formed in 2008 through the consolidation of other agencies.

Sephardi: Jews from the Mediterranean Basin (Iberian Peninsula, North Africa, and Middle East). After an influx from Morocco, Algeria, and Tunisia (former French colonial territories) in the 1950s and 1960s, Sephardic Jews are more numerous than Ashkenazi Jews within the French Jewish community.

Service public: A wide array of subsidized public services, which may be provided by government agencies and other public institutions whose employees may have civil service status or, increasingly, affiliated nonprofit or for-profit contractors that adhere to the public service mission and are subject to government regulations. Examples include the postal service, public hospitals, public transportation, the national railroad (SNCF), public schools and universities, public broadcasting, unemployment offices, utilities, and cultural institutions. Public Services are important to the French republican model because they reflect the principles of the common good, equality, social solidarity, and national cohesion.

SNCF: Acronym for Société Nationale des Chemins de fer Français—France's national, state-owned railway company.

Sorbonne: Originally a thirteenth-century residential college for poor students of theology at the University of Paris, with which it was traditionally synonymous. In 1968, the University of Paris was broken up into different independent institutions, several of which used "Sorbonne" in their names. A new wave of university restructuring and consolidation occurred in the 2010s. One of the institutions to emerge is Sorbonne Université (2018); it is one of several highly placed French universities in global rankings. The physical Sorbonne site in the Latin Quarter of Paris (Left Bank) is shared by several institutions.

Sun King: Louis XIV (1638–1715) was King of France from 1643 to 1715. He is known as the Sun King because he adopted the Sun as his emblem, positioned himself at the center of all things in his expansive practice of absolute monarchy, carefully cultivated an image of radiant splendor at Versailles, and personally identified with Apollo, the Greek god of the Sun and light.

Surrealism: International movement in literature and the arts founded in Paris by André Breton in 1924 (the term itself was coined by Guillaume Apollinaire) in reaction to the horrors of World War I and the corrupt and morally bankrupt bourgeois society that had brought about the war. Surrealism's aim was to emancipate the subconscious and its creative potential by opening art and literature to chance, dreamlife, automatic processes, games, liberated sexual desire, and non-Western influences. Although disrupted by World War II, Surrealism continued through the 1950s. Leading figures include the poets Paul Eluard, Robert Desnos, and Louis Aragon; the sculptor Alberto Giacometti; the painters Max Ernst, Joan Mirò, René Magritte, Salvador Dalì, Leonara Carrington, and Remedios Varo; the photographers Man Ray, Claude Cahun, and Dora Maar; and the filmmakers René Clair, Germaine Dulac, and Luis Buñuel.

Terroir: French term for a geographical and natural microregion with specific environmental characteristics (e.g., soil, topography, and climate) that affect the crops grown there. Together with traditional farming and production practices that may be specific to the area, these environmental factors give unique flavor and other distinctive characteristics to the food and beverages—for example, cheese and wine—that originate from the terroir, which are appreciated by food aficionados and may be fixtures of local identity. In France, terroir is more than food—it is a component of cultural heritage and a site of memory that harkens back to France's long history as a rural society.

TGV: Acronym for Train à Grande Vitesse (high-speed train)—successful high-speed passenger rail service was introduced in 1981 and regularly expanded (additional routes) since then. In 2019 (pre-COVID-19), the TGV system registered a total of 61.9 million passenger-kilometers traveled in France, an all-time high. Via TGV, Paris is 1:45 from Lyon, 2:14 from Bordeaux, 2:20 from Strasbourg, and 3:30 from Marseille.

Theatre of the Absurd: A current of post–World War II (esp. late 1940s–1960s) theatre prominent in France characterized by the abandonment of traditional modes of dramatic intrigue, characterization, dialogue, time, and space to express the futility of human language, action, ritual, and notions of individual freedom in a world devoid of meaning. Emblematic playwrights of the movement include Arthur Adamov, Samuel Beckett, Jean Genet, and Eugène Ionesco.

Third Estate: Under the feudal social hierarchy, the Third Estate was comprised of commoners, including peasants, manual laborers, tradesmen, and bourgeois of all professions; the other two estates, or orders, were the clergy and the aristocracy—both more privileged. As a sign of growing power and dissatisfaction, representatives of the Third Estate at the Estates General assembly in 1789 declared themselves a constitutional assembly and vowed to reform the monarchy—a decisive event in what was to become the French Revolution.

Third Republic: Regime of parliamentary democracy in place in France from 1870 to 1940. It was set up following France's defeat in the Franco-Prussian War and the collapse of the French Second Empire led by Napoleon III. It is known for advancing public education, the broader cultural dissemination and political normalization of moderate republican ideals, and the expansion of France's colonial empire in Africa and Southeast Asia.

Toubon Law: A 1994 law named for its sponsor, conservative minister of culture Jacques Toubon. It sought to protect the French language against the encroachment of English. Provisions stipulated that French must be used in government publications, the workplace, contracts, and advertising (other languages may be used if French translations are provided) and that 40% of the songs played by any broadcast radio station must be in French.

Tour de France: The world's premier bicycle road race: twenty-one stages crisscrossing France (with occasional stages in neighboring countries) over the course of three weeks in July, including grueling mountain stages and a finale on the Champs-Élysées in Paris. A major national sporting and cultural event that showcases the geographical diversity of France.

Trente Glorieuses: The period of "Thirty Glorious Years" from 1945 to 1975 known for postwar reconstruction, modernization, urbanization, economic growth, middle-class expansion, rising standards of living, the advent of consumer society, greater individualism, decolonization, the establishment of the European Community and of the Fifth Republic, and France's return to international prominence. A fixture of French nostalgia.

Tricolor: Name given to France's national flag since the French Revolution because of its three vertical bands of color: blue, white, and red. Blue and red were the traditional colors of the city of Paris, white that of the monarchy.

Troubadours: The medieval writers and performers of chivalrous and courtly love-themed lyric poetry in Old Occitan in southern France from the eleventh through the fourteenth centuries. The Trouvères were their equivalent in northern France (Old French).

Union libre: French term for couples living together outside of marriage or civil union. It is called "free union" because it is often construed as a rejection of middle-class societal and moral conventions and as a preservation of individual liberty and equality between two domestic partners. Very popular in France, including as a prelude to marriage or civil union for younger couples.

Verlan: A practice of slang with lower-class (*populaire*) origins and especially widespread among the young and in urban areas and disadvantaged suburbs that consists of inverting the syllables of a word (e.g., "verlan" itself is an inversion of the syllables of the word "l'envers" [the reverse]). It is often employed as a marker of group identity and belonging. Verlan has also given rise to practice of "double verlan" that further distorts the source word.

Vichy: The reactionary, traditionalist, and authoritarian regime (1940–1944) under the leadership of Philippe Pétain set up in France following the nation's defeat by Nazi Germany in the early phase of World War II. It was officially called the "French State" but is more commonly known by the reference to the resort town in central France where it was based. The regime is known for state collaboration with Germany, depriving French Jews of their civil rights and assisting in their deportation, and replacing the Republican motto of "Liberty, Equality, Fraternity" with "Work, Family, Fatherland."

Viticulteur: A member of the winegrowing (*viticulture*) profession—someome who cultivates and harvests grapes for the making of wine (*vinification* in French).

Vouvoiement–Tutoiement: French terms signifying the use of either the formal second person singular pronoun "vous" or the informal "tu" to address another person—a sometimes complex matter that involves factors of age, social status, etiquette, familiarity and closeness, and speaker intent.

Yellow Vests: Participants in the widespread political and social protest movement in France (first phase, 2018–2020), identified with the fluorescent yellow safety vests that they wore during their protest actions, which included occupying roundabouts, highway toll plazas, and major city intersections. The protests began as opposition to a new ecotax on gasoline and fuel, seen as putting an onerous burden on already financially strapped working people, but developed into a wide-ranging indictment of French democracy's failings, neoliberal economic policies, and President Emmanuel Macron.

Yé-yé: Style of French pop music in the 1960s that blended Anglo-American rock and roll influences and jazz inflections with the French chanson tradition. The name is a

French transcription of the English cry of "Yeah, yeah!" popularized by the Beatles and other rock performers. Songs ranged from bubblegum pop to winsome romantic ballads. While men were involved in *yé-yé* (e.g., Serge Gainsbourg, Johnny Hallyday, Claude François), the style was known especially for its women singers called "yé-yé girls" (e.g., Françoise Hardy, France Gall, Sheila, Sylvie Vartan).

FACTS AND FIGURES

Table 1: GEOGRAPHY

Location	Located in Western Europe, France is bordered by the English Channel to the northwest, Belgium and Luxembourg to the northeast, Germany and Switzerland to the east, Italy to the southeast, the Mediterranean Sea and Spain to the south, and the Atlantic Ocean to the west. The Mediterranean island of Corsica is considered part of metropolitan (continental) France, while thirteen separate territories—in the Atlantic Ocean, Caribbean Sea, South America, Indian Ocean, Pacific Ocean, and Antarctic region—make up overseas France. The latter include five dual departments and regions (i.e., with the same administrative status as the departments and regions of metropolitan France), five semiautonomous territorial collectivities, New Caledonia (special status), and two French-administered uninhabited territories.
National Capital	Paris
Time Zone	6 hours ahead of U.S. Eastern Standard
Land Borders	1,797 miles
Coastline	2,130 miles (includes Corsica)
Capital	Paris
Area	211,154 sq. miles
Climate	The climate throughout France is temperate and rainfall is frequent throughout the year. The southern part of the country has warm Mediterranean summers and mild winters. Temperatures in Paris typically range from 32°F to 75°F.
Land Use	52.7% AGRICULTURAL (1.8% permanent crops [incl. groves], 33.4% cultivated cropland, 17.5% permanent meadows and pastures); 29.2% FOREST; 18.1% OTHER (e.g., built-up [incl. urban, industrial], infrastructure [incl. roads], scrub, unused arable land, barren) (2018)
Arable Land	33.1% share of total land area (2018)

Arable Land Per Capita	0.27 hectares per person (2018)
Regions	Capital (area; 2019 population)
Auvergne-Rhône-Alpes	Lyon (26,915 sq. miles; pop. 8,042,936)
Bourgogne-Franche-Comté	Dijon (18,449 sq. miles; pop. 2,805,580)
Bretagne	Rennes (10,505 sq. miles; pop. 3,354,854)
Centre-Val de Loire	Orléans (15.116 sq. miles; pop. 2,573,180)
Corse	Ajaccio (3,351 sq. miles; pop. 340,440)
Grand Est	Strasbourg (22,178 sq. miles; pop. 5,556,219)
Guadeloupe	Basse Terre (628 sq. miles; pop. 384,239)
Guyane	Cayenne (32,252 sq. miles; pop. 281,678)
Hauts-de-France	Lille (12,280 sq. miles; pop. 6,004,947)
Île-de-France	Paris (4,637 sq. miles; pop. 12,262,544)
La Réunion	Saint-Denis (966 sq. miles; pop. 861,210)
Martinique	Fort-de-France (435 sq. miles; pop. 364,508)
Mayotte	Mamoudzou (144 sq. miles; pop. 256,000) [population figure is a 2017 estimate]
Normandie	Rouen (11,547 sq. miles; pop. 3,325,032)
Nouvelle-Aquitaine	Bordeaux (32,446 sq. miles; pop. 6,010,289)
Occitanie	Toulouse (28,078 sq. miles; pop. 5.933,185)
Pays de la Loire	Nantes (12,386 sq. miles; pop. 3,806,461)
Provence-Alpes-Côte d'Azur	Marseille (12,123 sq. miles; pop. 5,081,101)

Table 2:   POPULATION

Population	67,106,000 (estimate) (2017)
World Population Rank	21st (2017)
Population Density	104.8 people per square kilometer (2017)
Population Distribution	80.4% urban (2018)
Age Distribution	
0–14 years	18.53%
15–24 years	11.79%
25–54 years	37.78%
55–64 years	12.42%
65 years and over	19.48% (2017)
Median Age	41.4 years (estimate) (2017)
Population Growth Rate	0.4% per year (estimate) (2018)
Net Migration Rate	1.1 (estimate) (2018)
Languages	French (official) as well as over eighty recognized "languages of France," including twenty-six languages and dialects with ties to France's historical regions (the remainder are spoken primarily in its overseas departments and territories).

Religious Groups	(Estimates) (c. 2017)
Christian	55% (incl. 40–50% Catholic)
Atheist	25%
Agnostic/unaffiliated	12%
Muslim	5%
Jews	0.75%
Buddhists	0.75%

N.B. French law prohibits official collection of statistics on religious affiliation. Unofficial surveys are therefore highly approximative.

Major Cities	Consolidated metropolis population (2018)
Paris	7,025,026
Marseille	1,899,666
Lyon	1,398,892
Lille	1,174,273
Bordeaux	801,041
Toulouse	783,353
Nantes	656,725
Nice	540,281
Strasbourg	500,510
Rouen	492,681
Montpellier	481,276
Rennes	451,762
Grenoble	445,059
Toulon	438,985
Saint-Étienne	404,607
Tours	294,220
Clermont-Ferrand	294,127
Orléans	287,119
Nancy	257,431
Dijon	253,859
Metz	221,484
Brest	210,047

N.B. "Metropolis" is an official administrative and territorial entity in France. It includes the central city and closest surrounding suburbs. It is smaller than the greater urban area associated with each city, which is roughly equivalent to the American concept of "metropolitan area."

Table 3: HEALTH

Average Life Expectancy	82.0 years (2018)
Average Life Expectancy, Male	78.9 years (2018)
Average Life Expectancy, Female	85.3 years (2018)
Crude Birth Rate	12.1 per 1,000 people (2018)
Crude Death Rate	9.4 per 1,000 people (2018)
Maternal Mortality	8 per 100,000 live births (2017)
Infant Mortality	4 per 1,000 live births (2017)
Doctors	3.2 per 1,000 people (2017)

Table 4: ENVIRONMENT

CO_2 Emissions	5.5 metric tons per capita (2017)
Alternative and Nuclear Energy	50.1% of total energy use (2014)
Threatened Species	278 (2017)
Protected Areas	227,317 sq. miles (2016)
Total Renewable H_2O Resources per Year	3,247 cubic meters, per person, per year (2017)

Table 5: ENERGY AND NATURAL RESOURCES

Electric Power Generation	536,100,000,000 kilowatt hours per year (estimate) (2018)
Electric Power Consumption	436,100,000,000 kilowatt hours per year (estimate) (2017)
Nuclear Power Plants	19 (2018)
Crude Oil Production	15,000 barrels per day (2017)
Crude Oil Consumption	1,705,000 barrels per day (2017)
Natural Gas Production	166,900,000 cubic meters per year (estimate) (2017)
Natural Gas Consumption	41,880,000,000 cubic meters per year (estimate) (2017)
Natural Resources	Coal, iron ore, bauxite, zinc, uranium, antimony, arsenic, potash, feldspar, fluorspar, gypsum, timber, fish

Table 6: NATIONAL FINANCES

Currency	Euro
Total Government Revenues	$1,446,000,000,000 (estimate) (2017)
Total Government Expenditures	$1,515,000,000,000 (estimate) (2017)
Budget Deficit	−2.7 (estimate) (2017)
GDP Contribution by Sector	Agriculture: 2%; industry: 20.1%; services: 77.9% (2017)
External Debt	$5,360,000,000,000 (estimate) (2017)
Economic Aid Extended	$7,366,020,000 (2018)
Economic Aid Received	$0 (2017)

Table 7: INDUSTRY AND LABOR

Gross Domestic Product (GDP)—Official Exchange Rate	$2,730,000,000,000 (estimate) (2019)
GDP per Capita	$42,473 (estimate) (2019)
GDP—Purchasing Power Parity (PPP)	$2,835,746,000,000 (estimate) (2017)
GDP (PPP) per Capita	$43,761 (estimate) (2017)
Industry Products	Steel, machinery and equipment, textiles and clothing, chemicals, automobiles, aircraft and aeronautical equipment, processed food, refined minerals, metals, electronics, chemicals, plastics, pharmaceuticals. There is also a highly developed tourist industry.
Agriculture Products	Wheat, barley, beef, sugar beets, dairy products, cereals, wine grapes, potatoes.
Unemployment	8.6% (2020)
Labor Profile	Agriculture: 2.5%; industry: 18.3%; services: 79.3% (2016)

Table 8: TRADE

Imported Goods	Machinery, passenger cars, chemicals, mineral fuels and lubricants, textile yarns and fabric, iron and steel, plastic materials, meat and meat products, fruits and vegetables.
Total Value of Imports	$624,900,000,000 (estimate) (2017)
Exported Goods	Organic chemicals, cereals, pharmaceuticals, beverages, tobacco, clothing, aircraft and aeronautical equipment, industrial machinery, office equipment, road vehicles and parts, iron and steel, essential oils and perfume materials.
Total Value of Exports	$551,800,000,000 (estimate) (2017)
Import Partners	Germany 18.5%, Belgium 10.2%, Netherlands 8.3%, Italy 7.9%, Spain 7.1%, United Kingdom 5.3%, United States 5.2%, China 5.1% (2017)
Export Partners	Germany 14.8%, Spain 7.7%, Italy 7.5%, United States 7.2%, Belgium 7%, United Kingdom 6.7% (2017)
Current Account Balance	$−36,770,000,000 (estimate) (2017)
Weights and Measures	The metric system is in use.

Table 9: EDUCATION

School System	Compulsory instruction begins at the age of three, typically at a preschool/kindergarten (*école maternelle*). French students begin primary school at the age of six. After five years, they continue to four years of early secondary school (middle school), known as *collège*, and then to either a three-year academic program at a generalist lycée (LEGT) or vocational programs (two or three years in length) at a professional lycée (LEP) or in an accredited apprenticeship or on-the-job training program.
Mandatory Education	Thirteen years, from ages three to sixteen (+ mandatory two years of either additional schooling or professional training, through age eighteen).
Average Years Spent in School for Current Students	15 (2016)
Average Years Spent in School for Current Students, Male	15 (2016)
Average Years Spent in School for Current Students, Female	16 (2016)
Primary School–Age Children Enrolled in Primary School	4,309,942 (2017)
Primary School–Age Males Enrolled in Primary School	2,209,800 (2017)
Primary School–Age Females Enrolled in Primary School	2,100,142 (2017)
Secondary School–Age Children Enrolled in Secondary School	6,058,330 (2017)
Secondary School–Age Males Enrolled in Secondary School	3,092,949 (2017)
Secondary School–Age Females Enrolled in Secondary School	2,965,381 (2017)
Students Per Teacher, Primary School	18.2 (2016)
Students Per Teacher, Secondary School	12.9 (2016)
Enrollment in Tertiary Education	2,424,158 (2016)
Enrollment in Tertiary Education, Male	1,153,520 (2017)
Enrollment in Tertiary Education, Female	1,379,311 (2017)
Literacy	99% (2016)

Table 10: MILITARY

Defense Spending (Percentage of GDP)	2% (2017)
Total Active Armed Forces	307,000 (2017)
Annual Military Expenditures	$55,745,000,000 (2019)
Military Service	The French armed forces are all professional/volunteer. Compulsory military service ended in 2001. Young people (both men and women) must still register for possible conscription and participate in a mandatory day of "defense and citizenship." Plans are in the works for a longer period (four weeks) of mandatory "universal national service."

Table 11: TRANSPORTATION

Airports	460 total, including 129 open to commercial passenger flights (2017)
Registered Vehicles	42,792,103 (2015)
Paved Roads	100% paved; 600,192 miles (2019)
Railroads	29,640 miles (2017)
Ports	Major: 10 (incl. Marseille, Le Havre, Dunkerque, Nantes, Rouen, Bordeaux, Toulon)

Table 12: COMMUNICATIONS

Facebook Users	33,000,000 (estimate) (2017)
Internet Users	57,226,585 (2016)
Internet Users (Percentage of Population)	83.0% (2019)
Land-Based Telephones in Use	38,687,000 (2017)
Mobile Telephone Subscribers	69,017,000 (2017)

HOLIDAYS

Day/Date	Holiday
January 1	New Year's Day (*Jour de l'An*). Public holiday.
January 6	Epiphany/Three Kings Day (*Fête des Rois*). Christian celebration of the Three Kings' visit to the Infant Jesus; secular association with eating a galette (almond paste–flavored pastry cake) with a hidden bean or trinket.
February 2	Candlemas (*Chandeleur*). For Christians, it marks Jesus Christ's presentation at the temple; its secular version is that of a midwinter celebration featuring crepes and various rituals thought to bring good fortune.
February 3–March 9 (dates varies)	Mardi Gras (also called *Carnaval*). Festive celebration on the last Tuesday before the beginning of Lent (for Christians, the forty-day period that precedes Holy Week culminating in Easter Sunday). Children dress up in costumes and march in parades. The Carnivals of Dunkirk and Nice are France's most iconic *Carnaval* celebrations.
February 14	Valentine's Day (*Saint-Valentin*), primarily for couples in France.
March 8	International Women's Day (*Journée de la Femme*).
Middle March	French Language and Francophonie Week (*Semaine de la Langue Française et de la Francophonie*), a weeklong celebration of the French language and mutual cultural appreciation among the countries and regions of the world that share French as part of their heritage.
Middle March	The Spring of the Poets (*Le Printemps des Poètes*). Two-week celebration of poetry (esp. in the French language) sponsored by the Ministry of Culture. Since 2001, devoted to a specific theme—for instance, Beauty (2019), Courage (2020), Desire (2021), and the Ephemeral (2022).
March 21 (week of)	Celebration of French Gastronomy (*Fête de la Gastronomie*).
March 22–April 25 (date varies)	Easter (*Pâques*). Christians celebrate the Resurrection of Jesus Christ. Easter Monday (the day after Easter Sunday) is a public holiday.

April 22	Earth Day (*Jour de la Terre*). Annual show of support for protection of the planet and environment.
April 30–June 3 (date varies)	Feast of the Ascension (*Jeudi de l'Ascension*). Public holiday observed on Thursday, thirty-nine days after Easter Sunday. For Christians, it signifies the ascent of Jesus Christ into heaven after the resurrection.
May 1	Labor Day (*Fête du Travail*). Public holiday. Workers hold marches and people buy lilies of the valley to celebrate the return of spring.
May 8	V-E Day (*Fête de la Victoire*). Public holiday. Celebration of Allied victory over Nazi Germany in World War II (1945).
Second Sunday in May	National Celebration of Joan of Arc and Patriotism (*Fête Nationale de Jeanne d'Arc et du Patriotisme*). The celebration coincides with the date (May 8, 1429) of the liberation of Orleans by an army under Joan's command. It comes before the Catholic feast day (May 30) of Saint Joan of Arc.
Last Sunday in May (date varies)	Mother's Day (*Fête des Mères*).
May 11–June 14 (date varies)	Pentecost Monday (*Lundi de Pentecôte*). Public holiday observed on the day after Pentecost Sunday (for Christians, a celebration of the descent of the Holy Spirit on the disciples of Jesus after the Ascension), which takes place on the seventh Sunday after Easter.
June 21	World Music Day (*Fête de la Musique*). Concerts and free public performances of all musical genres throughout the day (including in the streets at night).
June 24	Saint John's Eve (*Fête de la Saint-Jean*). A celebration on the night before Saint John the Baptist's feast day that also harkens back to pagan rituals of the summer solstice (e.g., the traditional lighting of bonfires on the eve of the feast day).
Third Sunday in June (date varies)	Father's Day (*Fête des Pères*).
End June	Paris Pride (*Marche des Fiertés LGBT*). Formerly known as Gay Pride, the Paris march is at the center of one of the largest LGBTQI+ celebrations/demonstrations in Europe. Similar events are held in other French cities around the same time.
Late June–Early July	Celebration of Cinema (*Fête du Cinema*), currently a four-day celebration of the movies and cinematic arts, including thematic festivals and special ticket prices.
July (three-week period)	Tour de France bicycle race. Avignon Festival (*Festival d'Avignon*), celebration of theatre and arts.
July 14	Bastille Day (*Quatorze-Juillet*). France's national holiday, commemorating the storming of the Bastille prison in Paris at the start of the French Revolution (1789). Festivities include a military parade on the Champs-Élysées in Paris, picnics, open-air dances, and fireworks. Public holiday.

July 16–17	Commemoration of the Vel d'Hiv Roundup of 1942, when French police (at the behest of German occupation authorities) rounded up foreign Jews living in Paris (the victims were temporarily held in a bicycle stadium before being sent to other detention centers and camps).
Late July–Early August	Bayonne Feria (*Fêtes de Bayonne*), a celebration of local cultural heritage in French Basque Country that includes bullfights.
Early August	Inter-Celtic Festival of Lorient, a two-week celebration of Breton and Celtic cultures and heritage.
Late August	Sète Festival of Saint Louis (*Fêtes de la Saint-Louis*). A weeklong cultural celebration in honor of the patron saint of the Mediterranean port city that includes a tournament of water jousting on the royal canal.
August 15	Feast of the Assumption (*Assomption*). Public holiday. For Christians (esp. Catholics), a celebration of the Virgin Mary's bodily assumption into heaven upon her death.
Third weekend of September	European Heritage Days (*Journées du Patrimoine*), annual celebration of cultural heritage sites, institutions, and historical monuments.
First Saturday in October	*Nuit Blanche* (literally, "All-Nighter"), a celebration of contemporary art and culture in cities across France during which galleries, museums, and other cultural venues stay open all night and offer special programs to the public (many free).
November 1	All Saints' Day (*Toussaint*). Public holiday. A religious celebration honoring saints of the Catholic Church; additionally, a day of remembrance of family members and other loved ones who have died.
November 11	Armistice Day. Public holiday. A commemoration of the signing of the armistice that put an end to World War I in 1918.
November 25	Saint Catherine's Day (*Sainte-Catherine*). Now a mostly secular celebration for young women (traditionally below the age of twenty-five) who are not married, featuring fanciful bonnets worn by "spinsters" (*Catherinettes*).
December 6	Saint Nicholas Day (*Saint Nicholas*). For Christians, a celebration of the saint who is the inspiration for Santa Claus (*Père Noël*) and patron of school children. Children leave their shoes by the fireplace in hope of gifts of coins or other treats.
December 8	Lyon Festival of Lights (*Fête des Lumières*). Traditionally, a demonstration of gratitude to the Virgin Mary; now a seasonal four-day celebration (culminating on 12/8) that showcases local history and cultural heritage.
December 9	Day of Secularism (*Journée de la Laïcité*). This celebration of the French republican secular tradition takes place on the date in 1905 that the French Law on the Separation of Churches and State was promulgated.

December 25	Christmas (*Noël*). A celebration of the birth of Jesus Christ for Christians as well as a secular winter holiday. During Advent (period of forty days prior to Christmas), festive Christmas markets are held in public squares in cities (e.g., Strasbourg) and towns throughout France.
December 31	Saint Sylvester's Day (Saint-Sylvestre). Although a Catholic saint's day, this is also what French people typically call New Year's Eve.
* (date varies)	Eid al-Fitr, the celebration marking the end of the holy month of Ramadan (ninth month of the Islamic lunar calendar) and its requisite sunrise to sunset fasting—a major holiday for France's large Muslim community.

INDEX

Page numbers in *italic* indicate photos.

ABOUT THE AUTHOR

Michael F. Leruth received his PhD in French from Penn State University and is Professor of French and Francophone Studies at the College of William & Mary in Williamsburg, Virginia. He specializes in modern and contemporary French society and culture. He is the author of *Fred Forest's Utopia: Media Art and Activism* (MIT Press, 2017) and has published articles in leading journals, including *The French Review, French Cultural Studies, French Politics and Society, Modern and Contemporary France, Contemporary French Civilization*, and *Contemporary French and Francophone Studies*. His knowledge of French political culture and contemporary art is widely recognized. In 2018, he received a Plumeri Award for Faculty Excellence at William & Mary.

www.ingramcontent.com/pod-product-compliance
Lightning Source LLC
Chambersburg PA
CBHW050239290326
41929CB00048B/2943